W9-BND-616

Jews in the Eyes of the Germans

From the Enlightenment to Imperial Germany

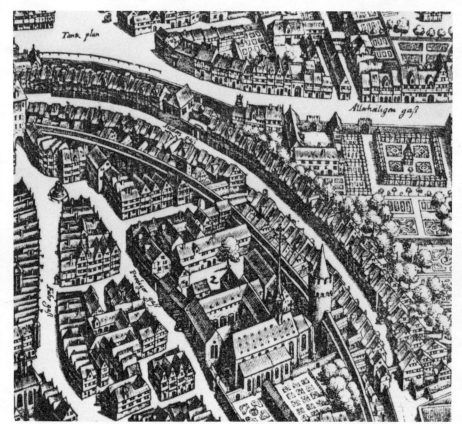

Judengasse in Frankfurt am Main

The Jewish quarter [was] called *Judengasse* ["Jews' Street"] because it comprised scarcely more than a single street and, in early times, had been hemmed in between the city wall and the moat as in a prison. . . . It was a long time before I dared to enter alone.

—*Goethe*

Jews
in the Eyes
of the Germans

From the Enlightenment to Imperial Germany

ALFRED D. LOW

ISHI A Publication of the
Institute for the Study of Human Issues
Philadelphia

Manufactured in the United States of America

Credits for portrait section (between pages 296 and 297)—Grillparzer: Courtesy of the Austrian Institute; Joseph II: Courtesy of the Austrian Press and
Information Service; Börne, Mendelssohn, Rothschild: Courtesy of the Leo
Baeck Institute, New York; Dorothea Schlegel and Rahel Varnhagen: Courtesy of the Nationalgalerie, Staatliche Museen Preussischer Kulturbesitz,
Berlin (West); the remaining portraits have been reproduced with the kind
permission of the German Information Service.

Library of Congress Cataloging in Publication Data:

Low, Alfred D
    Jews in the eyes of the Germans.

    Bibliography: p.
    Includes index.
    1. Jews in Germany—Public opinion.   2. Public opinion—Germany.
3. Germany—Intellectual life.   4. Jews in literature.   5. Anti-semitism—
Germany.   I. Title.
DS135.G33L67   301.45′19′24043   79–334
ISBN 0–915980–86–X

For information, write:

Director of Publications
ISHI
3401 Science Center
Philadelphia, Pennsylvania 19104
U.S.A.

To the victims of the Holocaust

Contents

Jews in the Eyes of the Germans

From the Enlightenment to Imperial Germany

Foreword

Books have their history. I conceived the idea for the present work while studying at the University of Vienna in the thirties. The manuscript was being typeset in Vienna in 1938 at the very moment that Nazi Germany annexed Austria. Aware that the printing had to be stopped, in the early morning of March 12—only hours after Chancellor Schuschnigg's resignation—I rushed to the printing shop to have the typesetting discontinued. Anti-Semitism was of course a cardinal article of faith in the Third Reich, and it was apparent that any attempt to disprove or even to qualify the Nazi claim that all great Germans were anti-Semites and thus forerunners of National Socialism would not be tolerated. Several years later in the United States, I rewrote the bulk of the work in English and then simply shelved it—as it turned out, for about a quarter of a century—while working in other fields. During the last few years I resumed work on it, reread the primary sources, acquainted myself with the secondary sources that had been published in the meantime, and rewrote the study in its entirety.

The present book differs from the early German version in scope and emphasis and to some extent in the assessment of individuals. While the original purpose of the work was primarily to refute the thesis that *all* great Germans were champions of Jew-hating, any work written after the Holocaust was bound to examine the depth and intensity of anti-Jewish sentiments among Germans in the eighteenth and nineteenth centuries.

Perceptive studies of German and Austrian Jewry in that period have been written. My own purpose has been to focus on the German-Jewish relationship in general and on German judgment of Jews and Judaism in particular. Although I have attempted to include literary figures to a larger extent than has generally been done, I have by no means confined myself to explaining the image of the German Jew

1

as presented in German literature. Instead, I have discussed German rulers, statesmen, politicians, philosophers, scholars, and political writers, as well as poets and novelists, who have dealt, not casually or incidentally but directly and exclusively, with the problem of German-Jewish coexistence or some aspects of it.

I make no claim that I have covered the topic of the German judgment of Jews completely; to meet the need for a shorter book on the subject, I was compelled to omit material from a number of sources. In any case, the very breadth of the undertaking makes gaps of one sort or another virtually unavoidable. But none of the omissions is likely to alter basically the picture of the German judgment on the Jews as here presented.

The primary topic of this study, the German judgment on Judaism and the German attitude toward Jews, has, to my knowledge, not been fully dealt with before. Perhaps both to Central European Jews and to Germans, the history of the German-Jewish relationship is still too painful a subject, the German image of Jews and Judaism too distorted, and the wounds inflicted too deep for calm assessment. These problems impose upon the student of the German-Jewish relationship the obligation to exercise great caution and restraint, but they constitute no argument for postponing the task. German embarrassment may never disappear. Meanwhile, the new rise or revival of anti-Semitism, however disguised, in other parts of the world, makes it all the more imperative that the particular question of the German-Jewish relationship be examined, and in as objective a manner as possible.

I have tried to do justice to all concerned: not only to the German and Austrian Jews who in the eighteenth and nineteenth centuries were the targets of defamation, but also to the Germans of that period. I have attempted to present as fairly as possible the German views about Jews and Judaism, without of course endorsing or condoning them. If the book has any bias, it is a bias against anti-Semitism and inequality and in behalf of humanity, against suppression and in behalf of liberty.

None has recognized more clearly the danger to which an uncritical judge may succumb than Jean Paul Friedrich Richter, who wrote to his Jewish friend Emanuel Oswald: "Unfortunately, I have read more about Jews than from Jews. That is, I regret that I know the oppressed almost entirely through the mouths of the oppressors. I regret that Christians are the portrait-painters of the Jews, for they are no more to be trusted than the Jews when they paint the portraits of Christians."[1]

The German Jew-haters have generally cared little for the great

Germans, whose entire *Weltanschauung* contradicted their own cru-
dity and vulgarity. Nevertheless, they made strenuous efforts to picture them as severe critics and bitter enemies of the Jews. "From
Luther on," the anti-Semitic historian Heinrich von Treitschke
claimed, "down to Goethe, Herder, Kant and Fichte, almost all great
Germanic thinkers were one in this feeling. Lessing stood quite alone
with his predilection for the Jews."[2] In the same vein as Treitschke,
but without limiting himself to German opinions, Houston Stewart
Chamberlain, the English writer who became a German citizen and
court philosopher in the imperial era under Wilhelm II, wrote later:
"Almost all prominent men from Tiberius to Bismarck have looked
upon the presence of Jews as a social and political menace"[3]—which
was surely a distortion of Bismarck's thought and practical legislation.

It was only fitting that most later anti-Semitic writers, such as
Adolf Bartels, the literary historian, Theodor Fritsch, the editor of
countless *Anti-Semitic Catechisms,* Alfred Rosenberg, the "theoretician" of the Nazi movement, and Adolf Hitler himself in *Mein
Kampf,* repeated these assertions. Hitler claimed Schopenhauer as an
anti-Semite and, in another context, laid the same claim on Fichte.[4]
Culling quotes from the works of great or widely known German
writers, the anti-Semites wished to demonstrate that the attitude of
these literary men toward the Jews was always marked by dislike and
repugnance.

These assertions were denied by others, Jews and German Christians. Among the more noted replies may be mentioned some late
nineteenth-century publications, the *Antisemitenspiegel* [Anti-Semitic
Mirror], published under the auspices of the League for the Defense
against Anti-Semitism, and the *Antisemitenhammer* [Anti-Semitic
Hammer], a collection of testimonies gathered by the German Christian author Josef Schrattenholz. But these anthologies were far from
comprehensive, and they were combative in character, polemics
rather than balanced and detached discussions. In the heat of battle
with a demagogic foe, truth could not easily emerge.

Though it must be apparent that the German judgment on Jews
and Judaism was shaped by the course of German history and the
developments in the German-Jewish sector, neither German nor Jewish history proper is the focus of this book. On the other hand, the
struggle for and against emancipation and the struggle centering
around anti-Semitism, which fill the pages of nineteenth-century German and German-Jewish history, are inseparable from German
thought about Jews and Judaism in general, are its very crystalliza-
tion, and are therefore dealt with in this study. I have considered it
my primary task to gather and analyze major sources relating to the

German evaluation of Jews and Judaism. Such an assessment, covering roughly the period between 1750 and 1890, is essential for coming to grips with the question of the breadth and depth of German anti-Semitism and for understanding the ultimate catastrophe.

In the very center of this study stands the intellectual, artistic, and political elite of Germany. Its judgment about Jews and Judaism shows fluctuations as well as persistent elements. The German evaluation was both heavily laden with prejudicial notions, inherited from previous generations, and influenced by a forward-looking and optimistic world view, by rationalism, liberalism, positive Christianity, and later socialism. The judgment on the Jews was of course affected by German self-interest, by a complex of economic, political, religious, and other considerations. German opinions about the nature of Judaism, about baptism and mixed marriages, varied, but there was agreement on the desirability of a homogenous nation and of cultural assimilation and ultimate physical merger. Germans looked at Jews and Judaism through different glasses. Beauty or ugliness, merit or demerit, achievement or failure, value or unworthiness, lay frequently in the eyes of the beholder.

In the span of German and German-Jewish history from the Enlightenment to the unification of Germany, emancipation is written with capital letters in the history of both Germans and Jews. Since the struggle for Jewish emancipation and the struggle against anti-Semitism in the late eighteenth and the nineteenth century were not confined to Germany and Central Europe but raged on a broad European scale, events taking place outside Germany and Central Europe were bound to affect developments in Germany, though they can be given only brief mention in this book.

The Jews were more vulnerable than most other national groups in the German states and in Europe at large. A dispersed national and religious minority, with a history of persecution and discrimination, the Jews in Germany were separated from other Germans religiously, culturally, and in part linguistically and were also economically and socially distinct from the mass of the German people; they still served as a lightning rod in times of political and social disturbances, of rapid economic and technological changes and deep cultural and sociological transformations. The fact that assimilation made notable progress throughout the nineteenth century and that the dividing cultural and national gulf between Jews and Germans narrowed substantially made little difference. Lessing had anticipated the judgment of German hostility when he let the patriarch in *Nathan der Weise* repeat: "The Jew is to be burned." Hatred between two different groups by no means declines in proportion to the diminishing of the natural or the ideological differences. It is not necessarily the difference, as often claimed, which creates dislike; instead, hatred, seeking an outlet, seizes on real or alleged difference as a justification.

Anti-Semitism is a complex phenomenon; it has religious and national, economic, social and political, psychological, and even philosophical aspects as well as causes. It varies from age to age, from country to country, from one type of social and economic order to another, and is shaped by the length of the historical road the Jews and their host peoples have traveled. It is a group hatred which assumes many forms and offers numerous rationalizations. It is not confined to the political Right, the Center, or the extreme political Left; at various times it penetrates all of them, even those groups which, by virtue of their philosophy, are most unlikely to embrace its various manifestations or to succumb to them. To lay bare its causes means to dissect anti-Judaism into elements which are probably found in all group hatreds. Still, anti-Semitism, in spite of similarities with other collective hatreds, is a rather unique phenomenon.

It is the rationalizations, the attempts to "explain" and justify the group hatred aimed against the German Jews, that are bound to attract the primary attention of the student of intellectual history. But it cannot be reasonably expected that, in addition to my main task, the analysis of the German judgment on Judaism, I offer also a novel thesis on the causes of the age-old phenomenon of anti-Semitism; the best I could have come up with would obviously have been a thesis on the causes of *German* anti-Semitism of the eighteenth and nineteenth centuries, with which I am here concerned. But even this would have presupposed a searching examination of the economic and social, besides the intellectual, history of Germans and Jews, which again would have transcended the framework of this book.

I have attempted to distinguish between the real and the alleged causes of anti-Semitism, its essence and its garb. We need not concern ourselves with particular accusations levelled against the Jews— accusations involving religious prejudice, which still lingered on among many Germans, centering on the crucifixion of Jesus and the allegedly insidious religious teachings of Judaism; accusations relating to multiple loyalties, on account, for instance, of support given by German Jews to persecuted Jews in Russia, Rumania, France, or the Middle East; charges concerning the economic activities of the Jews and their supposed exploitation of the Germans; assertions about the alleged racial inferiority of the Jews; the accusation that the Jews were conspiring to dominate Germany, Europe, and the world; or numerous other charges of similar caliber. But the historian must attempt to analyze them and decide whether, given the conditions in

Germany of the particular period, their authors were rank demagogues or true, though uncritical, believers.

Sympathy for the apparent underdog, the Jewish minority, which
was struggling for equality and liberty, should not lead one to reject
all the accusations uttered by spokesmen of the majority; the latter of
course need not always be wrong, the minority not always right, the
majority not always repressive, the minority not always oppressed.
Still, there is no great difficulty in discerning the extent, if any, to
which the accusations were justified, their frequent inherent contradictions, and their challenge to common sense; nor is it especially
difficult to assess the actual balance of power between Germans and
Jews in the eighteenth and nineteenth centuries. One should also be
able to reach a judgment as to the justice of the Jews' demand for
legal equality.

The period chosen in this study represents a distinct unit, extending from the age of enlightened absolutism and the last stages of the
Holy Roman Empire, with its multiplicity of petty states, to the unification of Germany and the aftermath, the beginnings of German imperialism; from the age of classicism, rationalism, and cosmopolitanism to
the Romantic era and then integral nationalism. As far as German
Jewry was concerned, it comprises an era of tremendous changes,
from the state of inequality of the eighteenth century to the egalitarian-
ism of the French Revolution and its liberating impact upon Germany,
to the first emancipation in Prussia in 1812, the radical innovations of
1848–1849, the complete legal emancipation of Austrian and German
Jews in 1867 and 1869 respectively, to the threatening revival of anti-
Semitism in the seventies. It was then that the German-Jewish novelist
Berthold Auerbach remarked: "Vergebens gelebt und gearbeitet" (I
have lived and worked in vain). The rise of political anti-Semitism in
Germany and Austria in the seventies and eighties foreshadows the
ultimate catastrophe of German Jewry and of much of the rest of European Jewry.

The period dealt with was one of progressive changes for both
Germans and Jews along several lines, toward liberalism, secularism, democracy, the national state, and emancipation. Still, progress
in their mutual relationship up to 1870, and even more until 1890,
was elusive. The cultural and social rapprochement between Germans and Jews did not solve the problem of peaceful and harmonious coexistence.

To some, the German judgment about Jews and Judaism offered
in this book will confirm that, most of the time, Germans entertained
prejudiced notions about—and knew little about—their Jewish neighbors; it will also offer ample proof that most Germans considered the

Jews as aliens and that coexistence was always an illusion. The biases of the nineteenth century will appear to them a mere continuation of earlier prejudices—some of them dating back to the Middle Ages—wrapped in new garb. Still, there were always some broadminded and cosmopolitan Germans who, in the interest of the German nation, of German *Kultur* in the best sense of the word, and of the German Jews themselves, came out for improvement of the Jewish situation and for justice and ultimately for emancipation and equality. And there were many who throughout their own lifetime displayed contradictory attitudes toward the Jews, vacillated, even veered from one extreme to the other. Rationality and irrationality, inclinations toward sociability and segregation, attraction and repulsion, were frequently strangely combined, often in the same person. Many of the political and ideological currents sweeping Germany were highly destructive, but they never completely submerged opposing opinions. What resulted was the prevalence at different times of different political and intellectual fashions, never total unanimity—neither full approval nor complete rejection.

If the anti-Semites' thesis that all great Germans were enemies of the Jews is spurious and untenable, so is the opposite one, developed by some friends of the Jews and some Jews themselves, who painted too favorable a picture of the relationship between great Germans and Jews and their thoughts about them. In spite of numerous genuine friendships and intimate connections between individual Germans and Jews, the German-Jewish coexistence was never idyllic or anything approaching it. The eye of friendship was perhaps never entirely closed, but the eye of hatred was always open. The student of the history of the German-Jewish relationship will see on almost all of its pages the harsh, intolerant features of hate. In the wild storm of time the waves of anti-Semitism often beat high; and even when calmer winds prevailed, those waves were always in threatening motion. The waters never stood still.

With a few notable exceptions, eighteenth- and nineteenth-century Germans did not preach the removal of Jews from Germany or their elimination in any form; they stood a world apart from twentieth-century Nazi barbarism. But the number of Germans who hoped for the disappearance and "death" of Judaism was quite large; they included adherents of the most diverse political and ideological currents. Here was an unquestionable link between the German attitude toward Jews and Judaism in the late eighteenth and the nineteenth century and the racial Jew-hatred of the Nazis. The deep roots of anti-Semitism to which this study points explain to a large extent the relative ease with which later Nazi racial anti-Semitism spread through German lands and the relative lack of resistance that the Nazi totalitarian juggernaut encountered in this crucial sector of the front.

As has often been said, the success of the National Socialist movement was due to a combination of unique circumstances and factors. Yet all accounts agree that virulent anti-Semitism was an essential ingredient—more, that it played a key role. It was the cement holding all other elements in their places, the very fundament of Nazi thought and practice. The anti-Semitic obsession, which first gripped the Nazis, and, secondly, only to a lesser extent, many other segments of the German people, must be traced back centuries, to medieval society and thought as well as to Martin Luther and his inveighing against Jews and their synagogues, the burning of which he recommended.

In the eighteenth and nineteenth centuries German anti-Semitism underwent a radical transformation, though it lost nothing of its fanatic intensity. To the time-worn religious "justification" of Jew-hatred, it added new dimensions, novel accusations of an economic, social and political, and ultimately "racial" type. Nineteenth-century Germany had apparently no less need for a scapegoat than earlier unenlightened ages, and perhaps even greater frustrations; these it unloaded upon the always small minority within its midst, a most convenient target which could be hit easily and without penalty.

In writing this book, it seemed to me especially important to have individual Germans voice their views directly and to cite significant quotations in full. Only in this way is the reader enabled to judge for himself, to perceive the main thrust of the opinions uttered and sense their flavor; only such direct quotation can revive for him the past dispute, involving mutual criticism, invective, and apology. The very purpose of this study would have been defeated by either shortening or paraphrasing some of the important quotes. Unless otherwise indicated, I have myself translated the German quotations; thus I am responsible for their accuracy.

Though I am aware that the term *anti-Semite* is of late nineteenth-century coinage and has peculiar racial overtones, I have nevertheless used it throughout as interchangeable with opposition and hostility to and hatred of Jews and Judaism, whatever its motivation. *Anti-Semite* at least has the advantage of brevity.

This book owes a debt to authors of monographs, some dating back to the nineteenth century, on the attitude of Germans toward Jews and Judaism and of general studies on German thought, on philosophers, poets and novelists, politicians, and other writers. To those authors who deserve more than a brief mention special reference has been made throughout the book, especially in the Notes.

My thanks go out to all those who have shown an interest in the progress of this work. Years ago Professor Harold J. Grimm of Ohio State University kindly read parts of the German manuscript; Professor George H. Blake of Marietta College also read portions of the early English version and made useful suggestions. I of course bear full responsibility for any errors of fact. As usual, I owe a special debt to my wife, Dr. Rose S. Low, for early encouragement and later for critical reading and many valuable suggestions. My daughter Suzanne has likewise made most helpful suggestions in regard to style and content, and my daughter Ruth has assisted in other ways. Special thanks are due to Janet Greenwood, Production Editor of the Institute for the Study of Human Issues, for her many useful comments and for securing the photographs included in this book, and to the German Information Service and the Leo Baeck Institute, both of New York City, for offering generous assistance in this matter. Dr. John Berens, Perry Raines, and Carol Schieffer have conscientiously typed the final version of the manuscript. Furthermore, I am most appreciative of the invaluable assistance rendered by the personnel of Marquette University Library and its inter-library service.

Alfred D. Low
January 1979

PART I

In the Mirror of Enlightenment and Classicism

It is amazing, how much anti-Semitism has cropped up among the enlightened thinkers and how a straight line leads from old radicalism and liberalism to the anti-Semites of the nineteenth and twentieth centuries.

—Carlo Schmid

CHAPTER 1

Enlightened Absolutism and the Jews

The Coming of the New Age

In the latter half of the eighteenth century Jews in Central Europe lived dispersed in cities and towns throughout the Germanies and the Austrian Empire rather than in a contiguous region. Toward the end of the eighteenth century there were about 175,000 Jews in Germany—less than one percent of the entire population—and about 75,000 Jews in German Austria, Bohemia, and Moravia and another 100,000 in Hungary. German Jewry had a long and tortuous history which went back to the Roman period. Molded by a common history of repression and persecution and linked by close cultural, religious, and linguistic bonds, narrowly confined by law to a few commercial activities and prevented from engaging in agriculture and the crafts, Jews for centuries represented a tight-knit national and religious group. They were held together by voluntary and involuntary, positive and negative forces, by their religious faith, their memory of national experiences stretching back to antiquity, and by their languages—Hebrew and later also Yiddish. They were also linked by their hope for ultimate liberation, their belief in a Messiah, their will to survive as a people, and their rejection of complete submergence among their host peoples. Their survival was largely due also to the continued hostility of their hosts and neighbors. It was helped by the discriminatory legal walls which surrounded them, by the anti-Semitism which throughout the ages had continually brought repression and persecution. Landless, separated from their ancient homeland, they were the pariah among European peoples. Recurrent expulsions encouraged maintenance of ties with kinsfolk in other countries and kept Jewish solidarity alive.

It was in the latter part of the eighteenth century that the Enlightenment began powerfully to affect Europe's political and cultural elite. This intellectual revolution found expression in Enlightened Absolutism and the French Revolution and in legislation which was to transform permanently not only France but much of Europe, including Germany. It was also to alter radically the character and outlook of German Jewry. During the era of the Enlightenment, the French Revolution, and Prussian state reforms—the latter a response to subjugation by France and to the spread of French equalitarian and libertarian ideas into German lands—many internal walls between Germans and Jews came down. But the removal of some, even of many, legal obstacles did not and could not solve the problems of social integration and coexistence between Germans and the small Jewish minority in their midst.

What was needed in addition to purely legal changes—which should have come about without procrastination and reservations—was the thorough reeducation of both Germans and Jews, the energetic removal of old prejudices of a primarily religious character, and a resolute struggle against new biases of an ethnic, social, economic, and sporadically even racial character. Furthermore, a change in the lopsided economic structure of the Jews would have facilitated social acceptance, as distinguished from mere legal equality. Both Germans and Jews had expectations which were perhaps unrealistic and, given the mutual dispositions, could not be fulfilled. Even Germans who favored the removal of legal inequality expected the Jews to quickly reach a level of acculturation and assimilation which would lead to the vanishing of German-Jewish culture and the separate religious-ethnic existence of the Jews. In the nineteenth century, destined to become the era of national growth and national political fulfillment for so many European peoples, including the Germans, it was not reasonable to expect that the Jews, who had shown such determination to survive, would be the only ones not affected by the mighty appeal of national revival. Actually the German Jews, eager for emancipation, chafing under persistent inequality, and persuaded of the superiority of German culture, lovingly embraced it, opting thus for the nineteenth century. But in doing so, the great majority of German Jews still spurned the idea of committing cultural and religious suicide and of completely abandoning their distinct religious-ethnic individuality.

The accession to the throne in 1740 of Frederick the Great in Prussia and of Maria Theresa in Austria represented a turning point in the history of the German and Austrian peoples. This was also the era of the Enlightenment; the ideas of the *philosophes* penetrated Central Europe and their thought began to be partially realized through the reforms of Frederick II and Joseph II. The transformation was deepened by an unprecedented intellectual and literary revival, which radically changed Germany's cultural and social life. It was an era during which the German people began to display a vigorous vitality in countless fields of human endeavor. The critical ideas of the Enlightenment, the revolutionary zeal of the Storm and Stress movement, and the lofty ideals of Classicism represented the quickly changing phases of the pulsating German spirit of those decades.

The great intellectual and political advances as well as the economic and social progress of the German people were accompanied by significant improvements in the Jewish sector. In the later decades of the eighteenth century Jews in German Central Europe moved closer to emancipation than ever before. The vanguard of the Jews began to move freely in Germany's economic, social, and cultural life. Enlightened rulers encouraged wealthy and enterprising Jews to establish factories and to engage in foreign trade. Educated Jews began to associate with German poets, playwrights, philosophers, and liberal aristocrats, and the residences of some wealthy Jews became social centers for a select group of German men and women.

The intellectual horizon of German Jews widened rapidly. For centuries they had led a bare existence in the ghetto, their intellectual life restricted to study of their holy books and commentaries. Now, with astounding speed, they developed an intelligentsia that could appreciate, and even contribute to, German culture. It was as if they wished to prove themselves worthy of the social and civil rights they claimed and to make amends for the centuries of social and cultural isolation and backwardness to which persecution had condemned them. Many of the great German writers and thinkers of the classical period entertained friendly relations with the Jews and favored the extension of greater rights to them.

Socially and economically, however, a deep gulf still separated the great mass of the German Jews from the German people. Because the trend of the period was on the whole favorable, both Germans and Jews, blinded by the rising sun of the Enlightenment, tended to overlook the broad areas still covered by the darkness of an unconquered past.

Joseph II and the Jews in Austria

Of the two great reform monarchs in German Central Europe, both of whom were devoted to the philosophical ideas of the age, Frederick the Great of Prussia pursued the more cautious domestic policy, while Joseph II of Austria, the son of Maria Theresa, was the more daring ruler. In the end the Habsburg monarch encountered bitter opposition in Austria and was compelled to abandon many of his reforms.

Herder called Joseph II "the man with great objectives." The attitude of the Habsburg monarch toward the Jews helps justify this epithet. The measures which the Emperor was to adopt in regard to the Austrian Jews grew out of his general domestic policy—the modernization of the Austrian Empire—and were, partly at least, motivated by economic considerations. The contemporary writer Johann Gottfried Zimmermann, with an eye upon the Jews, wrote in his book *Von dem Nationalstolze* [About the National Pride]: "The princes are praised everywhere for the toleration of antagonistic religions; the more money is needed at the courts, the more agreeable are the princes to all claims of philosophy, if they increase thereby their revenues."[1]

While Joseph II was to be admired by forward-looking, liberal elements in German Austria, he won no friends among the privileged classes or among many of the non-German peoples of the Austrian Empire. Nobility and clergy resented the Emperor's abolition of centuries-old class privileges. Hungarians, Czechs, and other awakening nationalities never quite forgave him for his policy of Germanization, an outgrowth of his centralism rather than of German national inclinations.

As Joseph II tried to impose German language and culture on these ethnic groups, he also tried to make Germans out of Austrian Jews. He met with less opposition from them than from other nationalities in Austria, whose position was not quite as precarious as theirs, who had been oppressed but not persecuted, and who lived not scattered throughout the realm but in compact settlements and on their own ancestral soil.

Throughout his co-regency (1765–1780), Joseph II worked along with State Chancellor Prince Wenzel Kaunitz and others in preparation of an edict of toleration. As long, however, as the Empress Maria Theresa lived, there was no likelihood of her making the slightest concessions to the demands of the time, and mother and son reached no agreement on policy toward the Jews. In her correspondence with Joseph in 1777 Maria Theresa's opposition to making religious concessions, not only in regard to the Jews but to all non-Catholics, emerged clearly. Without a "dominant religion," "tolerance, indifference" would spread, and "these were just the very means to undermine everything." Maria Theresa identified her unrelenting attitude as a defense of religion as such. She did not favor the spirit of persecution, she assured her son, but she favored even less indifference or religious latitudinarianism and expressed the fear that Joseph II did not share her views.[2]

By the time Maria Theresa's reign neared its end, only about 550 Jews lived in Vienna, their existence being sharply circumscribed by the *Judenordnung* of May 5, 1764.[3] Not covered by this regulation was the much smaller community of Sephardic Jews in Vienna, whose origin was Constantinople and who could claim foreign citizenship. The religious census of 1784 showed, in addition, a Jewish population of about 42,000 in Bohemia and 27,000 in Moravia and Austrian Silesia. Unlike the Jews in Vienna, Jewish men in these provinces had to wear yellow armbands and girls and women yellow ribbons in their hair. For Hungary the religious census of 1735 listed about 11,600 Jews, though their actual number may have been larger. Following the first partition of Poland in 1772, the part of Galicia annexed by the Habsburg monarchy contained about 250,000 Jews, many more Jews than had lived in the entire monarchy before.

Most likely it was a combination of factors which led to the proclamation of the Edict of Toleration of the Jews under Joseph II. The spread of the ideas of toleration and humanity, fostered by the age and also enunciated in German literature (as for instance in Lessing's *Nathan der Weise* [Nathan the Wise], in the writings of Herder, Wieland, and Klopstock, and in the plays of the Austrian playwright and actor Stephanie the Younger), the eminent role of the *Hofjuden* (Court Jews),* the cultural progress and usefulness of Jews to the economy of country and state—all this contributed substantially to the progress, toleration, legal improvement, and final equality of the Jews in Austria. The growing self-confidence of more wealthy and enterprising Jews such as Amschel Arnstein, a tolerated Jew of Vienna who dared threatening to leave Austria unless he obtained a remission of the so-called toleration tax, must have convinced the authorities that concessions were imperative. The preoccupation of the Austrian *Staatsrat* with the Jewish question came about rather suddenly, after the receipt on May 13, 1781, of a lengthy instruction from the Emperor Joseph II himself.

In view of Joseph II's impetuosity, his lack perhaps of careful preparation (he appears to have had wrong notions about the scarcity of tailors, engravers, sculptors, and workers in the textile business among Austrian Jews), the *Staatsrat* reacted rather cautiously, though

---

*The *Hofjuden* appeared in the era of Absolutism and mercantilism, rendering important functions to the princely ruler of the state and enjoying special privileges. While some relinquished Jewish tradition, others remained faithful and used their wealth and position to help their brethren.

one member, Baron Gebler, praised the Emperor's intentions as likely
to bestow honor upon the government. When the *Hofkanzlei* took up
the Emperor's proposals, some members questioned whether Jews
needed to study German for the purpose of keeping their books, since
they already knew the language. Fear was expressed that, if Jewish
children would enroll in Catholic schools, they would spread calumnies
about Christianity. Furthermore, in view of the opposition of master
craftsmen to taking on Jewish apprentices, it would be preferable if the
Jews learned these trades abroad!

Objections were also raised to opening up agricultural occupations
to the Jews and to increasing the number of the legally privileged
"tolerated" Jews. Only one member of the *Hofkanzlei,* Baron Joseph
Greiner, pointed out in a separate report that the negative reaction of
the *Hofkanzlei* amounted to the perpetuation of the status quo, since it
ran counter to the Emperor's proposal to bring about radical changes in
the situation of the Jews.[4] Greiner simultaneously drew attention to the
Netherlands, where the granting of complete equality had produced
most fruitful results. He also discussed the fears of others that equality
would bring about wholesale conversions to Judaism. The reports of
the *Hofkanzlei* and of Baron Greiner were taken up in the *Staatsrat*
during the month of September. There followed on October 1, 1781, an
imperial resolution which made the Emperor's intention known to the
public. It revealed that Joseph II had given much attention to the objections raised in the *Hofkanzlei* and the *Staatsrat,* and these were reflected in the final edict of toleration.

With the Edict of Toleration of 1781, decreed in the very year
when Lessing, the great preacher of tolerance, died, Joseph II began
to free the Jews from centuries of oppression. The most important
legal provisions affecting the Jews were issued between October 19,
1781, and January 2, 1782. First came a letter of the Emperor to
Count Blümegen, which liberated Jews from "humiliating and oppressive laws." Thereafter, on October 21, 1781, the yellow badge which
Jews had been compelled to wear outside of the ghetto was abolished.
This was followed by the annulment of the degrading body toll which
was imposed on them as well as on their cattle (December 18, 1781).
On January 2, 1782, the charter of toleration, in which Joseph's views
were most clearly articulated, was finally proclaimed.

In the charter Joseph II declared that since the beginning of his
reign it had been his purpose to have all his Austrian subjects contribute to public welfare "without any distinction in regard to nationality
and religion." All should enjoy liberty before the law, and none
should be hindered in earning an honest livelihood. Existing ordi-
nances relating to the Jews, particularly those in Vienna and Lower

Austria, were not always in harmony with these declared aims; the last ordinance, bearing the date of May 5, 1764, was therefore repealed. Joseph further proclaimed that it was his intention to make the Jewish people useful to the state, principally through providing better education of their young people and by admitting Jews to the sciences and the arts and to agriculture and the crafts.

The Edict of Toleration granted the Austrian Jews the right to send their children to elementary and secondary schools. The attendance at higher institutions of learning, which had not been forbidden, was now expressly permitted. Jews might attend public places of amusement. On Sunday and on other days of religious festivals they might also take walks in the forenoon. They were now permitted to learn all trades and to engage in wholesale business under the same conditions as Christian subjects and like them could establish factories. In Galicia Joseph II made a special attempt to win the Jews over to agriculture.

Theoretically at least, public service was now opened to the Jews. They were put on an equal footing with Christians before the courts, which meant suffering the same penalties as well as enjoying the same benefits: "The Jews are to be put on a full basis of equality with the Christians in matters relating to emigration; therefore, they are also to be punished in accordance with the laws, if they act contrary to them."[5]

Still, there was no thought as yet of full emancipation of the Jews. They could not become masters in their crafts, and acquisition of land was permitted to them only in Jewish communities. In Vienna public religious services remained forbidden, and the number of Jewish residents was not supposed to increase. With new rights the Jews also acquired new duties: they were made subject to military service.[6] They were also granted family names, by no means a mere curiosity but a sign of the newly attained civil position. No other contemporary European state called upon the Jews to render military service or gave them family names.

Although complete emancipation was neither aimed at nor achieved, the new laws represented a radical change for the better, a striking improvement over past policies. The novel measures breathed a fresh spirit and were a clear repudiation of the oppressive laws which had burdened the Jews for centuries.[7] The Emperor's main purpose in granting tolerance to the adherents of the various Protestant sects and the Greek-Orthodox elements had not been the extension of full equality either. Its real significance lay rather, as a leading Austrian historian, August Fournier, later remarked, in admitting non-Catholics to the purchase of houses and farms, to civil rights and rights of master of trade, to academic honors and to public service, all of which assured the state new talents and new economic resources.[8] The patents relating to the civil rights of the Jews showed, in the judgment of Fournier, the same regard for the practical interests of the state.

Pragmatism and utilitarianism were indeed the keys to Joseph II's policy toward the Jews, as the Emperor himself made quite clear in his instruction of May, 1781. Permitting economic diversification for the Jews instead of limiting them to a few branches of the economy was the means to make them most useful to the state. A radical change in their economic activities required not only the removal of legal prohibitions but also active retraining and reeducation. Reeducation was needed by Gentiles as well to make them accept the broadening of opportunities for Jews.

Joseph II also praised the "abundant advantage which occurs to both religion and state" from genuine tolerance, which was also in accord with "Christian love," and rejected every "pressure of conscience as harmful."[9] Religion, he confessed, must be a matter of the heart. In this sense, a decree of the Emperor, dated March 31, 1782, prohibited the baptizing of Jewish children before the eighteenth year without parental consent, since "mature judgment" could not be assumed before this age and "fear" or "allurement" might exercise improper influence.[10]

While Joseph II firmly believed in religious tolerance as such, he also considered it to be of "abundant advantage" to the state. In his mind the liberation of the Jews thus became linked with the interests of the Austrian Empire. Joseph II wished to make the Jews "useful members of the state" and to introduce them, "as far as possible, to agriculture and other useful crafts."[11] The Austrian Emperor recognized more clearly than many of his contemporaries the economic causes and aspects of the Jewish problem and tried to bring about a less lopsided, more balanced economic structure within Austria's Jewry.

Joseph II pointed to many real and alleged shortcomings of the Jews but attributed these, as well as what he considered their often harmful economic activity, to the harsh oppression which for so long had been their lot. He did not doubt their capacity for moral improvement nor their ability to become of greater economic utility to the state. "This magnificent nation," he wrote, "dispersed all over the world, yet more imbued with a national spirit than any other people; this nation which does not live together compactly in any country and still retains its character under all climates, has supported itself so far mostly by small trade. Since most of them circulate only a little capital, they must seek to make as much profit as possible, in order to be able to live on it." Therefore they charged higher rates of interest and, resorting to trickery, sold their wares often under false pretenses. In view of this situation it was necessary "that the Jews seize the hoe, instead of the wallet," that they contribute to the acquisition of home products and make themselves as "useful to the state" as they should and could.[12]

Like Prussia's Jews under Frederick the Great, the Austrian Jews, in general accordance with the doctrines of mercantilism, were induced to establish factories. Even the Austrian Empress Maria Theresa, though hostile to the Jews, had granted favors to those who wished to build factories, as the edict of May 6, 1774, showed. Her liberal son urged the Jews even more strongly to build factories and permitted them in the edict of September 18, 1775, to buy public buildings for this purpose.

Joseph II was convinced that it would be possible to harness the talents of the Jews for the purpose of developing the economy and thus enriching the state. Provided only that they were kept within certain "limits,"[13] the Jews would abundantly promote Austria's interests. This basic idea, which lies at the very source of the Edict of Toleration, crops up regularly. Although the Jews were not Christians, they were, Joseph II emphasized, "human beings," "consumers," and they paid taxes![14] He always judged the Jews from the point of view of their present and future economic usefulness to the state but also, in accordance with the ideas of the time, from the humanitarian standpoint.

Joseph II hoped to bring about a thorough assimilation of the Jews to German culture. Stipulations in the Edict of Toleration aimed at the replacement of Hebrew and Yiddish by German as the daily language for conversation and business. Jewish youth should be educated in German schools. In his regulations Joseph II turned repeatedly to school and study, which he considered the main vehicles for the Germanization of the Jews. They should cease to be Jews in everything but religion. Actually, in accordance with the prevailing trend of the Enlightenment in matters regarding Judaica, he saw in Judaism "a quintessence of foolishness and nonsense"[15] and looked upon it as an "evil which had to be made innocuous."[16] Though the Jews might keep their faith in a purified and enlightened form, Judaism as such should vanish and individual Jews should seek amalgamation with the German people.

The Austrian monarch thus demanded a price for the new rights, for the treatment of the Jews as "fellow creatures," namely their assimilation and amalgamation with the German element in Austria's polyglot state. This very element, in combination with the aristocracy of some other nationalities, dominated the Habsburg monarchy and was to continue to play an eminent political, social, and cultural role in the Empire. By insisting on the Germanization of the Jews, Joseph actually opened to them the door to joint control of the multi-national Empire, assigning to them a rather distinguished role in the monarchy, that of co-rulers. Still, culturally they had to become Germans. But before the educational work could be undertaken, an improvement of the status of the Jews in state and society was imperative. The centuries-old defamation had to be ended, and honor and dignity had to be accorded the Jews; this, in his view, was not necessarily equivalent to granting them immediate and full equality.

Closely related to this goal of Germanizing his Jewish subjects was his resistance to an increase in the Jewish population of the Austrian provinces. Although the Emperor did not intend to expel the Jews from any part of Austria, he was opposed to their further increase, particularly in certain parts of the monarchy, since this would only delay the assimilation of the more educated and enlightened among them.

Joseph II insisted that his edicts on the Jews be carried out. When news reached him that the yellow badge was still worn and the body toll still levied on Jewish travelers in some provinces of Austria, he demanded of Count Blümegen to enforce immediate respect for the law.[17] Repeatedly he stressed that the Jews ought to observe, as far as possible, the same laws as the Christians, and he insisted on the removal of all discriminatory special measures. Thus he remarked on May 19, 1788, in reference to the Galician Jews, that "all laws which exist separately for the Jews and are not valid for the Christians too should be eliminated with the exception of a very few, without further delay," and that the Jews should likewise be referred "to those laws which are designed for all my subjects." They should enjoy "full religious freedom" and "be treated like people possessing the same rights as all other citizens of the state." This way, he held, "all coercion and all contempt would cease quickly."[18]

In some respects—for instance in the destruction of the autonomy of the Jewish communities—Joseph II went too far; many of his well-meant reforms bore the stamp of imprudent haste. In other respects, judged particularly from the point of view of the present, Joseph II appears not to have traveled far enough or moved boldly enough. He may have given too much consideration to reactionary, though often broad-based, resistance to the movement toward greater equality.

Still, the Austrian Emperor had thrown down the gauntlet to the prejudices of the ages. He who blazed many a new trail had also the courage to chart a new policy in regard to his Jewish subjects. While it held out opportunities to the Jews as individuals, it offered no bright hope for Judaism as a religion and none for the continuance of Jewish nationality, since the rights of national minorities were still unheard of at the time. But Joseph II made a praiseworthy attempt to begin treating the Jews, pariahs for centuries, as the equals of the Christian subjects of the Austrian monarchy. The significance of his policy was not limited to Central Europe but paved the way for toleration of the Jews in all of Europe.

Frederick the Great and the Jews in Prussia

Although Frederick the Great pursued a more conservative Jewish policy than Joseph II, he too, indirectly, promoted the progress of Prussian and German Jewry. The philosopher on Prussia's throne always knew how to distinguish between idea and reality, between thinking and governing. As youthful crown prince, he wrote an "Anti-Machiavelli." As King, however, he followed Machiavelli's path when, without a declaration of war, he crossed the Austrian frontier with his army in order to wrest Silesia from the young Austrian empress Maria Theresa.

An enlightened but absolutist ruler, Frederick the Great considered himself the first servant of the state; yet his hand rested heavily upon his people. He carried out major reforms in Prussia as well as in the newly conquered provinces, without, however, like Joseph II, laying the axe to the feudal order itself. Nor did he initiate the emancipation of the peasants. But his economic policy, based as it was upon the development of industry and trade, resulted, like that of Joseph II in Austria, in the strengthening of the middle class and was to make Prussia's military establishment independent from outside sources.

Frederick II's attitude toward the Prussian Jews reflected his pragmatic conception of Prussian state interests. The Prussian King acted in accordance with the idea of tolerance whenever he found the Jews to be useful instruments of the state. The wealthy Prussian Jews enjoyed his benevolence and his support. The poorer elements, however, lived in a state of misery and oppression, hardly different from that of earlier centuries.

The life of Prussian Jews in the eighteenth century was regulated by four comprehensive bodies of laws, or *Generalreglements,* which bore the dates 1700, 1714, 1730, and 1750.[19] Only the last of these fell under the reign of Frederick II and bore his seal. Under the order of Frederick III of January 24, 1700, Jews were looked upon as targets of the tax collectors and were required to pay high protective tolls (*Schutzgelder*). Furthermore, Jews had to pay for the recruitment and creation of a regiment of foot soldiers. Still, because of the complaints by Christian merchants, the order pledged to reduce the number of Jewish families. Second and third sons of protected Jews were permitted to reside in the country, to marry and to carry on business, but all this was made contingent on a certain amount of wealth and the payment of a special tax. The *Generalreglement* of 1730 under Frederick William I limited the number of children per protective letter (*Schutzbrief*) to two, compelling all other children to leave the country when they attained adulthood, and prohibited Jewish clerks and servants from marrying.

Frederick II's accession to the throne did not result in any improvement of the lot of Prussia's Jews. "It seemed," wrote the German Jewish historian Ludwig Geiger in his *Geschichte der Juden in Berlin* [History of the Jews in Berlin] "as if only the name of the ruler had changed, not the principles of his government." The regulation of the *Generalprivilegium* of 1750 under Frederick II was based upon a distinction between ordinary protected Jews and specially protected ones. The *Schutzbrief* of the first-named extended only to the first child; the "protection" of the specially protected Jews did not extend to their children but was limited to their own life's duration. The collection of protection money was left to the Jewish community, which was made collectively responsible for theft, fraud, and bankruptcy by any one of its members. The regulations were petty, dishonorable, and offensive in many ways and the Jews pleaded that the edict, which was orally communicated to them, not be published, since it would only destroy their credit abroad and add to their shame; but law it became.

Frederick II's Jewish regulations breathed the same dislike of Jews in general which his father Frederick William I had shown for them, though his motives may have been different ones. He shared the contempt and the new prejudices of the Enlightenment and especially of Voltaire against the Jews and Judaism (this "religious superstition"), holding their ceremonial laws to be irrational and their orthodox rabbis an anachronism. Though he judged the economic activities of the Jews to be harmful in many ways, he was prepared to use the talents of those among them who were likely to further Prussia's economic and political interests.

The Jews, according to the regulation of 1750,[20] were still required to pay numerous taxes. Aside from the tax for protection, there was a tax for the confirmation of the chosen representatives of the Jewish communities, special stamp taxes, a silver tax, and many others. The authorities showed great inventiveness in burdening the Jewish population with novel and increasingly heavy financial burdens. They introduced a marriage tax, required another tax for issuing marriage certificates, and established a fee for the registration of the newly born. Freedom of movement for the Jews was severely curtailed by the charging of passage money (*Geleit*), which made the emigration of Jews from one Prussian province into the other more difficult.

To the exploitation was added dishonor. In 1787 the representatives of Prussia's Jewish communities complained in a memoir to Frederick William II, the successor to Frederick II, that the Jews, when paying the *Geleit,* were treated like cattle. In cities such as Magdeburg and Stettin Jews were forbidden to stay overnight. Even in the permitted districts they were closely watched, lest their number increase.[21] While Frederick II drew foreign artisans and agrarian settlers into the country, Prussia's borders were closed to alien Jews. Frederick's announcement, one of his earlier biographers, Reinhold Koser, observed, "that all Turks and pagans who wished to people the country would be welcome to him, suffered a sharp limitation in regard to the Jews." Not religious reasons, Koser remarked apologetically, "merely economic considerations" determined Frederick's policy of barring alien Jews from Prussia and of permitting the mass of his Jewish subjects to eke out at best a miserable existence and suffer an unstable status as second-class citizens.[22]

The attitude of Frederick the Great is well illustrated in his treatment of the Jews of the former province of Silesia, which he won from Austria after a prolonged struggle. Following a temporary improvement in their status, the old unfavorable Silesian regulations concerning the Jews, which dated back to the Austrian period, were, at the urging of the merchants of Breslau, reintroduced in 1744. The number of Jews in Breslau was then limited to twelve protected families and a few officials and religious ministrants; all other Jews were ordered to leave the city. To the petition of the Breslau Jews relating to trading rights, Frederick the Great replied thus: "They may retain the rights concerning their trade, but they cannot be permitted to bring masses of Jews into Breslau and to transform it into a complete Jerusalem."[23] In spite of all restrictions, the Jewish community of Breslau grew steadily, even rapidly, and obtained a new constitution from Frederick in 1754. In Upper Silesia, where few Germans lived and many Polish peasants were settled, industry and trade lay almost exclusively in the hands of protected Jews.[24]

At the time of the invasion of Silesia in 1740 Frederick had let himself be hailed as defender of Protestantism against the Catholic house of Habsburg. He who used to laugh at religious fanatics had rare fun making political capital out of religious fanaticism.[25] A rumor spread in Catholic Austria that the Jews of Silesia had betrayed the province to Protestant Prussia. Similar accusations in earlier centuries had been leveled against the Austrian Jews, especially during the wars against Sweden and Turkey; the very repression of the Jews made their loyalty to the oppressive rulers and the native population suspect. During the Seven Years' War, also called the Third Silesian War, Maria Theresa herself declared the recent charge as baseless.[26] The handful of Silesian Jews was caught between the Prussian hammer and the Austrian anvil, symbolic of the situation of Central European Jews in general.

When the Prussian authorities prepared themselves to revise in a more liberal spirit the *Generaljudenprivileg* of 1730, which had been issued in the era of Frederick's father, the drillmaster Frederick William I, Frederick warned them lest they grant too many new letters of protection to the Jews. Simultaneously, he issued the order to retain several particularly offensive regulations of that constitution, such as the provision regarding the collective responsibility of the local Jewry for a number of offenses committed by individual coreligionists. It was thus hardly surprising when Honoré Gabriel Mirabeau, while on a visit to Berlin, remarked that some of Frederick's regulations regarding the Jews were "worthy of a cannibal."

The Prussian Jews, according to the *Generalprivilegium* of 1750, were prohibited from engaging in crafts; access to agriculture remained likewise forbidden to them in any form. They could neither possess nor rent distilleries or breweries. Even some branches of commerce were closed to them. Yet they were free to further the exportation of Prussian goods, because manifestly such policy was in the interest of the state. Beginning in 1769 Prussian Jews were even obliged to buy porcelain wares at fixed prices from the royal porcelain factory and to sell them abroad. The clever system of making the Jews promoters of Prussian export bore fruits for the state but hardly for the Jews. They often were forced to sell the "Jew porcelain," as it was everywhere called, at great loss.

But Frederick was not always a "cannibal," and not to all Jews. The capricious and, according to Goethe, "self-willed, incorrigible" ruler showed a different side to some Prussian Jews. J. D. E. Preuss, one of the early biographers of Frederick the Great, observed that a few very rich and enterprising Jews enjoyed "influence, prestige and privileges" throughout the entire reign of Frederick II.[27] In the same vein the noted Jewish historian S. M. Dubnow wrote later: "Frederick II who, economically, let the mass of Jews perish in their small business, supported the great Jewish capitalists in their factories, banks, and renting enterprises."[28]

Many wealthy Jews, such as Veitel Ephraim and Itzig, were permitted to reside in Berlin. Jews from Berlin, Königsberg, and Breslau who were prepared to assume high financial risks served Prussia as army contractors during the Seven Years' War. Driven by the pressing need of this war, Frederick the Great carried out money-clipping on a grand scale with the help of Veitel Ephraim; people used to call the bad coins "Ephraimites" after the latter.

It was Frederick's economic policy that drove the Jews into manufacturing. An order of October 29, 1757, specified that only a Jew who established a factory could obtain a new letter of protection.[29] Jews who were ready to establish factories received public favors of various sorts. Thus, according to the historian Preuss, Frederick donated to the Potsdamer Jew Joel, who had erected a knitting factory in 1758, the castle of Glienicke near Potsdam, together with side buildings, garden, and lawn, for the manufacture of tapestry.[30] Since wealthy Jews were not always prepared to found factories producing goods that promised little return, the King was ready to purchase their cooperation through a more liberal policy toward their younger children. During the Seven Years' War the coin manufacturers were compelled to invest their acquired capital in textile factories and other industrial enterprises. Jewish factory owners were given a helping hand by the Prussian authorities, who, for instance, sent Christian waifs to work in the factory of Veitel Ephraim.

Frederick II wished to develop Frankfurt an der Oder and to transform the recently acquired city of Breslau into an important trading center. High transit tolls, amounting to 30 percent of the sale price of all goods, were introduced in Silesia for the traffic between Saxony and Poland in order to force the Jews of Brody and Lemberg, who provided the entire East with German goods, to visit the fairs in Frankfurt an der Oder or in Breslau, instead of the fair at Leipzig.[31] The historian Otto Hintze pointed out in his book *Preussische Seidenindustrie im achtzehnten Jahrhundert und ihre Begründung durch Friedrich den Grossen* that Frederick, in introducing the silk industry in Prussia, found the first useful tools for his endeavors in the French colony and among the Jews of the capital.[32]

Frederick the Great wished to make use of wealthy Jews to found not only the silk industry but also many other branches of industry. As he remarked: "We want these rentings of agrarian objects [cows] by Jews to cease and be no longer permitted, since protection is extended to them mainly for the development of trade, manufacture, commerce, goods, etc. Only to Christian people is reserved the occupation of agriculture; everybody must stay within his own field of activity [*Fach*]." The "field" of activity of wealthy Jews was industry and commerce, not agriculture.[33] Acquisition of land, however, was forbidden not only to the Jews but also to the German Christian burgher. It was not until the victories of Napoleon at Jena and Auerstädt in 1806 that this disability of the Prussian middle class was abolished. Then followed rapidly Stein's and Hardenberg's reforms, which put an end to many an anachronism in Prussia, including the inequality of the Jews.

As a result of Poland's first partition in 1772 a sizable number of Polish Jews became Prussian subjects. Among them were only a few wealthy individuals. Just as in the case of Silesia, the Prussian monarch wished to keep only wealthy Jews, who were engaged in trade and industry and promised to enrich the state treasury, and to settle them along the Netze River to trade with the Poles. Frederick II also took special interest in the Jewish population that lived before the gates of Danzig. This city, inhabited by Germans, had not fallen to Prussia, and Frederick, always thinking in terms of Prussian rather than German interests, was determined to carry on an economic struggle against it to further Prussia's trade. When the Jews residing around Danzig asked the King for a patent of protection, they stressed in their petition that through their trade they had already caused great injury to the city of Danzig. "This report was very favorably received by the King," since it fitted admirably into his policy. The King therefore immediately granted them the letter of protection.[34] Prussian state interests thus made Frederick the Great and the Jews around Danzig allies against this German city.

While Frederick wished to retain the rich West Prussian Jews, he issued an order to eject all "beggar Jews" from the new provinces, "successively and without haste." Little did he then think of his own words: "False zeal is a tyrant who depopulates the provinces. Tolerance is a tender mother who makes them flourish."[35] Frederick the Great let everybody be "happy after his own fashion," but these Jews had to look for happiness beyond the borders of Prussia. Such contradictions between the words and deeds of Frederick II were by no means rare. The official Dohmhardt opposed the sudden ejection of the West Prussian Jews and dared to present objections to the King: "His Majesty so far has made his government memorable by toleration of all religions; a sudden ejection would contradict not only a general feeling of humanity but also those lofty ideas."[36] But Dohmhardt's appeal met with a cold reception; about four thousand Jews were compelled to leave the country.

Frederick did, however, free moneyed Jews from the hard yoke that pressed upon their coreligionists, granting them the *Generalprivilegia* which Christian merchants usually received. "The rise of Jewry in Berlin," Constantin Frantz, an anti-Semitic writer of the late nineteenth century, remarked regretfully, in accusation of Frederick the Great, "does not date from yesterday. The beginnings extend rather back to the great Frederick."[37] By strengthening the social and economic position of Prussia's wealthy Jewry, Frederick the Great indeed made civil equality of the Jews with the rest of the population unavoidable. But this was a consequence of the policy upon which he embarked rather than its motive.[38] The Jewish historian Selma Stern, in a comprehensive examination of Frederick's policy toward the Jews, reached the conclusion that the Prussian King used the Jews as instruments of his mercantilist policy to his best advantage; he acted not for their own sake, since he still considered their economic activity occasionally harmful, but for the sake of furthering the interests of the Prussian state. Yet Frederick II paved the way toward the economic, cultural, and, ultimately, the political emancipation of the Jews.

That the anti-Semitic writings of Voltaire, especially *Le Dictionnaire philosophique* and *Le Traité de la Tolerance,* considerably influenced Frederick the Great and strengthened the traditional hostility toward Jews in Prussia can be taken for granted. Like Voltaire, Frederick derided and castigated what he considered childish tales of religions—revelations, miracles, and religious ceremonials—as well as ambitious priests and gullible masses. Voltaire's major interest in refuting not only Judaism but also Christianity struck a responsive chord in the Prussian King. Yet basically Frederick II, like Joseph II, was motivated by considerations of whether and to what extent the Jews of his state could be made into a pliable instrument of state policy.

Enlightenment had not only a negative but also a positive influence on Frederick II's policy toward the Jews. Though it may have deepened some prejudices, it eradicated many more. A great number of Frederick's ministers, sons of the proud Prussian aristocracy and of the educated bourgeoisie, had studied at the universities of Frankfurt an der Oder, Königsberg, and Halle and had become imbued with the ideas of Christian Thomasius, who was a pioneer of the ideas of the Enlightenment in Europe and had spoken out against the lie of

Jewish ritual murder. Such enlightened and humanitarian Prussian bureaucrats, increasingly independent even in matters of Jewish policy, dared to challenge the monarch and present more pragmatic and tolerant points of view.

Frederick the Great himself shared the views of the Enlightenment regarding state and religion: the religious conviction of the individual was less important to him than the obedience and fidelity of the subject to the ruler. As the King wrote in his political Testament of 1752, Catholics, Lutherans, Calvinists, Jews, and many other sects lived together peacefully in Prussia. He feared that preferential treatment of any of them would result in bitter wrangles, persecutions, and, finally, in the emigration of those persecuted, which would only enrich neighboring states. The government ought to be satisfied with any religion that impressed upon its adherents the need for fulfilling their duties to the state. A decided opponent of religious fanaticism on pragmatic, economic, and philosophical grounds, he favored instead toleration, which would guarantee each individual freedom of conscience. Though a proponent of tolerance and humanitarianism in theory, Frederick in practice did not show compassion toward those Jews at the bottom of Prussia's economic and social scale.

Frederick II, who surrounded himself with men of culture, appreciated knowledge and wit. He often received the Jewish philosopher Moses Mendelssohn and paid his respects to him. Frederick the Great had granted him a letter of protection, which enabled him to stay in Berlin. The French philosopher Marquis d'Argens, author of the *Lettres Juives* and a member of Frederick's French circle in Potsdam, had intervened in behalf of "son cher Moïse" with these words: "Un philosophe mauvais catholique supplie un philosophe mauvais protestant de donner de privilège à un philosophe mauvais Juif. Il y a dans ceci trop de philosophie, pour que la raison ne soit pas du côté de la demande."[*39]

On several occasions Moses Mendelssohn had praised Frederick the Great, but like other German authors he had also dared to blame Frederick for his predilection for French language and culture and his lack of regard, even contempt, for Germans and for contemporary German literature. In regard to German language and culture, Moses Mendelssohn—whose native language was not German but who had learned to write it brilliantly—was a greater patriot than Frederick, who, though occasionally pitted militarily against the French, as in the Seven Years' War, was at the same time convinced of the superi-

*A philosopher who is a bad Catholic requests a philosopher who is a bad Protestant to issue a letter of protection to a philosopher who is a bad Jew. There is in all this too much philosophy, for reason not to support the plea.

ority of French culture and civilization and wrote in French rather than in German, which he never mastered.

A plan to erect a monument in honor of Leibnitz, Lambert, and Sulzer was under study when Moses Mendelssohn died. When it was suggested that Mendelssohn be included in their company, Frederick II was consulted. He is supposed to have replied: "Why do you ask me? Don't you know that I esteem every religion and particularly the scholar and wise man?"[40] Yet while Mendelssohn was alive, the King had refused to comply with the wishes of the Academy of Berlin to make the Jewish philosopher a member. Frederick's rejection of Mendelssohn for membership in the Academy has been looked upon as proof of his general opposition to the Jews. But according to the historian of the Prussian Academy of Sciences, the Frenchman Barthélmess, Frederick's refusal to consider Mendelssohn had important diplomatic motives, not anti-Jewish ones. Frederick wanted Catherine II, Empress of Russia, to be made the new member of the Academy of Sciences at Berlin, hoping thus to gain her good will.[41] Under the circumstances it was hardly surprising that Mendelssohn lost.

In a letter to the French philosopher D'Alembert, Frederick remarked: "Jesus was a Jew and we burn the Jews."[42] Shortly before his death the Prussian King touched upon the Jewish question in a talk with another Frenchman, H. G. Mirabeau, who was soon to play a major role in the French Revolution. Mirabeau was generally very critical of Frederick's Jewish policy but seemed highly gratified about his conversation with the Prussian ruler: "Tell Dohm," he wrote to an acquaintance, referring to the German author of the much discussed book *Über die bürgerliche Verbesserung der Juden* [On the Civil Improvement of the Jews] (1781), "we have talked very nicely about the Jews and about tolerance. I advise the fanatics not to get angry about it."[43]

Dohm's "Über die Bürgerliche Verbesserung der Juden"

The rays of the Enlightenment did not banish all fanatics or every fanaticism, but the new era did give birth to new ideas and proposals, including new ideas about policy toward the Jews. This is splendidly demonstrated by the work of the Prussian administrative official, diplomat, and writer, Christian Wilhelm Dohm. He submitted his views on the situation of the Jews to the German public, demanding a humane and just solution to the pressing problem, only a few months

before the publication of the Edict of Toleration by the Austrian
Emperor Joseph II. A great admirer of Frederick the Great, to whom
he dedicated his main work, *Denkwürdigkeiten meiner Zeit* [Memoirs
of My Time], Dohm had succeeded in his long-held ambition to exchange teaching and writing for Prussian public service. He made it
his business to propagate, as he wrote, "the spirit of true humanity"
in all fields of human endeavor and to "fight against the old and the
new prejudices which separate men in such a sad manner."[44]

When in 1781 Moses Mendelssohn was approached by several
Alsatian Jews to write a memoir in behalf of their people to the
French Council of State, he had turned to Dohm, whose acquaintance
he had made in Berlin, and suggested that he undertake this task.
Since Dohm, as he revealed, had always taken a great interest in the
history of the Jewish people, Mendelssohn's request was very welcome. With great enthusiasm he turned to writing the "Mémoire sur
l'état des Juifs en Alsace." Dohm's study of the situation of the
Alsatian Jews aroused in turn his interest in the status of the Jews in
Germany, and this led subsequently to his reform proposals for the
improvement of their status.[45] In the second part of *Über die
bürgerliche Verbesserung der Juden,* which appeared in 1783, he joyfully recorded that "one of the noblest and generally most beloved of
our princes" had already given his "approval" to his plans, alluding
to Joseph II.

Dohm demanded full equality of the Jews with the Christian
population for humanitarian reasons as well as on the basis of natural
rights: "The oppressive condition under which the Jews at present
still live in most states, is only a relic of the unwise and inhuman
prejudices of the darkest centuries, and therefore does not deserve to
continue in our times."[46] Dohm tried to demonstrate from history
how the Jews have been "corrupt as human beings and citizens,
because one has denied them the rights of both." He wished "to
encourage the governments . . . to increase the number of their good
citizens by not causing them any longer to be bad ones." The "miserable and oppressive conditions" in which the Jews still found themselves almost everywhere "would explain, though not justify, an even
greater corruption on their part." Everything they had been reproached for had grown from the "political condition under which
they lived" and "any other human race placed into the same circumstances would certainly make itself guilty of the same offenses." The
Jews were bound to "feel dislike for other peoples who derived their
holy teachings from theirs and still persecuted them everywhere."

Viewing the Jews' shortcomings, he felt only guilt and shame.
"We always were the rulers," he wrote; "it was up to us to instill in

the Jews human feelings by giving them proofs of our own. We had to rid ourselves of our own prejudices to cure the Jew of his prejudices against us. If these today still deter the Jew from being a good citizen, a sociable human being, if he feels dislike of and hatred against Christians, if he believes himself not bound toward them by the same laws of honesty, then all this is our work. . . . We are guilty of the offenses of which we accuse him." The faults of the Jews, the result of oppression by European peoples through centuries, cannot and should not be reason "to justify the further continuance of a faulty policy." The solution of the Jewish problem lay, he held, in removing the unjust oppression and in granting equal rights, freedom in the choice of trade and profession, and free admission to business and agriculture.

Because prejudices against the Jews were still prevalent, Dohm believed it necessary to proceed cautiously in some fields so as not to produce a backlash. He seemed convinced of the tactical wisdom of moving slowly, of traveling "the middle of the road." Dohm advised that some types of agricultural work, as well as some branches of manufacture and military and civil service, remain forbidden to the Jews. Yet he looked upon such qualifications as strictly "provisional, temporary limitations," as "transitory regulations."*

Those who received Dohm's book in a friendly manner approved his criticism of the treatment of the Jews and paid him recognition for having turned the attention of the Germans to this urgent problem. H. F. Diez in his book *Über die Juden* [On the Jews] considered Dohm's description of the sad conditions under which the Jews still lived, "moving." "It would be an unspeakable shame for our era which boasts so much of its enlightenment," he wrote, "if barbarities, devised in the darkness of superstition, would continue much longer!"[47] The reviewer of Dohm's book in the learned magazine *Allgemeine Deutsche Bibliothek* observed that Dohm's "love for the most unfortunate of the co-citizens" did honor to his heart,[48] and the preacher Schwager in his discussion of Dohm's book in the *Minden'sches Intelligenzblatt* spoke in similar vein of the "heavy yoke of

---

*Dohm earned the gratitude of the Jews not only on account of *Über die bürgerliche Verbesserung der Juden*. Repeatedly he pleaded for their equality. His endeavors found a resounding echo around the conference table at the Congress at Aachen in 1818. Dohm was then associated with an English minister named Lewis Way, who on many occasions had already demanded their equality. In the year 1819 Way decided on publishing in Paris a petition and some other pertinent documents under the title *Mémoires sur l'état des Israélites, dédiés et presentés à leur majestés impériales et royales, réunies au Congrès d'Aix-la-Chapelle*. This time the booklet contained also "Remarques" and a special memorandum, both the work of Dohm. The "Remarques," which carry the date November 12, 1818, breathe the same spirit of far-seeing rational statesmanship and also of warm friendship for the Jews which had distinguished his earlier book.

slavery" that pressed upon the Jews and wished them a more fortunate lot.[49] The critic of Dohm's study in the *Ephemeriden der
Menschheit* held that it was the duty of the rulers to compensate the
Jews for the injuries which had been inflicted upon them and for the
miseries which they had suffered.[50] Even Professor Michaelis of
Göttingen, whose criticism of Dohm's work stirred Moses Mendelssohn to a reply, paid Dohm the tribute that he had become "the
advocate of the poorer elements among the Jews."[51]

As much as the reviewers extolled Dohm's high motives, commiserated with the Jews, and were willing to concede German responsibility for their current condition, the German public as a whole
remained cool to Dohm's practical proposals. Waitzel, in Rotteck's
and Welcker's famous *Encyclopädie der Staatswissenschaften* [Ency-
clopedia of Political Science], later summed up correctly that in spite
of the general praise bestowed upon Dohm, the expectation that Jews
be granted the right of citizens was declared to be absurd.[52]

Some of the critics suggested baptism as a solution to the Jewish
problem—a "solution" which of course church and state had held
out to the Jews for many centuries. H. F. Diez feared lest the Jews,
for religious reasons, would never become as good citizens as the
Christians.[53] Michaelis of Göttingen voiced the same view and therefore recommended conversion to the Jews.[54] The reviewer of Dohm's
work in the *Allgemeine Deutsche Bibliothek* hoped similarly that the
Jews would come closer to the Christian religion and thus bridge the
gap between Judaism and Germandom.[55] Many, as for instance Michaelis, looked upon the Jews as "foreigners"[56] and "aliens"[57] and
were therefore opposed to their increase.

The response to Dohm's appeal underlined, if not the religious
fervor of his critics, the widespread German conviction that the gulf
between German Christians and Jews could be bridged only if the
latter were prepared to abandon their religious identity, shed their
cultural heritage, and, in effect, commit suicide as a people. The
Jews' cultural and religious heritage was deemed not suitable to the
modern age and not adaptable to coexistence with German Christianity. The "tolerance" of the age, as far as Jews and Judaism were
concerned, was still a mere sham and illusion.

CHAPTER 2

From Gellert and Klopstock to Lessing and Herder

Influence of the Enlightenment and Classicism

In the later part of the eighteenth century hostility to the Jews was widely on the decline, at least in the intellectual realm. During the era of the Enlightenment and of Classicism the spirit of humanity, of tolerance and cosmopolitanism, prevailed. It was in this period that the flag of equality for the Jews began to be unfurled and the first serious discussions about their emancipation commenced. Beneficent as the influence of the Enlightenment was in many respects, it also had, as shall be seen, negative aspects and an adverse impact upon the German-Jewish relationship.

Positive, as noted, was the utilitarian and pragmatic outlook of Enlightened Absolutism, desirous to make the Jews as useful to the state as possible. This outlook was also in harmony with the prevailing ideas in France and England, their general policies, and their particular policy toward the Jews. In the mid-eighties of the eighteenth century the Academy of Metz posed in its literary competition the question "How to make the Jews more useful and more happy in France?" The question pointed to the dominant utilitarian bent that marked contemporary political thought in Western Europe. To it must be added the growing need of an expanding economy for manpower during the second half of the eighteenth century. England and Holland were frequently held up as examples of the benefits a more liberal policy toward the Jews was likely to reap. But the emergence of a more generous policy of Enlightened Absolutism toward the Jews and the new trends of thought about them cannot be fully understood unless the influence of the philosophy of the Enlightenment and Classicism upon contemporaries is more fully analyzed.

A feeling of guilt for past sins and a growing sense of justice and humanitarianism characterized the new era. Sensitive individuals, attempting to atone for the misdeeds and mistakes of centuries, began to display a more humane attitude toward the Jews. They extolled their noble qualities and attributed their less admirable traits, real or alleged, to the effects of their hard, oppressive past. These Germans expressed a belief in the desirability and the possibility of improving the character of the Jews—indeed of all peoples—by ending injustice, inequality, and oppression.

The German intelligentsia of the era of the Enlightenment included men who had freed themselves from many prejudices and were not afraid to upbraid their own people for intolerance. Many Germans, on the other hand, still opposed the Jews and met them, as Gellert observed, with "contempt" and even "violence," determined to keep them suppressed. "The mob among the Christians," the contemporary physician and writer J. G. Zimmermann observed, "sees in the Jews, without exception, a people dead to virtue . . . , sunk into greed, fraud and extortion."[1]

On the whole, however, the German Jews found more understanding and friendship among men of education, knowledge, and refinement than among the common people, who remained caught in the whirlpool of cultural, religious, and other prejudices. The more enlightened attitude of the thinkers and writers of the Enlightenment and of Classicism was in close harmony with their entire *Weltanschauung,* their cosmopolitanism, their belief in reason, in the dignity of man, in education, and in general progress. But even they had not entirely cast off the prejudices of the age. Their criticism of the Jews may have been in part apt, but it was no less often harsh. Neither Germans nor Jews were capable of looking at each other in a truly detached and impartial manner.

The era of the Enlightenment and of enlightened absolutism was also the period of a most impressive upsurge of the German spirit. A strong belief in the power of reason and in the possibility of rational reform of social and political life characterized the new age. A main feature of the new gospel was a belief in the capacity of the human character to move closer to perfection. Superstition and prejudice were believed to be receding before rationalism. According to the men of the Enlightenment, who trusted the future, hate between human beings was doomed: reason was to be the ultimate victor over crude passion.

Religious hatred and in particular religious persecution, which had raged in Europe for centuries, were now most severely condemned for the tremendous harm they had caused. To Johann Christoph Gottsched, a widely influential professor of literature at the University of Leipzig, nothing was more intolerable than religious hatred, nothing more contemptible than religious persecution: "I see as many hostile religious parties in the world as religions. . . . Through the irrational zeal of its protagonists, religiosity has become the sad cause of thousandfold unhappiness. Most of the blood the earth has drunk has been spilled on account of religion."[2] Religious fanaticism was considered the source of all evil.

The Enlightenment had a considerable influence on the relationship between Germans and Jews. The flourishing of individualism and cosmopolitanism, the simultaneous recession of national and religious exclusiveness, and the popularity of Deism, the religious fashion of the age, all tended to establish closer links between Germans and Jews. The struggle of reason against prejudices of every sort, the belief in the power of education, and the conviction that every individual and every people was naturally disposed to goodness, all explain the change in attitude, particularly of the German intellectual elite, toward the Jews.

The influence of the Enlightenment on the relations between Germans and Jews was, however, not entirely favorable. While it placed the Jew in a brighter light, at times it cast a new shadow on him. By reducing religious prejudices the Enlightenment had a beneficent effect upon the relationship between Germans and Jews. But by attacking traditional Christianity and, along with it, the Old Testament and ancient Judaism, it partly nullified its salutary work. The men of the Enlightenment were also inclined to see in traditional Judaism, of which they knew very little, the quintessence of blind superstition and stubborn irrationalism. They pitied the Jews as objects of greed, hate, and fanatic persecution, but they found little in their history, culture, and religion to stir admiration.

The Enlightenment in German-speaking countries was part and parcel of a European-wide intellectual movement, the heart and soul of which was France. It was there that the movement originated, there that it had its most prominent spokesmen, and there that it was to achieve its most impressive political results. Though the Enlightenment everywhere in Europe took on characteristic national garb, the influence of the French *philosophes* on the spokesmen and thinkers of the German Enlightenment in all social, cultural, and political matters, including attitudes toward the Jews, was quite apparent. Herder referred directly to the dispute between Voltaire and Pinto about the Jews,[3] and Dohm was deeply involved in the struggle of the French Jews, especially the Alsatian Jews, for equality against unrelenting opponents. For the next century France's impact upon the situation of the German Jews and upon German thought about them would be deep and penetrating.

The French Enlightenment had both pro-Jewish and anti-Jewish figures among its spokesmen. Judged from a strictly logical point of view, the men of the Enlightenment should have rushed to the defense of the Jews, a people oppressed for centuries; they should have unfurled the flag of equality and should have lived up to their faith in human progress and acted in accordance with their denunciation of the Dark Ages and of the repression by the Inquisition. Indeed the spirit of the Enlightenment found articulate expression in the writings of Montesquieu, especially in his *L'Esprit des Lois* [Spirit of Laws], which denounced the Inquisition and appealed for humane treatment of the Jews. To Montesquieu, as becomes clear in his *Lettres persanes* [Persian Letters], tolerance in a world marked by the greatest diversity of religious and political views and customs was simply a necessity. In the *Lettres persanes* he considered Judaism the "ancient trunk" that produced the two branches, Christianity and Islam. Publicly he also favored toleration of the Jews; his historic-philosophical view that culture was shaped by climate and environment excluded the notion of any innately evil and obnoxious national character.

But other champions of the French Enlightenment, though they condemned the Inquisition, did not show true compassion toward some of its main victims, the Jews. While Diderot's article on the Crusades was sharply critical of the massacres of the Jews, the articles of the *Encyclopédie* on Jews and Judaism showed little sympathy for them.[4] Mirabeau remarked aptly that only a few thinkers of the Enlightenment were pro-Jewish.[5]

Though Voltaire was frequently ambiguous, the major thrust of his thought was anti-Semitic. In his study *The French Enlightenment and the Jews* (1968), Arthur Hertzberg concluded that Voltaire, its leading spirit, was an anti-Semite and that for the following century he provided "the fundamentals of the rhetoric of secular anti-Semitism."[6] Voltaire certainly contributed to the ambivalence that marked the era of Jewish emancipation and laid the groundwork for its setbacks and its twentieth-century debacle.

One major reason for Voltaire's puzzling attitude was, as André Maurois has pointed out, the infatuation of the men and women of the Enlightenment with Classicism.[7] The *philosophes* idolized Greco-Roman antiquity as the golden age of humanity and adopted many ancient, pagan standards. Thus Voltaire turned against Christianity *and* Judaism—against the former because it had brought antiquity to ruin, against the latter because it had given birth to Christianity. Voltaire battled both religions for their enmity to antiquity and eagerly embraced in turn the hostility of the ancients to the Jews. He lumped Christianity and Judaism together as the enemy and made the Bible, which was holy to both, a major target; he ignored the fact that the Jews had been the primary target of Christian persecution for centuries. Similarly, Diderot's *Encyclopédie* contained a slur on Jesus, a "fanatical and obscure Jew." Diderot directed sharp attacks against the Talmud and criticized the Jews for their alleged sedition in Egypt, for their fanaticism and their blind respect for the authority of their rabbis, and, on the whole, for being "an ignorant and superstitious people."[8] This analysis culminated in the hardly startling recommendation that the Jews "be kept separate" from other peoples. Jews, who might have expected liberation during the Enlightenment, instead found themselves attacked and vilified by many of its spokesmen and were compelled to add another foe to the long list of traditional enemies.

It was perhaps equally paradoxical that in Germany it was the Romantic movement, on the whole hostile to the Jews, that tried to ward off these attacks. Thus the early Romantic Georg Hamann became the defender of religion in general and protagonist of Judaism in particular against non-German philosophers of the Enlightenment such as Voltaire and Henry St. John, 1st Viscount Bolingbroke. In defending the Old Testament and ancient Judaism, Johann Gottfried Herder competed with his close friend Hamann. In the *Briefe das Studium der Theologie betreffend* [Letters Relating to the Study of Theology] (1780) Herder asked the following question: "Where is such a magnificent people which the gods approached, as the Lord approached this people? Where is such a magnificent people which possessed such just morals and commands as were these commands of God?"[9] A great expounder of the Bible, Herder blazed a trail that biblical scholarship was subsequently to follow. Rationalist sophistry had tried to convince the world that the Bible was the creation of a primitive and backward people. Herder, a forerunner of Romanticism, blunted these attacks.

It was not only rationalism's assault on Christianity, the Bible, and ancient Judaism that cast a new gloom upon German-Jewish relations; the fashionable cult of Classicism had the same effect. With the Enlightenment, Classicism turned the thoughts of contemporaries back to antiquity, to Greece, which revered beauty and created a great literature and philosophy, and to Rome, its politics and its law. Toward the end of the eighteenth century the cult of antiquity—a result partly of the studies of Johann Winckelmann—reached a climax in Germany. The art and science, morals and politics of all nations were measured by the accomplishments of the Greeks and Romans.

Their civilizations constituted the model, and other nations necessarily fell short of this unattainable ideal. Schiller, in the poem "Die Götter Griechenlands" [The Gods of Greece] longed for the beauty of antiquity and regretted that its flowers had fallen before "the dreadful winds blowing from the North."

In contrast with Greeks and Romans, the Jews fared no better than the Nordic peoples. The opinions of many contemporaries about the Jews were unquestionably warped by their predilection for Greeks and Romans. This prejudice is exemplified even by the German-Jewish poet Heinrich Heine, who wrote toward the end of his life that his "Hellenic nature felt repelled by Jewish asceticism."[10] The German philosopher Hegel, who was to find in later years "great trends" in Jewish history, gave expression in his youth to his dislike of the Jews, offering the following rationalization: "The great tragedy of the Jewish people," he wrote, "is not a Greek tragedy."*[11]

The Changing Image of the Jew in Literature

While some of the *Dichter und Denker* lamented that the Jews were not ancient Greeks, the common people held other grievances against them. They were hardly influenced by the adverse comments of the young Hegel or those of the enlightened French *philosophes* but rather by Christian Germany's legacy of anti-Jewish attitudes. Early in the eighteenth century this legacy had crystallized in the treatise of Johann Andreas Eisenmenger, *Entdecktes Judentum* [Judaism Unmasked], which repeated all the age-old distortions and hate-filled condemnations of the Jewish religion and of the Talmud in particular. Eisenmenger charged that the Jewish religion was dominated by demons and unholy spirits and that it expressed hatred and contempt for Christians and Christianity. The masses were also receptive to hearing the Jews accused once again of unsavory business practices and questionable ethics, of usury, cheating, fraud, and economic exploitation. They doubted that Jews considered themselves Germans and, since the Jews prayed for the coming of the Messiah and for their return to Jerusalem, to Zion, questioned their loyalty to the German community.

---

*Goethe too was a "Hellene." Although he often showed his high esteem for ancient Judaism, once, while reading Homer, he exclaimed: "At the renewed study of Homer I now fully feel the unspeakable misery the Jewish debauchery [*Prass*] has brought upon us." (The anti-Semitic writer Max Maurenbrecher conceded that this deprecatory remark of Goethe about the Old Testament was unique.) Decades later Schopenhauer similarly regretted that European civilization had developed on a Judaeo-Christian basis rather than on a Greek foundation.

As we have seen, Christian Wilhelm Dohm was the leader in the defense of the Jews against such attacks and the pioneer in reforming policy toward them. But it was in the field of German public opinion and in German literature in particular that a change in the image of the Jews was first noticeable. A literary predecessor of the work of Dohm was the novel *Das Leben der schwedischen Gräfin von G.* [The Life of the Swedish Countess of G.] by the German poet Christian Fürchtegott Gellert—the "praeceptor Germaniae" (educator of Germany), as he was called. The novel had been published in the year 1746, three years before the publication of the drama *Die Juden* [The Jews] by the young Lessing. For the first time the German Jew appeared in a brighter, more favorable light. Gellert had lifted the ban that had prevented German poets, playwrights, and novelists from seeing the Jew as anything but a usurer and anti-Christ.

Gellert described movingly the self-sacrifice and gratitude of a Jew for his rescuer, a Swedish count who has been exiled to Siberia. The Jew alleviated the count's harsh imprisonment and finally helped him to escape. After many years their paths crossed again. "The Jew's heart was indeed like his honest and simple face, and his manners pleased because of his heart. He had already aged, and his gray beard and his long Polish fur gave him a very dignified appearance. The friendly manner in which we treated him and whereby we tried to show him our appreciation moved him particularly. . . . The honest man! Many perhaps of this people would have better hearts, if we, through contempt and shrewd violence, did not make them even more vile and fraudulent, and if by our conduct we did not compel them to hate our religion!"[12]

The Protestant minister, pietist, and writer Johann Timotheus Hermes was decisively influenced by Gellert. In the foreword of his novel *Sophiens Reise von Memel nach Sachsen* [Sophie's Journey from Memel to Saxony],[13] which achieved great popularity among contemporaries, he confessed his admiration for Gellert, whose novel had inspired him to picture likewise a noble Jew. One of the Jewish characters in his novel, which appeared more than two decades after that of Gellert, is a physician who with love and care attends to poor Christian patients and generously offers them his help in many ways.

Not all the Jews in Hermes' novel are favorably portrayed. Many return the hate of Christians with hatred of their own. But like Gellert before him, Hermes pictured some Jews as noble, honorable, and friendly and rebuked Christians for their harshness toward them and their suspicion against them. Similarly the satirist Gottlieb Wilhelm Rabener—who belonged to the circle of the so-called "Contributors of Bremen" (*Bremer Beiträger*) and was close to Gellert—bared in the satire "Life and Deeds of an Honest Bankrupt"[14] the anti-Semitic feelings and practices of many contemporary Germans.

Klopstock

Joseph II's emancipation of the Jews in Austria was favorably received by the many Germans who were imbued with the prevailing ideas of humanity and tolerance. The Austrian Emperor's liberating acts found a particularly enthusiastic echo in Friedrich Gottlieb Klopstock, the revered patriarch of German poetry and author of the great epic *Der Messias* [Messiah]. Klopstock, whose German national feeling is strongly expressed in his patriotic odes, shared, nevertheless, the cosmopolitan sentiments of his age and its belief in progress. Patriotic views and a freedom-loving disposition did not exclude but rather complemented one another.

Klopstock celebrated the North American War of Independence, praised the French Revolution, and extolled the liberating work of Joseph II, including the emancipation of the Jews:

> You call the priest to be again the disciple
> Of the great Founder, you make a citizen
> Of the yoke-laden man, you make of
> The Jew a human being. . . .

Klopstock commiserated with the Jewish people, his sympathy with the victims of oppression climaxing in condemnation of their tormentors:

> Who is not seized by the shudder of compassion when he sees
> How our mob dehumanizes the people of Canaan?
> And doesn't it indulge in it because our princes
> Lay upon them too heavy chains?
> You, Savior, loosen the rusty,
> Tightly fettered chain from their sore arm.
> They hardly feel it, don't believe it. So long
> Has it rattled on the miserable ones.[15]

Klopstock's dramatic production embraced six dramas. Three of these are grouped around the Germanic warrior-hero Arminius (Hermann), victor over the Roman armies. The other dramatic trilogy borrows its themes from the Bible. Klopstock's three biblical dramas are *Der Tod Adams* [The Death of Adam], *David,* and *Salomo.* In choosing subjects for his dramas Klopstock harked back to early Germanic history and also to Jewish history. In the foreword to *Der Tod Adams*, the playwright anticipated the objection of some readers to his borrowing the motive of his tragedy from the Holy Scriptures: "The great men which the Bible has preserved us," he wrote somewhat apologetically, "deserve as much to appear before us as the great men of paganism. . . . I do not understand why I should not esteem Salomon as highly as Titus."[16] In a similar manner the Swiss Salomon Gessner, powerfully impressed with Klopstock's *Der Messias*, found it necessary to defend himself because of his treatment of a biblical subject.[17] In his drama *Salomo* Klopstock puts the idea of freedom of belief into the mouth of the doubting biblical king.[18] Klopstock's dislike of religious compulsion also found lively expression in another of his works, *Die deutsche Gelehrtenrepublik* [The German Republic of Scholars], wherein he granted tolerance to everybody but "inquisitorially minded Christians."[19]

The poet of religion, which Klopstock shows himself to be, particularly in *Der Messias*, turns to religion as

> . . . holy friend of men!
> Daughter of God, most lofty teacher of virtue, peace.

Yet religion is a two-edged weapon:

> A sword in the hand of the raging! Priestess of blood
> and of strangling!
> Daughter of the first rebel! No religion any longer![20]

The most sublime is turned by the fanatic into the abject. A "horror of men" overwhelmed the poet whenever he thought of how "incapable people are to separate religion from bloodthirstiness."[21]

Klopstock's great epic *Der Messias*, the favorite book of the young Goethe and his sister, affected contemporaries very strongly. In content and style the epic closely follows the Holy Scriptures; whole sentences are patterned after them. Johann Gottfried Herder, in "Dialog zwischen einem Rabbiner und einem Christen in Klopstocks 'Messias' " ["Dialogue between a Rabbi and a Christian in Klopstock's 'Messiah' "] lets the rabbi praise Klopstock for having "built an Oriental monument on German soil, for the honor of our people."[22] *Der Messias* is a description of the redeeming work of Jesus. In grandeur of conception and development, it can be compared only to the greatest literary works, to Dante's *Divine Comedy* or Milton's *Paradise Lost*. The poem is saturated with the spirit of Christianity. Yet religion as conceived by Klopstock is not identical with divisiveness, it does not thrive upon hate or "bloodthirstiness," it is active love.[23] Klopstock's *Messias* does not arouse dislike or hatred of the Jews.

Like Klopstock's poem on Joseph II, the poem "The Eternal Jew" by Christian Friedrich Daniel Schubart, one of the most vigorous *Stürmer und Dränger** (members of the "Storm and Stress" movement), is another echo of the emancipatory effort of the Austrian Emperor. Schubart's son remarked about his father's poem that it was merely a fragment of a more comprehensive work, based perhaps on the most original plan Schubart ever devised. Schubart recounts in the poem how Ahasver in the Holy Land had driven Jesus from his threshold when the Savior wished to rest on his last journey. As punishment he must wander without rest all over the earth until Judgment Day, not to be delivered from his misery by death. Ahasver tells how often he has vainly sought death, how he has rushed into the grimmest battle, has tried to drown himself in the ocean waves and to be burned to death in the lava stream of the Etna. The bite of the poisonous snake has not killed him, and even sneering at the tyrant has not brought about the hoped-for punishment. Finally, an angel announced to Ahasver in a dream that God would not forever be angry with him:

> When you awaken, he will be here
> Whose blood on Golgotha you saw flow.
> And who forgives you too.[24]

Ahasver's personality is pictured by the poet in all its loftiness and fearfulness, yet it also evokes pity.

The same figure, the eternal Jew, reveals both Schubart's humane and friendly attitude toward the Jews and the animosity toward them of Maler (Friedrich) Müller, another vigorous member of the "Storm and Stress" movement. In Müller's "Das Leben Fausts" [Faust's Life] Ahasver strides across the stage stammering like an imbecile, and the contemporary Jews, such as Izick and Mauschel, are shrewd, greedy, and unrefined. They speak Yiddish, are unable to converse in German, and display questionable morals. Mauschel is ready to steal from the authorities to secure his rights. Unmercifully, both Jewish characters insist that Faust, who has become bondsman for two debtors, indemnify them. The naive philosopher, who does not know the world and abandons himself entirely to the realm of thought, is contrasted to the noisy Jews, representatives of the "trite

*A movement expressing individualism and rebellion, influenced by Rousseau and critical of tradition in literature and life.

and indifferent," avid for the material values of this world, who chase
in vain after tranquility and satisfaction.[25] These portraits of Jews
show that though "Storm and Stress" battled against outworn tradition, it did nothing to uproot traditional prejudice against the Jews,
even among its own members.

Wieland

Christoph Martin Wieland, poet, satirist, and critic of his era—the
"German Voltaire" as some contemporaries called him—launched in
1775, in the fourth issue of his widely respected magazine *Der
teutsche Merkur,* a strong attack on the oppressive conditions under
which the Jews were compelled to live. He recommended the article
"Gedanken über das Schicksal der Juden" [Thoughts about the Fate
of the Jews], of which he was most likely the author, in the following
footnote: "Forwarded by an anonymous person whom all well-
meaning readers of the *Merkur* will love, as I do, and with whom they
will wish to get acquainted."[26]

Reading about the "oppression of the Negro slaves" in Africa
had turned the writer's thought "to that almost countless mass . . .
which lives in the utmost moral wretchedness right among us who are
Christians . . . and who first of all should practice genuine compassion." "My heart bleeds," the author confessed, coming face to face
with Jewish misery. The Jewish people, "as if not sufficiently piti-
able, should also become the victim of our contempt, of our injustice,
our greed? Men! What is your opinion?"

He continued: "We hate the Jews because they speak another
language, have other customs than we have. We persecute them because God has punished them for their sins with blindness so that
they, for the sake of their redemption, cannot believe what we believe; we despise them because they acquire theirs [their property] in
a vile manner. We oppress them in order to enrich ourselves with
their belongings. Hearts of steel! Unwise slaves! Does not the welfare, all spiritual, even the greatest portion of your civil happiness
come to you through them? Where were you before the light which
rose among them shone upon you? . . . if God has rejected them, you
should know that he may well prop them up again on the right stem so
that they may bear better fruit than you."

The Jews had "purity of manners." Contempt for the Jews was
not only immoral and unwise but also unjustified. An impartial examination would show that the Jews do not lag in virtues behind other

peoples but rather surpass them. "Can we attribute the unity in which they live among themselves to anything else but the purity of their customs? Are they less good parents, less good providers, less true spouses than we? I fear lest we lose in this comparison. Can we observe these virtues without being convinced that the germ of all other civil virtues lies hidden in them and merely waits for the opportunity to break out most happily?"

The Jews, it was said, enriched themselves at the expense of the indigenous population. "If they are our clandestine parasites, we have made them this way by closing to them the door to legitimate trades. Necessity makes them what otherwise they would not be. And your own example? Who among you be without vices may throw the first stone upon them, you Christian usurers! And you are coreligionists . . . !"

The warm defense of the Jews is coupled with a bitter attack against the Germans. They were "unwise" because they "left a productive source of wealth," the capacities of the Jews, "unused" and held them down "in order to enrich themselves" at their expense. "You oppress these unfortunate ones in order to feed yourselves from their surplus. How great is the shame! How small the reward! What important things can you wrest from a mob that can enrich itself only clandestinely at your expense? Should not God punish this? And does the state profit thereby? Be human beings! Then you will reap honor and the fatherland will gain."

The author concluded his vigorous appeal with the demand that the Jews be given equal rights: "It appears to me, when I look upon these unfortunates, that the Lord has dispersed them among us in order to test our religion by a magnificent work of charity. Now then, let us be charitable toward them, toward the fatherland, toward ourselves! Let us accept them as brothers! Let us concede them privileges by means of which they may become useful members of the state! Let us give them hope that in this way they too may attain honor. . . . Then you will be right to punish them as transgressors. Grant them freedom and chain them by your laws. Treat them as you want to be treated yourselves!"

Two years before this article had appeared in *Der teutsche Merkur,* Wieland had sent a copy of his journal to the Jewish philosopher Moses Mendelssohn to interest him in the magazine and to request "the collaboration of the best of my contemporaries." "Is it true indeed," he asked, "that we have never seen each other? Does not each of us know the other's best part? . . . I greet you in the holy name of friendship. . . . Should we not know each other long enough to be able to read in the other's soul without need of an interpreter?''[27] In a letter to Zimmermann, Wieland had already confessed that he knew "few intellects in Europe whose applause could have pleased me so much as that of Herr Mendelssohn."

Wieland was also a great admirer of Joseph II, whose name appears often in his political writings. It was Joseph II who was portrayed as King Tifan in Wieland's work *Der goldene Spiegel oder die Könige von Scheschian* [The Golden Mirror or the Kings of Scheschian] (1772). Tifan is pictured as an ideal ruler, a model for the enlightened monarchs of the period. Tifan's laws on religion in his state "Scheschian" deserve particular attention, because they apparently reflect Wieland's own views.[28]

When Tifan ascends the throne, he finds his subject in a most primitive religious state, engrossed in dark superstition and deep prejudices and dominated by selfish, ignorant, and fanatic priests. Under Tifan, however, "an enlightened piety," a "rational religion, and one in accordance with the very best interests of humanity," gains ground. Superstition is "annihilated" and "fanatic fervor and intolerant principles" are "dethroned."[29]

From "this general toleration only those were excepted who were unwilling to grant to others who thought differently from them the tolerance which they claimed for themselves."[30] Tifan tried "to extirpate deeply rooted prejudices without resorting to violence" and attempted also to awaken in the new priests "sound reason" and "love of humanity." In every religion lay "some truth." "A mutual tolerance" appeared to Wieland, as he remarked in the annotations to this novel, founded on "natural fairness."[31]

Wieland won over the German reading public, which had been accustomed to turn primarily to French literature, to German writing. He was a German patriot and a cosmopolitan at the same time. He joyfully celebrated the beginnings of the French Revolution and exalted its noble principles—freedom, equality, and fraternity. Equality before the law, he particularly emphasized, would permit every citizen to compete for the position in which he could best serve the state—every citizen, "without regard to his birth, family name, and other accidental circumstances," whether he "descended in direct lineage from Nebuchadnezzar or Confucius."[32]

Prejudice and Tolerance

It was hardly to be expected that the Jews, who for centuries had been derided, oppressed, and persecuted, would, at the very dawn of a new age, suddenly be universally esteemed and loved, or even tolerated, by the entire populace. The thick, almost indissoluble, fog of prejudice lifted itself only slowly from German soil. According to his own account, Johann Heinrich Voss, the translator of the Homeric epics, had, while a young teacher, abandoned a Jewish boy in a heartless manner to the jeers and jibes of his Christian schoolmates and had even incited their mischief.[33] In his idyllic rustic epic *Louise,* however, he voiced approval of religious tolerance, including tolerance of the adherents of the Jewish faith.[34]

The writer and philosopher Georg Christian Lichtenberg, who also enjoyed a reputation as a mathematician and physicist, was not free from prejudices either. He did not love "the people of God," he confessed openly. Yet in his personal meetings with Jews he rejected any bias. In his satire "Timorus, die Verteidigung zweier Israeliten" [Timorus, the defense of two Israelites who, induced by the strength of the argumentation of Lavater and the sausages of Göttingen, have adopted the true faith],[35] Lavater is derided, and converted Jews appear in a very unfavorable light. They are thieves, blasphemers, and vagabonds. Yet Lichtenberg paints some Germans in not much brighter colors. In a surge for justice he even rebels against the unequal treatment of Jews and Christians. Thus he counters the accusation of thievery leveled against the Jews with the oratorical question: "Think only, what does stealing mean? . . . tell me only how could so many honest people at court and in the city, who take from the rich merchants their surplus, borrow and do not pay, how could so many honest guardians who embezzle the property of their wards, how could these be honest people? . . . why then does one insult this poor devil of a Jew from morning until night, and there nobody is roused? Because these persons possess not only enough knowledge to be able, if necessary, to defend themselves, but also enough power to counter emphatically such an empty calumny."

In spite of his dislike of Jews in general, Lichtenberg made some exceptions, such as Spinoza and Moses Mendelssohn; he also did not deny the injustice of the Christian world in individual cases. "A scholarly Jew of this locality, of the name of Amschel," he wrote to Ramberg, "will have sent to you an application of mine. I know, Sir, you do not love the people of God, as little as I, your obedient servant, do. But this man is an exception indeed. He is a man of cold blood and a very fine, observing intellect. He also has received here the Accessit [second-best prize] in two prize questions, and at the latter he lost the main prize for a strange reason—because his essay was too profuse, perhaps also because one does not love the people of God (this between us)."[36]

Mathias Claudius, the author of many lyric poems and of the *Botschafter von Wandsbeck* [Messenger of Wandsbeck], deeply influenced by Klopstock's religious poetry, testified on the occasion of Mendelssohn's death to the high esteem in which he had been held by the contemporary world. "I was not destined," he wrote, "to make Mr. Mendelssohn's acquaintance. . . . But like many others, I felt him to be a lucid scholarly man . . . I had a *tendre* for the Jew." And the son of a Protestant minister of Holstein added, "because of his great Father and for the sake of his religion."[37]

Author and publisher of books, Friedrich Nicolai stood in close company with Lessing and Moses Mendelssohn. Through his numerous writings and as a founder of magazines, he rendered great services to the German Enlightenment. His novel *Leben und Meinungen des Magisters Sebaldus Nothanker* [Life and Opinions of the Magister Sebaldus Nothanker], whose first volume appeared in 1773 and enjoyed immense popularity, was a battle cry against the high Lutheran clergy.[38] The hero, Sebaldus Nothanker, a minister who is imbued with ideas of the German Enlightenment, although generally somewhat passive, is a fighter in the realm of ideas.

Sebaldus Nothanker opposes every kind of religious fanaticism and believes firmly in the necessity of mutual tolerance. "God looks into the heart," he said, "and not upon the doctrine; one should therefore not condemn outright virtuous Jews and pagans."[39] Nicolai's views are expressed by Mackligius who first reproaches the "blind and obstinate Jew" but ends with the plea: "Let us, like the merciful Lord who sustains all of us, extend our tolerance not only to all Christians, but also to Jews and all other non-Christians."

This appeal appeared to be heeded by the poet Karl Wilhelm Ramler, the "German Horace." Ramler, whose odes Goethe and Lessing admired, wrote the poem "Sulamith and Eusebia, a Mourning Song at the Death of Moses Mendelssohn" for the *Berlinische Monatsschrift*.[40] On the occasion of the performance of Shakespeare's *The Merchant of Venice* in the Berliner *Staatstheater* in 1778, Ramler wrote a prologue to spare possible sensitivities and to prevent an anti-Jewish interpretation of the drama by the public.

Now since the sophisticated Berlin begins to appreciate more
  highly
The coreligionists of the wise Mendelssohn; now when we
  see men
Among this people whose prophets and first laws we honor,
Equally great in learning and arts,
Do we wish to distress this people by jeering? To give

New food to the old and unjust hatred? And
Redden the faces of those who are humanely inclined,
Who do not discriminate among poor Christians and Jews?
No, we don't want to do this! We describe also biblical
    Christians,
Depict, in abhorrence, persecuting Christians; we reprove
    the coercion
And cruelties of the monasteries against their own
    coreligionists.
Our play shows the ridiculous, the vice
Among the degenerated nobility and the tyrants of the world,
It sneers at the bad physician, insults the corrupt judge,
Punishes the greedy servant of the altar. In *Nathan the Wise*
The Christians cut a worse figure; in *The Merchant of Venice*
The Jews do. . . ."[41]

Lessing

Gotthold Ephraim Lessing was the author of the great drama *Nathan
der Weise,* in which a Jew presented the better character and Christians "cut a worse figure." Lessing, one of the most emphatic advocates of the emancipation of the Jews, was also one of the most
courageous personalities and keenest intellects of his day. During his
lifetime relentless opponents attempted to cast suspicion on his motives. After his death Jew-haters continued to revile Lessing and
slander him.

Some contemporaries of Lessing accused him of having accepted
one thousand talers from the Jews of Amsterdam for writing the play
Nathan.[42] Later, others pointed to Lessing's allegedly Slavic ancestry,[43] for the idea of tolerance could not possibly be German! While the
court preacher Adolf Stöcker, the political leader of the anti-Semites in
the newly unified German Reich, declared that Lessing's Nathan was
no Jew at all but a Christian,[44] the late nineteenth-century racial anti-
Semite Eugen Dühring indulged in completely unsubstantiated assertions about "Lessing's Jew-related or rather half-Jewish pen."[45] In the
twentieth century the leading National Socialist, Gottfried Feder, author of the twenty-five point program of the Nazis, severely reprehended the "foolish ferreting out of Jews [*Judenriecherei*] by little
informed *völkisch* people" who had allegedly discovered Lessing's
"partly Jewish ancestry."[46] Feder actually attempted to "rehabilitate"
the great man, who, because of his friendship for the Jews, could not
court popularity in anti-Semitic circles. But the German literary histo-

rian Josef Nadler, representing a different trend in *völkisch* circles, renounced Lessing and revived the "thesis" of the racial anti-Semite Dühring that Lessing was of Jewish origin.[47] He offered no evidence whatsoever to substantiate his claim.

Ideas of religious tolerance were rooted in Lessing's family. In 1669 Lessing's grandfather, the theologian Theophilus Lessing, had authored the treatise *De Tolerantia Religionum*. No external impulse such as the friendship with Moses Mendelssohn was needed to guide Lessing toward advocating toleration and conciliation. By the year· 1749 the twenty-year-old author had published the play *Die Juden*. He remarked later that this comedy was "the result of a very serious observation about the shameful suppression in which a people must sigh, a people which a Christian, one would think, cannot regard without some sort of reverence. From it, I thought, had once sprung many heroes and prophets, and now one doubts whether an honest man could be found among them."[48] Even in this youthful play, the "Jew-drama," as it was generally called, Lessing did not content himself with merely defending the Jews but attacked many of the Christians because of their hostile attitude toward them.

The content of the drama is the following: A baron and his daughter, while on a journey, are attacked by robbers. They are saved through the timely intercession of a traveler and his servant. The baron is convinced that the robbers were Jews but must finally admit not only that his suspicion had been unwarranted but also that his savior actually was a Jew. The traveler apparently voices the conviction of the youthful Lessing when he says: "When a Jew cheats, perhaps seven times out of nine the Christian has compelled him to do it. I doubt whether many Christians can boast of having dealt sincerely with a Jew; yet they are surprised if he tries to repay them with the same coin. If faith and honesty shall prevail among two peoples, both must contribute equally. But what if it were a religious matter and almost a deserving work to persecute the other. . . ?" The traveler rather believed that there were "good and evil souls among all peoples."

In Lessing's *Rettung des Cardanus* [Rehabilitation of Cardanus] (1754), an unprejudiced scholar from Milan, Cardanus, refuses to concede first rank to any one of the four contending world religions but wants to leave this question to the future. Contrary to many other Germans, including sons of the Enlightenment who were often sharply critical of Judaism and the Jews, Lessing questioned whether the Jewish religion had actually become fossilized: "What if the present state is only a longer Babylonian captivity? The arm, which then saved His people, is even today still strong. . . . Perhaps the God of

Abraham has permitted the descendants of this pious man to return to their heritage and to multiply, in order to let his power and wisdom brilliantly arise to shame their oppressors."[49]

It was on the very eve of the proclamation of the Edict of Toleration by Joseph II that Lessing's play *Nathan der Weise* appeared. His second "Jewish drama" has to this day remained the finest expression of the idea of brotherhood on German soil. Moses Mendelssohn, the intimate friend of the playwright, served as the model for Nathan. While Lessing knew many other Jews and entertained friendly relations with them, his long friendship with Mendelssohn surpassed in importance all his other Jewish contacts. For thirty years, until the latter's death, he lived in closest intellectual association with him. Several writings of both men bear the stamp of their joint intellectual labor. In *Nathan* Lessing has created an eternal monument to his friend.[50]

The core of the drama is the story of a ring, a tale Lessing borrowed from Boccaccio's *Decamerone* and enlarged upon. Sultan Saladin asks Nathan which of the three main religions, Christianity, Judaism, or Islam, he considers the true and right one. Nathan evades a direct reply to this delicate question by telling about a ring of inestimable value which a father had always left to his most beloved son. Once, however, a father who loved his three sons equally promised each of them the ring and in deep embarrassment ordered the fashioning of two additional rings. They turned out to be so much like the original that he himself was no longer able to recognize the genuine one. When the father died, each of the sons claimed to be the possessor of the genuine ring, which, however, could no more be identified with certainty than the true faith.

The judge to whom the quarreling brothers appealed based his decision upon the circumstance that the genuine ring possessed the miraculous power to make its owner beloved; since each of the sons loved himself most, the original ring probably had been lost, and all three of them were "cheated cheaters." He pronounced the Solomonic sentence that every one of them should try "to prove the magic of the stone in the ring" and to reveal through social consciousness, philanthropy, and acquiescence in God's will the genuineness of his ring—the truth of his religion.

Nathan observes in a talk with the Templar that "all nations have good men." The difference between them does not amount to much, and it is most important not to find fault with each other. When the Templar charges that the Jews always have looked upon themselves as the chosen people and have raised themselves above all other nations, Nathan does not lose his equanimity but rather offers him his friendship. Neither of them had selected his people. And he finally poses the question: "Are Christian and Jew more Christian and Jew than they are human beings?"

In his fight for tolerance and mutual understanding Lessing clashed with the fanatics of all religions. He severely criticized them in the figure of the patriarch. The Templar submits to the patriarch the case of Nathan and his adopted daughter Recha, without, however, mentioning them by name, so as to avoid casting any suspicion upon them. A Jew had picked up a small child who had been abandoned and without his help would probably have died. He had lovingly cared for her, brought her up in no particular faith and had taught her about God, "no more, no less" than satisfies human reason. The patriarch, having at first been friendly, is seized by religious fervor. In blind fanaticism he mercilessly repeats the death verdict against the Jew: "It doesn't matter, the Jew is to be burned."

In his historical-philosophical essay "Erziehung des Menschengeschlechtes" [Education of the Human Race], which appeared shortly before his death in 1781, Lessing made some further observations about Jewish religion and Jews. This time, however, it was less the moralist who spoke and more the philosopher of history. The different peoples of the world, Lessing elaborated, represented different stages in the religious evolution of humanity. At the same time they revealed the march of human reason through history, in accordance with a divine plan. Embedded in this conception of the religious development of humanity is the thought of the relative truth of all religions. Hegel's philosophy of a later period is to some degree anticipated by Lessing in this essay. One should, Lessing exhorted, neither ridicule any religion nor turn in anger against it. "Nothing in the best of all worlds would deserve this sneering, this anger of ours, and only the religions should deserve it? If God had his hand in everything, then probably also in our errors." God had chosen "a single people for his particular education; and just the least polished, the most intractable one, in order to start with it right from the beginning." God educated the Israelites "in order to be able subsequently to use particular individual members of it the better as educators of all other peoples."[51]

Lessing had been an untiring fighter for truth. He wielded his sharp sword against orthodox fanaticism, fought against excessive patriotism, upon which he looked contemptuously as a "heroic weakness," and battled against religious and national prejudices. Love of truth animated him when in his *"Rettungen"* he defended authors of the past against unjust yet widespread misinterpretations and distortions. The situation of the German Jews had similarly aroused his conscience and outraged his sense of justice from his early youth. He had rushed to their defense, anxious to "rehabilitate" the reputation of a much maligned and persecuted people.

Hamann and Herder

Johann Georg Hamann and Johann Gottfried Herder, the forerunners of the Romantic movement, approached Judaism quite differently from their classicist contemporaries. Hamann, the mystic East Prussian thinker who deeply impressed Herder and other contemporaries, was no Jew-hater.[52] To the contrary, he entertained most cordial relations with Jews. As one of his biographers wrote, "We find at Hamann's table occasionally Catholics, Lutherans and Jews in most loving company."[53]

Hamann's deep Christian piety and his thorough knowledge of the Bible and of the Hebrew language formed the basis for his understanding of Jewish antiquity. The Bible had for him the most intensely personal significance. He used to compare his own career with the history of the Jewish people, his own errors with the sins of the Jews. "I forgot all my books over it," he wrote about the Bible. "I was ashamed to have ever compared them with the Book of God, . . . yes to have ever preferred another book to this one. . . . I recognized my own crimes in the history of the Jewish people, I read my own life-career and thanked God for his patience with this his people, because nothing else than such an example could entitle me to hope for the same.[54] "The history of this people," he continued, was "in view of our religion of greater importance than that of all other nations."[55]

It was his opposition to the Enlightenment that brought the ancient world of Judaism close to Hamann and let him understand and love it. While some proponents of the Enlightenment drew their swords against all religions, including Judaism, Hamann defended the religious heritage, including the Jewish faith, against rationalists such as Voltaire and Bolingbroke. Hamann raised the question of why God had chosen this people and replied thus: "Not because of its virtues. The free-thinkers may let stand out, as sharply as they wish, its foolishness and malice, as contrasted with other peoples'. Did not God wish to transmit the Gospel through apparently ignorant and uncomely tools? . . . Whatever the contrary accounts of Voltaire and Bolingbroke, the first Book of Moses remains of great importance for its discovery of the early history of nations and of the human race."[56] One of the editors of Hamann's writings and letters, Moritz Petri, remarked about his struggle with the men of the Enlightenment: "With Deborah he sings a victory song over the enemies of the people of Israel—the enlightened critics of his time."[57]

The proponents of the Enlightenment loved to contrast the brilliance of classical antiquity with the darkness of the Middle Ages. Like other forerunners of German Romanticism, which was to turn back to Christianity the hearts and minds estranged by the Enlightenment, Hamann resisted this glorification of the pagan Greeks and Romans.

Hamann found the ancient Jews, whose entire life was molded by religious prescriptions, much more to his liking. And it was from the womb of Judaism that Christianity had sprung. In rare and bold contradiction to many of his contemporaries, Hamann preferred austere and solemn Judea to glittering and shining Hellas: "In the simple words of the language of Canaan is more wisdom and life than in the splendor of Greek classicism." Moreover, without a thorough knowledge of Judaism there was no hope of attaining a real understanding of pagan antiquity. One had, he remarked, to use the books of Moses and the prophets as a yardstick to measure by them and appreciate the ancient world of the pagans. Incidentally, "why does one always point to the Greeks and Romans? *Redemption does not come from the Greeks, but from the Jews.*"*[58]

A thorough student of the Bible, Hamann alluded repeatedly to biblical mottoes and used biblical parables. He even "judaized" his good Christian friends. He called the preacher Pitius "an honest Israelite," designated his friend Lindner as a "teacher in Israel," and spoke of another deserving man as a "master in Israel and Ashkalon."[59]

German Romanticism contained strong anti-Semitic ingredients. But Hamann, who blazed a path for Romanticism, revealed a rare appreciation of Judaism.

If anyone could be expected to agree with Hamann's enthusiastic judgment of ancient Judaism, it was Johann Gottfried Herder, poet, critic, philosopher of history and expounder of the Bible, a writer who richly influenced not only the greatest of his contemporaries but Germany's intellectual life for years to come. His *Vom Geist der hebräischen Poesie* [Spirit of Hebrew Poetry] (1782), as he called the main work of his Hebrew studies, shows his great knowledge of Hebrew literature. Hardly any other German thinker became as keen a student of Hebrew literature or displayed deeper insights, and none loved it more than he.

*Italics, A.D.L.

Although Herder did not look upon the Jews with an uncritical eye, it would falsify not only the letter but also the spirit of his writings to present him as an opponent of the Jews. Yet this was done by, among others, Houston Stewart Chamberlain,[60] the English writer who became an apostle of the German race. In fact, few demanded legal equality for the Jews more emphatically than Herder. "All laws," he wrote, "which consider the Jew like cattle, which do not trust him an inch . . . and thus call him daily, even hourly, a dishonest man, testify to the continued barbarism of the state which tolerates such laws of barbaric times."[61] Here was one of the sharpest condemnations of the very inequality under which the Jews of the late eighteenth century still lived everywhere in Germany.

Like his friend Hamann, Herder elevated the ancient Jews above the admired Greeks. "Which poet of Greece and Rome," he asked, "dare we place beside Isaiah in regard to the sublime morals and the all-embracing national spirit? And which king of the Egyptians, Scythians, and Indians sang and taught like David?"[62] At a time when the aesthetic and literary culture of the Greeks and the literary and political culture of the Romans were extolled, Herder paid his respects to the ethics of Judaism. He also criticized those who tended to belittle the ancient Jews as compared with the Greeks and Romans.[63] "Greeks and Romans," Herder wrote in the *Briefe das Studium der Theologie betreffend*, "have so many indecent things that the Hebrews do not possess; yet, in the case of the former, one interprets them away or hides them, in the latter [Hebrews] one discloses them and derides them."[64] Like Hamann, Herder opposed the one-sided and exaggerated cult of antiquity to which many representatives of the Enlightenment belonged. Both men attempted to repel the attacks of these classicists against Christianity, the Bible, and Judaism.

"The philosopher in the black robe," as Herder, a young minister in Riga, was called, had devoted himself enthusiastically to the study of the ancient Hebrew writings and had treated the literary works of ancient Judaism in a series of important publications. The writings of the Old Testament represented, according to Herder, different types of poetry. He highly praised David and Isaiah and the lamentations of Jeremiah and admired especially the Song of Solomon and the Book of Job. Herder also showed lively interest in the Talmud and the Midrash. He recognized the deeply human content and spiritual core in their seemingly childish and simple parables, legends, and allegories and gathered some of the most beautiful in his *Blätter der Vorzeit* [Leaves of Ancient Times].

In the foreward to these "poetries from the oriental tradition," the "Jewish Poetries and Fables," which appeared first in *Der teutsche Merkur* in 1781, Herder developed his program to familiarize the German people with the poetry of the Hebrews: the Germans should learn to appreciate and love it. German prejudices about Jewish poetry must be overcome and widespread misunderstandings removed: "The Hebrew nation, like all peoples which through language and tradition reach back into early antiquity, has its own mythology and poetry; it is, however, not so well known, appreciated and developed as the mythology of other peoples, even of some doubtlessly cruder and more uncivilized peoples." When the Bible fell into the hands of other nations, they often "ridiculed what they did not understand at all."[65]

In the *Älteste Urkunde des Menschengeschlechtes* [Earliest Document of the Human Race], which appeared in 1774, Herder had looked upon the Old Testament as reflecting in poetic form the notions of the Jews about the origin of the world and had wished it placed in the same category as cosmogonies of other ancient peoples.[66] This conception of Herder, however, pleased neither the orthodox elements nor the rationalists. To the former he appeared an atheist, to the latter a confused mystical pietist.

In his book *Geist der hebräischen Poesie* (1782), Herder tried, in accordance with his basic philosophical and historical ideas, to expound the peculiarities of Hebrew writings through the character of the people and the era that produced it. The Bible, he emphasized, must be read humanly, like a book written by man for man,[67] an idea which he later was to repeat frequently, particularly in his work *Vom Geist des Christentums* [On the Spirit of Christianity]. Several other of Herder's writings testify to his continued preoccupation with the Old Testament. He was driven to it by his theological training as well as his poetic and ethnic-historical interests. Herder's famous *Volkslieder* [Songs of Nations] contains masterpieces in translation from different languages, including Hebrew. After his death they were edited by Johannes von Müller and published under the title *Stimmen der Völker in Liedern* [Voices of Nations in Songs]. These songs of nations include the "songs of love," actually the Song of Solomon. Herder's translation of this song aroused considerable attention, for in it Herder, a Protestant theologian, dared to treat as a simple collection of erotic poems a book which had been considered a mystic announcement of Christ and of his relation to his "bride," the church.[68]

Herder ranks high not only in the fields of literary history and literary criticism but also as a general historian and especially as philosopher of history. In all these different capacities he discussed the ancient Hebrews and their writings. In his main work, *Ideen zur Philosophie der Geschichte der Menschheit* [Ideas on the Philosophy of History of Humanity], he presented his views on the historic role of the Jews during antiquity and the Middle Ages, particularly in two chapters, "The Hebrews" and "Alien Peoples in Europe."[69]

In the first of these chapters Herder emphasized the significance of the Jewish people in world history. The Hebrews possessed historic annals of events dating back to "periods in which most of the now enlightened nations could not yet write." Herder lent more credence to the Hebrews' own account of their history than to the slanders of alien Jew-haters like the Egyptian priest Manetho. "The great man" Moses, "the greatest which this nation has had," liberated them from "the contemptible oppression" under which they were forced to live among the Egyptians. "All the laws of Moses are admirably conceived."

But after a brief survey of their political history Herder reached a hardly favorable conclusion: "Considered as a state, a people can hardly present a more miserable figure than this one, excepting the rule of two kings." The reason for this was that a country with such poor internal and external conditions could "not possibly prosper in this locality on earth." Then too Jews in Palestine had not distinguished themselves as a people skilled in war—though in another passage he conceded that the Jewish nation had not lacked courage in war, as was shown in the epochs of David and of the Maccabeans and especially in the last terrible downfall of the state. Also, the Hebrews had not been creative in science and art; yet it could not be denied that "Hebrew literature was preserved through them, that in the Dark Ages science, medicine and philosophy, as attained by the Arabs, were transmitted also through them, and, besides, much good was created which could be brought about by none except a Jew."

Through Christianity the holy books of the Jews had reached the hands of many nations. Depending on how they were interpreted and used, they had had a good or a bad effect on all Christian eras. "Good was their effect, since Moses' law made the doctrine of one God the basis of all their philosophy and religion and since it spoke of this God in so many songs . . . with a dignity and loftiness, with a devotion and gratitude which little else in human writings approximates." A comparison of their holy books with the literature of other ancient peoples and with the Koran shows "unmistakably the superiority of the Hebrew books over all ancient religious writings of other nations, . . . not to mention the whole instructive history of the people and the pure ethics of their scriptures."

No other people on earth had spread out like the Jews. "No

people on earth has preserved itself in all climates so distinctly and in so vigorous a manner as this one. . . . The nationality of the Jews since its dispersion has proven itself by its presence useful or harmful to the peoples of the earth depending on how one has used it. In early times one looked upon Christians as Jews and despised or suppressed them jointly, because the Christians were subjected to the same accusations as the Jews, of hating other people, of being arrogant and bigoted. Later when the Christians themselves oppressed the Jews they enabled them by their industry and further dispersion to become almost everywhere masters of the money exchanges; thus the more primitive nations of Europe became voluntarily slaves of their usury. No doubt, such a spread-out republic of shrewd usurers held back for a time many a European people from an industry of its own and from commerce, because it considered itself superior to a Jewish occupation. . . . Nevertheless, they were indispensable to those times, and are still indispensable to some countries."

Intent on relating the history of the Jews "impartially," Herder does not close his eyes to what he considered either their shortcomings or their virtues. His high esteem for the Jewish people, nevertheless, is often apparent. Israel, he wrote, "was and is the most excellent people on earth; in its origin and continuity to this day, in its happiness and unhappiness, in its vices and virtues, in its vileness and nobility, it is so unique, so singular, that I consider the history, the manner, the existence of this nation the most convincing proof of the miracles and writings which we have from it and which we know of. Something like this cannot be invented, such a history with all that is connected with it and that depends on it, briefly, such a people cannot be feigned. Its development, not yet completed, is the great poem of the times."[70]

Historians, according to Herder, should strive for fairness, should overcome political, national, or racial prejudices and, in judging nations, must reject "false yardsticks."[71] "First of all," he wrote, "one should not have a pet race, a favorite people on earth. Such a predilection misleads one easily to ascribe to the favored nation too many good traits, to others too many evil ones. If the beloved nation were merely a collective name (Celts, Semites, . . .) which perhaps nowhere has ever existed, whose origin and continuation one cannot prove, one would then have written into the blue sky."[72] The zoologist should not establish *a priori* a "hierarchy" among the creatures which he is going to study; "all are equally dear and precious to him. The same holds true of the social scientist." Besides, nothing is more difficult than the characterization of an entire nation. "How I am always seized by fear when I hear an entire people or era characterized by a few words; what a huge quantity of differences are covered by the word *nation,* how little does he think, how little does he often know those whom he characterizes most verbosely."[73]

Although Herder at times blamed contemporary Jewry for some shortcomings, his criticism on the whole was of a constructive nature and was also softened by his ascribing many virtues to the Jewish character. He praised the "great talents" of the Jews, their sense of ethics and of honor. He commended them for their mutual solidarity as well as for their exclusion of disreputable individuals from their community. The Jew often is a much "stricter judge of honesty" than the Christian, whose concepts of rank and honor "from childhood on have been distorted and confused." The Jew also, Herder held, possessed a much more thorough knowledge of peoples and countries and knew how to distinguish between true and false values.

Jews were "free from many political prejudices" and other biases "which we discard with difficulty or not at all." They were also a people of a keen and penetrating mind. "Who surpassed Spinoza in the consistency which he brought into his system of morality and politics, even of theology? Will any intelligent man read without appreciation an Orobbio, Pinto, so many excellent judgments and parables of the rabbis, based upon the most acute remarks? Indeed, to the rabble of writers, because of hate and perversity, the most ingenuous parables appeared at times ridiculous, at times contemptible. How? Because they could not penetrate to their meaning and stubbornly clung to the phraseology, which often seemed childish." Exigency and trade had developed in the Jews an acuteness which only a dull eye could not discern. Herder rendered high praise to the magnanimity and charity of noble Israelites. Diligence too could not be denied to them, neither in the past nor in the present times: "Let Christians know their trade as well, work as assiduously as the Jews work at theirs."[74]

EMANCIPATION AND EDUCATION

On the other hand, the mass of the Jews, according to Herder, had not yet advanced far enough and engaged in practices which, though once economically beneficial, were now harmful, particularly in some countries. But with the removal of inequality these economically harmful effects would end. "Only a barbaric constitution," he wrote in this sense, could keep the Jew from contributing "to the best interests of the state . . . or could make his capabilities pernicious."[75] Herder referred to Montesquieu's remarks that the early barbarism in Europe had contributed to the corruption of the character of the Jews by violent and ugly behavior against them. "Following history," he added, "we cannot deny it." It was therefore "the duty of Europeans to compensate [!] for the debts of their ancestors and to render those, who became dishonest through them, again capable of honesty and deserving of it." How? Obviously and first of all by "our closing to them all sources of dishonest profit and fraud which we ourselves opened to them and still open in poorly organized states."[76] As long as this was not done, however, one ought to admit the Jews to some occupations only in a limited measure.

Was Herder, who demanded the emancipation of the Jews and their free admission to all trades, after all a proponent of the *numerus clausus,* of a qualified liberation? The contradiction is only an apparent one. Herder wished the economic restriction to last only as long as the "barbaric constitution" persisted. Only as long as, contrary to his wishes, the Jews continued to be treated as "slaves" instead of being raised to the status of "fellow citizens" would the admission of the Jews to various occupations have to be limited. Herder thought the Jews' economic activities harmful only in the state of their oppression and only in "poorly organized states." In these the Jews drew profit from "the most corrupt and most degenerated portion of the nation," from the young spendthrifts and from the "high and mighty" ones who, for their part, plundered the Jews. "The mighty prodigal lets them suppress others in order to be able to squeeze them; is the fault entirely theirs?" On the other hand, Herder emphasized that the medieval Jews had furthered economic growth and had had a beneficial effect upon their host nations and that they were "even now" indispensable to the economic prosperity of some countries.[77]

The granting of full equality for the Jews was for Herder a natural imperative. Political inequality was rejected not only on economic but also on moral grounds. "A time will come," Herder announced confidently, "when one will not ask any more in Europe who is a Jew or a Christian; for the Jew too will live in accordance with European laws and will contribute to the best interests of the state."[78]

At times Herder appeared to call upon the Jews, at other times upon the Germans, to initiate the move toward emancipation. First he turned to the Jews, admonishing them to remove "the dishonesty in their trade . . . before the state can accord them true honor." He conceded, however, that the Jews protected the dishonest among them less than did Christians who were "in partnership with them" or were "bribed." The Christians were then urged to assist the Jews with "caution and confidence" to attain "self-respect, which means honor." Christian attitudes and Christian law-making seemed to Herder the most effective means to bring about ultimate equality. The foregoing words are followed by the remark that all laws which are based upon inequality, which do "not trust the Jew an inch," testified only to the continuing barbarism of the state. While Herder thus pleaded for the emancipation of the Jews, he was well aware that the proclamation of their political equality formed only the beginning of better relations between Germans and Jews. Education of both would be necessary to produce further results.

Like Dohm, Herder seemed convinced that "vexation," past oppression, had left its marks on the Jewish character. The oppression of the Jews had brought to the fore their worst and their best, had revealed their weaknesses and their "great talents," all of which showed themselves clearly in their history. Herder did not embellish either the character of the Jews or the deeds and character of the Germans: "One often treated the Jews cruelly and squeezed tyrannically from them what they had earned by avarice and fraud, or by industry, good sense and order."[79]

Yet even what Herder considered their less attractive traits could be corrected. He firmly believed in the capacity for the development and improvement of the human race, of all peoples, and his philosophy was permeated by the belief that all nations and nationalities were basically good and possessed a healthy core. "Where there is evil, the cause of the evil is not the nature of the human species, not its essence and character."[80] No one believed with greater conviction than Herder in the great formative power of education. *Humanität*, in his opinion, was the ultimate goal of all human development, of education.

Herder observed character shortcomings among all peoples. He held therefore that the education of all nations was equally necessary and desirable. He wished to improve Jews *and* Gentiles, to "convert" both of them to "*Humanität*," and believed that "improvement" of the Christians should even precede that of the Jews. "Where Jews are, the improvement must begin with dishonest Christians who abuse the Hebrew. . . . The political conversion starts at the wrong end if it hits the Jew, not the Christian, for, according to the old proverb, where there is rottenness, there hatch insects and worms."[81]

The idea of education emerges repeatedly in Herder's discussion of the Jewish problem. The Jews, he had developed in his *Ideen zur Philosophie der Geschichte der Menschheit*, were a people who became "corrupt through education," because due to a combination of historical circumstances it did not develop its own political culture. It was to this idea that Herder reverted in his later essay in the *Adrastea*, when he pointed out the necessity of a "better education." "What else," he wrote there, could change the Jews, if not a "better education, morality and culture . . . which imperceptibly remove inequality among human beings." This better education conveys advantages to both sides. A means of such education was, in Herder's opinion, the joint schooling of Jewish and Christian youngsters. "While Jewish and Christian children are educated in accordance with the same principles of morals and science, they learn to know and appreciate each other, forget prejudices, which otherwise divided them. Common culture of the soul joins human beings of all times, areas, and nations."

"What a prospect would it be," Herder continued, "to see such a keen people loyally devoted to the fostering of scholarship, to the welfare of the state which protects them and to other purposes generally useful to humanity! They would not work as slaves but indeed as fellow citizens of civilized nations on the greatest colosseum, the edifice of learning, the entire culture of *Humanität*. . . . All nations would adore with them, they with all nations, the creator of the world, by perfecting his likeness, reason and wisdom, magnanimity and charity in the human race and extolling it." The vision of the equality of the Jews with other peoples held Herder captive.

DISCRIMINATION OR HUMANITARIANISM?

In spite of Herder's notions of the need for improving both Jews *and* Germans, his support for the joint education of their children and for the immediate removal of legal barriers, and his vision of a bright future for Jews and Germans, some have claimed him as a forerunner of twentieth-century German anti-Semitism. They have felt particularly attracted by a passage in Herder's work *Ideen zur Philosophie der Geschichte der Menschheit,* where Herder spoke of Jewish "parasitism."

"The people of God," Herder had written in the *Ideen,* "has been for millennia, indeed almost since its origin, a parasitic plant on the stems of other nations."[82] This remark, often torn from its context, must be evaluated within the larger framework of his ideas about German Jewry. Herder made the remark when he discussed the national character of the Jews, its excellences and its shortcomings. He extolled in this connection the "great talents" of the Jewish people. "Ingenuous, shrewd and industrious, it knew at all times how to survive, even under the most extreme pressure by other peoples." Immediately thereafter he said: "In their country they were once an industrious, diligent people."

It is obvious that Herder's use of the word "parasitic" had a different connotation than was read into it by the opponents of the Jews, since in this very context he praised their "industry." The anti-Semites thought of "parasites" as those living by the sweat and hard work of others. Also, the parasite lives off his host, whereas the Jew, according to Herder, is often exploited, subject to "the most extreme pressure by other peoples." In the *Briefe zur Beförderung der Humanität* [Letters for the Promotion of Humanity] Herder also remarked that the Hebrews "more than any other Asiatic nation influenced other peoples; indeed, in a way, through Christianity as well as through Islam they have become a foundation of the greatest part of world enlightenment." It was also due to the influence of the Jews that "no single Christian nation had formed its laws and state constitution from the bottom."[83] Was this a reference to the cultural "parasitism" of the European host nations and to the cultural originality of the Jews? In reality, on the basis of these remarks by Herder neither an anti-Jewish inference nor a derogatory inference in regard to any European people would appear to be warranted.

In the foregoing work Herder wrote: "The human race is a totality; we work and suffer, sow and harvest for each other." He demanded a "feeling of fairness toward other nations."[84] Thus he could hold no brief for oppression and persecution of any individual or group. As he remarked about Uriel Acosta: "From my childhood on, nothing has been more detestable to me than persecutions or personal insults of a human being on account of his religion. Whom does this concern except himself and God?"[85]

In the late twenties and thirties of the twentieth century, a leading German literary historian, Josef Nadler of the University of Vienna, repeated Houston Stewart Chamberlain's assertion of Herder's opposition to the Jews. Nadler purported to observe "very early gestures of rejection" of Judaism by Germans.[86] To prove his thesis he pointed to Herder who, in his magazine *Adrastea,* had recommended the migration of the Jews to Palestine. Thus the false impression was given that Herder, the German champion of humanity and humanitarianism, was a forerunner of anti-Semitism and National Socialism in particular.

Actually, in *Adrastea* Herder had favorably reviewed the pamphlet of an English author of the seventeenth century who had voiced his conviction that one day the Jews would return to Palestine. In this context Herder directed friendly and warmly encouraging words to the Jews: "Good luck thus if a Messiah-Bonaparte leads them there victoriously, good luck to Palestine! Fine, keen people, a miracle of the times!" Were these good wishes "gestures of rejection"? A few lines thereafter Herder praised the remark of a rabbi that Jews and Gentiles, although at times hostile toward each other, lived so closely and intimately together that their separation was almost impossible.[87]

While Herder wished the Jews a happy return to Palestine, he desired no less a peaceful and harmonious living together of Jews and Gentiles in other countries. In a concluding vision in the above article he sketched the outlines of a new era in which the Jews would live no longer as slaves but as free members of the human race, with equal rights, and would contribute to the general welfare, to learning, and to human culture in general. "Not on the bare hills of Palestine," he wrote, "of the narrow, ravaged country, everywhere their temple will spiritually surge from its ruins. . . . Their Palestine will then be there where they live and act nobly, everywhere."

The rejection of Jews by many Germans even in the era of the Enlightenment was quite real, but the name of Herder does not belong among the forerunners of anti-Semitism; quite the contrary. Nadler, however, attempted to introduce further "evidence" in support of his thesis. As he wrote: "It was Johann Gottfried Herder who in his book *Vom Geist des Christentums* [On the Spirit of Christianity] demanded strongly 'the attuning of Christianity to a German soul' "[88] and the turning away of Christianity from its Jewish origin. This book of Herder appeared in the year 1798, near the end of his life, and expressed thus his late views on Jews and Judaism. Did it have any real anti-Jewish tendency?

The reader will find here again one of Herder's basic ideas, the concept of the distinct cultural individuality of each national group. The cultural diversity of nations springs from the interplay of numerous factors, of major significance being geographic conditions, historical traditions, circumstances of time and place, national character, and the age and maturity of a people. In view of these differences and the resulting diversity of the prevailing philosophy and outlook of various ethnic groups, Herder was fully aware of the difficulty of making one people fully understand and appreciate the literature, thought, and life experience of another nation.

It is in this sense that the following remarks of Herder on the Bible should be understood: "What we call the Bible of the Old Testament is a collection of Oriental writings which belong in great part to the childhood of the world. All history tells us that the greatest peculiarity prevails in what different nations and epochs called spirit and divine; it obviously would therefore lead to a confusion of eras, peoples, and human reason to explain expressions of such a nature at random, in accordance with our linguistic use or with arbitrary construction."[89] Christianity could not rest upon "a terminology of misunderstood Jewish words." The apostles of Christianity who originated in Judaism "were bound to think, talk, symbolize as Jews." In order to fully comprehend early Christianity, it was necessary to transplant oneself spiritually into those early periods and to penetrate into the national character and language of the Jews. Then one will not find an "incomprehensible spirit" in the Bible and will not ridicule what before seemed incomprehensible. "Hundreds of objections which are made against the Bible will be abandoned if one looks upon each book of this collection naturally—that is, in accordance with time and place," and all derisions then will appear absurd.

What Herder clearly aimed at was bringing the Old Testament close to the heart and mind of the Germans. To achieve this it was necessary "to Germanize ancient Judaism." "One ought to talk," he admonished his contemporaries, "as the Apostles would have talked if Christianity had arisen among us."[90] Herder wanted the Germans to perceive the spirit of the Old Testament and to discard the linguistic peculiarities and everything merely incidental. To conceive of Herder's work as a "gesture of rejection" meant entirely misjudging his intent.

On the contrary, Herder stressed in this late work the Jewish origins of Christianity, criticized slurs against the Bible as an expression of gross ignorance, and was baffled by the prejudices people harbored against the Hebrew writings. Once again he expressed his enthusiasm for the ancient Jewish books. Thus he remarked about the Song of Solomon, Job, and the prophets: "The most typical beat of their heart finds an echo in mine." Herder saw God's spirit as a "unifier of peoples." Before Him "prejudices must vanish." He recommended to the different nations to observe the law of "harmony, fairness, appreciation of each other, freedom, peace." This law, he announced prophetically, "will reach the hearts of the peoples, in spite of all resistance; for the repugnance of the nations is always caused only by a few."[91]

Evaluating the drama *Nathan der Weise*, Herder praised Lessing's "teachings of the finest kind, toleration of human beings, of religions and of nations." All characters "finally call out to us, 'You nations, tolerate one another! You men of different customs, opinions, and characters, help one another, get along with each other: be human beings!' An eternal motto for our race in all classes, of whatever religion and national character. . . ."[92]

CHAPTER 3

Goethe, Schiller, and Kant

Goethe

The greatest German poet, Johann Wolfgang von Goethe, met Jews personally in a friendly manner. He esteemed many among them and invited some repeatedly to his house. Yet he remained indifferent to the struggle of the Jews for emancipation. It should be noted that he displayed a similar indifference toward his own people in their war for liberation from the French. He found among the Jews both admirable and reprehensible traits. Yet again he was also sharply critical of Germans and compared them repeatedly with the Jews.

A student of Spinoza, Goethe, according to his own testimony, owed much to the Jewish philosopher. He was no less influenced by the Old Testament. Goethe possessed a thorough knowledge of the Bible and other Jewish writings and in admiration of them vied with Herder, who had first introduced him to their treasures. He highly valued the ancient Jewry which had created them and disliked the "unjust, ridiculing and distorting attacks against the Bible."[1] He often remarked that he did not hate the Jews and that he "never had been an enemy of the Maccabean family."[2]

A few passages in his works and some of his utterances have been used by German anti-Semitic propaganda at various times. These passages must be judged within the framework of the totality of his observations. They convey the impression, if not always of friendship, definitely of interest in and respect for the Jewish people and its literary creations. His critical utterances on the Jews must also be juxtaposed with many angry and deprecatory remarks of his about the German people themselves.

National or religious hatred was entirely alien to Goethe's character. Eckermann reports a talk with Goethe in which the poet pointed out that he had not written any war poems during the War

67

of Liberation against Napoleonic France because it would have been like wearing "a mask" which would have "fitted me very badly": "How could I ever have written songs of hate without feeling hate? . . . How could I, to whom only culture and barbarism are matters of significance, have hated a nation which belonged to the most cultivated on earth and to which I owed a great deal of my own education?"

Goethe, as he often admitted, also owed a great deal of his education to the Jews, in particular to the Old Testament, to ancient Jewish history, and to Spinoza. He hated the Jews as little as he hated the French. "In general," Eckermann lets Goethe say, "there is something peculiar about national hatred. You will find it most vigorous and violent at the lowest stages of civilization. There is one stage, however, where it entirely vanishes, and where one in a way stands above the nations and feels the happiness or grief of his neighboring nation as if it had hit one's own nation. This cultural stage was appropriate to my own nature. . . ."[3]

Goethe, the great cosmopolitan who raised himself high above all "patriotic narrowness,"[4] took a deep interest in folk songs and in the poetic expressions of all nations, following Herder along this path. National literature, he thought, did not mean much any more, for the "epoch of world literature has arrived." His poem "Weltliteratur" [World Literature] ended with the exhortation: "Let all peoples under the same sky enjoy happily the same gift."[5] That Goethe did not wish to exclude the Jews, but, to the contrary, thought first of them, is shown by his alluding to them and their royal singer David in the very first line of this poem.

The poet of the *West-östlicher Divan* did not believe in an inherent natural difference between human beings: "Occident and Orient do not make for an essential difference in the character of men. An Oriental is from head to toe just as much a human being as an Occidental." Goethe strove ardently to reconcile these two separate worlds.[6] He wished to include "the Jewish stories" from the Bible and similarly from Josephus in the German *Volksbuch*. Goethe's testament to the German people lies embedded in the words: "Orient and Occident cannot be kept apart any longer."

During his long and active life Goethe made numerous and not always consistent observations on many topics, including the Jews. This consideration aside, some of the passages quoted in support of anti-Semitism have been torn out of context and distorted. Brief remarks about the Jews may be found in the first and second parts of *Faust*. In the first Mephistopheles tells Faust that Gretchen's mother, having had a presentiment of evil, had turned over the devil's ornament to a priest. The priest observed that the church had "a good stomach, had swallowed entire countries and yet had never overeaten itself; the church alone . . . can digest dubious property." Thereupon Faust replies: "This is a general custom; a Jew and a king can do it too."[7] The remark is no more hostile toward the Jews than toward kings and the church.

In the second part of *Faust* there is a brief reference to a Jew who insists upon repayment of his loans.[8] Goethe points several times to the money-lending activities of the Jews, as also in the poem "Brautfahrt" [Bridal Journey].[9] Jews present to the knight Kurt, who can as little rid himself of debts as of opponents and women, the "note of postponed debt." The money-lending Jew, of course, is not looked upon by his debtors in a friendly manner. Goethe felt repelled by the haggling which accompanied trading in eastern and southern Europe and the loud advertising of goods and judged it disapprovingly in the drama *Clavigo*.[10] In spite of some criticism of the Jewish merchant, Goethe in general did not indulge in malicious remarks about Jewish economic undertakings and Jewish wealth. At times he made joking remarks about the financial abilities of the Jews, asserting their superiority in money matters, at other times he made generally flattering observations about their skill. "One must be somebody to create something," Goethe said to Eckermann. "Dante appears great to us, but he has behind himself a culture of centuries; the house of Rothschild is rich, but it has needed more than a century to attain these treasures. These things all lie deeper than one thinks."[11] In no case, however, did he make the Jewish merchant or moneylender identical with the Jew as such. There were also scholarly people among the Jews, as for instance Master Abryon of Trier in *Reinecke Fuchs*.

Goethe's fine gift for observation is revealed in many of his remarks. He liked the Jews' national enthusiasm, which expressed itself "before the entire world." He carefully noted trait after trait of the Jewish character, as his communication to Madame Stein after a visit of Ephraim Veitel, the son of the Jewish financier, shows: "Soon I shall have gathered everything significant about the character of Jewry."[12] Similarly Riemer reported that Goethe endeavored to "conceive correctly the characteristics" of the Jews. In *Sprüche in Prosa* Goethe depicts the Jewish character as follows: "Energy the basis of everything. Immediate purpose. None, not even the most humble Jew, who did not reveal determined endeavor and, in particular, an earthly, temporary, momentary one. Jewish language has something expressive."[13] Interest in the alien and "enigmatic" in Judaism and Jews had already seized the young poet. When the young Goethe reviewed the "Gedichte eines polnischen Juden"

[Poems of a Polish Jew] (which he happened to find weak), he admitted that the title had made upon him a "very favorable" impression. He had posed to himself the question: "What kind of sentiments will stir in him, what remarks will he make, he to whom everything is new?"[14]

According to Goethe, Germans and Jews were in many respects alike. Germans, like Jews, he remarked once to his loyal Eckermann, could not perish, because they all were individualists.[15] Goethe, according to a letter of the statesman and scholar Wilhelm von Humboldt to his wife Caroline, asserted that the best advice to be given is "to disperse the Germans like the Jews all over the world; only abroad are they still tolerable."[16]

Once Goethe told Eckermann that it might take centuries before one would be able to say about the Germans: "It has been a long time since they were barbarians." The Germans were lacking in "freedom of taste and intellect," he observed on another occasion; then he held that they loved to be dominated.[17] At other times Goethe extolled what he considered German virtues. His observations about the Jews were equally varied.

The notion of the distinct individualism of Jews and Germans and the idea of the necessity of dispersing the Germans like the Jews over the entire globe emerge repeatedly in Goethe's remarks. "Germany is nothing, but every individual German is much, and yet they fancy themselves just the opposite. One must transplant and scatter the Germans like the Jews all over the world in order to develop in its entirety and to the benefit of all peoples the mass of good which is in them."[18] "The Germans," Goethe said another time to Reinhard, "like the Jews, are not easily discouraged and remain strongly united, even if they are destined to possess no fatherland any longer."[19] Like Greeks and Romans, Germans and Jews had not presented impartially their own history nor that of other peoples, because of a false patriotism which was always detrimental to historical truth. Goethe even compared Faust with a Jew, the Israelite king Ahab,[20] whose eternal restlessness and dissatisfaction with himself had not left him even in old age. In a talk with Reinhard, Goethe said: "The Germans, like the Jews, can be suppressed, but they cannot be annihilated."[21]

Goethe faced contemporary Jews with somewhat ambivalent feelings. He esteemed the intellectual elite of Jewry, whence came, according to Riemer, his most attentive and appreciative audience. This admiration contrasted strangely with a feeling of "contempt" for the mass of the Jews, which, as Goethe himself confessed, used to "stir" particularly in his youth. But this feeling, in his own words, was "more the reflex of Christian men and women" around him.[22]

The legacy of past prejudices, which had penetrated into every niche of German life, was much too recent even for Goethe to shake off entirely and completely. Still, his dislike of Jews had already been blunted in his youth by his interest in and curiosity about the customs of alien groups and peoples. He had also found in the Jewish national character appealing human traits, and the industry of the Jews, their "courteousness," and even their "stubbornness" in clinging to their traditional customs had made him acknowledge his "respect."[23]

Everything considered, however, the Jews of antiquity attracted Goethe much more than their descendants. Thus he remarked that the Jews in the period of the Maccabees looked best to him. In a letter to Zelter, Goethe referred to the "unsuitability of biblical subjects," because of their effect upon the audience. As those Jewish "heroes step into the present times, we are reminded that they are Jews and we feel a contrast between the forefathers and the descendants which confuses and irritates us." Whereupon Zelter fully consented: "One is accustomed to see the Jewish heroes mistreated. If the words are spoken 'It does not matter, the Jew is to be burned,' the effect is as certain as hard cash."[24] There is audible here a certain disdain of anti-Semitic prejudice. However, Goethe displayed little sympathy for the mass of German Jews in their quest for emancipation.

ON TOLERATION AND EMANCIPATION

How much the question of Jewish emancipation preoccupied Goethe is revealed in his correspondence with the poetess Bettina Brentano, *Goethes Briefwechsel mit einem Kinde* [Goethe's Correspondence with a Child], which Bettina published after Goethe's death. Goethe repeatedly asked his correspondent, who emerges as a great friend of the Jews, to transmit to him from Frankfurt one or another of the many pamphlets on the emancipation which were then being published by Jews and Gentiles.[25] Goethe himself inclined to the side that was opposed to the Jews. Bettina's enthusiastic advocacy of the Jews, with its apparent emotionalism, was perhaps bound to challenge Goethe and may have made him stress the arguments of the opposing side. He heaped ridicule upon the spokesman of the Jews, Israel Jacobsohn, and approved of a pamphlet against him.[26] Goethe's approval does not conclusively show that he endorsed it just on account of its anti-Jewish bent. As the literary historian Ludwig Geiger showed, this pamphlet contained a curious blend of conservative *and* progressive ideas.

"It is very strange," Goethe wrote in the midst of the turbulent Napoleonic era, "that just at a time when so many people are being killed, one tries most neatly to pretty up the remaining ones." "Please continue to send me," he asked Bettina, "from time to time news of this beneficent institution [Philantropinum in Frankfurt], of which you are the sponsor. It is only proper for the Jew-savior of Braunschweig [Jacobsohn] to look upon his people as they should and ought to become, yet one cannot blame the Prince-Primate for treating this people as they are and as they will remain for a while."[27] Harsh words which reveal Goethe's resistance to the emancipation of the Jews.

Although Goethe could not resolve to raise his voice in behalf of the Jews and, during their struggle for equality, stood aside as an indifferent and at times ironic onlooker, he did not aim at curtailing rights once they had been obtained, as did a good number of his contemporaries. Nor did he after 1815 support the reactionary movement which was eager to thrust the Jews back to their former status of pariahs.

In the postwar period Goethe suggested the celebration of the anniversary of the battle of Leipzig of October 1813 instead of the Reformation festival, which was considered sacred only by Protestants. That battle, Goethe remarked, "owes its glory also . . . to the Jews,"[28] fellow-combatants in the wars against France. Nobody had asked the man of the *Landsturm* about his religion. Since this day could be celebrated by everyone, whatever his faith, Goethe concluded, it would be even more than a national celebration, namely a festival of purest humanity. Such a view was in harmony with the spirit of the emancipation, as partly accomplished in Prussia and other German states, and was directly opposed to the anti-Semitism which again began to flood the German lands after the war of liberation.

In this era of reaction, the Jew was often presented on the German stage as the butt of ridicule. In Sessa's *Unser Verkehr* [Our Life] and in the plays of Romantics such as Achim von Arnim and Clemens Brentano, the Jew appeared as a contemptible creature. Goethe sharply condemned this abuse of the Jew. "It is a disgrace," he said, "to put in the pillory a people which has produced such excellent talents in art and science."[29] Goethe prevented the staging in Weimar of a play in which Jews were pictured as despicable. Moreover he was helpful in showing on the stage a noble Jew. According to his own testimony, Goethe had "actively assisted" Schiller in the latter's attempt in 1801 to adapt Lessing's *Nathan* to the Weimar stage. On several occasions Goethe demonstrated keen interest in Lessing's great drama and its message. In 1802 he congratulated the Weimar theater intendant that "such a drama" in which reason prevails "could be often repeated"[30] and expressed the hope that it would make a yearly appearance on the stage.

Can it be assumed that Goethe, who warmly recommended to the Germans the "sentiment of toleration"[31] toward the Jews, in another context judged "toleration toward the Jews" to be "menacing" to the civil order?[32] If we place the whole sentence in its context, it becomes clear that the "menaced" civil order was obsolete and deserved to be changed.

The assumption that Goethe's reference to the alleged "menace" to civil order was meant to be somewhat ironical is strengthened by another passage in *Dichtung und Wahrheit* [Fiction and Truth], where Goethe ridiculed the same citizens of Frankfurt am Main because of their intolerance toward the Jews. On the eve of the election day, Goethe wrote, "all aliens are banished from the city, the gates are closed, the Jews confined to their ghetto, and the citizen of Frankfurt fancies himself quite a bit that he alone may remain witness to such a great festivity."[33]

In Goethe's novel *Wilhelm Meisters Wanderjahre* [Wilhelm Meister's Wandering Years], the hero Friedrich makes the following utterance: "In this sense which one might perhaps call pedantic, but must recognize as consequent, we do not tolerate the Jew among us; for how should we not begrudge him a share in the highest culture, the origin of which he denies?"[34] This remark refers, as R. Eberhard in his study *Goethe und die Bibel* observed,[35] "only and exclusively" to the particular attitude of that peculiar religious humanitarian union to which Friedrich belonged, which stressed free Christianity; it did not reflect Goethe's own opinions. In the same novel "the Jewish people is rendered the honor" of figuring largely in the education of the Germans. Its history is made the basis, the "main subject" of the German curriculum, because the Jews, compared to other nations and religions, possessed many "advantages." "Before the ethnic tribunal," Goethe let the Eldest say, "before the tribunal of the God of nations, no question will be asked whether it is the best, the most excellent nation, but only whether it lasts, whether it has preserved itself. The Israelite nation was never very good, as its leaders, judges, officials, and prophets have made clear in reproaching it. Yet it still has to find its equal in independence and steadfastness, in courage, and, if all this does not count any more, in tenacity. It is the most persevering people on earth; it is, it was, it will be, in order to glorify the name of Jehovah at all times."[36]

YOUTHFUL IMPRESSIONS AND THE BIBLE

What were Goethe's earliest relations with the German Jews? Let us listen to Goethe himself: "To the matters which distressed the boy and perhaps even the young man," Goethe related in his autobiography *Dichtung und Wahrheit,* "belonged particularly the condition of the Jewish quarter, properly called Jewish street because it hardly consists of anything more than a single street, which in early times probably had been hemmed in between the city wall and moat as in a prison. The narrowness, the filth, the crowded conditions, the accent of a disagreeable language, all together made the most unpleasant impression, even if one looked into it merely as a passerby. It was a long time before I dared to enter alone, and I did not return after I had escaped the importunities of so many men, untiringly asking or offering to shop and trade. At the same time the old fairy tales of cruelty against Christian children by the Jews hovered dark over the young soul. And though one more recently thought better of them, yet the large, derisive, and obscene picture which could still be seen quite well on an arch beneath the tower of the bridge, in rudeness to them, testified very much against them; for it had not been made by private ill-will but by public order."[37] The inhabitants of the city of Frankfurt and of its ghetto were strangers to each other, separated by walls which no one could breach completely.

There hardly existed sharper contrasts than those between the overcrowded ghetto, without light and air, and the world of the carefully tended child of the Frankfurt councilor, no greater contrasts than those between the language of Goethe and the Yiddish of the ghetto Jews, between the young man striving for inner harmony and the Jews struggling for survival. Goethe himself has admitted that as a youth largely aesthetic impressions determined his attitude toward the Jews. "What in my early youth stirred as contempt against the Jews," he wrote, "was rooted in the enigmatic, the not beautiful."[38]

Goethe was bound to lose this fear when he met "pretty Jewish girls." The beauty of Jewish women is a subject to which he often alluded. Thus he remarked about the book *Judith:* "The Hebrew people is not to be despised, because it has beautiful women; should one not wage wars over such beautiful women?" Goethe rid himself also of his fear of the enigmatic, as his interest in the unknown and the mysterious awakened. "The Jews," Goethe wrote, "remained the chosen people of God and, however it happened, walked around, a living testament to earlier times. Besides, they were, after all, also human beings—active, pleasing—and one could not deny one's respect for the stubbornness with which they clung to their customs. Moreover, the girls were pretty and liked it well if a Christian lad, meeting them on the Sabbath on the Fischer field, showed himself friendly and attentive. I was therefore extremely curious to learn to know their ceremonies. I did not cease until I had visited their school several times, had attended a circumcision and a wedding, and had gained an impression of the feast of the tabernacles. Everywhere I was well received, well served, and invited to return; for persons of influence introduced me or recommended me."[39]

The accent of "an unpleasant language" had first made "a most disagreeable impression" on Goethe. But in the same way that he developed an interest in Jewish customs and traditions, he also became interested in their languages, Yiddish and Hebrew. Goethe even conceived a plan for a novel in which seven brothers and sisters, scattered all over the world, communicated with one another about their experiences and impressions in different languages. "The youngest, a kind of impertinent little nestling, because he had no access to or knowledge of other languages, had turned to Yiddish and, because of his terrible letters, made the others despair and his parents laugh at the splendid idea."

"As things of this sort, once begun, have no end and no limit, it happened also in this case; for a while I tried to master the baroque Yiddish and to write it as well as I could read it. I soon found out that I lacked the knowledge of Hebrew whence alone the modern, corrupted, and distorted form could be derived and with some certainty discerned. I therefore disclosed to my father the necessity of my studying Hebrew and tried very actively to obtain his permission, for I had an even higher ambition." He wished to read the Old Testament, which "because of its peculiarity had always very specially attracted" him, in its original language.

Goethe highly esteemed both the Bible and ancient Judaism. The Old Testament, the Jewish prophets, and the Books of Job and Ruth in particular found in him an enthusiastic reader. The Book of Job appeared to him "the most tender and most inimitable thing" and the Book of Ruth made him captive through its "unconquerable charm." "And so book after book," Goethe remarked on the literature of the Hebrews, "the book of all books should prove that it has been given to us in order that we might enlighten ourselves, that we might educate ourselves."[40] "As far as I am concerned," he admitted in *Dichtung und Wahrheit,* "I loved and appreciated the Bible; because to it almost alone I owed my ethical education, and the teachings, the symbols, the parables, all had impressed themselves deeply upon me and had become effective in one way or the other."[41] It is therefore not astonishing that Goethe always indignantly rejected attacks on the Bible: "Unjust, derisive, distorting attacks on the Bible," he wrote in another context, "displeased me."[42] He urged people to "renounce . . . every prejudice of selfish partisanship in regard to the Old Testament"[43] and to do justice to its greatness.

Various considerations led Goethe to reject attacks against the Bible. Goethe, the "great heathen," is supposed to have replied to a question of the pious Julie von Egloffstein whether he too read the Bible, "Yes, my daughter, only differently from you."[44] Goethe did not wish to deprive the masses of their faith in God and resisted every such attempt, yet as a man of scholarship, he defended freedom of inquiry and held that the Holy Scriptures would suffer as little "damage" as any other tradition "when we treat it in a critical sense, if we expose where it contradicts itself."[45] Another time, not quite consistently, he criticized that some "now jolted the five Books of Moses, and if the annihilating criticism is somehow injurious, it is in religious matters."[46] Goethe's wish to preserve the religiosity of the people was not the only motive for his opposing attacks on the Bible. It was for him personally an irreplaceable source, both of inspiration and of inner peace.

The young Goethe had not tolerated derision of the Bible and of Jewry because of its inherent "injustice." "Although I am not an anti-Christian . . . but rather a decided non-Christian," he had written to Lavater, then his friend, "your Pilate, etc. have made a disgusting impression upon me, because you oppose too turbulently the old God and his children."[47] Goethe felt not only repelled by attacks upon the ancient Jews but especially grateful to them for their Scriptures, to which he owed his spiritual and intellectual development and peace: "When the always stirring force of imagination," Goethe wrote, "led me at times in this direction, then into another, when the mixture of color and history, mythology and religion, threatened to confuse me, then I liked to flee into those oriental realms. I plunged into the first Books of Moses and found myself there among the scattered tribes of shepherds simultaneously in the greatest loneliness and in the greatest company."[48]

In *Dichtung und Wahrheit* Goethe devoted many a page to the Old Testament and expounded his own thoughts on it. To the self-posed question why he again presented these often-told stories so elaborately, he replied that he could not describe in any other way the "peace" which surrounded him "when outside wild and strange events took place."[49] The Jewish patriarchs strongly attracted Goethe, especially Abraham and Isaac. "As human, beautiful and gay as the religion of the patriarch appears," still traits of "wildness and cruelty" permeate it, "whence the human being may arise or into which he may plunge again." Jacob finds little favor with Goethe because he knows how to "preserve his advantage" and to acquire, through skill and sympathy, the best and largest part of the herd; he becomes "thereby the truly worthy tribal progenitor of the people of

Israel and a model for his descendants." Yet Goethe finds in Jacob also attractive traits which again win him his "affection." If Jacob has not acquired "our affection by cunning and greed, he wins it by his lasting and sacred love for Rachel." Goethe found the aptitude for business, which repelled him in the case of Jacob, again in Joseph, in whom, however, he admired this trait, because Joseph practiced it "in the larger meaning."

JEWISH HISTORY AND TRADITION IN GOETHE'S WRITING

Two earlier treatises testify to Goethe's continuous preoccupation with biblical questions. The first dates from the year 1773 and bears the title "What Was Written on the Tables of the Covenant?" The second essay, composed in 1779, is named "Israel in the Desert." In the latter the character of Moses emerges unfavorably. He possesses talent neither for generalship nor for government. Goethe, who later changed his view about him, was well aware that he denied Moses qualities which "so far have been highly admired" in him, yet claimed to esteem him, nevertheless. Moses had a "personality on which in such cases everything depends. The character rests upon personality, not upon talents."

Goethe developed the thesis that the migration of the Hebrews through the desert had lasted only two years, not forty years. Only such a supposition, he believed, could "save, justify and honor" the leader and general Moses, since otherwise he was bound to appear incompetent. Still, the characterization of Moses, everything considered, remains far from flattering, though it apparently was not written in a spirit hostile to the Jews.

On the one hand, Goethe sympathized with the Jews because of their oppression in Egypt. "One seeks to torment, to frighten, to molest, to annihilate the Hebrews." On the other, the Israelites and Moses cruelly slaughtered the first-born of the Egyptians and did not recognize any "further obligations" toward them. Goethe himself, however, had previously related the Egyptian plan to make the Jews construct prisons and dungeons for themselves and to kill them afterwards.

In later years Moses was to appear to Goethe as an admirable and magnificent figure. In the *Italienische Reise* [Italian Journey] he called Moses one of the great forerunners of Jesus.[50] In *Hermann und Dorothea* a dignified Elder, a judge who soothed aroused feelings and called upon opponents to be reasonable and to help one another, is compared to Moses.[51] According to Eckermann, in 1828 Goethe remarked that Moses had well understood how to liberate his people from disgraceful oppression, slavery, and tyranny.[52]

The German poets and playwrights showed a strong inclination to select themes from Jewish history. At times they posed contemporary German-Jewish problems; more often they merely borrowed settings from ancient Jewish history to treat timeless problems of general human interest. The Old Testament was a rich source of inspiration also for Goethe, especially in his first poetic strides. He was attracted by the characters of Joseph, Jezebel, and Ruth. "Description of biblical characters and events, only sketched in the Holy Scriptures, was no longer alien to the Germans," Goethe related in *Dichtung und Wahrheit*. The treatment of the story of Joseph had for a long time appeared desirable to him, and he finally plunged into it with great zeal. "I had not yet undertaken such a great work as that biblical prose-epic poem. It was . . . a rather calm period and nothing called back the force of my imagination from Palestine and Egypt."[53]

The language, the spirit, and the images of the Bible and of other ancient Jewish writings influenced Goethe in most varied ways.[54] The Hebrew language, for which Goethe had come to display increasing interest, stimulated the fancy of many German writers. Symbols and parables, lessons and events, derived from the ancient Jewish writings, had a beneficial effect upon German poetry in general and on Goethe himself, as he freely admitted.

The influence of the biblical language upon Goethe and the many biblical allusions in his poems and letters have often been pointed out. The prologue in heaven in Goethe's *Faust* shows a striking similarity to the Book of Job. Similarities to the Song of Solomon can be found in Gretchen's song in *Faust;* Goethe esteemed both books very highly. In his reverence toward the old Hebraic literature Goethe rivaled Herder, who first had opened his eyes to its beauty and depth. It was in the *West-östlicher Divan* that Goethe recalled the merits of Herder and Eichhorn in regard to Hebrew literature. "A great part of the Old Testament," he observed, was "written in exalted spirit, with enthusiasm, and belongs to the field of poetry." It was given to the world "that we might enlighten ourselves, that we might educate ourselves."[55]

Goethe looked upon the Bible and Jewish history as especially suitable to form the basis of the "enlightenment and education" of all peoples, including the German nation. This idea repeatedly cropped up in Goethe's works, as in *Wilhelm Meisters Wanderjahre*. Goethe had remarked that he owed to the Bible almost alone his moral discipline. The history of the Hebrews as embedded in the Holy Scriptures was to play a similarly vital role in the education of the entire German people.

Goethe wished to include the stories of Jewish tradition in the

German *Volksbuch*. He was convinced that Jewish history contained generally valid truths and universal values, in spite of occasional references to what he considered the particularism of the Jews and their religion. If contrasted with Islam and the Indian religions, the Jewish religion appeared quite favorable, though the "highest praise" was reserved for Christianity. "The Jewish religion," Goethe observed, "will always generate a certain strong self-will, but also free reasoning and lively activity."[56]

Jewish history preoccupied Goethe almost continually. As Riemer said: "Goethe had made the history of the Jewish nation from its first appearance the object of a special and thorough study, had conceived correctly its most characteristic features and had also put the peculiar qualities which nature, chance and fate have given them in the proper light. . . . This alone proves that he could not harbor any prejudice against them, which would have been unworthy of him as a scientist and a historian."[57]

Many of the contemporary Jews, Riemer continued, stood "through pure Deism, of which the enlightened among them may boast, already close enough" to Goethe. Also, he "owed so much to the ethics of Spinoza." This common way of thinking in religious and philosophical fields helped to overcome the "contempt" and "shyness" which had stirred in the young Goethe. Later, as Goethe observed, he developed "respect" for contemporary Jews, "when I learned to know many talented and sensitive men of this people."[58]

OTHER CONTACTS WITH JEWS

The noted literary historian Ludwig Geiger believed that Goethe, while in Frankfurt, had had little contact with individual Jews. But according to G. L. Kriegk in *Deutsche Kulturbilder* (1974), Goethe, after returning from his studies in Strassburg, represented in Frankfurt courts no fewer than seven Jewish clients.[59] Goethe's uncle, Jost Textor, had often served as the advocate of Jews of Frankfurt, but after becoming judge he transferred many of his clients, including Jews, to his nephew. Goethe's advocacy of Jews was no doubt a business affair, though he would hardly have taken their cases and pleaded them with energy and skill had he disliked them.

Goethe showed a fatherly friendship for David Veit, a Jewish student of medicine whom Rahel Levin had recommended to him. He also esteemed two Jewish disciples of Kant, Solomon Maimon and Lazarus Bendavid. His friend Zelter introduced him to David Friedländer, the leading spokesman for the emancipation of the Jews; Goethe came to know him as a fellow coin collector. Among the many persons who year after year made a pilgrimage to Weimar were several Jews, including Solomon Munk, later a famous Orientalist, and Eduard Simson, afterwards president of the Goethe Society and the first President of the Supreme Court in the new German Reich. Goethe procured a professorate for the poet O. L. B. Wolff. He was especially friendly with the noted jurist and university professor Eduard Gans, who once had devoted his efforts to the Society of the Science of Judaism but was later baptized.

Goethe was not free of contradictions. He termed the law prohibiting Jews from staying overnight in Jena "praiseworthy," yet in Weimar he opened his own house to Jews and invited many of them to repeat their visit. Thus Riemer observed: "Since Goethe also performed social honors in Weimar, the strangers who came to visit him—scholars, artists, famous travelers of whatever faith, including Jews and people who associated with them—were invited to his table."[60]

When in the year 1827 the Jewish painter Moritz Oppenheim came to Weimar, he presented several paintings to Goethe. The poet showed himself very appreciative, arranging for an exhibition of Oppenheim's paintings in his own home and later obtaining a teaching position for him. The Jewish playwright Michael Beer submitted his drama *Der Paria* [The Pariah] to Goethe, who recommended the play—the work of a "brave man"—for the Weimar stage. As he wrote, *"The Pariah* may stand aptly as symbol for the degraded, suppressed, despised humanity of all peoples and, as such a subject appears generally human, it is thereby highly poetic." Beer, according to Riemer, enjoyed Goethe's "most genuine approval." Riemer testified further that Goethe, "in poetry as well as painting and sculpture, was through instructive advice and artistic tasks in close intercourse with several men of Jewish descent. He turned his fatherly love and care especially to the young Felix Mendelssohn-Bartholdy, as the letters to Zelter show most touchingly."[61]

The twelve-year-old Mendelssohn-Bartholdy became Goethe's favorite. Zelter notified Goethe from time to time of the progress and the successes of the young artist, since the poet had taken a lively interest in the talented and handsome boy. "I am Saul," Goethe later wrote to the young Mendelssohn-Bartholdy, "and you are my David; if I am sad and gloomy, come to me and cheer me up with your string play." Similarly, Goethe admired the great Jewish composer of those days, Giacomo Meyerbeer, whom he held capable of writing a composition for his *Faust.* According to Eckermann, Goethe spoke of him as "a German character."[62]

Less fortunate was Goethe's meeting with the young Heinrich

Heine in October, 1824. Heine, although critical of Goethe in some respects, was, everything considered, an admirer of the German prince of poets. Goethe himself, who used words of praise sparingly, in turn spoke of Heine as a "gifted man" and a "talent."[63] Related in spirit to Heine, Ludwig Börne, a German-Jewish critic and journalist, vehemently attacked Goethe, though not the poet and playwright but rather the man who, in his judgment, looked coolly and indifferently at the struggle of the German people for freedom and equality.

When in 1778 Goethe had briefly stopped in Berlin, he had wanted, according to the poetess Karschin, to visit only Moses Mendelssohn, though the latter, like Lessing, had been critical of Goethe's youthful works. Goethe himself always recognized Mendelssohn's merits. That Mendelssohn later turned against Spinozism could hardly have endeared him to Goethe, and herein rather than in any hostility to the Jews must be sought the cause of his occasional criticism of Mendelssohn. Thus Goethe enjoyed Hamann's sneers at Mendelssohn's *Jerusalem,* spoke at one time of his "Jewish whistles," and stirred up Johann Jacobi to write against him. The literary historian Julius Bab correctly observed that a question of *Weltanschauung* lay at the bottom of this quarrel and that Judaism was not the issue.[64] If Goethe took a stand against the Jew Mendelssohn, at the same time he defended another Jew, Spinoza.

In *Dichtung und Wahrheit* Goethe referred thus to the struggle over Spinoza: "The break was so violent that as a result of it we lost . . . one of our most worthy men, Mendelssohn."[65] In another passage Goethe made reference to the "general admiration"[66] Mendelssohn had aroused. Goethe had found the importunities and the religious impetuosity of Lavater vis-à-vis Mendelssohn "irritating." When after Mendelssohn's death he heard mocking verses about the deceased, he remarked to Frau von Stein: "A poor Jew cannot even leave the world without being jeered at."[67]

The dispute that had excited the German intellectual world after Lessing's death focused on the question of whether Lessing in his last days turned to Spinozism, which according to the prevailing notion of the time was identical with the worst atheism. Moses Mendelssohn believed that he had to defend Lessing against this accusation. Goethe, however, having early freed himself from the prejudices that had engulfed Spinoza, concluded from the circumstance that he had led a "life pleasing to men and God," that it could not have sprung from "pernicious principles," and that he must have been misunderstood.[68]

Goethe valued Spinoza highly both as a thinker and as a man, and Spinozist ideas are deeply embedded in his works. He called Spinoza the "most unselfish" man who had ever lived on earth[69] and always maintained for him the affection one reserves for those whose spirit and thoughts have deeply influenced one's own philosophy. "I still remember well," Goethe wrote, "what calm and clarity came over me when I turned over the pages of the posthumous works of that remarkable man. I was still very distinctly aware of this effect upon me without being able to remember particulars; I therefore hastened again to the writings to which I had become so indebted, and the same peaceful air blew at me again. I abandoned myself to these readings and, by looking into myself, I believed never to have discerned the world so clearly." His attitude toward Spinoza, Goethe admitted, had produced a "great effect" upon his subsequent life.

That Goethe entertained friendly relations with many Jews was not entirely accidental. German Jewry, liberated from the ghetto, highly valued German culture, which in those days blossomed forth more splendidly than ever before. Jews often formed a more appreciative audience than did the Germans themselves. Riemer, by no means a friend of the Jews, wrote thus: "The educated Jews were for the greatest part more obliging and lasting in their admiration of Goethe's personality as well as of his writings than many of his coreligionists. As a rule they show more pleasing attention and flattering interest than an indigenous German, and their talent of quick perception, their penetrating reason, their peculiar wit make them a more sensitive public than, unfortunately, is found among the at times slow and dull genuine and original Germans."[70]

Among the educated Jews, Riemer continued, women stood out, "possessing those gifts in a even more amiable form; thus it came about that Goethe liked to read to them his most recent poetic productions, individually or in company, for instance in Carlsbad (1807, 1808, 1810), because he could always be certain to find some approval, as I can confirm from my own experience in the cases of Frau von Eibenberg, von Grotthus, von Eskeles, Flies and others."

Rahel Levin, "the greatest woman on earth," as Alexander von der Marwitz called her, was intellectually the most prominent among the many Jewish women who played a major role in the social and intellectual life of Berlin. An enthusiastic admirer of Goethe, she rendered great service to him and to German literature by propagating his writings in Berlin and throughout all of Germany. She was the first in the Prussian capital to grasp Goethe's genius. Goethe praised her remarks about *Wilhelm Meisters Wanderjahre* as being full of understanding and recommended them for print. When Goethe met Rahel in Karlsbad, he made this observation to Veit: "She is a girl of extraordinary intelligence, who always thinks, and of feelings."

For many years Goethe maintained close relations with the two sisters Sarah and Marianne Meyer, who later became the ladies von Grotthus and von Eibenberg. Their correspondence with Goethe dates from the year 1799 until 1810 and 1814 respectively, an indication of Goethe's lasting interest. "Dearest friend," he addressed Frau von Eibenberg; a deep affection drew him to her and caused him to bring the *Wahlverwandtschaften* [Elective Affinities] to a speedy conclusion.

In his personal relations Goethe made hardly any distinction between Jews and Gentiles. Yet, though he came to appreciate, even to love, several Jewish women, Goethe was an opponent of mixed marriages. When in 1823 he returned from Marienbad and learned that mixed marriages had been made legal, he said, "Do we everywhere want to lead in the absurd, to be the first to try everything grotesque?"[71] True, after his experience in Marienbad Goethe was in a very irritated mood. There the vitality of the old man had burst out again into the high flame of a great love; but he had been rejected and was deeply wounded. Unknown perhaps to himself, a touch of envy, of dislike of marriages of any kind, may have gripped the poet. His opposition to mixed marriages was probably rooted in the realm of the human-all-too-human; he expressed himself on this issue at the height of a traumatic personal experience. The rather emphatic assurance of the National Socialist literary historian Franz Koch that Goethe's rejection of mixed marriages was not the "thundering of a dejected old man"[72] seems merely to strengthen this assumption.

"I was opposed to our new Jewish law," Goethe remarked later. "I think the Superintendent should rather resign his office than tolerate the marriage of a Jewess in the name of Holy Trinity; every contempt of the religious feelings of the people brings unhappiness. But I do not hate the Jews."[73] One will observe that Goethe, unlike Adolf Hitler, who once claimed him as like-minded on this issue,[74] disavowed any hatred or any racial motive for his rejection of mixed marriages. He offered instead religious considerations as explanation for his negative attitude.

Actually, Goethe expressed opposition to mixed marriages just that one time, and it seems to have applied only to the common people. In the case of the social and intellectual elite, among whom marriages between Christian men and Jewish women were not uncommon, mixed marriages had never disturbed Goethe. As mentioned, the ladies von Eibenberg and von Grotthus were Jewish by birth but later married Christian German princes. Rahel Levin, whom he admired, was likewise linked in marriage to Karl Varnhagen von Ense.

Jew-haters have often maligned Germans whose *Weltanschauung* they abhorred and proclaimed them to be of Jewish descent, as for instance Lessing, Jean Paul, and Kant. Some have claimed Goethe also to be a descendant of Jews! They "discovered" among Goethe's ancestors the family Lindheimer, which promptly was declared to be partly Jewish. This origin was supposed to explain the cosmopolitanism in Goethe's outlook, the prevalence of human, antinationalist traits, and especially his interest in and friendliness toward Jews. A German writer, Eugen Dühring, one of the few racial anti-Semites in nineteenth-century Germany, was one of the first to point to Goethe's alleged "Hebraic stirrings."[75]

Most of the Jew-haters, however, recognized that in expounding this "thesis" they rendered the Jews only honor and brought shame and ridicule upon their own heads. They therefore made of Goethe no Jew—but rather a hater of Jews! They referred to some utterances of his, which they culled out of context, giving them an anti-Semitic coloring, while simultaneously suppressing numerous passages which were favorable to Jews and Judaism. One of their own, Houston Stewart Chamberlain, reprehended them for their inept deceptive maneuvers.[76] Nevertheless, other anti-Semitic writers persisted in their efforts to paint Goethe as an illustrious forerunner of anti-Semitic thought.

A SATIRE ON JEWS OR ON ANTI-SEMITISM?

Theodor Fritsch, editor of the long and widely known *Antisemitenkatechismus,* and Franz Koch, a National Socialist literary historian, quoted as proof of Goethe's allegedly anti-Semitic convictions a few lines from his youthful farce *Das Jahrmarktsfest zu Plundersweilen* [The Annual Fair at Plundersweilen] (1774). Yet the only words cited were those spoken by the biblical figure of Hamann, whom Goethe, of course, had let ride his anti-Semitic hobbyhorse. Hamann is pictured as a conceited individual, powerful yet insecure, a false and vengeful courtier. If Goethe intended to ridicule anti-Semitism, he could hardly have designed Hamann very differently. Yet through his mouth Goethe is supposed to have revealed to the world his most personal views on the Jews. Most likely, Goethe planned to write neither for nor against the Jews, neither for nor against their enemies. Nevertheless, one cannot read the Esther playlet without being struck by how closely it approximated a satire on Jew-hating.

Hamann, an intimate of King Ahasverus, is pictured by Goethe as haughty, intriguing, and hurt in his vanity. He cannot forgive the Jew Mordechai for alone refusing to prostrate himself before him, though the entire Persian realm lies at his feet. Filled with hatred against him and thirsty for personal revenge, he resolves to humiliate and punish all Jews for the "crime" of one of them.[77] Hamann calls forth all his persuasive powers to warn the King of the alleged Jewish threat to throne and altar. Yet the monarch remains calm and unperturbed. In the end all charges raised against the Jews are revealed as hollow and baseless.

The Jews, says Hamann in opening his oration, refuse to pay due respects to Ahasverus. But the King, not losing his equanimity, replies that this makes no difference as long as they sing the psalms, stay peaceful, and pay their taxes. Thereupon Hamann charges that the Jews have "a faith which permits them to rob the Gentiles." To the King this accusation, which he has never heard before, appears simply incredible. How could all this "now so suddenly" have surfaced? He has not heard recently about "murder and highway robbery" committed by them. The clever and adroit courtier, compelled to retreat, attacks anew along another front:

> The Jew loves money and fears danger.
> He knows how to carry money out of the state
> Through trade and interest, with little labor and without great risk!

Whereupon the King retorts,

> I know it only too well, my friend; I am not blind.
> Yet others, uncircumcised, do this even better.

All accusations so far have failed to make an impact. Hamann, however, does not relent in his attacks, pointing to the spectre of a bloody revolt which the Jews supposedly are plotting against the state and in which they scheme to avail themselves of "Judaized" groups; Persia's "Judaization" has allegedly attained a most menacing scope. But the King, undisturbed, counters that of all rebellions that had occurred, none had succeeded.

Finally, Hamann plays his trump card, accusing the Jews of plotting against the King himself. The monarch, now gripped by panic, commands that ten thousand gallows be erected. Thereupon even the Jew-hater Hamann feels compelled to curb the suddenly awakened bloodthirstiness of the King and warns him "against spilling innocent blood! A prince must punish, yet not rage like a tiger." The King thereupon admires Hamann's "magnanimity," since the latter does not want to hang all Jews but only the wealthiest, and promises him their "fortune and good chattels." "A sad present," replies Hamann hypocritically. He emerges thus as a slanderer and thief who first blackens the good name of his victims in order to annihilate them the more easily and to steal their property.

The original version of the Esther scenes in Goethe's comedy *Das Jahrmarktsfest zu Plundersweilen* is found in "Zwei ältere Szenen vom 'Jahrmarktsfest zu Plundersweilen.' " In complete disregard of all chronology Hamann and King Ahasverus are placed in the Christian era. Hamann appears in this earlier version as a rationalist and atheist. "Only reason" should guide men; "religion and sentimentalism" should be "destroyed." The rationalist and atheist is an opponent not only of Christianity but also of the Jews and Jewry. Hamann's anger is aroused by "the miserable false doctrines of the sentimentalists from Judaea."[78]

Goethe's earlier conception of Hamann as an enemy of all religion, of Christianity as well as of Judaism, is as interesting as the later one and also in many ways revealing. Anti-Semitism, personified by Hamann, appears to Goethe not only as hostile to the Jews but also to religion as such, for the Jew-hater Hamann is also an enemy of the Christians.

If there was any moment in Goethe's life which similarly exemplified his attitude toward the Jews, it was perhaps the courageous intercession of the young man on the occasion of a sudden outbreak of fire in the Jewish ghetto of Frankfurt, a mishap which he himself related in his autobiography *Dichtung und Wahrheit:* "In the very narrow Jewish street a violent fire had broken out. My general benevolence, the desire springing from it to help actively, drove me there, well dressed as I was." Under Goethe's direction the fire was localized and extinguished. Yet hardly was the worst disaster overcome when already "mischief" asserted itself. "Fleeing people, pitiful to look at, dragging their miserable belongings on their shoulders, did not remain unmolested. Mischievous youths squirted water at them and added contempt and rudeness to the misery. Yet the wickedness was put down, through reasonable persuading and inveighing against them, probably in consideration of my clean clothes, which I neglected."[79]

Without regard to himself, Goethe rushed to the help of the Jews when they were threatened by the flames and sternly opposed "the wild, rude manners" of the young "mischief-makers." The motives of the latter were a desire to vex and "pleasure at the misfortune of others," while Goethe's motives were a desire to help, compassion, and a strong feeling for justice.

Schiller

Perhaps no other poet made so deep an impression on the German Jews as Friedrich Schiller. The poet and champion of freedom was bound to produce a resounding echo among a still suppressed people. Schiller's youthful revolutionary fight against enslavement, which found expression in the battle cry "In tyrannos" in *Die Räuber* [The Robbers], could hardly have been alien to German Jewry, which impatiently longed for its charter of freedom. Marquis Posa's struggle for freedom of thought in the drama *Don Carlos* and the fight of the Swiss in *Wilhelm Tell* against the yoke of alien rulers and for human dignity and liberty appeared to the German Jews as their own fight. And if Wilhelm Tell's liberating deed seemed justifiable on the basis of the "eternal rights of humanity," which "stand above, high, inalienable," the Jews were bound to support wholeheartedly demands based upon these natural rights.

Schiller's native state was Württemberg. This was the state in which the powerful court Jew Süss (Jud Süss) had once lived, where he had exerted a decisive influence upon the affairs of state, and where he had to atone with his life for his own and his ruler's faults. Jew-hating in Württemberg had thus a historic significance of its own. In Schiller, however, the progressive spirit of the age overcame the local and provincial prejudices which may have formed part of his youthful environment.

Schiller's contacts with Jews were apparently neither frequent nor intimate. He highly valued two Jewish disciples of Kant, Lazarus Bendavid and Solomon Maimon, who were both contributors to his magazine *Die Horen*. As a letter to his friend Theodor Körner revealed, Schiller considered them among "the best humanistic writers" of his age. He had found high excellence in Maimon's *Streifereien in das Gebiet der Philosophie* [Excursions into the Realm of Philosophy].[80] A Jewish actor, Jacob Herzfeld, repeatedly played Wilhelm Tell on the Weimar stage to Schiller's great satisfaction.

The playwright concluded a contract with Michaelis, a Jewish publisher, for the publication of a *Musenalmanach* [Poetic Almanac]. He subsequently wrote to his friend Hoven: "You need not turn away, if I perhaps select a Jew (namely one who is truly circumcised) as a publisher. There indeed has appeared one as a Jewish bookseller, and he has an annual almanac of mine in publication. The Saxon Jews have much *Kultur* and are of some importance. This one, who calls himself Michaelis, is an enterprising young man who possesses knowledge, has good connections, and is held in good repute by the

Duke of Mecklenburg.''[81] He not only entered into business relations with Michaelis but recommended him to others.

Schiller's relations with Michaelis and also with a Jewish money-lender by the name of Beit did not remain happy. Yet it is noteworthy that, in spite of some unpleasant encounters, the playwright never criticized them as Jews.

Schiller's early familiarity with the Bible, to the study of which his pious mother had probably induced him, showed itself in his poetic works. The Bible had hardly less importance for Schiller than it did for Goethe. It was not accidental that Schiller chose for his serious plays topics borrowed from Jewish history. He wished to present dramatically the rebellion of Absalom. Also, in the harsh training of the *Karlsschule* he conceived the idea of a biblical epic, the hero of which, according to the testimony of his schoolmate Petersen, was to be Moses, the liberator of his people from an oppressive yoke. What the young Schiller wrote about his *Don Carlos* was equally valid for himself: "The most beautiful dreams of liberty are dreamed behind prison bars." His high appreciation of Moses also found expression in a later essay on him.

In spirit, language, and images the Bible produced rich fruits in Schiller's works. Its strong influence appeared in his drama *Die Jungfrau von Orleans* [The Maid of Orleans]. Like Joseph, Joan of Arc recognized the future in her dreams, and just as Samson tore the lion into pieces, Joan overwhelmed the tiger which broke into her herd. Passages from the Bible influenced Schiller in *Wallensteins Lager* [Wallenstein's Camp]. Numerous references to the Holy Scriptures can also be found in his drama *Die Räuber,* the language of which is saturated with biblical expressions. According to an authority on Schiller, Eugen Kühnemann, in *Die Räuber* the playwright's feeling for the Old Testament is stronger than for the New Testament.[82] The old Moor asks Amelia to read him the biblical stories of Jacob and of Joseph and his brothers to gain from them strength and peace of mind. Schiller's poems, too, bear the imprint of the Bible. The poems "An die Freude" [To Joy] and "Der Abend" [The Evening] disclose the influence of the Psalms.

The view has been expressed that in *Die Räuber* Schiller intended to paint Spiegelberg, one of the robbers, as a Jew. Spiegelberg, in contrast to the other robbers, who show human, amiable, and sometimes noble traits, is an unpleasant, even wicked character. Karl Moor's laughingly expressed surmise that Spiegelberg may be a Jew is, however, indignantly rejected by the latter. He furthermore remarks: "I am miraculously already precircumcised."[83] Ludwig Geiger expressed the opinion that the word "miraculously" precluded Spiegelberg's Jewish origin. It must also be borne in mind that the actual model for Spiegelberg was not a Jew;[84] three of Schiller's schoolmates from the military school lent their traits to Spiegelberg.

It was Schiller's adaptation of Lessing's *Nathan der Weise* that first brought success to this great drama on the German stage. Schiller valued Lessing very highly; among the Germans of his age Lessing had thought "most clearly, keenly, and at the same time most liberally" about art. Schiller did not close his eyes to what he considered technical weaknesses of the play *Nathan,* although its moral tendency was close to his heart.[85] After abridgements and various other modifications that left the characters on the whole unchanged, the drama was put on the stage in Weimar on November 28, 1801. Schiller thus rendered Lessing's *Nathan* great service and identified himself with Lessing's call for tolerance and friendship among the adherents of different religions.

Schiller, like Lessing, at times sharply criticized individual members of the clergy. But the German classicists Herder and Goethe, Lessing and Schiller, did not wish to assail religion as such or the Holy Scriptures in particular. The young Schiller refused emphatically "to let his wit shine at the expense of religion" and attacked those who wanted to "maltreat" and ridicule the noble simplicity of the Scriptures.[86]

Schiller the historian touched upon the question of the significance of the Jewish people in world history in the academic address "Was heisst und zu welchem Ende studiert man Universalgeschichte?" (What does world history mean and to what purpose does one study it?) with which he opened his lectures in Jena. He emphasized that his epoch was a great "debtor to past centuries" and that all previous ages had exerted themselves "to bring about our human century." "Our Christian religion, prepared by countless revolutions, had to grow out of Judaism."[87]

In the essay "Die Sendung Moses" [The Mission of Moses] Schiller, by implication, came out in support of the equality of the Jews, though the relevant passage, if examined only superficially, might create the opposite impression—that of an aversion against the Jews. This essay, in which Schiller's view of the Jews and their ancient history emerged most clearly, appeared in the year 1789. In it he emphasizes strongly the far-reaching cultural importance of the Jews and describes the establishment of the Jewish state by Moses as one of the "most memorable events" of history in general, since it produced effects which could be felt "until this moment." "Christianity and Islam both lean upon the religion of the Hebrews, and without this neither Christianity nor a Koran would ever have existed." It is

therefore "irrefutably true that we owe a great part of the enlightenment which we enjoy today to the Mosaic religion. For through it was
spread a precious truth which human reason, left to itself, might have
found only after a slow development, namely the doctrine of one
God; and it was long kept as an object of blind belief among them,
until it could mature in wiser heads to an idea. Thus a great portion of
the human race was spared all the sad detours to which the belief in
polytheism must finally lead," and the Hebrew constitution attained a
"unique excellence." For these reasons, the "nation of the Hebrews
must appear to us an important people in world history, and all evil
which one is accustomed to attribute to this people, all the endeavors
of witty fellows to belittle it, will not prevent us from being just
toward it."[88]

Even if it was asserted that the ancient Hebrews had been unworthy as a people, the merits of their lawgiver Moses cannot be
questioned or "eradicated, and just as little could the great influence
which this nation rightfully has maintained in world history be annulled." Although Schiller looks upon Judaism merely as an "un-
clean," ordinary vessel, as a "channel" which Providence chose to
transmit to humanity the "noblest" and most precious of all goods,
the truth, he nevertheless "values" and "reveres" it. Schiller attempted to steer what he considered a middle course; he wished to
avoid, in his own words, as much "ascribing to the Hebrew people a
value which it never possessed" as "depriving it of an excellence
which cannot be denied."

Schiller was of the opinion that the ancient Egyptians felt threatened by the rapid increase of the Jews and that they resorted therefore to repressive measures. On humanitarian as well as on political
grounds he emphatically condemned their cruel and unreasonable system of oppression. It was in this context that Schiller advocated the
emancipation of the Jews.

The Egyptians, according to Schiller, had "burdened the Jews
with heavy work, and having thus utilized them for the state, selfishness joined with politics to increase their loads. One reduced them
inhumanly to slave labor for the state and hired special task masters
to spur them on and to maltreat them. But this barbaric treatment did
not prevent them from increasing in even greater numbers. *A sound
policy would naturally have led to dispersing them among the other
inhabitants and to giving them equal rights.*"*[89]

In these words lay much more than a mere condemnation of the

*Italics, A. D. L.

"barbaric treatment" of the Jews by their Egyptian oppressors. By implication these words express Schiller's program for the solution of the German-Jewish problem of his age. A "sound policy," in harmony with the commands of reason and natural law, should not consist in separation and segregation aimed at continued oppression but should be based on dispersing the Jews throughout the entire state and on granting them full equality!

One can better appreciate Schiller's plea in behalf of the emancipation of the Jews if one takes account of the circumstance that he leaned heavily on the work of a thoroughly anti-Semitic writer, the contemporary philosopher K. L. Reinhold's treatise *Über die ägyptischen Mysterien* [On the Egyptian Mysteries].[90] But while Reinhold rejected Jewish emancipation and did not condemn the barbaric treatment of the Jews by the Egyptians, Schiller took the opposite position on these two points. Here is convincing proof that Schiller's stand for the emancipation of the Jews in ancient Egypt reflected his own thought. He approved of Jewish equality any time and everywhere.

In his essay "Die Sendung Moses" Schiller accepted a thesis which has an apparently anti-Jewish implication. Ancient writers, foremost among them the Egyptian priest Manetho and others who were hostile to the Jews, charged that many Jews of antiquity had been lepers. Though the youthful Schiller accepted this view, he had, he stressed, not intended to offend. According to Schiller, the extraordinary natural increase of the Jews had compelled them to live "increasingly closer." "What was more natural," he continued, "than the effects developed which are inevitable in such a case—the greatest uncleanliness and contagious diseases."[91]

Still, Schiller seemed bent on defending rather than attacking the Jews: "This plague therefore, a natural result of their crowded habitation, of their bad and scarce nutrition, and of the maltreatment which people accorded them, became again a new cause of it. . . . Any behavior toward human beings whom the anger of the Gods had marked in such a terrible manner seemed permissible, and people did not have any hesitation in depriving them of the holiest human rights. It is not surprising that barbarism arose against them, the more visible the effects of this barbaric treatment became, and that one punished them increasingly more severely for the misery which one had brought upon them."

As a historian Schiller may have badly erred in accepting the self-serving and patently hostile thesis of the Egyptian priest Manetho. But he made clear that he embraced it not out of hostility or dislike of the Jews but simply because it appeared plausible to him.

Schiller's condemnation of the "barbaric treatment" of the Jews by the Egyptians has an apparently universal significance. It testifies to the poet's abhorrence of the oppression of any people and, in particular, of the oppression of the Jews throughout their long history.[92]

Like Goethe and Schiller, the much admired novelist Jean Paul Friedrich Richter was linked with Weimar, though only briefly. Also like Schiller, he raised his voice in behalf of the Jews. His deep human culture and his personal amiability made him their friend and an energetic fighter for tolerance.

An intimate friendship linked him to a pious young Jew by the name of Emanuel Oswald. "My entire soul rejoices," Jean Paul wrote him, "that you are reading my work, dear friend. You and I belong together. Our acquaintance is brief, but our kinship is eternal."[93]

In the course of a brawl with Bavarian officers in 1795, Oswald had been beaten so severely that he suffered deafness for the rest of his life. In the unsuccessful trials against the perpetrators of the injury Jean Paul remained close at his side. His support of his injured friend and his general interest in Jews and Judaism did not remain unobserved. Because of his sympathy for the Jews, Jean Paul was identified by some as a Jew himself. In a letter of September 2, 1795, he related to his wife, half in earnest, half facetiously, his invitation to the princely palace, where he had found "all necessary sects," "magnetists and antimagnetists, Ultras, Constitutionalists, ladies who were friends and foes of the most recent age, anti-Semites and a few Jews, to whom I belong."[94]

In his essay "Über die Religionen in der Welt" [On the Religions in the World], Jean Paul raised his voice vigorously and emphatically against religious zealots and religious persecution. All religions, he developed therein, promoted more or less the perfection of man; each therefore had its justification. "We betray," he wrote, "not only stupidity, but also rudeness, if we misjudge the utility of many religions . . . and if we stigmatize their worshippers by unkind remarks. . . . The apparent difference of religions is nothing but difference in the degree of their spirituality. . . . Judaism ascended from one degree of spirituality to the other and the Christian religion itself did not always remain the same."

From his conception of the unity of all human life and of everything divine grew his deep humanity and his tolerance. Nothing appeared to him more disagreeable than to offend a man on account of his religious or national origin. "We shall be too much in heaven," he said, "to be still Christians. . . . In Judaism Christianity lay already as a seed."[95]

Kant's Critique of Judaism

Immanuel Kant, the "Alleszermalmer" (iconoclast), as the Jewish philosopher Moses Mendelssohn called him, was in his personal relations a friend of the Jews. He also anticipated and approved their emancipation. Yet he was not free of harsh moods and held a low opinion of the Jewish religion.[96] Kant set great hopes upon education and more liberal interpretations of Jewish religious doctrines, on "purified religious conceptions" which, as he believed he could observe, were gaining ground among the Jews.

The Jewish religion, Kant suggested in his work *Die Religion innerhalb der Grenzen der blossen Vernunft* [Religion within the Confines of Pure Reason], which appeared in the year 1793, was, "according to its original institution, the sum total of mere statutes upon which was based a national constitution." The Jewish religion, which has served the Jewish state and nation, is therefore "not really a religion at all." For true religion must be "founded on the purely moral belief." To Judaism, however, mere "moral additions," which really do not belong to it, had been attached. The Jewish commandments, Kant professed to know, required "only external observations"; the "moral intention in an act," which Christianity later emphasized, was not insisted upon.

Closely connected with this alleged lack of a "moral belief" was the reputed absence in Judaism of the doctrine of immortality. The belief in a future life, in which the deeds springing from noble motives are rewarded and the actions originating in base ones are punished, is, according to Kant, an ethical postulate. The idea of immortality, however, is alien to Judaism. Although it could not be denied that the Jews had given thought to a future life, the belief in a world beyond has, according to Kant, never fully belonged to Judaism.

In Christianity Kant perceived a religion founded upon morality. It appears to him therefore a "complete abandonment of Judaism whence it originated, based upon a wholly new principle, a thorough revolution in matters of belief." Yet later Judaism contained ethical writings. "Thus from Judaism—but not any more from old-fashioned Judaism . . . but from Judaism mixed with a religious belief which contained gradually developed and publicly accepted moral teachings, in a state of affairs in which already much alien [Greek] wisdom had accrued to this otherwise crude people—from such a Judaism Christianity raised itself suddenly, though not unprepared."[97] Though Kant evidently held no lofty conceptions of the Jewish religion, Christianity and "later Judaism" are occasionally placed upon the same plane.

According to Hermann Cohen, an eminent student of Kant and, at the same time, an authority on Judaism, Kant had neither been "an expert in questions of religion and of the science of Judaism"[98] nor had he studied the original sources. Kant's conception of the Jewish religion was gained from Moses Mendelssohn, whom he interpreted in a manner disadvantageous to Judaism. Another source for Kant was Spinoza's criticism of the Jewish teachings in his *Tractatus Theologico-Politicus* [Theological-Political Treatise]. Kant borrowed his conception of Judaism almost word by word from Spinoza. The juxtaposition of Jewish law and of Christian love, a cornerstone in the literature of the Christian Enlightenment and in Deism, had also strongly influenced his judgment. Only if one takes these sources into consideration will one properly comprehend Kant's view.

Still, it is undeniable that a dislike of the Jews colored Kant's judgment on Judaism and the Jewish religion. This emerges in his work *Anthropologie in pragmatischer Hinsicht abgefasst* [Anthropology Written with a Pragmatic Purpose], where, in a long footnote, he discussed some aspects of the Jewish question. This work was written in the winter either of 1795–1796 or 1796–1797. "The Palestinians who live among us," Kant wrote, "have since their exile, because of their inclination to usury, gained the not unjustified reputation of fraudulence. It is perhaps strange to imagine a nation of cheaters of which the by far greatest part does not seek any civil honors, which is held together by an old superstition recognized by the state in which they live, and which seeks the advantages of tricking the people among whom they find protection and cheating each other." These sharp accusations against contemporary Jews and their religion, which go beyond earlier more moderate statements, are followed by the explanatory remark: "Well, this cannot be any other way in the case of an entire nation of mere merchants who are not productive members of society (e.g., of the Jews of Poland)." Nowhere else did Kant voice a similarly hostile view. As a matter of fact, in his work *Der Streit der Fakultäten* [The Dispute of the Faculties] he stated, as shall be seen, almost simultaneously, his conviction of the capacity of the Jews to enjoy equal rights.

According to the *Anthropologie*, the causes of the special economic activities of the Jews, of their lopsided economic structure, do not lie "in their history after the loss of their country." Kant "supposes" that the Jews of Palestine already had been inclined to trade. Yet not racial disposition but historical and geographic reasons are given to explain "the origin of this peculiar constitution (namely a people of mere merchants). . . . Palestine was situated very advantageously for caravan trade."[99]

While the hostility of some of his remarks in the *Anthropologie* should not be minimized, Kant, taking everything into consideration, was not the opponent of the Jews that German anti-Semites have portrayed. His entire *Weltanschauung,* his personal relations with Jews, the reaction of contemporary Jew-haters to him, and, last but not least, his remarks in *Der Streit der Fakultäten* preclude such an inference.

This work, which appeared in 1798, had been written at about the same time as the *Anthropologie.* Although Kant continued to criticize the Jewish religion, he claimed that in the same Jewry from which had come to him many personal friends, disciples, and propagandists, healthy seeds were developing in a magnificent manner. Thus he remarked here that "purified religious conceptions are awakening now among the Jews" and that the "old rites" were being abandoned. "Enlightened Catholics and Protestants," he wrote, "will be able to look upon each other as coreligionists, yet without merging with each other, both in the expectation that the age and the policies of the government will gradually bring closer the formalities of belief . . . to the dignity of their purpose, namely of religion itself. Even in regard to the Jews this is possible without the dream of a general conversion of the Jews (to Christianity as a Messianic belief), if, as happens now, *purified religious conceptions** awaken among them and they discard the old rites which now do not serve any purpose but rather smother all true religious spirit." It is difficult to comprehend how Kant could express such contradictory opinions of the Jews almost simultaneously.

FOR THE "IMPROVEMENT" OF THE JEWISH STATUS

Kant holds that "the idea of a very keen mind of this nation, Bendavid [Lazarus Bendavid], to accept publicly the religion of Jesus (probably with its vehicle, the Gospel) is not only very fortunate, but is also the only proposal whose realization would soon turn this people, even without merging with others in matters of belief, into an *educated, well mannered people and one capable of all rights of citizenship.*† Its belief could also be sanctioned by the government." A purification of their teachings would ennoble the Jewish people, prepare it for its emancipation, and remove the last obstacles to its equality with the Christian population. It should be emphasized that Kant considered religious reforms necessary not only in Judaism but also in Christianity.[100] On the other hand, he claimed no interest in baptism but merely in the "purification" of the Jewish religion; he

*Italics, A. D. L.
†Italics, A. D. L.

thought that the abrogation of some ceremonial laws, such as Benda-vid suggested to the Jews, was necessary before the Jewish religion could be recognized by the state and equal rights granted to its adherents. Public recognition of Judaism had thus a special price tag for the Jews.

Lazarus Bendavid, whom Kant here quoted and whose utterances on Judaism had exerted considerable influence upon him, had published in 1793 the booklet *Etwas zur Charakteristik der Juden* [About the Characterization of the Jews].[101] He had demanded the dissolution of the "senseless" ceremonial law, a "hydra" which, as he asserted, was very harmful to Jews and Judaism. Kant gained from Bendavid's work the impression that progressive Jews themselves believed that reforms in Judaism were urgently needed.

If Kant, and also Fichte, spoke about the necessity of a moral improvement of the Jewish people and of necessary reforms in their religion, one should take into consideration that they merely repeated what some individual Jews were saying. Contemporary Jewish intellectuals conceded that on the whole their people lagged behind the Christians, though they did not consider the latter perfect by any standard. Lazarus Bendavid opened his work with the question: "What do the Jews have to do to make themselves fit for a civil reform?" And Moses Mendelssohn appealed to his people to imitate the virtues rather than the vices of their host nations.

Bendavid supported the idea of purifying and refining the faith as a Jewish command, as the "pure teaching of Moses." In the moral improvement and purification of Jewish religion Kant saw an approach toward Christianity; he remarked that Bendavid recommended to the Jews the "religion Jesu," while in reality the latter talked merely of the return to the pure teachings of Moses and of brotherly love.

Kant, the prophet of eternal peace among the peoples of the earth, forecast future domestic and religious peace between the Jews and the Gentile world. He was convinced that the Jewish people would soon become "capable of all rights of citizenship." In an essay on education he made the bold statement that true education could overcome all difficulties.[102] He never believed that its power would fail before racial and national barriers. According to Kant, no deep natural difference existed between the races and peoples of the world. "The various kinds of humanity," he wrote, "are branches of a single supreme and general kind."[103]

KANT'S RELATIONS WITH JEWS

Among the men who became Kant's disciples and rendered great services in propagating his philosophy throughout German lands and

Austria, Jewish thinkers such as Markus Herz, Solomon Maimon, and Lazarus Bendavid were very prominent. The correspondence between Kant and Markus Herz, one of his favorite disciples in Königsberg, constitutes the most important source of Kant's philosophical development. Kant also consulted Herz frequently in his capacity as a physician.[104] While Markus Herz spread the reputation of the great thinker of Königsberg through Berlin, another Jew, Lazarus Bendavid, propagated Kant's philosophy in Vienna.

Markus Herz warmly recommended to Kant a work of Solomon Maimon that won Kant's enthusiastic approval: "A glance which I cast upon it," Kant wrote to Herz, "made me soon recognize its excellence and that not only did no one of my opponents understand me in the central problem as well, but also that only a few had as much keenness for such deep investigations as Herr Maimon."[105]

This letter to Herz, though full of praise for Maimon, contained an acknowledgment of some philosophical opposition. Five years later Kant sent a letter to the philosopher Reinhold. Kant may have known about his bias against the Jews, since the following passage appeared to be geared to its recipient: "What for instance a Maimon really wished with his 'improvement' [*Nachbesserung*] of the critical philosophy— such as the Jews like to try in order to give themselves an air of importance at the expense of others—I never could really understand and must leave to the reprimand of others."[106] This utterance stands in direct contradiction to Kant's earlier praise of Maimon.*

In 1789 Kant had acknowledged that Maimon was taking "another way," that his work "to a great degree" was aimed against Kant himself. He therefore had refused to "accompany" the book with his "praise."[107] The philosopher, grown old, believed he deserved a rest in the edifice of his critical philosophy and became indignant if anyone dared to disturb its foundations. He demonstrated no less anger against the German Fichte than against the Jewish thinker Maimon.[108] Actually, he used the same word, *improvement,* in rejecting any modifications of his critical philosophy and considered both Maimon's and Fichte's efforts "superfluous." In the first case reference is to be found in the letter to Reinhold on Maimon, in the other in his utterance on Fichte's *Wissenschaftslehre* [The Theory of Science].

It is revealing of Kant's close relations with individual Jews, in

*Nothing was more distasteful to Maimon than giving himself "an air of importance." Kant himself had testified that Maimon, in view of the great virtues of his work, could have submitted it "without a second thought to the public." Maimon, however, in spite of this truly encouraging judgment, still hesitated over publication; it was not until the year 1790 that the book was finally published.

spite of his occasional lapses into anti-Jewish generalizations, that of the four specially dedicated copies of his main work *Die Kritik der blossen Vernunft* [The Critique of Pure Reason] (1781) he had sent two copies to Jews, namely to Markus Herz and Moses Mendelssohn; he always esteemed both men very highly. He accepted Mendelssohn's offer to enter into an exchange of thoughts with him "with pleasure."[109]

It was in the year 1777, on the occasion of a visit of Moses Mendelssohn to Königsberg, that they finally met. Kant then publicly embraced the Jewish philosopher before a gathering of students. On the day of Mendelssohn's departure he wrote regretfully to Markus Herz: "Today your, and as I flatter myself, also my dear friend, Herr Mendelssohn, leaves town. To have a man of such gentle temper, good humor, and great talents as a permanent and close companion would constitute that nourishment of spirit which I miss here so completely."[110]

A contemporary has described Kant's and Mendelssohn's first meeting, recording in this connection the somewhat hostile reaction of many students and, in contrast to it, Kant's own friendly and warm reception of Mendelssohn. The students had laughed "sneeringly" when they had seen the Jewish philosopher, who was physically slightly deformed. Yet their attitude changed quickly when they learned that the stranger was none other than Mendelssohn and when they observed Kant's friendliness toward him.[111]

According to Jacobi, Kant admired Mendelssohn's *Jerusalem* "like an irrefutable book."[112] After having read it, Kant wrote to Mendelssohn: "I consider this book as the announcement of a great reform which will not only affect your people, but also others. You have been able to combine your religion with a degree of freedom of conscience which one would not have attributed to it and of which no other can pride itself."[113] When the *Kritik der blossen Vernunft* appeared, Mendelssohn was already too set in his ways to be influenced by it. Kant was perhaps disappointed, having hoped that Mendelssohn would show greater interest in his work.

Kant's relations with Jews appeared so close to contemporary Jew-haters that they could not refrain from heaping abuse on him. One went so far as to declare that Kant held special lectures for his Jewish students on the Talmud,[114] which in anti-Semitic eyes of course doomed the philosopher and his thought.

Kant's ideas on politics and ethics were irreconcilable with civil inequality and with the suppression of any group of human beings. The moral duties of man toward his neighbor were, according to Kant, not contingent on his racial origin or religious affiliation. Thus

Kant praised the excellent intentions of the author of a work entitled *Leitfaden zur Ethik* [Guide to Ethics for All Humans without Distinction of Religion], a book which had stirred in him "impatient expectations."[115] "Difference of religion," he wrote in the famous little essay "Zum ewigen Frieden" [Toward Eternal Peace], "what an odd expression! Just as if one talked about different moralities. . . . There may well exist different religious beliefs, different religious books (Zendavesta, Veda, Koran, etc.), but only a single religion valid for all human beings and in all epochs."[116]

The difference of religions throughout history had had, according to Kant, only too often a divisive effect. Next to language, fate had availed itself particularly of religion "to hinder the mixture of peoples and to keep them apart." These differences, deepened by "hatred," had often served "as excuse for war." "Yet with increasing culture and the powerful mutual advances of human beings," linguistic and religious differences need not necessarily lead to separation but might rather produce "a larger agreement in principles," "harmony," and "peace."

Kant wished to eliminate war but did not hold it possible to attain this goal by eliminating or reducing linguistic, religious, or other differences of the nations. While he looked upon "eternal peace" as the ultimate goal of human development, he preferred in his own time rather the "separate existence of many neighboring states, independent of each other," to "their amalgamation by one power, surpassing the others and changing into one universal monarchy." The latter would be "a despotism without a soul," which "on the graveyard of freedom"[117] would end diversity and enforce uniformity.

While Kant readily acknowledged ethnic and religious diversity, he at the same time upheld the principle of equality of rights for all human groupings. Mere "tolerance" seemed to him irreconcilable with that principle, and he praised as "enlightened" and worthy of the esteem of "posterity" that prince who rejected the "arrogant name of tolerance."[118]

The era of the Enlightenment produced in different European countries different results. In France it reached its climax in the Great Revolution and brought emancipation to the French Jews. In Germany it generated an intellectual revolution the consequences of which, in combination with Prussia's defeat in 1806–1807, brought near-equality to Prussia's Jews. But Allied victory over Napoleonic France established ultraconservatism in most of Europe and largely deprived German Jews of the benefits that Enlightenment, in spite of some adverse effects, had brought them. The emerging emancipation in the German states was soon followed by a counter-emancipation.

PART II

The War of Liberation and the Emerging Emancipation

All recall those days [of the War of Liberation] that owe their glory not only to Christians, but also to Jews, Moslems, and pagans.

—Goethe

CHAPTER 4

Hope and Disappointment

From Frederick William II to the War of Liberation

The death in 1786 of Frederick the Great, under whose government the mass of Prussia's Jews had remained oppressed, brought to the throne his nephew Frederick William II, a less enlightened but also a less despotic ruler. In the very month of his accession, the Prussian King issued an order to the *Generaldirektorium* to the effect "that the situation of this persecuted nation [the Jews] be alleviated as far as possible." The results, however, proved disappointing, and when war with France broke out in 1792, any thought of improving the status of Prussia's Jews was shelved.

But the years that followed were by no means years of standstill in the struggle for equality. The emancipation of the Jews in France and in other European states which were annexed or dominated by the French inspired the Jews and their spokesmen in Germany and became the prime moving force in favor of Jewish equality. At the peace conference at Rastatt in 1798–1799 and at the gathering of the *Reichsdeputation* in Regensburg in 1803, the Jews submitted their pleas and pressed their claims. At the Congress of Rastatt, Dutch Jews approached the diplomatic representatives of the Great Powers in behalf of the German Jews and pleaded with them to bring their influence to bear upon the German princes. Two booklets, one by an anonymous writer, the other by Christian Grund, supported the demands of the Dutch Jews in favor of their German brethren. The German Jews submitted a petition of their own, dated November 15, 1802, to the deputation of estates gathered at Regensburg and asked for the right to vote; their plea was supported by the Austrian ambassador. But none of these moves actually brought the Jews closer to equality.

The opponents of the Jews closely watched their attempts to free themselves from the chains that had bound them for centuries. The anti-Semites were resolved to resist the emancipation by all means. During the years 1803–1805 some writers—Paalzow, Buchholz, Grattenauer, and others who remained anonymous—raised their voices in virtually all sections of Germany and particularly in Berlin. Grattenauer's pamphlet *Wider die Juden: Ein Wort der Warnung* [Against the Jews: A Word of Warning] (Berlin, 1803) was printed in no less than six editions.[1] Grattenauer even planned the publication of a special magazine, entitled "Die Juden." He quickly followed up his first pamphlet against the Jews with a second one, *Erklärung an das Publikum über die Schrift: 'Wider die Juden'* [Explanation to the Public of the Book 'Against the Jews']. His attacks were on the lowest intellectual and moral level. The same held true of the attacks by Buchholz, who insisted that friendship or even mere association with Jews was out of the question. Christians had to be protected against the Jews, Buchholz announced, though he had no objection to Jews rendering military service.

The outbreak of war between France and Austria in 1805 and the Prussian debacle in 1806–1807 silenced these voices of hatred. But after the War of Liberation they were to resound more forcefully throughout the German states.

When Prussia succumbed to French arms in 1806, the idea of a thorough reorganization of the state's social and political structure spread like wildfire. The new social and political reforms were to give Prussia a powerful impetus and were to strengthen her hand in dealing with the French. The liberation of the Prussian Jews in March 1812 was actually one of the links in the chain of reforms that was to bring about the resurgence of the Prussian state.

As Field Marshal von Boyen revealed later in his *Denkwürdigkeiten und Erinnerungen* [Memoirs and Reminiscences], Chancellor Fürst von Hardenberg's reforms had aimed at the "improvement of the internal state of the [Prussian] nation" and at reviving its spiritual force and physical welfare by dissolving oppressive privileges. Through these liberating reforms, among which the emancipation of the Jews figured prominently, the spirit, the initiative, and the enthusiasm of all groups should be aroused;[2] all should be spurred on to active participation in public life. These domestic reforms, according to von Boyen, produced a "feeling of gratitude" in all circles and reawakened national honor. The spiritual force thus generated saved the state.[3]

The emancipation of the German Jews in the era of the War of Liberation was accelerated by the success of the French armies and by the impact of French revolutionary ideas. Prussia's statesmen felt the need to win the deeper allegiance of all to the state, including the Jews. At the same time, equality suited the practical interests and moral demands of the Germans and Jews. Liberation of the German Jews seemed the necessary accompaniment of the breakdown of feudalism and the growth of the modern state.

But the obstacles which had to be overcome were staggering. Foremost among them were the prejudices of centuries and a deep-rooted conservatism that made many Germans stubbornly support preservation of the status quo. The rapid increase of Jews in Prussia due to the partitions of Poland—which brought into the state culturally more backward Jews, who were farther removed from German *Kultur*—tended also to postpone emancipation.

Equality of the Jews in Prussia was seriously considered only after the defeat of 1806. At about the same time attention began to focus on the liberation of the Jews in other German states. The battles of Jena and Auerstädt in 1806 therefore represent a milestone in the history of German Jewry; in their aftermath the concept of the equality of German Jews made great inroads. In January 1808 equal rights were granted to the Jews of the newly created Kingdom of Westphalia, whose ruler was Napoleon's brother Jerome. Equality was extended not only to the Jews already domiciled in Westphalia but also to those who immigrated there. The twenty thousand Jews immediately affected were given full civil rights.

While the emancipation in Westphalia, a French vassal state, was the first example of Jewish equality on German soil, abroad Jews had attained legal equality earlier. In the United States equality under the law was assured from the birth of the nation. In France emancipation was obtained in 1791, and soon afterwards it became the law of the land in Holland, Switzerland, and the Kingdom of Italy.

In Frankfurt am Main the emancipation of the Jews was decreed by an edict of the Grand Duke von Dalberg, formerly Prince Elector of Main, a liberal and a friend of France who had been made Prince-Primate of the *Rheinbund* by Napoleon. The old Hanseatic city of Hamburg was occupied by French troops in 1810; after its incorporation by France the Jews of Hamburg became full-fledged citizens. Jews were permitted to settle also in Lübeck and Bremen, where residence had been prohibited to them.

The emancipation in Prussia saw the light of the day under Hardenberg in 1812. This liberation in turn set in motion the emancipation in Catholic Bavaria, which, as a member of the *Rheinbund,* was already wide open to French influences. Yet the "full freedom of conscience" which was granted to the Jews in Bavaria in June 1813 was vitiated by many oppressive measures, and the Bavarian government did not conceal that it actually wished "gradually to diminish" the number of Jews in some localities. In Mecklenburg too the emancipation in Prussia had made a great impression; an edict of emancipation was proclaimed there in February 1813. In the Grand Duchy of Baden a decree of equality, though very much circumscribed, had been brought about in 1809.

Military considerations played an important role in the equalization measures. Reformers such as Wilhelm von Humboldt, vom Stein, and Scharnhorst may have differed in their attitude toward the Jews, but they were all agreed on the need of enlisting Prussian Jews in the military service and were fully aware of the military implications of the liberation.

Most revealing was the shift of position of Schroetter, a close collaborator of the Baron vom Stein, from an opponent of the Jews to the author of a much-debated emancipation project. This transformation of a Saulus into a Paulus was directly linked with vom Stein's understanding of military requirements. In a memoir to the king in behalf of the equality of the Jews, Schroetter pointed to their bravery in earlier epochs and also "in quite recent times, in the American as well as in the French revolutionary wars." Then he continued: "The Jew has fervent Oriental blood and a lively imagination. All this is an indication of manly strength, if it is utilized and set in motion. . . . The cowardice of the Jews originates, in my view, in the slavery in which they were held and in the contempt with which they were treated by all nations."[4] The soldierly capacity of the Jews, he observed, was already recognized in all civilized states. About 50,000 Jewish men fit to carry arms lived in Silesia and East Prussia and in the Marken. Prussia therefore could not ignore the Jews in considering the defense of the fatherland. The King had to be persuaded of the military usefulness of the Jews before a favorable decision about their emancipation could be reached.

The expectation of the German statesmen that the Jews would display martial courage and patriotic zeal was not to be disappointed. In 1813 Jews rushed to the colors. The historian Heinrich von Treitschke, hardly a friend of the Jews, admitted that considering all circumstances—"complicated historic facts" of which "the young Teutons, naturally, had no understanding"—the Jews acquitted themselves very well in battle against Napoleon's armies. This is the more noteworthy since it had been Napoleon's triumphal march across Germany to which, directly or indirectly, they owed their freedom in the German states.[5]

Hardenberg later praised the Jews for their enthusiasm and their patriotic sacrifices during the war. He extolled their "loyal attachment" to the state and the many "examples of heroic courage and of the most praiseworthy disregard of the risks of war" on their part.[6] Jewish wartime endeavors were similarly acknowledged in the memoir written in 1847 at the order of the Prussian government; it was based upon documents of the Ministry of War and was later submitted to the United Diet (*Landtag*). The memoir underlines that the Jews "had proved themselves in war as the other Prussians, had in time of peace not been inferior to the other troops, and Jewish religion in particular had nowhere shown itself a hindrance to military service."[7]

While young Jews who were fit to carry arms rushed to the colors, older wealthy Jews gave in full measure. "The Jews," wrote Rahel Levin, "give whatever they possess; upon them I called first." The Jewish merchants in Berlin gave the first patriotic donation in the amount of 700 talers. Even such a critic of the Jews as Julius von Voss, the author of *Der travestierte Nathan* [The Travestied Nathan], admitted later that "in that time the richest Jewish money-changers in Berlin let their sons volunteer and did not attempt to buy them free."

In spite of the peril of contagious disease, Jewish women volunteered to serve as nurses in the hospitals. According to Voss, other Jewish women joined patriotic societies, "brought help to wounded sisters," and "visited daily the hospitals in which the contagious typhus raged."[8] Hardenberg too testified that Jewish women "emulated the Christians in sacrifices of every sort."[9] The patriotic participation of the Jews in the War of Liberation made a strong impression upon contemporaries, including Goethe.[10]

But the voices of hostility were heard even during wartime. Writers of renown such as Arndt and Jahn voiced their enmity against Jews in private letters during the war years 1813–1815. So also did the statesman Baron vom Stein and Karoline von Humboldt,[11] the wife of Wilhelm von Humboldt, himself a friend of the Jews and a leading advocate of their cause. Ernst Moritz Arndt claimed that Jewish journalists hampered the continuation of the triumphal march against France.[12]

Actually, Jews offered substantial help. The Rothschilds transmitted English money to the Allies, a complex and difficult transaction at the time. "When Napoleon's star was declining," wrote the German historian Franz Schnabel, "the brothers Rothschild rendered great services to the coalition which was formed against the Emperor: they arranged the dispatch of English subsidies to the allies."[13] Similarly, Egon Caesar Conte Corti, author of a history of the Rothschild family, singled out financial measures of Nathan Rothschild that had given aid to the allies against Napoleon.[14]

German Victory and Ultraconservative Anti-Semitism

With the defeat of Napoleon in the Russian campaign, liberation from French domination made rapid progress. Yet along with it, reaction and anti-Semitism began to raise their heads everywhere. Though the emancipation of the Jews on German soil had been completed in neither a legal nor a geographic sense, now the Jews suffered one reversal after the other.

The Kingdom of Westphalia, a creation of the French, collapsed in 1813. Frankfurt am Main was liberated by the Allied troops in the same year, Hamburg in 1814. Everywhere the Jews were deprived of the status of equality to the applause of hostile German elements. Only in Bavaria did the "liberation edict" of 1809—depicted by the government as liberal but denounced by the Jews—remain in force. Here, so little had been given that no need was felt to take it back. This reasoning applied even more to the Jews of Saxony, who in this period of reform had remained pariahs, and this in spite of the Saxon King's loyalty to Napoleon and France.

The defeats at Jena and Auerstädt had dealt serious blows to the self-confidence of the Prussians, indeed of all Germans. The victories of 1813, however, raised their spirits to dizzy heights. Excessive and arrogant nationalism, accompanied by contempt for alien peoples, was left in their wake. Many Germans, intoxicated with victory, gave expression to xenophobia. The "fashionable" Jew-hating, as Wilhelm von Humboldt called it, fitted into this general mood.

The Romantic movement strengthened the newly awakened nationalism. Romanticism revived interest in religion, especially medieval religiosity, which bore the impress of zealous fanaticism and blind prejudice and which was inseparable from hostility against the Jews. By fostering nationalism and focusing interest on one's own ancestry, Romanticism also helped give birth to German Teutonism. The latter attitude of boastfulness and rudeness had a baneful effect upon the German character. Even the nationalistic German historian Heinrich von Treitschke was compelled to admit that Teutonic strong words and manners were inimical to freedom and proud individualism.[15] "An essential trait of the new Teutonism," he continued, "formed the deep-seated anti-Semitism. Since the violent agitation of the wars of liberation brought all secrets of the German soul to the surface, the old deep dislike of the Jewish [*orientalisch*] character was again loudly heard in the general excitement."[16]

Agitation against the Jews, revived during the War of Liberation, gained new impetus thereafter. On the German stage it commenced with the repeated performance of the one-act farce *Unser Verkehr* [Our Life] by K. B. A. Sessa, which gave vent to spite and malice against the Jews. Lessing had hoped that the German theater would send a message of understanding and brotherly love throughout the German lands. Yet Sessa was to attain greater applause from a wider audience than Lessing had ever enjoyed.

Sessa's *Unser Verkehr* is a grotesque distortion of Jewish life. Greediness is the domineering trait of the young Jacob, his father Abraham Hirsch, who trades old clothes, and his mother Rachel. The worldly ambition of the Jews lies in their desire to acquire land holdings and titles of nobility and to dispossess the indigenous aristocracy. The pretentious and coquettish Miss Lydia is as much derided as is the "German" youth, Isidorus Morgenländer. Although he has studied at many German universities, he is as much obsessed by money as his less educated brethren. Jewish family life appears devoid of any tender feeling. The janitor of the church expresses the bitterness of many a German Christian at the many converted and unconverted Jews who come "running into the Church," ready to take it over.

Speaking Yiddish, which was bound to arouse sneering and mocking on the German stage, Jacob reveals in the final scene of the farce his philosophy of life: "First come old rags; then comes wealth and with it taste and education and repute!—One begins with humility! With slyness one advances, with boldness one succeeds. . . . I shall trade until I have become rich—and should I trade all my life! [From the center of the stage to the audience]: Gentlemen! Have you anything to shop and trade?"[17]

Playwrights like Sessa, historians like F. Rühs, philosophers, like J. F. Fries, and jurists like Savigny and Eichhorn joined hands in the battle against German Jewry. These scholars, partly from the newly established University of Berlin and partly from the old University of Heidelberg, were supported in their attacks against the Jews by Professor Dresch of the University of Tübingen and academic dignitaries of the University of Göttingen. Eminent professors from German universities, centers of education and learning, did not disdain lending the prestige and authority of scholarship to a vulgar, virulent, and reactionary anti-Semitism.

Friedrich Rühs, historian at the University of Berlin, led off the new war of pamphlets with his booklet *Über die Ansprüche der Juden an das deutsche Bürgerrecht* [On the Claims of the Jews to German Civil Rights] (1815). Preoccupation with the Middle Ages, he admitted, had drawn his attention to the Jewish question. The lamentations of the Jews over excessive pressure were, in his view, generally exaggerated and unwarranted. The character of the Jews was not merely the result of oppression. "A spirit of speculation" could be observed among them in ancient Palestine, before their dispersal. Rühs claimed that the root of all evil lay in the authority of their rabbis and in the Jewish conception of being the chosen people—briefly, in their religion. But the Jews were not merely a religious society but also a people; they even formed "at the same time a state." The only rights which should be extended to them therefore should be the rights of aliens.[18] For the enjoyment of such rights they were to pay a special Jewish tax, as in times past.

At a moment when German victory was already won, Rühs no longer insisted on the duty of the Jews to carry arms for the defense of the country. But every Jew ought to wear a "national ribbon," a distinguishing mark like the "yellow badge" of the Middle Ages, so that Germans could no longer be misled by the German appearance, language, and general manners of the Jews. Rühs thus acknowledged by implication the advanced degree of assimilation of Jewry to German culture and the circumstance that many of the linguistic and cultural differences between Germans and Jews were vanishing.

The preservation of the national character of the Jews, Rühs continued, was "tied to their religion." As long as the Jews clung to that, they would continue to preserve their nationality. From this belief sprang Rühs' suggestion to the governments of the Christian states "to facilitate" the conversion of the Jews to Christianity. "Obviously," he remarked, "too little has been done in this respect by Christians, and on this ground we ought to reproach ourselves most seriously." Rühs thus rejected all violent means which "earlier zealots" had applied to bring about conversion. But the proposed special laws against the Jews included curtailing their economic freedom. The guilds should not be forced to accept Jews as members, and cities in which the Jews had formerly enjoyed no right of residence could continue to bar them. Rühs looked upon this flagrant discrimination as a legitimate and apparently "nonviolent" means to induce the Jews to embrace Christianity. Only baptism would lead to their "refinement" and open to them the doors to all the rights of German citizenship; it alone would bring about "real acquisition of the German national character" and thus effect "gradually the ruin of the Jewish people." This was what Rühs really aimed at: the destruction of Judaism and burial of Jewry!

Friedrich Rühs' booklet was reviewed by the philosopher Friedrich Fries under the title "Über die Gefährdung des Wohlstandes und des Charakters der Deutschen durch die Juden" [About the Threat to the Welfare and Character of the Germans by the Jews] in the *Heidelberger Jahrbücher der Literatur*. Fries, Professor of Natural Science at Heidelberg, asserted that the Jews represented a caste and that they formed a "state within a state," confirming the Rühs thesis. Two decades before, Fichte had offered the same analysis. Fries demanded the restoration of the yellow badge and recommended that the Germans suppress the Jews, "even destroy" them. But he claimed to have declared war only on "Jewry," by no means on the individual Jew.[19] In view of this and similar attacks by scholars it was hardly suprising that Rahel Levin blamed the common people less than the "professors Fries and Rühs . . . and even higher personalities with prejudices"[20] for excesses against the Jews. These men appeared to her the real culprits.*

The attacks reached a peak of scurrility with Hartwig Hundt von Radowsky, who recommended selling Jewish children to the English, who might use them, instead of Negroes, on their overseas plantations. The men should be castrated and their wives and daughters brought to houses of prostitution. Hundt von Radowsky was a worthy forerunner of the most vicious German racial anti-Semitism of the twentieth century. In a later "work," *Die Judenschule,* he contrasted Judaism, a "religion based upon hatred of men, upon cruelty," with Christianity, "a religion of humility, of love of humanity, of gentleness and of mildness." He apparently never measured his own "policy" concerning the Jews by these yardsticks.[21]

"Liberal" Foes

Enmity toward the Jews after 1815 was by no means exhibited only by reactionaries and conservatives, by religiously orthodox groups and Romanticists. It also infected liberal and even radical circles, religious rationalists, and exponents of the Enlightenment. Playing on their diverse instruments, members of these groups produced a symphony of hate which appealed to broad segments of the German public. The rationalist theologian Heinrich Paulus[22] and the "liberal"

---

*The pastor Johann Ewald came to the defense of the Jews with a booklet entitled *Ideas on the Necessary Organization of the Israelites in Christian States* (1816). The Jews also received support from Professor Lips, author of the book *On the Future Status of the Jews in the States of the German Confederation* (1819).

writer Johann Ludwig Klüber expressed sharp hostility to the Jews, Klüber including a special chapter on them in his contemporary work on the Congress of Vienna.[23] He reproached the Jews for their "religious haughtiness" and their concept of being the chosen people at the very time when the German nation under the influence of Teutonism and of German nationalistic philosophers boasted of the superiority of everything German.

"The Jews," Klüber wrote, "are a political-religious sect, under the strict theocratic despotism of their rabbis." They form a "completely closed society," dedicated to their own special education, "which excludes the gradual progress to a higher culture," and pledged to preserve a caste-like family spirit, characterized by complete physical separation from all Gentiles, as commanded by their laws. They believe that, after the arrival of the Messiah, all non-Jews will have to be "exterminated" (*ausgerottet*)! There followed almost an entire page of "sources" allegedly corroborating these grotesque charges, including the notorious J. A. Eisenmenger, *Entdecktes Judentum* [Unmasked Judaism] (1701), one of the bibles of German anti-Semitism. Such an accusation was bound to disseminate a vicious mood throughout the German states and to give sanction to virtually any excesses against the Jews.

Klüber's recommendations for a "new" policy on the Jews opened the door to the most shameful reaction. In support of this retrogressive course Klüber leveled further accusations which defied all credibility. He repeated charges that the Jewish religion commanded hatred of all non-Jews and that its religious and ethical teachings permitted the use of all sorts of exploitation of Gentiles. Klüber claimed that Jews were unwilling to defend the fatherland, since they did not recognize it as such, and incapable of doing so because they were cowardly. Rare exceptions aside, the Jews showed "poverty of spiritual nobility and true education of the mind." A continuing antagonism between the state and Judaism was unavoidable. The Jews were simply a disease in the body of the state. To give them complete equality "would be the same as turning a limited unavoidable evil into an incurable cancerous affliction" which would cause unrelenting pain and ultimately destroy the state.

Yet, strangely, Klüber proclaimed that the Jews should not be left in a state of complete hopelessness. He recommended that the state offer the Jews means for their spiritual, ethical, and political ennoblement, approve their rabbis and teachers, and offer protection to person and property, while at the same time taking measures against their increase, especially in the countryside. He did not object to their acquiring land and engaging in trade and commerce, within certain limitations. Nor did he ask that they be baptized. But he demanded the "repudiation and elimination of Talmudism and everything else the government declares irreconcilable with the welfare of the state."

Klüber's recommendations—the denial of genuine religious freedom aside—were perhaps a kind of anticlimax, in view of his preceding vilification of the Jews. His outbursts were a measure of the depth of anti-Semitism not only in his own mind but also in the minds of broad segments of the German intelligentsia after the liberation from France. He continued to talk in grandiloquent terms about "liberalism" and "humanity" while subverting these ideals in his own attitude toward the Jews.

Burschenschaften and Exclusion of the Jews

Teutonic anti-Semitism, strongly Christian in tone, reached down to the common people, in whom anti-Jewish prejudices were still rampant from earlier times. But it had its chief base among the intelligentsia; German students and their organizations exhibited special virulence. After the War of Liberation the German *Burschenschaften* had become the very nucleus of the anti-Semitic movement. Teachers of German youth such as Arndt and Jahn, Rühs and Fries, Oken and Luden, who were imbued with the narrow medieval spirit of religious and ethnic separatism and traditional discrimination, were largely responsible for the luxuriant growth of the new ideas.

Many of these men apparently felt instinctively that love for the German nation could not be awakened without simultaneously arousing hatred of all things alien. Love of Germany seemed indissolubly coupled with hatred of Judaism; the German Jews, a tiny, helpless minority in the German realm, served conveniently as a scapegoat.

Bitterness and disappointment over the lack of freedom and of national unity had gripped German students after the war. They were frustrated, confused, and torn by conflicting ideas. German nationalism and German freedom, Christianity and Romanticism—Treitschke spoke aptly of "the Romanticism of Christian reverie"[24]—colored their thoughts. Fichte recognized the dangers inherent in this trend when he warned students not to confound the conceptions of *German* and *medieval*.

Hegel too castigated the intellectual superficiality of the *Burschenschaften* and of Fries' politics and philosophy in particular. Against the followers of Fries, the disciples of Hegel—especially members of the Heidelberg *Burschenschaft* "Teutonia" led by the Catholic Friedrich Carové—supported the admission of Jews to student organizations.[25] But though neither the entire student body nor the entire German intelligentsia had succumbed to anti-Semitism, it had made devastating inroads into German territory.

To quote Heinrich von Treitschke again: "The *Burschen* felt themselves to be a new Christian order of knights and displayed their Jew-hating with a crude intolerance. . . . From the beginning one intended to exclude all non-Christians from the new youth league." Whereas German Christendom of the late eighteenth century, under the influence of pietism and humanitarianism, had approached the Jews in a more tolerant spirit, "fashionable" Christianity of the early nineteenth century turned its back on them. According to Treitschke, the exclusive Christianity of those days recalled in many ways the age of the Crusades.[26] Similarly, the famous criminologist and professor of law Anselm von Feuerbach, in a letter writen in 1813 to his friends Tiedge and Elise von der Recke, expressed his amazement that during the recent "crusade" against "the French infidels" the new German men, "in passing, had not preached and practiced a little murdering of Jews, as during the crusades of the eleventh and twelfth centuries." "Please do not show these lines to any new German man," Feuerbach pleaded with his friends after using a word of foreign extraction, "otherwise I am eternally damned! One really does not know whether one should laugh at the mad stuff or shed tears about it; but mad it certainly is and, if simultaneously coupled with lust for persecution, spying after patriots and popishness and obscurant religious fanaticism, it is, at the same time, malicious and foolish. . . . The persecution of Jews is quite in line with the spirit of the Christianity of these people."[27]

Hostility to the Jews flourished in both Catholic and Protestant regions of Germany. After the restoration in the States of the Church, Pope Pius VII decreed that the Jews were to be deprived of the freedom they had received during the short-lived French rule. Such an act was bound to increase enmity against the Jews in all Catholic countries. And a no more friendly or enlightened spirit was displayed in the overwhelmingly Protestant German states.

The anger and the frustration of the German students found a resounding echo in the Wartburg Festival of 1817, celebrated in honor of the tercentenary of the German Reformation. The books of some authors who were looked upon as traitors to the fatherland—some of them liberals, others conservatives—were lifted with a fork and cast into the flames. The *Code Napoléon* and other writings, among them the book *Germanomania* from the pen of the Jewish journalist Saul

Ascher, were burned. When Ascher's book was thrown into the flames, the students shouted after it three times: "Woe to the Jews!"

The cultivation of Teutonic manners sharpened intolerance and led to numerous anti-Semitic excesses, particularly the violent outbursts of 1819. Compared to earlier anti-Jewish manifestations, these attacks of anti-Semitism may have marked only a temporary surfacing of the anti-Jewish mood. The historian Treitschke, an opponent of the Jews, held them to have been quite unjustified. In 1879 he posed the question whether the outbreaks in that year of a deep, long-restrained anger against the Jews were "only a casual effervescence, as hollow and baseless as had been the Teutonic incitement of the year 1819?"[28]

The assassination in 1819 of the Prussian Councilor of State and playwright Kotzebue by a student named Sand brought the suppressed excitement to an explosion, the repercussions of which affected German Jewry. The bitterness of the educated classes this time reached the German masses. To continue with Treitschke: "The old racial hatred against the Jews broke out frightfully: in Würzburg, in Karlsruhe, Heidelberg, Darmstadt, Frankfurt, the mob conspired to storm individual Jewish houses, mistreated the inhabitants. . . . Here and there individual Teutonic students may have participated in the mischief. The derisive call 'Hep! Hep!', which was then first sounded, appears to have arisen in educated circles [It was to mean: *Hierosolyma est perdita;* Jerusalem is lost]."[29] Some students and teachers, however, rushed to the help of the Jews, at considerable risk to themselves. In Heidelberg students led by two professors, Thibaut and Daub, defended the Jews against the raging mob.

The furious agitation and the wild excesses made a deep impression upon the Jews. Rahel Levin, though claiming to have foreseen everything, was shocked and wounded. She wrote to her brother Ludwig Robert, who had witnessed the Hep Hep storm, "I am extremely sad, as I was never before, because of the Jews." "They [the Germans] want to keep them; but to torment them, to despise them, to call them 'Low Jew' [*Judenmauschel*] . . . to kick them with their feet and to throw them down the stairs. . . . The hypocritical new love for the Christian religion (God pardon my sin), for the Middle Ages with its art, poetry, and outrages, incites the people to the only atrocity to which, reminded of the old experiences, it still permits itself to be incited."[30]

The disillusionment of the German Jews was all the sharper because they had entertained such high hopes.

CHAPTER 5

German Statesmen and Jewish Emancipation

Changing Attitudes of Baron vom Stein

One of the great personalities of the era was Baron Karl Friedrich vom Stein. The patriotic and religious spirit of the Protestant sections of Germany found no keener expression in any German statesman of that time.[1] A reformer but no doctrinaire, vom Stein wished to change only those institutions which had proved hopelessly obsolete. Though decisively influenced by the French Revolution, he opposed the imitation of French concepts and institutions on German soil. In the period of reaction he abandoned many basic points of his earlier progressive program. The ultra-conservative waves that swept over Central Europe and the rest of the Continent after 1815 clearly affected vom Stein's later *Weltanschauung* and politics.

Vom Stein's policy in regard to the Jews underwent distinct changes, though personally he was never favorably disposed toward them. In the era of general reform, however, he suppressed his personal sentiments and approved their emancipation,[2] accepting the Jews into the Prussian state on the basis of almost full equality, as his municipal ordinance for Prussia showed. But after the War of Liberation, when the reform wave had subsided and Napoleon had been defeated, he proposed that the emancipation be revoked. The widespread acceptance of the Jews by the German states prior to the clash of battle and their rejection afterwards were clearly mirrored in the changing attitudes of the Baron vom Stein.

Vom Stein had originally entertained misgivings about granting equality to the Jews. While *Oberpräsident* in Münster, he feared the allegedly harmful influence of the Jews upon the peasants. He even expressed the view that the peasantry as a class might face dissolution and imagined that "instead of bondage to the landlords, a much worse bondage," one to "Jews and usurers," might develop.[3] He feared a "new consolidation in large estates; poverty forces to sell, while the rich, the usurer, the Jew, buys up and has the field worked by laborers."[4]

Yet vom Stein the reformer, whose ideas had aroused the bitter resistance of many Junkers, had seen the main cause of the peasantry's sufferings not in the actions of the Jews but rather in the peasants' lack of freedom, their bondage to the Prussian landed proprietors. Through his peasant reforms and his municipal ordinance—the latter embracing the emancipation of the Jews in the towns—he showed unmistakably that in his opinion the liberty of the Jews could well be reconciled with the freedom and prosperity of the German peasant.

Even in this reform period, however, vom Stein was no friend of the Jews. His criticisms of them abounded during this stage. They were by no means limited to his earliest years, the pre-reform era, or his later years, when once again he embraced more conservative views.

Vom Stein was not only sharply critical of the role of the Jews in the countryside, where they operated, as he charged, against the independence of the small peasants; he also took them to task for their allegedly detrimental influence upon the Prussian civil service. When vom Stein in September 1805 accepted the direction of the Prussian *Bank und Seehandlung* (maritime company), he expressed disapproval of his predecessors. Many bureaus, he remarked, "favor mainly Jewish bankers whose cunning, persistence, connections and lack of honor are pernicious in every state and have particularly detrimental effects upon the civil servants."[5] Thus vom Stein made the Jews the culprits of bureaucratic dishonesty, while virtually acquitting the corrupt Christian civil servants.

In view of such hostile remarks, vom Stein's support of the emancipation of the Jews as urban residents of Prussia is somewhat startling. Yet his municipal ordinance spoke an unequivocal language. The provision relating to the equality of the Jews in Prussian cities preceded by four years Hardenberg's edict of the emancipation of the Jews throughout Prussia. Paragraph 18 of Stein's municipal ordinance stipulated that "rank, birth, religion and personal circumstances have no bearing upon the acquisition of civil rights. . . . Soldiers, minors and Jews may be granted civil rights."[6] Through his municipal ordinance, one of his most statesmanlike works, vom Stein appears in the field of legislation concerning the Jews as the pioneer of emancipation in Prussia, the undisputed forerunner of Hardenberg.

That vom Stein was pushed along the road that pointed to Jewish equality testifies to the irresistible momentum of the movement, to the force of contemporary ideas, which overwhelmed the indifferent and temporarily even silenced some opponents. It would have contradicted logic if he, while attempting to create a new and strong Prussia with a view toward gaining independence, had left the Jews within Prussia in a state of oppression.

Friedrich Perthes has told of a meeting with vom Stein in December 1813. According to Perthes, vom Stein spoke in behalf of "full equality of the three Christian confessions" in the German cities "in all political matters" but specifically excluded the Jews: "No Jew could be accepted on the basis of equality."[7] If this testimony is correct, vom Stein apparently repented the inclusion of the pro-Jewish clause in his municipal ordinance just five years after its enactment and opposed the extension of his own measure to other German cities without substantial changes.

In spite of its enlightened façade under Frederick II, the old Prussian state had clung rigidly to many an obsolete institution, including the inequality of the Jews. Yet after its breakdown in 1806, the idea of the emancipation of the Jews had rapidly gained ground. Aside from the challenge posed by the liberation of the Jews of France and French-dominated countries, the deeper causes of the preoccupation of Prussian statesmen after 1806 with projects for the improvement of the Jewish status lay in the burning desire of Prussia and other German states for a war of revenge against France. This required marshaling all existing resources, including the Jewish population, against the French.

But the more immediate causes of the widespread interest in the Prussian emancipation projects lay in changes in the situation of the Jews in neighboring states. These changes were for the better in Westphalia and in the newly established Grand Duchy of Warsaw but for the worse in Russia. Prussian authorities were concerned lest the recent grant of equality to the Jews in Westphalia and the Grand Duchy might induce many wealthy Prussian Jews to move their residences and businesses to Westphalia, where immigrant Jews enjoyed full equality.[8] At the same time the increase in taxes levied upon the Russian Jews threatened to spur immigration of these Jews into the Prussian provinces. Prussia was thus threatened both by the flight of wealthy Jews and the influx of impoverished ones.

The Prussian Minister Schroetter first attempted to counter the immigration of Jews from Russia with expulsion, then performed a turnabout and adopted a policy of conciliation.[9] He proposed to King Frederick William III that the Jews be given a new constitution, which would aim at undermining their nationality and at accelerating their assimilation. If one wished that the Jews should cease being a state within a state, he argued, one would have to grant them all civil rights and impose upon them all civil duties, including military service. One must "educate them to be useful citizens."

According to O. H. Pertz, the earliest biographer of Baron vom Stein, Stein gave his approval to Schroetter's project for Jewish emancipation.[10] A later biographer, Max Lehmann, held that Stein himself submitted these proposals to the king.[11] There appears to be a consensus that in the days after the Prussian municipal ordinance became law, vom Stein continued to work in close collaboration with Schroetter on the improvement of the legal status of Prussia's Jewry.

Everything considered, Schroetter's proposal was a long step forward, particularly in view of the author's earlier hostile attitude.[12] Schroetter, whom Brand, a legal consultant of the city of Königsberg, had once called a "Hamann of the Jews," had changed his views about them. To a question of Frederick William III s to the capacity of the Jews for military service, he replied with conviction that the Jews would prove themselves good soldiers in war.[13] Yet Schroetter did not demand full equality for them in every respect.[14]

Schroetter hardly became an outright friend of the Jews. His contemporary, the statesman and scholar Wilhelm von Humboldt, certainly did not regard him as such, as emerges clearly in his classic statement on Jewish emancipation, where he subjected some of Schroetter's proposals to sharp criticism. Schroetter merely believed that now he could make the Jews useful to the Prussian state, something he had doubted before. In supporting Schroetter's project, Stein too had Prussia's interests at heart rather than those of the Jews.

The spirit in which Schroetter approached the Jewish problem is shown by the question he asked Brand in 1808, namely whether he knew a means "to kill" the Jews "in a bloodless manner, but at one stroke." Brand replied that he "possessed a very effective means to kill, not the Jews, but Judaism,"[15] and declared himself prepared to elaborate on this project. Many advocates of the emancipation of the Jews were prompted not by friendship for the Jews but by contrary motives. Full equality was frequently supported only as the most effective means of annihilating Judaism through cultural and national assimilation. Judaism was considered evil, individual Jews corrigible, and Germanization the cure.

In December 1813, after the decisive battle of Leipzig and its aftermath, vom Stein was already opposed to extending his own provision of municipal equality for Prussia's Jews to other German cities. In 1814, only six years after the promulgation of the municipal ordinance, he coolly rejected the pleas of the Jews of Frankfurt am Main, who had turned to him for help.

In the year 1812 a compact had been concluded between the Grand Duke Karl von Dalberg, the regent of Frankfurt am Main, and the city's Jewry.[16] The Frankfurter Jews were to receive full equality only after paying the city a final "compensation" amounting to twenty times the annual protection payment they had previously been obliged to pay. The agreement remained in force for only about two years, however, for on November 2, 1813, the Allied troops marched into the city and Karl von Dalberg resigned. A General Gouvernement was created and placed under the supervision of the Central Administrative Council for all conquered territories. Its chief was Baron vom Stein.

Vom Stein was a convinced adherent of local self-government. He was also well aware of Frankfurt's proud role in the old Empire and wary that Bavaria, which had her eye upon the city, might annex it. From the beginning he was thus very favorably disposed toward Frankfurt am Main. In his new capacity he therefore recognized on July 19, 1814, the independence of the city without further delay,[17] to the great displeasure of both Metternich and Hardenberg. Dalberg's city regime was thus replaced by the returning Frankfurt patricians and the old Lutheran majority. The new municipal authorities were ready to suppress again the city's religious minorities, Catholics and Jews, to reintroduce the old city charter,[18] and to reestablish the ghetto, to the applause especially of the lower middle class of the city.

Apparently prompted by the citizens of Frankfurt am Main, vom Stein in 1814 appointed a commission for the purpose of investigating the legality of the Jewish emancipation of the city. The decision reached by the commission was unfavorable to the Jews.[19] Thereupon the Jews of Frankfurt am Main turned to vom Stein for help. But he refused any intervention in their behalf and referred them coldly to the "justice and public-mindedness of the constitutional city authorities,"[20] their avowed opponents.

Vom Stein thought that the Jews of Frankfurt am Main raised excessive demands. But he was not uncritical of the new city charter. The city of Frankfurt, he said later, "created something entirely new, offended well established rights."[21] Whether he thought in this context of Catholics *and* Jews or merely of the first cannot be definitely ascertained.

At the Congress of Vienna Baron vom Stein was adviser to Tsar Alexander I and attempted to win him over to the concept of a German national state which, he pledged, would guarantee the "rights of all inhabitants of Germany.''[22] The possibility that he thought in this connection of the German Jews cannot be entirely excluded. The Jews themselves seem to have been convinced that Baron vom Stein was their opponent, but there is no conclusive evidence that he actively opposed Jewish demands at the Congress of Vienna.[23]

Vom Stein's Growing Hostility

In the postwar era vom Stein's growing opposition to the Jews cannot be questioned. That his hostility flared up again is revealed in a passage of a letter from Wilhelm von Humboldt to his wife Caroline: ''Your tirade about the Jews, my dear, is divine. I'd love to communicate it to Stein, who shares entirely your views, but proposes . . . still more heroic means, since he wishes to populate the northern coast of Africa with them.''[24] This plan of settling Jews in North Africa seems to have played no unimportant role in vom Stein's thoughts, for he often returned to it.[25]

Stein's ultraconservative views appear clearly in his last years. He had always adhered to a ''stationary political ideal''[26] and had only supported the enactment of reforms in a time of national emergency. The simple, pious peasant clinging to the soil had always attracted him more than the agile, enterprising, often, as he believed, morally corrupt urban citizen. He emphatically rejected the centralized, mechanized state, resting upon an elaborate bureaucracy. He opposed rapid industrial development and what he held to be its unavoidably destructive and pernicious effects, which included increasing competition, intensification of the social and economic struggle, and growing pecuniary power, the latter threatening primarily the peasants. This power, according to vom Stein, was wielded particularly by the Jews of the cities. He repeatedly voiced these exaggerated, one-sided views, especially in his later years.

Religious, moral, and political ''perfection'' of the state, he wrote, is ''miscarried if the population disintegrates into day laborers, small, impoverished landed proprietors, factory workers, and a medley of Christian-Jewish usurers, employers, civil servants whose goals in life are pleasure and acquisition.''[27] In a letter to Gagern of August 24, 1821, Stein attacked the bureaucrats, who formed a closed caste, did not possess any land, and therefore were indifferent if the bondage of the peasant to the landowner was supplanted by servitude to Jews and moneylenders.[28]

The same tune rang through many other letters and also oral

utterances, particularly during the years 1821–1822. In a letter to
Niebuhr of February 8, 1922, vom Stein denounced the new servitude
of the peasants to "Jews and usurers."[29] The Jews were admittedly
not the only usurers;[30] yet they figured prominently among them.
Stein condemned both again in a letter of February 19, 1822, to one
Dr. Schulz in Hamm.

Though for a brief historic moment vom Stein had paved the way
for Jewish emancipation, he later regretted his move as too hasty. In a
memoir of the year 1828, written under vom Stein's guidance, partly
formulated by him, and bearing his signature, the reactionary estates of
Westphalia demanded the abolition of the emancipation of the Westphalian Jews, again stressing vom Stein's favorite theme of Jewish
"usury." The opinion of the estates was delivered in reply to a request
by the Prussian ministers that they present their views on legislation
concerning the Jews and suggest "necessary modifications of present
laws." "Experience generally has taught," the estates held, "that the
goal of the various novel laws," which gave equality to the Jews, "has
not been attained and that they continue to remain a closed caste,
devoted to usury, particularly pernicious to the peasants."[31]

The memoir stressed the necessity of "improving the religious
and moral state of the future Jewish generation" and of "preventing
the evils which have sprung from the corruption of the present generations." The pronounced hostility and apparent unfairness were
hardly mitigated by vom Stein's holding out the possibility of the
Jews' "improvement." The gulf which separates vom Stein's opposition to the Jews from that of later racial anti-Semitism of the Nazi
variety was evidently deep. Yet no less deep was the gulf which
separated him from the contemporary friends of the Jews and consistent proponents of their emancipation.

The memoir of the Westphalian estates recommended instruction
in the German language as a means of improving Jewish youth. If the
Jews should not be able to establish their own schools, attendance at
the "Christian school" would be obligatory. German songbooks and
prayer books should be introduced into Jewish religious services.
Germanization of the Jews appeared to vom Stein and his like-minded
Westphalian friends as part of the solution to the Jewish problem.

The immediate task consisted in "eliminating the pernicious influence of the present Jewish generation upon the welfare of the remaining inhabitants." The Westphalian estates proposed for this purpose among other matters the following: "1) The abrogation of civil
rights extended to them [the Jews] prematurely by a foreign government. 2) The prohibition of [Jews] buying land or houses within the
next ten years. 3) The obligation of selling the rural estates which

they now possess within the next ten years, provided they themselves do not cultivate them.''

The trouble with the Jews, according to the memoir of the Westphalian estates, was apparently both their "corruption" and their lack of German culture. The goal of the estates was not social and ethnic separation of Germans and Jews but rather joint schools, which would lead to amalgamation and Germanization. Vom Stein and other German contemporaries made it quite clear that they disliked the Jews but conceded to the individual Jew, more or less graciously, that he was not irremediably lost; he still could be retrieved if he would only diligently search for ways to shed his "corrupt" ways and Judaic heritage at the same time.

In view of his life-long hostility, vom Stein's brief championship of Jewish emancipation in the era of Prussian reforms appears, everything considered, rather puzzling.

Hardenberg and the Project of Emancipation

The great work of reform in Prussia is also linked with the name of the Prussian Chancellor, Karl August Fürst von Hardenberg. The defeat of the Prussian army at Jena and Auerstädt represented a steep fall from the great heights it had attained under Frederick the Great. But the domestic reforms which followed closely upon the catastrophe were destined to give new wings to the Prussian eagle, to raise its spirits and steel its determination to resume the struggle. In March 1810 Hardenberg was entrusted with the conduct of the affairs of state for a second time. Under his chancellorship was decreed, among other reforms, the liberation of the Jews.

In the public service first of Hanover and later of Braunschweig, Hardenberg had manifested his friendliness to Prussia quite early. In 1792 he became a cabinet minister in Prussia and in this capacity took charge of the government of Ansbach-Bayreuth. These were two Frankish duchies which the childless margrave Alexander wished to transfer to Prussia. In 1803 Hardenberg went to Berlin, where he rendered long and faithful service to his adopted state. However, in March 1806, after Napoleon had openly denounced him, he was dismissed. This forcible removal from office made him a martyr in patriotic circles, just as two years later the discharge of vom Stein was to raise the latter's popularity.

Hardenberg has long been looked upon as one of the most determined protagonists of the enlightened liberal *Weltanschauung* in Prussia and in Germany as a whole.[32] He became a resolved opponent of Napoleon and of French desires for expansion, without, however, declaring war on the spirit of France's egalitarian anti-feudal reform. To the contrary, all his endeavors aimed at giving, with the support of princely power, the Prussian state a new healthy foundation, based upon liberty and popular participation in public life. He thus aroused the most bitter resistance of reactionary feudal circles, which, while continuing to cling selfishly to their class privileges, attempted to discredit him. They claimed that his moves to abolish feudal institutions and create a modern state were prompted merely by the desire to imitate French reforms. Resistance on the part of these circles also made itself felt against Hardenberg's policies toward the Jews.

Hardenberg had close social connections with the cultured Jewish circles in Berlin. He early perceived the striking contradictions between the important role the Jews played in the intellectual, social, and economic life of Prussia, and the sparse rights they could call their own. When Hardenberg accepted the chancellorship in 1810, therefore, he approached the matter of emancipation of the Jews with alacrity and resolve. He was not the initiator of the Jewish reform plans, which had already preoccupied previous cabinets, but he became the most emphatic advocate of Jewish liberty and equality. It was largely due to him that the Jews were freed from their chains. Smidt, an anti-Semitic representative of the city of Bremen at the Congress of Vienna, had no doubt about Hardenberg's leading role in bringing about the emancipation. The Jews, he maintained, owed "the excellent favors which by the edict of March 1812 were bestowed upon them in the Prussian estates, almost exclusively to the present Chancellor Fürst Hardenberg and the bureau personnel working under him." For a time, Jews wielded important influence in this circle.[33]

Smidt's remarks in their entirety must be taken with a grain of salt. The reference to the bureau personnel was particularly aimed at the University Professor Dr. Koreff, diplomat, mystic, and author and Hardenberg's private physician and personal friend, one of the most remarkable figures of those days. A converted Jew, he had considerable influence upon Hardenberg, though, contrary to some accusations, he never dominated the Chancellor. Karl Varnhagen von Ense related in his *Denkwürdigkeiten* how the Prussian Junkers sat in the vestibule of the Chancellor's palace and waited until the powerful Koreff let them enter to voice both their complaints and their wishes. No wonder that the Prussian noblemen, bitter enemies of Hardenberg's reforms in general and of his emancipation of the Jews in particular, were inclined to exaggerate the role of any converted Jew around the Chancellor, to raise suspicions about Hardenberg, and to attempt to discredit his hated political and social program. In fact, the Chancellor was by no means caught in the "web" of Jewish influence. To the contrary, Wilhelm von Humboldt reported that hostile criticism of the Jews extended even to the immediate surroundings of the Chancellor and could be expressed openly in his presence.[34]

In making this remark, von Humboldt probably had in mind Heinrich von Beguélin, who belonged to Hardenberg's circle of friends. As head of the Bureau for Revenues, Beguélin had written an opinion of Schroetter's reform program that took sharp issue with some of its features.[35] Later, when Hardenberg actively promoted the cause of emancipation of the Jews, Beguélin criticized the Chancellor's "strongly emerging benevolence" for them.[36] His wife Amalie, anti-Semitic like her husband, did not forgive Hardenberg his pleading for the Jews and even cast suspicion upon his motives. She claimed to know that an unknown Jew had once offered Hardenberg, then in dire financial need, a large sum of money at very moderate rates of interest. The Chancellor had allegedly not forgotten this help and had subsequently proved grateful through his activities in behalf of the Jews.[37]

In reality Hardenberg's Jewish policy corresponded to his liberal political and social thinking and formed part of the comprehensive reform program by means of which he hoped to build a new and vigorous Prussia. His main thought was to induce all segments of the population to take an active part in public life. The restoration and liberation of Prussia was, in his opinion, closely interwoven with the success of the reform movement. In 1807, after the catastrophe of Jena and Auerstädt, Hardenberg had written a memoir on reorganization for Prussia. He admonished the authorities to show high esteem for religion and to grant freedom of thought and teaching. The state should practice toleration toward its religious minorities, not intervene in matters of conscience, and should "tolerate every religious service which did not arouse public offense and did not disturb others." It should "not persecute" any religious sect that did not oppose the public order. "Every disturbance of the permitted religious service, every demonstration of disrespect should be prohibited and removed."[38] Hardenberg referred directly to the Jews and recommended as "the only effective means of ennobling them" efficient instruction of their children, the admission of Jews to all crafts, and imposition of all civil burdens upon them.

The main thoughts underlying Hardenberg's Jewish policy emerge here clearly. Equality before the law, economic freedom, and education were the means Hardenberg recommended for the solution of the

Jewish problem. In Austria and Prussia close attention was then being given to Napoleon's endeavors to win the active sympathies of Europe's Jews for France. Napoleon had extended a call for a Sanhedrin, a long-extinct, once-revered institution, which would include representative Jews from different states and which would meet in Paris. Hardenberg was apparently convinced of the necessity to meet the French wooing of the Jews with a Prussian counteroffensive—the emancipation. His specific reference to Napoleon's project for "taking hold of the Jews by calling a Great Sanhedrin"[39] may have been aimed at Frederick William III and influential circles whose resistance to emancipation would thus be lessened or overcome.

Hardenberg had pleaded earlier in behalf of the Jews. In 1792, while Prussian administrator in the duchies of Bayreuth and Ansbach, he had supported the improvement of their civil status. In a later memoir (1797) on the general state of affairs in these two Frankish duchies, he depicted the situation of the nobility, townspeople, and peasants and also the status of the Jews, of whom there were but six thousand. In his view the Jews in Ansbach and Beyreuth were heavily burdened by taxes. Once rich in these areas, the Jew had grown visibly impoverished. As Hardenberg wrote: "Politics and love of humanity strongly demand relief of the lot of that unfortunate group of people. Political pressure and the lowering of their civil status has worsened their moral character and has given their status its present harmful direction. With the political ennoblement of the Jews must also begin again their moral improvement. Only a new raising of their civil status can alter their character for the better. Even though the influence upon the present generation may not yet be very noticeable, it is still only fair to work also for future generations." The great obstacles which impeded civil improvement of the Jews should not be underestimated. Though Hardenberg refrained from giving the state administration of Ansbach definite orders, he promised every support to "ease the lot of this unfortunate nation and to make of them, without any tangible harm to the other citizens, useful human beings and to ennoble their destiny." The Prussian King Frederick William II, however, in a letter dated July 6, 1792, held, no doubt with reference to the war with France, that the matter of the emancipation in the duchies ought to be left to "calmer days."[40]

In the memoir of 1797 Hardenberg recommended that an "improvement of the civil state" of the Jews be inaugurated but wished at the same time that measures be taken "that they do not become harmful to the remaining inhabitants." "The Jews," it is said in another context, "carry on various forms of business, often contrary to the common welfare and the citizenry."[41] Hardenberg also believed that it would be "necessary" to examine their privileges again.[42] Their church constitution should be "established properly"— that is, in accordance with the welfare of the entire population. In spite of such critical comment, which largely reflected local opinion, he pleaded for a change for the better. But recommendation of full emancipation still lay in the future.

When Hardenberg again took charge of the chancellery in March 1810, he faced so many pressing problems that at first he could give only cursory attention to the Jewish question. But repeated presentations by the Jews of Berlin and by other Jewish communities in Prussia reminded him that a regulation of their status still awaited final decision.

In November 1810 Hardenberg intervened in behalf of a Jew against an order of the government of Kurmarken. The government had rejected the request of a Prussian *Schutzjude* (protected Jew) to have his daughter married to a Jew who was not entitled to reside in the state. The Chancellor, to whom the father had directly appealed, rescinded the prohibition by the government of Kurmarken in an opinion which contained a criticism of its decision: "I cannot let it go by without remarking that the literal interpretation of a law which has outlived itself does by no means pave the way to necessary reforms; that, indeed, every society appears alive only by the spirit of the application of the law which the age requires. Such a construction and application of a more lenient sort will excite people less than the contrary one, without entailing any disadvantages to the state."[43] Obsolete laws should be interpreted in a more liberal manner until new "better laws" would come forth in the near future.

At Hardenberg's suggestion the various projects on the emancipation were submitted to David Friedländer, the spokesman for the Jews of Berlin. Among them was a legislative proposal dated January 1811, but it proved as little successful as the previous project, which had originated with Minister Schroetter. Not until December of 1811 did Hardenberg turn his full attention to regulating the situation of Prussia's Jews. He then ordered the councilor Pfeiffer, an official in the Prussian Ministry of Justice, and the privy councilor Bülow to draft a new project on Jewish emancipation and to submit it to the chancellery. Hardenberg himself played a part in drafting the law. He not only provided inspiration and direction for the project but repeatedly intervened during its preliminary stages. With the document completed, Hardenberg had an audience with the King on March 6. Five days thereafter the Edict of Emancipation was proclaimed.[44] On the same day Hardenberg personally informed the heads of the Jewish communities of Berlin, Königsberg, and Breslau of the historic act.

The long-desired edict was celebrated by the Prussian Jews as their freedom's charter. In the words of the edict, "a new constitution, suitable to the general welfare" was given to the Jews. Almost all existing laws which had specially referred to them were abrogated. Jews were required to accept family names and to use the German language or any other living tongue for conducting their business and for legal documents. Admission to universities and appointment to municipal offices were open to those among them who would prove qualified.

The Jews were permitted to acquire land just like Christian citizens and would also engage in crafts and commerce. The imposition of special taxes on Jews was prohibited. Like German Christians, they were obliged to render military service. Various stipulations of a restrictive nature relating to foreign Jews remained in force. The edict announced that further regulations regarding religion and religious establishments would soon be forthcoming.[45]

Hardenberg had not achieved everything he wanted. The principle of full equality was not extended to holding public office, and though further edicts on admission to the civil service were promised, this promise was not fulfilled until the revolution of 1848. But by and large, the equality of Prussia's Jews with the rest of the population was established.[46]

Before the edict of Jewish emancipation was actually promulgated, great obstacles had to be overcome. The opposition to it had its seat in some of the ministerial departments themselves, particularly in the bureau of revenues, whose head was Heinrich von Beguélin. These civil servants, in league with some Junkers, criticized not only the emancipation of the Jews and its advocates but also those who dared to attack their class privileges, the freedom of their estates from taxation, their domination of the peasants, and their monopoly of officers' positions in the army.

Marwitz's Opposition and Hardenberg's Postwar Policy

The author of the memoir expressing their views, which was transmitted to Potsdam on June 10, 1811, was the Baron von der Marwitz. Its purpose was to kill the emancipation project in the last hour. After reading it, Frederick William III turned it over to Hardenberg, who returned it with marginal remarks. Filled as it was with the Junker's spiteful stubbornness and autocratic pretenses, the document was highly disrespectful to the King. Hardenberg insisted therefore on the immediate transfer of the author to the Spandau jail. The Baron von der Marwitz paid for his boldness with imprisonment for a period of three months.

In the memoir Baron von der Marwitz had voiced his "astonishment" that at the very time when unbearably hard burdens were placed upon the nobility, the Jews were liberated and freed from all pressures. The Jews, he complained, were treated too indulgently. One did "not any longer give them their name, because it was considered too bad for them. . . . In the order which permits them to acquire land"—the latter provision aroused especially Marwitz's anger—"they must be named: 'those professing the Mosaic religion.' " Frederick William III, judging by his marginal comment, did not seem to disapprove completely of this criticism. Hardenberg, however, made the following notation: "This entire tirade is as unjust as it is improper."

"These Jews," Marwitz continued, "if they are really loyal to their faith, are the necessary enemies of every existing state (if they are not loyal to their religion, they are hypocrites). They have the bulk of ready cash in their hands, and as soon as the value of the land will be so much lowered that they can acquire it with advantage, it will immediately pass into their hands; they as landlords will become the main representatives of the state, and thus our old and respectable Brandenburg-Prussia will become a very fashionable Jewish state."

"No comment is necessary," Hardenberg jotted down, "on these highly improper utterances."[47]

In the original draft by Marwitz the words "a Jewish state" had been followed by "the true new Jerusalem." On the advice of his more prudent Junker friend von Prittwitz, however, Marwitz had deleted the latter phrase. "We are too serious," Prittwitz had admonished Marwitz, interjecting a critical note, "to make jokes. . . . Besides, it causes, as bitterness, a dissonance with the rest." Yet he held the idea to be "striking and beautiful."[48]

The equality of the Prussian Jews with the remaining population was thus depicted by the opponents of the Jews as portending the predominance of Judaism in the state, and the worst consequences were anticipated. Since the Jews represented only a small minority and were unlikely to gain hegemony in Prussia, the anti-Semites attempted to arouse fear of this tiny group artificially. To spokesmen for the equality of the Jews, such as the Prussian statesman and scholar Wilhelm von Humboldt, the notion that the Germans could be seriously menaced by the handful of Jews in their midst seemed simply preposterous and "chimeric."[49]

Hardenberg remained loyal to his work. Wilhelm von Humboldt, in a letter to his wife Caroline, reported in 1815 that a lively discussion had evolved at Hardenberg's table on the consequence of the emancipation of the Jews. When some of his friends claimed to know of harmful effects of the liberation of the Jews on the rest of the population, Hardenberg defended his laws with warmth and resolution. Wilhelm von Humboldt praised Hardenberg's progressive, liberal views.[50]

After the wars of liberation Hardenberg continued to show interest in the struggle of the Jews for equality. At the Congress of Vienna Hardenberg, like Metternich, actively defended the interests of the Jews. Both statesmen pleaded especially for the Jews of Frankfurt am Main and of the Hanseatic cities Hamburg, Bremen, and Lübeck. Hardenberg strongly resisted the reactionary endeavors to force upon the Jews their old yoke. At the risk of being accused of interference in the internal affairs of other German states, he transmitted through the Prussian envoy to the Senate of Hamburg a letter dated January 4, 1815, warning that Prussia, since the Edict of Emancipation in 1812, could not be unconcerned about the lot of the Jews in the remaining provinces and cities of northern Germany, "because the immorality of which they were reproached would be prolonged through a lasting oppression and through malicious exclusion from rights to which they had a claim as human beings. Also the intention of this government to erase among them the vestiges of dishonor and opprobrium, which have only sprung from an oppressive, contemptible and slavish treatment, by granting them all civil rights and imposing upon them all burdens, was thereby thwarted. The history of the last war too proved that by loyal attachment they became worthy of the state which accepted them." The young men of Jewish faith had been "brothers-in-arms of their Christian co-citizens" and had "shown examples of heroic courage and of the most glorious disregard of the risks of war." Legislation in the neighboring states which was hostile to the Jews would also adversely affect the spirit of the Prussian Jews "and delay further progress."[51]

Hardenberg furthermore instructed the envoy to induce the magistrates and populations of the Hanseatic cities to remove all special laws against the Jews and thus to associate themselves with the spirit and institutions "which the Prussian state by its edict of March 11, 1812, has found in harmony as much with the demands of humanity and the needs of the age as with a reasonable system of government."[52] Hardenberg's liberation of the Prussian Jews led him thus to unfurl the flag of emancipation for the Jews in all German states. Yet he pleaded in vain.[53] The new stifling atmosphere in the Germanies after the victory over Napoleon was to doom his efforts both in the Hanseatic cities and Frankfurt am Main.

Beginning in 1815, Hardenberg, jointly with Metternich, intervened repeatedly on behalf of the Jews of Frankfurt am Main. Representing the two most powerful states in the German Confederation, Hardenberg and Metternich wrote on November 8 and 13, 1815, virtually identical letters to Frankfurt am Main. They reproached the patricians of the city for having asked the opinions of some judicial faculties of German universities about the legal status of Frankfurt's Jews. The opinions, as delivered, had been unfavorable to the Jews. Both statesmen pointed out that the diet of the German Confederation alone had jurisdiction in this matter.

By the year 1817, the cause of the Jews of Frankfurt am Main, who were still struggling for the equality which had been granted them by the previous ruler, Prince Karl von Dalberg, in 1811, had become a *cause célèbre* which preoccupied the cabinets of the great powers, of Austria, Russia, Great Britain, and also Prussia. Just before the German diet was to take up the complaint of the Jews of Frankfurt, the Senate of Frankfurt on November 6, 1817, sent letters to the heads of all member states of the German Confederation. It presented its case on the city's relations with the Jews and expressed the hope that the other states would recognize the sovereign right of Frankfurt am Main and therefore reject the Jewish claims. The Senate went to the extreme of accusing the Jews of Frankfurt of having plotted to establish a "Jewish state" in the city. The struggle which had been imposed upon the city was one to be fought "for the entire German nation."[54]

This memorandum was also presented to the Prussian King Frederick William III and made a considerable impression upon him. A few years earlier the Baron von der Marwitz, as mentioned, had warned him in a similar fashion not to turn the old and venerable state of Brandenburg-Prussia into a "fashionable Jewish state." The king then had taken sides with Hardenberg against Marwitz and his Junker friends. This time, however, he took a position contrary to Hardenberg's wishes.

Although Frederick William III made it clear that he would still leave it to Hardenberg's discretion to reply to the letter from the Senate of Frankfurt am Main, he did not conceal that he personally inclined to the position taken by the city of Frankfurt. "In any case," he remarked, "I wish that at the diet of the confederation the Jews not be supported by Prussia."[55] Hardenberg made the notation: "For the moment, ad acta." He referred to the stipulations of the Viennese Congress pertaining to the Jews of Frankfurt, which he interpreted in a sense favorable to them and which, in his opinion, imposed definite obligations also upon Prussia. But the difference of opinion between the King and Hardenberg limited the Chancellor's freedom of action and precluded further activities on behalf of the Jews.

While Hardenberg defended the interests of the German Jews beyond the borders of Prussia, he did not forget the Jews of Prussia themselves. Their emancipation in 1812, Hardenberg held, obligated the state not to tolerate any agitation against them. When the passions of many people were violently excited by the appearance of numerous anti-Semitic pamphlets, the Chancellor considered it the best policy to prohibit any further publications concerning the Jews. "To arouse hatred against the Jews," he wrote, "is as unstatesmanlike as it is immoral. It is certain that in the case of continued public insults against the Jews the lower mass of the population will feel called upon and justified to offend them and it will be impossible to avoid excesses by the one and the other party. This evil must be prevented. It also appears to me not to be to the honor of the Prussian state if intolerance is preached by the capital against a colony which the state protects."[56]

The German Jew of the postwar era was repeatedly exposed to the sneers and contempt of German theater audiences. As mentioned, Sessa's comedy *Unser Verkehr,* in which Jewish characters were thoroughly derided, won special applause. In spite of all endeavors on the part of a few leading Jews such as Israel Jacobsohn to prevent the staging of the play, the farce was finally presented in Berlin and also attracted large audiences in other German cities. Hardenberg himself disapproved of the incitement which these distortions of Jewish characters were bound to produce among Germans.[57]

While reaction cast its dark shadow over Germany, Hardenberg remained at the helm of the Prussian state. He was compelled to make many a concession, which cost him a good deal of popularity in progressive circles. After 1815 his support of the Jews was also severely curtailed. When in December 1817 the privy councilor to the Austrian legation, Jordan, left for Vienna, he carried instructions on the "Policy of the Prussian government concerning the affairs of the Israelites." The instructions breathed an unfriendly spirit, testifying to the mistrust in which the Jews were held by the authorities and to the belief in their corruption: the Jews ought not to be admitted to civil service or to the assemblies of the states, "because they obviously corrupt the spirit of both." Hardenberg made the annotation: "Accedo" [I accede].[58]

This remark expressed the accommodation to the prevailing temper of the times rather than a genuine change of his views and policies. He probably realized that the year 1817 was hardly the opportune moment for lending support to the demands of German Jews for rights which even the emancipated Prussian Jews had not yet attained. Hardenberg remained convinced of the necessity, justice, and humanity of the Jewish emancipation and also of its usefulness to the Prussian state. While Stein later repented his earlier moves in behalf of the Jews, Hardenberg steadfastly continued to defend his policies.

Wilhelm von Humboldt and Full Equality

Wilhelm von Humboldt, statesman and educator, linguistic scholar and author, the friend of Goethe and Schiller, deserved hardly less credit for the emancipation of Prussia's Jews than Hardenberg. Like his older brother, the great world traveler and scholar Alexander von Humboldt, Wilhelm von Humboldt as a youth had experienced strongly formative influences by Jews. "It has pleased me very much," Wilhelm von Humboldt wrote after the death of David Friedländer, the leading Jewish advocate of the emancipation in Berlin, to Friedländer's son Benoni, "that the deceased still thought at times of my brother and myself. We shall never forget how he influenced both of us. He guided us early to the right views on several important points affecting life and society."[59]

According to the testimony of Alexander von Humboldt, both brothers associated from their earliest childhood with prominent men of Jewish ancestry and faith, who excelled in philosophy and mathematics. "One of the greatest writers, the friend of Lessing, Moses Mendelssohn," Alexander remarked in a letter to the rabbi Mortara of Mantua (1855), "had exerted influence upon the education which I and my brother enjoyed in 'prehistoric' times."[60]

According to Henriette Herz, the young brothers had been introduced to her husband, the philosopher and physician Markus Herz, by the private tutor J. Christian Knuth. Both of them later heard Herz's lectures on philosophy. Wilhelm and Alexander von Humboldt joined the reading circle of Henriette Herz, where the *Tugendbund* (League of Virtue) was established. To it also belonged Christian Dohm, then already known as the spokesman for Jewish emancipation; Wilhelm attended Dohm's lectures in Berlin in 1785. The young Wilhelm developed great interest in Henriette Herz, who taught the brothers how to read and write Hebrew. In his correspondence with his wife Caroline, the former Caroline von Dacheröden (whom Wilhelm, incidentally, had met in the gatherings at Henriette's), Madame Herz was often mentioned. The young brothers had also frequented the salon of Dorothea Veit, the daughter of Moses Mendelssohn.

Wilhelm von Humboldt's attitude toward the Jews emerged most distinctly from a memoir on the reform project of Schroetter by the Bureau of Religious and Public Instruction, which he headed.[61] Aside from Humboldt, the memoir listed Nicolovius, Suevern, and Schmedding as contributors. The "present situation of the Jews among us," it said, was based upon "causes and connected with circumstances which are beyond the power of any single state to affect essentially and radically." The means to change the status of the Jews consisted of "amalgamation, destruction of their clerical organization and settlement. . . . But as long as these means are tried only in a single state, the amalgamation is never strong enough, and in the realm of religious ideas the contrast between Christians and Jews will necessarily continue, until people everywhere cease to think of Christianity on the low plane of opposition to Judaism."

There were difficulties which no legislation could entirely eliminate. But it is "clear and undeniable that that legislation on the Jews is better than any other, which makes separation less noticeable and makes amalgamation more intimate."

The wall of separation between Christians and Jews may be torn down with one blow or gradually. "Only a sudden and full equalization" is "just, statesmanlike and consistent. . . . Just: for no other possible legal ground may be thought of why the Jew, who wishes to fulfill all duties of the Christian, ought not to acquire also his rights. Statesmanlike: for the state should teach its citizens to esteem everybody, not merely the Jew. The state, furthermore, must eradicate the inhuman and prejudiced way of thinking according to which a human being is judged not on the basis of his individual characteristics but in accordance with his origin and religion; contrary to every true conception of human dignity, man was looked upon not as an individual, but as belonging to a race and necessarily sharing with it certain qualities. The state, however, can eliminate bias only by declaring loudly and distinctly that it does not recognize any longer a difference between Jews and Christians."

Finally, only an immediate, full equality of the Jews was also "consistent: for a gradual abolition confirms the separation which it wishes to eliminate in all not abolished points, doubles the attention in regard to the still existing limitation and runs thereby counter to itself."

Humboldt moved still other, heavier guns into position against those who supported only a gradual equalization of the Jews with

their Christian fellow citizens. "The state," he remarked, "is no educational institute, but a legal establishment." If one wishes to make
the granting of new rights dependent on the moral progress of a
people, one would have to consider that the "moral stage of a nation
can never be calculated accurately, while its development can even
less be foreseen mechanically." Humboldt, always fascinated by
comparative anthropology, had diligently studied the phenomenon of
national character, particularly that of the French, the Spaniards, and
the Basques, and was a recognized authority in this field. He noted
that the judgment on national characters required "a rare combination
of genuine philosophical sense and of the gift of rapid and keen observation." A conscientious man would "never connect" it with granting or denying rights.

"One becomes involved in the greatest difficulties, however, if
one tries to ascertain the progress of the nation. How, for instance,
shall one discern whether the Jews have become more deserving of
public esteem? Perhaps by considering individual acts? Or by public
reports of officials capable perhaps of a thousand things but not of
observation of human beings, on a subject about which even the
lonely monologue attains agreement only with difficulty? Or perhaps
by tables showing how many Jews have learned this or that trade,
have become agriculturists or soldiers?" To judge in accordance
with such "external appearances" would be "incompatible with the
most elementary feelings of human dignity." "If a state wished to be
consistent in this point, its legislation would have to distribute civil
rights in an unequal measure also among Christians, dependent on
the individual's cultural stage; an idea which, fortunately, has not
yet occurred to anyone." As far as political rights were concerned,
the difference in culture did not matter, only the difference in honesty did. "But is any experience sufficient to attach to an entire
people a stigma of depravity? . . . Does not a government which in a
new law pronounces such an anathema necessarily bring it about
that the better elements of the nation emigrate and only the scum
remains?"

"In my opinion no legislation on the Jews will attain its ultimate
goal save one which compels the use of the word Jew in no other
sense than the religious one, and I would for this reason alone vote
for the full equalization of Jews with Christians." In case the Jews
should not wish to assume the duties which all citizens bear, he
would, Humboldt asserted, after trying all means of persuasion,
"rather expel them from the state. . . . For to tolerate human beings
in the state who acquiesce in being trusted so little that they are
denied, even in case of higher culture, the civil rights otherwise com-

mensurate with their status, is most hazardous to the morality of the entire nation."

Humboldt raised the question whether "a complete and sudden equality" of the Jews with the Christians was not like "a jump from one extreme into the other." Such an assumption rested on a misunderstanding. "If an unnatural state of things changes into a natural one, one should not speak of a leap, at least not of a hazardous one." Humboldt questioned the claim that sudden emancipation of the Jews constituted a peril to the Germans. He "did not see the great danger," since all would have to obey the laws. He also derided the possibility that Jews could "dispossess" the Germans as a delusion. To the contrary, Humboldt discerned a serious danger for both Christians and Jews in the continuance of inequality.

After this masterful plea for the complete and immediate emancipation of the Jews, Humboldt turned to a detailed discussion of Schroetter's project for emancipation. He condemned most sharply the author's "rather petty timidity." The "physical well-being"of the Jews would undoubtedly "considerably gain" if Schroetter's project would be accepted and the degree of freedom attained might appear in some regards satisfactory. Yet the project pronounced "their moral degradation in an almost revolting manner. For while ascribing to the Jews an acute intellect . . . it deprives them of all confidence in their honesty, faith and love for truth."

Humboldt, a disciple of Kant, was apparently influenced by Kant's negative conception of Judaism and of Jewish religion as a mere ceremonial law. He seemed convinced that German Jewry would fully embrace German culture, would assimilate itself rapidly, and would finally abandon the Jewish religion. For these reasons, Humboldt, deviating from Schroetter, dissuaded the state from investing high rabbis for the Jews, unless they themselves asked for them, and urged the state to "further," through natural and just tolerance, "schisms" within Judaism; the Jewish "hierarchy" would then "break up by itself." Humboldt was apparently unaware that, while fighting prejudices against the Jews, he himself was perhaps a victim of all-pervasive, centuries-old prejudices about their religion. Nor did he anticipate that the policies he recommended might involve the state deeply in religious differences within Judaism, contrary to his own liberal, *laissez-faire* attitude.

With sharp logic, however, Humboldt showed the incongruity of Schroetter's ideas about the Jews. In regard to special measures to be retained, he criticized the provision that a Jewish deserter was to face a harder punishment than a Christian deserter. The principle of legal equality was always his guide. The acquisition of civil rights should not be presented to the Jews as an "extraordinary favor"; their "loss should be a penalty for the Jews only where the Christian must expect the same."

Humboldt had rejected Schroetter's conception of the state as an "educational institute" instead of as a legal one because he did not wish to make the granting of full civil equality contingent on the real or alleged progress of the Jewish community. On the other hand, as head of the Prussian system of education and as creator of the University of Berlin, Humboldt had always shown a most lively interest in problems of education, and he eagerly seized upon the idea of education, though in a different sense, one more friendly to the Jews. He considered not only Jews but also Christians far removed from ideal "refinement" and from a state of mind untarnished by prejudices. Thus Wilhelm von Humboldt wished to commence his "education" of both Jews and Christians without delay; and the best means of education was the full legal emancipation of the Jews.

True equality of the Jews appeared to him the ultimate goal, and prompt legal emancipation the most effective initial means to bring it about and to eradicate the bias of both Christians and Jews. In this sense he remarked that mere gradual abolition of legal inequality, taking unduly into consideration still prevalent prejudices, "worked against itself" in that it was educationally unsound: it "misguided public opinion" on the Jews and thus produced undesirable consequences. The following remarks should be similarly understood: "The state need not tolerate a prejudice offending the rights of many of its members, such as the lack of esteem of the Jews, but ought to declare itself outright against the same." Legislation should not trail the blind prejudices of the mob and thus "strengthen" them, but should begin to eliminate them by granting equality to the Jews, who longed for it and were ready to accept it.

For many years Wilhelm von Humboldt and the Chancellor Hardenberg were closely linked in the political arena. In many respects Humboldt decisively influenced the Chancellor.[62] How much he influenced him concerning the emancipation of the Jews cannot be proved with certainty, but probably to a considerable extent.

As representative of Prussia at the Congress of Vienna, Wilhelm von Humboldt, jointly with Hardenberg, took the side of the Jews. He reported from Vienna to his wife Caroline that he had recently been visited by an old Jew who offered him three precious rings out of gratitude for his services to his people. To the amazement of Gentz he had refused the present: "I merely told him that if one has come to espouse a cause as warmly as I have, the first condition was a clear conscience."[63]

Wilhelm and Caroline von Humboldt: Disagreements

From the correspondence between Wilhelm von Humboldt and his wife Caroline emerges clearly the prominent role that the Jewish question played in Germany. Wilhelm reminded his wife, who disliked Jews, that in early childhood he and his brother Alexander had entertained close relationships with individual Jews and had defended Jews whenever necessary; "Alexander and I, while still children, were held to be the bulwark of Judaism." Yet Caroline clung firmly to her preconceived notion: "You boast," she wrote in March 1816, "that you will never desert the Jews. It is your only fault that I know of. . . ."[64] She then raised bitter accusations against the Jews, reproaching them for usury and cowardice. "If I had anything to say about it, I would forbid them to trade for three generations, and all twenty-year-old youths, without exception save for reason of physical disability, would be soldiers. I'd bet that in fifty years the Jews as Jews would be destroyed. And I cannot be convinced that this would not be a gain for humanity; the Jews in their depravity, their usury, their inherited lack of courage, which springs from usury, are a stain upon humanity."

Caroline's charges against the Jews and their alleged cowardice stand in sharp contradiction to repeated acknowledgment, including acknowledgment by official sources, of Jewish fortitude and fulfillment of duty in the war against France. Even hostile contemporaries such as Julius von Voss testified to it.[65] Caroline, however, was only too ready to lend her ear to every rumor about Jews, plainly contradictory as these frequently were. She accused wealthy Jews of special greediness but charged them at the same time with buying off their poorer brethren from military service. Similarly, she claimed to "know" in advance that three of four houses to be sold in Berlin "will certainly be acquired by Jews."[66]

No wonder that her husband "joked about her tirades,"[67] particularly since he knew only too well of her intimate friendships with individual Jewish men and women. He also questioned her sources of information: "The Jews may well possess many houses, but so far own very few lands." "Indeed," he remarked, one could "do much that has been omitted . . . without abandoning what I always consider beneficial, namely granting them civil rights." Unlike some of his contemporaries, Wilhelm von Humboldt by no means regretted the emancipation as an error because of supposedly unfavorable experiences thereafter. Any possible blame should be directed against the state: "Why, for instance, does one tolerate the buying off from military service? Why does one not facilitate their learning of trades? The state need not resort so much to them in financial matters, and this is a cardinal corruption.'' It is one and the same situation which brought forth opposite replies from Caroline and Wilhelm von Humboldt; it aroused in Caroline an outpouring of prejudice and accusations and induced her husband to make constructive statesmanlike proposals for the further post-emancipation improvement of the Jews.

"My tirade on the Jews, beloved,'' Caroline finally yielded somewhat, "about which you joke so sweetly, is perhaps not in order.''[68] Whereupon Wilhelm replied in a resigned mood: "I can imagine your hatred of the Jews. It has everything which contemporary Christians have. I fully concede to be worse off with the old faith; one has no chance against the new one. I also, however, love the Jews only in principle; in practice I avoid crossing their way.''[69]

This, however, did not quite correspond to the truth and was probably written to conciliate his wife. Still, it was true that in his plea for the emancipation of the Jews Wilhelm von Humboldt was moved by general principles rather than by "love" for individual Jews. His attitude toward them was ultimately founded in his "old faith," in his conception of humanity and society in their entirety: it rested neither upon a vacillating political opportunism nor upon fleeting impressions or hasty conclusions drawn from personal encounters with individual Jews.

At one time Caroline suddenly perceived that there were "low-minded" people also among the Germans,[70] that there existed, as she put it, "also Christian Jews," and her opposition to equality seemed to have narrowed down to opposing a sudden emancipation of the Jews with the rest of the population: "I do not find it right to skip all stages with them and to let them enjoy all civil rights at once.''[71] Wilhelm von Humboldt could have referred his wife to his memoir on the Jews in 1808, in which he had demanded their immediate and unconditional emancipation, effectively refuting arguments for a more gradual extension of equality.

Caroline clearly exhibited the ambivalence of the Romantic age toward Jews and Judaism. Hers was a hate-love relationship toward the Jews, and she was unable to establish one on a more rational basis, free from exaggerations and unstable emotionalism. Some Jews were close to her heart. "We belong to each other,'' she assured Rahel Levin. She also could not separate herself from the daughter of Moses Mendelssohn, Dorothea Schlegel, or from Dr. Koreff, professor at the University of Berlin, the personal physician and friend of Chancellor Hardenberg. "Here, my dear,' she wrote Rahel from Vienna, "I leave only two human beings whom it costs me very much, infinitely much, to leave: Dorothea Schlegel, for I feel loved by her, and Koreff. I could talk to you about him, particularly if you had seen him, but I cannot write. This is the most marvelous character who has taken hold of me."[72] Varnagen von der Ense remarked in a letter to Rahel of June 26, 1815, that it had greatly pleased him to hear that Caroline von Humboldt and her daughters had prepared a room in their house for a visit of their private physician Dr. Koreff, for Koreff was a Jew and "the Humboldts are in general hostile toward the Jews."[73]

Prussian Military Leaders and Jewish Emancipation

The Jews as a people, as distinguished from individuals among them, were also rejected by the old prince Gebhard Leberecht von Blücher, Marshal "Vorwärts" (Forward!), as he was popularly called, and by the German military strategist August Neithardt von Gneisenau, who had played a major role in reawakening the spirit of the Prussian army after the debacle of 1806. In a letter to Gneisenau, dated July 10, 1818, Blücher voiced his vivid regret that his esteemed Prussian monarch Friedrich Wilhelm III had not yet granted the "promised constitution," while the Bavarian King had done so. "Since," he added, "schemers, Jews and female fortunetellers are placed on the agenda, I rather wish not to have anything to do with it any more."[74] Actually, the Jews' interest pointed clearly to a modern constitutional state rather than to the continuation of the absolutist princely regime. Throughout the nineteenth century reactionary feudal Junkers and their political followers leveled just the opposite accusation against the Jews, namely that they were destroyers of the old, venerable, historically grown constitution and propagators of "new legislation."

No other than the recipient of Blücher's letter, Gneisenau, though generally liberal-minded,[75] made this charge. The waves of reaction flooded even the liberal camp and left behind a residue of prejudice. Gneisenau replied to Blücher on July 15, 1818: "I consent from the bottom of my heart to what your Highness says about scheming and the Jews. It is a disease, indeed a fury of the age, to overthrow everything old and to introduce new legislation. The nobility is ruined by it and by the circumstances of the time, and Jews and contractors will take its place and will become our future peers of the Reich. This Jewish nuisance stirs my innermost feelings . . . like the vileness of the age which esteems only the man who can live high and throw big dinners; one accepts them from people who may be very depraved."[76]

What resounds here is the defiance and rancor of the nobleman against the wealthy bourgeoisie, which the Jews partly represented. A class hatred, which had assumed a national and religious garb, burst violently forth. The social rise of Jewry and the growing pecuniary power of the Jewish bourgeoise had aroused envy and jealousy even in reform-minded aristocratic circles. Oddly enough, Gneisenau elsewhere praised the memory of Lessing in his poem "Zum Tode Lessings" [To the Death of Lessing] (1781).[77]

The resurgence of Prussia after her defeat in 1806 was also linked with the name of Gerhard von Scharnhorst. An outstanding military leader, he met a heroic death in the War of Liberation. When the various Prussian ministries in 1808 had been invited to present their opinions on Schroetter's project for the emancipation of the Jews, Scharnhorst, as Minister of War, had stated his views.[78] With great perspicacity he had pointed to the shortcomings of Schroetter's plan and had demanded full and unconditional equality of the Jews with the rest of the population. The memoir was signed also by von Boyen, Scharnhorst's successor as Minister of War, by von Hacke, von Rauch, and von Duncker. This document breathed the spirit of liberty, equality, and fair play, sharply condemning the continued infringement of the natural rights of the Jews.

"We must take the position," it said, "that since the Jews are to be subjected by the new constitution to all obligations and performances required of Christian citizens, not excepting even the duty of conscription, which appears the most burdensome, they ought to receive for this and for the loss of so many freedoms enjoyed so far a treatment which closely approximates that of the Christian citizens, without making the fulfillment of their new duties more bitter and spiteful by causing hardships which do not hit the Christian citizen."

Equal rights for equal duties was Scharnhorst's watchword. He sharply criticized every deviation from this principle, rejecting for instance Schroetter's suggestion that Jews be forced to have their beards cut as an "importunate pretension." He similarly criticized Schroetter's exclusion of the Jews from civil service and held "the manner in which it is expressed not considerate enough."

Schroetter had also raised objections to the settlement of the Jews in the countryside. Scharnhorst countered thus: "When the state hopes to attain a vital goal by changing the character of the Jews, it will succeed in full measure only if as few exceptions as possible will be made in regard to the Jews." Referring to Schroetter's recommendation that military duties be imposed on the Jews, he recommended erasing the words immediately following—"and, to be sure, in the strictest sense"—and replacing them with the words:

"just as on the Christian citizens." The Prussian Minister of War showed greater confidence in the Jews than did Schroetter.

Like Wilhelm von Humboldt, Scharnhorst opposed a piecemeal emancipation which would extend over a lengthy period and demanded immediate equality for the Jews. Any "special legislation," although it might be presented as merely temporary, permitted the continuation of a state of inequality for an indefinite period and was therefore inherently discriminatory. By necessity, then, it impeded and delayed the work of liberation and education. His unequivocal rejection of all halfway measures made Scharnhorst stand out as a forthright friend of the emancipation of the Jews.

Another one of the signatories of this memoir of the "General Department of War" was Leopold Hermann Ludwig von Boyen, later Minister of War. Like Wilhelm von Humboldt, he had been a student of Kant at Königsberg and had been deeply influenced by Kant's philosophy of law. He had also greatly admired the Declaration of the Rights of Man, which the French had proudly proclaimed during the Revolution.[79] In view of his general *Weltanschauung,* his special plea for the emancipation of the Jews was hardly surprising. Yet a few years after the proclamation of their emancipation, von Boyen was slightly critical of the implementation of the edict, although he still approved its essence.

The emancipation of 1812, he wrote in his *Denkwürdigkeiten und Erinnerungen* [Memoirs and Remembrances], "gave the Jews who had lived in the Prussian state under various pressures most civil rights and became instantaneously the object of a noisy agitation, which Christian prejudice produced as much as Christian commercial envy. It obviously needs no further proof that the purpose of the law was just and truly Christian, yet, because the lawgiver ought to reflect upon the prevailing popular prejudices, the leap all at once was too great."[80]

Now von Boyen held that the lawgiver should ponder popular "prejudices," instead of disregarding them. This view differed from the philosophy underlying the memoir of the War Department of November 1808, which had borne Boyen's signature.

The counterthrust of the reaction after 1815 and the "noisy" attacks against the emancipation of the Jews cast their shadow even upon the enlightened liberal camp. It influenced the judgment of men who generally favored reforms, such as von Gneisenau and von Boyen.

CHAPTER 6

German Educators
and the Jews

Fichte on the French Revolution and the Jews

Statesmen and military leaders led the Prussian people from defeat to victory. But no one played a larger role in awakening the German nation than the philosopher and educator Johann Gottlieb Fichte. That Fichte was a sharp opponent of the Jews has been asserted by Jews as well as by their enemies. A Jewish contemporary of Fichte, the journalist Saul Ascher, countered the philosopher in the year 1794, when he wrote his pamphlet "Eisenmenger* II, Sendschreiben an Herrn Professor Fichte" [Epistle to Professor Fichte]. Contemporaries such as the fanatic pamphleteer Grattenauer, who early in the nineteenth century launched several booklets against the Jews, and the historian Friedrich Rühs, in his anti-Semitic treatise of 1816, claimed Fichte as a Jew-hater.[1] The German anti-Semites of the later nineteenth century and finally the National Socialists and Hitler[2] pointed proudly to Fichte as their illustrious forerunner. Was Fichte indeed an enemy of the Jews?

In his work *Beiträge zur Berichtigung der öffentlichen Meinung über die Rechtmässigkeit der französischen Revolution* [Contributions to Correcting Public Opinion on the Rightfulness of the French Revolution] (1793), Fichte touched upon the Jewish question. This book was imbued with the spirit of the French Revolution, which Fichte, then its defender in the German realm, wholeheartedly endorsed. Like other German thinkers and poets, Herder and Kant,

*Johann Andreas Eisenmenger (1654–1704), one of the most noted German Jew-baiters, published his bitterly hostile book *Entdecktes Judentum* in Frankfurt am Main in the year 1700.

Klopstock and Wieland, he greeted enthusiastically the early beginnings of the French Revolution and was an ardent admirer of the
egalitarian drives of the French nation. But though the French extended liberty and equality to their entire population, Fichte, rather
inconsistently, excluded the German Jews.

In the *Beiträge* Fichte raised the question whether a new revolutionary formation within the framework of the existing state—a union
of free citizens who concluded among themselves a new civil contract—would be a threat to the state and emphatically denied it. He
pointed to several already existing "states within the state," which
were perhaps harmful but did not actually undermine the existing
state. The Jews formed such a "state within the state." "Through
almost all countries of Europe spreads a powerful state which is hostile to all others, is continually at war with them, and in some states
presses very heavily upon the citizens: it is Judaism."[3] The separation of the Jews from the alien surrounding, commanded by their
religion and deepened by their national pride, prevented them from
developing friendly relations with their host nations. Their peculiar
economic and social position, their inclination to trading, and their
exclusive laws—all made their separation from Christians complete.
It was therefore not surprising that the Jews remained aliens and even
retained a hostile attitude to Christians.

"Could anything else be expected from such a people except
what we saw, namely that in a state where even the absolute king is
not permitted to take my inherited hut and where I obtain my right
against the omnipotent minister, the first Jew whom it pleases robs
me unpunished. You too see all this and you cannot deny it, and you
still talk words as sweet as sugar about tolerance and human and civil
rights, although you violate our basic human rights; you cannot satisfy enough your loving tolerance toward those who do not believe in
Jesus Christ by giving them titles, dignities, and positions of honor,
while you insult publicly those who, like yourselves, believe in Him
and deprive them of their civil honor and of bread earned in dignity.
Don't you remember here the state within the state? Don't you recall
the intelligible thought that the Jews, who are, beside you, citizens of
a state which is firmer and mightier than all of yours, will, if you will
give them also civil rights in your state, trample all other citizens
under their feet?"

That Fichte emerged here as an outspoken enemy of the Jews is
beyond dispute. Nevertheless, a few remarks are in order. Did Fichte
then truly believe that the individual German could keep his parental
hut against the wishes of the absolutist ruler and his rights against the

will of the omnipotent minister? This from the thinker who only a year earlier in his book *Gedankenfreiheit und die Prinzen Europas* [Reclaiming Freedom of Thought from the Princes of Europe] had declared war against kings and princes because of their suppression of liberty and had attacked the ministers who surrounded the throne? Who had wished to abolish princes and nobility? His work on the French Revolution was written with an ulterior purpose; as the literary historian Heinrich Houben cautioned, the very title of his book was "a disguise of the content."[4]

Fichte painted the "state of the Jews" in most suspect colors so that the new "state within the state," which was to arise through the new contract of some of its citizens, would appear the more innocent. Actually, at that very time he developed in the *Vorlesungen über die Bestimmung des Gelehrten* [Lectures on the Destiny of the Scholar] the idea that the purpose of the state was to develop a perfect society and that ultimately it had to make itself superfluous. In reality, Fichte was not much concerned about the existing state nor about its future. He did not seem unduly alarmed by the weakening of the state through "states within the state," namely by the Jews and others such as nobility, clergy, and the military. These latter groups too, he asserted, pursued their own interests, formed closed castes, and were "no less menacing" than the Jews and "almost as terrible." It is only because Fichte and his radical companions felt harassed that, to divert the attention of the ruling powers, he pointed to other dangerous associations, already existing "states within the state," of which the Jews were only one example. Modern racial anti-Semitism in Germany, which placed Fichte among its glorious forerunners, had to abandon an essential part of Fichte's thesis, namely that the Jews were as perilous to the German state as for instance the German military![5]

Fichte acknowledged that the Jews must possess human rights, but he denied them civil rights. "Far from these pages," he wrote, "be the poisonous breath of intolerance as it is from my heart. . . . They must possess human rights, although they do not acknowledge ours, for they are humans and their injustice does not excuse our becoming like them. Do not compel any Jew against his will and do not allow that it be done, where you are the neighbor who can hinder it; you owe this to him by all means. If you have eaten yesterday, are hungry again, and have only bread for today, give it to the Jew who hungers beside you if he has not eaten yesterday, and you will do well." But this is followed by an unpardonable outburst: "But to give them civil rights, I see no other means than that of cutting off all their heads in one night* and of placing others upon their bodies in which there is not even one Jewish idea. To protect us from them, I again see no other way than of conquering their beloved country for them and to send all of them thereto.''

A critic of Fichte's political philosophy has remarked that ''Fichte's hatred of the Jews was almost equal to that of the Nazis.''[6] However, Fichte's hostility against the Jews did not extend throughout his entire life but appears to have been limited to a rather short period. His quoted anti-Jewish remarks in the work on the French Revolution are limited to four pages. One will encounter the words ''Jew'' and ''Judaism'' only sporadically in other writings of Fichte. Even in the work on the French Revolution Fichte displayed a minimum of justice. Writing on commercial treaties, he pilloried the ''most cruel and malicious modification'' of such contracts: if namely ''the suffering party is obligated to accept a certain quantity of a designated ware and to pay for it at a fixed price, as is the policy of the government in several countries in regard to salt and as Frederick II compelled for a time every Jew to take a certain quantity of porcelain at his wedding.''[7] Instead of approving the discriminatory policy and legislation of the state against the Jews, as one might expect from a relentless Jew-hater, Fichte condemned this practice!

The Jewish problem had for Fichte, even in his anti-Semitic phase, only peripheral significance. It played a rather small role within the totality of his thought on social and national problems of the Germans or any other nation. In his work on the French Revolution Fichte entangled himself in numerous contradictions. One ought to refrain from all constraints against the Jews yet leave them in the state of pariahs! The German ought to share his bread with the hungry Jew! Were there hungry Jews, and did these impoverished ones represent the formidable danger to Germandom? Not the least inconsistency, however, lay in the circumstance that after all his violent outbursts he tried to assure the reader that he detested the ''poisonous breath of intolerance'' and that he did not wish to lend his hand to persecution: ''I do not wish to say that one ought not to persecute the Jews because of their faith, but that one ought not to persecute anybody at all for this reason.'' But at the same time the ''protection'' of the Germans required the removal of the Jews to Palestine.

Some of Fichte's remarks point to the chasm between his enmity

---

*It is only fair to point out that Fichte's unhappily chosen phrase about the cutting off of heads had with him never the literal significance which National Socialism later gave to it. Had he, in the age of the Enlightenment, been able to foresee organized, factory-like annihilation of Jews, he without any doubt would have expressed himself differently.

toward the Jews in 1793 and the deadly hostility of German racial anti-Semitism in the twentieth century. The latter never concealed its hatred, since its adherents never felt ashamed of it. Fichte tried to assure his readers that he did not harbor any "private animosity" against the Jews, called upon the Germans to treat them humanely, and even spoke of "German obligations" toward them. According to his own testimony, Fichte, "to his own peril and to his personal disadvantage," even protected Jews whom people "teased." German National Socialism later gloated at the spectacle of Fichte spouting anti-Semitism maliciously against the Jews but disregarded entirely his contrary remarks and deeds.

Most of those who have declared Fichte to be an uncompromising enemy of the Jews have overlooked the fact that Fichte himself expressly called the few anti-Jewish utterances in his work on the French Revolution youthful "one-sidedness" and "exaggerations"— he was thirty-one years old when he wrote that work. Those who have tried to capitalize on Fichte's brief and rather isolated outburst against the Jews have made little attempt to evaluate the numerous, brief remarks on Jews and Judaism which are scattered throughout his other writings and have also failed to take into consideration his later relations with individual Jews.

In a letter of March 1, 1794, addressed to the philosopher Reinhold, Fichte recanted much of his work on the French Revolution, published during the previous year.[8] In 1799, defending himself against the accusations of atheism, he remarked on the earlier book: "If a young man who had abandoned his fatherland . . . carried away by anger because of the exaggerations which the defenders of the lawless, arbitrary power of the mighty permitted themselves, had on his part likewise exaggerated a little . . . , if the same person since, turned into a man, had in a more mature, more thoughtful work on the same topic avoided all one-sidedness, is it then fair and just still to use that youthful and incomplete attempt of the young man as a yardstick of the political principles of the man?"[9] These words are rather conclusive and relate to the entire work, including the "exaggerated" remarks on the Jews.

FICHTE'S CHANGE OF HEART AND MIND

When in 1793 Fichte had ascribed so much evil to the Jews, he actually had not known them at all. He had, as he then admitted, "never entered into any relations with a Jew." When he later came to know them personally, the fog of bias which had blurred his judgment quickly dissolved.

Fichte experienced a decisive change in his feelings about the Jews when through Friedrich Schlegel he made the acquaintance of Dorothea Mendelssohn Veit, the daughter of Moses Mendelssohn and later Schlegel's wife. Fichte's relations with Friedrich Schlegel grew very close.[10] When Fichte became involved in a dispute in which he was charged with atheism, Schlegel thought of coming to his defense. Fichte stayed in Berlin with Friedrich and Dorothea Schlegel for several months. During these days Friedrich wrote to his brother August Wilhelm: "We live very intimately with Fichte, pleasantly and interestingly."

In joint excursions into the surroundings of Berlin, Fichte learned to know Dorothea better. His letters to his fiancée and later wife testify to the change that came over him. He openly confessed that Dorothea Schlegel had shaken his views on the Jews, which had scarcely been favorable: "I owe it to Madame Veit and to you,' he wrote in September 1800, "to recommend her to you urgently. The praise of a Jewess from my lips may sound strange, but this woman has changed my view that nothing good can emerge from this nation. She possesses an unusually rich intellect and knowledge, with little or indeed no exterior radiance, utmost lack of pretensions, and much kindheartedness. One gradually takes to liking her, but then from one's heart. I hope you will become friends."[11] Fichte's anti-Semitic intoxication had begun to vanish.

Fichte's changed attitude toward the Jews continued to show itself a year later. He had conceived the idea of publishing a new magazine and of winning for this enterprise the financial help of some wealthy Jews of Berlin: "I have so little abandoned the plan [to edit a magazine]," he wrote later to the philosopher Schelling, "that I have talked in definite terms about it, with Friedrich Schlegel and Madame Veit, in order to make the wealthy merchant houses here, a Veit, Levi, entrepreneurs of this matter."[12] He no longer had any hesitation in enlisting Jews in this venture.

Even before his personal acquaintance with Dorothea Schlegel, the Jewish philosopher Solomon Maimon had shaken Fichte's anti-Semitic prejudices. Solomon Maimon, an original thinker, represents the most important link between Kant and Fichte in the history of German idealistic philosophy and influenced the latter's own intellectual development in no negligible way. In view of Fichte's anti-Jewish outburst in 1793, it was an irony that it happened to be a Jewish philosopher who pointed the way on which Fichte was to journey. Kant himself, who disliked a further development of his philosophy, measured Maimon and Fichte by the same critical yardstick. In his declaration on Fichte's *Wissenschaftslehre* Kant stressed that the critical philosophy needed an "improvement" neither theoretically nor practically, aiming his shafts at both Fichte and Maimon.

That the two thinkers were moving in the same direction was observed not only by Kant. Fichte himself saw in Solomon Maimon an ally. He sent him a copy of the *Wissenschaftslehre* (1794) and assured him of his "unlimited esteem for his philosophical talent."[13] A year later, after the publication of his book on the French Revolution with its few poisonous pages on the Jews, Fichte appeared sobered in his relation with this Jewish thinker. He invited Maimon to become a contributor to his *Allgemeine Literatur-Zeitung*.[14] Fichte had come to welcome not only financial but also intellectual contributions of Jews to German papers and magazines.

Fichte's high regard for Maimon is reflected in a letter to the philosopher Reinhold, dated September 30, 1794: "My esteem for Maimon's talent is limitless; I firmly believe and I am ready to prove that through him the entire philosophy of Kant, as it has generally been interpreted, by you as well as others, has been turned completely upside down. He has done all this without anybody taking notice of it and while people look down upon him from the heights. I think that future generations will laugh at us."[15] Fichte's words underlined sharply the contrast between Maimon's actual importance and his lack of wide recognition and hint at the possible cause. Had not both philosophers, both opponents of the Jews, "looked down" upon Maimon? In this letter Fichte's sense of justice broke through to the surface.

Among Fichte's students at the University of Berlin were many Jews.[16] He was in frequent touch with them without displaying any anti-Jewish bias. Thus he related to his wife that he had found quarters in the house of the "Jew Borchard and that he had eaten at the Levin's at night."[17] In a letter of July 10, 1807, Fichte also notified his wife that he had sent her a letter from Memel through a Jew who had traveled to Krakau.[18]

Brief remarks on and references to Judaism can be found in many of Fichte's works. Two of these studies, *Aphorismen über Religion und Deismus* [Aphorisms on Religion and Deism] and *Kritik aller Offenbarung* [Criticism of All Revelation], were written in the years 1790 and 1791–1792 respectively—that is, before 1793, when his book on the French Revolution, containing the anti-Jewish passage, was published. Several other works in which Fichte referred to Judaism extend over the period from 1804 to 1813, the year of his death. In none of these writings did he express anti-Jewish sentiments; to the contrary, some of the passages in question, especially in later works, testify to his growing respect for Jews and Judaism. These remarks, scattered throughout his writings, exceed by sheer size the few pages published in 1793, to which anti-Semites have unceasingly drawn attention. Since the latter observations also span a long period of time, they appear more conclusive than the single hostile utterance, which was soon repudiated. In any case the thesis of Fichte's continued hostility to the Jews is a mere fiction.

In the *Aphorismen* (1790) Fichte referred to anthropomorphic conceptions of God, which prevailed in religions before Jesus, including the Jewish religion; in the latter "at the beginning more and afterwards gradually less." This points to a progressive development of the Jewish faith.[19] In his *Kritik* (1791–1792) Fichte again turned against anthropomorphism in religion,[20] to which the Jews, but also "some Christians of the Middle Ages and of more recent times," had clung. Thus the Jews, one among numerous religious groups and peoples, embraced at first a primitive, childlike, as yet unrefined concept of God.

Fichte evaluated the Jews from a traditionally Christian point of view. This is evident in a sermon the twenty-four-year-old preached in Dubrenski on March 25, 1786. God, he said, gave all men a certain incentive to improve. Many heathens and Jews, "thirsty after God," followed their blind leaders, "longing for a fatherly religion, perhaps with the warmest hearts, but without understanding. . . . The grace of God would incline also upon these hearts, he should offer also to them the possibility of cleansing their souls."[21] While the superiority of Christianity is not questioned and Jews and pagans appear on a lower plane, the friendly tone of the whole is undeniable.

Little hostility to the Jews was astir in Fichte before 1793, the year of his anti-Jewish outburst, and little animosity can be discerned thereafter. In 1793 Fichte had become a member of the Freemasons in Berlin and displayed a lively activity in the lodge of the capital. In an address delivered before it in April 1800, he voiced in truly cosmopolitan spirit the idea that differences in nationality and religion, as expressed in the writings of the Jews, Romans, and Arabs, should not matter fundamentally, that the simple human striving for religion alone should count.[22] At about the same time he castigated Clemens Brentano for his anti-Semitic satire "The Philistine."[23]*

Among later works of Fichte containing brief references to Jews and to Jewish religion but showing no hostility are the following: *Grundzüge des gegenwärtigen Zeitalters* [Fundamentals of the Present Age], 1804–1805; *Politische Fragmente* [Political Fragments], 1807–1813; and *Die Staatslehre* [Theory of the State], 1813. In

*See Clemens Brentano, Chapters 8 and 9.

Grundzüge Fichte stressed the Jewish origins of Christianity[24] and attempted to understand the ancient Jews in the framework of their age. The "strong, zealous, and jealous God of Judaism" was, in a certain sense, the God of the "entire antiquity." In another context, however, he compared the Jews with other ancient peoples, Assyrians, Medes, and Persians, and found them "by far more excellent."[25] The cultural history of the Jews proved that suppression at times can have healthy, "splendid consequences." Only after their dispersal over the countries of the earth had the Jews "freed themselves from their earlier, primitive superstition" and "raised themselves to better conceptions about God and the spiritual world."[26] Fichte discussed also the question of the authorship of the "so-called First Book of Moses." "It does not matter to me," he remarked, "how the essay has been preserved; fortunately it has been—and this is the main thing!"[27]

Regard for Judaism showed itself also in Fichte's posthumous *Politische Fragmente.* "Why," he asked there, "did Christianity have to develop from Judaism?" and replied "It was a very well finished theocracy . . . a civilizing of God as almost nowhere else."[28] The miracles performed by Moses were no fraud. Moses was "very enthusiastic and seized by love for his people, by the desire to make it a nation." In the *Staatslehre* Fichte stressed that ancient religions possessed an "inclination" to the doctrine of divine selection.[29] The Hebrews' belief that they were the chosen people was thus not a unique phenomenon. As before, he emphasized "the historic significance" of Judaism as a source of Christianity.[30]

AGAINST JEW-HATERS

In the history of the War of Liberation Fichte's name appears in capital letters. He was a member of the patriotic *Christlich-Deutsche Tischgesellschaft* (Christian-German Table Company) in Berlin, which in the days of spiritual and material preparation for the impending war played an important role. The *Tischgesellschaft,* in accordance with its statutes, excluded Jews from membership, but Fichte espoused neither its conservative political philosophy in general nor its anti-Semitic prejudices in particular. His rejection of anti-Semitism was apparently shared by other members, such as the poets Heinrich von Kleist and Stägemann,* who were rather favorably disposed to the Jews. It was in this circle that Clemens Brentano read his satire "Der Philister, in und nach der Geschichte" [The Philistine, in and according to History] which among other features had a distinctly anti-Semitic note; it soon

*For Kleist and Stägemann, see Chapter 8.

afterwards appeared anonymously in print. Rumor had it that it was either the work of the poet Achim von Arnim, who was known to dislike Jews, or of Fichte. Fichte, however, was not its author; he was not only not indifferent toward it but outright critical of it.

At the turn of the century Clemens Brentano had read the original version of his satire, then named "Die Naturgeschichte des Philisters" [The Natural History of the Philistine] in the circle of Schlegel and Tieck in Jena. According to an account by Tieck, Fichte had risen after Brentano's reading and had sharply criticized the poet, starting with these words: "Now I shall prove to you from this story that Brentano here is the foremost and worst of all Philistines."[31]

Fichte's youthful anti-Semitic outburst in 1793 was probably still remembered in some circles, and his name was therefore linked, though erroneously, with the anonymous anti-Semitic essay. Few knew of his criticism of Brentano's satire, which he had publicly uttered a decade earlier. Among them was Eduard Julius Hitzig and the novelist-poet Fouqué. They were convinced that Fichte's criticism of and hostility to Brentano's satire were just as sharp at the time of the reading in Jena.

Eduard Hitzig was the friend, helper, and publisher of many German poets, including Chamisso, E. T. A. Hoffman, Fouqué, and others. Although a converted Jew, he was nevertheless enraged at Brentano's work and urged his friend Fouqué "to lash" the "scoundrel." Fouqué, however, held that "silent comtempt of the jester" would be more effective and appropriate. Yet he too wished to deprive Clemens Brentano of "the fun of barking again," as he wrote Hitzig in his reply, and recommended a "serious admonition by Fichte." Fouqué and Hitzig seem to have been familiar with Fichte's hardly flattering thoughts about Clemens Brentano and his anti-Semitic literary outpouring.[32]

That Fichte now opposed anti-Semitic criticism—perhaps because once, as a young man, he himself had indulged in it—is also confirmed by the following episode. It shows clearly how far Fichte had traveled in the intervening two decades.

On January 18, 1812, Fichte was to preside at a meeting of the Christian-German Table Company. On this occasion he read verses, which, while voiced in jest, nevertheless reveal his critical attitude toward the very club of which he was a member. The Table Company, which according to its statutes excluded "Philistines" and Jews, was bluntly told by Fichte that the topics so far had been "trite." Neither allusions to Jews nor allusions to Philistines served the purpose of making people laugh. One should beware lest by ridiculing others "ridicule hit ourselves." He himself would not tease

Jews and Philistines. And in typically Fichtean fashion he closed the verses with the lofty appeal: "The thought which soars above the low grounds should purify itself and be filled with noble matters." Obviously, dislike of either "Philistines" or Jews lacked such nobility.

As rector of the University of Berlin, Fichte became entangled in a decision relating to a student brawl between several German students and a Jewish student. The incident tended to divide the student body and the senate of the faculty into two camps. The all too lenient judgment of the misdemeanor of two German students who were involved in this matter and the excessively sharp sentence against the Jewish student apparently challenged Fichte's sense of fair play; he sided with the Jewish student. Max Lenz, the historian of the University of Berlin, has recounted in some detail these student scandals, which embittered Fichte's administration and caused him ultimately to resign from the rectorate.[33]

The name of the Jewish student was Brogi; he came from Posen and was the son of a merchant. "Shabby in attire and also in spirits," as even benevolent people acknowledged, he was, on the other hand, according to Max Lenz, "not inaccessible to nobler feelings." He had been beaten with a hunting whip by a German student by the name of Melzer, also a native of Posen, an "insolent, even brutal individual." Fichte, who in his inaugural speech as rector had taken sharp issue with all brawling and dueling, wished to set a precedent but met unexpected resistance from his colleagues, who perhaps felt "sympathy with the Germanic bully." The senate sentenced Melzer to four weeks and Brogi to eight days of prison and pronounced a reprimand against Brogi but not against Melzer. Outraged about the sentence meted out to Brogi, Fichte sharply condemned the "mild treatment of the brutal disturbance of the peace." The great philosopher Boeckh and the famous physician Hufeland were likewise aroused about the leniency shown to Melzer and warned that this attitude of the senate majority could lead to new excesses. They were right.

The first outrage against Brogi was soon followed by a second one. This time he was slapped by a student named Klaatsch. Again Fichte wished to punish severely the rude violation of academic order, but once again he was deserted by his colleagues. He thereupon surrendered the conduct of the student trial and petitioned the Department of Instruction for release from the rectorate. The judgment of the senate, pronounced again over the sharp dissent of Boekh and Hufeland, according to Lenz, "lacked the dispassionate calm of the fair judge." The senate's sentence this time provided for fourteen days of prison for Klaatsch, eight for Brogi. Brogi, in addition, was threatened with expulsion should he become involved in new wrangles. No similar warning was given Klaatsch, although his record was already marred by previous punishment. Fichte called the new sentence of the senate "destructive of all discipline and highly unjust for the person of Brogi." A minority of the students took sides with Brogi. Fichte himself appealed to the Department of Instruction. The final decision of the authorities on April 24, 1811, supported the rector and expressed "recognition" of a man "who deserved honor for his zeal for justice." The University of Berlin had, however, in the judgment of its historian, "repudiated" Fichte, "this Messiah," although it had just elected him as its first rector.

Fichte's character appeared in the best light in the course of these quarrels. His incorruptibility, sense of fair play, and unwillingness to compromise in matters of principle emerge splendidly. He was not afraid of incurring unpopularity in order to promote justice. In 1793, in the midst of his anti-Semitic outburst, he had attempted to assure his readers that he had defended Jews "in peril to himself and to his own disadvantage." Eighteen years later, as rector of the University of Berlin, he indeed took the side of a Jewish student at personal risk.

Fichte lived long enough to see the Prussian emancipation of the Jews in 1812. He had learned to revise his conception of Judaism as much as of the Jews themselves. The German Jacobin who had turned German patriot but retained some of his earlier radicalism still anticipated toward the end of his days a "true realm of right, as it never has yet appeared in the world, . . . founded upon the equality of every human being."[34]

Arndt and the Burschenschaften

Ernst Moritz Arndt, German patriot and foe of Napoleon, devoted himself with great fervor to the cause of liberating the German people and the birth of a new Germany. His appeal to the Germans to take up arms against the French led to his proscription by the enemy. Preacher, poet, political pamphleteer, and university professor, Arndt was no scholar by nature but an active and passionate man. His energies were directed to the struggle against domination from abroad, while at home his targets were primarily reactionary and particularist tendencies. Himself the son of a freedman, he never showed any love for the Junkers. But in his political and national philosophy different strains of thought were hopelessly entangled in utter inconsistency.

Like the Baron vom Stein, with whom he was closely linked, Arndt was opposed to the Jews.[35] As a patriot and teacher who had the ear of German youth, he encouraged a spirit of hostility toward the Jews, attempting to perpetuate traditional anti-Semitism and to justify the age-old separation between Germans and Jews. In 1815, when the long-desired defeat of French arms had finally been achieved, Arndt published the tract *Über den deutschen Studentenstaat* [On the German Students' State]. From that state he excluded Jewish students, even though many such students had just sacrificed their lives for Germany's liberation. In this tract Arndt extolled the Middle Ages, during which the Jews had been banished from German life and in which "everything formed itself into exclusive societies and associations." He also placed "very great value" upon the racial "purity" of the German people, which, he thought, must be protected, since it was "youthful" and in political matters "naive and partly childish." While the Germans were in this respect inferior to Englishmen and Frenchmen, they surpassed in other ways all other peoples (the Frenchman for instance was looked upon by Arndt, with little sophistication and with apparent contempt, as a "being halfway between a Chinese and a Jew").

Did Arndt perhaps fear the allegedly evil influences of Jewish students upon their German fellow students, as vom Stein feared or claimed to fear the "sinister" influence of Jews upon German peasants and civil servants? Hardly. For none has revealed more mercilessly the vices of German students than Arndt himself. He thundered angrily against the "student philistines" and against the adherents of the duel, this "old hereditary evil at German universities," and denounced drunkenness, this "truly disgusting side of university life." "Here is the source," he wrote, "where the body and spirit of a great number of people is corrupted, the moral feeling is blunted, and the vulgar spirit is inhaled for one's entire life." Nevertheless, "the University as an idea" was claimed as a "creation of Germanic Christians." "Freedom and equality existed" nowhere in the world as in Germany[36]—but obviously they were not to be extended to the German Jews.

When Arndt wrote the tract *Über den deutschen Studentenstaat,* exclusion of the Jews from the *Burschenschaften* was not yet common practice at the German universities. The constitution of the first student union at Jena in 1815, which had been drawn up under the influence of principles enunciated by Jahn, the "father of gymnastics," did not mention Jews at all.[37] As one of the historians of the German fraternities remarked, "No Jewish problem existed" for the first *Burschenschaften*.[38] Jews actually played a notable role in establishing several student chapters, such as those in Berlin and Freiburg im Breisgau. The students in Giessen, however, took Arndt's book on the student state as their model and guide. The "black ones of Giessen" formed a religious-romantic student organization whose members at their gatherings partook of the Lord's Supper; Jews were not admitted to this chapter.

In Königsberg and Heidelberg the exclusion of the Jews was finally written into the bylaws as a basic rule for the student groups. Yet this victory for exclusion and anti-Judaism was gained only after bitter struggles. Many students in Königsberg pointed to the patriotic performance of the Jews in the recent war. Friedrich Wilhelm Carové in Heidelberg raised the question whether it was not "the most beautiful part of the German national character to honor the right also of foreigners."[39] For the moment, however, all endeavors to keep the doors of the *Burschenshaften* open to Jews were doomed. At a secret meeting in Dresden in 1820 the German students rejected the admission of any Jews as a matter of principle. Arndt's thought undoubtedly played a key role in their exclusion from the German *Burschenschaften*. Jews were soon barred also from Jahn's gymnastic associations.

Immediately after the War of Liberation the German students set themselves national goals. The loose German Confederation of thirty-nine states created by the Vienna Congress fell short of satisfying their national demands. Yet soon many students lost sight of the original aim, the national unitary state. The purpose and goal of the original *Burschenschaften,* a historian of the German student activities wrote, "may thus be summed up: to overcome within academic life and among all Christian-German students particularist phenomena of every kind and to place the members into the service of the national idea. But the *Landsmannschaften* [associations of students by German states] maintained themselves. Purpose and goal shifted. Christian-German meant finally only a rejection of Jewish and alien elements."[40]

The contemporary historian Heinrich Leo, though no friend of the Jews, confirmed this judgment in his autobiography *Meine Jugendzeit* [My Youth]. German Christianity, he wrote, had been conceived by the German students not in a positive but in a negative way; it had been thought of as being exclusively "in contrast" with Judaism.[41] Similarly, the Christian-German Table Company in Berlin, according to Clemens Brentano, had been created only to exclude Jews![42] Thus the conception of German Christianity only as a negation of Judaism reached from the prewar period to the postwar era, to the anti-Jewish German student organizations after 1815.

ABOUT CONTEMPORARY JEWS

Arndt's hostile remarks about the Jews, which continued through-out his entire life, were especially frequent during the years of the War of Liberation and in the period of postwar reaction. At the time of the Congress of Vienna Arndt published *Ein Blick aus der Zeit auf die Zeit* [A Glance on the Contemporary Era], in which his anti-Semitism sharply emerged. He wrote: "One should simply prohibit and hinder the importation into Germany of Jews from abroad. . . . The Jews as Jews do not fit into this world and into this state, and therefore I do not want their number to be unduly increased in Germany. I also do not wish this because they are an alien people and because I desire to keep the Germanic race as pure as possible," undefiled by "alien elements."[43]

Though the rejection of the Jews was here coupled with the idea of the alleged racial purity of the German people, hostility toward the Jews for racial reasons was reflected only sporadically in Arndt's writings. On the whole, it was also a rather rare phenomenon in nineteenth-century anti-Semitic literature in Germany, at least up to 1870. Even in the foregoing remarks Arndt was no racist toward Jews already resident in Germany. As K. Hildebrandt, a National Socialist admirer of Arndt, remarked, Arndt believed that the German people could "absorb the then relatively small number" of German Jews.[44] Arndt voiced a racially tainted anti-Semitism in connection not with German Jews but with Jews from abroad; logically, of course, such a position was anything but consistent.

However, it was quite obvious that Arndt did not love any Jews. Occasionally his hatred poured forth like a stream of lava: "The admission of alien Jews who covet our country is an evil and a plague for our people. A Jew unaccustomed for many centuries to faith and honesty, which calmer occupations bring about, spurns great pains and hard labor, wandering about in the uncertain hope of sudden booty rather than earning his bread by sweat. Unsteady in mind and will, roaming at large, waylaying, sly, cheating, and slavish, he suffers every disgrace and misery rather than perform the incessant labor that breaks the furrows, clears the forests, cuts the stones, or sweats in the workshop; like flies and gnats and other vermin he flutters around, always waylays, snatches at the easy and fleeting profit and, once having seized it, holds on to it with merciless claws."[45]

Arndt painted the Jews as corrupt and the Germans as the poor innocent victims of their practices. True, he believed that Christians "too adopt much of Jewish manner" and that "the honest, quiet, and loyal German city resident and peasant becomes a fraudulent and sly fellow.'' The Germans were thus not free of faults. But if they strayed from the right path, it was only due to their living together with the Jews and the Jews' contagious wickedness. The Jews too, Arndt implied, had merely been estranged from ''faithfulness and honesty.'' In spite of virulent and vicious criticism, Arndt neither held the Jews incapable of ''improvement'' nor thought that the Germans had no need of it.

Arndt wishes that an ''irreversible law'' be enacted, which would forbid immigration of alien Jews under any pretext and without exception, though they might prove that they would bring with them ''millions of treasures.'' He wished to keep even the wealthiest among foreign Jews away from Germany. This policy differed radically from that of Frederick the Great, who had been anxious to draw at least wealthy Jews into his state.

Arndt was ''not unconcerned'' whether, because of his remarks on the Jews, he was looked upon as ''a human being or a cannibal,'' and he also could not forget that he had been ''reproached for being a horrible and wild barbarian'' because of a few utterances on the Jews in his writings ''here and there.'' ''I do not belong to those,'' he assured his readers, ''who hate the Jews as Jews by all means or hold them to be a people wicked by nature. I know well what they have meant in world history and what great martyrs they have become.'' He pointed in this connection to passages from his book *Ansichten and Aussichten der deutschen Geschichte* [Views and Prospects of German History], which, he held, ought to make the Jews ''content'' with him. Christianity had sprung from Judaism, and Jews were the ''first messengers and apostles'' of Christianity.

Yet Arndt very much regretted the emancipation decrees, which shortly before had become the law of the land in many German states. The Jews thus affected were German Jews, not aliens. ''Indeed,'' he wrote, ''those did wrong who, without further consideration of such great differences and of such important consequences for the common welfare, granted to the Jews civil rights equal to those of the Christians.'' One could ''be sorry for the Jews, and ought to be sorry for them, but one cannot love them''; for love, he maintained, was only ''born from the sameness of nature and from sociability, which this people lacks.'' Neither could one bestow honors upon them. The Jew who stood ''outside Christianity'' was incapable of enjoying full citizenship in a Christian state, because he could not fulfill all civil duties.

Still, one should not treat the Jews with medieval ''rudeness and cruelty,'' but ought to consider those born in Germany ''German *Landsleute* [fellow countrymen] and defend and protect them as such.'' While one might have wished that this ''alien part'' had "never touched our wonderful and pure people," God had let them "be born among us and we are not allowed to drive them into the sea or into the desert." Every mixture of the German people with other peoples, with Poles, Italians, and Frenchmen, was to be regretted, and especially with Jews, because they were a "corrupt and degenerate people."

Originally they had been a noble nation. Considering all they had suffered, "it would have been a miracle" if they had remained noble. A few laws could not "suddenly" change the Jews and reeducate them entirely. It might take at least three generations to make the Jews as industrious and honest as the Germans. The Christian ruler, in the meantime, should not tolerate that Jews through "malicious and cruel treatment" be still further "trampled upon," "dishonored and dehumanized." Arndt definitely recommended conversion to Christianity. Baptism would bring about the Jews' amalgamation with the "stock of Christian peoples." "When the Jews accept Christianity, all Jewish peculiarity of character and form soon vanishes, as experience teaches, and one hardly recognizes any more the race of Abraham in the second generation."[46]

In 1815 Arndt strongly rejected, as we observed, foreign Jews, mostly from Poland and Russia. In a later work, however, his autobiography *Erinnerungen aus meinem äusseren Leben* [Reminiscences from My Eternal Life] (1840), he painted quite a different picture of the Polish Jews, one which breathes friendliness and impartiality. Some irony still rings in his voice, but the natural life of Polish Jews had apparently won the affection of this foe of the Jews. Witnessing a "splended Jewish wedding," he posed the question why these Polish Jews in manners and appearance surpassed to such an extent the German Jews as he knew them. Their unspoiled native life, their living closely together, and the agricultural work and the breeding of cattle in which they were engaged had produced, he held, their more vigorous and at the same time "more graceful" figures, "nobler" Jewish forms, and a "greater serenity and calm in their customs. . . ."[47] Arndt, himself not always placid but rather inclined to passionate outbursts, was apparently capable of expressing divergent opinions on the same subject, depending on mood and time.

Arndt was bitterly disappointed over the results of the Congress of Vienna. The widespread expectations of German national unity and liberty remained unfulfilled. He vented his anger in a letter dated July 8, 1815, in which he also sharply attacked the Jews: "Everything goes well, if only the scribbling pens will not destroy the labor of the swords. The Lord is visibly with us, but the Jews are again alive to commit fraud and to engage in political double-dealings."[48] The outburst defied all logic. In the days of the Vienna Congress the city-states and some German rulers were actually set to deprive the Jews of the freedom, which had been granted to them on the very eve of the War of Liberation. Far from being "cheaters," the Jews belonged among the "cheated ones."

In his personal life and relations Arndt did not display anti-Jewish prejudices. The Arndts were close friends of the beautiful Henriette Herz, the widow of Markus Herz, himself a famous Jewish physician in Berlin and noted student of Kant. "Frau Herz has written to me," Arndt remarked in a letter of June 3, 1819. "She wants to come to us from Italy toward the end of this month and stay with us for a few weeks. This would be something very welcome and desirable for my wife."[49]

Arndt appreciated personal virtues and merits in all individuals, whatever their national or religious origin.[50] On the eve of the revolutionary year 1848 he referred to the "excellent men" and "friends drawn from the Jewish people" whom he greatly esteemed. He remarked in this context that a cosmopolitanism had recently emerged which denied the existence of special national characters. A sort of cosmopolitan Judaism appeared to many perplexed and naive people to provide the ideal of the coming ages. Jews and converted Jews, particularly in Germany, were said to propagate these teachings. "I, however," he added, "while accepting perhaps a small portion of this accusation, do not think at all of making the Israelites responsible for it, for I know many excellent men of this race and love them as friends, who, much more than I myself, keep distant from every extreme and walk within much more narrow and limited confines of the Old Christian State and of its laws."[51]

Yet Arndt did not always speak so moderately and discreetly; he tended to veer from one extreme to the other. Only too often he made the Jews collectively liable for the deeds and attitudes of a few among them, who appeared to him as extremists. It was of course also unfair to label those Germans who pursued cosmopolitan tendencies "all-world Jews" (*Allerweltsjuden*),[52] a phrase which revealed disapproval of the Jews themselves.

OLD TESTAMENT AND ANCIENT JEWRY

The former student of theology and preacher remained throughout life an admirer of the Old Testament. "I lived with the patriarchs of ancient times," Arndt recounts of his childhood, "tending the herds of my cows, around the ponds, in the bushes."[53] In the judgment of the historian Friedrich Meinecke, for Arndt "the Bible was the spiritual food of the child, of the grown man and of the old man."[54]

Arndt's national feeling is saturated with Christian religiosity. Piety founded on the Bible was characteristic of the national awakening of the era. The Germans appeared to Arndt as the favorite people of God. Occasionally he spoke of the "German God."[55] "But he moved thus," a student of Arndt held, "within the circle of thought drawn by the Old Testament of a special divine providence which favored the German people."[56] The Old Testament conception of divine selection reappeared thus in Arndt, though with a significant modification. In an age of political and military setbacks and disappointments for the Germans, many of their thinkers and poets, including Arndt, created the idealized picture of an intellectually and morally superior Germandom in the hope that it would spur on the Germans in their struggle for liberty and independence. A later generation preferred to take for reality what was supposed to be a source of inspiration and an ideal.

Numerous Germans, including Arndt, have drawn a sharp distinction between ancient Judaism and modern Jewry. Respect was paid to the venerable Old Testament religion, but criticism was expressed concerning contemporary Jews. Arndt greatly valued ancient Judaism and sang its praises. His admiration for the old Jewish writings and the ancient Hebrews found distinct expression in his work *Versuche in vergleichender Völkergeschichte* [Attempts in Comparative History of the Nations] (1844).

"The children of Israel," Arndt wrote, had once been "the object of hatred by the human race and are still the object of derision. They have been looked upon in some countries as trash and as an abomination. And yet what benefactors of us all are they, like a great, bloody, historic sacrifice that God in his inscrutable wisdom has preserved as such and offered for the sake of the welfare of humanity."

While the great individualists among Chinese, Indians, and Persians are pictured only as mythical personalities, individuals appear in the Old Testament for the first time as "true human beings," with human urges and human shortcomings. "Here we have first in history the personality established in its holy rights versus heaven and God, a full human picture, full and genuine urges to good and bad; here displays itself for the first time the majesty of the moral world. The ancient Jews, the children of Israel, are thus extolled here and must be extolled and praised as happy. . . . These books of the Old Testament, what a kind of world book are they! One might say an eternal book for all ages and generations." He called—a high compliment in his eyes—old Judaism the "Protestantism of the old world."[57]

Arndt's high esteem for ancient Judaism and his recognition of its importance in world history emerge also in his letters to Christian Josias von Bunsen, Prussian ambassador to Great Britain. Arndt praised Bunsen's "beautiful book" *Zeichen der Zeit* [Signs of the Times], in which he had written with warmth about the Jews and their religion and had expressed his wish that one had more recourse in Germany "to the oldest, the Jewish sources of Christianity." It is not easy," Arndt commented, "to stress today orientalism versus occidentalism. . . . The bright and the translucid qualities of the otherwise so bitter and knotty Jewish trunk are depicted by you with great clarity."[58]

UNCEASING CRITICISM

Himself proscribed by the reaction of the postwar era, Arndt later turned against liberals and the Young German authors, whose works were condemned by the Frankfurt diet of the German Confederation. Among these writers was no Jew, though Heinrich Heine and Ludwig Börne were considered by many to be closely linked with them. In 1841 Arndt discerned in the contemporary theory of humanity and in the "hate against folkdom and Christianity" "very much of the Hebrew heritage." "Jews and associates of Jews, converted Jews and unconverted ones, sitting at the most extreme, most radical left, labor untiringly to destroy and dissolve" everything which appeared sacred to the German, "every patriotism and fear of God."[59]

At the same time that Arndt raised this accusation against the Jews, Young German Christian authors and other writers of liberal-progressive inclinations attacked most sharply the Austrian chancellor Metternich and Jewish moneyed power, which through its loans supported his archconservative regime. While Arndt and many like-minded contemporaries tended to make all Jews liable for the real and asserted radicalism that some of them displayed, many liberal and radical elements of the *Vormärz* blamed all Jews for what they judged to be the sins of a few wealthy Jews, who subscribed to political conservatism. The political opposition, whatever its colors, was burdened with the odium of Judaism, of close connection, if not of identification, with it. It was a favorite technique to accuse the political foe of being Jewish or having "Jewish" ideological or political ties. It seemed a sure means of discrediting him and of destroying his political appeal. People in all political camps—conservatives, liberals, and radicals—indulged in this game with great persistency, few scruples, and considerable profit.

In 1848 Arndt was elected to the National Assembly of Frankfurt. Seventy-eight years old, he was out of touch with the new generation. From his seat at the right center he subjected his epoch to sharp criticism: "A miserable kind of Christianity, half sentimental, half denying, breathes through our entire life and, naturally, permeates a great number of those who sit here in the council of the people: so-called preachers of humanity, whose teachings consist of two-thirds of cleansed Judaism and, in the remaining third, of one-third attempted paganism and of two-thirds diluted Christianity."[60] The abolition of the nobility, about which the assembly of Frankfurt deliberated, appeared to the old enemy of the Junkers to serve only the special interests of the Jews. Here too one discerns the widely practiced inclination of pointing to the Jews as a scapegoat. Arndt declared them responsible for political movements he abhorred and for conditions he found repellent.

After the War of Liberation Arndt, the German patriot, the author of the pamphlet "Der Rhein, Teutschlands Strom, nicht Teutschlands Grenze" [The Rhine, Germany's Stream, Not Germany's Border], had refused to accept the peace treaty which left Alsace and Lorraine with France. He did not make Metternich, the German statesmen, the rulers of Great Britain, Russia, and France at the Congress of Vienna responsible for this territorial settlement, but blamed among others—"Jewish journalists." In the revolution of 1848 the ideas of the parliament of Frankfurt appeared to Arndt too radical, too democratic and Jacobin-like, alarming him, who had once been suspected of Jacobinism. He reacted by largely identifying democracy with Judaism, aiming to discredit the former. In the period of reaction after 1848 the old man discovered once more that his heart still beat for freedom, as he thundered against the "oriental" autocracy of the Prussian King Frederick William IV. This was an apparent reference to the reactionary Prussian camarilla of the brothers Gerlach, who then guided Prussia and whose political theories of state and society were founded upon the teachings of the conservative jurist and political scientist Friedrich Julius Stahl, a converted Jew. In 1855 Arndt wrote to his friend Christian Josias von Bunsen, who had sent him his book *Zeichen der Zeit* [Signs of the Times]: "If only our master [Frederick William IV] would read it reverently! If he could only see the *Zeichen der Zeit* and could hear true prophets! But he has his Old Testament prophet Stahl*-Samuel, who paints the German King, as our age requires him, in Jewish [*orientalisch*] fashion and thus interprets him."[61]

During the course of his long political career Arndt attacked op-

*Friedrich Julius Stahl, a Jewish convert to Lutheranism, noted jurist, theoretician, and leader of the Prussian Conservatives in the 1850s.

ponents of the most diverse political orientations and *Weltanschauungen:* at times the Young German liberals and radical democrats, at other times Metternich, reaction, and autocracy. Almost every time he no doubt deliberately hit the Jews as well. Both the absurdity of anti-Semitism and its political abuse emerge in Arndt in no unequivocal manner.

Arndt considered the German Jews an evil to which the Germans would have to accommodate themselves until that distant time when the problem was solved. He never suggested that the Jews should be expelled or physically harmed, but he was unwilling to grant them equal rights. He recommended that they be converted to Christianity, which would facilitate their assimilation. Baptism and amalgamation rather than continued separation were his ultimate goals for them. But these proposals arose not out of love, for he rather disliked Jews as a collective, at least contemporary Jews.

Jahn

Very close to Arndt stood Friedrich Ludwig Jahn, the "father of gymnastics," also a great hater of Napoleon and of the French. He too was to gain great influence upon German students. Like Arndt, he had studied theology in his youth and had become a teacher and political writer; and, again like Arndt, he wished to prepare German youth spiritually and physically for the impending struggle against Napoleon. Imbued with patriotic spirit, he wrote the book *Deutsches Volkstum* [German Folkdom] (1811) to teach German youth about the customs and manners of their ancestors, and he gathered as many youths as he could on the *Hasenheide* at Berlin for play and sport. Like Arndt, he suffered in the reactionary postwar era, when he was suspected by the government because of his national and seemingly radical social views. In recognition of his services to the German people he was, like Arndt, elected to the National Assembly at Frankfurt am Main in 1848.

At times Jahn sharply attacked the Jews; on other occasions he spoke about them with greater restraint and a modicum of impartiality.[62] Compared to Arndt, Jahn took a more liberal attitude toward the admission of Jews to the German student associations.[63] Jahn's outbursts were never directed against the Jews alone. It was the indigenous nobility which aroused his special fury. In the fierceness of his opposition to the Junker class Jahn was hardly surpassed by Arndt or anyone else. The ecclesiastical dignitaries too aroused his ire. He despised bureaucrats, and, a sort of German Jacobin, he inveighed at times even against the standing army. But the Jews were never missing from among those he assailed.[64] Throughout his life he was involved in continuous skirmishes with them.

Jahn and Arndt constituted a nationalist and Christian as well as a kind of confused populist reaction against the German Jews. Their criticism of the Jews punctured the myth that anti-Semitism burst forth from, and found adherents only among, the extreme German Right. In the violence of their language, the duration of their hostility, and the apparent approximation of their anti-Semitism to racism, both men, but especially Arndt, must be considered forerunners of National Socialism. The teachings in general, and particularly the anti-Semitism, of Arndt and Jahn, Rühs and Fries, and numerous other university professors then and thereafter had a lasting and pernicious impact upon the education and philosophy of Germany's youth and her intelligentsia.

PART III

Hate and Love of Romanticism

Jew-hating begins with the Romantic School.

—Heinrich Heine

For centuries one has taught Christianity. What contrasts does it bring forth where Jews are concerned!

—Johann Heinrich Pestalozzi

CHAPTER 7

Romanticism and Religion

Romanticism and Judaism

Resistance to the prevailing ideas of the Enlightenment and Classicism had developed in the late eighteenth century and increased during the era of the War of Liberation. It was in this period that Romanticism embraced all phases of German culture. Romanticism supplanted the cult of reason of the Enlightenment with the cult of emotion. While individualism and cosmopolitanism continued to flourish in the Romantic period, they were increasingly replaced by the new ideals of German folkdom—a national and collective idea—and the pagan antiquity of Greece and Rome was dethroned in favor of the deeply Christian Middle Ages.

This intellectual revolution, which deeply stirred the German intelligentsia, intensified after the overthrow of Napoleon. The Allied victory prolonged the life of the feudal-ecclesiastic institutions in the victorious monarchies, especially Austria and Prussia. The growing resistance against any radical change of the social and political order found support in the Romantic movement. Its flowering occurred in the period when the conservative powers, having restored legitimacy, suppressed all national and liberal popular stirrings.

The deep influence of the Romantic movement extended to all branches of national life. It also affected decisively the relations of the German intelligentsia with the Jews. The cultivation of folkish and religious ideals in the era of Romanticism brought into sharp focus the national and religious differences between Germandom and Judaism. The cosmopolitanism of the Enlightenment was thrust into the background. Glorification of the Middle Ages revived a gloomy period of hatred and intolerance and aroused dangerous passions, for the medieval era had displayed not only deep-rooted piety but also a fierce religious fanaticism. It had been an era of oppression and enslavement of the Jews and of violent outbursts against them.

Heinrich Heine once remarked that the hate of Jews began with the Romantic School.[1] Though German hostility to the Jews can be traced farther back, it remains true that anti-Semitism reached great heights in the Romantic age, in a reaction to the recent emancipation of the Jews, incomplete as that was. In the time of the Enlightenment, when cool, critical reason and a hopeful cosmopolitanism had prevailed, opposition to the Jews had somewhat receded. Now, however, new fashions seemed to come alive in anti-Semitism, and hatred revealed itself as a source of bursting energy.

Still it would be false to assume that the entire German intelligentsia which was swayed by Romanticism hated Judaism. The recession of critical reason in the age of Romanticism, and to a lesser extent the recession of individualism and of universal cosmopolitanism, affected German-Jewish relations adversely. Yet Romanticism did not exhaust itself in mere negations. Understanding of the past flourished. While Romanticism contributed a good deal to the uncritical glorification of the past, it also helped lay the foundations for a more impartial and scholarly evaluation of the culture and history of entire peoples.

It was no accident that Hamann and Herder, the forerunners of German Romanticism, had looked upon the Jews in a more friendly manner than many of their enlightened contemporaries. More than once they defended them against such men as Voltaire, who sneered at Christianity and derided the Bible and also Judaism. It is not surprising that Friedrich Schlegel, a leader of German Romanticism, and Friedrich Wilhelm Schelling, its philosopher, enthusiastically praised the poetry of ancient Judaism and that Leopold von Ranke, the great teacher of German historians, wrote with warmth and sympathy about the Jews. Romanticism helped to awaken understanding of and appreciation for the ancient Hebrews and for Jewish history in general and furthered interest in the people from whose religion Christianity had sprung.

But historicism also had its reverse side. The search for the oldest cultural monuments of the German people contributed indirectly to the reawakening of Jew-hating. The rediscovery of old German laws, of German fairy tales and legends, of German songs and customs which dated back to the Middle Ages, reminded the Germans of the suppression of medieval Jewry and made rejection and dislike of Judaism fashionable once again. The sons of the Romantic era frequently saw the Middle Ages through rose-colored glasses and tended to extol and idealize them. It was hardly accidental that many Germans who gained fame for their rediscovery of old German cultural values and monuments—Jahn and Arndt, Arnim and Clemens Brentano, the brothers Jakob and Wilhelm Grimm—also happened to sharply oppose the Jews.

The German-Jewish novelist Berthold Auerbach was both enraged and distressed about the anti-Jewish tendency of the Grimm brothers' fairy tale "Der Jude im Dorn" [The Jew in the Thorn].[2] What is pilloried therein is the Jews' greed for money. The Jew who resorts to theft is finally hanged for his misdeed. The Christians' attitude toward him is always condoned, even their pure "wantonness." It is true that the brothers Grimm, who took their fairy tales from the popular tradition, did not invent this particular one; but they included it in a compilation that was primarily designed for children, even though such a tale was bound to arouse hatred of the Jews.

As in the fairy tale, so also in the folk song. Achim von Arnim and Clemens Brentano, sharp foes of the Jews, included some songs in their popular collection *Des Knaben Wunderhorn* [The Boy's Wonderhorn] which also cut across Jewish life and history. "Das neue Jerusalem" [The New Jerusalem], "David," and especially "Die Judentochter" [The Jewish Daughter] breathe a friendly spirit; the last-named tells the tragic love story of a Christian clerk and a beautiful Jewess, who prefers death in the sea to baptism. Two other songs, however, strike an unmistakably hostile note, "The Crucifixion of Christ" and "Jews in Passau";[3] the latter depicts the alleged desecration of the host, giving expression to an accusation which the medieval world had hurled against the Jews and which had caused them untold suffering. The cross that Romanticism helped to erect in German lands cast a long shadow upon German-Jewish relations.

Supported by Romanticism, Christianity, which had been thrust back by the Enlightenment and Classicism, once again penetrated the spiritual and also the social and political life of the German nation. This new flowering of the Christian religion awakened false religious zeal, while deepening the mutual alienation of Christian and Jew. By reviving numerous old memories, it tended to widen the gulf between contemporary Judaism and the Christian world. This "new faith," as the Prussian statesman and writer Wilhelm von Humboldt called it, embraced hatred of the Jews; against it the "old faith"—a humane Christianity which in theory and practice proved to be a religion of brotherly love—had little chance.[4] The latter, under the influence of the prevailing ideas of the eighteenth century, agreed very well with a more friendly and humane treatment of the Jews; Christianity and Jew-hating were by no means inseparable. But contemporaries who shared Humboldt's "old faith" were a minority.

German Romanticism, in its early phase, showed cosmopolitan traits and even later did not completely abandon universalism. The cosmopolitan, universal, and Christian traits of Romanticism all found expression in the dramatic piece *Die Mutter der Makkabäer* [The Mother of the Maccabeans] (1820) by Zacharias Werner, who, after a turbulent life, had become a priest. The scene of this drama of martyrdom is borrowed from Jewish history. Through Salome's spirit Zacharias Werner announces that God will prepare a pure sacrifice, which, unifying all peoples, will cleanse the world from sins.[5]

That newly awakening Christianity had such varied effects, that it could arouse dislike of non-Christian religions, of Judaism in particular, among many people, while making others profess brotherly love, was recognized by no one more clearly than by the great educator Johann Heinrich Pestalozzi. He expressed puzzlement that the teachings of Christianity had produced such contrasts in attitudes toward Jews.[6]

Yet the attitude of anti-Jewish Romanticists was not entirely negative. This held true for resolute and persistent opponents of the Jews such as Ludwig Tieck and Clemens Brentano; even these paid their respects to ancient Judaism. While they criticized later Judaism, denounced what they considered an obtruding Jewry, which allegedly threatened and dispossessed Christians in the economic and social fields, many Romanticists distinguished between the venerable lofty Judaism from which Christianity had sprung and contemporary Judaism, which aggressively demanded equality. In making this distinction, it was not brotherly love but rather Christian self-interest that pierced the fog of prejudice. Ancient Judaism—the source, after all, of ancient Christianity—had to appear respectable; for Christianity's sake, reverence for ancient Judaism was required.

The Prussian writer and political scientist Adam Müller, prominent among anti-Semites in his day, violently attacked contemporary Judaism and denied equality to its adherents. Yet he revered ancient Judaism. The ancient Jewish state appeared to him to have been free from internal disorders and violent revolutions and thus won the favor of this thoroughly conservative man. Therefore he did not object to having a partly "Jewish" base for his ideal state.[7] Like Müller, Ludwig Tieck considered emancipation for contemporary Jews "incomprehensible," yet recalled at other times the "indeed marvelous disposition of Providence"[8] which had let monotheism and Christianity develop within the framework of ancient Judaism. Judaism similarly bore a dual character in the writings of Clemens Brentano, who conceded ancient Judaism a high rank in world history and religious thought but derided recent Judaism and vented hate against contemporary Jewry.

Conversion and Equality

Although many Romanticists felt sympathy for and gratitude toward the descendants of the people among whom Christianity was born, only a few endeavored to focus attention on the close historical relations between Judaism and Christianity. Indeed, some would have liked to forget this relationship once and for all. Friedrich Schleiermacher, a Protestant theologian and personally a friend of the Jews, openly confessed that he "hated in religion this kind of historical relation."[9] This attitude also appears distinctly in a pithy remark in his "Aphorisms on Church History": "It is my credo that Christianity begins with Christ; no continuation of Judaism."[10]

Since Romanticism was deeply Christian, it was no wonder that conversion as a possible solution of the Jewish problem was once again seriously contemplated by numerous contemporaries. While Schleiermacher determinedly rejected the suggestion of a mass baptism of the Jews, he encouraged individual men and women—among them his friend Henriette Herz—to be baptized. Wilhelm von Humboldt looked upon the conversion of Jews to Christianity as an inescapable result of their expected assimilation to Germandom, but thrust it far into the future. It would follow emancipation and assimilation, not precede them. The adoption of Christianity by the Jews, Humboldt wrote in 1808, "which now, when they leave their oppressed brethren and devolve upon them the burden so far borne jointly with them," was excusable only under extraordinary circumstances, would later, after the attainment of full equality and complete assimilation, be "desirable, gratifying, and beneficial."[11]

Not only friends but also enemies of the Jews pointed to the desirability of their conversion. The latter rejected the Jews as a people, but as Christians they could not deny individual Jews admission to Christianity. Christianization would lead to Germanization and would remove religious and cultural obstacles which blocked a rapprochement between Jews and Germans.[12] But the Romantics hardly thought of conversion to Christianity as a means for solving the Jewish question in its entirety. Most Germans who toyed with the idea of baptism of the Jews had in mind primarily the conversion of single individuals. They knew only too well that baptism, which they asked in return for emancipation and full integration, would appear too high a price for most Jews to pay.

Some of the Romantics, however, renewed the age-old proffer of baptism just because of this conviction, in order to provide themselves with a perfect excuse for delaying emancipation. Achim von Arnim's Ahasver announced to the Jews that, until they were "all converted,"[13] he would not find any rest and that they themselves would be martyred and tormented. Another bitter foe of the Jews, Friedrich Rühs, likewise promoted the conversion of the Jews.[14]

Schleiermacher refused to sanction any religious change for "impure" motives. He recommended that equality be granted; this would preclude conversion induced by self-interest rather than religious conviction. Rühs, to the contrary, wished to maintain the existing inequality to lure the Jews to Christianity. Equality was to be their reward for conversion. Opponents of the Jews among the Romantics were generally torn between contrary impulses. Their religious leanings commanded them to welcome individual Jews into the pale of Christianity, while their anti-Jewish feelings prompted them to bar the Jews from the German-Christian folkish community.

The early German Romanticism did not exhibit the nationalistic limitations and the religious intolerance which became characteristic of the later movement. The Christianity of the early Romanticism still had a universal character. Its religion was directed inward rather than being founded upon hatred of those beyond the fence. The older Romanticists were still in close contact with Jews, and some among them pleaded for their emancipation, conditional as it may have been. This was true of Friedrich Schlegel, the philosopher Schelling, Friedrich Schleiermacher, and others. Among the Younger Romantics, however, Bettina Brentano, with her friendly attitude toward Jews, was rather an exception.

In contrast to these men and women there was an impressive number of Romantic poets and novelists, and of scholars who were strongly influenced by the Romantic movement, who denied equality to the Jews. The conservative jurist Adam Müller disapproved of Jewish emancipation.[15] So did the poet and novelist Ludwig Tieck, who doubted that the Jews could ever become Germans. Karl von Savigny, the founder of the German Historical School of Jurisprudence, rejected with the help of his "historical method" the claim of the Jews of Frankfurt am Main to equality. He recalled that in the

Middle Ages the German Jews had been *Kammerknechte** (Chamber Slaves) of the Empire.[16] What anachronism to grant them, in the era when renewed interest was displayed in medieval times, equality with the Christian population! A hostile mood was also displayed by B. G. Niebuhr, famous for his *Römische Geschichte* [History of Rome]. He voiced the fear that speculation at the stock exchange threatened to annihilate "all better feelings in the capital" and "to dissolve all classes into an ignominious Judaism."[17]

The opposition of the Romantic movement to the Jews differs in character, depth, and scope from twentieth-century National Socialist racial anti-Semitism. Still, there can be little doubt that many Romantics thoroughly disliked Jews and Judaism. This antipathy was reflected in their creative work; in their plays, poems, and novels the Jewish character was distorted, sneered at, and ridiculed. A wild, fanatic hatred, rising from vanished ages, raged in the works of Clemens Brentano and Achim von Arnim. In these writings as well as in many other Romantic poems and novels Jews appear as the scum of humanity.

The Prussian diplomat and writer Karl Varnhagen von Ense, who was closely linked with many of the leading figures of Romanticism, came out in sharp criticism of this anti-Semitism. Married to Rahel Levin, Varnhagen was an ardent admirer of the Jewish people who "gave to humanity Jesus, then Spinoza, and who daily yield the most extraordinary resources without growing poorer."[18] In a talk with the noted jurist Eduard Gans, he voiced bitter anger against "the stupid, narrow minds, the selfish opponents of the Jews." Varnhagen was inclined to see in a man's attitude to the Jews a yardstick of his human value. "An enemy and hater of Jews may have great and noble qualities, yet he carries a dark blot in his heart or in his mind and his life will not be without moments when he limps."[19]

While many Romantics disliked the Jews, they could not, oddly enough, entirely escape the peculiar charm of Jewish sociability. This was true of Achim von Arnim, Clemens Brentano, Caroline Humboldt, and others. Like Schleiermacher and Friedrich Schlegel, they met Jews socially in Berlin, where they used to attend their salons. The novelist Theodor Fontane spoke in later years of a "Berliner Jewish spirit," which had exerted a great influence upon the educated middle class and had displayed "its finest forms" in those days. This had also been "the proper time" for mixed marriages. People had

*In 1103 Heinrich IV took all Jews under his protection and their relationship to the King was termed as *Kammerknechtschaft*. Jews were placed under the jurisdiction of the monarch, who also had the right to levy taxes upon them.

found matrimony between Jews and Gentiles "quite natural."[20] Many
Jews, particularly in Berlin, were saturated with German culture and
had become increasingly alienated from Judaism in both its religious
and its cultural aspects. Jean Paul remarked about some socially
prominent Jewish women that there was so little of the Old Testament
in them that they all married into the New one.

In other parts of Germany, however—for instance, in Frankfurt
am Main—social prejudices were more deeply rooted. Bettina Brentano regretted the circumstance that so many "made keeping company with people dependent on the exterior rank" that they let themselves be "chained by prejudices" and even "boasted of them."[21]
Anti-Jewish feelings in general and social anti-Semitism in particular
were widespread throughout many parts of Germany.

Schleiermacher's "Über Religion"

One who personally contributed much to breaking down the social
barriers between Christians and Jews was Friedrich Schleiermacher.
The "church father" of modern German Protestant theology, preacher
and professor in Berlin, Schleiermacher brought about a genuine revival of Protestantism at the beginning of the nineteenth century. While
in Berlin, he participated actively in the intellectual and social life of
the Prussian capital. Its centers were the Jewish salons, where men of
culture and influence, statesmen and diplomats, poets and philosophers, artists and theologians, mingled with educated Jews. Many a
flirtation developed here between the German guests and the charming
and intelligent Jewish hostesses; sometimes permanent ties were knit.
"The Christian houses of Berlin," wrote Henriette Herz, glancing
backward, "offered nothing in intellectual sociability which approached or even resembled what those Jewish salons held out."[22] In
the same vein a correspondent from Berlin wrote to Schiller in 1797
that "the educated Jewish circles of Berlin" were the "only ones,
where one talked about literature"[23] and showed deep interest in the
works of Schiller and Goethe.

Schleiermacher too attended the Jewish salons and felt at home
there. The close friendship between him and the beautiful Henriette
Herz became the subject of much gossip in Berlin. A caricature
shown in the capital depicted Henriette Herz as a stately, majestic
woman beside a frail, diminutive preacher. Schleiermacher and Henriette Herz themselves asserted the purely platonic character of their
friendship.·

Schleiermacher maintained numerous other contacts with Jews. In letters to his sister Charlotte he denounced anti-Semitism as "an old bias,"[24] at another time as "one of the miserable prejudices."[25] To defend himself against reproaches aimed at his keeping close company with Henriette Herz, he emphasized that the Jewish families of Berlin were "the only ones" which kept an open house.[26] How strongly he wished to foster close social relations between Jews and Gentiles emerges also in his booklet *Von einem Prediger ausserhalb Berlins* [From a Preacher Outside of Berlin]. There he recommended to the clergymen of the capital "that they as human beings and members of the literary world associate themselves too, without hesitation, with those who do not shun the company of educated and informed Jews and that in their social life they do not take notice of this separation of religions."[27]

As a young preacher he was anxious to guide that part of the German youth and intelligentsia which had become indifferent to religion or even "despised" it back to its pure source. Although he rejected a mass conversion of Jews, as obviously motivated by political, nonreligious interests, he joyfully accepted individual baptism, if it was prompted by true conviction. Persuasion of an honest man or woman who was hesitant appeared to him a religious duty. He thus induced Henriette Herz to embrace Christianity. Henriette turned Christian only after the death of her mother; she wanted to avoid saddening her by leaving Judaism during her lifetime.

Satiated with German culture, alienated from Jewish tradition, many educated Jews abandoned the Jewish religion and adopted Christianity; like Heinrich Heine, they considered it the *"entrée billet"* to German and European civilization. Wilhelm von Humboldt and numerous other contemporaries, both Germans and Jews, became convinced that the ultimate disappearance of the Jewish religious community was unavoidable and might safely be left to the grindstone of time.[28] This was also Schleiermacher's view. Judaism appeared to him like an "indestructible mummy," reaching from immemorial times into the new age. Thus he remarked in his work *Über Religion. Rede an die Gebildeten unter ihren Verächtern* [On Religion: Talks to the Educated among Its Despisers] (1799): "For a long time Judaism has been a dead religion."[29] Few Germans were experts on Jewish religion and Judaism, and most often, due to traditional, old-fashioned theological training, they were biased against it; they also tended to underestimate its inner vigor and power of adaptation.

In any case, conversion hardly represented a realistic solution to the Jewish problem. First, German Jews rejected the idea of a mass baptism. Second, while some converts were moved by pure conviction, others were prompted by cool calculation. In either case the change of religion entailed some tangible advantages. Baptism swept away the legal discriminations which had hampered them in earning their livelihood and had wounded their dignity. But the hoped-for integration with the German-Christian people did not necessarily follow. All too often the new Christian appeared to Christians and Jews only as a converted Jew.

Truly religious-minded men could not look with equanimity at a baptism that was largely politically motivated. They disapproved of its motives and voiced fear as to its results. As long as the emancipation of the Jews was not attained, the motives of all converts to Christianity were bound to be suspect.

RELIGIOUS AND POLITICAL DEBATE

Religious considerations impelled Schleiermacher to come forward against the suggestion of a mass conversion of the Jews. In the year 1799 an anonymous booklet had appeared in Berlin, *"Sendschreiben an Probst Teller"* [Epistle to His Reverence Chief Consistorial Councilor and Provost Teller at Berlin, by Some Housefathers of the Jewish Faith].[30] It was an open secret that David Friedländer, the noted leader of the German Jews, was the author. Friedländer proposed the founding of a Jewish-Christian sect on the basis of a religious compromise by the Jews; the state was to reward their effort by extending civil equality to the members of the new association. Friedländer's suggestion was the expression of sheer impatience and even despair on the part of a wealthy, cultured elite of German Jews, who judged that they were now farther away from the goal of emancipation than ever.

However, the conversion plan was doomed to failure. The liberal Provost Teller politely but determinedly rejected the suggestion of the Jewish "housefathers." He demanded their acknowledgment at least of the doctrines of baptism and of the Holy Supper,[31] dogmas which the housefathers had declared unacceptable. People spoke ironically of the "dry," "waterless" baptism to which alone the Jews around Friedländer seemed prepared to submit.

Friedländer's *Sendschreiben* caused a considerable stir. In the midst of the excitement his discussion of a Jewish mass conversion aroused, there appeared Schleiermacher's likewise anonymous *Briefe bei Gelegenheit der politisch-theologischen Aufgabe* [Letters on the Occasion of the Political-Theological Task and the Epistle to the Jewish Housefathers, From a Preacher outside of Berlin] (1799).[32] Schleiermacher claimed that he did not know the real author of the *Send-*

schreiben. A "sad and desperate belief" revealed itself in this letter, he remarked, namely "that the Jews, in order to attain equality with other citizens, had no choice but to become converts to Christianity." Schleiermacher saw in the *Sendschreiben* the endeavor of some intelligent and educated Jews to use "Christianity as a means . . . of stepping into civil society." Friedländer, he recalled, had once rejected the suggestion of abandoning the Jewish ceremonial laws. And now this "mighty leap into Christianity, disregarding all possibilities lying in between? and with as little grace as happens here, which obviously shows that neither love for the new religion nor hate of the old one is the cause of this clumsy conversion."

"Reason demands that all ought to be citizens, but it does not require that all be Christians and therefore it must be possible . . . to be a citizen and non-Christian." Schleiermacher pointed to other countries in which non-Christians had already obtained citizenship, the United States, France, and the states annexed by France or dependent on her. It was also a "lazy reason of statesmen" which held "the vestiges of old barbarism indestructible." Why does one "import aliens from abroad as long as there exists in the interior a large human mass who are not yet citizens? Behind which dogma does this lazy reason hide if not behind that of an innate corruption of the Jews and behind the assertion that it is therefore dangerous to accept them into the civil community?"

SCHLEIERMACHER'S STANCE

Mass baptism of the Jews, Schleiermacher believed, would hurt the church. "Twenty or thirty years ago," he wrote in 1799, "both religious parties had been so much separated from each other and the Jews had been so devoid of life that the temptation to merge with the Christians and to carry on different activities in civil life could have hardly spread among many, nor could it have been strong and urgent with a few." From time to time there had been "some proselytes," but all of them, with the exception of the "lovebirds," had been "bad individuals of whom the Jewish communities had very much liked to rid themselves, ruined human beings, close to desperation, who had only a momentary advantage in view, and of these, thank Heaven, there are always and everywhere only a few."

"Quite different human beings," Schleiermacher continued, "are thinking now of conversion to Christianity—educated, wealthy people, well versed in all worldly matters." They wish to acquire rights and to become citizens. These enlightened Jews were "imbued with the wisdom of Kant," looked at religion "entirely indifferently," were primarily interested in Christian morality, and had only "their political purpose" in mind, the gaining of civil rights. The baptism of such people would hardly be "a special acquisition" for Christianity. It is always "highly dangerous if only a small portion of religion" exists in an enormously large religious society, as is already the case in the Christian church. The conversion of the Jewish "housefathers" would merely increase the number of such indifferent Christians and would thus bring religious society "closer to ruin."

Schleiermacher resented that he was suspected of being an enemy of the Jews merely because of his insistence on rigorous selection of newcomers to the church: "No, I had not expected to be so badly misunderstood by you. Am I supposed to be an enemy of the Jews? Did I also, perhaps without knowing it, secretly believe in their moral degradation? And all this merely because I do not wish to see them enter the Christian church! Did you forget that I likewise wish also the greater portion of Christians put out of the church? . . . On that point I shall therefore not defend myself any further."

The honesty of the Jews could not be questioned, Schleiermacher asserted. Their assimilation to Germandom had made tangible progress, and it was therefore only just to grant them the equality which so far had been withheld. "It is vain to deny that increasingly the Jews take a relatively equal part with the Christians in the formation of the age, that they visibly abandon alien characteristics in customs and manners, and, what is best, that that honesty tends measurably to grow among them which is the natural consequence of a secure prosperity, when better sociability and a sense of honor can influence the character. The more all this becomes reality, the more there disappears whatever might serve to support the alleged legitimacy of a political difference between them and the Christians, the more does the preservation of this differentiation look like an entirely unjustified partiality."

It was in the well-understood interest of the church to free itself from the suspicion of proselytism. The church, according to Schleiermacher, did not wish to maintain the existing inequality. Not only would the church not resist the equalization of the Jews with the Christian population; to the contrary, it wished to "plead fervently with the state," indeed to "conjure" it, to alter a situation which makes some Jews turn to Christianity out of "impure motives," for the purpose of gaining political equality.

There were, admittedly, others who desired to become Christians for different reasons—for instance, those who had fallen in love with an adherent of the Christian faith and wished to marry. Wrote Schleiermacher: "Perhaps, in most cases, it may not be advisable for a Christian to conclude a marriage with a Jew (or vice versa), but certainly it is nowhere written in the Holy Books that it is un-Christian or forbidden by religion. . . . The church does not know anything of such a prohibition and on its part would have to declare that it did not have any objections, if the state abolished the respective law.''

The "Jewish housefathers'' had declared themselves ready to abandon certain Jewish ceremonies in the supposed interest of the state. They had created thus the impression that the observation of Jewish ceremonies and the fulfillment of civil duties were in parts irreconcilable. Schleiermacher followed in their path and in that of Kant when he asserted "that the unlimited authority of the ceremonial laws constituted a political obstacle'' to granting equality to them. However, the Jews did not need to abandon entirely the ceremonial laws, he held, but should merely declare that they would not shun any civil duty on the ground that it contradicted their ceremonial law. Furthermore they should formally and publicly renounce their belief in the Messiah, a belief which expressed their hope of again becoming a nation. (Similarly the state should not grant full civil rights to French refugees who declared their intention of returning later to the fatherland.) Schleiermacher wished fervently for the assimilation of the Jews to Germandom. Like most of his contemporaries he entertained no doubt that Germans were in the right when they demanded that the Jews cease to be Jews, nationally and culturally speaking and partly even religiously. He did not rise to the idea of national minority rights, the spiritual child of a later age.

In conclusion Schleiermacher demanded that those Jews "who accept both points''—the abandonment of the belief in the Messiah and of parts of their ceremonial law—should establish a special church, a "changed Judaism." "Do not laugh,'' he wrote, anticipating objections to his proposition; "I am fully serious about this sect.'' The educated Jews were already aware of the "sharp difference between them and the others; the separation, in reality, has already existed for a long time and it seems an impropriety that it has not yet constituted itself externally.''

Schleiermacher, the greatest Protestant theologian since Martin Luther, acknowledged the great progress of German Jewry and encouraged the baptism of individual Jews. On religious grounds he opposed mass conversion, an academic project in any case, rather than one of immediate practical significance. While not prejudiced against the Jews, he held a bias against Judaism,[33] the ceremonial of which, in his opinion, ought to be modified before emancipation could be granted.

The Schlegels on Ancient and Contemporary Jews

Like his friend Schleiermacher, Friedrich Schlegel, theoretician and leader of German Romanticism, poet, critic, and literary historian, was a frequent visitor of the Jewish salons in Berlin. He met there his later wife, the daughter of Moses Mendelssohn, Dorothea, who was then married to the Jewish banker Veit. The thirty-two-year-old woman—mother of two sons, both of whom were to achieve fame— was won by the fiery courting of the brilliant twenty-five-year-old man, who, after his fight with Schiller, had emerged as one of the most promising writers in Germany. Friedrich Schlegel assured his sister in later years that he had found his youth again in Dorothea's arms. In 1798 he dedicated to Dorothea his essay "Über Philosophie" [On Philosophy], which was published the following year in the *Athenaeum*. Dorothea appeared as his feminine ideal in his novel *Lucinde*, which, because of its imputed immorality, was to arouse considerable feeling.

Herself a writer, Dorothea followed Friedrich Schlegel, whom she greatly admired, through his various transformations. Spurred on by Romanticism, which glorified Catholicism, she entered with him the fellowship of the Roman Catholic Church. The pair settled in Vienna, where he accepted the position of an imperial *Hofrat* (Privy Councilor) at the Austrian Court-Chancery. The marriage of Schlegel, the German "knight" of Romanticism, with Dorothea symbolized the spiritual and social closeness of the German and Jewish intelligentsia of the era.

Schlegel met many Jews in the salons of Berlin and Vienna and learned to esteem them. He was also a great admirer of Lessing and edited some of his works. He prefaced the drama *Nathan der Weise* with a few verses in which he gave thanks to Lessing for the light he had sent into the world.[34]

In 1821 Schlegel offered lectures on world literature at the University of Vienna, in which he exalted ancient Hebrew literature. Like Hegel, he admired the "loftiness" of the Mosaic document, which, in his view, constituted a "pivot of all history of the human spirit." He praised its "excellence," its superiority over all other Asiatic traditions. The Hebrews' "higher perception and knowledge of God showed itself in the songs of David, the allegories of Solomon, and the prophesies of Isaiah, with a splendor and a majesty which, even if judged only as poetry, arouses admiration" and "repels every reviling attack; a fiery, flaming source of divine enthusiasm, in which the greatest poets, including those of recent times, have found encouragement and inspiration."[35]

In his capacity as Counselor of the Austrian legation at the diet of the German Confederation in Frankfurt am Main, Schlegel had to acquaint himself with the legal dispute between the city and its Jewish community. The Jews of Frankfurt am Main were struggling to retain the equality which had been granted to them under the previous regime of Grand Duke Karl von Dalberg, while the city authorities were determined to wrest the new liberty from them. In their struggle the Jews were supported by the Austrian and Prussian governments, though neither exerted itself very strongly in their behalf.

Schlegel himself, however, pleaded emphatically for the Jews and their emancipation. In a memoir dated January 1816, "Bemerkungen über die Frankfurter Angelegenheiten" [Remarks on the Affairs of Frankfurt],[36] he sternly reproached the Lutheran majority of the city for its narrow policy of suppression of the Catholic *and* Jewish minorities. The magistracy of Frankfurt had "shown definite dislike" of Catholics and Jews in 1812. He criticized the authorities of Frankfurt am Main for their insolent attitude toward Austria and Prussia; they had not even acknowledged receipt of the presentations by these states, which bore the dates of November 8 and 13, 1815, respectively. Schlegel recommended in conclusion a more resolute policy of the Great Powers toward Frankfurt, since yielding was interpreted only as weakness.

Schlegel did not plead for full equality for the Jews of Frankfurt am Main, though he supported most of their demands. He held that it might later be determined to what degree the Jews ought to be admitted to civil positions and offices. Schlegel probably thought in this connection of some of the limitations which remained in existence for the Prussian Jews, even after the Edict of Emancipation of 1812. "But," he continued, "it is in every respect highly improper that the magistracy, arbitrarily and without any previous discussion, has excluded the Jews from the most insignificant of all civil rights: namely participation in the election of those who represent the citizenry and should form their council. . . . If in the future the Jews should not have someone from their midst in any office of the city or in any civil council, who possessed the indisputable right to speak in behalf of his community, the encroachments and complaints in this area will never cease."

The city authorities of Frankfurt had not stopped at denying voting rights to the Jews. The new constitutional project revealed the clear intention of "depriving" the Jews entirely of passive civil rights and of "thrusting them completely back into the old state of affairs": they would be forbidden to engage even in crafts and other civil occupations. This plan must be the more sternly disapproved, "since the civil improvement of the Jews can only be effected thoroughly by guiding and encouraging them much more to turning to trades and civil occupation and not, as is set forth here, by excluding them constitutionally from crafts and by prohibiting their access to them, which is a manifest retrogression into barbarism." He recommended in conclusion to his own government "to vigorously oppose with all necessary measures and stern reprimands the arrogant attitude of the magistracy of Frankfurt." Schlegel was to remain deeply concerned about the status of the Jews of Frankfurt am Main.[37]

Like Friedrich Schlegel, the deeply religious poet Novalis (Friedrich von Hardenberg) highly esteemed the ancient Jews. At the time of the Babylonian exile, he wrote, "the Jews received a genuinely religious tendency, a religious hope which, miraculously, thoroughly changed them and preserved them in a most remarkable fashion until our time."[38] While he valued the Jews of antiquity, he did not forget their descendants, as his verses "On Joseph's Death" (Joseph II) attest:

On Joseph's death I saw the tear of tolerance flow,
And, full of cheerful hope, superstition began to sing
Jubilantly a song of joy around the overturned throne.[39]

In 1801 August Wilhelm Schlegel, Friedrich Schlegel's elder brother and, like him, one of the leaders of German Romanticism, composed the poem "Die Warnung" [The Warning], which takes the Eternal Jew as its subject.[40] Ahasver enters a tavern in which two rough companions drink to excess and boast of crimes committed against Christ's pictures and crosses, as if these outrages were the boldest and most heroic deeds. The Eternal Jew vainly warns them to cease their mischief and mockeries. He too had once treated Christ in an insolent and overbearing manner, and he was still paying heavily for his sin. When the two thugs disregard his warnings and continue their evil deeds, a blood-red cross appears on the forehead of the Jew; it is only then that "the frenzy of desperation falls upon them." But it was too late, "the scoffers did not live long."

In this poem August Wilhelm Schlegel used Ahasver merely as a prophetic warner.[41] The atmosphere of awe and fear found in many poems on Ahasver here also grips the Eternal Jew. The rudeness of the impudent, arrogant fellows is turned against Jesus as well as against Ahasver.

CHAPTER 8

Divided Counsels

Schelling and Tieck

Friedrich Wilhelm Schelling, the philosopher of Romanticism, enjoyed a very high repute among his contemporaries. In his younger years he treated Judaism in a critical if not outright hostile manner, but as a mature man he judged the Jews in a more friendly spirit and endorsed their emancipation.

Schelling's father had turned to the study of Oriental languages, especially the writings of Solomon and the apocryphal books of the Old Testament, and the young Friedrich Wilhelm Schelling followed in his footsteps. He was among the first in Württemberg to teach himself in accordance with the better principles of Hebrew philology and was on his way to becoming an Orientalist.[1] The editor of his letters voiced his opinion that readers would find in them "many a gold nugget" of explanation of the Book of Job and of the prophets Isaiah and Jeremiah.[2] Schelling became so preoccupied with the Jewish writings that "envious people" tried to label him "a mere Hebrew,"[3] though he possessed an excellent knowledge of other classical languages.

In 1797, as a youth of twenty-two, Schelling visited Berlin. His impressions of the Prussian capital and its inhabitants, especially of the Jews, were quite unfavorable. He alleged that "the talent" in Berlin was very "poor" and that the "vermin" of young scholars and writers, "particularly among the Jews,"[4] was unbearable. What irony that later it was a Jewish thinker, Spinoza, who decisively influenced Schelling's philosophy of nature. Like Goethe, Schelling experienced a calming and satisfying influence emanating from Spinoza and enjoyed the light of gaiety that filled Spinoza's life and illuminated his writings.[5] The philosopher and racial anti-Semite Eugen Dühring regretted Schelling's "prepossession"[6] with the Jewish thinker.

Much later, in 1848, the year of the Revolution, Schelling again came face to face with the Jewish question. The young king Maximilian II had just ascended the throne of Bavaria. A progressive monarch who appreciated and patronized the arts and was devoted to the spread of knowledge, he surrounded himself with liberal counselors. He had decided to emancipate the Jews, but before doing so, he turned to Schelling, his revered teacher, requesting his opinion on the subject. "Dear Privy Councilor," he wrote, "I take advantage of a few free moments to write to you these lines and to transmit to you the enclosed draft about the emancipation of the Jews. I would be very grateful if, at your earliest convenience, you would communicate to me your view on this so important question. . . . I do not remember quite distinctly an utterance of yours about the lot, the destiny of the Jewish people. Minister Lerchenfeld believes that this law is a postulate of the age and at the same time the best and safest way to make the Israelites loyal citizens of the state. I am not clear about this point. I wish to hear your opinion on this question, esteemed teacher, to have your judgment, also from a world-historical, philosophic viewpoint.—Goodbye, do write soon to your faithful disciple and friend Max."[7]

As becomes evident from references in the later correspondence, Schelling replied to the monarch, but the answer seems to have been lost. The spirit of his reply, however, is not difficult to surmise. The monarch and his counselors had in principle decided in favor of the emancipation of the Jews and a legislative draft to this effect had already been prepared. At such a moment Maximilian II would hardly have turned to Schelling if he had reason to believe that his former teacher would offer any objections. On the contrary, the monarch apparently expected Schelling's approval, and the latter's reply appears to have fulfilled his hope. Soon thereafter the Bavarian *Landtag* passed the emancipation bill in the form in which it had been submitted by Maximilian's government. In a later audience the monarch granted to the Rabbi Daub, Maximilian remarked, "I do not wish that anyone of my subjects be oppressed; to me they are all equal."

The spirit that moved Schelling concerning the Jewish question may be inferred from a letter of his to the historian Waitz, written only three months after the royal inquiry. This epistle may serve as a substitute for the missing letter to Maximilian. Schelling referred to the deliberations of the German Constituent Assembly at Frankfurt am Main and stated his opposition to the establishment of a hereditary monarchy: "I could not get accustomed to the idea of making a strong monarchy of Germany or of us Germans a nation in the narrow and exclusive sense as, for instance, the French are. Were this to be our destiny, I would have had to abandon long ago every feeling of esteem for my own nation; the Germans, it appears to me, are rather destined to be a nation of nations and thus to represent, compared to the others who admittedly in folkish respects had to be superior to us, humanity again. Only thus I conceived the enigmatic course of history which has compelled us to attract quite alien races and nationalities or to leave them in a part of our realm."[8]

In 1854, the year of his death, Schelling pleaded on behalf of a Jewish scholar, though without success. He who in his early days had vented his dislike of Jewish writers concluded his life warmly recommending a Jewish scholar. "On how much regard I may still count," he wrote bitterly about the lack of response, "I had occasion to learn when I sent to the Academy, with a recommendation, the book of a scholar here—of a Jew, admittedly, who, however, possesses a great knowledge of medieval Hebrew, philosophy, and poetry—and did not even receive a reply. I was not astonished at it; the contrary rather would have astonished me. Nevertheless, I did not want to fail to encourage a fine and qualified man."[9]

The anti-Semitic current in Romanticism appeared particularly strong among the younger Romanticists. One of their prominent representatives was Ludwig Tieck. "It is inconceivable to me," he wrote, "how people can promote the emancipation of the Jews. Through their law they are and remain aliens, while living in our midst; they cannot adopt the manners of our nation. One cannot possibly concede to an entirely alien people the same rights as to one's own people! Would one do it, for instance, to a Negro colony, if one lived among us? What the Jews have accepted of modern education is only external, and most of them, if they would be honest, would have to admit that they consider themselves much better than the Christians. Everywhere they intrude these days; everywhere they hold the floor continually. If this goes on, we shall in the end be only a tolerated sect."[10]

What Tieck called the "intrusions" of the Jews were largely an expression of their desire to attach themselves closely to the German community in all cultural, social, and economic respects. The Jews wished to participate as equals in German life and to rid themselves of the "strangeness" for which Tieck and others like him reproached them. If Tieck is to be believed, it was largely fear that the handful of German Jews might suppress the entire German people which determined his hostile attitude to their plea for equality. Tieck professed to discern in the emancipation of the Jews danger of the subjugation of the Germans. The latter, although a vast majority in the German states, would then become only "tolerated." For Tieck, the only alternative to the enslavement of the Jews was enslavement of the Germans. He could not conceive of a state based upon the domination of none and the equality of all, including the ethnic and religious minorities. The question must be raised, of course, whether the Germans ever seriously feared being dominated by the tiny Jewish minority in their midst. Or was fear merely the convenient pretext for opposing the demand for equality and keeping the Jews in a state of subjection?

Like other German Romanticists, especially Achim von Arnim and Clemens Brentano, Tieck disliked contemporary Judaism and agreed with these anti-Semitic contemporaries in rejecting the emancipation of the Jews. Again like many of his Romantic friends, he showed high esteem for ancient Judaism, from which by "a miraculous disposition of Providence" monotheism has sprung, to be transmitted down to the present age. Ancient Judaism was respectable, since Christianity emerged from it. "This Jewish nation," Tieck wrote, "which lived without commerce, without navigation, without community with the remaining peoples, without science and art, had admittedly to sacrifice the largest and best parts of its life to be able to preserve this one indefinitely precious treasure." "This people" had shown a "stubborn, vigorous will," and "enclosed in its heart its firm and simple belief," and had avoided "all ornament, all embellishment."[11]

In spite of such excellences which Tieck found in ancient Judaism the thought that similarly admirable traits might be found or developed among the descendants and that they too might be worthy of equality, strangely, never occurred to him.

Bettina Brentano: A True Friend

In contrast to Tieck and his allies, Bettina Brentano, the child genius of German Romanticism, displayed a truly apostolic activity on behalf of the Jews. The Jews of Frankfurt am Main appreciated Bettina's services in their behalf and sent her a copy of their magazine *Sulamith,* which bore a dedication to her as "their protectress and little helper in need."[12] The Primate Karl von Dalberg saw in her likewise a "little friend of the Hebrews." Her work *Goethes Briefwechsel mit einem Kinde* not only reveals her great admiration for Goethe but shows also her intense preoccupation with the Jewish question. Bettina took the role of an advocate of the Jews, defending them with fervor and enthusiasm against what she considered unjust attacks; she did not hesitate to blame Goethe for his "cold letters."[13] Untiring, she attempted to win his sympathy for the Jews of Frankfurt am Main by recounting their struggle for justice and their striving for education and knowledge. When Goethe asked Bettina for some of the numerous writings on the dispute, she promptly sent him a number of these booklets.[14]

Among the materials Bettina forwarded to Goethe was the picture of a Jew. "One would have liked to have been with him," she wrote with romantic exuberance—the sort of sentimentalism that let some like Bettina love the Jews and let others hate them—"in order to suffer with him all torment, to compensate him for everything with a thousandfold love." Goethe should hang this picture on the wall of his bedroom. At the same time, she admitted her fear of communicating his views on the Jews to the Primate Dalberg, "because," she wrote, "I do not agree with you and have also my reasons. But I do not deny that the Jews are a greedy, immodest people; if one extends to them the finger, they draw one to themselves with the hand that one may tumble head over heels. This comes from their having been so long in misery. Their kind is still humankind, which some day is supposed to enjoy freedom. People want to make of them absolutely Christians, but do not wish to let them out of the narrow purgatory of the overcrowded ghetto. It was quite a victory when the Christians decided to send their children to school with the poor Jewish children. The Jews are indeed full of vice; that cannot be denied. But I do not see at all what can be corrupted among the Christians; and if . . . all humans ought to become Christians, one should let them into the heavenly paradise." She assured Goethe finally: "Love does not blind me."[15]

But her love was genuine and it emanated also from her work *Die Günderode*. Bettina recounted therein the episode of her acquaintance with an old Jew named Ephraim, whose majestic beauty as much as his rare intellect had aroused her interest and admiration. She sincerely wished to alleviate the lot of the Jews, which appeared to her extremely harsh and burdensome: "The Jew's way is to sneak through the thorns and thistles with which the Christian blocks the road to him, and he must fear lest he wake the dogs which pursue him into the bushes; in the end he does not know whether to march forward or backward and often perishes in the sweat of his labors or, which is even sadder, does not find his God any more in his own heart."[16]

How much justice for the Jews was close to Bettina's heart is also shown in the following passage from a letter of hers. "On Sunday," she wrote, "Bang preached here. I promised to hear him, if he wished to preach on the Jews, on how the Christians barricade their un-Christian hearts against them so that the Jews cannot even perceive Christianity.''[17] Just as Bettina wished to attend the church only if the preacher spoke about tolerance, she interested herself in education only if it concerned "poor Jewish children." "Molitor,"* she wrote, "has sent me an educational project. . . . He must believe that education interests me in general; this, however, was only because of the poor Jewish children who had there received a little human treatment together with the Christians. . . . This alone appeared to me education: namely to get children of the same age, of equal capabilities, early accustomed to having also equal human rights whether they are Jews or Christians.''[18] Like Herder and Pestalozzi, Bettina Brentano pleaded for the joint education of Jewish and Christian children and spoke strongly in behalf of "equal human rights."

Bettina maintained her friendly attitude toward the Jews in later years and continued to believe in the need for harmony between Christians and Jews. Envy and superstition should be overcome and harmony should reign among all men, regardless of national and religious origins. When in the year 1840 Frederick William IV ascended the Prussian throne and the city of Berlin undertook preparations for the festival, Bettina sent a letter to the first mayor of Berlin, criticizing the project of erecting on this occasion a tower-like structure on which the forty progenitors of the royal house of Hohenzollern were to be painted. "Oh why," she wrote, "don't you rather have painted on this tower Turks, pagans, Jews and Christians, Egyptians, Canadians, Arabs . . . who, all uniting under the scepter of a magnanimous king, give the country the highest prosperity and free the spirit from the slave chains of envy, superstition? . . . Why not paint on it peasants, burghers, Jews and Christians all of whom . . . shouting with joy call Jehovah or Our father, thou art in Heaven?''[19]

Clemens Brentano and Achim von Arnim:
Enemies of the Jews

Bettina's brother was Clemens Brentano, one of the promising stars of German Romanticism.[20] He ridiculed the endeavors of German Judaism to obtain political emancipation and to assimilate itself culturally. Like the Prussian Junkers, he and Achim von Arnim, his

---

*Joseph Franz Molitor, German Christian cabalist in Frankfurt am Main, taught at an institution for the uplifting of the Jews which was founded by Prince von Dalberg.

brother-in-law and fellow writer, fell into reveries about the feudal state and rigid class society of the Middle Ages. The Jews then had eked out a miserable existence and, virtual outcasts, had suffered oppression and humiliation. The relegation of the Jews to the very bottom of the social structure seemed to exert a special fascination upon many Romantics.

Clemens Brentano was one of the most active members of the Christian-German Table Company, which, as mentioned before, was founded in Berlin toward the end of the first decade of the nineteenth century. Its membership embraced artists and diplomats, authors and Prussian Junkers, but specifically excluded Jews. It was in this circle that Clemens Brentano read in 1811 his anti-Semitic satiric essay "Der Philister, in und nach der Geschichte" [The Philistine in and according to History]. According to Karl Varnhagen von Ense, "the company" went "out of its senses, rejoiced greatly and cried out with pleasure. . . . All members rose, surrounded Brentano and flattered him, rendering homage indeed."[21] Since many requested a copy of the essay, he decided to have it printed. The edition of two hundred copies was quickly sold out. Surprisingly, the tract, which contained also some critical side-glances at Prussian policy, had been passed by the Prussian censor. The license was later revoked, but only after the entire edition was out of print.

The satire was aimed primarily against the flat intellectuality of the Enlightenment. The author argued that Philistines and Jews, while displaying different traits of character and even showing hostility to each other, were both representatives of a cold, barren rationality which could only harm humanity in life as well as in the arts and sciences.

In a manner characteristic of Christian Romanticism, Brentano distinguished ancient Judaism from its contemporary successor. He assigned to ancient Judaism, the cradle of Christianity, a high rank in religious and world history. But while in general Brentano approached ancient Judaism respectfully,[22] he vented all his bitterness against contemporary Jewry. The Jews of Berlin were a particular target of his vituperation. He reminded the wealthy and educated Berlin Jews, in whose salons the elite of the Prussian capital met, of their lowly and, as he held, shameful origins, their trading in old clothes and rabbit furs. He also made numerous allusions to the questionable economic and financial activities of the Jews, their greed for money,[23] their social and intellectual ambitions, and their connections with the world of Enlightenment.

In his concluding words Brentano recalled that the Table Company had been founded "to the sole anger of Jews and Philistines, because they should not enter," and demanded that all members once again "render the laws against them more strict." He did not seem to be embarrassed ascribing purely negative goals to the Christian-German Table Company.

Although Clemens Brentano had been very prominent in patriotic circles before the War of Liberation, he did not consider it his duty to put down the pen and take up arms;[24] he also strongly dissuaded Arnim from volunteering for the struggle.[25] While many German Jews gave their blood freely for Germany's liberation, Clemens Brentano sketched the figure of the Jewish spy Gänsefett in a play designed to expose Jews to ridicule and contempt.

Yet Brentano did not shun all social intercourse with Jews. He frequented especially the salon of Sara Levi and learned to know better two other Jewish women, Dorothea Veit-Schlegel and Rahel Levin. In 1799 Dorothea had moved with Friedrich Schlegel, her later husband, to Jena. There she became the confidant of Clemens Brentano and closely acquainted with his work. He dedicated *Godwi* to Friedrich Schlegel and Dorothea. In an unprinted letter of the year 1801 Brentano bared to Dorothea "his torn soul."[26] Soon after these delicate revelations, however, he called her a "common, ugly Jewish female."[27] The beginning of differences with Friedrich Schlegel, as well as unstable and unaccountable Romantic moods, may partly explain such excesses; the rest was Clemens Brentano.

Anti-Semitism was nevertheless not the deepest cause of his later estrangement from Dorothea and Rahel, although he himself pointed at the time to the Jewish descent of both women.[28] He had been well aware that they were Jews at the beginning of his relationship with them, and his knowledge did not deter him later from making frantic efforts to reknit the bonds of friendship.

Brentano's relations with Rahel Varnhagen were even more puzzling than his relations with Dorothea Schlegel. His reverent courting of Rahel, his sudden switch to arrogant and insolent behavior toward her, and again his undignified courting of her friendship follow each other in bewildering succession. Neither Karl Varnhagen von Ense, Rahel's husband, nor she herself appear to have been without blame in the relationship with Brentano, yet his behavior was plainly repulsive.

In the year 1811 Brentano recounted to Varnhagen that his sister Bettina had for some reason complained about Rahel and had allegedly called her a "nasty intruding Jewess."[29] In October of the same year, however, Brentano, according to Varnhagen, spoke about Rahel in quite a different tone. By then he had succeeded in winning her confidence. Yet the friendship did not last long.[30] Brentano sent Rahel, incomprehensibly with Varnhagen's knowledge, a truly insolent letter in which he attempted to explain her stimulating effect upon many a great intellect. The root of everything which was "not beautiful" in her character[31] ought to be looked for in her Judaism. After the receipt of this letter Rahel remarked tersely: "I have been offended during my life only three times, once by a woman, the second time by a man, the third time by Clemens." She blamed herself for having believed she possessed "an especially exquisite manner to compel respect even from crazy people."[32]

After all he had blurted out, Brentano was still anxious for a reconciliation with Rahel. Again he turned to her, reverently and full of flatteries, and begged anew for her confidence and friendship. While in Prague, Rahel, oddly enough, agreed to see him again. On several occasions she had stressed her spiritual kinship with the Romantic poet. When they met, he was unable to speak from sheer excitement. For a whole week they saw each other daily. From Vienna he sent her an enthusiastic letter. Yet new letters followed in which he reproached her again for her Judaism. What she lacked, he asserted, was "an invisible Christianity."[33] Their relations at long last were severed for good. Unfavorable, even hostile references to Rahel, "Madame de Maintenon-Rahel," are found in some of Brentano's works, as in *Aloys und Ismelde,* where Rahel's salon is sharply criticized for alleged immorality.[34]

From the year 1815–1816 dates an unpublished talk by Brentano, found in the Varnhagen collection in Berlin by K. Krüger. "The historic deformation of Judaism," Brentano wrote, "follows from a rebellion of this tribe against its flowering and fruit (Jesus); they therefore have sprouted out into a stale, sickly, ugly weed. . . ."[35] The degeneration of Judaism thus had religious causes and aspects rather than social roots; it was the result of the "rebellion against his [Jesus'] divine mission."

Clemens Brentano's irreconcilably anti-Semitic phase seems to have lasted until about 1815–1816. Thereafter, a growing religiosity, an inclination to Catholicism in particular, made him repent his earlier outbursts against the Jews. When at the end of the twenties a new edition of his writings was under consideration, Brentano disavowed his *Philister.* Brentano, according to the literary historian R. Steig, "felt differently now than before. . . . What he had once written down in sociable, intimate familiarity did not appear to him suitable for wide publicity."[36] In the same vein, after 1831 he began to rewrite the fairy tale "Gockel" to blunt its anti-Jewish satirical points. The designation "Jew" was to be supplanted by the inoffensive "Morgenländer" (one from the East). During his residence in Frankfurt am Main, which began in July 1829 and lasted until 1832, Brentano once more attached himself closely to Dorothea Schlegel and her son Philip and became, like Dorothea, a member of the Society of the Rosary. "The Jewish woman and the anti-Semite found each other in the pale of the church,"[37] an anti-Semitic student of Brentano remarked regretfully.

The great change that finally came over Brentano found vivid expression in his work *Tagebuch einer Ahnfrau* [Diary of an Ancestress]. Toward the end of his days, the Jew-hater Brentano seemed to be completely converted: full tolerance had become his watchword. His medieval chronicler Jacob von Guise tries to prove the existence of a "close kinship of the people of God" with the people in the Hennegau. Without the assumption of such an affinity "the history of that people would hardly be a sacred history and would concern us little." The Eternal Jew is now the object of "great compassion," and the Christian woman recounting her meeting with him tells how she crossed herself after the old man fled, but prayed: "May the blessing reach him!"[38]

Bettina Brentano's husband was the nobleman Achim von Arnim, one of the leading figures of the Younger Romantics. Jointly with his brother-in-law Clemens Brentano, Arnim edited the collection of folk songs *Des Knaben Wunderhorn*. Though he shared Brentano's anti-Jewish moods, he seemed just as incapable as Clemens of avoiding Jewish salons in Berlin. Both abhorred Judaism and disliked Jews in general yet could not bring themselves to break with them socially.[39]

His marriage in 1810 with Bettina Brentano, who has pleaded so warmly for the Jews, seemingly had no influence upon Arnim's attitude to them. Just as little did Wilhelm von Humboldt's emphatic defense of the Jews dissuade his wife Caroline from showing relentless opposition to them. Among Germans, the Jewish question even divided members of the same household.

That the opponents of the Jews were often terrified by the picture of the Jew which they themselves had painted is also shown by a remark Arnim made in 1830. He complained that "the Jews had by now taken possession of most periodicals"[40] and added: "Perhaps they really may plot something." His opposition to the Jews "perhaps" was not unjustified!

Arnim, a leading member of the Christian-German Table Company, played a main part in the exclusion of Jews from this association. In May 1811 the Jewish journalist Saul Ascher accused him of intolerance in Zschokke's *Miscellen*. Indeed, Arnim was generally held to be an enemy of the Jews. He once warned Wilhelm Grimm not to engage in business relations with a Jewish publisher.[41] Another time he wrote to Görres that he felt well in little Wiepersdorf and was only disturbed by the loneliness of the place and by thoughts about the Jews![42]

Arnim's hostility to the Jews emerged in his encounter with a young Jewish student, Moritz Itzig.[43] When Arnim appeared in the salon of Itzig's aunt in Berlin, apparently without special invitation, Itzig took him to task for his contradictory behavior in criticizing Jews and at the same time seeking their company and challenged him to a fight. Arnim, however, refused to engage in a duel with a Jew. Though the dispute was much talked about in Berlin, it had no heroic aftermath but merely a simple epilogue in court. The trial could not be brought to a conclusion, since Itzig, who had volunteered for military service, had fallen at Lützen. His military superior, a Captain von Rexin, praised his "conscientious fulfillment of duty" in a letter to Itzig's wounded brother. He had "highly esteemed him as a soldier," he wrote, "admired him as a philosopher, and loved him most dearly as a man."

Arnim himself survived the war. When Clemens Brentano in a hardly patriotic spirit warned him not to take up arms, Arnim replied that he too considered it "most unreasonable" to don the soldier's uniform.[44] Berlin society seemed to condemn Arnim's attitude toward Itzig. An echo of this mood reverberated in the following verses, which have been attributed to the martial poet Stägemann:

> At home remained the nobleman,
> The Jew remained on the battlefield.[45]

Kleist

One of the most gifted German dramatists of the era was Heinrich von Kleist. A passionate hater of Napoleon, whom he nevertheless admired, he urged the German people to shake off the alien French yoke. Strongly nationalistic, he was, however, not entirely immune to the cosmopolitan ideas of his age.

The lonely, unhappy poet was fond neither of his occupation, Prussian public service, nor of the society of Berlin. "I rarely attend social meetings," he wrote on February 5, 1801, to his beloved half-sister Ulrike. "I would prefer the Jewish ones, if they did not behave so pretentiously with their knowledge."[46] But he came to frequent the houses of Mesdames Ephraim, Levi, Herz, and Cohen.[47] Most important, however, became his relationship to Rahel. "You have as much expression in your words as in your eyes,"[48] he wrote her shortly before his death. The visit which he announced did not come about.

The general agitation of the era thrust Kleist, an essentially apolitical writer, into the midst of the political struggle. When he appeared in Berlin in 1810, he was in close company with Achim von Arnim, Clemens Brentano, Adam Müller, and some ultraconservative Prussian noblemen who united in the Christian-German Table Company and fought strenuously against the reforms of Chancellor Hardenberg.[49] Kleist accepted the editorship of the *Berliner Abendblätter,* which often served as mouthpiece for this reactionary group.[50] Yet basically Kleist shared neither the political opinions nor the anti-Semitic views of his companions.[51] When the government began to harass the paper, Kleist showed himself receptive to its admonition. He would hardly have done so if heeding it would have run counter to his genuine convictions.

The literary historian Reinhold Steig, himself an anti-Semite, claimed to have found proof of Kleist's hostility to the Jews in his poem "Der Weltlauf." The poem, which appeared in the *Berliner Abendblätter* on December 8, 1810, contained a concealed criticism of Hardenberg's agrarian policy. Kleist pilloried the evil business of usurers and grain speculators, who exploited the misery of the people, yet no single line referred to the Jews.[52]

In reality, no one scolded his own people more severely than Kleist. He asserted that the Germans carried on trade and business by "clinging with immoderate and ignoble love to money and property."[53] These were the words he used in his draft of the "Katechismus der Deutschen" [Catechism of the Germans], which he wrote for the planned magazine *Germania.* Kleist advised the Germans to remain bitter enemies of the despot Napoleon, but not to hate the French or to hate them only "as long as he [Napoleon] is their Emperor"[54]; except for the Corsican conqueror, the Germans should not hate anybody in the entire wide world.

Filled with doubt of himself and of God, Kleist shot himself at the Wannsee in November 1811, after having found in Henriette Vogel a willing companion for the double suicide. Reinhold Steig has asserted that the Jews, supposedly Kleist's sworn enemies, pursued him with their hatred beyond the grave. The accusation turned out to have no basis whatsoever.

The death of Kleist, whose true greatness was recognized only after his death, at first awakened little sympathy. On the contrary, on December 27, 1811, Kleist's memory was slandered in an article of four columns which appeared in the *Morgenblatt* in Berlin under the title: "Public beatification of a murder and suicide in Germany in the year 1811." In one of his studies on Kleist, Steig made the sensational statement that the author of that defaming article had been no one else than Saul Ascher, a Jewish journalist in Berlin. This, of course, positively proved the deadly enmity of *all* Jews against Kleist! Again, the hate of Kleist by "the Jews" could have only one reason: Kleist must have attacked them, must have been their foe! This inference apparently freed Steig from the scholarly obligation to adduce compelling proof of Kleist's asserted animosity. Unfortunately for Steig, the literary historian Heinrich Houben, in a report of the *Berliner Gesellschaft für deutsche Literatur* in 1904, proved beyond the shadow of a doubt that the reviling article had been written not by Ascher but by one Christian Friedrich Weisser, a Christian German journalist of the *Morgenblatt*.[55]

Kleist was the author of the patriotic dramas *Die Hermannsschlacht* [The Battle of Hermann] and *Prinz Friedrich von Homburg*. Through these plays he sought to encourage the German people to throw off the French yoke. He presented to the Germans the battle of their ancestors against the Romans in the Teutoburg Forest as an exemplary heroic encounter. It was in 1811 that the poet conceived the plan for a tragedy, "The Destruction of Jerusalem." Little is known about the details of this project, but it appears that he thought of the tragedy as a counterpart to the *Hermannsschlacht,* as another patriotic drama, this one glorifying the struggle of the ancient Jews for freedom and independence. Their courage and heroism were to raise the spirits of the Germans and strengthen their self-confidence.[56]

The comparison between the Germans, who were suppressed by the French, and the ancient Jews, who suffered under the Roman yoke, had occurred to Kleist earlier. In his previously mentioned "Appeal" to the German people, he let a Jewish contemporary of Titus display overconfidence on the eve of the destruction of Jerusalem: "Indeed? This powerful state of the Jews is to perish? Jerusalem, this city of God, protected by his own Cherubim; Zion, it should sink to ashes?"[57] Kleist thus culled various episodes from the pages of Jewish history to inspire the Germans or, as in the latter case, to alarm them.

The Faculties of Political Science and Law:
Adam Müller and Carl von Savigny

Linked with Kleist in the German-Christian Table Company with its distinct anti-Jewish and anti-Philistine leanings was the political scientist, economist, and journalist Adam Müller. Achim von Arnim called Müller the organization's "lawgiver"; as such he must have been largely responsible for its statutes, and for the exclusion of Jews. He was a sharp opponent of the reform program of Chancellor Hardenberg and sought to blame it on alleged Jewish influence upon Prussia's leading statesman. Adam Müller played no minor role in helping to phrase the memoir of the Baron von der Marwitz and of the States of Lebus,[58] to which reference has been made, but there is no agreement on the exact role he played. J. Baxa, a biographer of Müller, found in the memoir only "thoughts"[59] of Müller; he held this to be especially true for the anti-Semitic ideas in the memoir of Marwitz. Another student of Adam Müller claimed, however, that, "angered" by the ill success of his application for a post in the Prussian civil service, he had himself composed the memoir of Marwitz of February 11, 1812, and had personally "transcribed" it.[60] In any case, Adam Müller's name was prominently linked with one of the sharpest attacks against Prussia's Jewry on the very eve of their emancipation.

While Müller like many other Romantics criticized contemporary Jewry and rejected the concept of equality for the Jews, he too frequented the Jewish salons of Henriette Herz, Rahel Levin, and Madame Cohen. He also had social relations with Eduard Julius Hitzig, David Ferdinand Koreff, and Ludwig Robert and praised the latter repeatedly and emphatically. And he was often seen as a guest in the Viennese salons of Mesdames Arnstein, Eskeles, Pereira, and Marianne Saaling and in the homes of Dorothea Schlegel and other Jews.

Rahel Levin especially made a lasting impression on Müller, though at times he was somewhat critical of her. In a letter to Gentz of June 28, 1810, he referred to the "agile and pliable intellect of this miraculous little animal." He conceded that "she was still witty . . . like a thousand others put together" and regretted having missed her in January 1822, when he had passed through Berlin.

K. Krüger, the author of the dissertation "Romanticism and Jewry," written in the Nazi era (1939), took Adam Müller to task for his "sympathy for Judaism." He had gone so far as to apply for a credit of 550 florins to the banking house of Arnstein and Eskeles, "one of those Jewish money institutions the morals of which he could not condemn sharply enough in theory."[61] As Krüger learned when he consulted the Austrian state archives, however, the Jewish banking house Arnstein and Eskeles had to write off a bad debt. And it was Müller, who previously had raged about the moral laxity of Jewish financial magnates!

In weaving wreaths to ancient Judaism, Müller surpassed even his fellow Romanticists of the Table Company. His esteem for the Jews of antiquity found special expression in his *Elemente der Staats-*

kunst [Principles of the Art of Government], which he himself designated as his most important study and which was generally looked upon as the political manifesto of the Company.[62]

Like Hamann and Herder, the forerunners of Romanticism, Müller extolled the merits of the ancient Jews as compared to the much praised Greeks and Romans. "To what avail," he asked, "is the rediscovery of Greek and Roman antiquity, to the gay commotion of which we can never return?"[63] The teachings of the Greek and Roman philosophers had supplanted "the belief in Christ and the faith of the Middle Ages."[64] "Our age" had forgotten Moses, one of the greatest lawgivers of all times, because of its "fashionable fondness for Greek and Roman antiquity."[65] Müller placed Moses, the great educator of his people, high above all other champions of liberty, both in ancient and recent history.

Adam Müller shared Edmund Burke's conception of the state as a historically grown formation, as a natural organism. He rejected any sudden and arbitrary revolutionary changes, which would cause only harm to the living political entity. In ancient Judaism Müller believed he had found an ideal organic state. The Jewish state of antiquity had shown most varied political forms, including democratic and monarchic features, all of which fitted into the framework of the same basic Mosaic Law. Müller saw therein "a remarkable proof of living legislation." The ancient Jews had remained God-fearing peasants. Although the geographic location of their country had favored the development of commerce, they had not created a merchant state. National disunity—a consequence, Müller held, of the growth of trade and commerce—had not split them in two. The Jews could thus give expression to the "great idea of the fatherland."

An all-pervading religiosity, a strong national feeling, a preponderance of agriculture over industry and commerce and of the conservative peasants over the eternally discontented middle class of society and its followers, a constitution permitting slow and gradual transformations—all this Adam Müller professed to discern in the ancient Jewish state. Ancient Judaism, however, was not merely Müller's political model and ideal for the contemporary period. It had also infused its spirit and life into the Middle Ages, which in turn has become the source of inspiration to the Romantics in many fields, including politics.

While land, according to Roman law, was unlimited personal property, the Mosaic religion taught that the Jews had received their land merely as usufruct from Jehovah. Müller seemed convinced that the national-religious Jewish laws had in many ways shaped the growth of the medieval feudal order in Europe. He saw in history a contest between Jewish and Roman conceptions of law. Roman law had furthered the rise of the third estate, of the middle class, "while clergy and nobility, or canon law and so-called feudalism, represent the very ancient Mosaic law in progressive evolution."[66] Müller's own ultraconservatism found sustenance in ancient Judaism as well as in the Middle Ages—the latter, in his view, being largely shaped by the former. Yet any sympathy for the Jews which he may thus have awakened in feudal Junker circles was heavily outweighed by his and the German nobility's deep-seated hostility to social, economic, and political change, including the emancipation of contemporary Jewry.

After Adam Müller's hopes of becoming a Prussian civil servant had been shattered, he had left Berlin for Vienna. There, like Friedrich Schlegel, he had succeeded in entering the Austrian public service. In his capacity as Austrian Consul-General in Leipzig, it became his duty to represent the interests of Austrian visitors to the Leipzig fair, including the interests of Polish Jews. On one occasion, Jews from Brody stayed too long in the city and were arraigned before police authorities. It has been alleged that Müller was remiss in his consular duties and did not adequately defend these Jews.[67] Whatever the truth of these allegations, it is undeniable that Müller wrote at that very time articles with a distinctly anti-Jewish bias.[68] In 1816 he published in the *Deutsche Staatsanzeigen* another anti-Semitic article. "Our age," he wrote, "wants to reform the Jews and does not want to understand that the Jews are only mighty and pernicious because we have become pagans."[69] While Christians were reprimanded for this supposed paganism, the main reproach was clearly aimed at the Jews. Similar accusations had been hurled against the Jews by more vulgar writers such as Grattenauer, Buchholz, Paalzow, and numerous others during the anti-Semitic war of pamphlets in the years 1803–1805.

"No power in the world," Müller continued, could "prevent the growth of this corrupted, but always venerable people. . . . Even today they are the chosen people and internally more powerful than all pagans. . . . If the system of our enslavement to money extends to land and agriculture, well, then they will dominate also our agriculture; they will be the only proprietors of land."* Then follows what may be interpreted as prognosis or simply as a threat: "The honest Christian housefather will see no other exit than to annihilate [*vernichten*] them or to become their slave." Ruin of the Jews or enslavement of the Germans—these seemed the inescapable alternatives to

---

*The same idea, similarly expressed, is indeed found in the anti-Semitic memoir of the Baron von der Marwitz of February 1812, which was discussed earlier and which Müller possibly coauthored.

Adam Müller as they were to Ludwig Tieck and many others.* "En-slavement"—that is, subjection to Jewish domination—would neces-sarily also lead to a form of Judaization: "The entire unpleasant busi-ness of our trade and commerce will have to conform to Jewish ways in order to survive." Christian society, instead of reforming the Jews, will be "reformed" by them.

Müller's move to Vienna had not diminished his hostility either to Hardenberg or to the Jews. In a letter to Prince Metternich, dated December 12, 1815, he vented his antipathy against both. He appar-ently did not know that Hardenberg and Metternich had jointly sup-ported the Jews at the Congress of Vienna and that the former had sided with the latter again when a dispute arose between the Jews and the Hanseatic cities and Frankfurt am Main. In his epistle Müller repeated the clichés of the Christian-German Table Company and criticized Hardenberg's philo-Semitic attitude. The latter, he charged, had in financial matters "availed himself too exclusively of the Jews."[70] While conceding that the important role Prussia had played for three years "could not have been performed without the compli-ance of the Jews in pecuniary respects," Müller did not intend to weave patriotic wreaths for the Prussian Jews but rather to draw attention to their allegedly enormous economic power, a power which he vastly exaggerated. "The Jews," he wrote, "were not only in possession of all money, but all capitalists in Prussia, on account of the ubiquitous letters of reprieve, lived at their discretion." He was unable to explain why the Prussian Jews, supposedly in control of such overwhelming economic and financial power, were compelled to carry on such a prolonged and desperate struggle in behalf of their emancipation and to suffer so many reverses.

Did Adam Müller with this letter to Metternich pursue a definite goal? Did he who in Prussia had fought in the vanguard of the anti-Semites and suffered defeat wish to resume his struggle against the Jews in his new surroundings in Austria? In his letter Müller warned Metternich not to forget that every emancipation would "necessar-ily" lead to a deterioration in the situation of the Jews by arousing an anti-Semitic reaction. He appears to have nursed the thought of be-coming its spokesman.

The new Judaism, Müller asserted, was "corrupted." The dete-rioration of the Jews, however, was, in his view, the product of a peculiar historic evolution, not of a racial peculiarity. In the *Elemente der Staatskunst,* Müller had developed the thought that Moses had

---

*In this exaggerated antithetical form this idea emerged in the Nazi era to "justify" some of the unspeakable atrocities of that regime.

instilled in the Jews a healthy pride but that later, when the powerful empires of Cyrus, Alexander, and the Romans had brought misery and suppression to the Jewish people, pride had turned into arrogance to overcompensate for their humiliation.[71]

Like other Romanticists, Adam Müller approved of the conversion of individual Jews to Christianity—especially to Catholicism, wherein he, once a Protestant and then a convert himself, had found refuge. Contemporary Judaism as such was degenerate, but individual Jews could still be saved by baptism.

Linked in extreme conservative political thought with Adam Müller was Friedrich Carl von Savigny, leading spirit of the influential Historical School of Law. Professor of Law at the University of Berlin, Savigny pointed to the *Volksgeist* as the source of all the legal institutions of a nation. Thus Savigny opposed any rational creation of law as a presumptuous interference in historical custom. These ideas were crystallized in his review of a book by D. B. W. Pfeiffer, *Ideen über eine neue bürgerliche Gesetzgebung in deutschen Staaten* [Ideas about a New Civil Legislation for German States] (Göttingen, 1815). Savigny developed herein some of his own thoughts about the immediate postwar era, including the legal status of the German Jews.

Pfeiffer had criticized the exclusion of Jews, Turks, and pagans and had rejected it as barbaric discrimination by the state between natives and aliens and even more so between Christians and Jews. Not so Savigny, who took Pfeiffer to task on this ground. In Savigny's opinion, Germany had long lost the true concept of the citizen—a result allegedly of a misunderstood, ill-applied humanitarianism. Yet without true citizens, no healthy vigorous state could exist, and therefore, Savigny claimed, the erection of visible frontiers between citizens and aliens cannot be rejected absolutely. "Harshness and inhumanity of course shall be permitted in no case. . . . But the obliteration of all boundaries is quite unnatural." As he asserted, especially "the Jews, because of their innate nature, are and remain alien to us, and to disregard this could merely misguide us into the most unfortunate confusion of political concepts; not to mention that this civil and political emancipation, in spite of the humanitarian intention, can in the end be anything but beneficiary and can lead only to the perpetuation of the unfortunate national existence of the Jews, and possibly even to their further spread."[72]

Unlike his colleague Hegel, Savigny definitely rejected Jewish emancipation, while simultaneously claiming to reject also barbarism and "inhumanity." In the immediate postwar period he also offered an advisory legal opinion on the much-debated status of the Jews of Frankfurt am Main that was unfavorable to the Jews.[73]

German Historiography and the Jews

The master of German historiography Leopold von Ranke was well aware of the role of the Jewish people throughout the ages and their importance in world history. Ranke found the study of Jewish history "satisfying and instructive." He valued the Bible highly and "read particularly the Old Testament again and again."[74] In the year 1825 he accepted an invitation to join the University of Berlin as professor of history. In the Prussian capital he entered into friendly social relations with Varnhagen von Ense and the latter's wife, Rahel Levin, who made a deep impression upon him.

Leopold von Ranke was national-minded but at the same time a good European who held firmly to the common European culture and civilization—a culture which, in his view, showed the marks of the "Germano-Romanic" spirit. His political credo was embedded in the words: "The seclusion of nationalities from each other is at present no longer feasible; they all belong jointly to the great European concert."[75]

In his first year at the University of Berlin Ranke, in a survey of Western European history, dealt briefly with the Middle East, considering Assyrians and Babylonians, Jews, and Egyptians, the three major peoples of the area. According to E. Schulin, who has researched *Rankes Nachlass,* Ranke in his lectures in 1826–1827 and in 1833, turning to the Near East, had singled out "Semites and Egyptians" as the most important nations of the region, holding that the letter were most likely of non-Semitic origin.[76] As Ranke wrote, "The first world-historic event in that region is the rise of the Jewish people."[77] In his view, this included all of Jewish history as recounted in the Old Testament, from the migration of the patriarchs via the exodus from Egypt to the conquest of Canaan. The Orient meant for him the area of the Near East, as known through the Scriptures and Herodotus. Among the ancient peoples, Ranke showed genuine interest only in the Hebrews, the Greeks, and the Romans. When he later turned away from antiquity, he conceded: "I have at times a deep and strong longing for antiquity in the way that one recalls the gayer and more vigorous years of one's youth."[78] Ranke also felt attracted to the Middle East as the region where Jesus was born and lived. Not long after 1843 he conceived the idea of visiting the holy places to write a life of Jesus. He still clung to his plan even in advanced years.

Schulin, in a study of *Die weltgeschichtliche Erfassung des Orients bei Hegel und Ranke* (1958), spoke of the preference shown by Ranke for the Hebrews over the other peoples of the Middle East. The philosopher Hegel, who especially in his youth tended to deprecate if not abhor ancient Judaism and Jewish history, and the quickly rising historian Ranke, who extolled this history—both of the University of Berlin—thus pulled in different directions.

In spite of Ranke's deeply religious conception of world historical development, the historian in him early subordinated religious to political history. In his work of 1834 on the papacy he argued that the Christian religion signified the reawakening of the oldest, the aboriginal religious conscience. The latter had been preserved through the Jewish people, who had transmitted "pure monotheism."[79]

In the first volume of his world history, Ranke, referring to the biblical story of the rescue of Lot, noticed that a trait expressed itself in this legend that reached "above the national." The stories of the blessing of Abraham by Melchisedek and of the prevented sacrifice by Isaac were the "most splendid episodes" of the five Books of Moses and belong to "the most beautiful story ever written." Other peoples had excelled in art, science, or politics, but the Jews of antiquity were outstanding in their lofty moral feelings and the sublime ethics of their social life: "A more exalted inauguration of moral life in human society could not be thought of."[80]

In Jewish history there emerged, Ranke held, basic contesting forces which shaped events in an almost classic form. He saw in "some great biblical figures the 'models,' the first personifications of eternal types in history": "One will have to yield high praise to the Books of Samuel and of Kings about the presentation of secular history and, if we are permitted to use this word, political history. How a people, attacked from all sides, changes its constitution, renounces the republic, and subjects itself to the unifying force of the kingdom has never been better pictured. The natural struggle between clerical impulses and the tendencies of a full independence inherent in secular power, as it emerges here, is symbolic for all ages."

One could recognize in the struggle of Saul with Samuel "the German Emperor in contrast to the papacy. Similarly, the two kings, the warlike, soaring David and the peaceful, wise Solomon, are models for all centuries. Rehoboam and Jeroboam, they bespeak the discord between central power and provincial independence, as it has repeated itself numerous times. They are, however, not thought of as models, but rather have the reality of historic phenomena. One is satisfied and instructed, if one studies them."[81]

Anti-Semitism, awake at all times, found an echo in the field of historiography. The German historian Heinrich Leo, a former liberal, had in his *Geschichte des jüdischen Volkes* [History of the Jewish People] (1828) attempted to explain Jewish monotheism, as well as other qualities of Jewish thought and Jewish national character, as the result of a particular characteristic of the Jews, namely their supposedly destructive reason. Ranke, generally conciliatory, became incensed over such an insupportable and insulting thesis: "Have you ever read his [Leo's] *Jewish History*," he asked Heinrich Ritter in a letter, "where he traces this people's monotheism, hierarchy and skill for moneyed business from one principle, namely from the abstracting, truly destructive reason of this people. If he continues to irritate me any longer, I shall take him thoroughly to task and make an example of him."[82]

CHAPTER 9

The Image of the Jew
in Romantic Literature

Jewish Character Maligned:
Clemens Brentano and Achim von Arnim

Virulent anti-Semitism was displayed by Clemens Brentano and Achim von Arnim not only in their attitude toward Jews but also in their literary works. Brentano's hostility is mirrored in his satire *Der Philister* and in his festive play *Victoria und ihre Brüder und Schwester* [Victoria and Her Brothers and Sisters with Flying Colors and Burning Lunt: A Play with Music] (1813).[1] In this play the Jews pictured by Brentano are spies, thieves, and imposters. Emmes Gänsefett is the illegitimate child of a mother who made a living by trading hare skins and a father who was an informer. Both had been guillotined during the Revolution on charges of espionage. The son follows in their footsteps, carrying on as a thief and good-for-nothing. This comedy, like Clemens Brentano's other plays and those of Arnim, no less an enemy of the Jews, received scant contemporary attention.[2]

Brentano's animosity against the Jews also emerged in his fairy tales "Gockel and Hinkel" and "The Fairy Tale of the Tailor Siebentot at One Stroke."[3] In the latter the facetious and the fabulous are so closely interwoven that it is impossible to separate the different strains and to draw meaningful conclusions as to Brentano's attitude toward the Jews. But in "Gockel and Hinkel" his enmity appears undisguised. Three old Jews, "great philosophers of nature," reveal themselves in the end to be "imposters" and "old scoundrels." The cheaters are punished by falling into a wolf trap. Brentano recounted here also a story about the ring of Solomon which he borrowed from the Kabala and the Talmud.[4] Neither Brentano nor Achim von Arnim, as a matter of fact, avoided Jewish topics. Arnim did not deem

206

Jewish subject matter unsuitable when he used the Jewish Golem legend in *Isabella von Ägypten* [Isabella of Egypt]. Clemens Brentano availed himself of another Jewish theme in his *Romanzen vom Rosenkranz* [Romances on the Rosary].[5]

The spirit of Christian Romanticism pulsated in Arnim's double drama *Halle und Jerusalem* (1811). From the imagery of the Romantic movement he borrowed fairies, ghosts, and the Eternal Jew Ahasverus. The medieval hatred of Jews found here a dreadful resurrection. Of all the Jewish figures in the drama only Ahasverus does not appear in a dismal light. Because of his hard-heartedness he has been doomed to wander to the last day, but he already repents his sins and, in spite of occasional lapses into the old belief, thinks and acts like a Christian. He is presented as a prophetic warner and a propagator of Christian doctrine and, obviously for this reason, appears in a better light than the other Jews. Old Jerusalem is for Arnim merely "the city of sacrilege, which haughtily annihilated everything of magnificence that was born in it." The Jews of Jerusalem are incendiaries;[6] their rabbi incites them "to set aflame the church of Jerusalem."

Achim's Nathan does not feel any pity for his own suffering brethren. He rejects Ahasverus' plea for a donation to ransom the Jews whom the Turks have thrown into dungeons, whereupon Ahasverus retorts bitterly: "Until you Jews have all been converted, I shall not find any rest. I must wander through all countries, must see you martyred, tormented, flayed. How thus you are made ridiculous!" While the persecuted appear ludicrous, no word of indignation is uttered about the inhumanity of the persecutors.

Was it accidental that Arnim selected the name of Nathan for his Jew? Did he wish to juxtapose to Lessing's noble creation of Nathan the Wise his own conception of Judaism, his Nathan?[7]

Hardly less hostile to the Jews was Arnim's novel *Armut, Reichtum, Schuld und Sühne der Gräfin Dolores* [Poverty, Wealth, Guilt and Repentance of the Countess Dolores] (1810).[8] In an episode of this work an impoverished noble family and a newly rich Jewish family are contrasted, the latter cutting a bad figure. As in *Halle und Jerusalem,* the Jews are objects of derision and contempt and get the worst of it. They are depicted less unfavorably in Arnim's *Isabella von Ägypten.* [9]

Droste-Hülshoff and Hebel on Tolerance

The devastation often caused by the flood of anti-Semitism is pictured by Annette Freiin von Droste-Hülshoff, the greatest German woman writer of the nineteenth century, in her short story, *Die Judenbuche* [The Beech of the Jews].[10] The feeling of justice is still alive in a boy when he defends an innocent old Jew against his mother, who, without reason, suspects him of engaging in fraud. Yet in the end he murders the old man.

While Droste-Hülshoff asked for forbearance toward the people's fateful hostility to the Jews, the dialect short story writer Johann Peter Hebel, editor of the *Rheinischer Hausfreund,* demanded understanding and justice for the Jews. The Jews' disinclination to engage in hard physical labor, in agriculture and the crafts, for which they were so often criticized, could easily be explained, he suggested in his essay "Die Juden," by their characters as "Orientals."[11]

Although Hebel thought that rejection of hard physical labor by an entire people could have demoralizing effects, he nevertheless expressed a certain admiration for the "character and vigor" of the Jews, who had "remained so faithful to their old country." Prohibitive laws, which had kept Jews away from agriculture and the crafts of their host peoples for centuries, had probably shaped their occupational inclinations more than any original "oriental" disposition. But, whatever the validity of Hebel's analysis, a sincere liking of and sympathy for the Jews emanates from his lines. A humane spirit is characteristic of many of Hebel's stories, including those relating to Jews and Jewish life.[12]

Hebel's story "Sanhedrin"[13] shows that the author wished equality for the Jews, approved of their assimilation, and saw in their religion and their character no hindrance to either. The story tells of Napoleon's regulations concerning the Jews of France and of the Kingdom of Italy and relates the calling in 1806 of a general assembly of Europe's Jews in Paris. The Emperor posed questions to the Sanhedrin, as the assembly, modeled after the ancient Hebrew institution, was called. The questions showed that he was not thinking of sending the Jews away to Palestine, as some had feared, but rather of their staying and their "close association with the other citizens in France and the Kingdom of Italy."

Hebel reported approvingly the answers of the Sanhedrin to these questions. "The Great Sanhedrin recognizes that Christians and Jews are brothers, because they revere one God." The Jew must practice "justice" and cultivate "brotherly love," as it "is commanded in the law of Moses," and "just as much toward the Christians, because they are his brothers, as toward his own co-religionists within and outside of France." The "country where an Israelite is born and brought up or where he is settled is his fatherland, which he must serve and which he is also obligated to defend." One ought to instill into youth "love of labor." And mixed marriages were not forbidden.

Critical Sounds: Grabbe and Hauff

Anti-Semitic clouds, which hovered over wide areas in Germany in the era of Romanticism and the *Vormärz,* cast a shadow in the poetic work of the dramatist Dietrich Grabbe, of the youthful narrator of fairy tales and short stories Wilhelm Hauff, and of the lyric virtuoso August Graf von Platen. Friendlier rays broke through in the poems of Adalbert von Chamisso and Friedrich Rückert and the novels of Karl Immermann.

In his drama *Napoleon oder die hundert Tage* [Napoleon or the Hundred Days] (1831) Grabbe caricatured the Jewish soldier of the War of Liberation, picturing him as a coward and a generally ludicrous figure. It is puzzling that in the end Grabbe let the Jew fall from an enemy bullet, thus dying for the Germans.[14] In his opposition to the Jews Grabbe was not alone among contemporary playwrights, poets, and writers. Yet Hauff and Platen were by no means critical only of the Jews but also of their own people; at times they also expressed themselves about the Jews in a more friendly vein.

In his contemporary satire *Die Memoiren des Satan* [The Memoirs of Satan] the Swabian poet Hauff presented some Jewish characters in a hardly favorable light. Although the writer was critical and derisive also of the weaknesses of the Germans, the criticism of Jewish life was distinctly hostile. The Jewish parvenu was especially repugnant to Hauff. Satan meets with a company of unrefined but wealthy Jewish upstarts, who are enjoying themselves on the day of rest. "How the times have changed," Hauff comments ironically, "through education and through money. These were the same human beings who only thirty years ago were not permitted to set foot on the broad promenade, but modestly took the sidepath. . . . The same who every night were shut in their dirty ghetto by the mayor and the high council of the city of Frankfurt. And how differently did they look now! The women and the young ladies sat overladen with ornaments and precious stones; the men, though they could not conceal the pointed elbows and the bent knees of their race, though they sought in vain to copy the quiet solid bearing von der Zeile [a main street in Frankfurt am Main] . . . had put on their Sabbath dress and let heavy golden chains hang over the chest and belly, stretched out all ten fingers, studded with shining diamonds—as if they wanted to announce: Is this not something quite solid? Aren't we the chosen people? To whom do God and the world, Emperor and King, owe money, to whom else but us?"[15]

That Hauff was not always caught in such an unfriendly mood is shown in his short story "Jud Süss" [Jew Süss]. The love between a German, Lanbeck, and a Jewish woman, the beautiful sister of Jud Süss and the equally tragic fate of the Jew himself are the themes of the narrative. The Jewish girl is pictured as a most noble and beautiful character and Jud Süss himself shows very human and pleasant traits. This powerful man, who steers Württemberg's ship of state, almost arouses sympathy in his lonely heights. He watches over his sister with tender love and through promises as well as threats seeks to induce the young Lanbeck to marry the girl, who has been compromised through him. Yet Lanbeck thinks of "his proud father, of his distinguished family, and so great was the fear of dishonor, so deeply still rooted were the prejudices against those unhappy children of Abraham that in this terrible moment they even overwhelmed his tender feelings for the beautiful daughter of Israel."

Jud Süss is overthrown, sentenced to death by hanging on a huge gallows in an iron cage. "The manner," Hauff concluded his story, "in which this unhappy man could deal with Württemberg and his punishment is equally striking and incomprehensible at a time when one had already long left behind the beginnings of civilization and Enlightenment." "One would be tempted," Hauff added with irony, "to accuse Württemberg of that day of the most disgraceful barbarism, had not a circumstance existed which men who lived at that time often repeat and which, though it does not justify the deed, still appears to demonstrate its necessity. 'He had to die on the gallows,' they say, 'not only for his own heavy crimes but also for the deeds of infamy and plans of mighty men.' Kinship, reputation, secret promises saved the others. Nobody, however, could save and wished to save the Jew, and thus people put, as the old legal councilor to the states Lanbeck said, 'on his bill what the others had consumed.' "[16]

Hauff might easily have painted Jud Süss in dark colors. That he instead focused attention upon the human traits of the powerful man, condemned his punishment, and pointed an accusing finger at many other guilty people attests to his impartiality. Although Hauff sharply blamed Jewish weaknesses, he was also critical of the Germans and their treatment of the Jews.

Poems, Satires, and Dissonances: Chamisso, Platen,
Rückert, and Immermann

Adalbert von Chamisso, who became one of the most popular German lyric poets, also achieved fame as a botanist and world traveler.
Once he deplored to Madame de Staël that he was looked upon by
Germans as a Frenchman and by the French as a German. During his
entire life he felt as if he stood between the two nations, belonging to
neither. The creator of Peter Schlemihl, a man without a shadow who
is excluded from all human company, himself knew well the misery of
homelessness. No wonder that by some form of *Wahlverwandtschaft*
(elective affinity) he felt drawn to the Jews, whom fate had likewise
deprived of their country.[17]

The intellectual and spiritual life of North Germany and especially of Berlin in the late eighteenth century and the beginning of the
nineteenth century was, as noted, under the cosmopolitan influence
of Jewish and French circles in Prussia's capital. It was this atmosphere which surrounded Chamisso; it was there that the *Nordstern-
bund* (North Star League) was founded, in which young literary
forces joined hands—the poets Fouqué, Chamisso, and Ludwig Robert, the brother of Rahel Levin; Rahel herself; Karl Varnhagen von
Ense, who later became her husband; and Julius Eduard Hitzig, the
friend of Chamisso and also of E. T. A. Hoffman and later the publisher of their works. It was in Hitzig's home that the young poets
gathered and discussed poems and essays for the almanac they
planned to publish.

An intimate friendship bound Chamisso to Julius Hitzig, a convert to Christianity, who always remained loyally at his side. In accordance with Chamisso's last wish, Hitzig was entrusted with publishing the posthumous edition of his works. He often had decisively
intervened in Chamisso's life. Chamisso found Antonie Piaste, who
was to become his tenderly loved wife, in Hitzig's house, where she
had grown up with Hitzig's older daughters like a sister.

In several poems Chamisso touched on Jewish life and Jewish
history.[18] The poet, who called himself Ahasverus,[19] always felt attracted to Judaism and was greatly interested in Jewish culture. His
poem "Abba Glosk Leczeka," of deeply human content, cuts across
Jewish life. Abba Glosk Leczeka is a Jew who in his wanderings has
stopped for a visit at the house of the Jewish philosopher Moses
Mendelssohn. The inconspicuous beggar proves himself not only a
keen thinker but also a man who passionately clings to goodness and
truth.[20]

The poet and playwright August Graf von Platen-Hallermünde was critical of the *Schicksalstragödien* (tragedies of destiny) which were very popular in his time. The central theme in these plays was the change in the ownership of a certain object which brought bad luck and even death to every one of its possessors. In two literary comedies, *Die verhängnisvolle Gabel* [The Sinister Fork] and *Der romantische Ödipus* [The Romantic Ödipus], Platen ridiculed this type of tragedy. In the latter he turned his criticism also against Heinrich Heine and the playwright Ernst Benjamin Salomon Raupach, whom he, apparently misled by his biblical names, held to be a Jew. Platen gave this literary struggle an anti-Semitic twist by pointing in rather crude fashion to Heine's Jewish ancestry and to Raupach's alleged Jewish descent. An epigram of Karl Immermann, unflattering to Platen, had been applauded by Heine. This seems to have been the immediate cause of the dispute, in the course of which both Platen and Heine violated accepted standards.

Though in the heat of battle Platen made some anti-Jewish remarks in *Der romantische Ödipus*[21] he did not display persistent enmity against the Jews, as his praise of Lessing's *Nathan* proves:

> I have read many German tragedies, this one
> Appeared the best to me, though without spirits and ghost;
> Here is everything, character and soul and the picture
> Of noblest humanity, and the gods vanish before the only God.[22]

Platen's poem "Auf Golgatha" [On Golgotha] is also conceived in a spirit friendly to the Jews. A pilgrim to the holy place meets an old man, the Eternal Jew, who arouses deep compassion in him; he deems his punishment too "severe." To the question of the pilgrim how long he would have to drag his tired bones all over the earth Ahasver gives this reply:

> Until you emerge,
> God-like as he himself.

This "holy interpretation"[23] was perhaps Platen's answer to the contemporary Jewish problem: The liberation of Judaism was linked with the education and inner transformation of the Christian world. The improvement of the Christians was the condition of the redemption of the Jews.

While Platen at times expressed himself critically in regard to the Jews, the poet and university professor Friedrich Rückert denied having adopted a hostile position toward them when he wrote his early poem "Der nächtliche Gang" [The Nocturnal Walk].[24] A Jewish reader on whom this poem had made a painful impression turned to the revered poet for an explanation. Rückert dismissed any anti-Jewish interpretation and professed at the same time his rejection of the anti-Jewish agitation which was then zealously carried on.

Some people believed they could discern hostility to the Jews also in Rückert's poem "Vom Bäumlein, das andere Blätter hat gewollt" [Of the Little Tree Which Had Wished Other Leaves].[25] Such a conclusion appears farfetched. The poet would hardly have expressed possible dislike of the Jews in one of the "Five Little Fairy Tales for My Little Sister To Fall Asleep" (Christmas, 1813); Rückert, a great admirer of Lessing,[26] in reality ridiculed all nationalistic and religious narrowness, as his poem "Bekehrungseifer" [Zeal for Conversion] attested to:

> Don't let your view be narrowed
> By the self-appointed fanatics,
> Who do not recognize anything alien
> And who hate everything out of love.[27]

Karl Lebrecht Immermann, in two of his most important works, *Die Epigonen* [The Epigones] and *Münchhausen,* presented satiric pictures of contemporary Germany in which light and shadow fall upon the German Jews. In *Die Epigonen* (1836) a Jewish salon lady, Madame Meyer, is slightly derided.[28] And a Jew from Hameln who joins Hermann, a friend of Madame Meyer, as a traveling companion, is also unfavorably characterized.[29] In another episode of *Die Epigonen* Hermann meets with a group of youthful "demagogues" and lets the students know his mind. Yet Hermann, suspected to be a revolutionary himself, is arrested. He then becomes a witness to an "ingenious talk" between two gendarmes, one of whom reveals to the other that "all devilishness," the entire spectacle of "demagoguery and of Teutonic revolutionary machinations" of the students, stemmed from the Jews. When the other officer attempts to place the burden of responsibility for all this on the French, he is told that "all" Frenchman are in reality "secret Jews." Napoleon had converted his entire army in Egypt to Judaism. "If the trash got the upper hand," they would "kill all children and drink their blood."[30] Immermann ridiculed here the utter irrationality of anti-Semitism and the ignorance of the Jew-haters. The Jews in Germany are blamed by their opponents for everything disagreeable under the sun, even for the alleged conspiracies of the Teutonic students who actually were so hostile to them in those days.

Brief ironic references to the moneyed power of the Jews, to the Rothschilds and their alleged greed for money, and at the same time to the cupidity of the German princes are found in another satiric work of Immermann, *Münchhausen*.[31] They are, however, too brief and too general to permit one to draw meaningful conclusions in regard to Immermann's attitude toward Jews.

The *Weltanschauung* of the Romantic period, which displayed numerous contradictions, brought also to the fore strikingly different attitudes and views on the German-Jewish question. On the whole, however, the emotional and intellectual climate of Romanticism ran counter to the spirit of social and political progress in the field of German-Jewish co-existence.

Austria in the Biedermeier Era

From Joseph II to Ferdinand I

While there were always close cultural and political ties between the German states and Austria, they became pronounced in the period of the joint struggle against Napoleon and of the Congress of Vienna. Germans such as Clemens von Metternich, Friedrich Gentz, Friedrich Schlegel, Adam Müller, and Friedrich Hebbel made their way to the Austrian capital and entered Austria's state service or engaged in other endeavors. Frequently, attracted by the Romantic religious fashion of the age, they entered the fellowship of the Roman Catholic Church. Their attitudes toward Jews and Judaism, formed in their early lives in the states of the Holy Roman Empire, were expressed in theory and practice or in poetic garb in the new Austrian environment.

The enlightened absolutism of Joseph II in Austria had breached the wall of centuries-old prejudices. The Austrian Emperor had given Austrian Jews undreamed-of liberty of movement and held before them the promise of complete equality. Yet it was not friendship for the Jews but rather Austrian state interests, his belief of the usefulness of the Jews, that had made him sign the Edict of Toleration. The struggle over this reform and most of the other reforms he introduced deeply split public opinion in his own time and for generations to come. The proponents and friends of Josephinism pleaded, among other things, for full restoration of the Edict of Toleration and in later years recommended its extension to produce complete equality.

Opposition to the Edict of Toleration, subdued during Joseph's lifetime, rose sharply after his death. The Catholic bishops of Austria, resentful of what they judged to be Joseph's anti-Catholic measures, formed the spearhead of this opposition. In 1790, after the Emperor's death, they expressed to his successor Leopold II their grievance about the tolerance granted to non-Catholics and particularly to the Jews. They voiced fear lest the admission of Jewish children into Christian schools would lead to the conversion of Christian youngsters and proposed that the Edict of Toleration be abolished or made ineffective. But the high expectations with which the opponents of the Jews had looked upon the accession of Leopold II were not to be fulfilled during his brief reign.

With the accession of Francis II, later Francis I, in 1792, however, a thorough political change took place. Austria, waging war against revolutionary and republican France, turned her back on Josephinism and embraced ultraconservatism and reaction. In all provinces of the Crown the Austrian government began not only to harass Jacobins but also suspected and persecuted all those who looked with favor upon Joseph II's reforms.

The liberation of the Jews of France in the year 1791 had caused a strong echo everywhere in Europe, and when Napoleon called a "Great Sanhedrin" of Europe's Jews to Paris in 1806–1807, the Austrian government feared the impact of this French move upon its own Jewry. Its concern was hardly justified. Most Austrian Jews were religiously and culturally dominated by orthodox rabbis or by mystic-enthusiastic Chassidim. They suspected the ideas of the Enlightenment and of the Revolution as much as the Austrian government itself, though politically they had much to gain from them. A handful of well-to-do, educated, highly assimilated Jews in Vienna and a small number of their coreligionists in German Austria posed a sharp contrast to the orthodox mass of Jews in the Slavic and Hungarian areas of the multinational Empire. While this sophisticated and wealthy elite looked eagerly toward legal equality, they were socially already the equal of the best in Austrian society and the least receptive to French wooings. Dedicated to Austria and to German culture, they felt and acted like Austrian patriots. Equality attracted them, but not under the French tricolor.

In spite of Vienna's fear lest Paris might win the allegiance of Austria's Jewry, the emancipation of the Jews by Prussia in 1812, on the eve of the German War of Liberation, had no counterpart in Austria. And when France was finally defeated and Napoleon banished to St. Helena, meeting the spirit of the age even half-way in any sector, including that of Jewish policy, did not appear imperative to the Austrian government.

Under Francis I, the Jews were to suffer many setbacks. Humiliating and annoying laws vexed even the most privileged of Austria's Jewry, the residents of Vienna. In the year 1804 the number of "tolerated" Jewish families in Vienna had reached 119. Actually, a larger number of Jewish families had come to live in the capital, though illegally—"tolerated" by the Viennese police, who were rewarded for keeping silent. The Jews were not permitted to possess any houses in the capital, nor could they engage in any trades, though some branches of commerce were open to them. A Jewish physician in the city was restricted to a Jewish clientele. Jews were also subject to the payment of special taxes. Since an imperial edict of the year 1802, the widow and children of a "tolerated" husband and father automatically lost at his death the right of residence in Vienna and had to leave the capital.[1]

During the long reign of Francis I ultraconservatism was at times carried to absurdity. Even the slightest change in the rigid political structure or in the position of the Jews was considered a dangerous step, likely to lead ultimately to violent revolution. In this period the great majority of Austrian Jews had little to hope for. Jews in Bohemia and Moravia, Galicia, Hungary, and Slavonia lived in dire misery, hedged in by laws which hampered them in earning a livelihood and even set a limit to their natural increase.

In spite of occasionally soothing words, the Austrian government did little to alleviate the lot of the Jews. The government repeatedly declared itself in favor of equality for the Jews in principle, but it failed to implement its noble proclamations. On the other hand, bent on maintaining law and order, it would not tolerate anti-Jewish agitation. The Vienna police, for instance, prohibited the performance of a comedy with a distinctly anti-Semitic tone. Abroad, Metternich and Gentz often pleaded in behalf of the Jews of Frankfurt am Main and several Hanseatic cities in the name of Austria's government but stopped short of using their full influence and power in the Jews' behalf.

The imperial resolution of January 22, 1820,[2] stressed the preservation of the legal status quo, opposed the increase of Jews, and rejected the extension of tolerance to other Austrian provinces. Closer social relations, more intimate cultural exchange with the Christian population, and Germanization of the Jews appeared desirable goals to the Austrian government, yet it rejected the most effective measure for their realization—extending equality to the Jews.

During the reign of Francis I only a few Austrian statesmen raised their voices in behalf of full equality for the Jews. A majority seemed to favor maintaining the status quo of inequality. Some even urged that the Jews be compelled to return to the ghetto.

When liberalism first entered the political arena, it was hardly less critical of the Jews than conservative Christian circles. Friedrich Hebbel's poem of the early forties, "Der Jude an den Christen" [The

Jew to the Christian], clearly expressed the disappointment of the Jew who, pleading for freedom, has "appealed to the most recent, proud age" only to have it coolly turn its back on him.[3]

The hopes of Austrian Jews ran high when Ferdinand I ascended the throne in 1836, but they were soon disappointed again. The new decrees that affected the Jews showed no improvement, though the harsh laws were administered with greater leniency. Both the more tolerant spirit of the age and the wealth of the Jews affected this change. How contradictory the attitude of the Austrian government was and how much it lacked clear objectives in its Jewish policy are revealed by its negative attitude in regard to the Union for Promoting Crafts Among the Native Israelites. The government curtailed the activities of this organization in Vienna, though the Jews had repeatedly been blamed by the authorities as well as by public opinion for their heavy concentration in trade and commerce. All in all, Austria's Jews chafed under numerous restrictions that still lay heavily upon them.

Metternich and the Jews

The era of the *Vormärz** in Austria was the era of Prince Clemens von Metternich, the controversial Austrian statesman who gave his name to an entire political system. Metternich entertained very good personal relations with Jews. Although many Jews belonged in the camp of the opposition, the Austrian Chancellor generally did not express anti-Jewish sentiments. The Viennese Rothschild family was a financial pillar of his system. Yet, dedicated to the maintenance of the most rigid status quo, Metternich did nothing to improve the lot of the mass of Austria's Jews.

Salomon Rothschild, representative of his family in Vienna, had access to superior sources of information through his own and his brothers' international contacts. Thus he was able to furnish Metternich with vital facts and figures which the Chancellor would receive through his own state couriers only at a later date.[4] During the *Vormärz* the house of Rothschild was at the height of its influence and power and through its financial transactions helped to shape the course of events. Metternich was inclined to grant many a wish that the Rothschild brothers uttered.

*The period 1815–1848; before the March Revolution of 1848 in Austria and the Germanies.

At the Congress of Vienna, Metternich, like Hardenberg, had pleaded in behalf of the Jews. Due to the efforts of both men an urgent warning had been sent to the Hanseatic towns which were preparing to rescind the emancipation that had only recently been granted to the Jews. Repeatedly Prince Metternich also took the side of the Jews of Frankfurt am Main, at times at the specific request of the Rothschilds of Frankfurt and Vienna. Yet in the end these interventions were not crowned with success. It was somewhat ironic that Austria, while defending the rights of the Jews in other German states, clung in its own provinces unyieldingly to the status quo, which often was highly unfavorable to the Jews and always fell short of granting them full equality.

In the year 1815 some of the wealthiest Jews of Vienna and Prague petitioned Emperor Francis I to bestow equality upon them and separately appealed to Metternich for support of their plea. But the archconservative Emperor, who wished to keep everything just as it was, was frantically opposed to innovation in any area, including the field of Jewish legislation.

In 1818 Metternich penned a memorandum, "Über die Judenfrage in Österreich," which was prompted by a document, "Mémoire sur l'état des Israélites, par un Ministre du saint Evangile," submitted to the European monarchs gathered at the Congress of Aachen.[5] On that occasion representatives of the Jews of Vienna had likewise turned to the Austrian monarch, asking him to examine the state of legislation in regard to the civil conditions of the Jews. In response to both documents, Metternich stressed that the edict of Emperor Joseph II was still "in full force" in all German territories of Austria, though the Hungarian constitution prevented the implementation of parts of Joseph's legislation. In large communities Jewish children were free to choose between Jewish and Christian schools. In the military service, to which Jews were subject, all ranks and branches were open to them, except those, like the cavalry, which required a Christian oath. Many distinguished Jews had acquired titles of nobility which placed them at the same rank as Christian noblemen.

Jews could choose any trade. If there were hardly any Jews in the ranks of the civil service, the cause, Metternich claimed, was that all those aspiring to enter it had already become Christians. In several places it had been necessary to take precautions regarding the implementation of the edict of Emperor Joseph II, because the Jews had abused the concessions which had been granted them. Devoted to small trade, assisting each other with immense sums of capital, they preferred, according to Metternich, to make a profit through legal and illegal commerce rather than to attempt to succeed through other means. The laws of Emperor Joseph II had, however, "produced real benefit." The best proof lay in the genuine difference which existed between the Jews of Galicia and those of old Poland.

One of the greatest difficulties regarding a change in the position of Austrian Jews derived, Metternich held, from their large numbers. "Precipitous reforms" would not guarantee that the Jews would renounce their old habits and adopt new ones.

This document, in accordance with Metternich's basic ideas about preserving the status quo, was marked not by hostility toward, but by mistrust of, the mass of the Jews and by opposition to radical, "precipitous" change. The doubts expressed as to a rapid transformation of Jewish "habits" and of their occupational patterns reflected wide-spread prejudices which Metternich took into account and which, in no case, he was ready to combat. At the same time he approved of the progressive legislation of Joseph II, which partly was still in force, and did not consider the situation of the Jews in Austria unbearable. While Metternich emerges here as anything but a reformer, he was, as far as the mass of Austria's Jews were concerned, neither an enemy nor a reactionary: his credo was rather the preservation of the Jewish status quo, to be tempered by improvements for the Jewish social and economic elite.

Dim clouds hung over Europe after the July Revolution of 1830; Prince Metternich then contemplated intervention in France. The Rothschild family, which had much to lose from a new conflagration, showed concern about the possible outbreak of a European war and worked for the preservation of peace. The Parisian Rothschild advised his brother in Vienna to influence "his" Prince Metternich to maintain peace. As he wrote: "Much beloved brother! . . . . I send a courier to you, not for business reasons, but merely to forward to you for Prince Metternich a speech of the ministers here, which should make a great impression in England and Germany. You see, their principle is peace and nothing but peace. . . . I urgently entreat you now, dear Salomon, give Prince Metternich no rest, let him strengthen the cabinet here, and harass him to maintain peace. . . . He knows that you are a straightforward, frank and honest man, who certainly operates always with candidness and truthfulness, and that all my reports, which I hitherto have communicated to you for his information, have been confirmed."[6]

Salomon Rothschild and Metternich rendered each other many favors. At Rothschild's request Metternich assumed sponsorship of the railway between Vienna and Bochnia and made two members of Rothschild's family Austrian Consuls-General. Princess Melanie, Metternich's wife, praised the loyalty of the old Salomon to her husband.[7]

Prince Metternich and his wife were often dinner guests at the Rothschilds' and occasionally were also invited to other Jewish houses, such as Louis Amschel's.[8] Altogether, Metternich maintained numerous contacts with Jews during his long career.

After pleading in behalf of the Jews at the Congress of Vienna, Metternich continued to support them in their struggle to gain civil and political rights. Thus he intervened in their behalf in Modena in 1831 and in the Papal States in 1833. In 1837 Salomon Rothschild sent from Paris an urgent plea to Metternich for the improvement of the situation of Austria's Jewry. Immediately after the receipt of this letter Metternich summoned a state conference for the discussion of the Jewish question. During the Damascus affair of 1840, which outraged Jews and Gentiles everywhere, Metternich stood at the side of the Jews. Both Metternich and Rothschild, as the former had keenly discerned, had reason to fear revolution. In January 1848, the Chancellor told Salomon Rothschild: "If the devil catches me, he'll get you too."[9] When the March Revolution erupted, both Metternich and Rothschild hurriedly packed their suitcases.

In spite of the great influence of the Rothschild family upon Metternich, it was, nevertheless, sharply circumscribed; the brothers Rothschild did not succeed in placing the emancipation of the Jews upon Austria's agenda. What they helped to achieve was the attainment of equality for a thin upper crust of wealthy Jews.

Metternich cared as little as Bismarck would later about the political past of his co-workers. He did not hesitate to try to win to his side writers of the opposition, including those of Jewish background, by extending advantageous offers. Thus Metternich agreed with Rothschild's suggestion that the much feared satirist Moritz Gottlieb Saphir be bribed. Salomon Rothschild wished to rid himself of Saphir, who had cost him a great deal of money, by helping him get government employment.[10]

Metternich succeeded in availing himself of Saphir's facile pen, but a few years earlier he failed to win a stronger character, Ludwig Börne. Börne's father had been representative of the Jews of Frankfurt am Main at the Congress of Vienna. Attempting to secure for his son a position with the Austrian government, he had contacted Metternich. The Austrian Chancellor had praised Ludwig Börne and had expressed his interest in employing him. Börne was to live in Vienna with the title, rank, and income of an imperial councilor, without any obligations to perform regular work. Metternich assured the father that anything his son wished to write would be free from censorship and that he could resign from the position after a few months if he should not find it to his liking. In Austrian public service he would have an excellent opportunity, the Chancellor ventured to say, to work for progress and humanity.[11] Metternich did not seem to have any hesitation in trying to engage the liberal writer for the propagation of his own arch-conservative political ideas, in spite of Börne's well-known Jewish background. In an entry in her diary on January 26, 1838, Princess Melanie reported that she had read aloud to her husband Börne's *Pariser Briefe* [Parisian Letters]: "They are of course as mischievous as possible; the style is of a devilish extravagance and unusually witty."[12]

In spite of, or because of, his political opposition to Heinrich Heine, Metternich apparently followed Heine's literary career with interest. On February 13, 1834, he wrote to Apponyi, in a partly sarcastic, partly admiring manner, about the "bad German literature" which had established itself in Paris, including Börne's *Pariser Briefe*. Heine too, he wrote, "is going to publish a new work, which will be extraordinarily strong."[13] On the occasion of Heine's death he praised the poet as "intellectually eminent," a personality "endowed . . . with great intellectual gifts," but caught in a "morass of immorality."[14] There is an apparent ambiguity of feelings on Metternich's part toward Heine, which, in view of the latter's irreverence toward certain religious and political values and Metternich's own ultraconservatism, is hardly surprising.

"The Pen of Europe"

Friedrich Gentz, the "pen of Europe," was one of the leading political publicists of his age. A man of the world, brilliant and opportunistic, he underwent a radical change in his political views, including his attitude toward the Jews. The once fiery apologist of the French Revolution became known as one of the most persuasive advocates of Metternich's governmental system. A frequent visitor to Jewish salons, he similarly gave exuberant expression to his admiration for Jewish women, but later vented criticism of the Jews in the most unrestrained manner, though he did not remain their enemy.

Early in the nineteenth century Gentz, with many other members of Austria's aristocracy and intelligentsia, frequented Jewish salons in Vienna and found the company of Jews very entertaining and stimulating. Without it, he admitted, he would have left Vienna long ago. "The Arnstein family," he wrote to his friend Karl August Brinkman, "is the greatest and in a way the only resource of all aliens who arrive here, and an inestimable one for those who, like me, acquire a greater claim to services and demonstrations of friendship, by older acquaintance, by the connections with Berlin and Jewish culture, which we have often little valued and which I now esteem daily. How pleased I was when I saw united here, besides your charming friend Henriette Pereira and her excellent mother, also Madame Levi, whom I always loved and esteemed; Madame Ephraim, whom I—to my eternal shame—never gave a glance and whom I find to be one of the most interesting women I have ever seen; Madame Eskeles, on account of whom I often teased you and whom I now know to value; Frau von Eybenberg, who is here my consolation, my friend, my support—how I appreciated seeing besides these witty, likeable, in every respect praiseworthy women, everything else that Vienna contained of vivacious, sociable and tolerable company! This house is in more than one sense of the word a little world. Without it I would have been again far from Vienna; with it, however disagreeable everything else may be, one cannot easily despair entirely or sink to ruin."[15]

Yet times changed. Two years later Gentz permitted himself a furious anti-Jewish outburst. In a private letter to Brinkmann, the same correspondent to whom he had earlier confided his "reverence" for Judaism, Gentz wrote in September 1804: "So that not one of our letters omits the Jews, I wish to treat only briefly of one of the most horrible of this depraved breed, since you call upon me to talk about him. I mean the beast—Salomon Bartholdy." And with amazing frankness he continues: "This rogue, without disputing it in the least, has brains—just this, however, is the mortal sin of the Jews. They all have brains, more or less; only he remains still to be born in whose body beats a heart, in whom may be found a spark of true feeling." Gentz appeared to have forgotten how much true feeling he previously had discovered in Jewish salons when he had extolled the "amiability," "goodheartedness," and "sociability" of their prominent Jewish hostesses.

New converts often show greatest zeal. Gentz, the former defender of the French Revolution who had turned into a protagonist of legitimism and reaction, had grown angry with the Jews, the "born representatives of atheism, of Jacobinism, of the mode of Enlightenment." However, the Jewish financiers with whom Gentz later was closely associated apparently did not fall into any of these categories.

Gentz made the Jews, whom the French Revolution had given equality, the natural protagonists of revolutionary ideas. Since, in accordance with his new world outlook, the ideas of the French Revolution were the cause of all wretchedness in the world, the Jews appeared to Gentz to be ultimately responsible for every evil on earth: "Every misery in the modern world springs, if one pursues it to its deepest roots, obviously from the Jews. They alone have made Napoleon Emperor."[16] Yet, in another outburst of passion, Gentz, who in Vienna had been converted to Roman Catholicism, made Protestantism, not Judaism, responsible for all depravity in the world, tracing the root of all misery back not to the French Revolution but to the Protestant Reformation.

In spite of occasionally vehement attacks on the Jews, he displayed at other times greater equanimity. With characteristic "frankness" Gentz referred repeatedly to his "pleasant money-deals"[17] with Jewish financiers. He did not conceal that the Jewish banker Lamel had made him presents and that in May 1818 the financier Parish had invested on his behalf in the Austrian state loan. Several Jewish financiers were intent upon ingratiating themselves with Gentz, since it was well known what great influence he wielded upon Metternich, who himself possessed little knowledge of financial matters, and upon the Minister of Finance, Count Stadion.

Soon Gentz began to plead earnestly in behalf of Jewish causes. At the Congress of Aachen in 1818 he was very active in behalf of the Jews. In spite of his heavy burdens as secretary of the Congress, Gentz, after several discussions with the Frankfurt Rothschild, prepared a memoir in support of the Jews of this ancient *Reich* city. "Then probably," wrote a historian of the Rothschild family, the foundation was laid "for the intimate understanding, so fruitful for both sides, which on the one hand was to procure Rothschild an important political source of information and the connection with Metternich and on the other hand was to enable Gentz to lead his extravagant life and indulge in his expensive late love with Fanny Elssler."[18]

Basically, in spite of occasional sharp anti-Jewish outbursts, Gentz harbored consistently and truly anti-Semitic views as little as Metternich. This emerges clearly in a letter to his friend Adam Müller—himself critical of the Jews—who had asked him for his opinion about the Rothschild family. Had Gentz been a Jew-hater, he would hardly have expressed himself in as restrained a manner about the Rothschild brothers as he did, especially to a man who, as he probably knew, showed hostility toward Jewish financiers. "The Rothschilds," he remarked, were a special "*species plantarum*. They are ordinary ignorant Jews, of good deportment, without any notion of a higher connection of things, but endowed with an admirable instinct which people are used to call luck. . . . I relate to you *con amore* about these people and their business; for they were my relaxation in Aachen and, at the same time, I have learned much from them."[19] When the publishing house Brockhaus prepared in 1826 a new edition of the popular *Konversationslexikon,* Gentz was approached to write an article about the house of Rothschild. He acquitted himself of this task with a hymn about the Rothschild brothers[20] for which he was promptly rewarded.

While Metternich and Gentz tried to make life as harsh as possible for liberal German writers and fought them every inch, they could not but secretly admire the writings of Ludwig Börne and Heinrich Heine. Thus Gentz reported that Metternich had been "delighted" by a satiric fragment which had Talleyrand as object. "After he had gloated long, I told him," Gentz related, "that he owed the fun to the devil in person [Heine]. Yesterday's article is of an incomparable atheism . . . : but what censorship could overwhelm him and what Cato could read him without enjoying himself every second?"[21]

Nikolaus Lenau and Anastasius Grün

Among the most distinguished representatives of the poetry of the Austrian *Vormärz* were Nikolaus Lenau (as Nimbsch von Strehlenau called himself) and Anastasius Grün. Lenau, the greatest Austrian lyric poet of the nineteenth century, was much applauded in liberal circles throughout Germany. He was friendly to the Jews and had close relations with many of them, including the Viennese professor of history Romeo Seligmann, the banker Adolf von Hefs, and one named Jokel, who later took baptism and became a Catholic priest. Lenau loved passionately and hopelessly Sophie Löwenthal, wife of the Jewish banker. An intimate friend of Lenau's was the Jewish writer August Ludwig Frankl, who remarked on Lenau's attitude to the Jews: "Never came a disagreeable word on the Jews, or even only a joking expression about them, from Lenau's lips."

Nikolaus Lenau felt drawn to the Jews by a kind of special affinity. His brief, restless life was not a happy one. To Lenau the Eternal Jew became a symbol of death and of the yearning for it. Two of his poems, "Der ewige Jude" [The Eternal Jew] and "Ahasverus, der ewige Jude," testify to his preoccupation with this legendary figure.[22] The conception of Ahasverus is conventional throughout, but the poet's compassion for his suffering, his "heart's pain," is pronounced.

Lenau's poem "Der arme Jude" [The Poor Jew] reflects his deep sympathy for the harsh lot of many a contemporary Jew. The small Jewish peddler appeared repeatedly in the poetic works of the age, as in the poems and narratives of Karl Beck, Karl Gutzkow, and Anastasius Grün. In Lenau's poem, the poor Jewish dealer in old clothes, who wanders from door to door, ekes out only a miserable existence. Exposed to the burning summer heat as well as to the biting winter cold, he is expelled by the authorities, driven by hunger, coldheartedly rejected at many a door, chased from other houses by dogs, and doomed to continue his wanderings. He is to the poet a symbol for the entire Jewish people.

In the Austrian Empire of this period lived not only a mass of oppressed and impoverished Jewish artisans and small traders but also a few very wealthy and influential Jews who enjoyed rights and freedoms and were even raised to the rank of nobility. With his eyes fixed on them, Lenau turned to the poor Jew:

> A Jerusalem of paper
> Your brethren build,
> But for you it is closed,
> You must wander, starve, freeze.[23]

The poet of freedom, who threw down the gauntlet to kings, noblemen, and all "crowned trash," defied no less the Jewish finance of the day which supported Metternich's ultraconservative policies and thus helped the ruling powers to keep radical, liberal, and national movements submerged. On the occasion of naming a well in honor of Rothschild, Lenau wrote these verses:

> Not the source alone, the pure one,
> Which flows from the mountains,
> The stream of the ages too, the muddy one,
> Should call itself the Rothschild spring.[24]

Though Lenau had a keen eye for the deep social differences within Jewry, he believed that in spite of their prominence and influence, even the wealthy Jews were not entirely happy. If the poor Jew suffered from hunger and misery, the rich Jew was unhappy because he was slighted and because he still lacked political rights:

> Those have fared well,
> You sell old clothes,
> But all of you, alas,
> Have remained a bent people.[25]

In Lenau's poems the Jewish peddler is presented not as a villainous usurer but as a pitiful wanderer who arouses the reader's sympathy. Karl Gutzkow had sketched a no less friendly and sympathetic picture of the small Jewish peddler in an episode of his reminiscences *Aus der Knabenzeit* [From My Boyhood].

In one of Lenau's greatest poetic attempts, the *Faust* (1836), brief mention is made of the Jews. Mephistopheles in the "Waldgespräch" [Forest Talk] with Faust wishes to have "a Jew on the spot." Faust asks him what he plans to do with him and Mephistopheles replies:

> I would sharply drill the Jew and plague him
> For his people's faults in past days.[26]

The Jews "messed up" (*verpfuscht*) the world. The "traitors to nature" brought about a cleavage between man and nature. This, according to Mephistopheles, is the Jews' true "fault"—not the crucifixion of Christ, which leaves him cool. Mephistopheles, of course, is the bitter enemy of all religion, of Christianity, and of the Bible. Thus he persuades Faust to throw the Holy Book into the fire before finally surrendering to him. However, when Faust sees the Bible burning, his heart pains, though he has long rejected the Scriptures. Mephistopheles scolds Faust for having been "silly" long enough, for having dreamed "long-faded pages of Jewish history." The opposition of Mephistopheles to the Jews is rooted in his hostility to religion in general and to Christianity in particular.

In the epic *Savonarola* (1838) Lenau has pictured in Tubal a Jew carried to the verge of insanity by grief over his slaughtered children. Like Shylock a hater of the Christians, the old Jew Tubal believes in Jehovah as a stern god of vengeance. Shakespeare makes Shylock's hatred of Christians humanly comprehensible. Lenau too is full of compassion and understanding. He describes movingly how the poor, half-insane Jew demands in burning hate vengeance for bitter injustice and merciless punishment.

When the guard on the high tower hears the Jew's steps from the street, compassion seizes him, and he feels "beautiful brotherly sympathy":

> You poor Jew! Is it a surprise
> If your mind has gone astray,
> And if the gruesome trash of insanity
> Buzzes angrily from your lips?
>
> Were you not miserable and despised,
> Oppressed from youth on, chased?
> Until they robbed and slaughtered
> Even your children in the end?[27]

In great lamentation, Tubal relates the heart-rending story of the murder of his children. After the Jew in bitterness has hurried into the night, the stranger says:

> He is no fool, he is only miserable,
> Because he suffered terribly,
> Because the picture of calamity pursues him in
> Torment from the grave with every step.
> Although the old Jew may rage
> In his horrible, wild speeches,
> In the broken mirror too
> The picture of our age shows itself.

Lenau's friend was his compatriot, the poet Anastasius Grün. This pen name had been chosen by Count Anton Alexander von Auersperg. In the collection of political poems, *Schutt* [Ruins, "Five Easters," 1836], which on its publication was greeted joyfully in progressive circles, Anastasius Grün also dealt with the Jewish question. The poet depicted Jerusalem after the Crusades, when the crescent again cast its shadow over the Holy Land.

A tired wanderer rests near a little church. It is a Jew, "a branch from the miracle tree" "which, though felled long ago, has not yet withered." He has traveled through all countries, has learned to know many peoples, yet has remained basically the same. The Jew of the *Schutt* sells to pilgrims at the grave of the Savior rosaries, Madonnas, and little crosses. But in spite of all his adaptability and adroitness, he is a proud and stubborn man. He has not learned any of the alien tongues, he boasts, and has carried only his own language through the entire world: "It is the nature of parrots to lisp the language of the tormentor who holds them captive." He had no fatherland, and his brethren, dispersed in all directions, have had to struggle through life.

> And, still, we are one people! Made one by
> Common misery, common distress.

It is pride of national character, an amazing resilience, and a bold defiance of all persecutions, he holds, that have preserved the Jewish people throughout centuries, have made it "immortal" while the "nations' sarcophagi" have floated by. In spite of centuries-old oppression, the Jew of the *Schutt* has not been crushed and has not become a slave; his sense of justice is as keen as ever. With biting irony, he pillories the injustices meted out to his people. It is not surprising that the Jew of the *Schutt* remains suspicious and that a brief "moment of peace" does not make him abandon his caution.[28] He wishes to test the love that one so suddenly professes for him.

In an era in which Austrian authorities were hostile to the memory of Joseph II, the liberal poet and politician Anastasius Grün recalled the great Austrian reformer and liberator of the Jews.[29] Grün condemned the persecution of the Jews and expressed admiration for their tenacity and inner strength.

Grillparzer

The playwright and poet Franz Grillparzer, one of the greatest sons of the polyglot Austrian Empire, disdained narrow nationalism. Although he described himself as a good German—which did not exclude his Austrian patriotism—he detested all chauvinism. Grillparzer even went so far as to see in the awakening Czech nationalism—for instance, that of Palacký—a mere imitation of the German "foolishness." "This clamor of nationality," he asserted, originated with the Germans and with German professors in particular, "learned fools, who have incensed the mind of a quiet, reasonable people to insanity and crime. There is the origin of your Slavomania, and if the Czech rages loudest against the German, he is nothing but a German translated into a Czech."[30]

Franz Grillparzer's contacts with Jews were numerous and friendly, and he expressed his admiration for many of their great sons.[31] Jewish history repeatedly caught the imagination of the playwright in his search for suitable dramatic themes. He cast an illuminating light upon the Jewish question in two dramas, *Die Jüdin von Toledo* [The Jewess of Toledo] (completed 1851) and the fragment *Esther*. In *Esther* he wanted to express "ideas of tolerance"; in *Die Jüdin von Toledo* he wished, among other matters, to remind his fellowmen of the great debt of Christianity to Judaism.

Grillparzer looked with repugnance on the conversion of Jews. Not hostile but rather friendly to the Jews, he, like the playwright Friedrich Hebbel and like the theologian Schleiermacher before them, suspected the purity of the motives, the depth of the religious commitment, of those who became Christians. Grillparzer's rejection of converted Jews found expression in the following verses:

A Christian stands at heaven's gate.
Saint Peter does not let him enter;
At that moment a cohort
Of converted Jews rushes in.

Even in heaven the baptized Jews demand precedence. While mockingly rejecting their claim to priority, Grillparzer reveals his liking for the "Old Believers":

> Perhaps your people is chosen,
> In spite of stock-jobbing and rag-shops.
> Old Believers I like quite well,
> But not the converted Jews.[32]

While in some states the Jews were suppressed by the Christians, Grillparzer held that they were gaining the upper hand in economically advanced countries—a view which, though much exaggerated, reflected widespread popular belief:

> In civilized countries, and in primitive and crude ones,
> Different people fight each other with power and cunning;
> In crude ones, the Christians persecute the Jews,
> In civilized ones, however, the Jews the Christians.[33]

Grillparzer ridiculed and criticized not only Jews but also Germans: "One must step on them [the Germans], if one wishes to make them grow."[34] He often poured biting sarcasm on the "Old-Germans" and "Super-Germans," turning thus to the former:

> You look magnificent in the shining armor of your ancestors,
> You stand here vigorously—but now stride for once.[35]

In the year 1837 Grillparzer dedicated the poem "The Statue of the Emperor" to the memory of Joseph II. He praised the freedom which the Habsburg Emperor had granted to Austria's religious minorities, Protestants and Jews. He let Joseph, from his statue on the Josephsplatz, disclose to the people of Vienna that to him religion was "one, . . . as man, as God."

> And in the breast, the innermost life,
> I did not grudge to anyone his consecrated altar.
> To the exterior world the lie is given,
> In inner life man be true to himself.[36]

He warns his people lest they fill "the world with murder" as their ancestors did, "piously deceived."

Grillparzer favored giving the Jews equality with the Christian population. Emancipation appeared to him just and "equitable." But he was disappointed that the Jews were not better assimilated. He turns to them thus:

People did justice late to your race,
Which hate and vengefulness burdened with shame.
Now you have all civil rights
You always remained, however, Jews.[37]

Grillparzer most sharply condemned the medieval persecution of the Jews. In a chapter of his *Historische und politische Studien* [Historic and Political Studies], which deals with the "Centuries of the Crusaders," he pilloried the "rapaciousness" which induced the "mob and fanatic adventurers" to undertake crusades. "The mood of the crusading army," he wrote, "reveals itself only too soon; the lamentations of the Jews of Cologne and Mainz, the smoking ruins of the plundered cities of Hungary, testify loudly to the divinity of their mission. Humanity was avenged early enough on these murderers and incendiaries; almost all fell under the swords of the Bulgars and Magyars."[38]

Grillparzer admired those who did not harbor any prejudices against the Jews. Thus he praised the "freedom from prejudice"[39] of the Spanish poet Lope de Vega in his character presentation of the Jewess of Toledo. Grillparzer delved into the same dramatic subject, giving in his "Jewish plays," *Die Jüdin von Toledo* and *Esther,* proof of his impartiality and displaying keen insight into the Jewish psyche as well as compassion.

In his youth he had found his journey through Germany, begun in Vienna in 1826, "highly unpleasant"[40] because two Jews had occupied places in the carriage. Yet no less severe was the antipathy of the young man toward the Saxons.[41] In the Jewish ghetto of Prague he found only "dirt." "And yet," he remarked, "I saw three of the most beautiful girls I have ever seen, in this Jewish quarter, and all three obviously Jewish. The one almost Greek and ideal, the others human, womanly. . . . But extremely pretty."[42] The beauty of Jewish women has found many admirers, among them Goethe, Friedrich Hebbel, and Friedrich Nietzsche.

Grillparzer's frequent meetings with Jews preclude any anti-Semitic bias. He enjoyed friendly relations with Frau von Pereira, the sisters Lieben, the aesthetician Ignatz Jeiteles, and the poet Ludwig August Frankl. On his journey to France and England in 1836 he met many Jews. In Paris he visited Ludwig Börne repeatedly. There he met also Heinrich Heine, the composer Giacomo Meyerbeer, Dr. Koreff,[43] and the Parisian Rothschild, to whom he presented a letter of recommendation. "Among the men in Paris," he wrote in his autobiography, "two German compatriots, Börne and Heine, interested me most. I concluded with the first-named nearly a friendship. Börne certainly was an honest man, and what was politically stirring in his writings sprang probably from his belief that the Germans were so insensitive that one had to beat them with cudgels to leave even the vestige of a small impression."[44] In the *Studien zur deutschen Literatur* [Studies on German Literature] (1834) Grillparzer wrote: "When this Börne fights, there is something in him which reminds one of Lessing."[45] In his autobiography Grillparzer referred also to his meetings with Heine in Paris. "I hardly ever have heard a German writer talk more intelligently."[46]

"DIE JÜDIN VON TOLEDO"

In Grillparzer's play *Die Jüdin von Toledo* the King orders the people to arm themselves to meet the invading Moors and to pray in the churches for victory in the impending battles.

> Garceran: Already, without your call, your word has been obeyed.
> The bells ring far on the borders.
> But the zeal, erring, as so often,
> Turns against those believing differently,
> Whom trade and profit have dispersed throughout the country.
> Already here and there a Jew has been maltreated.
>
> King: And you, do you tolerate it? indeed, great God!
> I will protect him who trusts me,
> Their religion is their concern, mine what they do.[47]

The King has met Rahel and has fallen in love with her. Indignantly he rejects Garceran's objections that Rahel is only a Jewess:

> I myself don't love this people, yet I know
> What disfigures them is our work;
> We cripple them and get angry if they limp.
> Besides, there is some greatness, Garceran,
> In this tribe of restless, flying herdsmen:
> We others are of today; they, however, reach
> To the creation's cradle. . . .
> Thus Christian like Moslem traces his origin
> Back to this people as the oldest, first,
> So that they question us, not we them.
> And though it has forfeited, like Esau, its right,
> We crucify the Lord ten times a day
> Through our sins, our misdeeds,
> And those have done it only once.[48]

The play shows the character development of the King, tracing his change from the passionate lover to the man who follows the call of duty. The victim of this character transformation is Rahel, who belongs to a still despised and suppressed people. After the King has learned about her assassination by the magnates of the realm, he first flies into a rage. At Rahel's burial, however, his sorrow and eagerness for revenge abate and he even grants a pardon to the murderers. A general reconciliation takes place thereafter, whereupon Esther speaks these bitter words to her father:

> Look, already they are gay and cheerful
> And arrange marriages for the future.
> They, the great ones, have for the feast of reconciliation
> Slaughtered a victim from among the small ones
> And extend to each other the still bloody hand.[49]

The Spanish playwrights, especially Lope de Vega, greatly influenced Grillparzer, who had turned to the most thorough study of their works. Even in his choice of subjects he followed closely in Lope de Vega's footsteps.[50] But his treatment of the themes, the problems posed, and the solutions suggested were his very own. In his *Studien über das spanische Theater* [Studies on the Spanish Theater] Grillparzer extolled Lope de Vega's relative "freedom from prejudice." "Incidentally," he wrote, "it is strange that Lope de Vega takes rather decidedly the side of the Jewess of Toledo. She is pictured as very noble, and he removes from her, for the onlooker, even the stain of Judaism by having her ask before her violent death to become a Christian. Another proof of his freedom from bias. Indeed, even in his title *Las Pazes de los Reyes* lies perhaps a hidden irony. . . . In the third act the guarantee of peace is the death of the Jewess, least guilty among all."[51]

Grillparzer touched upon Jewish problems in still another play, *Esther*,[52] which, regrettably, remained only a fragment. In May 1868 the poet wrote to Frau Auguste von Littrow-Bischoff about the planned scene in *Esther* in which Hamann presents to the King "how the differences of religion in the state could not be tolerated and what dangers might spring from them. Here would have come a great scene on the right of the state in regard to religion, on the role of religion in the state, on freedom of religions, political rights and church laws. This, for instance, was just the point which cooled all my desire for further work; for this could then not have been played under any conditions, perhaps—rather, quite certainly—not even have been printed."[53]

Like Goethe in his comedy *Das Jahrmarktsfest zu Plunderswei-len,* Grillparzer saw in Hamann, the personification of anti-Semitism, only a vain, vengeful, and evil courtier. "Mardochai," he wrote to Frau Auguste von Littrow-Bischoff, "who continuously denies to Hamann the reverence which he proffers only to his God, does not prostrate himself before him, does not lie on his knees, as is customary at Susa, and arouses thereby the anger of the mighty, who hold him to be a fire worshiper or a Jew. Since Hamann cannot destroy Mardochai alone, he transmits his hate to all Jews and decides to annihilate these stubborn people, and Bigthan, who comes from Babylon, where a great dislike of them may also have stirred, strengthens him in his evil plans."

Hebbel

The playwright Friedrich Hebbel entertained friendly contacts with many Jews and always showed great interest in Jewish affairs. For two of his dramas he chose Jewish history as a background. He found the Jews no more free from faults than members of any other group, yet it appeared to him unfair to look upon the wounds which Christianity had inflicted upon them as their "sins." The Jew appeared to Hebbel, he remarked once, "just as bad as man."[54]

Hebbel's friendly attitude toward the Jews and his perceptive understanding of their position in society are revealed most fully in his poem "Der Jude an den Christen." He wrote it in 1839, but did not give it to his Jewish friend Samuel Engländer for publication in his Viennese journal *The Salon* until eight years later. The poem, Hebbel wrote, "discussed in my way, therefore without any needling and stinging, the simple ideas of humanity of this century; nevertheless, it was deleted by the censor. Indeed, dear friend, one can be suspected here of having invented the sun, the moon and the stars."[55]

In this poem the poet has pictured the deep disappointment of the contemporary German Jew who hopes for final liberation by the "most recent proud era," only to see how it "counts silently the wounds":

Pale and bleeding I sank to your feet,
I pointed silently to the past,
I called, encouraging myself even while dying,
Be thou my Savior, newest, proud era!

You stood quietly before me, looking seriously at me,
Your glance, although clouded, still appeared commiserating,
So that my heart, longing so far in despair,
Swelled for the first time with soft hope.

Alas! You only counted silently the wounds
Which have destroyed me slowly to the core,
You shuddered to find them all undressed . . .
And turned away, deeply incensed.

Now your slate pencil, to prove to all eras
That no man can call me brother any longer,
Engraves me trait for trait in stone and iron!
Then you severely repeat the old curse.

Oh, drag my picture out from the dark
Tabernacle, torn and disfigured!
Oh, place it with all its faults
In bright sunshine before the entire world!

What could one gather from the bodies of your martyrs
If they were dragged torn to the light?
Only how hard their rack had been—
One did not deem their wounds to have been sins![56]

Mea culpa! Similarly, Grillparzer let the King in *Die Jüdin von
Toledo* say, "We cripple them and are angry if they limp."
    A passage from Hebbel's diary from the time when he made the
acquaintance of Felix Bamberg shows that Hebbel was occasionally
seized by an anti-Jewish mood: "He is a Jew," he wrote, "but it is
lucky for his nation that I have come in touch with him; for my liberal
views about the Jews have changed in general and very much needed
support through acquaintance with respectable Jews."[57] In his diary a
few months before, Hebbel had remarked: "The emancipation of the
Jews under the conditions which the Jews prescribe would in the
further course of history lead to a crisis which would necessitate the
emancipation of the Christians."[58] Yet on several occasions Hebbel
pleaded for equality for the Jews and held it "beneficial in every
respect."
    When in 1848 the emancipation of the Jews was placed upon the
political agenda, Hebbel too took sides. In political reports, which he
wrote in those days for the noted *Augsburger Allgemeine Zeitung,* he
took issue with those who identified the "corrupt" press with the
"Jewish" press. "Jews like Christians," he wrote, "sin against reason
and history not because they are Jews or Christians, but because and
insofar as they are men without education and without knowledge. . . .

Therefore, one must guard against making an entire nation responsible for the excesses of a few single individuals who do not belong to it . . . unless one wants to arouse in the dull, prejudiced mass brutality of the most unlimited sort."[59]

Hebbel did not slacken in his attacks on the anti-Semites and in his defense of the Jews. What he thought about the Jewish problem emerged nowhere more clearly than in his masterly discussion in 1861 of two anti-Semitic brochures, a discussion which bore the following title: "The Jews and the German State." "Almost ten years ago," Hebbel wrote, "a thin brochure appeared in Augsburg, from a 'German,' as it said in the title, which set itself the task of giving an insight into the dangerous doings of the Jewish kin and thus saving Europe from certain catastrophe. 'Israel infandum scelus audet, morte piandum' (Israel dares commit an infamous crime which can be redeemed only by death), sounded the motto, and on hardly twenty and seven pages topics were discussed which once had called for volumes and which naturally found a treatment just as summary as it was brief. 'German and Hebrew. The domination of the Jews in the world. The Jews in Poland, Germany, Norway, etc. Two sorts of Jews. Open and secret Jews. Jewish conspiracy. The Jews as future nobility. Theater-Jews. Jews in journalism. Jews in Parliament. Frankfurt am Main, a warning example for all of Christendom!' The proof was also furnished completely by the bold accuser and the terrifying result emerged that there did not exist any mortal sin of which the descendants of Abraham were not capable and which they had not often committed. . . . His conclusion or rather his judicial opinion that one should wipe this damned race off the face of the earth or at least chase them out of Europe and at the very least out of Germany would therefore have been well justified and, considering the pathos with which it was announced, would have certainly aroused the governments from their slumber, if in his ardor, unfortunately, he had not forgotten that *superbia, avaritia, luxuria, ira . . . individia* [arrogance, avarice, luxury, ire, envy] were held duly in contempt by the remaining inhabitants of the planet and lacked victims. But herein his achievement was deficient and the Jews probably owe it to this circumstance that the worldly arm has not yet been raised against them. . . . "[60]

This criticism of anti-Semitism in Hebbel's later years shows that the playwright's early liberal views on Jews and Judaism had changed little. The crude post-revolutionary anti-Semitism had appeared to Hebbel "ridiculous" and "dirty"; the anti-Semitism of a more intellectually inclined Jew-hater ten years afterwards still seemed to him "false and unjust." He took anti-Semitism as an infallible symptom of intellectual narrowness. "His thinking," he remarked when meeting a Jew-hater, "moved within the most narrow sphere; when, for instance, he discovered one of my acquaintances to be a Jew, he spoke of it as if he had found out that he was a murderer."[61] According to Hebbel's own testimony, he broke with a friend because of the latter's anti-Semitism.[62]

Hebbel was to experience personally the recklessness of anti-Semitic calumnies. His close relations with Jews made him suspect in the eyes of some Bavarian anti-Semites, who summarily declared him to be a Jew. He was "counted as circumcised,"[63] as he himself related.

In Vienna Hebbel was to enter into a closer relationship with several Jews. The literary historian Adolf Bartels, a prolific anti-Semitic writer, asserted that he "gradually gained a position for himself in Vienna, partly with the help of young Jewish friends."[64] Intimate friendship over many years linked him with the Jewish authors Samuel Engländer and Emil Kuh. Hebbel called Samuel Engländer "remarkably important" and praised his "ingenuously visible style."

Engländer was Hebbel's closest friend before the Revolution. Emil Kuh came closest to him thereafter. Kuh had fallen in love with an actress and wished to adopt Christianity for her sake, to the great sorrow of his parents who were devoted to Judaism. Hebbel tried strenuously to dissuade Kuh. Like many educated Jews who ardently sought assimilation and tried to forget their Jewish past and associations, Kuh was filled with a kind of hatred for everything Jewish. This attitude found expression in a collection of his poems which he sent to Hebbel. The latter, confirming its arrival, replied: "I congratulate you on the publication of the poems, yet do not ask me to subscribe to your view on the Jews; for you know that many years ago I broke with a Christian friend when he uttered similar opinions. And then I think too highly of man . . . not to hold him capable of overcoming by the smallest moral effort the little hindrances which race may perhaps put in his way. Ponder these thoughts in their entire depth and reconcile yourself with your people. It does no good to tear oneself away from the soil to which one belongs, and I do not like to see you on this road."[65] Emil Kuh, however, had made up his mind to be baptized. Hebbel later remarked that he should be forgiven for his conversion "because he let water be poured upon his head out of love for a beautiful girl so that he could marry her." Yet, he remarked in this context, generally he "hated renegades." Another friend of Jewish ancestry was the later Austrian Minister of Justice Julius Glaser. Jointly with Emil Kuh he edited Hebbel's works after his death. The two men thus built the playwright his first monument.

Hebbel greatly esteemed Börne and Heine. In December 1836 he recommended Börne's work to Elise Lensing; he could not think of any "better reading." After Börne's death he wrote to her: "You will have learned from the papers that Börne has died. His death has stirred me painfully. However one may judge him, one will not deny him a noble, rich, and, in spite of all acidity, deeply refreshing mind, and still less manliness, courage, and the noble strength of self-sacrifice. He was more likeable with his defects than others with their virtues. . . ."[66] In 1843 Hebbel visited Heinrich Heine in Paris. "With Heine," he wrote, "one can talk about the deepest things, and I experienced again the joy of a discussion where one needed only to touch the other fellow, gently with the tip of the finger, if one wished to have one's very own thought rise from his mind . . . this is very rare."[67]

It was Heine's *Buch der Lieder* [Book of Songs] that made Hebbel revise his early critical judgment about the poet. After a penetrating analysis of Heine's humor Hebbel remarked conclusively: "One may come to the help of the eye, but not of the tongue. He who does not feel that songs like the "Fisher-Girl," the "Pilgrimage to Kevlaar," the "Sea-Lily," and others surpass entire volumes of didactic poems and similar ones, no one will be able to make him comprehend it."[68]

"JUDITH" AND "GENOVEVA"

In two great dramas, *Judith* and *Herodes und Mariamne,* Friedrich Hebbel chose Jewish history as a background. The two plays are in some ways also similar in content: both Judith and Mariamne feel offended in their human and womanly dignity, since Holofernes and Herodes respectively treat them as inferiors rather than as equals.

The Jews in Hebbel's *Judith* do not exhibit ideal traits but rather show human weaknesses. Against them the superman Holofernes stands out impressively. Although the great moment finds the Jews unprepared, the heroine Judith too is raised high above her race.

In Hebbel's drama *Genoveva* (1840–1841), the theme of which the poet borrowed from medieval legends, an old Jew appears in the last scene of the second act. Like Shakespeare's Shylock and Lenau's Tubal in *Savonarola,* the Jew of Hebbel's *Genoveva* is a violent hater. None of these is an ideal character like Lessing's Nathan; all harbor feelings of revenge in their hearts for the bitter injustice they have suffered. Yet Hebbel, like Shakespeare and Lenau, seems to comprehend the hatred of the Jew and makes it understandable. The

Jew of Hebbel's *Genoveva,* even with death staring him in the face, prefers cursing to praying.[69] Though people have often beaten him and humiliated him, he has remained silent. For he has longed "for disgrace and shame and undeserved torture"; they had been his "treasure," through which he had hoped to regain the liberty that Judea lost to Rome. The servants kill the Jew and leave his corpse to ravens and vultures. By stoning him to death they have filled "the measure of time" and the Jews' "sins" "have been paid for." "Come Christians," the old Jew sneers at them with his last breath, "stone me, yet hurry, hurry, hurry! Else I die."[70]

When Franz Dingelstedt, theater director in Munich, wished to cut the scene in *Genoveva* in which the old Jew appeared, Hebbel pleaded with him to save it: "Once again I wish to draw your attention to the Jew whom you already have condemned. I believe what makes an effect in this piece is the concentrated presentation of the Middle Ages, and they in a way are personified in the Jew."[71]

In the comedy *Der Diamant* [The Diamond] (1847), which he wrote immediately after *Genoveva,* Hebbel pictures the Jew Benjamin as a shrewd man who never forgets his advantage. Driven finally by mere greed, he swallows a stolen diamond rather than return it. With the exception of the royal family, however, and of the simple and honest peasant Jacob, all other persons of the comedy are just as cunning as Benjamin himself.

Though the literary historian Adolf Bartels claimed Hebbel for anti-Semitism, at the same time he denounced Hebbel's text for an opera—"A stone's throw or sacrifice for sacrifice,"[72] which he wrote for the composer Rubinstein but which Rubinstein did not set to music—as a "real Jewish piece." Bartels' anger was understandable, for the song of the Jewish wedding entertainer Joel was distinctly friendly to the Jews and hostile to anti-Semites:

If a little boy who went
To buy fruit has run away,
Surely, the Jew caught him
For the bloody Easter torture.

If before the sunrise
A melancholic toad
Plunges itself into a well,
The Jew has mixed the drink.

For he is the whipping boy,
Whom one beats with special pleasure,
Instead of the bad thief,
Because everywhere he is up to tricks.[73]

The situation of the Jews in the Austrian *Biedermeier* era up to the March Revolution of 1848 was one of slow improvements. Their advances, moderately encouraged by Metternich and Friedrich Gentz, in spite of the latter's early anti-Jewish attitude, were also reflected in a growing German-Jewish relationship. The Austrian poetry of Nikolaus Lenau and Anastasius Grün and the plays of Franz Grillparzer and Friedrich Hebbel mirror both the contemporary acceptance and the contemporary criticism of Jews; they furnish deep insights into their social and cultural role and the persistence of opposition to them but reveal at the same time the growing support of German Austrians for tolerance and emancipation.

PART IV

The Struggle for Equality in the Vormärz

For no other people, having learned how slavery hurts, will persecute brothers from blind prejudice.

—Karl Gutzkow

CHAPTER 11

Toward Jewish Emancipation

The New Age and German Jewry

After the French Revolution, there ensued a drift toward ultraconservatism everywhere in Europe. The historic pendulum swung from Revolution to Reaction. In the new era the liberties of the peoples of Europe were in a dismal state. Upon Austria and the German states the Austrian Chancellor Metternich bore down especially hard.

But the ideas of liberalism, democracy, and nationalism continued to make progress, and no successful policy could be based upon their mere suppression. The outbreak of Revolution, which struck France again in July 1830, as well as the progress of liberalism in England in the early thirties, sent reverberations across the Rhine into Germany. Once again the eyes of both the German people and of Germany's Jewry turned to the West.

The Congress of Vienna had assured all Christians of whatever denomination the enjoyment of civil and political rights in all states of the German Confederation. It had also held out the promise of civil betterment to those who professed the Jewish faith, though it made this contingent on the adoption of as uniform a procedure as possible, to be determined by the federal Assembly. Until such time as such a procedure was arrived at, the Jews were to retain the rights already granted them in the individual states. Prussia favored a solution of the Jewish question patterned after its own progressive model of 1812. Austria, with a recent liberal tradition going back to Joseph II's Edict of Toleration of 1782, and Hanover, where progressive British influence made itself felt, worked at the Congress of Vienna on a forward-looking draft. But with rivalry growing between Austria and Prussia and the German states apparently unwilling to bow to the pressure of the larger powers, the text finally adopted by the Congress was less than satisfactory. After what the Jewish historian S. M. Dubnow called the "era of the first emancipation," there followed in German Central Europe the setbacks of the Restoration and of Romanticism and thereafter the slow progress of the *Vormärz*. The latter was marked by unceasing disputes concerning the German Jews, during which the demand for equality was often drowned out by shrill hostile voices. In the history of Jewish emancipation in nineteenth-century Europe, Germany occupied a special place. Nowhere else was the debate about Jewish emancipation conducted for so long or with so much passion.

France and Germany represented striking contrasts in regard to the emancipation of the Jews. In France the law of November 11, 1791, conferred, at one stroke, unconditional equality on all French Jews. In Germany, with its multiplicity of states, emancipation was neither complete nor general. It turned out to be a long-drawn-out process, involving numerous relapses. In France the enlightened state, acting with deliberate speed, deprived the opposition of any opportunity of being heard throughout the country, thus diminishing its chances of success. In Germany the opposite was the case: during this period voices of dissent were loudly raised, while the voices of friendship and statesmanship often weakened. And German liberalism became tainted with lack of conviction and resolve in regard to Jewish emancipation.

The German Jews suffered in the age of Restoration. In many states their newly won freedoms were eroded. But in the early 1830s German liberalism resumed its forward march and began cautiously to plead for an improvement in the status of the Jews. German nationalists too, struggling to overcome provincial barriers and achieve political unity of the German people, linked arms with the forces of liberalism and democracy, welcomed Jewish aid, and began to give support to the cause of Jewish equality and freedom. Unburdened by centuries of local attachments and prejudices, the Jews adopted the German national point of view more readily and willingly than their Christian neighbors.

German liberalism of the *Vormärz* unfurled the flag of the Enlightenment and paid tribute to the ideals of freedom and the dignity of the individual. It demanded an end to the feudal order and feudal privileges and the replacement of the inherited establishment with new political and social institutions. It called for the equality of all before the law, the separation of church and state, and freedom of belief and conscience, all in the framework of a constitutional monarchy. This program logically included the emancipation of the Jews.

Liberal Shortcomings

Yet not all those who rallied to the banner of German liberalism during the *Vormärz* were prepared to live up to the liberal creed, to shed their own prejudices against the Jews and to disregard those of their constituents. The inconsistencies of the German liberals in regard to Jews and Judaism were perhaps more pronounced and widespread than in any other areas of liberal thought and practice. They revealed the shortcomings and weaknesses of the liberal movement and portended the meager aid German Jewry could expect from so hesitant an ally. Many liberals apparently held with Kant that Judaism was a "rigid framework [*Hülle*] of customs, rules and national hopes." According to this view, Judaism was not really a religious faith; German Christians could deny Jews "religious" freedom without compunction. This view of Judaism as being no true religion, or at least, as in Hegel's judgment, as representing an allegedly low state of religion, was entertained by a good number of German liberals. It was only a modern version of the centuries-old Christian belief of the inferiority of the Jews' religion. The secular credo of the German Enlightenment and of German liberalism in regard to Judaism did not differ markedly from the traditional faith of medieval Christianity: thus Judaism was still relegated to lower levels of religious development.

Not only Judaism as a religion but also individual Jews were considered by many German liberals as below par. The liberal leaders in southern Germany, K. Rotteck, C. Welcker, and the theologian H. E. Paulus, though great admirers of the advanced social and political institutions of Western Europe, reflected in their attitude toward the Jews a policy of hesitancy, if not of appeasement, in regard to the prejudices of the mass of the population, peasants and artisans. Rotteck denied the Jews emancipation, since their religion was "hostile to other nations" (*völkerfeindlich*). Paulus in his work *Die jüdische Nationalabsonderung* [The Jewish National Separation] (1831) similarly blamed the Jews for the continuing separation, rather than the Germans for withholding equality. Such opinions were part of the reactionary echo to the 1830 revolution which was widely heard in the states of the German Confederation and also resounded in the liberal camp.

According to the theologian Paulus, as long as Jews, in accordance with the rabbinical and Mosaic faith, remained Jewish, they could not receive civil rights in any state, since they considered themselves a nationality distinct from all other peoples. The Jews would have to prove that in each country in which they lived, "each [!] Jewish inhabitant belonged only to that nationality, and to no other."

Paulus admitted that there was an "enigmatic contradiction" in that no "thoughtful person" would wish another human being to be discriminated against on account of religion; still one could not contemplate, "without many doubts," the admission of Jews to the offices of a judge, state official, professor of law, etc. Paulus seemed satisfied that the inequality of the Jews could be terminated only "by virtue of their own decision." Citizens of the Jewish or Moslem faith or heathens could not have equal claims to civil, military, and church offices in Christian states. "The more we are governed in a Christian manner, the better."

Only in some parts of Germany did the new bourgeoisie act in accordance with its general liberal professions. In the Prussian Rhineland the spokesmen of the liberal middle class in the *Landtag* demanded the emancipation of the Jews in 1843. Rhenish particularism and Catholicism, fighting the Prussian government, saw in the Jews an ally against Berlin. The Catholic Church of the Rhineland supported emancipation of the Jews; it hoped that equality for the Jews would establish a beachhead in the struggle against the "German-Christian," meaning Protestant, principles of the Prussian state and bring about equality also for Catholics. This agitation in behalf of the Jews failed, however, due to the unyielding resistance of the Prussian king Frederick William IV.

Jewish Religion, Nationality, and Equality

During the nineteenth century, Jews consistently and overwhelmingly denied that they were a nationality; they considered themselves primarily, if not exclusively, a religious community, held together by common religious-ceremonial conceptions and by a history of enforced separation and persecution. Some enemies of Judaism and Jews, such as the theologian Paulus, looked upon them as a culturally and ethnically alien group and scorned amalgamation, whether through conversion, mixed marriages, or cultural assimilation. Others, though hostile to Judaism as a religion, opened the doors of *Deutschheit* (Germanism) to individual Jews who embraced Christianity.

Whatever the true character of Judaism, liberal Germans were often impatient with it and its adherents and their continued survival as a group. They looked with intolerance upon the non-German elements in their midst. The prevalent concept of the nation-state, which Germans increasingly embraced, required cultural and ethnic conformity from all inhabitants. The concept of basic and equal rights for national minorities lay in the distant future. And the ideas about the Jews of most liberal and radical Germans—not to mention conservative Germans—strongly suggested their cultural submergence and the ultimate demise in Germany. All this was bound to affect the self-image of German Jews, to exacerbate their defensive attitude, and to increase their insistence that theirs was simply a religious association.

Most German liberals backed the German national movement; liberalism and nationalism complemented each other. Some among the national-minded liberals, however, accused the Jews not only of being a special ethnic group—strongly implying that, as long as they remained one, equality was out of the question—but sporadically even introduced the concept of a special Jewish "race." Representative Mittelmayer in the Chamber of Deputies in Baden spoke on June 3, 1831, of the "peculiarity of Jewish racial purity."

As nationalists, German liberals tolerated no competition between German patriotism and allegiance to an alien nationality—for instance, the Jewish one. Nineteenth-century national thought strenuously rejected the notion of a two-fold loyalty or the multiple loyalties of a pluralistic society. The less willing the liberals were to grant complete equality to the Jews, the higher the pricetag they attached to emancipation—namely the ultimate renunciation of the Jews' cultural identity. German Jews may have held erroneous conceptions as to the true character of this identity (which in essence was both national and religious), but many of them instinctively clung to their right to nourish their distinctive culture. They tried to ward off all attempts to have it obliterated by progressive and liberal "kindness," by the hidden intolerant bent of the ideology of the nation-state, or by harsh admonitions, just as in earlier centuries they had resisted annihilation through outright persecution.

Though German liberals moved only gradually toward democratic concepts, long remaining critical of the German masses as likely to be irresponsible, some sought refuge behind seemingly modern notions of democracy, popular sovereignty, and even "human rights" in order to rationalize their delays in regard to Jewish emancipation. The liberal deputy from Hanover, Professor Friedrich Dahlmann, was convinced that emancipation of the Jews constituted a political risk that was not permissible in view of the weaknesses of German society. It was partly fear of the German masses which made the wealthy and educated progressive German bourgeoisie proceed cautiously in the matter of Jewish emancipation, to prevent the outbreak of social disturbance which might engulf the entire German people.

Early in the nineteenth century Wilhelm von Humboldt had re-

248 The Struggle for Equality in the Vormärz

jected the course of political gradualism in favor of immediate and full emancipation of the Jews. Gradualism tied the legislative process to the necessarily slow advancement in "education" toward equal citizenship. But during the *Vormärz* the friends of the Jews and champions of their emancipation turned to gradualism as the only realistic alternative—an unmistakable sign of the relapse which had occurred. As the First Chamber of Hessen-Darmstadt was told by the government in 1823, it was the latter's intention to "pursue meticulously that gradual course, that must never be overlooked in the development of human capacities, and thus attain its goal by a longer, perhaps, but all the safer route." In fact, the longer route ultimately turned out to be neither a "safer" nor a surer route toward the goal of full and irrevocable emancipation.

The "Christian-German" State and Frederick William IV

While the religion of reason had thrust differences between traditional religions into the background, Romanticism strengthened the pre-revolutionary religious foundations of the state. And in 1840 with the accession to the Prussian throne of Frederick William IV, "the Romantic on the throne of the Caesars," the Christian-German theory of the state was loudly proclaimed.* The monarch dreamed of a European, of a universal mission for Protestant Prussia. The state was to be strengthened from within by the church. Once again the Jew was to be excluded and emancipation pushed into the distant future.

The new stress on German nationality in close alliance with Christianity did not close the door to individual Jews who took baptism. Many Jews, impatient and despondent about obtaining equality, were willing to embrace Christianity as the price for being accepted into the German state and German society. And even well-meaning Christians, unconvinced that Judaism had much to offer to Jews either politically or spiritually, encouraged their individual conversion. It was ironic that such recommendations of baptism emanated frequently from those who, in principle, extolled tolerance, favored a cosmopolitan outlook, and were skeptical of many, if not most, religious doctrines. But they held Judaism to be morally stunted—a position hardly different from that of the medieval church, which had looked upon the Jews as backward and stubborn (*verstockt*). Many

---

*For a discussion of the implications of this concept for the Jews see Friedrich Julius Stahl in Chapter 16.

liberal Germans, new theologians, freethinkers, and atheists may have kept their distance from, or may even have repudiated, the church, but, where Jews and Judaism were concerned, they often shared old-fashioned attitudes, in particular traditional anti-Semitism, which was intricately linked with it.

AGAINST METTERNICH AND THE ROTHSCHILDS

Liberals judged Jews and Judaism not only from the theological point of view, but also on the basis of political and economic pragmatism. To many liberal authors the ultraconservative system Metternich had devised, which was based upon the suppression of popular movements, deserved sharp condemnation. So did the Rothschild family, which was known to be well disposed to the Austrian Chancellor and had lent support to his government through extensive loans. Jewish writers themselves, such as Moritz Hartmann, Karl Beck, and Ludwig Börne, sharply attacked the Rothschild brothers and other wealthy Jews as Metternich's financial allies. Ludwig Börne condemned the Rothschild family as the "greatest brokers for all government loans, who furnish the princes with the power to resist freedom."[1]

Many German writers also criticized the Rothschilds. Inveighing against wealthy Jews meant unleashing an attack in the direction of least resistance. The Rothschilds and other rich Jews may have been influential, but they were never powerful, never entrenched, always vulnerable. Criticism of Jewish wealth was often tainted by anti-Semitism. Many of the liberal and radical writers who launched these attacks or joined the anti-Semitic chorus would have indignantly denied that they gave expression to even latent anti-Jewish sentiments, but knowingly or not, they contributed to the spread of anti-Semitism throughout Central Europe.

Among those who sharply attacked the "Jewish moneyed power of our age" was the historian Christoph Schlosser, generally not a hater of Jews. He castigated rich Jews like the Rothschilds, who "fight everything noble" and resort to "crude, bribed violence" against the new generation.[2] Sharp criticisms of "Jewish moneyed power" were also uttered by the Austrian poets Anastasius Grün[3] and Nikolaus Lenau,[4] both of whom were generally friendly to the Jews.

JEWISH WEALTH

By pillorying wealthy Jews, these critics stirred up dislike and hatred against Jews at a time when the old anti-Semitism was not yet buried. This tended to revive the old prejudices and to give them a new "liberal," respectable garb. The development of a more favorable, friendly attitude toward the Jews among the liberal German intelligentsia was thus stunted. The picture of German-Christian reaction in closest embrace with Jewish finance seemed to make a strong impression on the nascent liberal and the more radical democratic movement.[5] That this same German reaction and ultraconservatism condemned the mass of the Jews to live in misery, in a state of legal inequality, was scarcely noticed by many German democrats and radicals.

Many Jews had attained positions of power and prestige in the growing economy of the German states and Austria. Envy and competition attributed their economic successes to sharp business practices. Even liberal authors such as Franz Dingelstedt[6] and Hoffman von Fallersleben pointed accusingly to their "usury."[7] The young dramatist Georg Büchner alluded in an episode of his dramatic fragment *Wozzeck* to the alleged general Jewish greed for money,[8] and Wilhelm Hauff in his *Memoiren des Satan* described how "the Jewish money devil" seized Rebekkah, the Jewish salon lady of little refinement.[9] The Austrian poet Anastasius Grün, however, defended the Jews against these reproaches. Thus he lets the Jew in the *Schutt* retort:

> You scold that we turn our eyes to Mammon;
> As we are seeking him, you seek him too!
> You merely grope clumsily after him;
> We beckon with a light magic rod.[10]

The German-Jewish poet Karl Beck expressed the same thought in his poem "Der Trödeljude" [The Jewish Peddler]. The Christian, he held, did "not bear ill will" against the Jews on account of misdeeds against Jesus.

> He bears a grudge against you until death,
> Because your hand acquires gold
> and goods more rapidly and luckily.[11]

On the whole the economic role of Jewry, important as it was in Germany's economic life, was greatly exaggerated, while the misery of numerous Jews was widely ignored. The Christian-German writer Eduard Beurmann, like Wilhelm von Humboldt before him, mercilessly inveighed against those Germans who masked their intolerance with their pretended fear of the Jews. "I do not believe," he wrote, "that anybody fears a Judean Reich in Germany; I do not believe that Rothschild is planning to ascend the vacant Jewish throne. . . . Oh no! You know it well indeed, you scholarly, Christian orthodox, book-learned, consistorial professors, you know it very well that Germany has nothing to fear from the people of Israel; you know as well that the Jews won't eject the Germans from Germany, that Germany will never become Jewish. Israel in Germany, however, wishes to become German, not only in name, but also in every civil form, and then you pore over the Bible and the Talmud, the Christian teachings and Judaism, the intellectual emancipation and nationality, briefly all scholarly moss-clad, moldy intolerance, only to prove that the Jews can never become Germans in Germany, that they must remain eternally Jews."[12]

"Judaization" of Germany?

The enemies of the Jews persisted, however, in conjuring up before the eyes of the German people the imaginary menace of Jewish domination of Germany as well as the threat of a "Judaization" of the Germans. Alexander von der Marwitz had done so on the eve of the War of Liberation. About two decades later Wolfgang Menzel's denunciation of several contemporary writers, grouped together under the name *Jungdeutschland* (Young Germany), as a "Young Palestine" opened one of the main anti-Semitic offensives against Judaism. This slur by the literary critic was the less excusable since the great majority of the young liberals referred to as *Jungdeutsche* were German-Christian writers. Wolfgang Menzel accused them of spreading subversive and immoral ideas and the reactionary Bundestag in Frankfurt am Main responded to his denunciation by promptly prohibiting any further publication of their writings.

Menzel's crusade against *Jungdeutschland* made a considerable impression upon Prince Metternich. The Austrian Chancellor likewise gave the fight against the Young German writers an anti-Jewish twist, though only in private. Though Metternich himself did not share any anti-Semitic bias, in the case of the Young German authors the temptation to capitalize on anti-Jewish prejudice proved to be too strong for him to resist.

When the liberal government of Württemberg protested against Austria's proposal at the diet of the German Confederation to suppress the works of the Young German authors, Metternich instructed the Austrian envoy in Stuttgart to bring his powers of persuasion to bear upon the government of Württemberg. "Your Excellency knows," he wrote to the Austrian envoy, "that the matter in question concerns a number of young immoral literates, partly of Jewish ancestry." In the same spirit, reflecting Metternich's stand, the Austrian envoy to the Vatican voiced in a letter to the Viennese chancery his gratification over the resolute move against the "bels esprits du Nord de l'Allemagne"; they were in close association with other writers "qui ont abjuré le Talmoud."[13] The myth of the Jewish origin of a majority of the Young German writers was in full swing.

In reality, neither Heinrich Heine nor Ludwig Börne belonged to the Young German group, though its members, like many others, admired both men. The reactionary diet had not included Börne's writings in its ban against the Young Germans. As far as Heine was concerned, he jested that the German government, against his will, had employed him jointly with the Young Germans and that he often had requested his release, without avail.[14] Even the anonymous anti-Semitic author of the pamphlet *Jeune Allemagne* (Stuttgart, 1836), which was sharply critical of the Young German writers, virtually acquitted Heine. Heine, he wrote, could "certainly not know that people would admire and imitate, even exaggerate him to this extent, and therefore I am far from burdening him with all the sins of his following."[15]

It was the propagation of a liberal political and social philosophy that aroused opposition against the Young Germans, and it was on this ground that they were persecuted. To destroy their effectiveness among the German public, they were also accused of being Jews or of Jewish descent. The Young German writers recognized the main source of these attacks. "The general storm which mounted against Young Germany was partly stirred up by anti-Semitism,"[16] Gutzkow aptly wrote. Once again, Jews were dragged into a struggle which was not theirs to face public anger and vilification.

Actually, notes critical of the Jews and Judaism vibrated audibly through the Young German orchestra. Although Gutzkow pleaded for Jewish emancipation, he often censured the Jews and once even caused his friend Gabriel Riesser, the leading proponent of the Jews and their emancipation, to enter the arena as his opponent. The Young German Theodor Mundt ridiculed in *Madonna: Konversationen mit einer Heiligen* [Madonna: Conversations with a Saint] the uncouth Jewish parvenus "Itzig son" and "Itzig father" because neither showed appreciation for the beauties of nature, and he scoffed at their Yiddish language and "half-emancipation."[17] Another Young German, Alexander Count von Württemberg, was a distinct foe of the Jews. In his work "Ahasver and Bonaparte," the Eternal Jew, an orthodox servant of Jehovah, shields the Corsican conqueror, in order to embarrass, through him, the Christian nations. While the critic Wolfgang Menzel assailed the "Israelitic-French Party"[18] and Young Germany, allegedly allied with it, Alexander Count von Württemberg attacked Frenchmen and Jews together and claimed to discern in the drives of Napoleonic France to subdue Europe "Jewish" plans for the domination of the world!

Blows fell upon German Jewry from all sides, both Right and Left. The Jews found themselves thrust into the very center of a primarily literary struggle of their host people, though it had apparent social and political overtones. Anxious to improve their lot and to secure liberty and equality, German Jews were frequently puzzled about the nature of the attacks that were directed against them and about the offenses they supposedly had committed. Their cardinal sin was being different from Germans in religion, culture, and appearance.

These very differences made them a target for the Germans. Since many Germans also hated the French, contemporaries such as Wolfgang Menzel and Alexander von Württemberg went one step further and tried to identify Jews with Frenchmen. This fashion appeared to be general and widespread. The anonymous author of *Jeune Allemagne* (1836) gave, characteristically, a French designation to the group of Young German writers to draw attention to their pretended un-German character. "Frenchmen and Jews," he complained, "stir the unholy fire which consumes our best strength. . . . " He reached the conclusion that the Young Germans "unquestionably" must be Jews and Frenchmen.[19]

While many bridges spanned the deep waters that divided the German and Jewish worlds, the prejudice that separated the two peoples was like a wild stream that grew to menacing dimensions in stormy weather. As Karl Gutzkow remarked, "an abyss lay between Judaism and Christianity"[20] which none could easily overcome. In his words, the fear and shyness of the child, the envy and jealousy of the adult, had to be conquered before a German Christian could safely reach the other shore.

Old Fears and Old Hatreds

It was very revealing that Theodor Mundt, looking by chance at the "terrible"[21] Hebrew letters, which seemed so mysterious to him, was seized by a sort of "fear of ghosts"! Many Germans dreaded what appeared to them alien in German Jewry. Most of them never rid themselves in their later life of a religiously colored anti-Semitism based upon early childhood stories of Jewish culpability for Jesus' crucifixion. Gutzkow, for instance, related in his memoirs *Aus meiner Knabenzeit* that the Jew was first "a word of terror" to the child. (Goethe had similarly described his early fear of the Jew in *Dichtung und Wahrheit*.) Even later, when Gutzkow had learned to know Jews better, the picture of the crucifixion of Christ by their ancestors did not entirely vanish from his mind. "The hatred against Jews," Gutzkow frankly admitted, "had already been instilled into us Christians, when we learned to read. At the first religious instruction in the Bible we saw how Christianity sharply separated itself from Judaism. . . . Briefly, the dislike of the Jew by the Christian is a physical and moral idiosyncrasy which is as hard to conquer as the repugnance which some feel against blood and insects. But it is this way and it will vanish perhaps only through the emancipation. The disgrace strikes home at the prejudice of our parents, the carelessness of our educators, the curse of two thousand years of the historic past."[22]

Although many of the authors of the *Vormärz* and public opinion in general grew friendlier to the Jews, the shrill voice of anti-Semitism was clearly audible in the works of poets, playwrights, and novelists such as Hauff and Platen, Fallersleben and Dingelstedt, men of thought and action such as Bruno Bauer and the younger Friedrich List. Hatred of Jews and opposition to them were alive also in this era, in spite of a steady progress of liberal ideas. Old philosophies vanished and new classes and ideas emerged, but anti-Semitism remained the steady pole in the "flux of phenomena."

In the period of the War of Liberation and thereafter, social prejudices had been banished from the salons of Berlin and Vienna, where German statesmen and artists, diplomats and poets, aristocrats and financial magnates, had freely mingled with Jews and with the charming and intelligent Jewish hostesses. Outside the salons, however, exclusion continued. In his contemporary satire *Memoiren des Satan,* Wilhelm Hauff let Ahasver say: "I believe it is part of the curse which hangs over me that I become ridiculous as soon as I dare to enter higher spheres of society."[23] Though the writer ridiculed the Jewish parvenu, he poured bitter mockery upon his own people too. Theodor Mundt in his work *Madonna* similarly derided the unrefined newly rich Jews.[24] Wilhelm Müller, the philhellenic poet of the Greek songs, described in the poem "Der ewige Jude" the lonely Ahasver in his suffering and repentance, as he is shunned by all.[25] Ahasver's experience reflected the continuing isolation of Jews in many parts of Germany.

Yet neither the uncouth parvenu who intruded into the best society nor the loner, shy and withdrawn, was the prevailing type among the German Jews of the period. German Jewry in the age of Romanticism and the *Vormärz* lived in increasingly close social and intellectual contact with the Germans. Gutzkow praised in his *Rückblicke* [Memoirs] the "great importance of Berlin's Jewry for German culture in general and for art and literature in particular." The Jewry of Berlin, he wrote, "was once the most exclusive society, guarding and preserving the classical tradition as well as reflecting the continuous agitation and fermentation of the age."[26] The social and intellectual life of the time pulsated in its circles, and divisive prejudices were looked upon with little forbearance. But the meeting of minds at the highest social and intellectual level did not bridge the gulf that still separated Germans and Jews on other social and cultural levels.

Emancipation in the realm of ideas continued to make progress during the *Vormärz* but without attaining its fulfillment. In the eyes of Theodor Mundt and others the liberation of the Jews was only "half" achieved.[27] A few Germans pleaded for full equality of the Jews. Many, however, wished to preserve the status quo, while some even wanted to send them back into the ghetto. But on the whole, both German Jews as well as many German liberals inclined to be optimistic, underestimating the strength of the forces of reaction and the depth of anti-Jewish feelings among broad segments of the German people.

Anti-Jewish agitation in the 1830s and 1840s was fostered by, and addressed to, members of the most diverse social and economic strata of the German people. Merchants of the upper class, master craftsmen, and small merchants all took part in these anti-Jewish propagandistic activities. Similarly anti-Jewish were artisans, who organized exclusive organizations such as the participants in the Frankfurt congress of tailors. Karl Marlo-Winkelblech, who organized the congress of artisans and trade employees in 1848, opposed equality for the Jews and spurned parliamentarianism as identical with "Jewish moneyed aristocracy."[28] These populist groups continued the tradition of Frankfurt's anti-Semites, such as the "democrats" Friedrich Funk, author of the *Eulenspiegel* (1832) and Wilhelm Sauerwein, who in 1831 had published the tract *Beleuchtung der Judenemanzipation: Ein Wort an das Volk*. In Hamburg, artisans in union with German disciples of the French utopian socialist Charles Fourier unleashed through pamphlets and dailies a Christian-German attack on both capitalism and the Jews.

Before, during, and after 1848–1849, conservatives too aimed at winning partisans to their cause by exploiting anti-Semitism. In Catholic Bavaria, Pius Clubs and Leagues for Constitutional Monarchy and Religious Freedom roused artisans against the Jews in 1849. In the countryside, according to reports of the police, peasants were incited to follow the example of the anti-Semitic city mob and "move against the Jews." When Jewish emancipation was debated in the Rhenish *Landtag* in 1843, one H. E. Marcard of Westphalia engaged in anti-Jewish agitation with a pietist Jew-hater, V. A. Huber. Marcard claimed that the Jews derided the Christian faith; he even attempted to revive the myth of the Jewish desecration of the host. Accusations that Christian blood was spilled for alleged ceremonial purposes were heard again in the Rhineland in 1834 and led to outrages and excesses. In a report of the Prussian Minister of the Interior of 1844, Silesian district authorities were urged to supervise priests, for "they incited against the Jews."

Anti-Semitism thus asserted itself vigorously during the *Vormärz*, reaching from the heights of the German intellect down to the very bottom of society.

Jungdeutsche and "Young Palestine"

Wolfgang Menzel

The contradictions of the era of the *Vormärz* and its ambivalence toward the Jews are well reflected in the changing attitudes of Wolfgang Menzel to Jews and their cause of legal and social equality. Menzel, the "literary pope" of Württemberg—as the noted critic was derisively called by some of his opponents—and originally a liberal, was at first by no means the Jew-hater that he later revealed himself to be. The leading Jewish proponent of the emancipation of his people, Gabriel Riesser, wrote later in his *Jüdische Briefe zur Abwehr und zur Verständigung* [Jewish Letters for Defense and Understanding]: "I am not inclined to deny the gratitude which I have come to owe this man from earlier times not only in my own behalf, but in the name of all my coreligionists. He has pleaded the cause of civil equality of the Jews as a writer and as the people's representative, and, especially in the first-named capacity, with rare warmth and enthusiasm." Menzel's "support in this matter" had been very much appreciated.[1]

The young Menzel had been an ardent member of the *Burschenschaften* and admirer of Jahn and had early exhibited some anti-Jewish disposition. But after shedding his youthful exuberances and ideological vagaries, he had come to support the emancipation of the Jews. In several articles of his *Literary Magazine* in 1833, he also had highly praised Heinrich Heine and Ludwig Börne. At that time he still enthusiastically admired the "free-born sun child" Heine and scoffed at Börne's anti-Semitic foes, who "fear the little Jew and move against him into the field with spear and sticks like the seven Swabians against the young hare at Bodensee."[2] He vigorously attacked the enemies of the Jews and criticized most sharply the anti-Semitic "screamers,"[3] whose leader he was later to become. "The old rabbi who burned himself and his entire family in his own house could be judged happier," he wrote in regard to Heine, "than a contemporary highly gifted author of Jewish ancestry. The more witty he is, the more human, the more he is above every prejudice, the more certain it is that the dogs of all Christian-German capitals run after him and condemn him to the lifelong spiritual murder of having to keep dogs against his wish. Lessing's amiable wisdom has not been appreciated; people hardly remember that *Nathan* has ever been written—Nathan, compared to whom the great fighter for light and right in Heidelberg [Paulus] plays no better role than the patriarch. But how shall wisdom and love of humanity reach the people, where such demagogues of mob wisdom confuse the natural sense for nobility and justice. I consider it a sacred duty as a German, as a Christian, as a human being of the nineteenth century, to oppose them. If ultimately we do not return to the Jews their human rights undiminished, we deserve to lose ours for eternity."[4]

Even if men like Heine and Börne at times erred, Menzel continued, "there is still so much nobility in them, so much of the sacred poetic fire which shines through the centuries, and in their mistakes is so much of the spirit of the age, that the noblest judge, when they appear before him, will rise to pay respects to their genius. The literary rabble clamoring 'Hep! Hep!' should deservedly be thrown out of the house."[5] Strangely enough, the same man who condemned anti-Semitism, pilloried its practitioners, and demonstrated both unusual perception and a keen sense of justice soon thereafter leveled sharp accusations against the Jews in the worst anti-Semitic manner.

"For several years now, uninterruptedly," Gabriel Riesser charged in 1837, Menzel had hurled many an invective "as poisonous as they are unjust" against the Jews.[6] Menzel's attacks against German Jewry began in earnest in 1835. Simultaneously, he also turned his back on liberalism and, like many an overzealous neophyte, denounced the Young German authors to the reactionary German diet at Frankfurt am Main. His political transformation as well as his growing hostility to Goethe went hand in hand with his aggressive outbursts against the Jews. Menzel's bizarre dislike of Jews, Frenchmen, and Goethe together made him perform logical somersaults. Believing Jews and Frenchmen to be allies, he thundered against the "Israelitic-French party."[7] Then again he thought he had discovered a kinship between Goethe and the Jews and leveled bitter accusations against both.

Goethe and the Jews appeared to Menzel the real culprits in the death of the unfortunate Charlotte Stieglitz, which had made a considerable impression upon contemporaries. In 1834 this beautiful and talented woman, who happened to be a great admirer of Goethe, had committed suicide. Decades before, Goethe's youthful work *Die Leiden des jungen Werthers* [Werther's Sufferings] had caused a wave of suicides. According to Menzel, Goethe's guilt in this case was thus "proven" beyond any doubt. And Goethe's fame, of course, had been spread by Jews. In Menzel's distorted view, they too were thus responsible for the tragic end of Charlotte Stieglitz!

Menzel had never forgiven Karl Gutzkow, once his literary "adjutant," for turning his back on his teacher. When the twenty-four-year-old Gutzkow published his much-debated novel *Wally, die Zweiflerin* [The Doubtress] (1835), which was said to preach not only atheism but also the "emancipation of the flesh,"[8] Menzel declared open war against him and soon thereafter Gutzkow's book was prohibited.

Just as previously Menzel had added an anti-Jewish dimension to his criticism of Goethe, he now vented anti-Jewish feelings while fighting the *Jungdeutschen*. The attack on them and on Gutzkow in particular merged in his mind with the struggle against Jewry. Casual and incidental connections of the Young German authors with Jews led him to assert that they had forged an alliance. In *Wally, die Zweiflerin* Gutzkow had pictured a Jewish woman among many other characters, and he had also written a short story entitled "Der Sadduzäer von Amsterdam" [The Sadducean of Amsterdam]. All this served to "discredit" him in Menzel's eyes, making him appear a close associate and friend of the Jews. Gabriel Riesser charged that Menzel "used the hatred of Jews as a weapon against his mortal literary foes, as he successfully used the political fears of the rulers for the same purpose."[9]

Menzel specifically accused the Young German authors Gutzkow, Laube, Mundt, Kühne, Wienbarg—Christian Germans all—of being either of Jewish descent or at least closely affiliated with Jews. On October 23, 1835, six weeks after his public denunciation of *Jungdeutschland*—at which time Jews had not yet been singled out—Menzel referred to Gutzkow and Wienbarg with these words: "I should like to know what advantage the Jews expect from such literary lackeys in the somewhat delicate question of their emancipation, since one hears everywhere that the so-called Young Germany was really a Young Palestine and since all loathsomeness, which lies in the unlimited importunity, in the Gallomania, in the malicious impotent hate of Germans and Christians in the new propaganda of Frankfurt,* is generally blamed on Judaism." These imputations were as false as

*Meaning Frankfurt Jews.

they were unfair. Menzel made no effort to dispel these deceptions of public opinion; on the contrary, he seemed to endorse the prejudicial views.

At the very moment when he coined the slogan "Young Palestine"—which provided the spark that rekindled anti-Jewish sentiment—he reminded his readers that he had earlier pleaded in behalf of the Jews: "It is well known to all with how much ardor I have always taken up the cause of that [Jewish] emancipation."[10] While Menzel did not now directly criticize emancipation, his intemperate attacks were bound to block the road to full equality.

Menzel's "almost incomprehensible inconsequences" in his attitude toward the Jews puzzled many contemporaries, including Jewish writers such as J. Weil and Berthold Auerbach.[11] Ludwig Börne ridiculed him as a "Juden- und Franzosenfresser" (one who devoured Jews and Frenchmen), and Gabriel Riesser accused him of having discovered "a magic formula" by means of which every political opponent could be defeated—namely by denouncing him as a Jew, irrespective of the truth. Whatever hateful phenomena could be observed or invented in politics, aesthetics, or religion, according to Riesser, Menzel proclaimed them to be "Jewish" and "ascribed [them] to the Jewish character, Jewish hatred, Jewish occupancy, Jewish impudence, etc."[12]

In a study on Menzel in 1952, E. Schuppe pointed to Menzel's foreign policy ideas of German expansion, his endorsement of imperialism and war, and his frequent expressions of racism. All this, added to his persistent later attacks against the Jews, marked him as a forerunner of National Socialism.[13]

The Novels of Karl Gutzkow and Ahasver Poetry

Wolfgang Menzel had abused Karl Gutzkow as a "lackey" of Jewry. From the other side Gutzkow had been reproached for his overly critical attitude toward the Jews which some interpreted as anti-Semitic. A man of wide reading, a playwright and journalist, historian and student of politics, philosopher, theologian, and literary historian, Gutzkow was also a man of character and conviction. Increasingly involved in literary and political struggles, he frequently quarreled even with his friends, including Jewish writers. Though throughout most of his life he battled courageously and steadfastly for the emancipation of the Jews, differences with some of his Jewish friends over means and methods gave rise to suggestions that Gutzkow inclined to anti-Semitism. Close friends ridiculed such accusations, but Gutzkow himself was puzzled and irritated and became rather embittered.

In *Wally, die Zweiflerin,* Caesar, the hero of the novel, leaves Wally and marries Delphine, a Jew and the only appealing character in the work. The remarks made by Wally about the marriage of Caesar and Delphine seemed to lend ammunition to the anti-Semitic agitation which arose over the book. In fact, it appears that Gutzkow saw in intermarriage a way toward reconciliation of the differences between the two religions and their adherents.

Joel Jacoby, a former friend of Gutzkow and fellow traveler of Gutzkow and other radical writers, became in the late thirties a turncoat, deeply involved in clandestine activities in behalf of the Prussian government. Gutzkow painted a highly unfavorable portrait of him in the third book of his novel *Seraphine.* He denounced the spinelessness and treachery of the character; the circumstance that the man in the novel happened to be a Jew was, as the literary historian Heinrich Houben thought, quite coincidental.

In 1838 discussion of the Jewish question shifted from its practical and secular aspects to a seemingly abstruse theological and literary theme by focusing on Ahasver, the Eternal Jew. Poems and plays on the Eternal Jew and Jewish suffering became the fashion of the day. In earlier years Ahasver had been paid tribute by numerous writers, such as Klingermann in his drama *Ahasver* (1827), Duller in *Antichrist,* B. Auerbach in *Spinoza,* and the Frenchman Edgar Quinet in *Ahasverus* (1834). As Gutzkow disclosed in his *Rückblicke* [Memoirs], he himself was for some time susceptible to influences of the contemporary literary style, the so-called *Judenschmerz* (pain of Jewish suffering), which to a large extent was identical with the Ahasverus cult. Gutzkow apparently felt personally attracted to the figure of Ahasver, considering himself like the Eternal Jew in having been expelled and persecuted since his early youth. He welcomed in the *Telegraph* "Klagen des Juden" [Lamentations of the Jew] by Joel Jacoby, and the following year published a longer essay about what was perhaps the most important of all Ahasver epics, the work by Julius Mosen.

But it became increasingly clear to Gutzkow that logical separation of the poetic theme of Ahasver from analysis of the contemporary Jewish problem had become imperative. Some of the younger Jewish writers, driven by both conviction and self-interest and often as passionate and irreverent as Gutzkow himself, were to question his views on the proper method of achieving equality.[14] The dispute generated verbal fireworks which deepened their differences.

Gutzkow was not alone in criticizing the superabundance of Ahasver poems and lamentations over past Jewish oppression being produced by both Jewish and Christian writers. Other contemporaries, among them the German novelist Karl Immermann, were likewise irritated at what they believed was a sentimental turning back of enlightened Jews to Judaism, a resurgence of Jewish interest in their own historic and cultural roots. The hero of Immermann's novel *Münchhausen* hears in his dream one Jew talking to the other: "That they have given us citizenship, that is now the sorrow of our people; they paint pictures about sorrow and write verses about it."[15] The noted Hamburg physician Dr. Steinheim, himself a Jew and a personal friend of Gutzkow, spoke similarly about the repulsion he felt when reading Jacoby's "Klagen eines Juden." Other Jews, however, may have interpreted these criticisms to represent anti-Semitic sentiments or a striking indifference toward past Jewish suffering or an apparent inclination to preserve such inequality as still existed. While Gutzkow's attitude toward the Ahasver theme, judged from an aesthetic, political, and tactical point of view, was quite comprehensible, he overlooked the fact that in the eyes of many the issue had become fused with the Jews' struggle for equality, though logically it was quite distinct from it.

Gutzkow's critical essay on Ahasver appeared in the *Telegraph* in August 1838.[16] He was apparently not unsympathetic to the idea of creating a "modern" Ahasver but believed that the conception both Jewish and Christian poets entertained of the Eternal Jew was too narrow and unrelated to the problems of the age. Ahasver's crime, Gutzkow pointed out, was the crime of an egotist who judged matters only by standards of success; he mocked Jesus at the moment of his apparent failure. The Eternal Jew represented "the evil in Judaism"— which still delayed the emancipation. All this was accompanied by sharp and unjust stabs which were bound to arouse amazement and bitterness in the Jewish camp and especially among his Jewish friends in Hamburg, with whom he was intimately linked.

Gutzkow found himself compelled to write a postscriptum in the *Telegraph* in which he recalled that he had always lent his pen to the struggle for Jewish emancipation. To oppose it revealed both heartlessness and lack of political acumen. But people had interpreted his comments about a legend as hostility toward equality for the Jews. Following a line of thought with which he may have become acquainted through Gabriel Riesser's writings, he criticized some younger Jewish poets. Aroused over the long delay of civil equality, he charged, they turned back to Judaism, hated Jesus, underestimated the bigotry among the hostile Christian masses, and, on top of that, demanded apologies from Christianity. They overestimated the influence of educated Christians upon the uneducated, wished to rush historic developments, and looked upon everything from their own narrow, selfish point of view.

Though apparently shooting beyond the target, Gutzkow was seriously concerned that repetition of the Ahasver legend—which, as he emphasized, was Christian rather than Jewish—would deepen the gulf between Christianity and Judaism. He admitted that he would have done better to restrain his "inner urge" to elaborate upon the figure of Ahasver, since "Judaism at present was an open wound; the slightest touch of it already was painful to its German adherents."

"URIEL ACOSTA"

Karl Gutzkow was the author of *Uriel Acosta* (1849), the "Jew-drama," as it was called in its day. Two years before, he had used the same theme in the short story "Der Sadduzäer von Amsterdam," though he had furnished a different setting and offered a different psychological motivation of the main characters. In *Uriel Acosta* Gutzkow posed with great clarity the dilemma of many an intellectual Jew, torn between loyalty to his people and the attraction of an alien culture that was superior in many respects. At the same time the play was of universal human interest. The drama, as the playwright himself noted, gave "a harmonic accord to the intellectual wars of liberation of all peoples." It was also a call for toleration of all religions.

Uriel Acosta is a young scholar who has "illuminated" the Holy Scriptures "with the torch of reason" and in the course of his searching inquiry has become detached from Judaism. Yet when his old teacher De Silva suggests that he "take the side of the Christians," Uriel spurns his advice. Though he no longer shares the religious conceptions of his people, which appear intolerant to him, and he despises their ignoble occupations of trade and money-changing, he still sympathizes with them, is ready to suffer their torment, and will not desert them in their misery. Facing the threat of excommunication from the Jewish community, Uriel nevertheless professes to be a Jew:

> Am I a Christian? Shall an insolent sneer
> Open to me the backdoor of false compassion?[17]

At the same time he gratefully recalls the broad liberal education he has received from the Christian peoples. It is Uriel Acosta's tragedy that the Jews of his day live in cultural isolation from the rest of the world and treat their thinking sons with harsh intolerance, demanding from them heavy intellectual sacrifices. By conversion to Christianity Uriel Acosta could avoid the ban that hangs threateningly over him.

But out of noblest motives he rejects his personal deliverance, preferring the excommunication to severing his last ties with his people.

Gutzkow's support for the equality of the Jews also found expression in this drama. Through the fine character of De Silva, the wise Jewish scholar and physician, Gutzkow appeals to the generosity and the sense of justice of the Dutch people. Having themselves experienced "how slavery hurts," they would not forge "slave chains for other sufferers!"

In his autobiography *Rückblicke auf mein Leben*, Gutzkow told of his unhappiness when, as a freshman at the University, he had just learned that Börne, whom he revered, was a Jew and that he had felt similarly when he heard about Heine's Jewish descent. "Their appearance," he remarked later about both, "dazzled; but one did not let rest the eye long upon them with satisfaction. There was much to overcome before one could get accustomed to these two personalities; for with the Germans no small obstacle . . . was bound to be their Israelitic ancestry. . . . It took a long time until unconditional devotion could follow."[18] Gutzkow himself finally overcame his early "German-Christian" anti-Semitism. It was "through literature, the value of which I could not deny, that I came to tolerate the nationality."[19]

Early an enthusiastic disciple of Börne, Gutzkow remained his ardent admirer. In his biography of Börne, he pointed to the Jewish element in his endeavors and writings, without attributing everything to this background.[20] Gutzkow condemned the shameful living conditions of the German Jews, especially those of Frankfurt am Main, with utmost severity: "As the situation of the Jews in Germany was and still is," he wrote, "it must be a miserable feeling to be born among them. Even the play of a child has its restrictions; for what the Christian boy does not learn to hate and mock at through his own innocence, the hatred and mockery of his parents will teach him. . . . He is susceptible to numerous aversions, which the Christians permit against the Jews in civil intercourse, in society and locally. That must cut deeply into a nobler being and must leave wounds which can never heal, since the status of the Jews still does not seem to improve."[21]

Gutzkow was intimately linked in friendship with several Jews— with Gabriel Riesser, the leading advocate of the emancipation of the Jews in German states, with the scholar Steinheim, with the church historian August Neander (whose name before his conversion had been David Mendel), with Ludwig Assing, the model to his Ben Akiba in *Uriel Acosta,* and with many others, among them Berthold Auerbach, August Lewald, Zacharias Löwenthal, some of them converted either to Protestantism or Catholicism but most still Jews. When Gutzkow later was accused of opposing the Jews, he countered with the assurance: "Many of my dearest and best friends are Jews." The writer, though grown bitter in his old age, turned tender and sentimental when he remembered his first love, a very beautiful Jewish girl.[22] He had expressed his feeling in verses which, unfortunately, had fallen into the hands of her mother.

DISPUTE OVER TACTICS

Gutzkow pleaded repeatedly and with fervor in behalf of the Jews, calling upon the Germans to "open to the Jews every trade. Do not shudder if it is said that their educated people could become druggists, as if they thought of poisoning you; do not tremble when they bake bread, draw beer, if they are engaged in the wine trade. Take them into your company; do not exclude them from the clubs that are devoted to sociability. Let them read your bad journals in the same room where you sit bored over them. Let them become not merely physicians and lawyers, but also police officers, judges; let them become ministers, if they have the patent of nobility or the genius for it. . . . Then the difference of religion, the only means of distinction, will not disturb any longer."[23]

In a chapter "Religion und Christentum," in *Gesamtbild unseres Jahrhunderts* [Panorama of Our Century], Gutzkow had early come to grips with the arguments for and against emancipation. It was his conviction that in spite of all progress a deep dislike marked the relationship between Christians and Jews. To uproot its causes, he demanded separation of church and state, the existence of an organic Christian state being to him a contradiction in itself. In a later edition of this work he added the words: "The Jews have a right as human beings, Christianity aside." Yet he entertained no doubt that the Christian fear of the Jews, irrational as it was, was quite real. The Germans, in his view, were fearful of the cunning, skill, and the financial power of the Jews. Following their emancipation, Jews might make use of the new freedom to gain ascendancy in the industrial life of the nation; they might exploit the people in the countryside through usury and other means, enter the civil service, and inundate the press and literature. He also found blameworthy the manner in which the Jews wanted to gain their objectives. Jews, he advised, should mingle with Christians, intermarry, reform their religion, especially relinquish their religious observances in regard to food and drink, and celebrate Sunday instead of the Sabbath.[24]

The German Jews were bound to suspect the conviction and steadfastness of those German allies in the fight for emancipation who questioned their tactics, raised doubts about the wisdom of their alleged

haste and intemperateness, and demanded intolerable "concessions."
Except for a few Jewish friends who knew Gutzkow's past, knew that
on the whole his attitude toward emancipation was positive, and continued to trust him, his stance was bound to incur disapproval. While
in a discussion of an essay by Steinheim about Jewish emancipation in
Schleswig and Holstein, Gutzkow urged Christians to understand the
feelings of the Jews, he also appealed to the latter to put themselves in
the place of the Christians and try to understand their prejudices! Such
prejudices, he warned, could not be as rapidly eradicated as Riesser,
Steinheim, and others held possible: "Our religious instruction has
furnished us with an idiosyncrasy against Judaism that we cannot suppress overnight. . . . We have imbibed hate against the Jews since we
learned to read. . . . We are of the opinion that we ought to combat our
prejudice and that in the course of this century it will be virtually
eradicated . . . but it presupposes great heroism to overcome it as
rapidly as those spokesmen wish. We are no heroes; the least in the
mass; even less as lawmakers versus those who not even in principle
have raised themselves . . . to the acceptance of Jewish equality."[25]

While Gutzkow himself strongly supported such equality everywhere in Germany and in the rest of Europe, the more moderate tactics
which he recommended to the Jews were anything but acceptable to
them. They insisted on immediate and unconditional equality—the
only course which, even in an earlier day, had appeared logical and
consequent to Wilhelm von Humboldt—and rejected the view that they
were not yet prepared to assume civil responsibilities. Gutzkow also
expressed doubts that Jewish education, which looked toward the past,
was adequate for the life of German Jews in the nineteenth century;
and he found shortcomings in the education against Jew-hating. Since,
in any case, education of both Jews and Germans was a long drawn-out
process, Gutzkow warned the Jews not to believe that the solution of
the Jewish question merely awaited a "magic touch." In the heat of the
argument he even considered the alternative to Jewish slavery not
Jewish equality but German enslavement!

Although this view was not a characteristic or a permanent feature
of his thought on the Jewish question, it again raised doubts about
Gutzkow in the minds of a good number of Jews. M. Philippsohn,
editor of the Zeitung für das Judentum, leveled against Gutzkow the
accusation that he had deserted the cause of emancipation. Thereupon
Dr. Steinheim, rallying to the defense of Gutzkow, sent an article to the
Address-Komptoir-Nachrichten in Altona which had reprinted Philippsohn's charges. Steinheim pointed out that Gutzkow wanted only to
"designate and explain, but not to justify" the prejudice, "this
monster," into whose forehead he had burned the "sign of Cain."

Lamenting the shortcomings of Christian education and religious teachings, Gutzkow addressed himself to all educators and especially to teachers of religion, some of whom aroused hatred and foolishness among their students instead of teaching them ethics and reason. Taking the pulse of the average German, Gutzkow was both appalled at and impressed by the intensity of anti-Semitic sentiments and feared that the Jewish demands would only irritate the masses and be offensive to them. "The prejudice against the Jews does not arise from a wretched heart, nor from miserable hatred and zeal of oppression," and the Christian was "no such infamous tyrant as he is mostly painted by the Jew."[26] Whatever excuses the author made for the anti-Semitism of the mass, its persistence was undesirable to both Jews and forward-looking Germans, and Gutzkow's tendency of leaning over backward to comprehend a reactionary and reprehensible phenomenon was a questionable way of combating it effectively. His wish that, for the immediate future, Jews, out of regard for such sentiments, refrain from becoming teachers and civil servants was likely to perpetuate bigotry rather than destroy it.

No wonder then that Gutzkow's latest, overly cautious position, his limited acceptance of equality, aroused Gabriel Riesser, the eloquent spokesman of German Jews, who was his personal friend. Riesser bluntly called Gutzkow's toleration of still existing prejudices "cowardice."[27] He reminded Gutzkow that in his novel *Wally* he himself had not shown consideration for the religious convictions of numerous pious Christians and that he himself had encountered prejudice when, jointly with the Jews, he had become the target of the anti-Semites. Yet now he posed as defender of this prejudice. Gutzkow admittedly lamented it but still painted it *con amore*. If the prejudice was really as bad as he pictured it, one would have to castigate it the more mercilessly, instead of tolerating it, and the Jews then would be justified to close ranks more firmly than ever.

In his reply, published in Number 4 of the *Telegraph*, in 1842, Gutzkow paid highest tribute to Riesser's noble endeavors and polemical talent, yet criticized him for the irritated manner in which he had taken him to task, endorsing the wrong formula: "He who is not for me is against me." Again he stressed that he had never thought of his description of the prejudices of the Christians as a defense. What separated Riesser and him was only a difference of methods, not of principles. Jewish writers had become annoyed with him and he himself had "become so fearful to write about this subject that I have promised myself never again to touch upon it." The extant prejudice, unfortunately, was deeply rooted, being a "prejudice of religion." "There lay a gulf between Judaism and Christianity which cannot be bridged with phrases, one which only education and humanity can overcome." But one ran in vain against the iron wall of bigotry and would continue to do so until the "mass has become more mature or until through accomplished emancipation, which I support wholeheartedly, it has grown more indifferent in regard to what separates the faiths."[28] It was noteworthy that in an increasingly secular age a secular writer such as Gutzkow pointed the accusing finger at the religious rather than any other roots of Jew-hating.

Gutzkow believed it was necessary to proceed cautiously and gradually with the emancipation in order to avoid "increasing" anti-Semitism "through too rapid legislating at the top."[29] Having himself overcome his early anti-Jewish sentiments only with difficulty, he knew that the roots of anti-Semitism, which he considered a "disgrace,"[30] lay deep in Germany's soil. Nothing was further from his mind than to excuse the anti-Semitism of the masses. Though he felt that for the Jews some tactical moves, such as desisting from pressing their cause and especially avoiding some selected occupations, were in order, concessions to anti-Semitism were, in his view, to have definite limits: "Otherwise . . . liberate the Jew from all pressure under which he lives, contrary to his and our humanity. Leave the Jew every freedom to choose a profession and to do what he wishes."[31] In order to avoid any further misinterpretation, he reminded his readers once more that "for ten years" he had "written in the main in behalf of the civil emancipation of the Jews."[32]

Gutzkow's attitude toward the Jews emerged particularly clearly in an essay in the *Säkularbilder* [Images of the Century], "Jews and Emancipation." He developed there the views of the advocates of Jewish emancipation as well as of their enemies. "The result of this weighing of pro and contra," he wrote, "remains the full conviction of the necessity of the emancipation in every respect, theoretically and practically." The Jews were "long ours and strive to mingle with us." "Let us emancipate them now, you fearful Christian people, you who know how to tie together cruelty and religion in an odd manner," he appealed to the Germans. "Then Christ's prophecy will most strikingly be fulfilled."[33]

Jungdeutsche and Their Critics

The literary and political struggle over Jewish emancipation which Menzel's intervention against the Young Germans precipitated had a deeply divisive impact. Hermann Marggraf, in a contemporary description of the German-Jewish situation, pointed to the polarization which had taken place in the Germanies. Two camps had emerged, each offering a different analysis of the role of "our Jewish writers," the character of the Jews in general, and the problems of Jewish emancipation. There were those, he charged, who, like Menzel, "scented everywhere a Jew and in each Jewish writer a literary Shylock, who is avid for Christian flesh." But there were also the members of the other category, "which in behalf of the Jews would cut into their own Christian flesh" and fight for Jewish equality.

Menzel, he held, was correct in his view that the "Jewish element" had "consolidated" itself in literature more than was in its own interest. Marggraf voiced his regret that Jewish skepticism, instead of turning against Jewish orthodoxy, had allegedly turned against Christianity, and he asked Jewish writers: "Why are you getting mixed up in our internal affairs?" Actually, David Friedrich Strauss, Bruno Bauer, and Ludwig Feuerbach, who were leaders of this movement in biblical scholarship, were all German Christians, not Jews. Yet Marggraf apparently accepted the thesis that the modern "Jewish" criticism of the Scriptures was a revenge for medieval persecutions.

There follow critical remarks about the eroding Jewish wit, an appeal to the Jews to free themselves from their prejudices—no comparable appeal to German Christians!—and a call for "emancipation" of the Jews from the yoke of their rabbis and from the Talmud, so that "Jewish youth can then be educated as a young Europe, not as a young Palestine." Marggraf had a long list of complaints against the Jews, focusing on their alleged arrogance and forwardness and their proclivity to look for gain, though he gave them credit for their sociability, their women, and their family life. In return for the Jews improving their ways, he suggested that they be granted more civil functions. While acknowledging the injustice of past centuries, he tended to minimize it by pointing to "heretics" who had suffered even more.[34]

Like many of his German contemporaries, Marggraf did not wish to seem entirely out of step with the progressive tendencies of his era. Yet he was more afraid to be looked upon as friendly toward the Jews and especially toward the German Jewish writers whose criticism of German Christianity and theology and of German literature and culture in general he found objectionable, if not intolerable. While claiming to oppose only emancipation, his criticism actually undercut the unstable legal and political ground upon which German Jewry uneasily rested.

Heinrich Laube, one of the noted writers of the *Vormärz* and later Director of the Viennese *Burgtheater,* depicted in his novel *Die Krieger* [The Warriors][35] the fate of the Polish Jew Joel, a fighter for the freedom of Poland in 1830–1831. Though Joel makes sacrifices for the liberation of his country, the Poles show little gratitude to him. Joel loves the daughter of a Polish nobleman, who tolerates Joel's enthusiasm for Polish liberty and independence but vents his own contempt for the Jews when he rudely rejects Joel as suitor for his daughter. While the liberal novelist chooses Poland as the scene for this work, the reference to the situation of the Jews in the German realm becomes quite clear.

In this novel Laube criticized the ambiguity of a liberalism which had not yet freed itself from anti-Semitic prejudices. The German volunteer who, at the outbreak of the Polish war of liberation, had rushed to Warsaw to fight for liberty and independence is so shocked by the brutal treatment of Joel by the Poles that he begins to doubt the justice of their cause and decides to return early to his own country. Joel himself remains in the Polish army and is seriously wounded in the battle of Ostrolenka. While searching for his son, who still lies on the battlefield, Joel's father is attacked by a group of rebellious Polish peasants, who accuse him of espionage. His defense turns into an outcry against the wretched situation of Polish Jewry.

Another of the Young German writers was Gustav Kühne. He too espoused Jewish emancipation. In an essay on Moses Mendelssohn, Kühne criticized the treatment which had been accorded the Jews in Prussia under Frederick the Great. Christianity, he expounded, had always been able to discover in the Jew all the evil and ugliness it had wished to see in him. During emergencies, when the entire population had been called upon to fight against foreign aggression, people had granted rights to the Jews; but when the menacing flood had receded, Kühne wrote with an eye to the War of Liberation, earlier pledges were forgotten. The entire population, both Germans and Jews, had been deceived. Placing the Jewish question into the larger framework of the age, he wrote: "Because of the reaction in the epoch of restoration, everything suffers—sound reason most of all."[36]

Emancipation in England—the Political Echo in Germany

The seeming improvement of the situation of the Jews in England in 1833 found a hearty echo in the writings of Fürst Pückler-Muskau. He praised the liberation of the Jews in England and saw in it an example "for the world." "Hail thou, noble people," he harangued the British, "who had already led the way in so many things and who have now put the axe to that stupid barbarism with which we in the whole of Europe have persecuted so long, to our eternal disgrace, a numerous class of our fellow citizens, first corrupted them in order to accuse them of this corruption afterwards. It is a beautiful ultimate victory of humanity and justice, raised as an example to the world, and we would like to remain silent about the voices which at the same time have been heard in our countries. I do not know how other Christians will think about it, but as far as I am concerned, I can say that since I came to reason, I never met an educated Jew without being ashamed, because I felt vividly that we had no reason to despise his coreligionists, but he had reason to despise ours. We shall not remain where we are. Today's era, with all its shortcomings and birth pains, cuts down a hateful prejudice, and although it may, by an awkward approach, produce a momentarily successful reaction, in the end, in accordance with divine law, it still must reach unerringly the point to which it steers—the realm of reason."[37] Pückler-Muskau believed in the ultimate victory of rationality and of equality for the German Jews despite temporary reverses.

In the early thirties the Jews' struggle for emancipation was resumed in several German states, largely under the impact of advances of liberalism in France and Great Britain. Yet the tone emanating from the tribunes of the legislative assemblies of some German states drowned out the voice of brotherhood and conciliation. Even some German liberals joined the anti-Semitic chorus at times, while others did not commit themselves on the issue of Jewish equality.

One of those who pleaded for only moderate concessions to the Jews was the deputy and historian Christoph Dahlmann, a leading figure of German liberalism in his day. In December 1832 he demanded greater rights for the Jews of Hanover but refrained from asking for full equality.[38] The attitude of German liberalism to the Jews was still one of distrust, caution, and hesitation.

The granting of equal rights to the Israelites, Dahlmann stressed, "still remained within the jurisdiction of the state." The government which contemplated it had to take the people's mood into consideration. "A differentiation in the treatment" of Christians and Jews was at times "by no means unfair"; everything hinged on whether the Christian population would tolerate a "judge, a military superior, a clever competitor of this people." On the other hand, he considered mixed marriages desirable. A university professor himself, Dahlmann was favorably inclined toward admitting Jews to the academic profession. Narrowness of knowledge often stemmed, he held, from reli-

272 The Struggle for Equality in the Vormärz

gious prejudices: "It appears to me very beneficial to the freer movement of the sciences, if some men who stand outside our church
confines hold this danger [religious prejudice] constantly before our
eyes."[39] Although Dahlmann held full emancipation to be premature,
he wished to overcome the status quo of inequality and to move
gradually toward greater rights for the Jews. Yet suspicion of the
Jews as well as doubts about the readiness of the Germans to accept
them as equals colored his views.

Another rising star on the firmament of German liberalism of the
period was the politician and historian Karl von Rotteck. His attitude
toward the Jews was on the whole negative and hostile. "I cannot
give political equality to the Jews until they, by genuinely drawing
closer to us, have proved to us their will and their abilities to join us
really as brothers. . . . But I wish that the way to fraternization be
paved."[40] Affiliation with a different religious association should have
no bearing on one's citizenship: "Whether one believes in Moses,
Christ or Mohammed . . . ought to be without influence on the claim
to political equality." A different situation would exist, however, "if
a sect . . . because of its belief or its cult is driven to contempt of or
hostility against people in the same state who have different beliefs."[41] Rotteck claimed that the Jews' lack of will to assimilate
themselves and, beyond that, their religion itself prevented the Germans from granting them equality. While he did not recommend that
the Jews seek outright conversion, he appeared to have considered it
essential for their assimilation to German *Kultur* and for their acquisition of political equality. His opinions about Jewish religion and its
commands differed little from Christian views on Judaism uttered in
earlier centuries. His views on other contemporary questions were
influenced by his concepts of the law of nature and of reason. These
noble philosophical views, however, exerted hardly any influence
upon the policy he recommended in regard to the Jews.

Closely linked with Rotteck was Karl Theodor Welcker. A university professor and politician like Rotteck, he too suffered personally from the reaction in Germany, making many a personal sacrifice
for his convictions. Jointly with Rotteck, he was editor of the leading
liberal organ in Southern Germany, *Der Freisinnige*. He later edited
with Rotteck the *Staatslexicon,* which was dedicated to the propagation of the philosophy of liberalism. For many decades this great
work was a source of enlightenment to the German middle class on
social, political, and economic questions and a means of its political
education.

While Welcker and Rotteck saw eye to eye on many contemporary
problems, they differed in their attitude toward the Jews. Welcker's

position was much more favorable. Though, like Dahlmann, he pointed to the Germans' fear of Jewish competition, he remembered that in 1814 and 1815 the Jews had fought "shoulder to shoulder with our warriors." While Rotteck held that the Jews lacked the will to assimilate, Welcker observed that they showed "interest in the state and in the attainment of its purpose." He had learned "with pleasure," he wrote, that the majority of the Second Chamber in Baden had spoken in behalf of the full civil equality of Jews with Christians and "thus sought to erase the infamy of wishing to place on native inhabitants and fellow citizens . . . equal burdens of taxes and of national defense but of denying them equal rights. . . . The state acts contrary to its own purpose if it abridges for a single class of its population the possibility of free and vigorous development."[42]

CHAPTER 13

Hegel, Left Hegelians, and Anti-Semitism of the Left

Hegel's Early Anti-Semitism

Hardly any other German thinker has influenced German and European intellectual development during his lifetime and posthumously as decisively as the philosopher Georg Wilhelm Friedrich Hegel. In Germany his writings have served as an arsenal from which the Right and the Left and those between the extremes of the political spectrum have borrowed their weapons. His thoughts on Jews and Judaism have had an impact on both German and Jewish writers. In his attitude toward the Jews Hegel underwent a change similar to that experienced by Fichte before him, though he was never as sharply opposed to the Jews as Fichte.

People have blamed the young Hegel for displaying a "naive anti-Semitism."[1] But as a mature thinker Hegel discarded his early prejudices and demanded equality for the Jews. He criticized the state's policies, which he held responsible for the separation of the Jews from the rest of the population, and considered further "exclusion" of the Jews from civil rights unjustified, a violation of their human rights, and also "foolish" (töricht).

His *Fragmente theologischer Studien* [Fragments of Theological Studies], written in younger years, reveal distinctly anti-Jewish sentiments. The ancient Hebrews found little favor in his eyes. Biased because of his Hellenistic world view, he could hardly render justice to the Jewish people. Like Kant, he was not truly knowledgeable in regard to Judaica; his conception of Judaism rested heavily on secondary sources, such as Spinoza's criticism of the Jewish religion and

Moses Mendelssohn's views of it. To top matters, he relied on Kant in considering Judaism a body of statutory law. The Jews, Hegel asserted in his *Fragmente,* had not remained culturally independent from the influence of alien nations. While the period of the political "independence of other peoples" had been "a state of happiness and of more beautiful humanity," the short span of independence for the Jews had been "one of entire passivity, one of complete ugliness." Even the often admired social laws of the Jews found a severe judge in Hegel. The treatment of sex in the books and laws of the Hebrews "engaged" the author; but in general the Jews had fought over only material goods, over houses, women, vineyards, for they had had no share "in anything eternal."[2]

The lofty figure of Moses, which had strongly attracted Goethe and Schiller, made as little impression upon the young Hegel as did the great Jewish prophets, who, in his opinion, were merely "impotent fanatics." Similarly, he saw in the heroic struggle of the Maccabees only fanaticism. Although the Hebrew language had preserved "some deep childlike sounds" and though the stage of development characteristic of the Jewish people recalled in many respects the childhood of a nation, Hegel did not believe that the Jews as a people had lacked opportunity for further development. Their education and formation was not simply arrested and therefore incomplete; their national character was rather "deformed." The Jew has to struggle against this deformity and·"suffers from it." "Pure human beings, well-formed individuals,"[3] were, according to Hegel, in the minority among Jews.

The ideas of the young Hegel about ancient Judaism were closely related to the picture that the Enlightenment painted. Judaism represented to him forces of retardation, as it appeared to other contemporaries of the Enlightenment and to many Deists. The German-Jewish historian Hans Liebeschütz pointed out that Hegel, just as Spinoza and the Deists, aimed his critical shafts at what he considered lack of freedom in Judaism. All feared the influence of the spirit of Jewish legislation exerted via Christianity upon modern times. Besides, Hegel appears to have been influenced in his judgment of ancient Judaism by his dislike of contemporary Christian theologians. As Wilhelm Dilthey, noted German philosopher and historian, summed it up succinctly: Hegel had "dealt with Judaism summarily and in a hateful manner out of opposition to [Christian] theologians."

The utterances of the mature Hegel on Judaism sounded quite different. While in the *Phänomenologie des Geistes* [Phenomenology of the Mind], one of Hegel's early writings, Judaism was not classified as a religion, in his *Philosophie der Geschichte* [Philosophy of History] Hegel looked upon Judaism as a religion. Judea now took its place in the Oriental world. The characteristic feature of this world is that the Spirit has not yet attained its self-consciousness. In the first period, in China and India, the Spirit is identified with the existing world. In the second period the Spirit separates from the world and becomes a force opposed to it. Persia represents the first stage in this period, Judea the second and Egypt the third; Judea itself represents a watershed. The Greek world in turn is the antithesis to the Oriental world.[4]

There are substantial differences between Hegel's position in this work and that of his early writings. Though in some respects he returned to thoughts he had expressed earlier, now he appreciated the religious significance of Judaism. He classified it among the "ethnic religions." In his words, it was not "our own" faith. Judaism is one of the stages in the process of the development of self-consciousness of man as well as of the knowledge of God. It belongs to that stage in the dialectical development of religion that he calls "the religion of the Spiritual Individuality." Differently from in the *Frühschriften* [Early Writings], Judaism and Greek religion are on the same level, though Greek religion still represents a more advanced step.

In the *Frühschriften* Judaism is rejected by Hegel in preference to two other religions and cultures, Christian and Greek. But with the introduction of the dialectical method several changes occur. While Judaism was first considered a nonspiritual entity, it later becomes one of the partial manifestations of the total spirit. While Hegel was first critical of the concept of the chosen people, he later holds that Judaism is no longer a Judeo-centric culture but rather a theocentric one. While he previously upheld the notion of the "enslavement" of the Jewish people to God or to his laws, later the concept of the "sublimity" of God holds the center of the stage.

Dialectics and "Great Trends" in Jewish History

In his *Philosophie der Geschichte* Hegel discarded the indignant and hostile tone of the work of his youth. His dialectics had led him to see in all ideas, in all religions, merely stages in the development of the human intellect. "In every religion is divine presence, a divine relationship. . . . " Now it was his opinion that the Jewish religion had of necessity to confine itself to the Jewish people, had "necessarily to acquire an element of exclusion." While in his *Fragmente theologischer Studien* the patriarch Abraham had aroused his disapproval, in his *Philosophie der Geschichte* Hegel was to esteem him greatly: "The narratives about the patriarchs attract us." Hegel felt himself drawn to the study of the oldest Jewish writings and legends and also to the later history of the Jews. "The Jewish history" has "great trends," though some aspects of it continued to disturb him. The development of Christianity in the womb of the Jewish people gave "to it its significance and importance in world history."

A critical glance at Moses aside, the entire chapter in the *Philosophie* breathes a spirit of appreciation. The Jews receive much praise; Hegel places them high above the Phoenicians, among whom "spiritual matters were still confined," while in Judaism they were "completely purified." Neither the Persians nor the Indians reached the religious and spiritual heights the Jews attained. The "conception that God is master and creator of nature makes God's position a lofty one, inasmuch as all nature is his adornment. . . . True morality and integrity can now emerge, as also a historical view may appear here for the first time."

The individual in Judaism never comes to full realization of his "independence"; he attains no value. The family, however, is independent, autonomous. The worship of Jehovah is tied to the latter. Hegel found in the Jewish religion "inwardness, pure heart, penitence, devotion." He was critical of the "exclusion of other people's minds." Yet in another context he believed he could discern the "necessity" for such exclusion.

Many of these ideas are further developed in his *Philosophie der Religion*. The Jewish religion appears here again as a "religion of sublimity," Greek religion as one of beauty, Roman faith one of utility. Hegel seemed now convinced that the "exclusive" character of the Jewish religion was determined by the peculiar history of the Jewish people. Yet the awakening from particularism to universality also occurred, according to Hegel's *Philosophie der Geschichte,* in Judaism. In the latter stage "the Jewish God" could be comprehended only through abstract thinking: "That contrasted with the limitation to one nation." The preservation of the Jews through centuries could be explained by a "fanaticism of stubbornness," by an "admirable firmness."[5] In the *Vorlesungen über die Philosophie der Weltgeschichte* [Lectures on the Philosophy of World History] the relation in Judaism between God and men was no longer based on tyranny.[6] Hegel thus has abandoned some of his earlier negative beliefs about Jews and Judaism.

In the *Vorlesungen über Ästhetik* [Lectures on Estheticism] Hegel

held that "religious interest prevails" in the epic poetry of the Hebrews. He extolled "the loftiness of the Jewish phantasy in their conception of the creation, in the stories of the patriarchs, the migration
through the desert, the conquest of Canaan and in the further course of
national events,"[7] and praised their keen, intuitive perception.

Hegel for Emancipation

Hegel's conception of Judaism, as well as that of many other German thinkers, including Kant, had been decisively shaped, as stated,
by Spinoza's *Criticism of Judaism*. In his chapter on Spinoza in the
Vorlesungen über die Geschichte der Philosophie [Lectures on the
History of Philosophy] Hegel held that "the Jew" Spinoza had abandoned the dualism of Descartes. Through him the "Eastern [*orientalisch*] conception of the absolute identity had been introduced into
European thinking." Hegel described Spinoza's circumstances of life
and painted the picture of a pure and noble character. Spinoza had
been born in the Netherlands, "a country highly interesting for general culture, which first in Europe gave the example of a general
toleration."[8]

Hegel was a friend of the poet Heinrich Stieglitz, a half-Jew, to
whom he dedicated the only poem he ever wrote. The Jewish critic
Moritz Saphir, according to Grillparzer, was a very frequent visitor in
Hegel's home.[9] Hegel also was closely befriended by the noted jurist
and university professor Eduard Gans, one of his most original disciples.[10] Gans, once one of the proponents of the "Science of Judaism," later changed his views and embraced Christianity. In a letter
of October 3, 1826, Hegel assured him that "he had often missed the
company of his dear and esteemed friend." He also enjoyed intimate
fellowship with a Jewish banker named Bloch.[11]

Hegel greatly influenced the thinking of numerous contemporaries, including Jews. Among those who became his disciples, or were
decisively influenced by him, some at least temporarily, were, to mention only a few, Heine, Marx, Lassalle, and Friedrich Julius Stahl—
men of different political persuasions.

As little as Hegel in personal relationships entertained anti-
Jewish prejudices, so little did he tolerate anti-Semitism in public life.
This attitude emerges clearly in his work *Grundlagen des Rechts oder
Naturrechts* [Principles of Law, or Natural Law]. Hegel approved
therein the attitude of the Prussian government, which, at least in
theory, adhered to Jewish emancipation as proclaimed in the old

Prussian provinces before the War of Liberation. One would perhaps, Hegel argued, have "the formal law" on one's side, if one pleaded against the emancipation of the Jews, who formed not only a special religious association but also were an alien people. Yet in their clamor the opponents of the Jews "ignored that they are first of all human beings and that this is not a shallow, abstract quality."

Hegel believed in a future "reconciliation" between Jews and Gentiles in matters of "mind and thought" and proclaimed that the Jews had human and civil rights. "The separation of which the Jews were accused," he wrote, "had been perpetuated, and the excluding state had been rightly incriminated and reproached: for it had denied its principle, the objective institution, and its power. This exclusion, asserted by its adherents to be very much justified, had proved foolish also in practice; the policy of the government, however, had been shown to be wise and meritorious." "Man counts," Hegel writes in the same work in another context, "because he is man, not because he is a Jew, a Catholic, a Protestant, a German, an Italian, etc."[12] In the *Vorlesungen über die Philosophie der Geschichte* he castigated the "terrible beginning" of the medieval Crusades, when the crusaders killed and plundered thousands of Jews, and condemned the "excesses and cruelties" of the Christian host which "dripped with the blood of the murdered inhabitants of Jerusalem."[13]

In his *Rechtsphilosophie* [Philosophy of Law], which appeared posthumously, Hegel sharply criticized the *Burschenschaften* and the "superficial pap" (*seichter Brei*) of the ultranationalist politics and philosophy of Fries, one of the spiritual ancestors of anti-Semitism. Hegel inveighed against the "generals [*Heerführer*] of superficiality," who discarded thought for direct perception. It was not surprising "that such a view takes on the form of piety." It was characteristic that "superficiality"—this is the steadily recurring word—"parades" with a great deal of oratory. "Most characteristic, however, was its hatred of law and justice."[14]

Religious interest in Judaism is the key to Hegel's attitude toward the Jewish people. From his early days he clearly shared with the Enlightenment its antagonism to Judaism as a religion—an antagonism mainly directed at it as the matrix of Christian tradition—as well as its active sympathy for humanity and tolerance of every individual. His hostility to the Prussian anti-Semitism of his time and his support for the Edict of Emancipation of 1812 are unmistakable. Assimilation of the Jews and their reconciliation with the Gentiles appear to him possible and desirable. Still, underlying some of his thought on Judaism is a certain ambivalence which explains some of the contradictions in his writings on the Jews.

Left Hegelianism and the New Theology

After Hegel's death, his philosophy continued to have a powerful impact upon Germany's intellectual life. So did that of his disciples of both Right and Left. Among the Left Hegelians were theologians, students of the history of religion and philosophy, and secular writers as well as men of action. They attempted, theoretically and practically, to come to grips with the Jewish problem, with Judaism as a religion, and with the contemporary complex question of Jewish emancipation. David Friedrich Strauss and Bruno Bauer focused on the problem of Judaism as a religion, while Bauer, Arnold Ruge, and the young Karl Marx also faced up to the acute problem of Jewish emancipation, though in quite negative and hostile terms.

The alleged advantages of the tactics of gradualism aside, it was also national antipathy and continuing religious prejudice which held back liberals in their support of Jewish equality. Enlightenment and rationalism had not succeeded in uprooting the anti-Jewish prejudice and Hegel's dialectics were merely to refurbish it. True, according to Hegel, Christianity even in its most advanced Protestant forms was not yet fully developed; it was merely a step in the march of the spirit toward absolute divine truth. But it was superior to Judaism; Hegel had regarded Old Testament monotheism as a stage Christianity had definitely left behind.

DAVID FRIEDRICH STRAUSS AND LUDWIG FEUERBACH

Theologians in general, including those of the extreme Right and of the extreme Left, had little liking for Judaism. Some of Hegel's leftist disciples and interpreters also castigated Christianity. David Friedrich Strauss, Max Stirner, Arnold Ruge, and Bruno Bauer criticized Christian beliefs that men were sinners and needed a Savior—an opinion which, in their view, expressed hostility toward and contempt for man. The Christian radicals repeated a thesis earlier asserted in Jewish theological criticism. It was therefore not surprising that some Germans took the radical theologians to task for the alleged "victory of Judaism over Christianity." One critic dubbed David Friedrich Strauss's criticism "Jewish skepticism." Johann Sep, a Catholic deputy in the Bavarian *Landtag,* voiced the suspicion that a baptized Jewish writer, F. Nork, had given Strauss the basis for his "un-Christian work." By speaking out openly, the Young Hegelians could have prevented the abuse of their thesis for the political purposes of the Jew-haters, but partly because of their indifference to the contemporary Jewish struggle for equality, they ignored this matter.

Anti-Semites blamed the Jews for the criticism of Christian theology by the Young Hegelians, though the most noted of these critics were Germans. On the other hand, the scholarly skepticism toward religion turned itself into a new form of Jew-hating. The theological criticism by Friedrich Daumer, Bruno Bauer, and Arnold Ruge focused on what they considered the misanthropic character of Christianity as compared to the love of life in ancient Greece; they held Judaism, the "Asiatic" matrix of Christianity, responsible for this flaw. Thus Jews and Judaism became the target of attack by theological conservatives and theological liberals and radicals alike.

In *Das Wesen des Christentums* [The Nature of Christianity], Ludwig Feuerbach developed the thought that the basic principle of Jewish religion was "egotism," that "utility" was the "supreme principle of Judaism."[15] Personally, however, he did not harbor any enmity toward the Jews. He had married a Jewish woman, and he highly esteemed the Jewish philosopher Spinoza.[16] The key to the seeming riddle of his attitude toward Judaism must be sought in his philosophy.

Feuerbach saw in egotism the basis of all religions. He conceived of it as a "necessary, unavoidable egotism" and attempted to prove that in practice the adherents of all religions revered their deities only on account of their supposed usefulness to man. Utility therefore was important in every religion. "I understand under egotism," he wrote another time, "the love of man for himself; that means for the human kind, the love which is the impetus for the satisfaction and development without which he is not and cannot be a true, accomplished man."[17] Not only egotism but also utility forms, according to Feuerbach, an essential element of every religion, not of Judaism alone.

Feuerbach believed that occasionally the nationalistic-egotistic limit in Judaism was burst wide open. Yet universalism was "not really . . . the essential character of the Jewish religion." It was to be found rather in Christianity, which in his view was "the Jewish religion purified from national egotism."[18] The miracles of Christianity, however, had only the welfare of the Christian as object. Therefore Feuerbach still spoke of the "limitation of Christianity." One may compare this to the national "limitation" of Judaism. Feuerbach, who designated himself an atheist, was hardly less critical of Christianity than of Judaism. Christianity at one time appeared to him as nothing less than "spiritual Judaism" and Judaism as "earthly Christianity."[19]

In spite of Feuerbach's novel terminology, the close relationship between these views and Hegel's thought on Judaism is striking. So also is the influence of Feuerbach upon Karl Marx's thought on the religion of the Jews, though the young Marx's pronounced hostility to Jews and Judaism is absent.

BRUNO BAUER AND KARL MARX

Issues of religion and nationality and Jewish equality figured large in the dispute which Bruno Bauer, a disciple of Hegel, unleashed in 1842. He declared himself for the equality of the Jews in principle but actually questioned and opposed every one of their moves in the struggle for emancipation. Bauer, a Left Hegelian theologian and professor of the history of religion at Bonn, treated the Jewish question in a series of articles which appeared in the *Deutsche Jahrbücher für Kunst und Wissenschaft* in November 1842 and were reissued as a brochure in 1843. He further wrote an essay "Die Fähigkeit zur Befreiung zeitgenössischer Juden und Christen" [The Capacity for Liberation of Contemporary Jews and Christians] which he published in the collection of articles *Einundzwanzig Blätter aus der Schweiz* [Twenty-one Pages from Switzerland], edited by F. Herwegh. At the time of the publication of his first anti-Jewish essays Bauer already had a reputation as a historian of religion and Christianity, and this may have helped in the dissemination of his views.

Following Hegel, Bauer judged the religion of the Hebrews to represent a low stage of religious evolution and the appearance of Jesus a turning point in the history of religion. A decisive difference between Judaism and Christianity is that while, according to Judaism, religion is beyond man, Christianity raises man himself to the level of God. Christianity thus liberates man. Therefore, according to Bauer, a Christian can more easily become an atheist than a Jew. Following Hegel, Bauer holds that the Jew was subjugated to, and always obeyed, an extraneous power.[20]

In his second article Bauer continued to maintain that Christians were nearer to total emancipation than Jews. Though Bauer pointed to the insoluble contradiction of emancipating the Jews in a "Christian state," he did not recommend baptism to the Jews. He rather wanted to subject the "Christian state" to a "total transformation" and have it freed from all religious and clerical ties. Then equality for all citizens would become possible and emancipation of the Jews would be attained. Yet the Jews too—and they were the primary target of his unrelenting biased criticism—would have to renounce their "privileges" and abandon their "nature," which "excluded everything." Lacking true knowledge of Judaism and steeped in prejudice, Bauer aimed his shafts at the Mosaic law. He made emancipation of the Jews contingent on a twofold revolution—a revolution of state and society and of Judaism. On the surface this position appeared balanced, an impression which, in spite of his partiality, he wished to maintain.

In his criticism of Christianity Bauer pursued several objectives. Christianity, in his view, had definite Jewish characteristics, all of which he disliked. His criticism of Christianity is thus always a criticism of "Judaism." The state, Bauer asserted furthermore, had the right to reject Jews; he held them responsible for the narrow outlook from which the contemporary Christian state still suffered.

Bauer's opposition to and criticism of Christianity did not make him more tolerant toward the Jews. On the contrary, in his attack on Christianity he made use of the widespread animosity against the Jews, just as another freethinker, Voltaire, had done. In his struggle against emancipation, Bauer advanced a combination of diverse justifications—theological, philosophical, historical, and economic. He appealed to all those who bitterly resented the cultural, economic, and social progress of German Jewry and were determined to resist the full emancipation of the Jews by any means.

In his tract *Die Judenfrage* [The Jewish Problem] Bauer first made reference to "freedom, rights of humanity, emancipation and indemnification" for the injustice of two millennia, rights that are likely to find a sure echo in "every honest man." He who, like the author himself, challenges the Jews' claims to these rights is likely to be considered an *"Unmensch"* (barbarian), "a friend of tyranny." But Bauer merely wished, he assured the reader, to subject Judaism to the same kind of criticism as Christianity. The Jews should not be "privileged"—a theme to which he regularly returned. They too must suffer "the pains of criticism" and be subjected to its fire.

In a seemingly "dialectical" reversal, Bauer attacked not the oppressors of the Jews throughout the centuries but the victims. "The Jews have been oppressed, since they pressed first and have placed themselves against the wheel of history." According to Bauer, the exclusion of the Jews from Christian society must be traced back to their self-exclusion. Thus the European nations were virtually acquitted from any past wrongdoing. While Bauer conceded the Jews diligence and tenacity, he was quick to assert that these traits had "nothing to do with the interests of history." He claimed first-hand knowledge in regard to these interests and also concerning the direction in which the "wheel of history" was rolling and was supposed to roll. He believed that the cause of Jewish tenacity could be found in an alleged lack of capacity for historic evolution, the "completely unhistoric character of the Jews," their Oriental character—all a palpable tautology. Bauer cannot forgive the Jews for living in eternal separation from other peoples. Because they did so, their very religious, cultural, ethnic, and linguistic peculiarities were their own fault and not the fault of the discriminatory host nations. Unwilling to accept the religious and cultural differences between Germans and Jews, the "libertarian" Bruno Bauer displayed his cardinal article of faith, intolerance.

Bauer also mistrusted the educated and enlightened Jew. The latter's assurances were illusory and could not be believed, "since as long as he wishes to be a Jew, he cannot deny his nature, his exclusiveness, the thought of his special mission, domination." Jewish domination of the world was a theme to which the author often returned; it held a special fascination for him.

According to Bauer, the emancipation of the Jews was possible only if it was not a liberation merely of the Jews but of all human beings, and if it was not tied to baptism. The Germans could not liberate the Jews, since they were not free themselves; "the serf can't emancipate." The question of emancipation was a general one; the Jews were not the only ones who suffered. Oppression and persecution were also the lot of others who for the sake of a higher ideal quarreled with their era. Bauer countered the charge that the Jews had been victims of Christian oppression for centuries with the assertion that in the absolutist state "nobody" enjoyed basic civil rights. He simply ignored the special oppressive laws to which the Jews alone had been subjected for centuries; many such laws still burdened them exclusively at that very moment.

Contempt for the Jews hardly abated on a single page of his tract. Jews, contrary to widely held views, were not fighters for truth. They had not creatively participated in the history of humanity, not even in the history of their own nation. The Jews had by no means refuted Eisenmenger, a notorious Jew-hater of the early eighteenth century, and had not dealt with him in a "scientific" manner. It was not Eisenmenger and like-minded Jew-haters who had attacked the Jews but, Bauer claimed in his usual perplexing reversal of reality and make-believe, the Jews who had attacked Christianity. Compared to Jewish prejudice as aimed against Christianity, Christian bias against Jews and Judaism was of a minor nature. Bauer's charge of Jewish "stubbornness" simply repeated well-known, centuries-old theological prejudice.

The Jews, according to Bauer, were an alien caste. To the Jew only the fellow-Jew was a brother and a neighbor; all other peoples were without rights. Anyone who denied this was merely an apologist for Jews and Judaism. The Jewish people had always been arrogant; in their wars they had displayed harshness, primitiveness, and cruelty and had never been truly courageous. Nor did Bauer discern ethics and true humanity among them. Thus he went on in his endless philippic against the Jews, never discovering any virtue among them but every possible vice on earth. Few pieces of anti-Semitic writing in the nineteenth century were equally malicious and none at the same time claimed such "philosophical" and scholarly respectability.

It was all the more puzzling and ironic that such a broad-sided attack emanated from one who was considered a radical in regard to virtually all theological dogmas. Called the "Messiah of atheism," the "Robespierre of theology," Bauer had lost his chair at the University of Bonn. But in the matter of opposition to the Jews and their long-delayed emancipation, he stood arm in arm with the most obsolete medieval theology.

In 1844 the conservative theologian Friedrich Wilhelm Ghillany rushed to Bauer's side with his pamphlet *Das Judentum und die Kritik, oder es bleibt bei den Menschenopfern der Hebräer und bei der Notwendigkeit einer zeitgemässen Reform des Judentums* [Judaism and Criticism]. He did not entirely exclude the possibility of emancipation but, as the grotesque title of his tract indicated, made it contingent on the reform of Judaism. The tone and spirit of the pamphlet was viciously hostile. Ghillany claimed not to be insensitive to "humanism," but in view of the alleged antihumanist character of Judaism, anti-Semitism, in his opinion, was the justified defense of humanity against the Jews. He submitted in all seriousness that faithful Jews prayed for the resumption of human sacrifices in the restored temple.[21]

German Jews, both scholars and men of action, took Bauer's attack seriously. Abraham Geiger, Samuel Hirsch, Gotthold Salomon, Gustav Philippsohn, and Gabriel Riesser all crossed swords with Bauer. Among the Jewish critiques of Bauer's theses on Jews and Judaism was one from the socialist Karl Grün, *Die Judenfrage: Gegen Bruno Bauer* [The Jewish Problem: Against Bruno Bauer]. Grün accused Bauer of dishonesty in his polemic against the Jews. Actually, he asserted, the Jews no longer clung to the Messiah concept, emancipation having become their "Messiah." Grün also stressed that the prayer for a return to Jerusalem had never had any political significance. He was prepared to accept the declaration of the Jews that they no longer looked upon themselves as an alien nation and that they did not wish to leave Germany. Grün also pointed to the liberation of the Jews in France and the creation of a *Rechtsstaat* in North America, Belgium, and the Netherlands. The existence of a "Christian State" had been all but abandoned in these modern states.[22]

The young Karl Marx participated in the debate with the tract *Zur Judenfrage* [About the Jewish Question]. Due to his later paramount authority Marx was destined to have great influence on German socialist and communist thought and practice. Marx's general praise of Bauer, in spite of his differences with him, reflected, in view of the latter's patent anti-Jewish bias, Marx's equally strong anti-Jewish prejudices. Marx interpreted Bauer's views correctly in letting him thus address the Jews: "You Jews are egotists if you demand a special emancipation for yourselves as Jews. You ought to work as Germans for the political emancipation of Germany and as men for the emancipation of mankind and consider your particular sort of oppression and ignominy not as an exception to the rule but rather as confirmation of it."[23] Here was the extreme leftist point of view, shared by Bauer and Marx. It held out hope for ultimate liberation to all oppressed groups, provided only that revolutionaries of the oppressed nationalities, in a spirit of sacrifice, subordinate their "selfish" considerations to the common interest.

Marx called the secular basis of Judaism "practical need, selfishness," the secular cult of the Jews, "haggling," their "secular god," money. The "practical dominance of Judaism over the Christian world," he claimed to know, had reached its unambiguous and normal expression in North America! He repeated Bauer's statement that it was the Jews who possessed "monstrous power" and exercised political influence on a large scale. Whatever their ulterior motives and ultimate purposes may have been, both Bauer and Marx obviously undercut the Jews' demand for emancipation.

The basis of Jewish religion, Marx claimed, apparently repeating Feuerbach's thesis, was "egotism." Money was the "jealous God of Israel," exchange the actual God of the Jews. "The baseless and irrational law of the Jews is only a religious caricature of morality and law in general." Marx, less interested in theological niceties than Bauer, did not, however, point to Christianity as being on a higher level than Judaism.* But Marx's essay reached its climax in the words: "The social emancipation of the Jews implies the emancipation of society from Judaism." Marx thus identified Judaism and capitalism—a generalization fraught with momentous consequences. "Judaism" kept Germany and Germans in chains! The liberation of the individual Jew and German thus required the destruction of "Judaism."[24]

For apparent reasons, contemporary or later socialist and communist criticism of Marx's views would have been considered iconoclastic; therefore it did not occur. Thus the Jewish self-hatred in Marx in the end strengthened and perpetuated Christian hatred of Judaism and also of Jews, rationalized the dislike of both by radicals and "socialists," and laid the foundation for "socialist" anti-Semitism.

---

*"Christianity is the sublime thought of Judaism, Judaism is the vulgar application of Christianity." See also: "Christianity had its origin in Judaism. It has dissolved itself back into Judaism."

CHAPTER 14

Scholars, Poets, and Men of Action in the Forties

Alexander von Humboldt: A Friend

Among progressive Germans who steadfastly clung to their principles and made no compromise with the continuing bias was Alexander von Humboldt, one of the great German scholars of the nineteenth century. This great nature philosopher and famous traveler was a warm and loyal friend of the Jews. Since his "earliest youth in Germany," he wrote to Rabbi Mortara of Mantua, he had been connected "with excellent men of the Jewish faith and of Jewish descent."[1] Moses Mendelssohn and his disciple David Friedländer had exerted an important influence upon the education of the young brothers Humboldt. Alexander's relations with the Jews remained no less intimate in the following period. He esteemed the juridical scholar Eduard Gans and was also a friend of Dr. Michael Sachs. Repeatedly he gave encouragement and support to Jewish scholars, effecting the call of a Jewish professor to the University of Berlin and procuring for another a seat in the Academy of Berlin.[2]

When the Jewish scholar C. A. Slonimsky, author of a biography of Humboldt in Hebrew, sent him a copy, Humboldt replied: "Unfortunately, I am unfamiliar with Hebrew literature, but from earliest youth I have been most intimately connected with the noblest men of your coreligionists and have been a vigorous and persistent fighter for the rights which are their due and which are still largely denied to them. I am not indifferent to the honor which you have bestowed upon me."[3] He highly valued Hebrew poetry. In a letter to Dr. Emil Loew, Humboldt wrote: "You are indisputably correct if you call the poetry of the Hebrews by far the best of all Oriental nature poetry."

On a later occasion, Humboldt tried to dissuade Loew from being baptized: "Stay with your brethren, who after having suffered such a remarkable martyrdom through the centuries are standing on the threshold of freedom. Dedicate your strength and your mind to the labor of their history of a thousand years, and the success can and will not fail. The results which you, young friend, will gain from the source of free knowledge will solace and calm you for so many a sad experience of the fog-gray present age, which stands before the onset of a bright morning of freedom."[4]

When Heinrich Heine in a personal matter turned to Humboldt, the latter disclosed to the poet "his old admiration" for his "magnificent 'Book of Songs' which breathes a deep natural feeling," and thanked him for his "personal confidence in a purely human matter."[5] He equally esteemed Ferdinand Lassalle, later one of the prominent leaders of German socialism—the "child prodigy," as he then called the youthful fighter of the revolution of 1848. Humboldt pleaded successfully in his behalf with Frederick William IV and followed Lassalle's later career with keen interest. Humboldt succeeded also in procuring from the King an annual pension for Rahel Levin.

His admiration for Hebrew poetry found special expression in his great work *Cosmos*. The nature poetry of the Hebrews, he wrote there, was "a reflex of monotheism." Nature "appears to the Hebrew poet always in relation to a ruling spiritual power. It is to him something created . . . vivid expression of the omnipresence of God in the works of the external world. For this reason the lyric poetry of the Hebrews is, judged merely by its content, magnificent and of solemn seriousness; it is sad and longing . . . dedicated to the pure contemplation of the divine, metaphoric in language, but clear and simple in thought; it pleases itself in parables which almost rhythmically return, always the same. . . . One could say that in the 104th Psalm alone the picture of the entire Cosmos is presented."

In the same work Humboldt asserted his belief in the basic unity of the human race—there existed only "*Abarten*" (varieties) of the one human race, not separate races. He also rejected the assumption of superior and inferior human races as unscientific and "disagreeable." "If we wish to designate an idea," he wrote, "which is visible through all history in increasingly broad vitality, it is the idea of humanity: the endeavor to tear down the walls which prejudices and one-sided views of all kinds have erected in a hostile manner and the treatment of the entire human race, irrespective of religion, nationality, and color, as one great, closely related tribe, as an entity existing for the attainment of one purpose, the free development of internal strength. . . ."[6]

In 1843 the Prussian minister Eichhorn sought to extend the discriminatory legislation that applied to the Jews of Posen to all Prussian Jews. In this critical moment Alexander von Humboldt intervened decisively in behalf of the Jews. "I have read, dearest Count," he wrote to one of the most prominent royal councilors, Count Stolberg, "with sorrow, . . . the motives of which and tendency you share with me, the proposal which arrived yesterday. . . . I consider the planned innovations . . . to be in conflict with all principles of political wisdom, causing most malicious interpretations of motives; they rob rights which already have been acquired through a more humane law of the father, and are contrary to the leniency of the present monarch. It is a perilous pretense of weak humanity to wish to interpret the old laws of God. The history of dark centuries teaches which aberrations such interpretations encourage. The fear of harming me should not deter you from making use of these lines; first of all, one must have the courage to express one's opinion. . . ."[7] Simultaneously he wrote to a Jewish friend in Berlin: "You see, my friend, that my somewhat impetuous defense of the people who are always in distress will not remain entirely in vain."[8]

When in 1847 a new law affecting the situation of the Prussian Jews was enacted, Alexander von Humboldt criticized it as severely as he had previously condemned the legislative project of 1843. He was especially enraged that the Jews could no longer become extraordinary professors of history, professors of pagan and Greek mythology and of Oriental languages. He regretted that the Ministry of Education, as the proposed measure showed, was trailing far behind the people of Prussia in "intellectual growth."[9] When a German-Jewish writer sent him his work *Humanity,* Humboldt replied to him in November 1856: "Its propagation is the more desirable since in the German fatherland itself the progress of religious tolerance and of equality of political rights is not exactly splendid."[10]

A letter of gratitude from the Jews of Westfalen to Humboldt testified to the great esteem in which he was held in Jewish circles. Repeatedly and unhesitatingly he had thrown the weight of his prestige into the scales in their behalf. Like his younger brother Wilhelm, Alexander von Humboldt is one of the most splendid figures in the history of German-Jewish relations.

Liberal and Revolutionary Poetry

At first Franz Dingelstedt, poet and journalist, was, like Alexander von Humboldt, a critic of the political order of the *Vormärz*. But later he made peace with it. His vacillations were reflected in his changing attitudes to the Jews. In his satiric poem *Lieder eines kosmopolitischen Nachtwächters* [Songs of a Cosmopolitan Watchman] (1841) he pilloried the persecutors of the Jews but at the same time recommended a new persecution!

The Jew, Dingelstedt charged, has wrested "shrewdly the hilt from the unskilled hand" of the Germans:

> Emancipate this tough people, as you once
> Barricaded it! The fashion changed indeed!
> It has long grown to a multitude
> And as a power stands opposed to you.
>
> It drives away the peasant from his soil.
> It scares the merchant from the market!
> And half with gold and half with slavish wit
> It buys the watchword from the spirit of the age.
>
> What can emancipation help the tribe which
> Never emancipated itself from usury?
> What you want to give to it, it has long taken,
> While you debate over principles.
>
> Whatever you seize, you will seize Jews,
> Everywhere the favorite people of the Lord.
> Go, shut them into old quarters
> Before they shut you into a Christian ghetto.

Were the Jews, who had not yet attained full emancipation, indeed a menacing "power," as their enemies had asserted for so long? Friendly voices, Dingelstedt charged, had been bought "with gold." Dingelstedt aimed unabashedly at arousing fear, prejudice, and suspicion among Germans. The emancipation of the Jews was presented as the beginning of the oppression of Christians, and equal rights for all were turned into privileges only for the Jews.

Yet strangely enough Dingelstedt prefaced these bitterly hostile lines with verses which were directly opposed to them in content, tone, and spirit. While the second half of this poem sounded like a song of hate, the first part expressed sympathy for the Jews and anger at their oppressors. In the first half the poet, passing through Frankfurt's Jewish quarter, recalls the old times, when Israel had pitched its "tent" there. There are now only sad-looking, desolate houses.

From their low doors an eternal darkness yawns at the stranger. Neither the rays of the sun nor the glowing of the moon pierce the windows. The gaunt pale figures in front of the houses seem to fit into the crooked, angular streets. An all-pervading humidity hovers over them.

> How the gables hang over, very threateningly,
> Blackened by vapor, bent by the weight of the age!
> How they throng together for protection and defiance,
> As if force had driven them hereto!

> The Jewish ghetto!—O barbaric times
> When one forced a people in here like slaves,
> And when at night a merciless iron lock
> Hung at the door, on both sides.

> When every one of the Reich's Chamber Jews
> Carried his sign with the claw,
> And when the Junker with the bold right arm
> Beat unpunished the Hebrew's face![11]

While Dingelstedt bitterly criticized here the cruel age when Jews had been forced into the ghetto, his recommendation in the last verse was to "shut them into the old quarters" and to restore the "barbaric times."

In the year 1849, however, under the impact of the revolution, Dingelstedt sang a song of "conciliation." It was on the occasion of the one hundredth anniversary of Goethe's birth that he wrote the poem "Goethe und Börne." The German poet and the liberal Jewish journalist who had been so critical of him because of his supposed indifference to the lot of the common people embrace each other in the poet's dream. In the midst of the debates of the Frankfurt constituent assembly in the *Paulskirche* in 1848, the poet is overwhelmed by slumber. In his dream Goethe and Börne, both sons of Frankfurt am Main, enter the assembly hall, one from the right, the other from the left, and meet in the center of the hall.

> Soft tones whisper, touching their hearts,
> Sons of the same mother, don't you want to be brothers?

Finally, the

> Walls break down, also those which separated you,
> Hirschgraben, Judengasse, La Chaise and Fürstengruft.*

*Names of streets in Frankfurt a.M.

They are mere "shadows," "dissolved in morning air."

Thundering applause greets Goethe and Börne when they march arm in arm through the assembly hall:

> When I was awakened by it, conscious of reality,
> The twenty-eighth of August beamed at me.
> I saw clearly conciliation and fulfilment in the dream.[12]

Comparable to the sharp criticism of German Jewry in Dingelstedt's *Lieder eines kosmopolitischen Nachtwächters* in the early forties was another attack which emanated at about the same time from the liberal side, namely from Hoffman von Fallersleben in his *Unpolitische Lieder* [Nonpolitical Songs] (1840–1841). Fallersleben was the author of the song "Deutschland, Deutschland über alles," which placed German loyalty above loyalty to the *Stamm* (tribe, land) and was to become the German national anthem. Though he was a German patriot, a cosmopolitan note sounded throughout his works, just as it did through the works of other liberal writers of the age. Thus Fallersleben wrote:

> You are a German! I like this very much.
> You are also a man, I like this even better.

Yet such cosmopolitanism did not express itself in his attitude toward the Jews, which, as a matter of fact, was as contradictory as the position of Dingelstedt.

In his two little volumes, *Unpolitische Lieder,* Hoffman von Fallersleben gave vivid expression to the disappointments of German liberalism after the accession to the throne of Frederick William IV. These songs also included bitter accusations against contemporary Jews, though no group was to suffer more from the failure of the King to speed up progress more vigorously, in accordance with the hope he had earlier aroused. Just as Dingelstedt changed his tune, so also Fallersleben. The poet turned to the Jews with these harsh verses:

> To Israel!
> You steal from under our feet
> Our German fatherland!
> Is this your suffering, this your penance?
> This the edge of your open grave?
>
> O Israel, turned away from God,
> You have made yourself a God,
> And are, taught by this Lord,
> Intent on usury, lying and cheating.

If you don't want to abandon this God
May Germany never listen to you!
If you don't wish to hate your enslavement,
You shall never march through freedom's door.[13]

The Jews' abandonment of their allegedly reprehensible practices is considered a condition of their being granted "freedom" and equality. Thus, by implication, the existing inequality appears to be justified.

The voice of hostility is at times subdued by more friendly tones, as in Fallersleben's poem "Israel." The Jews have every reason to lament the fall of the ancient Jewish state, the poet says, "for it never will return."

No Messiah can save you,
But God feels pity,
And awakens through your sufferings
Love in Christians and in pagans,
And love saves you.[14]

Ferdinand Freiligrath stood in the forefront of the German revolutionary poets of his day. But he had found his first poetic themes in the Near East, in the Arabian desert, to which fantasy, aroused by the reading of the Bible, had carried him. That too is the scene of his poem "Kreuzigung" [Crucifixion]. Germanic warriors serve in Rome's army, which is stationed in Palestine and Syria. While Christ is nailed to the cross, the soldiers amuse themselves by throwing dice.[15] For centuries the Jews had been burdened with the accusation of blood-guilt for the crucifixion of Jesus, but Freiligrath pointed to Jesus as a Jew and presented a Roman legionnaire of German ancestry as his executioner.

The "Wirtschaftspolitische Bismarck"

Friedrich List was both one of the leading economic theoreticians in Germany as well as a man of great practical abilities. He became an untiring promoter of the German customs union and of railroad construction in the German states. In the latter project he was given firm support by many German Jews. As he himself attested, "Prussia's first merchant, the highly esteemed Josef Mendelssohn," backed him in his endeavors to establish a company to build a railroad between Leipzig and Dresden.[16] On a petition for the construction of one railroad, addressed to King Frederick William III by leading Prussian businessmen in 1835, about half the signatures were those of German Jews: "W. Beer; Jakobson; Ries; Mendelssohn & Co.; Bendermannsen; M. Magnus; Oppenheim Söhne; Josef Max Frenckel, Gebr. Behrend; Ossent & Poppe."[17] In January 1836 List wrote to his wife that he had been the guest of Rothschild in Frankfurt: "He was very friendly and gave me letters for the South."[18] Soon thereafter he informed her: "Today I am invited for dinner to the home of the first banker [Oppenheim]."[19] The help List found among Germany's Jews was to speed the economic unification of Germany, which in turn paved the way to the political unification of 1871. List's suicide in 1846 may be partly blamed on the inadequate support given him by his fellow Christians.

Except in some youthful remarks, List by no means displayed the "particular dislike" of Judaism and Jewry attributed to him by a noted German historian.[20] How little he inclined to anti-Semitism is indicated by the fact that he was offered the editorship of a new daily paper in Köln by the Jewish financier Oppenheim of that city. List was forced to decline the offer because he had just broken his leg.[21] A few months later, in another letter to Oppenheim, he again expressed his regret: "Yesterday Mr. Isidor Obermeyer gave me a picture of Köln and of you personally that made me again regret the serious mishap which prevented me last year from accepting your honorable offer. . . . Obviously, there is the place for the first national German paper." That this paper would be in Jewish hands—those of Herr Oppenheim—did not frighten List in the least. While voicing his regret to Oppenheim, he recommended for the editorship of his planned paper another Jewish journalist, Moses Hess, whom he introduced as "an important talent."[22]

In a chapter of his main work, *Das nationale System der politischen Ökonomie* [The National System of Political Economy], a classic in economics, List referred briefly to the ejection of the Jews from Spain in 1492 as an "evil of fanaticism." Spain, he wrote, "was in possession of all elements of greatness and of prosperity when fanaticism in union with despotism readied itself to suffocate the soul of the nation. This dark work was begun with the ejection of the Jews and concluded with the expulsion of the Moors, as a result of which two million of the most industrious and wealthiest inhabitants were driven from Spain with their capital."[23] "The spirit of enterprise, industry and trade," List remarked in conclusion, struck root only "in the soil of political and religious freedom."

List—the *wirtschaftspolitische* Bismarck (the Bismarck of political economy), as he was later dubbed—helped create in the German economy a unity upon which Bismarck later built territorial and political unity. List was one in the impressive line of great German economists and economic historians of the nineteenth century— Wilhelm Roscher, Karl Lamprecht, Lujo Brentano, and even Werner-Sombart—all of whom, contrary to their anti-Semitic contemporaries, gave recognition to the part played by German Jews in the development of the German economy.

Bismarck in 1847

Opposition to the emancipation of the Jews in Prussia found its expression on the eve of the 1848 revolution in the speeches made by the deputy Otto von Bismarck in the *Vereinigte Landtag*. The "tolle [mad] Junker," as Otto Jöhlinger in his study *Bismarck und die Juden* (Berlin, 1921) observed, was no friend of the Jews. In Jöhlinger's words: "In the circle in which Bismarck was born and in the circle in which he learned to know Johanna von Puttkamer, his later wife, one did not love Judaism."[24] Bismarck's early remarks about the Jews were quite negative, and he wished to restrict their rights. The speeches against the Jews in the *Vereinigte Landtag* on June 15 and 25 and in November 1847 reflected the reactionary and romantic view of the "Christian State" in which Jews could expect no equality but only subordination.

Prussia was a Christian state, Bismarck expounded on June 15, 1847. He conceded that this ideal was not always realized, but he did not believe that Prussia would come closer to its purpose with the help of the Jews. Christianity would only be diminished if the people were shown that the Christian faith was not required of its rulers. The Jews were anxious to become generals, ministers, even minister of religion; Bismarck, however, opposed these demands, admitting that he was "full of prejudices." The thought of a Jew as representative of his holy majesty made him feel deeply "depressed and downhearted." He shared "this feeling with the mass of the lower strata of the people and was not ashamed of their company." German Jews no longer lived in the era of Jewish persecutions; the only thing they were still excluded from was the "haven of bureaucracy." He would be prepared to join the ranks of those who wished the emancipation of the Jews if the Jews themselves only tore down the bars which separated them from the Germans.[25]

On June 25, 1847, Bismarck, speaking of a different motion before the house, which would have given the Jews equal rights without reservation, questioned whether full emancipation was desirable and constituted progress.[26] And on November 15, 1847, Bismarck addressed the assembly about Christianity and civil marriage, stressing the blessing of the church, which, in his view, was necessary for its validity. Yet later Bismarck introduced civil marriage in the *Reich,* just as he was to bring emancipation of the Jews to its legal completion in 1869. The mature statesman thus abandoned his early opposition, opening the door wide to changes which the modern age and the interests of nation and state seemed imperatively to demand.

Anti-Semites, nevertheless, have often quoted Bismarck's views, as expressed in 1847, in support of their allegations that he showed unchanging hostility to the Jews. Though an analysis of the early views of Bismarck proves that he opposed full equality and was swayed by prejudice, as he freely admitted, he was at no time a fanatic. Even in his speeches in 1847 there are hints that he would not wish to close the door to full emancipation forever, though he pointed to the Jews rather than to Germans as the alleged obstacle to equality. He did not oppose the marriage of Jews and Christians on principle and certainly not on racial grounds.

In any case, Bismarck later clearly repudiated the opinions about the Jews that he had voiced in the *Vereinigte Landtag.* In a circle of friends he facetiously spoke about having heard "many a bad speech" there and, as he smilingly added, "had also himself given one." Similarly, in a talk in November 1880 with his physician Dr. Eduard Cohen, a Jew himself, he remarked in reply to the question whether he was prepared to stand by everything he then said: "By no means. *Tempora mutantur.* Man grows with his goals."[27] Even Prussian conservatism did not stand still.

Joseph II (1741–1790; became Holy Roman Emperor in 1765 and Emperor of Austria in 1780)

Below: Frederick the Great (1712–1786; became King of Prussia in 1740)

Moses Mendelssohn
(1729–1786)

Gotthold Ephraim Lessing
(1729–1781)

Johann Wolfgang von Goethe (1749–1832)

Left:
*Rahel Varnhagen
(1771–1833)*

Immanuel Kant (1724–1804)

*Right: Friedrich Schiller
(1759–1805)*

*Baron Karl vom Stein
(1757–1831)*

*Above: Alexander von Humboldt
(1769–1859)*

*Wilhelm von Humboldt
(1767–1835)*

*Johann Gottlieb Fichte
(1762–1814)*

*Below: Friedrich Schleiermacher
(1768–1834)*

Dorothea Schlegel
(1763–1839)

Below left: Clemens Brentano
(1778–1842)

Right:
Salomon Mayer Rothschild
(1774–1855)

Above:
Franz Grillparzer
(1791–1872)

Heinrich Heine
(1797–1856)

Above: Fürst Otto von Bismarck
(1815–1898)

Facing Page

Top: Friedrich Hebbel (1813–1863)

Bottom left: Georg Wilhelm Friedrich Hegel
(1770–1831)

Bottom right: Ludwig Börne (1786–1837)

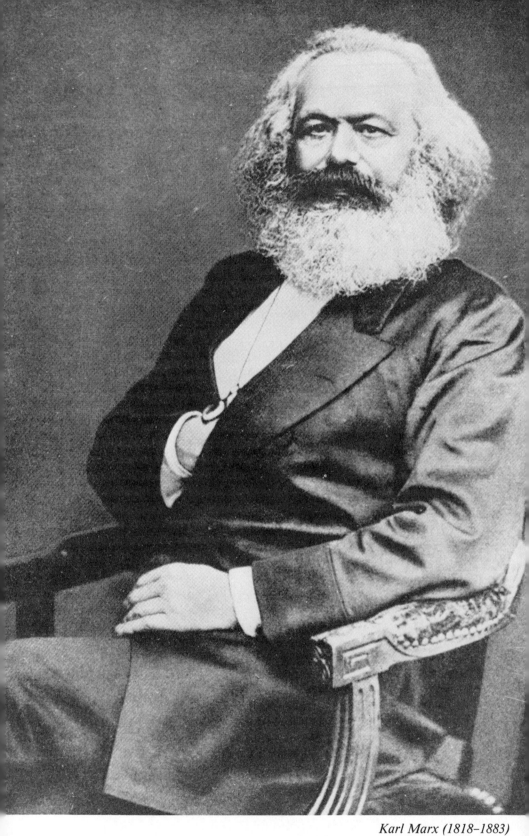

Karl Marx (1818–1883)

Friedrich Engels
(1820–1895)

Below: Richard Wagner
(1813–1883)

Right:
Heinrich von Treitschke
(1834–1896)

Left:
Ferdinand Lassalle
(1825–1864)

*Left: Arthur Schopenhauer
(1788–1860)*

*Right:
Friedrich Nietzsche
(1844–1900)*

PART V

The Era of Fulfillment: Unification and Emancipation

You are very much mistaken, dear Dahlmann, about the general enthusiasm of the whole of Germania for political unity. . . . In northern and northeastern Germany, if you discount the effervescence of the big cities and the Teutonic fury of the Jews, there is no trace of enthusiasm at all for it.

—Frederick William IV

From the Revolution of 1848/1849 to 1870

The Revolution of 1848/1849 in the Germanies

The political pressure which had lain so long and so heavily upon many European peoples appeared to be forever removed during the revolutions of 1848/1849. Once the chains of autocracy were shaken off, a deep enthusiasm prevailed in Central Europe. The Jews too strove for political freedom and German national unity, at the same time demanding full equality with the German-Christian population.

The great majority of the Jews hailed the coming of the revolution. They had only to gain from the creation of a modern constitutional state and the enforcement of human rights. Yet they did not think merely or primarily of themselves. In his sermon in Vienna on March 18, 1848, immediately after the fall of Metternich, Rabbi Mannheimer posed the question as to the duties the new hour imposed upon the Jews and outlined the Jewish position: "For us? Nothing! Everything for the nation and the fatherland. . . . Now, nothing for us! No word of Jewish emancipation, if others don't speak it for us. . . . First the right to live as men, to breathe, to think, to speak; first the right of the citizens, afterwards comes the Jew!"

Gabriel Riesser had clearly expressed Jewish wishes and hopes when he had written earlier: "Offer me with one hand the emancipation to which all my innermost wishes point, with the other the realization of the most beautiful dream of the political unity of Germany in union with its political freedom, and without hesitation I choose the latter! For I have the firm, deepest conviction that the latter contains the former."[1] Not merely as Jews, but also as German patriots and devotees of liberalism, most German Jews greeted the year 1848 as the beginning of a new era. Their seemingly selfless attitude was rooted in abiding faith in the progressivism of the new age.

Like others during the revolution, Jews displayed a spirit of sacrifice and courage. Although several wealthy Jewish financiers, including Salomon Rothschild,[2] remained in the conservative camp, in Vienna and Berlin Jewish blood was shed in the streets. Many Jews in Vienna were among the early March victims of the fighting and were buried in a mass grave jointly with the German Christian victims of the shootings. When General Windischgrätz in October 1848 took the city of Vienna after a bloody siege, the young radical journalist Hermann Jellinek, brother of the Viennese rabbi, was among those shot under martial law.

The poet and playwright Franz Grillparzer, in general averse to all excesses, was impressed by the boldness of a young Jewish fighter for liberty who, in the center of the Ballplatz, face to face with armed soldiers, harangued the multitude. "The young man," Grillparzer related in his *Erinnerungen aus dem Jahr 1848* [Remembrances of the Year 1848], "began his speech, of which I understood the beginning only with difficulty, 'My name is N. Burian; I was born in Galicia, and am nineteen years old.' In part I could not understand the rest; in part I feared that the soldiers would at any moment attack the young people with the bayonet. . . . But the entire scene made a grandiose impression upon me. The unconcern with which the young men stood like lambs for a sacrifice, taking no notice of the armed soldiers, was something magnificent. These are heroic children, I said to myself."[3]

In March 1848 Emperor Ferdinand decreed a constitution for Austria that also emancipated the Jews. During the next months most of the German states were to follow this example. In August 1848 the Jewish question was also debated in the German National Assembly in Frankfurt am Main. Paragraph 16 of the "Basic Rights of the German People," as accepted by the assembly, read thus: "The enjoyment of the civil and political rights is neither conditioned upon nor limited by religious belief. It must not curtail civic duties." The equality of the Jews was proclaimed for the projected unified German state over the opposition of just one delegate, Robert Mohl. His lone voice, however, preserved the historical continuity of German anti-Semitism. It represents the tenuous bridge between the Jew-hating of the *Vormärz* and the rising hostility toward the Jews that followed the failure of the revolution.

Anti-Semitism was far stronger and more deeply rooted in Germany's soil than the single vote indicated. During the first months of the revolution public opinion was plainly averse to every form of reaction, and the Jew-haters did not dare unfurl their banner. With other reactionaries, they sought cover and bided their time. Soon, however, the revolution had spent its force, and ultraconservatism and reaction quickly regained much of the lost ground. At that moment the opponents of the revolution sought a convenient scapegoat and focused on German Jewry—so often the target of hostile forces in prerevolutionary days.

During the "mad" year anti-Semitism had begun to raise its head with increasing boldness. Had the Jew not gained from the revolution? Had he not benefited more than the German? Did Jews not stand in the front line of the struggle for freedom and national unity? Those who raised these questions—the opponents of a modern constitutional state and the protagonists of the absolutist princely regimes of the *Vormärz*—saw opposition to the Jews as a welcome means to discredit liberals, democrats, and radicals generally and to reduce their political attractiveness for the people at large. So they created the myth of the "Jewish" revolution. Reactionaries spread rumors that it had been begun by Poles, Frenchmen, and Jews and had been led by alien elements. At the same time, they sought to divert the attention of the aroused mob from pressing political and social problems to the wealth of some Jews, who were pictured as unscrupulous financiers and exploiters of the German-Christian population. Thus the Jews were charged both with having created the revolt against the old order and with being the main supporters of the social and political establishment that the revolutionaries were set to overthrow. The incongruities of these accusations disturbed the accusers as little as, generations later, the contradictory charges that Jews were fighting to overthrow capitalism and that they were its most stubborn defenders.

Anti-Jewish agitation quickly bore fruit. In the very midst of the years 1848–1849 anti-Semitic outbursts spread like wildfire. They occurred in Austria—in a most violent form in Pressburg—as well as throughout Germany, especially in Baden. Even freedom's intoxication could not completely silence the voices of opposition to the Jews.

But the dispute about the Jews and their emancipation, though highly significant, did not provide the only or main attraction during the revolutionary turmoil. Many other urgent problems preoccupied the Germans. The struggle between the *Grossdeutschen* and *Kleindeutschen,* between republicans and monarchists, liberals, democrats, and conservatives, between the people and the princes, the forces for social change and for the status quo, tended to push the Jewish question to the sidelines. Still, the Jewish issue was often intertwined with other disputes and promptly exploited by anti-Jewish circles.

The Post-Revolutionary Era: Frederick William IV

Reactionaries accused the Jews of having "made" the revolution. Old Arndt raised contrary charges against them—namely of being responsible for the postrevolutionary Prussian reaction. Arndt assailed especially the converted Jew Friedrich Julius Stahl, theoretician of the Prussian Christian-German state, and criticized the "Oriental" autocracy of Prussia's King Frederick William IV.[4] He seemed to have forgotten that during the days of the *Vormärz* he had attacked the Jews because of their agitation in behalf of revolutionary and radical causes. In reality, Jews played no part in the Prussian government of the postrevolutionary or any subsequent period. The political philosophy which underlay the Christian-German state was exclusive in regard to the Jews and hostile to their basic interests. That philosophy was rather the theoretical handiwork of a single Jewish convert to Lutheranism, Stahl, who had cut his ties with the Jews long ago and denied emancipation to his former coreligionists.

Frederick William IV, the "Romantic on the throne of the Caesars," had promised equality to the Jews, assuring them that he did "not adhere to the blind prejudices of previous centuries." But after the revolution of 1848–1849 he thundered against the Jews, against "the existence and the influence of that despicable Jewish clique with its tail of silly and foolish yelpers," who were a "misfortune for Prussia." "The insolent rabble by word, letter and picture daily lays the axe to the root of the German character."[5] While Arndt tried to make the Jews responsible for the new reaction of King Frederick William IV, the latter sought to explain the revolution of 1848 as a mere machination of the Jews. "Jewish" became simply the by-word for any political thought which anyone, whatever his political and ideological bent, objected to and despised.

Did the accusations that the Prussian monarch hurled against the Jews spring from his sincere concern for German interests, for the "German" character? Had Frederick William IV, who in his absolutist monarchical pride had refused to receive the imperial crown from the hands of the popular representatives, the German National Assembly at Frankfurt, the right to pose as defender of Germany and to condemn the Jews, ardent spokesmen for the national state? What in the views of the Prussian monarch was the true, the genuine German character?

Germans gave a variety of answers to the question of what constituted its essence. Yet the great majority of educated Germans had already abandoned the narrow particularism revealed in a letter of King Frederick William IV to the historian Dahlmann. The Prussian's first loyalty, the king insisted, should be to Prussia and only thereafter to Germany, and he suggested similarly that the citizen of Hanover, Saxony, or Bavaria be first a patriot in regard to his own state. Dahlmann was very mistaken if he believed that there prevailed in Germany a "general enthusiasm for the whole of Germania."[6] In northern and northeastern Germany, if one discounted the "effervescence of the big cities and the Teutonic fury of the Jews," there was no trace of enthusiasm for it. To the contrary, "the rebellion of the Jews and of the big city population and its consequences have caused a heavy setback in the countryside, where one feels more intensely Prussian, Pomeranian, Hannoverian, and Saxonian than during [the last] 50 to 100 years."

In regard to the political future of Germany, the Prussian monarch and the Prussian Jews stood at opposite poles. When in March 1848 Frederick William IV had promised to his people the fulfillment of their national and political desires, he had been moved more by fear of the revolution than by genuine conviction. Like the conservative Prussian Junkers, he clung to a political past in which narrow provincial loyalties prevailed, and he detested new revolutionary formations. After the German revolution had spent its first force and the old establishment had regained its courage, Frederick William preferred remaining King of Prussia by the grace of God to becoming Emperor of Germany by the grace of the German people. It was no surprise that the monarch saw in the German Jews, many of whom were fervent advocates of a united German national state, his bitter opponents; in his eyes they were the gravediggers of German political tradition. Linked with the liberal, progressive, and nationalist, the politically conscious and articulate German bourgeoisie and intelligentsia, the Jews struggled against discredited absolutism and for a greater unified German state, while the monarch and the Junkers were still unwilling to look beyond the narrow confines of Pomerania and Prussia.

Jews in the Struggle for German National Unity

The Jews faced few obstacles in conquering old-fashioned German particularism. Unlike the indigenous Pomeranian Junkers, they were not tied down to any localism by tradition, sentiment, or interests. Unburdened by romantic notions of the past, which for them held memories only of oppression, they embraced the concept of a united Germany, which held out new hopes to them, and looked expectantly toward a better future.

As the twentieth century was to prove convincingly, national unification did not constitute a guarantee of equality for the German Jews. The preservation of political and territorial particularism in Germany, on the other hand, was not *per se* connected with continuing legal inequality. Historically, however, the formation of a unified *Reich* more or less coincided with the proclamation of full emancipation for the German Jews, just as the period of a loose confederacy embracing many German states coincided with the age of inequality for them.

The era of the drive toward German national unity happened to be an era of struggle for equality for the German Jews. While the Jews fought for the unification of Germany and continued to make economic and cultural progress, the German people became increasingly, though perhaps never fully, reconciled to the concept of Jewish emancipation. Lofty idealism and realistic self-interest moved both Jews and Christians and ultimately created the Reich. It was in the new imperial Germany that the Jews were to attain full legal equality.

During the revolution Frederick William IV and the composer Richard Wagner stood on opposite sides of the barricades; yet both testified to the enthusiasm of the German Jews for the unification of Germany. While Frederick William castigated them for their nationalistic endeavors, Wagner, after unification, addressed the Jews half in earnest, half sneeringly, as "guarantors of the unity of our Reich."[7]

The anti-Semitic writer Constantin Frantz, who gave support to German particularism long after the unity of Germany had been attained, did not forgive the Jews either their participation in the German national movement before 1870 or their influence thereafter in strengthening the centralistic and unitarian forces of the new state: "The Jews," he wrote reprehensively in 1874, "belong to the most energetic friends of the *Reich* and strive for the continuous widening of its jurisdiction."[8] Wherever a fight raged for stronger centralism and greater uniformity in the *Reich* against the old centrifugal, tribal tendencies, the Jews, according to Frantz, stood on the side of the former. In this development of a centralized state, Constantin Frantz, blinded by his particularism and even more by his hatred of the Jews, saw no "towering upsurge" of German nationalism but only a symptom of "Judaization"!

In German Central Europe as well as in the rest of nineteenth-century Europe nationalism and liberalism were long closely linked. While in the era of the War of Liberation German nationalists had still excluded German Jews, after 1848, in the words of the novelist

Gustav Freytag, they welcomed them as "dear allies" in the political and social struggle. The liberal Austrian politician Hans Kudlich, author in 1848 of the bill for the emancipation of the peasants, not only felt himself to be both a patriotic Austrian and good German but also knew how to combine the ideas of liberalism with his national idealism. He saw no place for anti-Semitism in the national-liberal camp. When he was proclaimed, quite undeservedly, by German anti-Jewish circles in Bohemia as their intellectual father, he vehemently protested against this "mendacious and impudent" assertion. "My entire life," he wrote, "is a proof that one can be a good German, a liberal, and a friend of the people, without excluding the Jews from the nation."[9] He considered them co-fighters in the German cause. Gustav Freytag in Germany similarly used the word "ally" (*Bundesgenosse*) to describe the relationship of the German Jews to the Germans.

Hostility against the Jews, however, was deeply rooted even in some liberal circles. Neither German liberalism nor the German national movement after 1848–1849 was entirely immune to anti-Semitism. The joint struggle of the German liberal bourgeoisie and German Jewry for the unitary state against conservative and reactionary Junkers did not prevent the survival of anti-Jewish sentiments and thoughts even in the German middle class. Competition of a material and also of an intellectual nature tended at times to deepen the gulf, which had separated German Jews and German Christians for many centuries. The spirit of intolerance, which had not been banished from the liberal camp during the *Vormärz,* did not entirely vanish in the more liberal fifties and sixties. It merely changed, taking on cultural and ethnic rather than religious characteristics, though the latter were not entirely submerged. The noted pedagogue Diesterweg found the "cruel prejudice" of anti-Semitism "even among writers and teachers,"[10] and Baron Josias von Bunson, Prussian diplomat and author, remarked: "Even among liberal-minded Christian men in Germany principles have been voiced against the freedom of religion which suit the seventeenth century rather than the nineteenth. Why this retardation of the Germans in the chorus of humanity? Leaders of progressive political parties boast of being exclusive in regard to Jews."[11]

Hans Kudlich blamed the enemies of the Jews for having "disfigured and soiled" the "pure, noble conception of German nationalism with inhuman and un-German anti-Semitism" to such an extent that "the word *national* [was looked upon] in Germany as equivalent to *anti-Semitic*."[12] This remark, though perhaps exaggerated, contained a kernel of truth. Yet *national* and anti-*Semitic* were not yet identical,

306 The Era of Fulfillment: Unification and Emancipation

as is shown by the attitudes of national-minded writers such as Scheffel, Dahn, and Freytag and of the German-Swiss novelist Konrad Ferdinand Meyer.*

From the War of 1866 toward Unification and Emancipation

German and Austrian Jews who demonstrated self-sacrifice in the struggle for liberty and national unity continued to display national spirit thereafter. When in 1866 a fratricidal war over supremacy in Germany broke out between Prussia and Austria, Jews fought and fell on both sides. "It looked," the novelist Theodor Fontane remarked in his historic work *Der deutsche Krieg von 1866* [The German War of 1866], "as if they had promised each other to erase the old conception of their unwillingness to wage war and their incapacity to do it."[13]

Aside from military contributions to the victory of Prussia and the development of the unitary German state, some Jews rendered other "services," which Bismarck himself "highly" appreciated. The money Prussia needed for engaging in war against Austria was lent to the government by the Jewish banker Bleichröder. When Bismarck was later attacked because of his close relations with Bleichröder, he publicly stated in the *Reichstag:* "It is true that Bleichröder brought me in the year 1866 the means for waging war which nobody else wanted to advance to us. This was a deed for which I was obligated to feel gratitude. As an honest person I don't like to be spoken ill of, nor have a Jew say that I have used him and then held him in contempt, in spite of services rendered which I, as a statesman, had to value highly."[14] At Bismarck's suggestion Bleichröder was later raised to the rank of nobility. Jewish capital thus helped to erect the house of German unity, while German capitalists cautiously stood aside, fearful of making a bad investment.

Since the doors of emancipation had been opened to the Jews, their economic functions had undergone significant changes. The number of those who continued to choose trade as an occupation was still relatively high. After centuries of social, political, and economic anomaly a return to "normalcy" could not be quickly expected, especially not in view of the hindrances erected by the still hostile outside world. Only a small number of Jews served in public administration

---

*Konrad Ferdinand Meyer, according to the testimony of Karl Emil Franzos, a Jewish writer who was his friend, did not harbor any anti-Semitic prejudice but rather opposed it. (*Vossische Zeitung,* November 12, 1903)

and as army officers. Many Germans reproached the Jews because of their lopsided concentration in some economic fields yet made the quick removal of this condition impossible by raising legal and extra-legal obstacles that prevented Jews from entering certain professions and occupations.

Karl Gutzkow had criticized the authorities for closing all public careers to the Jews in the 1830s. In 1862 the German pedagogue Diesterweg complained in the Prussian *Reichstag* that Jewish teachers were not hired. The Viennese physician Theodor Billroth, later one of the most outspoken converts to the cause of Jewish emancipation, originally gave distinct expression to his antipathy against Jews in his book *Über den Unterricht und das Studium der medizinischen Wissenschaften* [About the Instruction and the Study of the Medical Sciences]; his early attitude was an indication of the widespread anti-Semitic mood in Austria, which affected the exclusion of Jews from the study of medicine.[15] People also wished to keep the doors of jurisprudence closed to them. Leopold von Gerlach, minister of King Frederick William IV of Prussia, remarked in a letter to the cabinet councillor von Niebuhr: "One matter which you can communicate to His Majesty is the intrusion of Jews into jurisprudence. The King does not wish that they should become judges. Their intrusion into private law practice and into the notarial branch is highly dangerous, because with their capabilities, industry and corporative sense they might easily gain hold of the entire matter."[16]

Many German Jews displayed great intellectual receptivity. Schopenhauer found the "apostles" of his philosophy, as he called them, among the Jews, praising Dr. Julius Frauenstädt and Dr. David Asher.[17] Half a century earlier Immanuel Kant had bestowed almost the same praise on Solomon Maimon, also a Jewish thinker. Gutzkow stressed the "high significance of . . . Jewry for German culture in general." Were he to describe in detail the artistic-literary realm of German life, he said, he would have to write on "the more recent phase of Jewish cultural development."[18] If one is to believe Friedrich Nietzsche later, Jews were more appreciative of Wagner's music than were the "Aryan races."[19]

The German Jews played a significant role in Germany's cultural life not merely by providing an appreciative audience but also as interpreters of German culture. And aside from rendering such services, they made substantial progress in original creativity. "The Jews," Gustav Freytag wrote in countering Richard Wagner's attack upon them, "have also in times of repression, under very unfavorable circumstances, contributed an impressively great number of important names to our science and art. If we only look back to Baruch Spinoza, how long is the line of strong talents from their old families!''[20]

Jews flocked to the free professions. Many a son of a wealthy Jewish merchant turned his back on business and began to study law or medicine or to prepare himself for a teaching career; others turned to scientific careers, to scholarly or literary writing, or to journalism. Gutzkow held that if the state would open public careers to the Jews, fewer among them would turn to literary occupations. "There is an intelligentsia here," he wrote, "that wants an outlet; it throws itself into the press and pushes it beyond its proper limits." Yet Gutzkow tried to excuse what he considered to be an excess or occasional overzealousness: "The overexcitement as well as the deficit," he wrote, "stems from oppression."[21] He also thought that some of the greatest radicals were German Christians.

The so-called "Jewish press" could reflect merely the views of individual Jews, never the varied views and the diverse shades of opinions of German Jewry in its entirety, which was sharply divided. Jewish opinions in the religious sphere, just as in the social and political realms, ran the gamut from extreme conservatism to radicalism, paralleling the wide range and variety of views of the Germans on those matters. The "Jewish" press, incidentally, was liberal rather than radical. Helfert, a historian of Austrian journalism and himself an anti-Semitic writer, admitted that the radical triumvirate of the Viennese press in 1848 was formed by three Gentiles.[22]

The German-Jewish middle class of the mid-nineteenth century, especially its upper echelons, lived in favorable economic circumstances. It had no major material interests in any radical social change. Though equality was not yet attained, it appeared close. The majority of German Jews thus joined the ranks of moderate progress. Their leading spokesman, Gabriel Riesser, for instance, voted most often with the Right Center in the National Assembly at Frankfurt am Main in 1848. The Jewish intelligentsia, on the other hand, unquestionably contributed revolutionary forces, and very potent ones—Karl Marx, Ferdinand Lassalle, Johann Jacoby, and many others—to German radicalism. Yet many liberal and even radical Jews stood in league with many good German Christians against domestic reaction and the perpetuation of a multiplicity of outmoded German states and, like them, were imbued with democratic-national ideas of liberty and unity. Johann Jacoby, in the view of the poet Uhland, had, during the revolutionary years 1848–1849, not committed any greater "sins" than he himself.[23]

In their great majority, Jewish journalists expressed moderately liberal views. In the series of his widely disseminated anti-Semitic articles in 1879–1880, the historian Heinrich von Treitschke admitted that "our journalism" owed "very much to Jewish talents. . . . In this field the alert adroitness and keenness of the Jewish intellect early found a fertile field."[24]

The opposition press, particularly the press of the liberal and progressive opposition, was only too often vilified by its enemies; it was denounced as the "Jewish press" even though many papers were neither owned by Jews nor had any Jewish contributors at all. Liberal and progressive views were frequently and unjustifiedly labeled as simply "Jewish." Accusations against German journalists to the effect that they were in Jewish pay or descended from Jews were quite common and found an echo also in the novel and in the drama. In Wilhelm Raabe's novel *Die Kinder von Finkenrode* [The Children of Finkenrode] the editors of the liberal *Chameleon,* six Christian Germans, are branded by their enemies as a "Jewish gang." "You know, Weitenweber," the hero writes from his new location to a fellow journalist, "that we of the *Chameleon* fare the same as many other editors: One stamps us a savage, cantankerous Jewish gang which sells body and soul."[25]

In Gustav Freytag's comedy *Die Journalisten* [The Journalists] the journalist Schmock, who at times wrote for the Left, at times for the Right, is pictured as the prototype of the corrupt, servile, cheap journalist. Yet the characterization does not contain a specific anti-Jewish note.[26] Freytag knew from his journalistic experience many Jews whose intellectual honesty appeared to him beyond all doubt. Revealing in this respect was his eulogy for his colleague and friend Jacob Kaufmann. Freytag gave him credit for having been one of the first journalists who had supported the concept of the unitary German state: ". . . the Jewish boy from Bohemia who on his own became a German patriot, to whom acquisition and personal comfort meant infinitely little compared to the great thoughts for the propagation of which he lived . . . even on his deathbed considered it natural that the man who lives for the freedom and education of his people must value the material goods of this world as minor things."[27] Yet Freytag did not set a monument to this noble journalist and thus shared responsibility for the widespread belief, reinforced by his novel *Soll und Haben* [Debit and Credit], that he generally disliked Jews.

Germans and Jews joined in common endeavors, striving toward joint political, social, and national goals, and were also linked in common cultural pursuits. Intimate friendships and close associations were thus bound to develop among them. As Gustav Freytag aptly described it, the Jew has "associated himself peacefully with the Christian neighbor as companion in politics, as friend in social intercourse and in the home, as confidant, perhaps even as teacher in scientific research. He has had a drink with him and has laughed with him, was honored best man when his Christian friend gave his daughter in marriage, and laid mourningly his wreath on the coffin of the Christian; he has sent his sons into battle for the fatherland and has felt as a good German does in love and aversion.''[28] Close relations had been established between many Jews and many groups of the German people, especially the intelligentsia, and no one thought of renouncing the "living association with the Jews,''[29] as Felix Dahn called it—neither Schopenhauer nor the anti-Semitic composer Richard Wagner, neither Freytag nor Keller, neither Storm nor Dahn.

Yet "the living association with the Jews," indissoluble as it appeared to many, was by no means untroubled. Prejudices on both sides, though more distinctly on the side of the dominant, only recently repressive majority, created numerous misunderstandings. The Jewish problem never ceased to be a fruitful topic of conversation in the salon as well as in the tavern. The novelist Gottfried Keller described in his short story "Die missbrauchten Liebesbriefe" [The Abused Love Letters] the following conversation, typical of many a German company: "Those who had attained any success and were, at this moment, hundreds of miles distant, perhaps even sleeping the sleep of the just, were most thoroughly demolished; everybody claimed to have the most accurate news about their actions, there was no infamy which was not attributed to them, and the refrain in each case was the remark, which was supposed to sound drily: 'He incidentally is a Jew!' Whereupon it was replied in chorus as drily: 'Indeed, he is supposed to be a Jew!' ''[30]

During the political struggle for the unification of Germany and the numerous wars which prepared for it, most of the energies of the German people had been channeled into the service of German patriotism. The fight against Denmark, Austria, and finally France seemed paramount and made all other issues appear to be of secondary importance. But the voice of hostility did not remain silent even in those days. In 1864 the noted biblical scholar David Friedrich Strauss felt compelled to remind the Germans that a work like Lessing's *Nathan der Weise* was not "given merely to aesthetic enjoyment" but constituted a "warning." The struggle between "fanaticism" and bigotry on one side, "tolerance" and "enlightenment"[31] on the other side was still raging and its outcome was not assured. The closer the complete equality of the Jews appeared, the more desperate became the attempts of the opponents of the Jews to thwart the final act of redemption.

While in 1848 the equality of the Jews had in principle been recognized in virtually all German states, in the postrevolutionary era it was to remain a dead letter. In some German states equality even as a mere principle had been rescinded with the stroke of a pen, jointly with many other basic rights of the German people which had been granted in 1848–1849. In the Austrian Crown possessions the authorities again forbade the Jews to possess real estate, and their freedom of movement in Tyrol and Styria was sharply curtailed.

Yet with the progress of German liberalism the last obstacles in the way of Jewish equality were removed. The rising "New Era" in Prussia and the weakening of the rigid absolutism in Austria after the defeats of Magenta and Solferino in 1859 brought about changes in the policy of these states on Jews and Judaism. The emancipation of German-speaking Jewry finally became a reality in Austria in 1867 and in the North German Confederation in 1869. With the acceptance of the law of July 3rd, 1869, which was signed by Bismarck, the equality of the German Jews appeared to be established forever.

CHAPTER 16

Politicians, Political Writers, and Pamphleteers

Bismarck and the Jews prior to Unification

In the fifties and sixties Otto von Bismarck's political star rose rapidly on the German firmament. In the course of a long and active political life his attitude to the Jews had undergone radical change. The first period extends from his early political appearance to his entry into public service as Prussian ambassador to the *Bundestag* in Frankfurt am Main. The noted German-Jewish journalist Maximilian Harden, who knew Bismarck intimately, was not minimizing his early anti-Jewish position in the *Vereinigte Landtag* in 1847 when he wrote much later in *Die Zukunft*: "If one thinks that in the same session of June 15, 1847, a liberal Herr von Vincke spoke of the avarice and cowardice of the Jews, then one will find the speech of the *märkisch* knight who wished to close to the Jews only the haven of bureaucracy remarkably moderate."[1] Actually, Bismarck's letter to his bride about the foregoing speech on the Jews confirmed not only his lack of fanaticism but even of any deep concern about the issue. On June 15, 1847, he wrote: "Yesterday boring Jew-debate. . . . I gave a long talk against the emancipation, said many bitter things, do not walk any longer through the Königstrasse, since the Jews are going to kill me in the evening."[2] And three days later in another letter to his bride, he referred thus to the discussion about marriages between Jews and Christians: "I am indifferent about it. I must go to the wool market."[3] The issue certainly did not stir his innermost feelings.

The great change in general outlook and political philosophy came over Bismarck while he was serving in Frankfurt am Main. His growing maturity is also reflected in his new attitude to the Jews. Whatever he had said about the Jews in Frankfurt and in the post-Frankfurt era stands in direct contradiction to the content and tenor of his speeches about the Jews in 1847. Frankfurt offered him the opportunity of learning to know Jewry in different activities, to get acquainted with the great Jewish banker at the famous Frankfurt stock exchange, the Jewish intellectual and writer as well as the small peddler; it was in Frankfurt that he became impressed with the equal self-assurance of both the German and the German-Jewish bourgeoisie.

In his correspondence of 1853 Bismarck came out strongly in behalf of the Jews of Frankfurt am Main. Frankfurt citizens demanded then that Jews be deprived of the civil rights they had recently secured. The struggle was reminiscent of the earlier disputes that had arisen in Frankfurt after the War of Liberation. Judging the issue from the point of view of Prussian interests, Bismarck refused to support the motion of Frankfurt citizens, who were not only hostile to the Jews but also happened to be pro-Austrian. In a confidential report (Nr. 218, Dec. 5, 1853) relating to Frankfurt am Main, he referred to the "Austrian-Catholic Party" and its anti-Jewish proposition and suggested that Prussia should not support the complaint. He voiced the suspicion that Austria wished to use the anti-Jewish resolution as leverage in its financial negotiations with the house of Rothschild and expressed the view that, in spite of a speech by the Austrian representative Herr von Prokesch, which was full of praise for the Jews, "Jewish sagacity" would not be deceived by this maneuver.[4] Bismarck's letters to his wife from Frankfurt show his close contact with the Frankfurt Rothschild (May 18, 1851). Though the latter, according to Bismarck, had distinctly Jewish traits, Bismarck apparently displayed a genuine liking for him, which was returned by the old man. Though Bismarck made fun of his Yiddish pronunciation, he had respect for him, and the Frankfurt Rothschild was made Prussian court banker.

Once Bismarck had entered upon his career as a statesman, he refrained from making public statements about the Jews and the Jewish question. It was under Bismarck's stewardship in 1869 that the last bars to full legal emancipation fell with the adoption of a law of the North German Confederation. Only the representative of the two Mecklenburgs voted against the measure in the *Bundestag*.

Theoretically, emancipation in North Germany was widely accepted even before the law of July 3, 1869, was passed. That law consisted of a single article: "All still existing limitations of the . . . civic rights which are rooted in differences of religious faith are hereby annulled. In particular, the capacity for participation in representation on the community and state level and in serving in public office shall be independent from religious faith."[5] For Prussia, admittedly, the law created no novel situation, though the progress made in North Germany in its entirety was noteworthy. Bismarck subsequently complained at times about the alleged ingratitude of the Jews who ignored this particular achievement, though his assertion that no other statesman had done as much for them was a patent exaggeration.

In his *Gedanken und Erinnerungen* [Thoughts and Reminiscences] Bismarck asserted that in religious respects he had always been tolerant. While he wrote at length about Catholicism, the Jesuits, and *Kulturkampf* in this work, he had nothing at all to say about Judaism—an interesting contrast to Hitler's *Mein Kampf*. Obviously, the role which he assigned to the "Jewish question" in German life was a subordinate one; to him, it was just one of numerous problems. The emancipation of 1869 was in his view the last word to be said on the subject.

Riehl and von Rochau

German thought after the March Revolution had circled around the problem of the failure of German liberalism during the year 1848–1849; it also touched upon the role of the Jews in German life. Two writers, one a conservative, the other a liberal, dealt with these problems and reached different conclusions.

Wilhelm Heinrich Riehl, originally a student of theology and a deputy in 1848, became Professor of Political Science and History at the University of Munich. An opponent of liberalism, the author of *Die bürgerliche Gesellschaft* [Middle Class Society] (1851), he postulated that the only alternative to radical democracy and socialism was the "historic society." There existed in Germany four estates—the aristocracy, the bourgeoisie, the peasantry, and a fourth estate that was ill-defined. This fourth group, stronger in Germany than in other European countries, exhibited a lack of patriotic sentiment and of historical consciousness. Vengeful against state and police, the "intellectual proletarian" of the fourth estate becomes embittered against both state and society. Most prominent in this group were Jewish intellectual proletarians whose hatred of state and society had created extreme negativism. Such figures had emerged during the recent revolution. Said Riehl, they have "abandoned genuine Judaism, have not turned toward Christianity and do not wish to want to know anything about the Germanic state or about Hebraic Theocracy." Having rejected a school of rigid restrictions within Judaism, they were unable to acknowledge any historic limitations in the peculiar German social and political structure which demanded caution and restraint. It was of course true that not every Jewish writer belonged to this group, and there existed, Riehl also conceded, "uncircumcised literates."[6] Still, Riehl expressed sharply the conservative resentment of the prominence of Jewish intellectuals and of enlightened Jewry during the 1848 revolution and of their continued resolve to work toward the realization of modern trends in Germany, such as secularism, liberalism, and democracy. Unlike the Prussian King Frederick William IV, Riehl blamed the Jews not for their striving toward national unification but rather for their endorsing a sort of rootless cosmopolitanism. Different German judges blamed the Jews for different, at times even for contrary, political sins.

While Riehl singled out the Jews as a disturbing and revolutionary element, Ludwig August von Rochau, who opposed both radicals and conservatives, believed he could detect—as did later the philosophers Eduard von Hartmann and Nietzsche as well—what he considered the conservative character of Judaism and the conservative interests of German Jewry. In 1853 Rochau published what became a classic pronunciamento of German liberalism, *Grundsätze der Realpolitik* [Fundamentals of Realpolitik]. In spite of his disappointment over the immediate outcome of the 1848 revolution and the setbacks of the liberal bourgeoisie, he discerned in this class great potentialities, enlightened opinion, intelligence, and wealth. These endowments, he was convinced, would help in staging the inevitable comeback.

Unlike many contemporary Germans, Rochau believed he could detect in Judaism, "this historically personified conservatism," conservative rather than radical traits. Judaism, contrary to its innermost nature, has been driven into "determined opposition" to state and society; prevailing policy had made "of a born friend the most bitter enemy." In France the Jews were peaceful citizens as well as good patriots, while in Germany they often preserved "the most revolutionary spirit." "Each of these contrary phenomena is just as natural as the other; unnatural is the policy which sacrifices its imperative interest to an arbitrary whim."[7] The solution to Jewish "radicalism" lay obviously in a more liberal government policy.

Hermann Wagener and the "Kreuzzeitung"

The prevailing temper of the times in Prussia, the German state destined to become the leader in German political development, was an ultraconservatism which found expression in the views of the *Kreuz-*

zeitung and of its editor, Hermann Wagener. A member of the Prussian Chamber of Deputies, he was concerned that the Prussian constitution of 1850, granted by Frederick William IV, was too generous to the Jews and gave them too many rights. In 1856 he moved in the Lower House for the abolishment of paragraph 12 of the Constitution, which had removed religion as a bar to political and civic rights. In an essay on "Jewry and the State" Wagener tried to justify his position in the Chamber of Deputies while protesting the imputation that he was an anti-Semite. Taking a conservative and traditionalist stance, he opposed the concept of the modern state, which was built on abstract philosophical foundations and upon the concept of the natural rights of man and which stressed the importance of good citizenship irrespective of religious affiliation. Wagener held that the strictest dissociation of the Jews from other peoples was the very foundation of Judaism.[8]

Wagener's position differed little from that of the conservative group he helped found in 1861 and from that of Friedrich Julius Stahl, leader of Prussian conservatism in the fifties. Neither Stahl nor Wagener wanted to extend political rights to non-Christians; both rejected full equality for the Jews. While the emancipationists emphasized the principle of equality of rights and duties, Wagener proposed the application of principles based upon a mere correlation between rights and duties. Specifically, he wanted to return to the prerevolutionary legal status of the Jews, to that of 1847, which still contained a number of inequities.

Similar to Wagener's attitude in the early fifties was his position on Christianity and Judaism, as expressed in the first volume of the conservative *Politische und soziale Enzyklopädie* [Political and Social Encyclopedia], which appeared in 1859. Christianity was here juxtaposed with Judaism; the former centered on the inner world of man and on the individual's consciousness of himself, the latter on the consciousness of a public national entity.

A contemporary Jewish critic, Immanuel Heinrich Ritter, accused Wagener of making Judaism appear once again as the archenemy of Christianity in order to bestow upon Christians the right to suppress Jews and Judaism (see *Beleuchtung der Wagener'schen Schrift, Das Judentum und der Staat*). Ritter aimed the main shafts of his criticism against the very core of Wagener's treatise, the concept of the German-Christian state, which precluded equality of the German Jews. If, according to Wagener, equality was attained by the Prussian Jews, the period of Jewish exile would come to its end.[9] However, the concept of the Jewish diaspora, the state of oppression of Jews in their dispersion and their inequality with the Christian population resulting from their collective punishment for the crucifixion of Christ, had been an integral element of Christian theology for centuries. It extended into the nine-teenth century, influencing especially traditionalist religious circles. Ritter quoted Wagener to the effect that the concept of the Jewish diaspora meant "battling against the Lord. In the idea of emancipation lies therefore an anti-Christian element. To the Jew not only the reli-gious door is closed but also the national one. . . . The secret of patri-otism is not accessible to him." The widespread German opposition to having Jewish state officials did not, according to Wagener, rest merely upon prejudices of the mob; "it rests upon the sentiment of reality of the divine command." Wagener thus gave prejudice and continued inequality divine blessing!

While writing the essay "Judaism and the State," Wagener had disclosed that he had had the help of an anonymous expert. One perceptive writer has ventured the guess that the expert was none other than Bruno Bauer, whose radical ideas in the early forties were discussed earlier in connection with the stance of leftist Hegelianism toward the Jews. Bauer had prompted Karl Marx to write his tract *Zur Judenfrage*. Now Bruno Bauer had surfaced again. But his views were not quite identical with those of Hermann Wagener. While Wagener wrote in a measured tone, preserving a calm decorum, Bruno Bauer's writings about the Jews exude fanaticism; they burst the dam and, for this period, reached unusual heights of unadulterated racism.

In 1859 Wagener's *Encyclopedia* also contained an article by Bruno Bauer on "Die Juden als Fremde" [The Jews as Aliens] which was of interest from several points of view.[10] Both in scope and program it went far beyond the generally conservative tone and con-tent of the *Encyclopedia*, assuming an extremist character. Bauer, incidentally, appears to have wished to hide his identity as the author of a previous pamphlet on the Jewish question, one which had caused considerable stir during the emancipation debate in the early 1840s. He had a compelling reason to conceal his authorship: the writer of the early pamphlet had been a leftist radical, while by 1859 Bauer had veered all the way to the extreme Right, far beyond even the position of Wagener and the *Encyclopedia*. By the latter date his radical begin-nings were apparently embarrassing to him. Perhaps it was equally embarrassing that throughout all his political somersaults he had steadfastly clung to one thing—his anti-Jewish position. The element of consistency in Bruno Bauer, the raft to which he firmly clung while casting all his other early theoretical and political ballast overboard, was his dislike of the Jews.

There are strikingly similar, if not identical, elements in Bruno Bauer's two essays about the Jews, though they were written about sixteen years apart. According to both essays, Jewish law was never really alive; it was a "chimerical" law. Also, while other peoples changed in the course of history, the obdurate Jew preserved his identity. Both the extreme leftist and later the extreme rightist Bruno Bauer agreed on the thesis of Jewish "obstinacy." This was hardly a novel thesis; rather, it was as old as the religious antagonism between Christians and Jews.

In an article in 1853 Bruno Bauer had given expression to racism when he had claimed that the "aristocratic" nations in history had descended from Germanic stock. He then attributed the French Revolution to "Roman-Gallic blood." Speaking about contemporary Jewry, Bauer saw in Jewish "isolationism" and "exclusiveness" manifestations of Jewish racial consciousness. Wagener too spoke of Jewish isolationism, but like the young Bruno Bauer he conceived of this phenomenon as religious not racial. Not so Bruno Bauer in 1859! According to Bauer in the latter year, the blood that flowed in the veins of the Jews was different from that of all the Christian peoples of Europe. The Jew according to Bauer was a "white Negro," who lacked the crude and uncouth nature and the capacity for physical labor of his black brother but compensated for them by his mental agility. In view of the racially determined traits of the Jew, conversion to Christianity no longer represented a solution to the Jewish problem. Though Bauer subscribed in practice to the view of Wagener, the editor of the *Enzyklopädie*, that a return to the restrictions of Jewish life of the year 1847 was in order, this opinion seemed like an anticlimax in view of the apparent racism to which he had given expression.

At times it seemed as if the full implications of the racist world outlook had not yet dawned upon Bauer or that he was still hesitant to draw all the possible conclusions inherent in it. In any case, hostility to Jews and Judaism reached towering heights in Bruno Bauer.

Friedrich Julius Stahl, the Christian-German State, and Contemporary Criticism

The doctrine of the Christian-German state, which was in vogue in the forties and fifties in the Prussia of Frederick William IV and which found expression in the views of Wagener and many other contemporaries, was fully elaborated by none other than Friedrich Julius Stahl, son of a Jewish merchant in Würzburg. A convert to Lutheranism, he held that Christian doctrine conformed fully to reason and was also revealed by specific divine inspiration. Very early in the regime of

Frederick William IV, Stahl received a call to the University of Berlin to teach law. In 1849 he was elected to the first chamber of Prussia and later assumed the leadership of the parliamentary Conservative Party in the *Herrenhaus,* the upper chamber. The historian Treitschke, who had many harsh words to say about contemporary Jewish intellectuals, praised Stahl as one who "became fully a Christian and a Prussian" and conceived of Christianity in "a broad and liberal sense."[11] Actually, Treitschke, who turned his back on liberalism and increasingly embraced anti-Semitism, was hardly the best judge to assess the extent of Stahl's liberalism on the subject of Jews and Judaism.

Stahl's booklet *Der christliche Staat und sein Verhältnis zu Heidentum und Judentum* [The Christian State and Its Relationship to Paganism and Judaism] was published in 1847 in a Protestant church journal on the occasion of the deliberations of the Prussian diet of 1847 on the status of the Jews. Stahl regretted his inability to support the full emancipation of the Jews. Such a move, he claimed, would amount to denial of the Christian state. The function of the state is to protect the rights of citizens. But beyond such legal obligations, the state must safeguard religion, mores, and *Volkstum.* And the Jews, of course, did not share in the Christian principles of life.[12]

According to Stahl, "a consequence of the Christian state is the restriction of political rights to members of the recognized Christian churches." Jews could enjoy civil rights, which pertained to all inhabitants without regard to creed, but not political rights, which were "based on the adherence to state religion." "Legal equality in civil law, second-class citizenship in public law" was, according to Stahl, "the solution of the problem, one may say for all times." Admission of non-Christians to public office would merely undermine the Christian philosophy of state.

Stahl charged—and Wagener and Bruno Bauer later repeated— that Judaism had long ago chosen isolation. Christianity, past and present, has merely responded to its wishes. Discrimination against Jews was justified because of this self-imposed Jewish isolation. The latter in turn was rooted in the Jews' belief that they constituted a national community. In some respects Stahl preferred Orthodox Jews to contemporary Reform Jews, who were rationalists and endorsed the Enlightenment and modern political concepts such as popular sovereignty and even democracy. On the other hand he conceived Reform Judaism as the bridge leading eventually to Christianity. Through the mouth of this neophyte, sincere as he may have been, German Christianity of the mid-nineteenth century supported once more the prohibition of the Jew's entry into the German state and German society on the basis of equality.

320 The Era of Fulfillment: Unification and Emancipation

A broadside against the conception of the Christian-German
state as developed by Stahl and championed by Wagener and others
was fired by the liberal writer Ludwig von Rochau in his work
Grundsätze der Realpolitik (1853). As he wrote: "One of the most
inconceivable perversions resulting from a false church policy of the
Prussian government was the stubborn denial of constitutional equality of the Jews with the Christians."[13] Rochau claimed that the
treatment of the Jews violated both the word and the spirit of the
Prussian constitution. "Other slights and manifestations of the lack
of official good will are likewise the order of the day," he said. Thus
there has been brought about a situation in which a class of the
Prussian population "numbering hundreds of thousands and, in view
of their agility, their loyalty to each other and their wealth, possessing a political significance far exceeding their mere numbers, have
been pushed into opposition against the state itself." In creating this
situation, people had not acted in accordance with reason but rather
from prejudices and antipathies.

It was senseless to assert that one must protect the state against
"Judaization." Against the increasing penetration of Jews into all
areas of the national economy and their growing influence over public
opinion and upon the press, nothing could be achieved by mere
"petty chicanery." Rochau also ridiculed the idea that the Jewish
spirit had an influence upon the character of the state or Judaism
upon Christianity. Nowhere in the world did Judaism have any vestige of an independent political character: "The Jews support the
Opposition, which exists also without them, not as a community of
faith or of origin, but as an oppressed group conscious of the discrimination it encounters." Though possessing a "formidable power of
resistance" throughout history, the force of aggression of Jewry always was and remained virtually zero. Just as Jewry allegedly never
made proselytes, as little had it succeeded in imposing its character
upon other peoples. Only in the most recent era did the massive core
of Judaism exhibit "unmistakable symptoms of disintegration."
Rochau entertained little doubt that the cause of progress and the
interests of the state were served by this process of dissolution. Yet
Prussian government policy under the guise of preventing the "Judaization" of the state actually rendered more difficult the "Germanization" of Jewry. The latter, he held, should be the goal for the Jews.
This view was shared by most other German liberals.

CHAPTER 17

Schopenhauer
and Wagner

"Optimistic" Judaism and Schopenhauer's
Philosophy of Pessimism

While in the late forties and early fifties the young Bismarck, Hermann Wagener, and the older Bruno Bauer supported the "German-Christian" state of Frederick William IV, Arthur Schopenhauer turned the minds of the German intelligentsia and bourgeoisie away both from Christianity and from the progressive, democratic, and revolutionary legacy of 1848–1849. His thinking about Jews and Judaism was shaped neither by the ideology of the "German-Christian" state nor by that of the liberals and democrats of the 1848 revolution nor any other contemporary ideology. His attitude to both Christianity and Judaism was simply rooted in his philosophy of pessimism. Though Schopenhauer condemned past persecution and favored moving toward equality and assimilation of the Jews, he did not want emancipation to go too far or to move too rapidly.

The generation of the 1850s turned eagerly to Schopenhauer's philosophy of pessimism. It accepted his minimizing the significance of politics and his stress on philosophy and art as the means to achieve human salvation. His philosophy was to make a powerful impression upon the intellectual life of Germany, especially through its impact on Richard Wagner and Friedrich Nietzsche.

In his work *Parerga und Paralipomena* (1851) Schopenhauer said that it was "the fate of the small Jewish people" always to wander: "Driven from its soil, it has still preserved itself for almost two thousand years and roams about homeless, while so many great and glorious peoples . . . have entirely vanished. Thus this *gens extorris,* this John without land among peoples, may still today be found all over the earth, nowhere at home and nowhere alien, and maintains . . . with an unequaled stubbornness its nationality; indeed, it wishes to take roots somewhere to secure again a country, without which, indeed, a people is a ball in the air." Until that time, he continued, the Jewish people lived "parasitically upon the other peoples and upon their soil, but is nevertheless imbued with the most lively patriotism for its own nation."

The designation "parasitic" was in this connection not used in a deprecatory sense, any more than when Herder had used the term. Schopenhauer placed a time limit upon the "parasitic" existence, while the genuine Jew-hater has always looked upon parasitism as an essential, permanent character trait of the Jews and has questioned their capacity and will for a self-sufficient existence. Anti-Semites also have regularly criticized the international links existing between Jews of different countries and transcending all borders. Though Schopenhauer also stressed the ties that link Jews, he did not do so to vilify Judaism; on the contrary, he rather admired it. Jewish "patriotism *sine patria* [without fatherland]" was "more exciting than any other."[1] "The fatherland of the Jews is formed by the remaining Jews, . . . no community on earth holds together as firmly as this one."

Jewish solidarity was so strong, Schopenhauer claimed, that even the converted Jew felt himself to be a Jew and also was considered one by his fellow Jews. It was "a very superficial and false view to look upon the Jews merely as a religious sect": the concept of a "Jewish denomination"[2] was directly misleading. Rather, "Jewish nation" would be correct: "The Jews have no creed at all; monotheism belongs to their nationality and state constitution and is a matter of course with them."[3]

Schopenhauer believed to discern numerous faults in the Jewish character but also pointed to many a weakness in the German national make-up. He once called the Germans "materialistic and dull" and ironically asked whether he should be pleased to belong to the German people rather than to some other nation and whether he should indulge in praise of Germans and of the German character. The Jews' faults, according to Schopenhauer, were not incorrigible. They were due "mainly to the long and unjust oppression which they have suffered": this excused their weaknesses, though it did not "erase" them.

Many Germans—among them Goethe, Wilhelm von Humboldt and Schleiermacher, Hebbel and Grillparzer, some secular-minded, some religious—opposed the conversion of the Jews to Christianity, although they desired their assimilation. Schopenhauer, however, because religious affiliation was to him a matter of little consequence, defended the conversion of thoughtful Jews. In Schopenhauer's thought about the Jews different and unreconciled elements stand side by side. His plea for limited emancipation and his insistence at the same time that the Jews be treated like "aliens from abroad" are difficult to harmonize. Equally contradictory are his indifference to Christianity as a religion and his simultaneous emphasis on the "Christian" state in which Jews could not enjoy full equality. But he still held fusion between Germans and Jews as a "desirable" goal. As he remarked: "I must indeed praise the thinking Jew who, abandoning old fables, juggles and prejudices, quits, through baptism, an association which brings him neither honor nor advantage, even though he should not be very serious about the Christian faith. Is every young Christian who at confirmation says his credo serious about it? In order, however, to spare him this step and to make an end to this whole tragicomic confusion in the gentlest way in the world, certainly the best means is that one permit and foster marriage between Jews and Christians. Then Ahasver will finally find his rest." Assimilation and blending in the religious sphere and through intermarriage were Schopenhauer's recommendations for a solution to the problem of German-Jewish coexistence.

But this "desirable result"—the elimination of the entire "tragicomic confusion"—would be thwarted "if one carried the emancipation of the Jews so far" that they "attained participation in the administration and government of Christian countries. . . . Justice requires that they enjoy equal civil rights with others; but to admit them to the administration is absurd; they are and remain an alien, oriental people; they must therefore always be treated as aliens. . . ." Assimilation would only be threatened by too radical and complete an emancipation.

Whatever Schopenhauer's motivation, his rejection of full equality as well as the inner contradiction of his position is undeniable. Justice, to which Schopenhauer appealed, demanded not merely equal civil rights for all but also the admittance of the Jews to public service. Continued inequality could hardly expedite the assimilation which Schopenhauer obviously desired; to the contrary, it was bound to delay it.

Schopenhauer's judgment on Jewish religion was hardly more favorable than that on full emancipation of the Jews. The thinker undoubtedly was often carried away by his bitter disposition, but with all due allowance for his temperament and perhaps also for his philosophy, he undeniably disliked the Jews as a group.

To a substantial degree, his critical attitude toward Judaism stemmed from his philosophy, his pessimistic *Weltanschauung*. "The basic difference among religions," Schopenhauer wrote, "lies in whether they are optimistic or pessimistic." In the New Testament he found only pessimism. Original Christianity was based—like Brahmanism and Buddhism, which Schopenhauer highly esteemed—on recognition of the emptiness of earthly happiness, on contempt of it, and on "turning to a quite different, even contrary existence." The philosopher of pessimism and renunciation did not oppose original, pessimistic Christianity but contemporary, gay, optimistic Christendom. Judaism shared with contemporary Christianity an optimistic philosophy: "The Old Testament is optimism." Schopenhauer saw in contemporary Christianity a kinship with Judaism. "The rationalists of the present time" sought "by all means to erase and to interpret away" the pessimistic core of Christianity, "to reduce it to a sober, egoistic, optimistic Judaism, adding merely better morals and a future life."[4] Schopenhauer's criticism of contemporary Christianity, which he looked upon as a deviation from the originally pessimistic state, was also aimed consistently at optimistic Judaism.

Schopenhauer's terminology revealed his belief in a close connection between Judaism and contemporary Christianity. He used the term *Judaism* where one would have expected the word *Christianity*. In the work *Über die Universitätsphilosophie* [About the Universities' Philosophy], in which he especially assailed Hegel, this identification emerged clearly in his assertion that this philosophy propagated "Judaism," while nothing but Christianity was meant.

For many years Schopenhauer preoccupied himself with the study of Sanskrit and Indian culture. In accordance with Hindu religious conceptions, he was a great friend of the animal world and did not forgive Judaism its alleged indifference toward animals. Neither did he forgive Christianity on this account: "The important role which the animals have played at all times in Brahmanism and Buddhism, compared to the total nullity in Judaeo-Christianity, makes it fall short of the former in regard to perfection."[5] He rebuked Spinoza too for his "contempt of animals": "Spinoza could not get rid of the Jew in himself."[6] Yet he still accorded him unique recognition: "In spite of everything, Spinoza remains a great man."[7]

Schopenhauer defended the individual's right to commit suicide and criticized monotheistic religions, including Judaism, on the ground that they forbade suicide "because of their obligatory optimism."[8] It also detracted from the "merits" of Judaism that it did not possess the idea of immortality; indeed this shortcoming made it the "crudest of all religions."[9] In another context, however, he observed that "even the Jews" had given expression to the thought of immortality and the transmigration of souls.[10]

While burdened with many shortcomings, Judaism, according to Schopenhauer, nevertheless had one great advantage: "That Judaism is the only purely monotheistic religion is a merit which some incomprehensibly have sought to conceal, having maintained and taught that all peoples revered the true God, though under different names. However, not only is much incorrect in this, but everything."[11] Another time Schopenhauer spoke of the "monotheistic" beliefs as "Jewish religions."[12]

Hegel, Ranke, and later also Nietzsche discerned "great trends"[13] in Jewish history. Schopenhauer, however, found it essentially poor. Connected with his general lack of historical comprehension was his evaluation of the Bible, which was rooted in the tradition of the Enlightenment, with its built-in hostility to the Scriptures. He condemned Moses for having killed the Egyptian overseer of slaves, condemned the expulsion of Hagar by Abraham, and even reproached the Jews for having fled from Egypt and for having "stolen" temple treasures! He uncritically accepted the accounts of ancient anti-Jewish writers. Yet all these criticisms are to be found in a dialogue which ends with the disputants agreeing that they really had resorted to "sophistries" and had delivered "unlawful cuts" against each other and that dispute made "even the honest man unfair and malicious."[14]

Once Schopenhauer blamed the Jews for having acquired the control of foreign countries by robbery and murder,[15] only to observe elsewhere that "the role of the Jews in settling in the promised land and that of the Romans in establishing themselves in Italy is essentially the same, namely that of an immigrant people which wars continuously against its neighbors who had preceded it, and finally subjugates them."[16]

There are moments when Schopenhauer seemed to grasp the rich treasures of the Bible. As he wrote: "Who, without knowledge of Hebrew, wants to know what the Old Testament is like must read it in the Septuagint as the correct, most genuine and at the same time most beautiful of all translations; it has there quite a different tone and color. The style of the Septuagint almost always is noble and naive at the same time; it has nothing ecclesiastical and no presentiment of Christianity."[17]

In general, however, Jewish culture did not come close to the achievements of the ancient Greeks and Romans, not to mention the Hindu-Brahmanic civilization. Like the youthful Hegel before him, Schopenhauer regretted that modern European culture had grown more upon a Jewish[18] foundation, less upon Greek civilization, that it was not based at all upon Hinduism, and that contemporary European peoples considered themselves, in a way, heirs of the Jews.[19]

In spite of this at times naively anti-Semitic illumination of Jewish history, Schopenhauer was not a real enemy of the Jews. He sharply criticized as "cruel" the "expulsion of the Moors and Jews from Spain and their annihilation."[20] Religious fanaticism appeared to Schopenhauer as much a "bloody madness" as the religious war "in majorem Dei gloriam."[21] "Indeed, this is the worst side of religions that the believers of each consider everything permitted against the other, and that therefore they carry on with the utmost infamy and cruelty against each other; thus Moslems against Christians and Hindus; the Christians against Hindus, Moslems, Negroes, Jews, heretics, etc." Schopenhauer thus condemned every persecution of a religious nature or of any other sort, though, in his opinion, the Jews too had once been guilty of it.

While Schopenhauer's judgment on Jewish religion was unfavorable, his personal relations with Jews were at times close and generally friendly. An intimate friend of his youth was Josef Gans. Schopenhauer assisted the poor colleague, provided for a time for his maintenance by paying his tuition and furnishing him even with pocket money. He once took Gans with him to Weimar to visit his mother, the poetess Johanna Schopenhauer. Another old friend of Schopenhauer was the Jewish attorney Dr. Martin Emden, his legal counselor in financial matters, who represented him in several cases before the court. Schopenhauer often praised the ability, talents, and honesty of Dr. Emden, his "only, special friend," as he called him. He deeply regretted his passing: "Oh, my best friend for many years, Dr. Emden, died today! I am in deep mourning about this irreplaceable loss of mine. This belongs to the sufferings of old age; one loses one's friends!"[22]

Fame and recognition long eluded Schopenhauer. It was to the credit of two men, two indefatigable heralds of his philosophical greatness, that ultimately the light of glory shone upon him in his last years and cast some rays of joy upon this expounder of pessimism. These two, Dr. Julius Frauenstädt and Dr. David Asher, were both Jews and also belonged to his circle of personal friends.[23] When in 1840 Julius Frauenstädt published a favorable comprehensive essay on Schopenhauer's philosophy in the *Halle'sche Jahrbücher,* the silence surrounding Schopenhauer was broken. Frauenstädt and Schopenhauer later learned to know each other and entered into closer relations. Schopenhauer jokingly but aptly called the interpreter of his philosophy, who was twenty-five years his junior, his "trumpet" and his "dear old apostle." In his testament he bequeathed to Frauenstädt all his scholarly manuscripts and the copyright of all later editions of his writings, the works of Kant from his library, and Kant's bust—indications of the high esteem in which he held him.

The other herald of Schopenhauer was Dr. David Asher, who published many essays on his philosophy. Schopenhauer enjoyed most Asher's "Open Letter to the highly esteemed Dr. Schopenhauer from Dr. David Asher" and conferred upon him the unique praise that none among those who had written about his philosophy had recognized its real significance and merits as he had done.

The Jew-Hatred of Richard Wagner

Although the great German composer Richard Wagner entertained close relations with individual Jews during almost his entire lifetime, he was a relentless opponent of Jews and Judaism. Under the circumstances, it is puzzling that he found among the Jews deep appreciation of his music, an enthusiastic reception, and strong support. "I believe," Friedrich Nietzsche held later, "that the Semitic races show greater understanding of Wagner's art than the Aryan ones."[24] There were times when Wagner himself held similar opinions. It was the more unexpected that in 1850, with the publication of anti-Semitic articles, he declared war against German Jews and that he renewed the attack in 1869, on the eve of their full emancipation in Germany, with the republication of the anti-Semitic pamphlet.

Wagner's hostile articles *Das Judentum in der Musik* [Judaism in Music] began to appear in September 1850 in the musical journal *Neue Zeitschrift* under the pseudonym Karl Freigedank.[25] They were published in book form in 1851 and reprinted as late as 1869. The immediate cause of the publication in 1851 appears to have been Wagner's growing ill-feeling toward Meyerbeer—to whom, according to his own testimony, he owed so much—and also toward his former friend Ferdinand Hiller. The music critic Uhlig, criticizing Meyerbeer's and Hiller's works, had spoken of their "Hebraic art sense."[26] Wagner's reading of Uhlig's critical review seems to have triggered his anti-Semitic tract.

The reprinting of this pamphlet in 1869 hit even Wagner's anti-Semitic friends like a lightning out of a clear sky.[27] Cosima Wagner—according to Wagner's authoritative biographer Ernest Newman, "as venomous an anti-Semite as Germany could show at that time"—questioned the wisdom of Wagner's step, and von Bülow remarked that the *Meister* himself had made "fraternization with the world" impossible. Yet Wagner held that "a world incurably evil had entered into a conspiracy of hatred against the one truly righteous man in it" and that therefore the reopening of his attack on the Jews was necessary and justified.

Wagner's decision to republish his pamphlet was prompted by a question Madame Marie Muchanoff addressed to him: she asked why the press was so hostile to him. Wagner replied that the journals and magazines were in Jewish hands. Apparently in an excitable mood, he had early in that year begun a quarrel with his Gentile friend Eduard Devrient on the occasion of the latter's publication of his work *Erinnerungen an Felix Mendelssohn-Bartholdy* [Remembrances of Felix Mendelssohn-Bartholdy]. Now Wagner burst forth with his anti-Semitic tract, releasing his accumulated fury.

In a sharp rejoinder to Wagner's accusations against the Jews, the novelist Gustav Freytag hurled the reproach against him that he himself, in the sense of his brochure, appeared "as the greatest Jew."[28] In 1888 Friedrich Nietzsche, in his work *Der Fall Wagner* [The Wagner Case], went beyond Freytag by questioning Wagner's German ancestry. Nietzsche alleged that Wagner's stepfather, the conductor Ludwig Geyer, was his real father[29]—and rumor had it that Ludwig Geyer was of Jewish descent. Others who questioned Wagner's pure German origin pointed also to his allegedly un-German appearance.[30] In mature years Wagner himself seriously thought of the possibility that Geyer had been his real father.[31] Wagner's self-doubts about his origin may offer a psychological explanation for his outbursts against the Jews and his continuous preoccupation with the Jewish problem.

"DAS JUDENTUM IN DER MUSIK"

In his revolutionary phase Wagner had pleaded for the emancipation of the Jews. In his articles *Das Judentum in der Musik* in 1850, however, he tried to disavow the recent past and asserted that in reality he had always disliked the Jews. "When we fought for the emancipation of the Jews," he wrote, "we were, in a way, more fighters for an abstract principle than for the concrete case. . . . Our fervor for the equality of the Jews stemmed much more from the suggestion of a general idea than from real sympathy; for in spite of all our oratory and writing in behalf of the emancipation of the Jews, in actual contact with Jews we always felt instinctively repelled!"[32] This, however, did not fully correspond to the facts. Before the revolution Wagner had been in contact with many Jews, who apparently attracted him. Even in his anti-Semitic pamphlet he admitted that fate had brought to him "sympathetic friends" from among the Jews. His regard for them had allegedly long kept him from publishing his articles. And later, in a letter to Madame Muchanoff, he praised the "great talents from the circle of Jewish society whom he had come to know and truly to enjoy."[33]

The question on the agenda, according to Wagner's tract of 1850, was not the emancipation of the Jews but the emancipation of the Christians from the Jews! It was not the Jews who were oppressed but, he asserted, the Christians. Wagner claimed that the Jews actually were lords and masters over the German people. The Jew "dominates and will dominate as long as money remains power." Wagner was willing to concede that the historic misfortune of the Jews and the "rapacious vulgarity of the Christian Germanic rulers" had created this situation; but he gave Jew-hating a populist, "democratic" sanction: the plain people, according to Wagner, instinctively looked upon Jews as the enemy. "Our era" had only "popular dislike for the Jewish character."

There followed other offensive ramblings on what Wagner called Jewish speech and its alleged influence upon Jewish music. "The Jew speaks the language of the nation in which he lives from generation to generation, but he always speaks it like a foreigner." Therefore, in these languages the Jews can only imitate, repeat, not artistically create. And European culture has allegedly not succeeded in removing the peculiarities of "Semitic pronunciation"[34] even though Jews and Christians have lived together over two millennia. Jewish speech still sounded to Wagner's ears "alien and unpleasant, . . . hissing, shrill, buzzing, grunting," apparently anything but human. And since the Jew was thus incapable of adequately expressing his sentiments and views through speech, he was even more handicapped in rendering them through the song. "Everything which repels us in his exterior and his language has when he sings the effect of alienating us unless we should be captured by his completely ridiculous appearance."*[35]

A Jew, according to Wagner, could never be a hero on the stage, since he would always seem "ludicrous." Yet Wagner himself let Jewish singers appear in Bayreuth. "Long is the list of Jewish male and

---

*Then and later Wagner was compelled to admit so many exceptions to the "rule" that little remained of it. He often conceded that many Jews had taken deep root in Germany's cultural life. He thus characterized Moses Baruch, upon whom he placed great hopes: "Obviously a very gifted writer of Jewish origin, full of talent and wit, who appears immersed in the very German life." Another one of many German Jews who, according to Wagner, had sunk deep roots in German soil and in its culture was Giacomo Meyerbeer. Such remarks stand in sharp contradiction to numerous vilifications in his pamphlet and would appear inexplicable if Wagner had not expressed himself on many subjects in a flagrantly contradictory manner and if the composer's character did not exhibit many incongruities.

female singers," Grunsky, an anti-Semitic authority on Wagner's relations with Jews, admitted, "who were permitted to play in Bayreuth. Among the most noted were Paulni, Rebekka-Mailhac, and Lilly Lehmann-Kalisch."[36] Continuing his philippic in the anti-Jewish articles, Wagner claimed that the Jew, in spite of his natural shortcomings, had, due to his financial power, managed to attain domination over public taste in the field of music. Also, the educated Jews had endeavored to shed all conspicuous characteristics of their low-class coreligionists but had thus become merely the most lonely and most heartless of all men, "so that we have lost even the former sympathy for the tragic fate of his tribe." The educated Jew stood "alone and aloof in the midst of a society which he does not comprehend, with whose inclinations and endeavors he does not sympathize, whose history and development have remained indifferent to him. . . . Our entire European civilization and art has remained a foreign tongue for the Jews." The Jew's drive toward art was rooted only in superficialities; he had never had an art of his own.

In spite of his professed disdain for all Jewish artistic creation, Wagner asserted high esteem for Henrich Heine and Ludwig Börne. In the thirties Wagner had written his contributions for the *Dresdener Abendzeitung* and for Lewald's *Europa,* as again Grunsky admitted, "distinctly in Heine's style." He had then thought in a sympathetic manner of *Jungdeutschland.* Even in his anti-Semitic pamphlet he expressed admiration for the Jewish writers who, in his opinion, were linked with this movement. Heine had been a true poet: "At the time when poetry became a lie with us, it was the mission of a very talented Jewish poet to bare this extreme barrenness and Jesuitic hypocrisy of our poetically pretentious versifiers with biting ridicule. . . . No deception held up before him."[37]

"Still another Jew must be named," Wagner continued, referring to Ludwig Börne, "who appeared among us as a writer. From his special position as a Jew he stepped among us seeking salvation. He did not find it and had to become aware that he could find it only through our development toward true humanity. To become a human being jointly with us means for the Jew, however, first of all, to cease being a Jew; Börne had fulfilled this. But the case of Börne teaches also that this salvation . . . costs sweat, misery, full suffering and pain." Turning to the German Jews, Wagner concluded his pontificating thus: "Take part, without any regard, in this work of salvation by self-destruction; then we shall be one and without difference! But consider that only one thing can be your salvation from the curse which burdens you: the salvation of Ahasver—ruin!"

Wagner sounded the trumpet call for the destruction of Judaism.

The call was addressed to the Jews, and the destruction asked for was spiritual, not physical. But in practice it had no esoteric overtones, and the German mob translated such admonishments to remove the "curse" in due time with brutal directness.

The anti-Jewish thrust of Wagner's remarks aside, what the composer here asked of the Jews in grandiloquent words, fraught as they were with plain threats, was essentially full blending with the German people, their unqualified assimilation. It was a demand admittedly contrary to the policy of racial anti-Semitism but equally contrary to national, religious, and cultural tolerance of and coexistence with the Jews. Wagner posed his demand in a hostile manner. In the few lines which have just been quoted the word *salvation* crops up no less than six times, a circumstance which throws full light upon Wagner's conception of Judaism and the Jews. Judaism in his eyes was an evil, and the unfortunate Jew who was burdened with it must seek redemption.

In a letter to King Ludwig of Bavaria, Wagner assured him of his personal compassion for the "unfortunate" Jews. If the assimilation of the Jews in Germany was at times making only slow progress, the fault, according to Wagner, lay not with the Germans but with the Jews. The Jews did not seek deliverance with sufficient earnestness, according to Wagner, because they did not understand the true character of Judaism.

In several letters relating to the pamphlet *Das Judentum in der Musik* [Judaism in Music] Wagner similarly referred to the noble and positive intention which inspired his publication—his plan to further the assimilation of the German Jews. Thus he wrote in a letter from Jena to Marie Muchanoff in 1869: "Perhaps I expected a hopeful acceptance. . . . As it has been thought possible . . . to bring about a more beneficent form of the church by an appeal to the lower oppressed clergy, I similarly thought of the great talents of heart and mind from the circle of Jewish society whom I have learned to know and truly to enjoy. Certainly I am of the opinion that everything which oppresses the genuine German character from that side burdens in an even more terrible measure the witty and sensitive Jews themselves. . . . If the Jewish element is to become assimilated with us in such a way that it matures jointly with us toward the higher development of our nobler human gifts, it is clear that not concealment of the difficulties but only the most open exposure of them can further it."[38]

Was the publication of Wagner's pamphlet and his trumpeting once again of crude and vulgar anti-Semitic slogans not likely to produce the opposite result, to hinder the full assimilation of the Jews in Germandom? Wagner must have known that reprinting this booklet would only encourage the Jew-haters, alienate the Jews, and widen the gulf between Germandom and Judaism. When his tract was more critically received than he perhaps had anticipated, Wagner attempted to soft-pedal its anti-Semitism, to give it an innocent character, as the above letter shows.

In another letter, addressed to the Jewish pianist Tausig, Wagner beat a complete retreat. When Tausig, on the occasion of a performance of *Lohengrin,* sent a telegram to Wagner, informing him that Berlin Jewry had forgiven him for the attack and had become reconciled to him, Wagner replied that, if his writing had been excused as "over-hastiness," he was not yet fully consoled, because he had experienced many a kindness from Jews. His work, correctly read and interpreted, offered an opportunity for a really ingenuous Jew[39] to show true greatness. But Wagner's "repentance" came too late to prevent the damage already done to German-Jewish relations.

Richard Wagner's anti-Jewish tract could hardly be considered anything but ingratitude. For the number of Jews who in various capacities had unselfishly helped Wagner and his work was legion, and, though there were also several Jews among his opponents, the great majority were Germans. Wagner showed especially little consideration for Giacomo Meyerbeer, who had repeatedly pleaded on behalf of his music. In 1837 the young Wagner had written a most flattering letter to Meyerbeer: "Should I deny that it was just your works which showed me the new direction? It would appear here in any case a very improper occasion to indulge in awkward praises of your genius; only so much that I saw in you fully solved the mission of the German who took the excellences of the Italian and French school as model to make the creations of his genius universal."[40]

Meyerbeer in turn had warmly praised Wagner's *Rienzi* and his *Der fliegende Holländer* [The Flying Dutchman] and deserved much credit for the staging of both operas. After completing the *Flying Dutchman,* Wagner had thanked him enthusiastically: "I shall not be permitted to speak to you till eternity of anything else than of gratitude! gratitude! . . . if I should be recognized by the world as a disciple not quite unworthy of my revered master, it could be achieved only through you, my lord and master. God make every day of your beautiful life a joy and never sadden your eye with sorrow! This is the sincere prayer of your most loyal disciple and servant."[41] In 1840 he still admitted that "Meyerbeer has remained indefatigably loyal to my interests." In his anti-Semitic pamphlet, however, Wagner lists Meyerbeer only in passing.

Yet even in this tract Wagner expressed himself with some warmth[42] about Felix Mendelssohn-Bartholdy. He highly valued the latter's talent but, in spite of honest efforts, was unable to come close to him. What Wagner did not reveal was that Mendelssohn, like Robert Schumann, had remained cool to his various approaches and had not reciprocated his esteem.

WAGNER, JEWS, AND ANTI-SEMITES

The publication of *Das Judentum in der Musik* naturally aroused bitterness in Jewish circles. But though Wagner himself and his anti-Semitic companions were inclined to ascribe occasional bad luck to a Jewish "vendetta," the Jewish public in general showed itself more impartial than the composer. A relatively large number of Jews remained among the most enthusiastic admirers of Wagner. The composer's indisputable anti-Semitism did not keep them from attending his operas and expressing their admiration.

Even after the publication of his booklet Wagner's relations with individual Jews remained close. The anti-Semitic writer Grunsky had to admit that "Wagner proved gracious to individual Jews. . . . Wagner accepted Jews whom life or art led to him."[43] Among these were the composer Joseph Joachim, the pianist Carl Tausig, the friend and helper Angelo Neumann, and the conductor Hermann Levi. Levi and Heinrich Porges were two of Wagner's pall-bearers.[44]

Wagner was committed to Levi not only because of his competence and devotion but also because of his position as *Kapellmeister* (conductor) in Munich. Yet it rankled him that Levi was a Jew. Thus when Levi was at Wahnfried in 1882, Wagner tactlessly suggested that he submit to baptism. Levi, the son of a rabbi, resented Wagner's behavior, especially after Wagner had also been rude enough to show him an anonymous letter which made offensive reflections on Levi's relations with Cosima. He hurriedly left Wagner's household and asked to be released from his obligation to conduct *Parsifal*. Yet Wagner, appealing now to his "dear best friend," his "alter ego,"[45] prevailed upon him to return, though still proclaiming that Levi's way of looking at things "made relations difficult."

Actually, Wagner had plotted against Levi. In a letter to King Ludwig of Bavaria, he had referred to alleged complaints "as to his most Christian of works being conducted by a Jewish conductor," clearly attempting to remove Levi from his post. In his reply, however, while seemingly congratulating Wagner for not making any "distinction between Christian and Jew," the King added significantly: "There is nothing so nauseous, so unedifying as disputes of this sort: at bottom all men are brothers, whatever their confessional differences." But Wagner, in a subsequent letter, continued to exhibit his fanatic anti-Semitism.

For years Wagner lost no opportunity to make the lives of his Jewish collaborators, including Joseph Rubinstein and Hermann Levi, miserable by tactlessly haranguing them about Judaism. As he now alleged to King Ludwig, these two men had been the source of great tribulation to him. "These unfortunates" lacked the foundation of Christian education which gave the "rest of us" a sense of oneness, and thus they suffered and often comtemplated suicide. He had to exhibit "great patience" with them; indeed, "if it is a question of humanity towards the Jews, I can confidently claim credit on that score."[46] The correspondence reveals Wagner's hypocrisy and lack of sensitivity. It also casts much light upon the often strained relations between Wagner and his Jewish friends. Some of them managed to preserve their dignity; but others showed little regard for theirs. Their devotion to the genius and his creations would perhaps be comprehensible if Wagner had shown more than a fleeting "repentance" for his anti-Semitic pamphlet and had refrained from further anti-Jewish utterances.

It would have been consistent on Wagner's part to avoid Jewish company altogether and to exclude them from the circle of his friends. Instead, he surrounded himself with many Jews, exploiting their devotion and their enthusiasm for his music. They received, as the philosopher Eugen Dühring—himself an enemy of the Jews, yet critical of Wagner—charged, "indulgence" for the cardinal sin of their Judaism. The Jews, Wagner remarked in a letter to King Ludwig of Bavaria, had an instinct for the genuine and really precious in the field of art and had thus given him support. Instead of showing some appreciation for this gift, which richly benefited him, Wagner traced it back to their mercantile experience as traders of pictures, jewels, and furniture! Thus he attempted to deprecate their admittedly fine qualities and skills by pointing to the allegedly contemptible cause!

Originally a democrat and a revolutionary, an internationalist and an admirer of the French—whose revolution in July 1830 had made him, according to his own testimony, a rebel—Wagner had played a leading role during the revolution in Dresden in May 1848. Yet soon the friend of the French turned into their enemy, the internationalist became an intense nationalist, the democrat showed aristocratic leanings, and the advocate of Jewish emancipation reversed himself and displayed the flag of anti-Semitism. The revolution of 1848, he asserted soon thereafter, had been "entirely un-German":[47] "Democracy in Germany is a purely transplanted matter. This transposed French-Jewish-German democracy exists only in the press." Rejection of the French and of the Jews blended in his thought with repudiation of democracy. In the same sense Wagner later designated the revolution of 1848 publicly as an article of export from rationalist France; it had allegedly been imported into Germany by the Jews.[48]

Wagner the Romanticist had become the enemy of Rationalism, whose representatives appeared to him to be Jews and Frenchmen. Rationalism and intellectualism, according to Wagner, were destructive. In his *Bayreuther Blätter* he asserted in 1879, at a time when the anti-Semitic movement was again making rapid headway, that the Jews planned to destroy Germany "through the power of the pen."[49] In the same way that he pictured attacks against himself as originating with the Jews, he also maintained that attacks against "Germany" issued from them![50] He and Germany had the same sinister enemies!

In "Religion and Art" (*Blätter*, Oct. 1880) Wagner lamented that everything in the world was rotten—politics, property, gold, and, above all, Jewry and what it stood for. He regretted blood mixtures by which ignoble races tainted the nobler ones and showed himself an admirer of the "Aryans." Only the "pure" race was virtuous; the Germans could be a shining example of it if they would only rid themselves of the Jews. He had been shocked, he revealed, by the "frivolity" of so-called statesmen who had proclaimed the legal equality of all German citizens, irrespective of religious belief. Here as elsewhere Wagner embraced Count Arthur de Gobineau's racism (*Essai sur l'inégalité des races humaines*) lock, stock, and barrel, extolling as usual the Germans and deprecating the Jews. He contrasted idealism, proclaimed to be characteristic of the Germans, with materialism, which he asserted to be typical of the Jews. Yet, as in his earlier pamphlet, he held out the hope of "salvation" to the Jews through destruction of their Jewishness. Its annihilation was imperative, since the Judaization of the "so-called Romance" peoples had made frightening advances.[51]

In his last years Wagner remained, true to form, hostile to the Jews. Although he continued to contradict himself, in general he displayed the same anti-Jewish tendencies. Opportunism led him at times to minimize the Jewish issue, yet anti-Semitism prevailed among his sentiments and dominated his writing.

Nevertheless, Wagner was not directly linked with the political organization of German anti-Semitism which took shape in the newly formed German *Reich*. He assured Angelo Neumann, a Jew whom he called his "friend and benefactor": "I stand completely aloof from the current anti-Semitic movement."[52]

In the summer of 1881 Wagner refused to sign an anti-Semitic petition to the *Reichstag* which was organized by Dr. Bernhard Förster, later Friedrich Nietzsche's brother-in-law; Nietzsche spurned him on account of his views. Yet the reason Wagner advanced for his abstention was hardly a philo-Semitic one: after the failure of an earlier petition against vivisection, he explained, he had sworn never again to sign any of these documents. Wagner's biographer, Ernest Newman, an admirer of the composer but critic of the man, suspects that he may have felt that he could not in "ordinary decency" take the field so openly against the Jews, when one representative of the race—Rubinstein—was an inmate of his own household, another—Neumann—was organizing a touring Wagner theater that would mean large receipts for the composer of the *Ring,* and a third—Hermann Levi—was attracting all Munich to his performances of the Wagner operas.[53] Though Wagner did not associate his name with the anti-Semitic petition, he apparently took care that this should not be misconstrued as a philo-Semitic gesture or even as a testimonial of neutrality.

The republication of Wagner's anti-Semitic brochure in 1869 had made its author a hero in anti-Jewish circles. Many of those close to him were enemies of the Jews—Cosima, Houston Stewart Chamberlain, Glasenapp, and Gobineau,[54] to name only a few. Strangely enough, however, Wagner at times was sharply attacked by anti-Semites not only before but also after 1869, and apparently on different grounds. Some, as stated, seem to have suspected him of being a Jew; for others, bitter opponents of the composer, the "Jew" Wagner offered an easier target than the German Wagner.

Conjectures about Wagner's Jewish origin became more numerous in the seventies, according to Ernest Newman, author of the standard biography of Wagner. "A cartoon in the Vienna *Floh* of 1879 shows him surrounded by children of markedly Jewish cast of features: on the piano is a bust of the Jew Offenbach, while Wagner's own nose is made exaggeratedly Jewish." A drawing in the Vienna *Kikeriki* of 1882 showed an audience of Jews applauding *Parsifal.* About 1880 the Viennese journalist Spitzer published a malicious but amusing novel, *Verliebte Wagnerianer* [Enamored Wagnerians], in which Wagner unmistakably figures as the composer Goldschein, an obviously Jewish name. In 1876 another Viennese journalist, Ludwig Speidel, had said bluntly in an article in the *Fremdenblatt* that Wagner, who was born in the Jewish quarter of Leipzig, was of Semitic origin. In contemporary literature Wagner was repeatedly referred to as the rabbi of Bayreuth. "It was in 1878, be it recalled," Ernest Newman continues, "that Cosima asked Wagner point-blank whether he now thought that Geyer was his father."[55]

The relation of the Jew-haters to Wagner worsened during his last years. This is the more astonishing since Wagner's attitude toward the Jews underwent hardly any change. Occasional articles in the *Bayreuther Blätter* still showed an undisguised anti-Jewish tendency. Yet the anti-Semites, who earlier had proudly extolled Wagner as one of their great champions, attacked him unceasingly and even accused him of being of Jewish descent. The conspicuous demonstration of anti-Semitism apparently was to them no convincing proof of his German origin. Others who did not go so far as to declare him a Jew, as for instance the philosopher and racial anti-Semite Eugen Dühring, charged that he had been bribed by the Jews and that he had betrayed his better self, his anti-Semitic convictions. Dühring did not stand alone; the reproach that Wagner was a slave of the Jews (*Judenknecht*) was hurled by many anti-Semites. A decade before, Wagner had prophesied that the Jew would dominate as long as money would rule. Now some opponents of the Jews asserted that Wagner himself was living proof of this thesis.

The opposition between Wagner and the Jews, Eugen Dühring charged, "faded more later," because Wagner did not want to renounce Jewish financial contributions. His own journal, Dühring continued, "the *Bayreuther Blätter,* used at the end of the seventies such soft language concerning the Jews that, though it came to write many long pages on them, it principally avoided the expression 'Jews.' Indeed, it even said that those of the 'alien element' who attached themselves to Wagner were thus lifted into a higher spiritual sphere and thus the contrast was balanced. Jews contributing to the Orphism of Bayreuth were thus absolved from their Jewish characteristics. This is more than indulgence." It was therefore not astonishing "that in the end nothing of importance emerged from the rifts between Herr Wagner and the Jews."[56] Such an anti-Semitism apparently was too academic for the former professor Eugen Dühring. In any case, it was an act of historic justice that the weapon of anti-Semitic slander, which Wagner himself wielded relentlessly, ultimately boomeranged and that he himself was hurt by it.

A French literary historian of note, Gabriel Monod, who had met Wagner during the Bayreuth festivals in 1878 and had conversed with him at length, wrote later in an article which appeared in *Moniteur Universel:* "After seeing him at close quarters, at one moment irresponsibly gay . . . , at another vehement, respecting neither titles nor powers nor friendship, always letting himself be carried away by the first thing that comes into his head, you find yourself unable to be too hard upon him for lapses of taste, of tact, of delicacy; if you are a Jew, you are inclined to forgive him his pamphlet *Das Judentum in der Musik*, if a Frenchman, his farce on the capitulation of Paris, if you are a German, all the insults he has heaped on Germany. . . . You take him as he is, full of faults—no doubt because he is full of genius."[57]

Richard Wagner was later made the hero, the spiritual father, of National Socialist Germany. He became the mentor of the Führer and was praised as forerunner of the Third Reich. What the Frenchman Monod and other contemporaries, equally critically inclined, were prepared to forgive as "faults" of Wagner, the new Germany proclaimed to be unparalleled "virtues." And Wagner's anti-Semitism fell into this category.

GUSTAV FREYTAG AGAINST WAGNER

One of the strongest voices raised in the defense of the Jews in the wake of Wagner's attack against them was that of the novelist, playwright, and historian Gustav Freytag. In 1869 Freytag published a sharp reply in the leading magazine *Die Grenzboten,* which he himself edited. "We hold a serious attack against the Jews among us in no way timely," he wrote, "not in politics, not in society, not in science and art; for in all these fields our co-citizens of the Israelitic faith are valuable allies toward good goals; in no area are they predominantly representatives of a trend which we must hold socially injurious."[58] This was also true, contrary to widespread prejudices, in the fields of business and trade. "In trade and commerce the Jews have long been regarded as the main speculators in daring deals at the exchange and in enormous usury; they have passed on this reputation to Christians too. Now our princes and heads of the old country gentry protect unsavory business deals. . . . The Rothschilds have been almost reduced to the level of old Frankish business people, and reputed Jewish firms of our capitals belong to the most honorable opponents of the modern swindle of stock-jobbing."

The intellectual and cultural progress of German Jewry during the last decades had been extraordinary, Freytag reported. "He who with a lofty feeling wished to contemplate the advances of our nation in the last hundred years may first of all look upon the transformations which our Jewish co-citizens have undergone under the liberating development of modern knowledge. They themselves have every right to enjoy their energetic vitality and capacity for education; we too may say with some satisfaction that only the last remains of an old tradition and intolerance are to be overcome, in order that our people may encompass fully the hearts and minds of the German Jews. It is natural that during this period of transition occasionally something striking or not praiseworthy in their character may come to light, and they must acquiesce if such weaknesses or perversities from the time of their oppression are spoken of occasionally, with or without good humor, as Jewish characteristics. We, on the other hand, will find it also natural if they are especially sensitive about such discussions, for they . . . still feel the aftereffects of harsh pressure."

Freytag believed that the feelings of the Jews often lacked "rich and beautiful expression." He criticized Heine's "tasteless dissonances" but lauded at the same time his "genuine gaiety" and his "liberating humor." And as a historian he attempted to explain any shortcomings: "Who can say that full expression of beautiful feeling is denied to their national character, since their harsh fate on earth forced them until the present to hide secretly all their vigorous emotions in the locked-up home against hate and ridicule, and how should the gay love for life and the hearty, secure enjoyment, the basis of all humor, thrive in an oppressed and persecuted people. It appears to us that it would be more honest and more Christian to ascribe the capable sides of the Jewish character, which have evolved in a long millennium of servility and isolation, to their national strength than to blame the lack of national vitality where the valuable achievements of individuals among them showed perhaps common weaknesses." The resolute rejection of Wagner's tract, the attempt at a just evaluation of the Jewish character, and the recognition of the importance of the Jews for the German people, of their being a "valuable ally" in art, science, social and political life, show Gustav Freytag as an enlightened man and a champion of the Jews. Still, in his earlier novel *Soll und Haben* he had deeply etched portraits of bad Jews who made a lifelong adverse impression upon generations of German readers of this most popular novel.

CHAPTER 18

The Image of the Jew in German Literature

The Novels and Stories
of Freytag, Dahn, Reuter, and Storm

In *Soll und Haben* Freytag glorified the solidarity, industry, and "nobility" of the German middle class. In a country which in the nineteenth century still extolled the image of the landed aristocracy, praised the rural population for its steadiness and reliability and for being rooted in the soil, and frowned upon the more agile city population, it was perhaps a revolutionary deed to glorify the honest work of a German merchant house, of the urban bourgeoisie. But the contrast in the novel is not between the German merchant and the landed German gentleman but between Germans and Jews, the honest house of Schroetter and the disreputable firm of Ehrenthal.

Besides Ehrenthal there appear in Freytag's novel other questionable Jewish characters, such as Veitel Itzig and Schmeie Tinkeles.[1] The Jewish businessmen with their unsavory practices and their easy consciences offer a repelling contrast to the Germans of the respectable business houses. It was odd that Freytag did not see fit to depict at least one honest Jewish merchant among his many Jewish characters. In his reply to Wagner, Freytag recalled the "old Frankish" solidity of the Rothschilds and also stressed that many of the Jewish firms of the big cities were highly respected and enjoyed an excellent reputation. Yet in his novel Freytag lets the greedy Veitel Itzig even resort to murder, a crime much more common among the German Christian population than among Jews.

One Jewish character of the novel, however, has amiable and noble traits, namely Bernhard, son of the merchant Ehrenthal. In his utmost honesty and pure naiveté, the shy young scholar, an expert in ancient languages, is the exact opposite of his unscrupulous father. Yet the love of the old man for his son is genuine. On the insistence of the sick son the old Ehrenthal sacrifices a huge profit that is already within his grasp. Both the good Jew, Bernhard, and the bad character, Itzig, are expendable and die. Death is also the fate of two noble Jews, father Isaac and daughter Miriam, in Felix Dahn's novel *Der Kampf um Rom* [The Struggle for Rome].

Though Freytag was no Jew-hater, the stereotypes created by him, as well as by Felix Dahn and Wilhelm Raabe in their widely read novels, made an indelible impression upon readers and strengthened the German's sense of superiority as well as his belief in the inferiority of the average Jew. The literary creations of these most popular German novelists contributed powerfully to deepening rather than narrowing the cultural and social gulf between Jews and Germans and ultimately facilitated the inroads of anti-Semitic political propaganda.

The persons of the novel *Soll und Haben,* Freytag explained later, were "all freely . . . invented. . . . For the action of the novel I did not lack in experiences which I had made here and there. . . . And I had particularly learned to know thoroughly the usury of Jewish merchants, since as attorney of a dear relative I had to fight at court against some of them for many years."[2] At the same time Freytag admitted that his inclination to "create in contrasts" had also influenced him in the drawing of his characters. This is true of other works of his. The author of the *Ahnen* [Ancestors] pictured in glowing terms the German forefathers and their descendants. The Germans of his novels are always magnificent, bearers of progress and culture, pioneers on alien soil. The non-German nationalities, Slavs, Frenchmen, and Jews, are pictured as fully "contrasting" figures. Though a political liberal and often a fighter for humane and progressive goals, Freytag, like many other contemporaries, was also caught in the web of a national-religious bias which affected the portraits he painted of Jews.

Freytag was a friend of the German-Jewish short-story writer Berthold Auerbach, whom he portrayed as a very amiable character in his *Erinnerungen aus meinem Leben* [Memoirs of My Life]. He considered the publication of his *Erzählungen aus dem Schwarzwald* [Tales from the Black Forest] a "literary event," told how he had served as witness in the Jewish synagogue at Auerbach's wedding, and expressed regret that his later criticism had deeply hurt Auerbach. In the *Erinnerungen* he also drew a portrait of the Jewish journalist Jakob Kaufmann, one of the "most ingenuous and most pleasant men." Freytag praised his extraordinary "modesty and selflessness" and his "oddly sound judgment in political matters."[3]

In his early years Freytag had embraced the great principles of tolerance and equality. In 1843 the twenty-seven-year-old university lecturer (*Privatdozent*) had visited his uncle, the pastor and teacher Neugebauer. The occasion for the visit was the pastor's celebration of his fiftieth year in office. The gathering at the festive table included a Protestant minister, a Catholic priest, and a Jewish rabbi. This sight inspired the young Freytag to write a poem in which he compared the three religions to three different sorts of wine. The "bad period on earth" when one felt "dismal fear" in the presence of the adherent of another religion has passed. Now all three wines stand in peaceful mixture on the table.

> Now you ask, what has brought together the wines?
> Honest, brotherly love has done this,
> Love which soars high above the clouds,
> Love which beats in every heart.
> Therefore, though the wine may be very different,
> We all can agree in the One.
> Shake hands therefore and raise the cup:
> "Long live the brotherly love at today's meal."[4]

In his fine *Bilder aus der deutschen Vergangenheit* [Sketches from the German Past] Freytag painted a picture of the situation of the German Jews in the Middle Ages in which his impartiality emerged splendidly. Here, he clearly condemns the crudeness and cruelty of the German forefathers. Compassion and a sense of justice are reflected in the two chapters "Jesuits and Jews" and "On the Crusades." "No warlike people," he wrote in the former, "has more heroically resisted brutal force than these defenseless ones," who had "given most magnificent examples of persevering heroic courage."[5] In the chapter on the Crusades Freytag condemned most sharply the "anti-Jewish agitations" during which "men, women and children were slaughtered." "Persecutions of Jews, admittedly not the first ones of which the Germans were guilty, have recurred since then with a terrible regularity almost every time the mob has been stirred up by religious fanticism or by a sudden national catastrophe. For centuries these incitements were a shame to our people; only Protestantism chained them. Even today the urge is always alive where medieval conditions reach into the present."[6]

Freytag, living in the ethnic "frontier" region, disliked Poles in general, including Polish Jews. He was the product of border regions of Germanic and Slavic civilizations with all their national tensions, prejudices, and fears. Freytag's attitude to the Jews, though by no means consistently critical, was shaped by the frontier mentality. Emigration of Polish Jews into Germany would, in Freytag's view, only complicate the problem of the assimilation of the German Jews. Since he wanted assimilation, the German Jews, the potentially good Jews, had to be kept apart and away from the mass of "bad" Polish Jews, who, he held, displayed all the unfavorable traits of the Jewish character.

The nationalism of Gustav Freytag lacked, as he once conceded, truly cosmopolitan interests. The same could be said of Felix Dahn, who after the war of 1870–1871 worried about "regression into cosmopolitanism." A very popular novelist of his time, Dahn, also like Freytag a historian, presented in his works the heroic age of the ancient Germans and praised their virtues. In his much read novel *Der Kampf um Rom*, the heroic tale of the courageous but doomed East Gothic people, he has left very favorable sketches of two Jews, father Isaac and his daughter Miriam.

The "sun-king Totila," the handsome young hero of the Gothic nation, saves a beautiful Jewess, Miriam, from the Romans. Her father, the old Isaac, gratefully remembers his courageous deed, and Totila often visits him and his daughter. Like the Jews of Naples and other Italian cities, Isaac supports the Goths in their fight against the Romans and warns his co-religionists, especially the Jewish builder Jochem, not to leave for hostile Byzantium. Challenged by Jochem because of his service for the Goths, Isaac pledges loyalty to them for the rest of his life: "For the children of Israel owe gratitude to them and to their great king, who was wise as Salomo and whose sword was like Gideon's. . . . This great king has rebuilt our synagogues. . . . And I will remember this as long as my days will last; and I shall serve loyally his people till death, and one shall say again far in all countries: loyal and grateful as a Jew."[7]

Miriam loves Totila, yet in noble self-sacrifice she rescues his bride in besieged, burning Naples. Fearing for the life of the beloved one, she prays to his God. Shyly, "she dares enter the basilica St. Mariae, from which in peaceful days people had chased away the Jews with curses. But now the Christians had no time to curse."[8] Miriam also rescues Totila from mortal danger by rushing to his side to warn him and thereby giving her own life to save his.[9] From that hour on "Miriam has buried herself in his heart forever." Another Germanic warrior, who has earlier helped her to bury her father, lays her body next to his and holds nightly guard at her resting place.

Love between the sexes which bridges the differences between peoples and religions was a topic which repeatedly attracted Dahn. This is shown in his poem "Die Jüdin" [The Jewish Girl]: In Aachen, the city in which German Emperors are crowned, the handsome Rhenish count is married. While he rides with his following through the streets of the city, people cheer him from all sides, flowers are strewn his way, and a wreath of purple granates falls upon his scarf. He catches a glimpse of a beautiful Jewish girl who has thrown the wreath toward him from her hiding place, and even during his wedding night he cannot forget her.[10]

Though in both cases, the novel and the poem, the theme of love between Germanic men and beautiful Jewish women ends on an unhappy note, this was, considering the times, probably unavoidable. Dahn treated the topic with great tenderness and apparent deep sympathy. The nobility of the characters of Isaac and Miriam and their loyalty to the cause of the Goths clearly go hand in hand, and both father and daughter die a glorious death for the Germanic people. Their close association with the Gothic cause is bound to endear them to the German reader. The book thus carries a rather obvious message to both Germans and Jews: to the first the need for tolerance, to the latter for patriotism and dedication to Germany.

The contrast between Gothic virtues and Roman weaknesses, with definite ethnic and racial overtones, runs like a red thread through the novel. But though Dahn glorified the Germans, he did not, for contrast's sake, vilify the Jews; rather he focused upon the virtues of both.

Dahn appears to have been intimately linked with some Jews. When an editor of the reactionary and anti-Semitic *Kreuzzeitung* claimed to know that Dahn had professed to be an enemy of the Jews, the latter in a note to the paper did not hesitate to protest vigorously. Simultaneously he turned to the editor of the *Allgemeine Zeitung des Judentums,* Karpeles, whom he knew personally, and requested the publication of his letter: "This false imputation has aroused me most deeply; among my closest friends are Jews whom I judge to be the most excellent men I know. How should I renounce association with them? Promptly, I sent my most emphatic protest to several papers, and I shall be very grateful to you if you would give my lines the widest circulation. . . ."[11]

One of the best liked German novelists, who wrote in dialect, was Fritz Reuter. In his novel *Aus meiner Landmannszeit* (1862–1864), in which personal experiences are heavily interwoven, he created one of the finest Jewish characters in nineteenth-century German literature. In his younger years Moses had traveled from one village in Mecklenburg to the other, bringing joy and happiness into every house with his colored clothes and dresses. Always selfless and ready to help others, he enjoyed a fine reputation in the entire district. When he died, Jews and Christians alike followed his coffin and sincerely mourned his passing. His old Christian friend testified at the open grave that Moses, who had always remained a pious Jew, had led the model life of a good Christian. "The old man," Reuter wrote, "had gone through life like an honest and just man, and honest and just he went out of it. He died firm in his religious belief. . . . I believe that he has come to his patriarchs, though Christians followed him to the cemetery."[12] Reuter loved the idyllic life of the little towns in Mecklenburg; in his works was no room for hatred of any human being.

This becomes apparent in his narrative "Schurr-Murr." The author relates in this story his memories from his native city Stavenhagen. Like Gutzkow and other German writers, Reuter found "a secret charm" in peddling, which at the time of his writing had already disappeared. He described the "gay excitement" which came into every house when "Moses Joel" opened the door. "Hope, hate and love, frivolity and consideration—the novel with its poetry entered into the daily monotonous drudgery of the little house, and who called it into life? Who is the bearer of its poetry? The Jewish peddler."*[13]

Reuter was befriended with a Jewish physician, Dr. Michel Liebmann, a fellow citizen of his native Stavenhagen. When the novelist learned from the daily paper that his friend had conceived the plan of establishing a hospital, he sent him 250 talers for this purpose and attached the following note: "I send this gift to you because for many, many years I have known of your loyal, distinguished work in your profession and your love and friendship for me. To you, the Jew, I owe, perhaps, more than to many a Christian man, dressed up in his religion. . . . Your old friend, Fritz R."[14]

The character of Ahasver, a popular figure in the Romantic era, was treated by the Westphalian writer Levin Schücking in his novel *Der Bauernprinz* [The Peasant Prince] (1851); it was separately published in the year 1874 as a short story under the title "Die drei Freier" [The Three Suitors]. The well-known legends of the Flying Dutchman, the Wild Hunter, and the Eternal Jew, all of whom suffer a similar fate, have here been woven into the narrative. The burning desire for sociability and love on the part of these mysterious figures, who are doomed to an unsteady migratory existence, finds expression

*The novelist Jeremias Gotthelf (Albert Bitzius) sketched a less favorable picture of endeavors by the Jew in the countryside in his work *Uli der Knecht* [Uli the Manservant] (1841), a novel about the life of a German peasant. The Jewish cotton merchant, whose father has "carried spun cotton to the country in a box," has a very unfavorable reputation; he is held to be an untrustworthy braggart who tries to deceive people by appearances. He is a speculator and exploiter.

in this short story. The keeper of the inn, where the three guests, after a hundred years of painful wandering, have their meeting, feels compassion for Ahasver, who, though he appears to him a Jew, "still is a human being."[15] The innkeeper had concluded that he probably was a Jew "from the manner . . . in which the pious churchgoers, much like Christian Samaritans, passed by the poor devil, cold and indifferent." Ahasver appears here as a youthful Armenian prince, traveling under different names and guises.

The popular poet and short-story writer Theodor Storm, while corresponding with the novelist Gottfried Keller, seemed critical of the Jews. Storm voiced his anger at the poet Georg Ebers, who had made a derogatory remark about the poetic value of the short story, a genre which Storm cultivated and in which he excelled. Storm commented on Ebers' supposed Jewish descent. Keller questioned the authenticity of his information and remarked that in any case "Ebers' Judaism has nothing to do with the matter."[16] However, too much importance should not be attached to this one utterance by Storm, who was friendly with several Jews.[17] In an autobiographical sketch he professed his liking for the Jewish people and the "sympathy" he always had reserved for it; nothing would make him change his love for them.

Storm also described an episode from his childhood. As a boy he had written a drama "Mathatias the Liberator" for a school celebration and had presented it on that occasion. A Jewish merchant from a neighboring town who entertained close business relations with his father had appeared at the festival; the young Storm recognized him in the audience and felt as if he read the play just for him. Then he had come to his last verses:

> Your star sank, Juda's star
> Shines in new splendor and at your grave
> Burns the deserved torch of death.

"These were my last words for Mathatias. When I had left the lecturer's chair and had wedged my way through to the Old Testament picture, the great-grandson of it took my arm silently into his. We stepped together down the great spiral stairs. . . . Then, since the speech festival was terminated for the forenoon, we went into the market and sat down in the shadow of a linden tree in front of a house. . . . Opposite us in the sunlight one booth after the other was erected; but the otherwise so busy merchant, though he had not yet completed his usual business with my father, did not turn his eyes upon these industrious activities. Starting from my talk he involved me, as he loved to, in various religious-moral talks: 'Indeed,' he exclaimed, in the sharp accents of his people, 'I merely say: Do right and don't be afraid of anybody!' Soon afterwards, however, he appeared to be reminded by the . . . stroke of the bell from the near steeple of the value of time, for, as if he wished to shake off all gray theories, he suddenly rose and patted me tenderly on the shoulder. 'Come on!' he said smilingly, 'we will go and we will cheat the old man a little.' "

"But this was only a jest, my old friend. I can say nothing else after you into the grave, in which you now rest for a long time in the little Jewish cemetery in the neighboring town, than that you certainly have sold my father good Netherlandish cloth at Christian prices.— Who knows whether the friendliness which you once showed to the boy has not laid the seed for that liking which I have always preserved for your noble people and which even the dirtiest Jewish usurer has not undermined."[18]

According to Storm, an outgrowth of that sympathy for the Jews was his poem "Crucifixus," in which the poet severely blamed some disciples of Jesus for casting the terrible "picture of the crucifixion" in iron and stone instead of erasing the memory of it:

> Thus, a horror to every clear eye,
> It reaches into our age;
> Perpetuating the old outrage,
> A picture of implacability.[19]

Such "implacability" contradicted Storm's deep humanity, which the youthful author of the drama "Mathatias the Liberator" professed just as much as the old man who glanced back upon his life.

The Novels of Raabe and Keller

One of the most popular narrators of his day was Wilhelm Raabe. The novelist was held by some to be an enemy of the Jews because of his highly unfavorable characterization of a Jew in his novel *Der Hungerpastor* [The Hunger Pastor] (1864). Yet few other German novelists have created as many favorable Jewish characters as Raabe.

Raabe's best known novel, *Der Hungerpastor*, pictures the character development of two boys, a German and a Jewish youngster, Hans Unwirrsch and Moses Freudenstein, who at first are close friends. Their paths, running along parallel lines, later abruptly part; physical and spiritual hunger carries them to different goals. Moses, ambitious and personally ruthless, is baptized and rises to become a professor at the university.

Yet even in this novel Raabe's attitude toward the Jews is by no means entirely unfavorable. He blames bitterly the "infamous tormenting" of the little Moses, the "wretchedness," the "vileness," the "cowardice" which people display toward him, when they "offended him in his human dignity." "In those past days," Raabe wrote, "there still prevailed, primarily in little towns and villages, a disdain of the Jews which, fortunately, one finds no longer in as severe a form. The old as well as the young ones of the people of God had much to suffer from their Christian neighbors; the old terrible Hep Hep, which caused unspeakable misery, has been exceedingly slow in dying away in the world." When the novelist in another context recalled the age when the Jew Moses Mendelssohn, upon entering Berlin, still had to pay toll like cattle, he remarked: "The battle of Jena, which cast aside so many a vileness, so many a nonsense, made an end also to this scandal."

Der Hungerpastor introduced other Jewish characters who appeared in a more favorable light—for instance, Moses Freudenstein's father, who deeply appreciated Hans Unwirrsch's defense of his son against the other boys who beat and ridiculed him. The novelist showed furthermore how early experiences—exclusion from play and similar hurts to his dignity and self-esteem—burned themselves into Moses' memory and shaped his character and outlook. After that his thinking circled around the forging of weapons of diverse kinds, including education and wealth; he wanted to be able both to avenge himself for past injury and to prepare for future defense. Raabe, to avoid any misunderstanding, chose as the motto for his novel Sophocles' words: "We are here not to hate, but to love."[20]

Der Hungerpastor is only one of many works in which Raabe included Jewish characters and dealt with the problem of Jewish-Gentile relations, past and present. At the age of twenty-three, in an episode in *Die Chronik in der Sperlingsgasse* [Chronicle from the Sperlings-Street] (1856), the novelist presented the Jews, with their inextinguishable love for their lost native land, as a model for the not-yet unified German people.[21] In the novel *Die Leute aus dem Walde* [The People of the Forest] (1863) Raabe spoke of the great importance of the Bible for the "star-gazer" Heinrich Ulex, one of the finest characters in his works. He related "how one Sunday morning Ulex made the poetry of the sunny Orient in the book full of wisdom rise in the wintry north and tied the sayings and narratives of the Jewish seers and prophets to the events, the hopes and fears, the joys and pains of his own existence."[22] In the same novel Raabe also described the rescue of a

Jewish family from an anti-Jewish mob, "drunken soldiers, journeymen and loose wenches. This mob used the occasion to offend and to most crudely vilify the innocent promenaders. The police seemed to be preoccupied elsewhere . . . and no one restrained the raging mob from going from words to misdeeds. The two poor girls were most to be commiserated; they suffered all the torments of hell. . . ."

In *Der heilige Born* [The Holy Well] the novelist tells of an anti-Jewish minister whose child is saved by a Jewish peddler. Although the minister could "not tolerate" the Jews and looked upon them as parasites, "he would have shared his bed with this Hebrew who gave life again to his sick child if he had asked for it. He shared his table with him."[23] A touching love story between a young German and the teen-age Jewish girl Jemina is told by Raabe in the short story "Die Hollunderblüte" [The Lilac Flower]. Jemina dies from her love and is buried in the old Jewish cemetery in Prague, whose black humid soil has "devoured so many badly tormented, mistreated, despised generations of living beings, beaten by fear."[24]

The Baroness Salome in Raabe's short story bearing the same name is a lady remarkable for both her beauty and her intelligence. The legal councilor Scholten, her fatherly friend, criticizes her for temporarily abandoning herself to a melancholic mood, though he admits that, in spite of her material well-being and social standing, she is entitled to complain. "I am willing to believe that occasionally she has reason to get angry at her crooked-nose kinsfolk and at the dear acquaintances among the Christian-German smellers with their cocked-up noses." Her readiness to help, her self-sacrifice, and her determination and courage are revealed in a terrible fire which burns half the mountain village to ashes. Under risk to herself she rescues many children from the flames.[25]

In the short story "Hoexter und Corvey" Raabe depicts the struggle of the largely Protestant German town of Hoexter against the Catholic bishopric Corvey, to which the town is subjected and to which it must pay rent. The Jews of the town of Hoexter are placed in the midst of the religious struggles of the sixteenth century. Defenseless and exposed to robbery and murder by a fanatic mob, they lead a life dominated by fear and terror. Raabe describes the bitter quarrels between Protestants and Catholics and their final reconciliation at the expense of the Jews. The jointly arranged pogrom with its unspeakable cruelty forms the tragic ending.[26] This short story not only shows Raabe as a masterful narrator but also reveals his deep sympathy for the Jews, their vulnerability, and their sufferings.

As a citizen of Switzerland, the novelist Gottfried Keller was especially suited to recognize the importance of patriotism and progressive nationalism and to combine it with an international humanitarian outlook. In his poem "Nationalität" [Nationality] he warned lest nationalism become excessive and be abused by tyrants for their selfish, vile purposes.[27]

In the autobiographical novel *Der grüne Heinrich* [The Green Heinrich], Keller describes the sociable evenings at Frau Margaret's. The Jews are depicted as amiable characters, while the Christian mocker in his "insolence" and with his "wanton, useless heart" is presented in an unfavorable light. As Keller writes: "It possibly came from her [Frau Margaret's] joy in thriving industrious activity that several old-clothes Jews had been received into the circle of the favored ones. The tirelessness and steady attention of these men who frequented her house and deposited their heavy burdens, pulled full purses out of a modest cover wrapper and committed them to her charge without asking for any guarantee by word or letter, their fair kindness and curious modesty, aside from an undeniable shrewdness in trade, their strict religious customs and biblical ancestry, even their delicate attitude to Christianity and the shameful misdeeds of their forefathers, made these much tormented and despised people highly interesting to the good woman, and they were well received at the evening gatherings when they made coffee or baked a fish in Frau Margaret's kitchen."

"When the pious Christian woman gently reproached them that it had not been so long since the Jews had been bad fellows, had robbed and killed Christian children and had poisoned wells, or if Margaret asserted that twelve years ago the eternal Ahasverus had once stayed at night in the 'Black Bear' . . . , then the Jews smiled good-naturedly and nicely and did not let themselves lose their good humor.—Since, however, they also feared God and had a sharply defined religion, they belonged still more in this circle than two other persons in it."

These two were declared atheists, the one a wise, simple joiner, the other "an aged tailor with gray hair and wanton, useless heart, who could have played more than one evil prank. . . . His attitude toward the Jews, compared with that of the coffin-maker, was also highly significant." While the latter treated them benevolently, the tailor "tormented them whenever he could and persecuted them with genuinely Christian insolence, so that the poor devils at times became really angry and departed from the company."[28]

Keller often pleaded in behalf of the Jews. That he also stood up for them against his friend Theodor Storm shows that in matters of truth and justice he was unwilling to compromise.*

*See p. 346.

Keller's position in regard to the Jews emerged most clearly in an address he wrote in 1862 in his official capacity as public servant of the city of Zürich. With warmth and resolve he welcomed the full equality of the Jews of the canton, the fulfillment of human rights for these so long oppressed people: "The great council, which has been elected by you, dear co-citizens, has, with a few paragraphs, freed the Jewish people, despised for millennia, from its old limitations in our canton, and we have not heard any voices raised from your midst against it. You have thus honored yourself, and you may with this law, commanded as much by love towards men as finally by consideration of foreign policy, step forth calmly before the God of love and reconciliation on the next day of prayer. It will then depend on you to make the written law a living and fruitful truth by meeting in a friendly manner, also socially, the alienated and persecuted ones and by helping them, whenever they show good will, to begin a new civil life. Where inveterate contempt and persecution have not succeeded, love will succeed; the rigidity of this people in morale and opinions will loosen itself, its weaknesses will be transformed into useful capacities, its manyfold talents be turned into virtues, and one day you will have enriched the country instead of hurting it, as the blind spirit of persecution fears."[29]

Educators, Playwrights, and Poets

While notes of hostility to the Jews run unceasingly through the utterances of some, such as Richard Wagner, other contemporaries expressed themselves in a manner that was critical but not always unfriendly or unfavorable, stressing the necessity of peace and harmony between Jews and Germans. Foremost among them, aside from many of the novelists—Freytag and Dahn, Reuter and Raabe, Storm and Keller—were the student of religion David Friedrich Strauss, the educator Adolf Diesterweg, the playwright Otto Ludwig, and the poet Josef Viktor Scheffel.

On the occasion of the eightieth anniversary of the completion of Lessing's *Nathan der Weise*, David Friedrich Strauss still demanded full emancipation for the Jews, though he had traveled far from his Left Hegelian idealism to political arch-conservatism. The sense and the significance of the play *Nathan*, he wrote, "will not be mistaken as long as the struggle between fanaticism and tolerance, between bigotry and enlightenment, continues." Such plays were presented not merely to provide aesthetic enjoyment and contemplation but "rather as a guarantee and admonishment at the same time that the serious and honest struggle will not lack in ultimate meaning; that humanity, even though slowly and with setbacks, will step forth from the dawn to the light, from slavery to freedom; that, however, only he counts as a human being who in a wider or narrower circle has helped with all his strength as Nathan or lay brother, as monk, as Sittha or Recha, to speed the coming of God's realm."[30]

The noted German pedagog Adolf Diesterweg followed the path of the many great German educators who had been friendly to the Jews. On March 4, 1862, he delivered a speech in the Prussian *Reichstag* in favor of admitting Jews to the teaching profession. He denied that such an innovation would make the school lose its Christian character. Jewish teachers, he held, showed great educational capabilities: "I say, gentlemen, if you could recognize the sufferings, the difficulties which a Jew who prepares himself for the teaching profession has to overcome, you would have to assume: that must be a man of excellent pedagogic talent; otherwise he would not master the enormous difficulties."[31] Like Herder, Pestalozzi, and Bettina Brentano before him, Diesterweg favored the joint education of Christian and Jewish children: "What the children learn if they sit together is tolerance and humanity; these are the great virtues and qualities that the state authorities have the duty to further." Nothing was morally more dangerous than to arouse in a Christian child hatred and derision of the Jews: "A Christian child who looks with contempt upon Jewish children is corrupted for the true love of humanity and of the fatherland."

Otto Ludwig, novelist and playwright, with Friedrich Hebbel representative and theoretician of poetic realism, depicted in his drama *Die Makkabäer* [The Maccabees] (1852) the heroic struggle of a desperate people who have taken up arms to meet a threat to their very existence. The limitless ambition of Lea, the mother of the Maccabees, who fervently wishes for her favorite son Eleazar the office of High Priest, forms, according to Ludwig, the nucleus of the drama.

The description of the Jews is hardly favorable. They are irresolute and capricious, revering their leaders at one moment only to reject them the next. But the Jews as a mass form a springboard from which the main actors of the drama, Lea and her son Juda, reach heroic heights. The playwright has shown the Jews not only in their weakness but also in their strength. A hopeless heroism, admirable in its stubbornness and deep faith, stirs the Jews; they refuse to battle on the Sabbath, preferring to let themselves be slaughtered without a fight. In the end Lea turns out to be a tragic figure, torn between love for her children, whose lives are threatened, and her newly awakened love for her people. In this bitter struggle patriotism gains the upper hand. Juda Maccabeus, a powerful figure, suffers much from the faults he wants to rid his people of.[32] The silent energy of Juda is set against the indolence and loquaciousness of the other Jews.

While Ludwig in *Die Makkabäer* went back to ancient Jewish history, in another dramatic attempt, *Jud Süss oder Der Jakobsstab* [Jew Süss, or The Rod of Jacob], he turned to the recent history of German Jews. Unfortunately, *Jud Süss* is only a fragment, like so many other works of Ludwig. The playwright had been led to this topic by Wilhelm Hauff's short story of the same name, whose basic features he preserved. Jew Süss, the mighty dictator of Württemberg in the first half of the eighteenth century, does not object to the marriage of his beautiful sister Lea to the young Christian Lanbeck. He rather hopes thus to win over Lanbeck's father, the leader of the patriotic party, which has been hostile to him. But the young Lanbeck is torn by violent conflicts—by his love for Lea on the one hand and by obedience to his father, who violently opposes his son's marriage to a Jew, on the other. Heartstricken, the young man finally renounces his love. Lea, unable and unwilling to survive the betrayal of the loved one, drowns herself in the waters of the Neckar. Lanbeck, who has sacrificed his love, remains unwed.

Maltreatment and oppression have left their mark on the originally noble character of Jew Süss. His seemingly cold, cynical nature, his utter reserve coupled with contempt for man, testify to the hard, painful road he has trodden. He has suppressed all warmth of feeling, which the Christians used to counter only with sneers, and no one would surmise that a passionate heart pulsates behind the rigid, impenetrable mask. Left by Lea, for whom he had reserved his better self, tormented by persecution and sneers, Jew Süss, in half-mad derangement, tears his clothing and with the rod of Jacob in his hand departs from the stage, bitterly accusing the Christians: "Whatever I have done, it is you who have brought me to it." He wants to go peddling again, "a poor, despised, persecuted Jew."[33]

The noted German poet Emanuel Geibel, who lived for many years in Munich, was one of the leading figures of the circle of Munich poets. A master of poetic form, Geibel liked to give Old Testament color to current conflicts. In the poem "Menetekel,"[34] he foresaw in 1846 the impending revolution. His verses "Ein Psalm wider Babel" [A Psalm against Babel][35] in the *Heroldsrufe* [Herald's Calls] were written in behalf of German unity and against France. On the occasion of the death of the composer Felix Mendelssohn-Bartholdy he set a poetic monument to him, expressing admiration for the "rich" composer, who had carried in his breast a basic tone for every pain and every joy and who always, "at times with joy, at times with great lamentation," struck the proper tone:

> Who shall from the nearby altars,
> A priest, henceforth guard against vulgarity?[36]

In the epic poem "Judas Ischariot" Geibel offered a novel conception of the character of Judas. Not only the miracles of Jesus but also the simple clarity and purity of his life and his thoughts had convinced Judas of Jesus' divine origin. When he, nevertheless, turned away from Jesus, it was because of his deep patriotism. As a youth he had witnessed in silent fury how the Romans "domineeringly and defiantly" marched "with an iron foot" through the country. His heart had then beat angrily. He had cursed them, "imprecated evil upon the head of the oppressors," and called upon the Messiah for help. Now, however, Jesus taught love, reconciliation, and gentleness. To Judas, Jesus' doings and will were incomprehensible. He had expected a high priest and prophet whose words, "dipped in flaming fire, would spark the souls to the holy war."[37]

Another of the poets of the Munich circle was Count Adolf Friedrich von Schack. A friend of Geibel and of Paul Heyse, he was also an artist of form and a virtuoso of verse. In "Nächte des Orients" [Nights of the Orient] the poet offers a gripping description of a bloody persecution of the Jews during the Middle Ages. A young beautiful Jewish girl, one of the many victims of the mercilessly cruel persecution of her tribe, laments her bitter fate to a sympathetic listener. Her father and her brothers have been killed in a bloody pogrom by a plundering and murdering horde. She herself has succeeded in fleeing with her mother on a foggy night and, luckily, has found refuge in the home of a rabbi. The pogrom, however, advancing like a wave, has reached her new asylum and threatens again to drive her and her mother away.

> . . . does not murder and horror prey
> Always upon us? Already I foresee
> How they again will chase us from here.
> Oh rescue is for us only there in the grave below.[38]

In the meantime the knights hold council and ready themselves for the new drive against the Jews. Even the knights who had first opposed the pogrom take part in the outrages, in the course of which the girl is killed in the arms of the man who wished to save her.

One of the most popular patriotic German poets was Josef Viktor

Scheffel. Like Felix Dahn and Gustav Freytag he brought Germany's past closer to the German people, though in a strongly idealized form. Scheffel pointed to the ethnic difference between Germans and Jews as one of the roots of anti-Semitism, without, however, wishing to excuse it.[39] In his poem "Deutschland," which is filled with national pathos and pride, he rejected anti-Semitism as the "devil's work":

Prosit. The German Reich may live!
May it strengthen itself daily anew,
Rich in boldness, like the eagle!
Yet may God guard it against class hate
And racial hate and human hate
And devil's work of that sort![40]

The image of the German Jew in German novels, plays, and poetry of the period before and immediately after German unification was rather blurred, though on the whole it showed some improvement over earlier periods. Still, some stunted and evil characters contributed powerfully to the ugly German stereotype of the Jew. That stereotype nurtured and strengthened past prejudices, which might have been diminished if not destroyed by a more equitable and balanced presentation. The German image of the Jew thus reflected the gulf that still separated the two peoples and at the same time further widened that gulf.

PART VI

Imperial Germany and the Rise of Anti-Semitism, 1870–1890

Outside of Germany, little sympathy will be given to the revival of a passion [anti-Semitism] of a past era.

—*The Times*, London, 1880

CHAPTER 19

Bismarck, Nietzsche, and Counter-Emancipation

In the New Reich

The year 1870–1871 was a watershed in German history; it marked both the fulfillment of the age-old dream of national unification and the beginning of an era of German expansion beyond a strictly national framework, an era in which newly united Germany began to acquire a dominant position in Europe and a "place in the sun" in the world. This year was also a turning point, since for the next decades the forces of liberalism and democracy, reduced in power and prestige, would barely hold their own. For German Jews, realization of a centuries-old dream, emancipation, was followed by bitter disappointment. They were forced to question the nature of the equality, freedom, and citizenship they had achieved and, in view of the rising opposition against them, the kind of future they could look forward to in the *Reich*.

The seriousness of these questions is revealed in an analysis of the attitudes of two illustrious figures of the new era to Jews and Judaism—Chancellor Bismarck and the philosopher Friedrich Nietzsche—as well as the attitudes of some writers on the Jewish question, such as the historians Heinrich von Treitschke and his opponent Theodor Mommsen, and of outright anti-Semitic and frequently ultraconservative authors such as Eugen Dühring, Constantin Frantz, and Paul de Lagarde. Bismarck and Nietzsche were politically and intellectually at opposite poles, the one creator of the new unified Germany, the other virtually self-exiled from the new *Reich*, with its worship of power and nationalism. But as far as the Jews were concerned, both men opposed the surge of anti-Semitism, and both supported the completed legal emancipation, though the Chancellor was not above making tactical use of the anti-Semitic movement for his own political purposes in the struggle against German liberalism.

In spite of the unquestionable thrust of the anti-Semitic movement, beginning with the Founders' Scandal of 1873 and the economic crisis in the late seventies, in the first two decades of the new *Reich,* when Bismarck remained at the helm, anti-Semitism did not become a major political force in Germany. It was a potential threat rather than an immediate menace to German Jews and to the *Reich* itself. But the preoccupation of both men with anti-Semitism—the Chancellor and the intellectual who disapproved of the new era and became one of the great dissenters of his time—is a clear indication of its dangerous potential. It was destined to retreat in the nineties, but it would return powerfully after 1918, with frightful consequences.

Bismarck: The Mature Statesman

In the fifties and sixties, Otto von Bismarck had shed his outmoded political views of the prerevolutionary era and gradually taken up the cause of national territorial unification, while never abandoning Prussia's interests. On the eve of the completion of German national unification, in 1869, the emancipation of the Jews in the enlarged North German Confederation had become a reality. Yet for tactical reasons, the Chancellor preferred not to become more directly entangled in the political struggle that involved Jews, their German supporters, and the anti-Semites.

After the unification of the *Reich,* Bismarck was locked in battle with the Catholic Center Party during the *Kulturkampf,* and thereafter with the Social Democrats over the anti-socialist law. But his most protracted struggle, beginning in the days of the Conflict* in Prussia in 1863, was with the liberals, especially the *Freisinn.* Some of the prominent leaders of the party such as Rudolf Virchow and Eugen Richter were not Jews; but since the *Freisinn* supported Jewish emancipation and appealed through its general philosophy to many educated, well-to-do Prussian Jews and other German Jews, Jews flocked to the party and played an outstanding role in its leadership. In 1881 Moritz Busch jotted down Bismarck's remarks about the Jewish deputies Ludwig Bamberger and Eduard Lasker; after making critical observations about members of the liberal party, Bismarck said: "I

---

*A constitutional struggle pitting Bismarck as Chancellor against the liberal majority of the Prussian *Bundestag.*

make a distinction in the case of the Jews. Those who are wealthy are not dangerous; they are not going on the barricades and they pay their taxes promptly. The ambitious ones are those who do not yet have everything, especially those of the press, yet even here Christians are probably the worst, and not the Jews.''[1]

Busch, himself an anti-Semite, reported also a talk by Bismarck in military headquarters on September 25, 1870. The Jews, Bismarck observed, had in a way "no real home, they are generally European, cosmopolitan, nomads. . . . There are also good, honest people among them.''[2] He referred specifically to one he had known in Pomerania and in this context praised such Jewish virtues as respect for parents, marital fidelity, and charitableness. Another time, in 1892, he added to these virtues diligence, frugality, sobriety, enterprise, and abstinence from gambling, from dissoluteness, and from drinking.

Though Bismarck made some critical remarks about mixed marriages in the *Vereinigte Landtag* in 1847, he later expressed himself in a quite different vein. The later remarks were published during Bismarck's lifetime, after he had personally examined the proofs of Busch's work. According to Busch, when the talk turned to the Jews and mixed marriage, the Chancellor had facetiously observed that the Jews would have to be made "innocuous through intermarriage" and that the results were not bad. Bismarck had thereupon pointed to some noble families such as Lynar, Styrum, and Gusserow and remarked, "All quite intelligent nice people." While discussing the advantages of marriages between prominent Christian-German baronesses and rich and talented Jews, he expressed the opinion that the reverse would be better, namely "bringing together a Christian stallion of German upbringing with a Jewish mare. Money must circulate again, and there is no such thing as an evil race. I do not know what I shall advise my sons one day." In 1892 Bismarck expressed himself similarly to Hermann Hoffmann: "The Jews bring to the mixture of the different German tribes a certain *mousseaux* [sparkling], which should not be underestimated." And Busch added that, while the talk was jocular, it was "not without a serious foundation" and that it disposed of the accusation against the Chancellor that he harbored prejudices against the Semitic race.

In 1847 Bismarck had based his opposition to completing the emancipation of Prussian Jewry on religious grounds, the alleged incompatibility of full equality for the Jews with the concept of the German-Christian state. But the mature statesman relinquished this stand and emphasized that the German government had no state religion—a change of position comparable to that on mixed marriages. The noted Jewish journalist Maximilian Harden, in an article "Prinz

Bismarck und Antisemitismus" [Prince Bismarck and Anti-Semitism], published in 1893 when Bismarck was still alive, could thus rightfully deny that the Chancellor had been anti-Semitic. Stressing that Bismarck had never been a man who soft-pedaled his views, Harden wrote: "He has wooed the applause of anti-Semites as little as that of the philo-Semites, and he makes no secret of the fact that even today he can't associate with either of the two parties. He believes that certain Jewish qualities, especially in the field of finance, which is difficult for Germans, could be useful to the German spirit if it does not permit itself to be overwhelmed by them. He sees no possibility of removing Jews who happen to be here in a legal manner; therefore he wishes to strengthen the productive groups and in general expects good results from the gradual mixture and intermingling of the races."[3] He did not share the view of those who held either the Jews or the anti-Semites to be the "most dangerous enemies of the Reich" and considered either view a great exaggeration. These people reminded him of one who, while not daring to strike out against surrounding beasts, "heroically" fights off a swarm of gnats.

If Bismarck was guilty of a gross underestimation of anti-Semitism—one shared by most contemporaries, Germans of varied political persuasions, and also by Jews—the comparison of anti-Semites on the one hand, and Jews and philo-Semites on the other, was hardly a lesser blunder. The Jews represented no danger to the stability of the German *Reich* which Bismarck had founded, the former decidedly did.

BISMARCK AND EMINENT JEWS

While Bismarck thought that Jews were not gifted as painters, he conceded that there were great Jewish composers, such as Meyerbeer, Mendelssohn-Bartholdy, and Halevy. When a storm was raised in Germany over erection of a monument in honor of Heinrich Heine, who had criticized Prussia's expansionism, Bismarck raised the question whether Heine, after all, had been "so wrong." And he remarked that if he had been in Heine's shoes, he too would have glorified Napoleon I: "Could it have pleased me if I had been born a Jew that at 8 p.m. one closed the gates under the most pressing emergency decrees?"[4] And he finally reminded all present that Heine was a poet of songs with whom only Goethe could be compared and that the song was a specifically German form of poetry.

Just as in 1847, however, Bismarck in the unified *Reich* continued to oppose immigration from Eastern Europe into Prussia and Germany; such immigration apparently would have slowed the assimilation of German Jews. Yet his opposition to further Jewish immigration should not be interpreted as a symptom of Jew-hating or particularly of hostility to German Jews.[5] Nor was Bismarck by any means hostile to foreign Jews; he repeatedly criticized the Rumanian government for its discriminatory policy against the Jews. Prussian and German state interests, rather than personal sympathies and considerations, prompted Bismarck to take such a course as early as 1868.[6] Finally, at the Congress of Berlin in 1878, Rumania was asked to endorse equality of the Jews as a condition of her being accepted into the European family of nations. When Russia's spokesman Prince Gortschakoff warned that the Jews of Berlin, Paris, London, and Vienna should not be confused with those of Serbia, Rumania, and some Russian provinces, Bismarck as presiding officer observed that the regrettable condition of the Jews might perhaps be traced back to the limitation of their political and civic rights.[7] Here was a most valid argument, which, incidentally, reflected a reasoning contrary to that expressed in his Berlin speech in 1847! The same point of view had previously been voiced at the Congress by Waddington, the French delegate.

During the years 1880 to 1884, a Hamburg Jew, Dr. Eduard Cohen, was the family physician in Bismarck's house and thus had an opportunity to converse with the Chancellor; these conversations he promptly jotted down. He recorded Bismarck's complaint that he had been vilified by all sides, that some called him an anti-Semite, while others accused him of being a friend of Bleichröder.[8]

Bismarck was convinced of the superiority of Germans to most other European peoples; but this belief on the whole was free from an arrogant and offensive nationalism. Because of his very self-assurance, Bismarck was never genuinely fearful of any possible "domination" of the Germans by the handful of Jews among them. Though he frequently uttered critical remarks about the French, he made no similar negative observations about the Jews.

While in France, Great Britain, and other countries the Jew-haters did not organize themselves politically, in Germany anti-Semitism turned into a political movement. Austria too followed this road. In Berlin the court preacher Adolf Stöcker, appealing primarily to small artisans and merchants who were hit by the economic misfortunes of the seventies, fathered the anti-Semitic movement. Under the guise of "Christian Socialism" the party obtained as many as sixteen seats. It comprised most disparate elements. At times it marched politically with the conservatives; at other times it promoted a distinct social program of its own. In 1880 the anti-Semites made much propaganda with a petition which appealed to Chancellor Bismarck to prohibit Jewish immigration and to exclude Jews from high public office.

Though the petition allegedly bore a quarter of a million signatures, Bismarck never gave it official acknowledgment; to the contrary, a spokesman for the government, Graf zu Stolberg-Warnigerode, declared that "nobody intended to alter anything regarding the equality of the religious faiths in civic matters."

Bismarck had personal relations with a number of Jews. Certainly no greater ideological contrast could exist than that between Bismarck and the Jewish radical socialist Ferdinand Lassalle. Still, Lassalle felt deeply Prussian and German. Bismarck claimed that he met Lassalle only three or four times, but many have asserted that their relations were more intimate than that. Oncken held that these relations, begun in October 1863, lasted until February 1864.[9] In the famous *Reichstag* speech on September 17, 1879, Bismarck, who said few good things about any member of the parliament, praised the memory of Lassalle, drawing a sharp line between him and contemporary Social Democrats. "He was a much nobler character than his epigones. That was an important man with whom one could talk."[10] Politically, Lassalle had nothing to offer to Bismarck. In the latter's words, "what he had was something which, as a private citizen, attracted me extraordinarily, . . . he was one of the most ingenuous and amiable men with whom I ever associated, a man, ambitious in the grand style, by no means a republican. He had a very distinct national and monarchical point of view. Lassalle was an energetic and witty man whose conversation was very instructive; our talks lasted for hours and I always regretted when they reached their end. . . ." Bismarck added that he "would have enjoyed having a man of his talent and ingenuous character as a neighbor on his estate [*Gutsnachbar*]."

Among the numerous German-Jewish politicians whom Bismarck came to know was Ludwig Bamberger. After a radical youth and many years abroad, he had returned to Germany, convinced of Prussia's mission and Bismarck's accomplishments, and had propagated both in southern Germany. With a considerable knowledge of and expertise in economics, he played a major role in the introduction of the gold currency and the founding of the German *Reichsbank* and in 1870 entered into close relations with Bismarck. In 1871 he joined the National Liberals. Because of Bamberger's assistance in laying the foundation of the *Reichsbank,* it was assailed by haters of the Jews and of the Chancellor as "*Bismarck'sche Reichsjudenbank* [Jewish *Reichsbank*]."[11] Bismarck's struggle with the Social Democratic movement and his adoption of a new economic policy led to the break between the Chancellor and Bamberger.

Though Bamberger came personally close to Bismarck, in German politics Eduard Lasker played the greater role. While one of the founders of the National Liberal Party, Lasker remained loyal to Judaism—as also did Bamberger. A member of the Prussian *Landtag* from 1865, Lasker split with the Progressives after Königgrätz, approving indemnity for Bismarck for violations of the constitution committed during the Conflict. With Bamberger and the jurist Martin Eduard von Simson, also of Jewish descent, he played a major role when the foundation of the *Reich* was laid in 1870–1871. Though in agreement with the Chancellor until 1873, he often parted company with him thereafter. He died on a journey to America in 1883; the special tribute paid to him by the American House of Representatives was probably taken as a personal insult by Bismarck, who accused the deceased in an exceptionally bitter outburst of having made life for him more difficult than any other political figure—which did not fully accord with the facts. In any case, Bismarck's opposition to Lasker had primarily political roots, and anti-Semitism did not figure in it. According to the noted economic historian Gustav Schmoller, Lasker upheld the ideal of the absolute *Rechtsstaat,* while Bismarck represented the demands of practical politics: "They could not fully understand each other, but the fatherland can be grateful for having had both and for having seen them cooperate, at least for a time."[12]

Bismarck always showed a special liking for the politician and jurist Martin Eduard von Simson, who was of Jewish descent on both sides but had been baptized in his early youth. Twice in his life von Simson had the honor of offering the German imperial crown to a Hohenzollern king, in 1849 and during the Franco-Prussian War. In 1848–1849 he served as President of the Frankfurt National Assembly. In 1879 Bismarck appointed him President of the Supreme Court. Bismarck also had a close business relationship with the industrialist Moritz Behrend, the founder of the Varzin Paper Factory. In 1881 he discussed the growing anti-Jewish agitation with Behrend and disavowed any agreement with it: "I decidedly disapprove of this fight against the Jews, whether it is wrapped in religious garb or even refers to origin." He permitted Behrend to make use of this statement in the press.

During the course of his many-sided career Bismarck had come to know Jews in many capacities; as a landed proprietor he met Jews in the countryside, and as Prussian envoy to the *Bundestag* in Frankfurt am Main he encountered Jewish merchants and bankers. His relations with Bleichröder aside, in Berlin he met Jews who were active as politicians and journalists. The Jewish question preoccupied him continually throughout his career. Jöhlinger, a political conservative who admired Bismarck, made in his comprehensive study of the Chancellor's relationship with the Jews the point that, from the moment he turned statesman and accepted the chancellorship of Prussia, Bismarck never said or wrote anything unfriendly about them. This, as he held, was the more remarkable since the men of his entourage were to a large degree anti-Semites; at Bismarck's table sat men who in their heart were on the side of Stöcker.

BISMARCK AND THE RISE OF POLITICAL ANTI-SEMITISM

The financier Gerson Bleichröder, who administered the private finances of the Chancellor, was thoroughly trusted by Bismarck, who entertained close relations with him. In the course of a talk with Anton Memminger, the editor of the *Bayerische Landeszeitung,* Bismarck praised Bleichröder for his role in the Austro-Prussian war of 1866.[13] It was on the basis of Bismarck's recommendation that Bleichröder was raised to the rank of nobility. Bleichröder's political services, based upon intimate associations with the Rothschild banking house in Paris and the special role he played during the war of 1870, probably contributed heavily to his receiving this conspicuous honor.

The close relationship of Bismarck to Bleichröder became the target of numerous attacks by both haters of Bismarck and anti-Semites. One Otto von Diest-Daber, in numerous pamphlets, especially *Bismarck und Bleichröder: Deutsches Rechtsbewusstsein und die Gleichheit vor dem Gesetze* [Bismarck und Bleichröder: German Legal Consciousness and Equality before the Law], vilified both the Chancellor and the "Grossjuden Bleichröder."[14] In the notorious five essays called the "Ära-Aufsätze," the *Kreuzzeitung* in June and July 1875 had unleashed a sharp attack against both men, denouncing the monetary policy of the *Reich* as a "Jew-policy." Diest-Daber's accusations were later repeated in numerous other anti-Semitic tracts, especially in the *Reichsglocke,* whose editor was H. Joachim Gehlsen; his paper was indeed as hostile to Bismarck as it was to the Jews. Gehlsen himself conceded that "the opposition of wide circles to Bismarck was identical with that to the Jews."

Many anti-Semites such as Theodor Fritsch considered it their duty to oppose the so-called Bismarck-cult. Another notorious Jew-hater, Ahlwardt, looked upon hatred of Bismarck and hatred of the Jews as two sides of the same coin. One anti-Semitic writer in his tract *Die Wahrheit über Bismarck* [The Truth about Bismarck] judged the Chancellor to be a descendant of the Jews, a view shared also by the anti-Semite Carl Paasch; the latter, "refining" this thesis, suspected that Bismarck might be a "secret Jew." Another hater of both the Chancellor and the Jews was the one-time professor Eugen Dühring.

It is perhaps disconcerting that Bismarck did not reject anti-

Semitism in an unambiguous manner. The key to Bismarck's attitude toward both Jews and anti-Semites, however, lay in politics pure and simple. According to the *Bismarck-Erinnerungen* [Memories of Bismarck] of the Freiherrn Lucius von Ballhausen, Bismarck said that "the anti-Jewish agitation had been inopportune. He had taken a position against it, but beyond that he had not done anything because of their [the anti-Semites'] courageous attitude against the Progressives."[15] In other words, Bismarck tolerated the Jew-haters because of their opposition to the liberals, rather than on account of their agitation against the Jews. Jöhlinger, writing in 1921, considered Bismarck's attitude toward the anti-Semites "correct," judging it from a narrow political point of view. In view of the ravages of anti-Semitism in twentieth-century Germany, however, this position clearly can no longer be defended. The Chancellor's policy was perhaps tactically comprehensible, but it was neither ethically acceptable nor, taking a long-range point of view, politically sound. Nor was anti-Semitism, in spite of the views of Jöhlinger and others, devoid of any chances of success in the era of Bismarck. It was on account of Bismarck's occasionally ambiguous utterances about anti-Semites that many Jews suspected him of anti-Semitic leanings. But Jews more closely associated with the Chancellor, such as Ludwig Bamberger, A. Kohut, M. Behrend, and Maximilian Harden, sharply disputed such interpretation.

What were Bismarck's relations with the anti-Semitic agitator and court preacher ("Hetzkaplan") Stöcker? Bismarck never invited him for a conference and never personally received him. Stöcker himself revealed in his book *Dreizehn Jahre Hofprediger und Politiker* [Thirteen Years as Court Preacher and Politician] that their relationship consisted "in having no relationship with each other." He denied that the Chancellor ever took a "friendly stance" toward the anti-Semitic Christian Socials. According to Stöcker, "the very struggle against Judaism was the cause of the enmity of Bismarck" against him.[16]

Bismarck first believed that Stöcker would confine his battle to fighting Social Democrats. According to Moritz Busch, who, like Lothar Bucher, had voted for Stöcker, Bismarck in a talk on November 12, 1881, disclosed that he had first disliked Stöcker's anti-Semitic agitation, which was to him "inconvenient and went too far," but that Stöcker was fearless and courageous and had a "big mouth which cannot be shut up [*ein Maul, das nicht totzumachen ist*]";[17] yet agitator and court preacher did not go together. Stöcker himself castigated Bismarck bitterly; he accused him of having loosed lightning bolts against everything and everybody except Judaism and the Jewish press.[18] And he charged Bismarck with cowardice on this ground.

Rumors circulated that Bismarck considered applying the anti-socialist law to Stöcker and having him expelled from the country, and Stöcker himself claimed that Bismarck had wished to banish him from Germany. As the so-called pyre-letter (*Scheiterhaufenbrief*) disclosed, Stöcker in 1888 indulged in political intrigue with the avowed intention of arousing discord between the young Emperor William II and Bismarck.[19] Bismarck himself, in a long letter to Prince William on January 6, 1888, warned him against Stöcker: "I have nothing against Stöcker; he has, as far as I am concerned, the weakness as a politician that he is a priest and as a priest that he engages in politics."[20] After his political retirement, Bismarck frequently continued to take issue with Stöcker in the columns of the press.

A semiofficial attack on the anti-Semitic movement, apparently inspired by Bismarck, had earlier been made in an article in the *Norddeutsche Allgemeine Zeitung* on September 25, 1885. The writer had pointed out that in the summer of 1885 "the attitude of Bismarck toward the conservative anti-Semitic movement became hostile. Bismarck was prepared to accept defeat by the Progressives in Berlin rather than victory of the anti-Semitic movement in the capital and the country. The civic equality of all citizens, irrespective of religion, could not be altered, and even a policy of fanaticism, which might help anti-Semitism, would not be successful. Bismarck often stated that the anti-Semitic goal could not be achieved by peaceful reform."[21] In the article the Chancellor apparently let loose all the guns of a semiofficial journal against the anti-Semitic movement, against the "*Stöckerei und Muckerei*" (bigotry).[22]

In the same vein was an article in the *Hamburger Nachrichten* (July 22, 1892), reporting a conversation of Bismarck with Hermann Hoffman, his "Eckermann." Again the point was made that the anti-Semitic agitation could hardly lead to practical results: "The fact is that the Jewish people are superior to many other segments of the population in regard to acquisition of money. This fact could not be erased unless one wished to resort to such measures as the Massacre of St. Bartholomew or the Sicilian Vespers, which even fanatical anti-Semites declared impermissible."[23] Bismarck might have and should have rejected anti-Semitism on moral grounds and would have made a stronger case and appeared more consistent if he had. Still, for Bismarck, the rejection of anti-Semitism on so-called practical grounds, the repudiation of mass murder—the possibility of which, though mentioned, was hardly seriously entertained—disposed of this issue.

In the talk with Hermann Hoffman, Bismarck also pointed out that one could not expel the Jews. Any exclusion from positions in the civil service and as judges would push the Jewish intelligentsia even more into the fields of economics and finances. It would also be harmful to impose limits upon the Jewish drive for acquisition and accumulation, since this would hinder other segments of the population and harm the national welfare: "The well-to-do Jew appears to be an especially reliable taxpayer and a loyal citizen. . . . Likewise, one must not close one's eyes before the good sides of the Jews. There is much in them that we don't have: motives and movements which, without the Jews, would hardly exist in our national life to the same extent. If I were still minister, I would recommend in regard to the Jews the principle: 'La recherche de la confession est interdite.' "[24] According to the *Neue Freie Presse,* Bismarck believed that the Jews were, as a result of natural disposition in money matters, frequently smarter and more skillful than Christians. Furthermore, as long as they had not become rich, they were more modest and thrifty than their Christian competitors. In conclusion, Bismarck held the Jews to be useful members of the state and found it unwise to disturb them.

Academic and Literary Anti-Semites

In the new *Reich* anti-Semitism grew by leaps and bounds, intellectually, socially, and politically. While it is not the purpose of this study to render an account of the history of the political movement, reference must be made to the expression of anti-Semitic thought by prominent and widely read German writers, who cannot be completely separated from political anti-Semitism.

The noted historian and widely popular publicist Heinrich von Treitschke shed his early liberalism to fight aggressively for Germany's national unification under Prussian aegis. He became an admirer of Bismarck and a champion of intransigent German nationalism and expansionism and also turned into a sharp opponent of the Jews. The Professor, who had the ear of Germany's academic youth and shaped its political education, preached a pervading anti-Semitism, making Jew-hating once again fashionable in educated circles. At different times he feared that Germany's existence was threatened by South German particularists, by Catholics, by socialists, by a vengeful France or a jealous Britain. But though Jews were not the only group that Treitschke, during his long career, singled out as a menace to a strong and unified Germany, he never failed to give them conspicuous mention. At the height of the anti-Semitic agitation in 1879–1880 he made them the primary target in a series of wide-ranging journalistic attacks.

Only some Jews, Treitschke claimed in *Deutsche Geschichte des neunzehnten Jahrhunderts* [German History of the Nineteenth Century] had manifested patriotic zeal during the War of Liberation; others had demonstrated a "readily comprehensible sympathy" for France.[25] But Jews had not infrequently displayed an "astounding mendacity and presumption" about their numerical participation in the war. On the whole, Treitschke ignored or minimized past Christian outbursts against the Jews. The overall impressions he conveyed were of unwarranted Jewish aggressiveness, lack of patriotism, reluctance to assimilate—all of which explained and justified occasional outbursts of German impatience and wrath.

To Treitschke, German national development was deflected by what he called "the intrusion [*Einbruch*] of Judaism." Unlike the Jews in the West, who were descendants of Sephardic Jews, the German Jews were of Polish stock. In contrast to finer spirits among German Jews who pleaded for the abandonment of Jewish separatism and to such talents as F. Mendelssohn-Bartholdy, Veit, and the pious Neander, other Jewish writers "boldly insisted on the display of Jewish peculiarities." "These Jews without a country, vaunting themselves a nation within the nation," exercised a harmful influence upon the still inchoate national self-esteem of the Germans. He castigated Heine and Börne, largely blaming them for the alleged decline of German literature, but praised Friedrich Julius Stahl, the Bavarian Jew who had become a convert to Lutheranism and a champion of the Prussian monarchy and conservatism. In spite of his secular leanings Treitschke supported the "Christian-German state" conception of Friedrich Wilhelm IV on the eve of the 1848 revolution and rejected Jewish demands for full equality in Prussia. Proud of his own descent from Czech Protestants who had found religious refuge in Saxony, Treitschke was not unsympathetic to religious toleration. But for him this idea, coupled with the notion of equality of all religious values, was confined to Christian denominations. As the historian Hans Liebeschütz has made clear, Treitschke in the last twenty-five years of his life, when he was writing his *Deutsche Geschichte des neunzehnten Jahrhunderts* no longer believed in the equality of Judaism with Christianity.[26] This absence of true religious tolerance was reinforced by his concept of the nation state, which aimed at national homogeneity and at the assimilation of religiously and nationally disparate elements such as the Jews.

Treitschke's vanishing liberalism partly preceded, partly coincided with, the renewed attack against German Jews in the new *Reich,* spearheaded as it was by the Christian Social Labor Party under the leadership of Adolf Stöcker. The financial crisis of the seventies, fear for the cohesion of the just unified *Reich,* and anxiety over diversity and dissension spawned these attacks. Treitschke actually never met Stöcker personally, and in a strict sense of the word they were never truly political associates. But when returning to Berlin in 1879, Treitschke gave his blessing to the anti-Semitic movement without formally identifying himself with it. There could never be any doubt on whose side Treitschke was. While Stöcker appealed to the lower German classes in the new *Reich,* Treitschke opened to anti-Semitism the auditoria of the German universities. The *Vereine deutscher Studierender* [Leagues of German Students], which exerted considerable influence upon the German fraternities, became the vehicle of Treitschke's anti-Semitic program, adding racist overtones to it. Though Treitschke himself did not directly approve of racism, he was responsible for many ideological and political excesses. Students of his, including Hermann von Petersdorff, testified to his role in stirring up anti-Semitism among Germany's academic youth.[27]

Of the deep changes which Treitschke observed after a journey abroad and which he listed in his article in the *Preussische Jahrbücher* in 1879, none was so "alienating" as the deeply emotional movement against the Jews.[28] But, he claimed, there existed in Germany a "reverse Hep Hep": everybody could, without fear, say the harshest things about Germans and other peoples, but he "who dared to talk in a just and moderate manner about an undeniable weakness of the Jewish character was stigmatized" almost by the entire press as "a barbarian and religious persecutor." The historian was aware that the English and French disdained the "German prejudice against the Jews." But in the West the number of Jews were smaller; into Germany, on the other hand, there pushed from the East every year "a large number of ambitious youths who made their living by selling pants, youths whose children would one day dominate Germany's exchanges and the German press. The problem of amalgamating with this people grows."

"What we have to ask of our Israelitic fellow-citizens is simple: they ought to become Germans . . . for we do not wish that after a millennium of Germanic customs there should follow an era of mixed Germanic-Jewish culture." It would be sinful to forget that many Jews, baptized and unbaptized ones, were German in the best sense of the word. But recently, Treitschke concluded, powerful groups of German Jews did not want to become Germans; they displayed a "dangerous spirit of arrogance," and the impact of Jewry upon German national life had shown itself "again harmful in many respects." The loud anti-Semitic agitation was perhaps "a brutal and hateful, but still natural reaction of Germanic popular sentiment against an alien element." Even among the most educated elements of German society, "from among men who would scornfully reject every notion of clerical intolerance or national arrogance, one hears today unanimously: 'The Jews are our misfortune!' "

"Among reasonable people there can be no talk about a withdrawal or even a mere diminution of the emancipation; this would be an apparent injustice, a departure from the good tradition of our state and would only sharpen rather than blunt national tension." Perhaps the task of amalgamation between Germans and Jews can never be fully solved. But the contrast can be "alleviated if the Jews who talk so much about tolerance will become really tolerant and display some reverence toward the faith, the customs and feelings of the German nation." Treitschke concluded with the pious hope that out of the ferment of these troubled years there might emerge a stronger national sentiment.

Among the replies to Treitschke's articles was one by Harry Bresslau, Treitschke's Jewish colleague at the University of Berlin, who in measured but unambiguous manner accused him of lending the authority of his name to the anti-Semitic agitation and of being unjust and offensive toward Jewish fellow citizens. Another reply was written by the Jewish historian Heinrich Graetz, whom Treitschke had personally criticized. As Graetz countercharged, Treitschke had directed a broadside against German Jewry in its entirety; Graetz also raised the question whether forty million Germans were actually in danger of being corrupted by a mere handful of Jews.[29] He denied Treitschke's accusation that he was hostile to Christianity; he had merely depicted the thousandfold sufferings of the Jews at Christian hands through the centuries. Treitschke himself had branded past persecution of the Jews "Christian tyranny." As far as his own criticism of the great Germans was concerned, he had, after giving due credit to the greatness of Luther, Goethe, and Fichte, condemned Luther for his anti-Jewish agitation and criticized others for their negative attitudes toward the Jews.

On November 12, 1880, almost a year after the "Jew-debate" had started with Treitschke's first article in the *Preussische Jahrbücher,* there appeared a statement in the Berlin press which was signed by seventy-five distinguished Germans.[30] It lamented that "racial hatred and medieval fanaticism were now revived against our Jewish co-citizens in different localities, especially the largest cities of the *Reich.*" It had been forgotten how many of them, through diligence and talent in the crafts and trade, in arts and sciences, had brought benefit and honor to the fatherland. "The command of the law as well as the demand of honor that all Germans are equal in rights and duties are thus violated. . . . If now envy and jealousy are preached by the leaders of this movement only *in abstracto*, the mass will not hesitate to draw from this talk practical consequences. The legacy of Lessing is undermined by men who should announce from the pulpit and from the lecturer's chair that our culture has overcome the isolation of that tribe which once gave the world the adoration of one God."

"It is still time to oppose the confusion and to avert national shame. The passion of the mob, artificially fanned, can through the resistance of prudent men still be defeated. . . . Our call goes out to Christians of all parties, to whom religion is the happy message of peace; our call extends to all Germans who treasure the ideal heritage of their great princes, thinkers and poets. Defend in public declarations and calm enlightenment the foundation of our joint life: esteem for every faith, equal rights, equality in competition, equal acknowledgment of notable endeavors of Christians and Jews."

At the very moment the statement of the seventy-five notables appeared in the press, the distinguished historian Theodor Mommsen published the pamphlet *Auch ein Wort über unser Judentum* [Another Word about Our Jewry] (1880). He started out by lamenting the derision of Jews which had been heard in Germany to the astonishment of the entire civilized world. Before the establishment of the new unitary state, religious and tribal differences had been ignored, but now there raged a war of everybody against everybody. After the *Kulturkampf* and the recent civil war over financial and monetary questions there had appeared "a new deformity of the national sentiment, the campaign of the anti-Semites."[31] It represented a harmful retrogression, and no one had the right to look on in silence at this "suicidal agitation of national sentiment." An illusion had seized the masses "and their real prophet was Herr von Treitschke." What did he mean by demanding that "our Israelitic fellow-citizens should become Germans?" They are German just as he and I. He may be more virtuous, but does virtue make the Germans?" The just unified German nation had "with the war against the Jews entered a dangerous road." Mommsen ridiculed the German fear of the Jews as one "of the most silly perversions." Against any possible shortcomings of the Jews must be weighed capacities and excellences the possession of which has largely contributed to the anti-Semitic agitation. In the ancient Roman Empire the Jews were an element of national decomposition*; in Germany simi-

---

*In his polemics with Mommsen Treitschke quoted this phrase from Mommsen's *Römische Geschichte* (III, 550, Treitschke, *Deutsche Kämpfe*, N.F. 125). In his rejoinder Mommsen underlined its positive meaning: He had not intended to accuse; to the contrary he had meant to compliment the Jews. It is hardly surprising that numerous anti-Semites (among them Adolf Hitler) have followed Treitschke's path in attempting to distort Mommsen's saying.

larly, by "decomposing" numerous Germanic tribes the Jews worked toward the creation of a common German nationality. "That the Jews have been working in this direction for generations, I do not consider a misfortune and I generally believe that Providence has understood far better than Herr Stöcker why for the development of the Germanic metal it was necessary to add a few percent Israel."

Mommsen expressed finally the hope that tolerance would return, "not the one which is natural, the one toward the synagogue, but the more essential tolerance toward the Jewish characteristics for which they should not be blamed, since they were given them by fate. . . . " The German nation of course was obligated to uphold the principle of equality as well as to battle open or covert violation of the law through administrative manipulation. "This obligation of ours . . . does not depend at all on the good behavior of the Jews." Treating them unfairly and making them feel alien carried a danger "both for them and for us." The civil war of a majority against a minority would be a "national calamity."

There followed, however, a more controversial part of Mommsen's remarks. Since it was "difficult and perilous" to remain outside Christianity, he recommended to those Jews whose conscience permitted renunciation of Judaism and adoption of Christianity that they consider this step: "The entry into a great nation costs a price." Baptism would break down all barriers between the Jews and the rest of their Germanic fellow citizens. Though Mommsen deserved full credit for his principled defense of the Jews and his spirited criticism of Treitschke's accusations, the recommendation relating to baptism reveals the weakness of German liberalism. It was out of tune with the concepts of secularism, the modern *Rechtsstaat,* and in violation also of cultural and ethnic pluralism; the latter concept was not acknowledged by the modern nation-state of the nineteenth century.

The different strains of German anti-Semitism in the last third of the nineteenth century are represented by personalities such as the historian Heinrich von Treitschke, the political writer and civil servant Constantin Frantz, the philosopher Eduard Hartmann, the political economist and philosopher Eugen Dühring, the orientalist and theologian Paul de Lagarde, and the popularizer Julius Langbehn.[32] Frantz's opposition to the Jews and Judaism was a revived Christian anti-Semitism, based upon the concept of the Christian state. While some of the foregoing writers were still deeply rooted in the Christian heritage, others had moved far from Christianity, though traditional Christian thought and a kind of religious resentment of Jews as the brazen people, clinging obstinately to their faith, still appeared to stir them. Lagarde, preaching German Christianity, opposed traditional

Christian faith and rejected Jews on a variety of grounds, advancing religious, nationalistic, and partly racial reasons. Extreme nationalism, mingled with a varying dose of racism, dominated the thinking of Treitschke and even more of Dühring, Lagarde, and Langbehn. Racism was not entirely absent from the thought of any of these men, though they were not always conscious of it and often articulated their views in a far from consistent manner. Many of the writers, at least at some stage of their careers, had embraced a liberal political philosophy; and though they had long ago abandoned liberalism, a modicum of liberal thought survived in the heap of ultraconservative and nationalistic ideas.

All the foregoing writers rejected the concept of what they called a Jewish "state within the state," of a "Palestine" in Germany. Some asked for complete and earliest amalgamation and disappearance of the "Jews as Jews"; this demand was posed by friends of the Jews such as Theodor Mommsen and enemies such as Treitschke and Hartmann. Possessed of an anti-Semitism of a greater, fanatic, intensity were men such as C. Frantz, Lagarde, Dühring, and Langbehn. The new anti-Semitism had unquestionably pathological traits—which the *Weltanschauung* of these authors clearly reflected.

Virtually all the above writers also opposed the emancipation of the Jews and proposed reversion to an earlier state of inequality. Some, like Frantz, looked back to the Middle Ages as an inspiration for shutting the Jews once more into the ghetto; others, like Treitschke, disclaimed such intent, though with little conviction. Still others, like Lagarde, wanted to remove at least some Jews to Palestine or elsewhere, while fanatics like Dühring and Langbehn spoke of the destruction of Jewry and, raising the ante, made a distinction between the imposition of immediate restrictions and an ultimate solution, leaving the latter deliberately indeterminate.

All these writers claimed that Jews dominated Germany, that Germans needed to be "liberated," and that "dejudaization" was imperative. Most were resentful of the demonstrations of solidarity of German Jews for oppressed Jews abroad and claimed to be fearful of Jewish "world domination." The inability of apparently intelligent men, some rabble-rousers aside, to see the German-Jewish situation realistically and in perspective, not to mention with some detachment, is perhaps one of the most appalling lasting impressions made upon the student of German-Jewish history and German anti-Semitism. While the fear of Jewish "world domination" was surely abused by some, who quickly perceived its usefulness as propaganda, there can be little doubt that this fear was a symptom of a genuine and ravaging sickness to which many Germans succumbed.

The paranoid fear of Jewish world rule and Jewish hegemony was only one of numerous fears of the "alien" Jew which gripped generations of Germans and served to rationalize a boundless hatred of the Jewish "infidel." That the Jews dominated their host peoples was merely one charge among many indictments flung at the Jews in the course of history by many peoples—from the killing of Jesus, the *foetor Judaeorum* of antiquity, to the poisoning of medieval wells, to the ritual murder of Christian children and desecration of the host, to alleged responsibility for the spread of the plague, etc. Most though not all of these accusations had lost their credibility and therefore their usefulness in enlightened, rationalist, nineteenth-century Europe, but the myth of Jewish world domination turned out to be an effective, if not perfect, substitute for the earlier accusations.

Most of the writers mentioned above were politically of the Right, none of the Left. But socialism was by no means immune to anti-Semitism, and Jew-hating had also penetrated liberal and radical democratic circles earlier in the nineteenth century. In view of the absence of strong religious ties and the prevalence of freethinking among many writers, one must add to the phenomenon of traditional Christian anti-Semitism a Jew-hating that was rooted in intolerance toward an alien nationality—national anti-Semitism—one based upon hatred of the Jewish "race"—racial anti-Semitism—and an "enlightened" anti-Semitism, which repudiated Jewish "superstitions," was critical of the alleged religious backwardness of the Jews (though sustaining itself through old-fashioned theological opposition to Judaism), and rejected especially the Old Testament and the Talmud. Whatever the past intellectual orientation of the aforementioned writers, their prevalent ideological and political philosophy was conservatism, which was closely tied up with an increasingly ultranationalist outlook.

Some of the writers cited reprimanded the Jews for their reluctance to embrace assimilation and German *Kultur,* while others rejected their Germanization and preached cultural and ethnic separation to them. Some favored mixed marriages and baptism to bridge the existing gulf; others spurned these means to a goal—complete amalgamation—of which they disapproved, hoping to keep the German people "pure."

The revulsion against the Jews to which such writings point disappointed and hurt German Jewry and discouraged the German partisans of preserving the status quo, the recently accomplished legal equality of the Jews. It testified to the deep roots of German anti-Semitism, which Bismarck's legislation had been unable to extirpate; the flourishing anti-Semitic literature cast a dark shadow upon the outgoing century. Deep pessimism marked the thought of many about the future of the Jews in Germany and in Europe in its entirety. The noted Swiss cultural historian Jakob Burckhardt foresaw a change of legislation in the *Reich* which would modify the full equality of the Jews.[33] The philosopher Friedrich Nietzsche was even more fearful, both for the future of the Jews and for the future of Europe.

Nietzsche and the Revaluation of All Values

Friedrich Nietzsche, one of the giants of the nineteenth century, was a complex and unhappy man and one of many contradictions. But in spite of such well-known phrases and slogans as "will to power," "master morality," and "superman" (*Übermensch*), he was not a genuine forerunner of National Socialism. Instead, he was a resolute foe of militarism, nationalism, bigotry, doctrines of German superiority, racism, German imperialism, and, last but not least, anti-Semitism. He broke with Richard Wagner because "he became *reichsdeutsch*," and he did not forgive either him or his own beloved sister Elizabeth an anti-Semitism that was repugnant to him. After resigning his professorship in classics at the University of Basle in 1879, he spent ten years in wandering, to Switzerland, northern Italy, and the French Riviera. Except for very short visits he avoided his native country, since in his view it had come to worship idols.

While not uncritical of the Jews, he held them, both as a people and as individuals, in great esteem. In *Menschlich-Allzumenschliches* [Human-All-Too-Human] he wrote: "The whole problem of the Jews exists only with the national states, insofar as it is here that their vigor and higher intelligence and that capital of spirit and will that they have accumulated must show its weight in a manner which inspires hatred and envy. . . . Thus the literary obscenity is now getting out of hand in all contemporary nations—and actually in direct proportion to the manner in which these nations give themselves a national bearing—to make the Jews the scapegoats of all possible internal and external troubles and to lead them to the slaughter block. As soon as the preservation of nations is no longer at stake, but only the generation of a European mixed race that should be as strong as possible, the Jew is just as useful and desirable an ingredient as any other national group."[34] Thus Nietzsche decried anti-Semitism and traced it back to insecurity and inferiority. He also warmly advocated intermarriage between Jews and Gentiles.

"Unpleasant, even dangerous qualities," Nietzsche continued, "can be found in every nation and every individual. . . . It is cruel to demand that the Jew should be an exception. These qualities may even be dangerous and revolting in him to an unusual degree. . . ." Yet Nietzsche raised the question: "How much must one forgive a people in the total accounting, when they have had, not without the fault of all of us, the most painful history of all peoples and when one owes to them the most noble man (Christus), the purest sage (Spinoza), the most powerful book, and the most effective moral law of the world?"

Though Nietzsche used a terminology which became highly fashionable in the Nazi era, he castigated "Aryan humanity" and especially Manu's provisions for the oppression of outcasts, those of allegedly inferior races. As Nietzsche wrote, "Perhaps there is nothing that outrages our feelings more" than the notion of "pure blood, . . . the opposite of a harmless concept."[35] Anti-Semitism and German nationalism and power were both branded again. "Power makes stupid . . . , the Germans, once called the people of thinkers— do they still think at all today? . . . *Deutschland, Deutschland über alles,* I fear that was the end of German philosophy."[36] What Nietzsche was interested in was not naked power but rather "cultural power," such as France developed after her defeat on the battlefield in 1870–1871.

For many centuries the roots and the ideology of Jew-hating were "religious" and "Christian." It was only among eighteenth-century agnostic or atheistic Frenchmen and among some nineteenth-century German "freethinkers" and atheists that anti-Semitism became fashionable. Nietzsche turned his guns against both "Christian" anti-Semites, such as Richard Wagner and Bernhard Förster, and agnostics like Eugen Dühring. It was while polemicizing against the first that Nietzsche insisted on the Jewish origins of Christianity. While religiously oriented Germans extolled the early Christians, distinguishing them sharply from the Jews, Nietzsche deprecated the early Christians and pictured Christianity as the miscarriage of Judaism. Christianity appeared to Nietzsche as refuse, as waste matter of Judaism. This view of Christianity was perhaps grotesque or perverse, but, unlike the view held by contemporary Christian Jew-haters, it was not rooted in anti-Semitism.

Though at opposite poles in matters of religion, neither German Christians nor Nietzsche did and could deny or minimize the historical ties between ancient Judaism and early Christianity. German Christians, however, claimed that there had been a radical break between ancient Judaism and early Christianity, while Nietzsche proclaimed their close relationship. The former, disliking ancient Judaism, wanted to shift it as far back as possible in order to extol early Christianity, which they considered qualitatively as being in a different category. Nietzsche, appreciating ancient Judaism, placed early Christianity, in comparison with it, in a dimmer light.

Closely linked with Nietzsche's hostile views about Christianity, but not revealing any dislike or lack of appreciation of Judaism and the Jews, was his evaluation of the Old and New Testaments. He admired the Old Testament: "There are many things and speeches in so grand a style that Greek and Indian literature has nothing to compare with it. One stands in awe and reverence before these tremendous remnants of what man once was. . . . The taste for the Old Testament is a touchstone with respect to 'great' and 'small.' " He believed that the New Testament was not in the same class as the Old Testament. "To have glued this New Testament, a kind of rococo of taste in every respect, together with the Old Testament into one book, that is perhaps the greatest audacity and 'sin against the spirit' that literary Europe has on its conscience."[37] And in a similar vein Nietzsche wrote: "I do not love the 'New Testament.' The Old Testament—yes, that is something entirely different: all respect for the 'Old Testament.' In it I find great human beings, a heroic landscape, and something of what is among by far the rarest things on earth, the incomparable naiveté of the strong heart; even more, I find a people."

In his last book, *Antichrist,* just as in earlier writings, Nietzsche was sharply critical of racism and, contrary to Wagner's views, stressed the environmental influences upon man. Quoting the anti-Semitic slogans to keep East European Jews out of Germany, Nietzsche seemed to advise German Jews themselves to oppose further immigration, since it would merely impede the process of intermarriage and assimilation.[38] Though Nietzsche referred once to the ugliness of many immigrated Polish and Galician Jews, at other times he extolled the "beauty of racially pure Jewish women."

In the same notes to the *Antichrist* Nietzsche praised the ancient Jews who in the Old Testament had represented the dignity of death and a kind of consecration of passion most beautifully; to these Jews "even the Greeks could have gone to school!"[39] For Nietzsche there could be no higher praise. In another context he again compared the Jews with the Greeks, the Romans, and the French, all of whom possessed the genius of becoming culturally fertilized and giving birth to a new civilization. He hesitated to place the Germans in the same favored category.[40]

It is perhaps not surprising that Nietzsche, subjected to incessant, mounting racist propaganda in the eighties and attempting to rebut the charges, occasionally used terms such as *Aryan* and *Se-*

mitic. But he never adopted their later familiar racist connotations. In his notes to *Der Wille zur Macht* [The Will to Power] he tried to prove that the Old Testament and Islam too were in no way inferior to "Aryan" religions. Also, continuing his sharp criticism of the Manu law book, because it was based on the concept of "Aryan" racial supremacy, Nietzsche wrote: "The whole book rests upon the holy lie—power through lies. . . . Here the most cold-blooded circumspection was at work . . . the Aryan influence has corrupted the entire world."[41] Nietzsche's term *master race* in *Der Wille zur Macht* was used in the context of rule by a future race of philosophers and artists of diverse national origins, internationally mixed, consisting of individuals cultivating iron self-control.[42]

Characteristic of Nietzsche's notes of this period is an epigram in which he considered it a "mendacity" to raise racial questions "in the medley of Europe today" and proclaimed it as a maxim to keep aloof from the "mendacious race swindle."[43] "Value of anti-Semitism: to drive the Jews to set themselves higher goals . . . Contra Aryan and Semitic. Where races are mixed, there is the source of great cultures."[44]

Although there can be little doubt about Nietzsche's hostility to anti-Semitism, "the lowest level of European culture, its morass,"[45] the Nazis made a desperate effort to enlist him as a glorious forerunner of anti-Semitism. They resorted to short quotations torn out of context, attempting to give them a meaning radically different from the one that Nietzsche had given them. One scholar of the Nazi era, A. Bäumler, has gone so far as to claim that Nietzsche's published works were merely "poses,"[46] while the true Nietzsche appeared allegedly only in the notes. Yet the fact of the matter is that the notes do not reveal Nietzsche's racism either. Oehler, *Friedrich Nietzsche und die deutsche Zukunft,* and Härtle, *Nietzsche und der Nationalsozialismus* (1937), similarly distorted Nietzsche's thought on the Jews. Many of these Nazi interpretations of Nietzsche rest in turn on the laborious attempts of his sister, Frau Förster-Nietzsche, to pervert the true message of her brother, to make him appear as an anti-Semite—though he abhorred the movement—and thus posthumously to "reconcile" Nietzsche with her husband Förster, a noted anti-Semitic leader.[47]

Though he did speak of a master race, Nietzsche, unlike the Nazis, actually extolled and favored race mixture. In no case did he consider the Germans a master race. He held that the Slavs were more gifted than the Germans and thought that the latter had "entered the line of gifted nations only through a strong mixture with Slavic blood."[48] Nietzsche's doctrine of the master race had a sort of aristocratic bias, but no racial one; he thought rather of an international mixed "race" of artists and thinkers. He expected art, philosophy, and religion to elevate men. It was the spirit, not blood, which according to Nietzsche, lifted men—men of diverse ethnic and racial backgrounds—and entitled them to privilege.

In the first third of the nineteenth century, closely linked with Romanticism, there had begun a surge of interest in old Hindu literature and in Sanskrit. In the last third of the century popularizers attempted to exploit the results of the new knowledge of ancient Indian civilization in juxtaposing the "Aryan" character to the Semitic one. Anti-Semites in particular took the lead, borrowing their intellectual weapons from this armory. Nietzsche was well acquainted with the new literature, including the works of Arthur de Gobineau and Paul de Lagarde. The hero of Nietzsche's own work becomes of course Zarathustra, the Iranian-"Aryan" religious founder. But when the publisher Theodor Fritsch, one of the principal champions and organizers of anti-Semitism, turned to Nietzsche for literary contributions, in the belief that the creator of Zarathustra would be the most likely ally of his movement, Nietzsche rejected his plea in two magnificent letters and forbade him to send any further issues of the *Antisemitische Korrespondenz.* The creator of an "Aryan" God did not wish to become a party comrade.

ON ANCIENT AND CONTEMPORARY JUDAISM AND CHRISTIANITY

Nietzsche sharply distinguished between ancient and modern Judaism. His attitude toward ancient Judaism was shaped by his negative attitude toward Christianity. He could not forgive ancient Judaism for having been the womb of Christianity. According to Nietzsche, Christianity originated in Jewish resentment (Ressentiment). Judaism has created Christianity through revaluation of morality; in place of the morality of the masters, of the strong and powerful ones, Christianity constituted the morality of the poor, of the sick, of the slaves. This was what Nietzsche called the "slave revolt in morality."[49] It was the resentment of the weak and enslaved Jewish people that created Christianity. Nietzsche saw in its emergence the struggle of the small oppressed minority against its oppressor. Christ gathered the impoverished around himself; similarly, the "Aryan" Zarathustra was called in the Avesta the "shepherd of the poor."

In a comment about ancient Jewry Nietzsche wrote: "The reality upon which Christianity could build was the small Jewish family of the diaspora, with its warmth and tenderness, with its readiness to help, unheard of in the entire Roman Empire and perhaps misunderstood, with their support of each other, with its negation . . . without envy of everything which is above and which has splendor and power."[50] In the creation of Christianity lay the "world historic significance" of Judaism. Nietzsche did not doubt that Jesus was a Jew, the prototype of the spiritual Jew of his era. He appeared to Nietzsche as the "purest human being," but he was also the "holy anarchist," the revolutionary.[51] Pontius Pilate was to him the representative of the Roman ruling class and thus shared the morality of the masters. In the struggle of Rome against Judea and of Judea against Rome, Nietzsche held that Judea had won a spiritual victory over the power state Rome.[52]

What shaped Nietzsche's thought about Jews and Judaism was his notion that the Jews had dared to revalue all values. He, the philosopher who changed values, saw in the Jews the first people altering traditional values.[53] It is in this crucially important area that Nietzsche felt a strong affinity between himself and the Jews. Further common ground lay in the attitude to life itself.[54] The affirmation of life at any price is the core of the Dionysian philosophy of life to Nietzsche. The highest expression of the will to life is love, but not one tied to a certain object. And Nietzsche saw this love arise out of suffering. "The song in honor of love which Paul has mused upon is not Christian, but a Jewish blazing of the eternal flame, which is Semitic."[55] Nietzsche, physically often suffering, discerned in the Jews a people who suffered throughout history the same pain, had the same longings and the same capacity for love. This love of life appeared to him to be even stronger among the Jews than in the case of the honored people of his youth, the Greeks. In their clinging to life, the Jews as a people were "like the Greeks and even more so than the Greeks."[56] To exemplify their love of life, he referred to Jewish martyrs of the ancient Maccabean era as well as to thirteenth-century martyrs who, according to the chronicler, while laughing and dancing, mounted the funeral pyre.

In three epochs of world history Nietzsche saw the struggle against aristocratic values, a revolution which, as a cultural philosopher, he disapproved of: in the moral slave revolt of ancient Judaism, which led to Christianity, in the German Reformation, and in the French Revolution, which, according to Nietzsche, was "the daughter and continuer of Christianity." As he reproached ancient Jewry for its revaluation of all values, brought about through Christ and Paul, he similarly blamed the Germans for Luther and the French for Robespierre and Marat. Nietzsche applied the sharp scalpel of criticism not only to Jews but also to the Germans and to the English, to great and recognized poets and musicians, and finally to Wagner himself, though until the end he acknowledged in him the creative genius. And in spite of his criticism of all these peoples and men, he in a manner loved all of them and their creations. He also believed in the future of the Germans. And in spite of his occasional criticisms, he highly esteemed the Jews.

THE ANTI-ANTI-SEMITE

Nietzsche admired Jewish intellectuality ("The Jews have intellect").[57] When he informed those close to him of a Dr. Georg Brandes, holding lectures about his philosophy at the University of Copenhagen, he added significantly: "Of course, a Jew." He thought that the root of the peculiar Jewish intellectuality lay in Jewish history, which every Jew carried in him. All the passions, virtues, decisions, renunciations, struggles, and victories of the Jews had ultimately to express themselves in great intellects and their creations.

Hardly anything in Nietzsche's upbringing and surroundings had predestined his sympathy toward or liking of the Jews. To his mother, herself the daughter of a Protestant minister and wife of another, a Jew was a being from another world. Erwin Rohde, a friend of the young Nietzsche, was not free from anti-Semitism, and Peter Gast, the beloved disciple, called Berlin a "gravel Jerusalem" in a letter to Nietzsche.[58] Nietzsche's earlier encounter with Wagner, a modern apostle of opposition to the Jews, was hardly likely to improve matters. His sister Elizabeth finally married Bernhard Förster. Brother and sister had been unusually close to each other, and to Nietzsche, isolated as he was, Elizabeth's encouragement and faith in him had been a source of strength, especially after his resignation from the university. Under these circumstances the marriage was a serious personal blow to Nietzsche. Now Elizabeth would emigrate with her husband to Paraguay and would be lost to him. But to top matters, Förster was a prominent leader of the anti-Semitic movement, which Nietzsche had come to loathe. His aversion to anti-Semitism had been established long before Elizabeth's marriage, at the time of his break with Wagner and the publication of his work *Menschlich-Allzumenschliches* (1878). Nietzsche's ideas were clearly irreconcilable with Förster's and with the anti-Semitic *Weltanschauung*.

As Nietzsche wrote to his sister: "You have gone over to my antipodes. . . . I will not conceal that I consider this engagement an insult—or a stupidity—which will harm you as much as me." And to his mother he confessed: "The whole affair [the marriage] went through and through me. And since your son is in poor health, he was consequently sick all the time. . . . For my personal taste such an

agitator [Förster] is something impossible for closer acquaintance."
When Nietzsche learned that Förster had decided to concentrate on
his colonial work in South America and to "step back" from his
racist propaganda—this turned out to be false news—he was pleased,
"since every negative striving contains the danger of corrupting an
originally noble character." Torn between love for his sister—though
his feelings about her had long since become ambivalent—and his
own intellectual integrity, in 1886 he wrote to her in Paraguay, calling
himself an "incorrigible European and anti-anti-Semitic" and suggest-
ing that Förster return to Germany and head an educational institution "which would actively oppose the drilling of State slaves"; this
of course presupposed that his brother-in-law would shed his personality and be reborn as another man. At the same time Nietzsche wrote
to his mother that "because of this [Förster's] species of men I could
not go to Paraguay: I am so happy that they exile themselves voluntarily from Europe. For even if I should be a bad German—in any
case I am a very good European."[59]

Most revealing regarding his attitude to the Jews and to anti-
Semitism are two letters in which Nietzsche referred to his growing
"influence" in Germany and Europe. "In the *Antisemiten-Korrespon-
denz* (which is sent only to reliable *Parteigenossen*) my name is mentioned in almost every issue. Zarathustra, 'the divine man,' has
charmed the anti-Semites; there is a special anti-Semitic interpretation of it, which made me laugh very much."[60] Anti-Semitism was
thus one of the major issues in Nietzsche's life and thought, especially so since his particular relationship not only with his sister but
also with Wagner forced him to come to grips with it. In both cases
Nietzsche behaved in an admirable and uncompromising manner,
though his attitude required personal sacrifice. Once he went so far as
to suggest that the government "expel the anti-Semitic squallers from
the country." This anti-anti-Semitism was so pronouced that, when
insanity began to descend upon him, he scribbled across the margin of
his last letter to the historian Jakob Burckhardt: "Abolished [Kaiser]
Wilhelm, Bismarck, and all anti-Semites," and his last note to Overbeck ended in an even more violent manner: "Just now I am having
all anti-Semites shot."

A great admirer of Wagner and his music, Nietzsche always considered the days he spent in Wagner's house in Tribschen as some of
the happiest days of his life. The breach with Wagner developed
gradually; it was not precipitated by Wagner's art but rather by the
Bayreuth establishment and everything Wagner had come to stand
for. In Nietzsche's later view, Bayreuth had become the Holy City of
anti-Semitic "Christian" chauvinism.[61] Deeply affected by Wagner's

music, Nietzsche had long ignored the Master's fanatical prejudices and excesses of Teutonic worship and what Nietzsche considered his ostentatious pretensions of Christian piety. He apparently had come to be repelled by many a contradiction in Wagner, such as the sympathy for all beings which rises out of *Parzifal* and the contempt of entire classes of people. It was the irreconcilability of their *Weltanschauugen*—with anti-Semitism figuring prominently in Wagner's world view, while meriting no place at all in Nietzsche's—which was ultimately responsible for Nietzsche's break with the composer. In *Der Fall Wagner* [The Case of Wagner] Nietzsche, in a notorious footnote, had raised the question of Wagner's descent and had hinted at the composer's possibly Jewish origin.[62] In reading the proofs he had considered deleting this passage but had let it stand. But this allegation was a blow against Wagner and his entire philosophy rather than a ground for Nietzsche's growing aversion toward the composer and his own ultimate turn-about. Nietzsche's sister had already hinted that Wagner's anti-Semitism was the root cause of the alienation of the two men.

Anti-Semitism was part and parcel of what lay at the source of their troubled relationship and generally divergent philosophies.[63] According to Wagner, the peak of culture had already been reached, and the time had come to link up with a *völkisch* past, symbolized by Lohengrin, Tannhäuser, and Hans Sachs. For Nietzsche, however, culture was only in an incipient stage, pointing to the *Übermensch* of the future. Wagner, self-satisfied, retreated to the Romantic fields of the *völkisch* and Christian past; Nietzsche, looking ahead, saw a future for all peoples, including the Jews, whose extraordinary talents he did not want to forgo. But it was not easy for Nietzsche to break with Wagner, whom he considered one of the greatest Germans of his century, along with Goethe and Heine. In *Ecce Homo* there is a highly critical reference to a young man who once appeared to Nietzsche as a possible disciple, the Prussian Junker Heinrich vom Stein. The gist of it is that he had waded not only in the Wagnerian "morass" but also in that of the anti-Semitic writer Eugen Dühring.[64] Thus in Nietzsche's mind the Christian anti-Semite Wagner and the agnostic Jew-hater Dühring were linked, and their joint pupil Stein, in spite of his closeness also to Nietzsche, was therefore sharply rebuked.

As one who looked deep into the human soul, Nietzsche probably sensed that anti-Semitism was an arch-reactionary as well as, in some respects, a deeply revolutionary movement. An anti-revolutionary par excellence, Nietzsche was also bound to become an anti-anti-Semite. Yet this anti-anti-Semitism was not a private affair. Nietzsche did not wish to remain *au dessus de la mêlée;* to the contrary, in his letters he indulged in criticism of anti-Semitism at the risk of repetition. He urged those close to him to renounce Jew-hating; on its account he broke with his anti-Semitic publisher; and for the same reason he even risked family discord. And he did all this not because of his liking for individual Jews or because of his esteem for the Jewish people as a whole. Rather he saw in anti-Semitism a new slave revolt against European culture, a movement destined to become the antipode of his own philosophy and the archenemy.

The participants in the anti-Semitic movement were for Nietzsche the failures, the *Schlechtweggekommenen*.[65] This apt and comprehensive term included the envious, the avaricious, those who hated intellectuality, adventurers and bandwagon riders, factory owners and impoverished people, pious Christians and atheists, arch-conservatives and reactionaries, and all too frequently even those claiming to be liberals and socialists! Anti-Semites, according to Nietzsche, begrudged the Jews their intellect, money, and position. An opponent of socialism, he saw in the anti-Semitic movement a narrowly circumscribed kind of "socialism." While others, especially Wagner, pretended to spurn Mammon, Nietzsche—and, incidentally, Bismarck too—admired the Jews' business acumen. He rejected anti-Semitism also because of its hostility toward spiritual and cultural values. "The struggle against the Jews has always been a symptom of the worse characters, those more envious and more cowardly. He who participates in it now must have much of the disposition of the mob."[66]

It was also the *Kulturphilosoph* in Nietzsche, the opponent of the anti-cultural slave revolts, who battled the anti-Semitic movement. He opposed anti-Semitism the more resolutely as he discerned in it a movement that was on a collision course with his own mission as it became especially evident in his last creative period—to fashion a future led by a cultural elite, which was to be recruited from all peoples, including the Jews.

THE CULTURE OF THE FUTURE

Zarathustra rejects the revolution that "destroys pictures," that is hostile to culture. But Nietzsche demands a revolutionary change of the world. (He had earlier rejected mere liberalism of the old school as a "mediocrity.") Revolutionizing the world meant to him the inclusion and enhancement of the *entire* world, in all its economic and intellectual aspects. The culture of the future was to include not merely some races and peoples but all. In this sense Nietzsche spoke somewhat grandiloquently of "grosse Politik," opposing it to an ordinary revolution, and extolled "Gesamtkultur" rather than traditional national culture. It was as a "good European" that he sat in judgment of old and new cultures. Bent on preserving European culture, Nietzsche, the anti-revolutionary and "aristocratic radical,"[67] as Georg Brandes called him, saw in the Jews "the most conservative power in our so much threatened and insecure Europe. They can't use either revolutions of socialism or militarism." Apparently, in Nietzsche's view, the Jews stood politically on the same side as he himself! He did not seem to think that they could seize domination in Europe even if they wanted it; and it was "certain that they do not aim at it and are not making plans accordingly."[68] The myth of the Jewish conspiracy found no support in Nietzsche.

Had the Jews, a non-European people by ancestry, a right to live and work in Europe? (Nietzsche characteristically had broadened the question, not confining it to Germany.) He concluded that "Europe owed a lot to the Jews [*manches zu danken*]." It owed them "the high style of morality."[69] Aside from the importance of ancient Jewry in world history, Europe owed the Jews something more basic and important. "In respect to logical thinking, to cleaner mental habits," Europe was "not inconsiderably" indebted to the Jews: "Everywhere where Jews have reached a position of influence, they have taught others to distinguish more distinctly, more sharply, to write more clearly and more neatly."[70] There was no question in his mind as to the right of Jews to live anywhere and everywhere in Europe.

When modern Jewry had entered the doors of European civilization, it had helped substantially to shape it. The lover of Hellas, the "Aryan"-European philosopher who deep down remained alien to every sort of Orientalism, acknowledged that it was European Jewry that saved Greek culture for Europe: "In the darkest periods of the Middle Ages, when the layer of Asiatic clouds was already hanging over Europe, Jewish freethinkers, scholars, and physicians held high the banner of enlightenment and intellectual independence under the harshest conditions and defended Europe against Asia; one owes it not the least to their endeavors that the more natural, rational, and, in any case, nonmystical explanation of the world could finally achieve victory again and that the ring of culture which links us now with the enlightenment of Greco-Roman antiquity remained unbroken. If Christianity did everything to orientalize the Occident, Judaism substantially contributed to occidentalizing it again and again, which in a certain sense means making Europe's mission and history a continuation of the Greek one."[71]

Jews had contributed to the development of European culture both in science and in literature. Throughout his life Nietzsche held Heinrich Heine in greatest esteem. As he wrote, "Germany had produced only one poet besides Goethe: this is Heinrich Heine—and incidentally, he is a Jew." With Heine and Jacques Offenbach, he once remarked, the Jews, in the field of art, had touched genius. Another time he asserted that with their achievement "the potentiality of European culture had really been surpassed."[72]

Nietzsche was no racist; he was strongly influenced by doctrines which, in direct opposition to racism, stressed the role of climate, environment, and especially historical fate upon the character and physical appearance of man. He was aware that in the course of their historical development the Jews had "lost two castes, those of the warriors and of the peasants"—and this had shaped their outlook and character. According to Nietzsche, the crisis of culture would be met only through a regeneration of humanity, a concept irreconcilable with racism. In the early eighties, Nietzsche, while touring Italy, entered into close relations with the Austrian Jew Paneth, a gifted natural scientist, and discussed with him the possibility of regenerating the Jewish masses and, on the eve of the appearance of cultural and political Zionism in Europe, the question of the rebirth of Palestine.[73] But the thought of a regeneration of the Jewish masses was apparently to Nietzsche of primary interest only as part of his program for the higher development of mankind.

Nietzsche remained concerned with what he considered a "European problem," the creation of a new European master race which was destined to rule over all Europe. As far as the development of this new "race" was concerned, he wished to include, not to exclude, the Jewish element. The Jews, in his view, were "just as suitable" for the creation of a "vigorous European mixed race" as any other national group. The creation of such a race was Nietzsche's real objective. The Jews were admirably equipped to make a contribution to this mixed race, since, as he wrote, they possessed "capabilities which as ingredients of a race that is to carry on *Weltpolitik* are indispensable."[74] Nietzsche's *Weltpolitik,* however, was a cultural one, not identical with traditional chauvinistic, militaristic, and imperialistic policy.

Looking into the future, he anticipated with prophetic vision that to the "plays to which the next century invites us belongs the decision about the fate of Europe's Jews." By intellect and intuition Nietzsche feared that decision. Europe, he held, was "threatened with the loss of a part of its most European beings." And he raised the question: "What would remain of European rationality if one deducted from it the Jewish one?"

CHAPTER 20

Political Parties
and the Theorists

The Liberal Parties

The unexpected revival of anti-Semitism in the mid-seventies shook
the German Jews out of their euphoria. The *Israelitisches Wochen-
blatt* raised the question: "What lies at the root of this agitation . . .
which once again places the Jewish question upon the agenda?"
Many Jews were stunned not only by the widespread appeal of anti-
Semitism but also by the relative scarcity of true, reliable friends.

For about a decade German Jews formed a virtual alliance with
the National Liberal Party, which, however, soon split into two.
Thereafter, a majority of German Jews appeared to return to the
progressive *Freisinn,* the left wing of the liberals. In the eighties,
then, they were to a large extent once again in the camp of opposition. Still, Jews never supported the Progressives as closely as they
had backed the old National Liberals. A minority even moved to the
Free Conservatives on the Right, a few to the Catholic Center, and
some small groups to the rapidly rising Social Democractic Party.
Still, the program of the liberal *Freisinn* held greatest attraction for
the German Jews. With the exception of the Social Democrats, it was
the only party which programmatically opposed the revival of the
ideology of the Christian-German state and consistently supported the
separation of church and state. Yet the German *Freisinn* split subsequently into the *Freisinnige Volkspartei* under the liberal leader Eugen Richter* and the *Freisinnige Vereinigung* under Heinrich Rickert.
Both groups were denounced by their anti-Semitic opponents as *Ju-*

*For the views of leading liberal deputies such as Richter and R. Virchow on the Jews
see "Debate in the Prussian *Landtag,* November 1880," pp. 392–395.

denschutztruppe (guard for the protection of the Jews). Even after the rise of Zionism among the German Jews and the spread among its adherents and the Social Democrats of the slogan "Los von [away from] Rickert und Richter," Jews gave the *Freisinn* credit for frequently being their champion.

The Kulturkampf: Catholics and Jews

The position of German Catholicism toward Jews and Judaism in the latter half of the nineteenth century was considerably more critical than that of German liberalism and at times outright hostile. Traditional religious antipathy, a novel anti-Semitism rooted in class and cultural differences, and resentment of the support given to Bismarck and the liberals by some Jews during the *Kulturkampf* shaped the outlook of Catholics. So also did the spread of a more liberal philosophy among many Catholics, as well as growing awareness that both Catholics and Jews were minorities in the new *Reich*.

The Catholic Center was formed as a great political party in 1870–1871, in defense of the Catholic minority. Following the anti-Catholic legislation of the *Kulturkampf* and Bismarck's shift after 1879, the political pendulum swung in the opposite direction. Formerly a target of government policy, the Center was suddenly transformed into the pillar the government looked to for support. The Center Party had been viewed with suspicion by leading German Jews, but its support for the protection of all religious groups and its battle for religious schools and religious teaching and for keeping the day of rest undisturbed seemed to correspond to the interests of many Jews.

The coolness of German Jews to the Center Party can best be understood against their historical background. Determined to preserve and expand the legal equality obtained on the eve of the Franco-Prussian War, the German Jews were politically linked with the National Liberals. Both this party and the Progressives to its left, who happened to be anticlerical, supported the legal equality of the Jews as well as its implementation in public and private life. Given the heavy concentration of Catholics in southern Germany and in the Rhenish region, the Center Party stood for regionalism, whereas the Jews, for whom provincialism had always been an enemy, propagated instead "the great idea of German unity." Leaning to a liberal *Weltanschauung* and opposing ultramontanism, which, in their view, was historically linked to oppression and to recent opposition to emancipation, they seemed convinced that the interests of both Jews and Germans demanded definite limitations on Roman clericalism. The new doctrine of papal infallibility persuaded many Protestants and Jews that intellectual freedom too was at issue in the emerging *Kulturkampf* in the new *Reich.*

Yet soon countercurrents made themselves felt. There were "irreconcilables" both in the Catholic camp—anti-Semites—and in the Jewish one; the latter were persuaded that their interests and aspirations and those of the Roman Church could not be harmonized. Yet the bulk of German Jewry and a substantial number of German Catholics—especially Ludwig Windthorst, the leader of the Center Party—discovered a broad area of common interests. Bismarck's method of fighting the Center Party also alienated a good number of Jews. The Jewish deputies of the National Liberal and the Progressive parties showed a great deal of restraint during the debates on the Catholic Church and remained in the background. Of the four Jews in the *Reichstag,* none voted for the so-called May laws, the most restrictive of all anti-Catholic measures of the *Kulturkampf* period. Nevertheless, beginning a series of articles on German Jews on August 11, 1874, the Catholic Party organ, *Germania,* accused all Jews of being liberals and enemies of the Church; it called them grain speculators, Jews of the exchange, and terrorists. The series, entitled "Zur Judenfrage," constituted the opening round of the anti-Semitic agitation which rapidly increased in the late seventies and early eighties. This movement was largely supported by Protestant and conservative elements.

The sharp attacks of the *Kreuzzeitung* on the economic policies of the Prussian and German governments, frequently coupled with anti-Semitism, were followed by several other ultraconservative and orthodox papers, such as the *Reichsbote, Die deutsche Eisenbahnzeitung* of Herr Gehlsen, which later changed its name to *Reichsglocke,* and *Die deutsche Landeszeitung.* On September 14 the Catholic *Germania* complimented the latter paper for assailing moneyed power and Judaism in particular. It clearly revealed its goal of diverting attention from the Roman Catholic Church and the *Kulturkampf* to the struggle against the Jews: "The *Kulturkampf* too is partly and in many of its phenomena exclusively a consequence of Jewish activity [*Judenwirtschaft*]. Therefore we are pleased also on account of the *Kulturkampf* that the Jewish question has recently been clearly and decisively posed." Jews in turn considered the attacks by *Germania* in 1875 unwarranted and the charge that they were a determined and influential element among the opponents of German Catholicism exaggerated.

Ludwig Windthorst, leader of the Center Party, held that during the *Kulturkampf* the overwhelming majority of Jewish writers had assumed a hostile position toward Catholicism. Yet he seemed to understand the complex Catholic-Jewish relationship in Germany and on the whole displayed a fair attitude toward the Jews; he was especially inclined to exculpate Jewish orthodoxy.

Even at the height of the dispute it appears that a sizable number of Jews voted for the Center. In spite of religious and also ideological differences, the minority status shared by Catholics and Jews in the *Reich* established a certain community of interest which was understood by many Jews and Catholics. In 1879, on the occasion of reports about the settlement of disputes of the *Kulturkampf* era, the *Allgemeine Zeitung des Judentums* observed that the Jews had "only to win, if an acceptable peace" would be concluded and praised the Center for its support of the emancipation of Rumanian Jews. When finally a reconciliation between Bismarck and the Center took place, the Jewish paper assured its readers that "at present one need not fear any adverse impact of the domination of the Center upon the principle of equality."[1]

The Debate in the Prussian Landtag, November 1880

In the debate on the Jewish question in the Prussian *Landtag* in November 1880 the Center stood for preservation of the equality of the Jews. During the electoral campaign for the *Reichstag* in 1884 the *Allgemeine Zeitung des Judentums* again acknowledged that the Center had come out in principle against any restriction of emancipation but warned that some among the candidates of the Center party were anti-Semitic. Toward the end of the century Jewish-Catholic relations had improved sufficiently so that some German-Jewish circles—and a Jewish liberal paper, the Hamburger *Israelitisches Familienblatt*—considered the Center as the *Alternativpartei* for Jews.[2] But the voices of hostility were not entirely repressed in any camp, including that of Catholicism. Anti-Semitism reverberated especially loudly among Catholics in the neighboring Habsburg monarchy, where Roman Catholicism was dominant and where the clash between rising nationalities and the Jews produced additional tension because of the latter's important economic role and their leanings toward Germans and Magyars.

On November 13, 1880, the deputy Dr. Hänel had presented in the Prussian Assembly an interpellation regarding the agitation against

Jewish citizens, which had led to regrettable excesses and had given cause for alarm. In consequence of this agitation a petition was launched, addressed to the Chancellor and posing a number of demands. It asked that the immigration of Jews be completely prohibited; that Jews be excluded from all higher (*obrigkeitlichen*) positions and that a "proper limitation" be put on their employment in the field of jurisdiction; that the Christian character of the elementary school be strictly preserved by employing only Christian teachers and that in all other schools Jewish teachers be utilized only in exceptional cases; and that official statistics be introduced to keep track of the Jewish population. Dr. Hänel and cosignatories of the interpellation asked the Prussian government what position it took in regard to such demands, which, if granted, would quash the full legal equality of Jewish citizens.[3] In his reply, the Vice-President of the Cabinet, Graf zu Stolberg-Wernigerode, stated categorically that existing legislation enunciated the equality of all religious beliefs and that the cabinet did not intend to permit a change of this constitutional requirement.

Deputy Reichensperger of the Catholic Center Party approved the goverment's declaration in support of the principle of equality. He and his political friends of the Center, he underlined with reference to the *Kulturkampf,* had come to fully appreciate the significance of that principle. However, he advised Jewish citizens to demonstrate "more prudence and moderation" and warned that the actual possession of freedom was not a permanent solution, that it was still possible to raise the question "whether the expectations which had been tied [!] to the emancipation of the Jews had been fulfilled. . . . "

The same theme of moderation coupled with more or less subtle admonishments was also played by the Conservative deputy Heydebrand und der Lasa. Though he emphasized that he did not wish to hurt a single Jewish fellow citizen, he raised the question "whether or not a segment of our German Jewry itself bore some responsibility for the present unrest." True, in the past the Conservative Party had expressed doubts in regard to Jews filling high office and judicial posts. But after the emancipation had become the law of the land, the Conservatives had accepted it and had decided to "respect the constitutional rights of our Jewish fellow-citizens," like those of all others. Yet in the present transitional stage it appeared to him useful, if not imperative, that "Jewish co-citizens would show more tact and moderation"; they should desist from attempting "massive penetration" of the civil service. The speech set definite limits on the Jews and contained ominous warnings.

Rudolf Virchow, eminent scientist and leading Progressive, considered the government's answer to the interpellation "correct," though he felt that it could have been warmer. Pointing to the emancipation of Prussian Jews in 1812 and the specific promises that had been held out to Prussian Jews in Paragraphs 8 and 9—the right to academic posts and rights to serve in school and community positions and in offices of public administration—Virchow continued: "We are not accustomed, after having obtained rights, to being told: 'You ought to behave quite modestly for a long time.' . . . We [of the Progressive Party] are amazed that men who have rights shall not make use of them." And German Jews had been given additional rights in 1848! Should Germans tell them now: " 'You were given rights in 1848, but be wary of utilizing them fully' "?

Ludwig Windthorst, leader of the Catholic Center, the second largest group in the House, and the most formidable opponent of Bismarck in the *Reichstag,* held that the liberal interpellation was not justified but found the answer of the government satisfying. Windthorst voiced doubts that the problem of the social position of the Jewish fellow citizens in the Christian state—an "exceptionally difficult" problem—ought to be openly discussed. Considering the moods which prevailed among the masses of the people, he held such procedure to be "extremely dubious and hazardous." "Gentlemen," he continued, "the entire content of my thought lies in these short words: no anti-Jewish agitation, but also no agitation against Christians and especially none against Catholics. Political and religious toleration is the only basis on which the state and civil society can prosper. This toleration we owe all to our fellow citizens, including the Jews, and especially to them, since they are in the minority." But turning to the Jews, he admonished them that this toleration should not be one-sided but "mutual." He conceded that the prominent Jewish members of the Progressive Party had not been *Kulturkämpfer.*

One of the eminent figures in the Progressive Party was the deputy Eugen Richter. Contrasting the vituperative speech of the Center deputy Bachem on the third day of the debate with the address of Windthorst two days before, he thought it would have been better for the Center Party not to have followed the speech of their leader with that of a speaker of second rank. He charged that because "one could not battle the liberals on their principles, one had called racial hatred to one's help." He denounced the anti-Semitic movement as "antinational." It was also a sad sample of "courage" to turn against the Jews, "a small minority," comprising even in Berlin only one thirtieth of the entire city population, especially if one knows that the anti-Semitic movement has "supporters and friends, powerful people who rejoice at it."

THE POLITICAL ANTI-SEMITISM OF ADOLF STÖCKER

The anti-Semitic court preacher Adolf Stöcker began his address in the *Landtag* with a belligerent thrust, claiming that millions of people supported his cause. But he quickly moved to the defensive; he was fully aware of the great responsibility which "at this moment" lay on his shoulders. Yet his correspondence showed that the citizens of Berlin, the artisans who felt the social pressure, were at his side, not at the side of the *Fortschritt*. For him the Jewish question was not a religious problem, not a racial one, not a legal one, but a social-ethical problem; and he agreed in this respect with Deputy Bachem of the Center. It was obvious that he hoped, as far as anti-Semitism was concerned, to build bridges toward others and to broaden his political base. The Jews were "of a different tribe and religion, in their thought, feeling and ambitions not always one with the German kind," and they played a role among German Christians that far outweighed their numbers. It was not their wealth that was in question, but the way it had been acquired and the influence purchased with its help and protected by it. Thus Stöcker created a thicket of insinuations and innuendos.

It was this Jewish influence that the Christian Social movement opposed. Stöcker saw no solution in the formula "that we should grant tolerance to the Jewish people just as the latter should do to the Christians." Nor did the other formula, that the existence of Prussia was tied to the political equality of the different faiths, apply, since Judaism was no faith! With this statement Stöcker, whatever his claims, laid the axe to the emancipation and equality of the Jews.

Anti-Semitism did not score a victory in the Prussian *Landtag* in 1880. The *Fortschritt,* rising to the challenge, acquitted itself creditably. Still, the events which preceded the debate in the *Landtag* and the anti-Semitic waves which were to follow it beyond the following decade were bound to raise questions about the genuineness of freedom and legal equality for the Jews and the long-range future of German-Jewish relations. It could hardly be overlooked that anti-Jewish feelings and criticism of German Jewry were by no means confined to the extremist followers of Deputy Stöcker but were widely shared by Conservatives and Catholics. On the other hand, Stöcker, in typically demagogic manner, veered back and forth between brazenness and apparent moderation. A deep gulf still separated German anti-Semitism of the eighties from the fanatic, racist Jew-hating of the twenties and thirties of the following century.

The Roots of Socialist Anti-Semitism

Anti-Semitism also penetrated the German and Austrian Social Democratic parties. Jew-hating built a bridge which linked individuals of different ideologies, denominations, and social and economic status—members of the upper and middle classes, the peasantry, and the growing proletariat—in joint opposition to the Jews. Socialist anti-Semitism—theoretically perhaps a contradiction, if not an absurdity—was a phenomenon which was not confined to the socialist parties of Central Europe, the *Reich* and the Habsburg monarchy. There was a strong anti-Semitic current also in the French and Russian socialist movement and among socialists of other European countries. Such anti-Semitism persisted despite the absence of any socialist doctrine which would have permitted or "justified" it. The fact is that, side by side with a theological-medieval, an "enlightened," a feudal, a bourgeois anti-Semitism in Germany, anti-Semitism sprouted also in the socialist movement.

German socialist anti-Semitism may have been strengthened by Marx's own anti-Semitism and that of some French and Russian socialists who were Jew-haters. In France, Charles Fourier, the utopian socialist, and several of his followers, such as Alphonse Toussenel and Pierre Leroux, came out in opposition to the Jews. Toussenel and Leroux each published a pamphlet bearing the same title, *Les Juifs, rois de l'Epoque* (1845 and 1846). Similarly, Pierre-Joseph Proudhon, in *Césarisme et Christianisme,* claimed that Jewish policy in economics was entirely negative, entirely usurious. Proudhon sounded at times as if he were possessed by medieval spirits when he asserted for instance that "the evil principle, Satan, Ahriman, was incarnated in the race of theirs [the Jews]."[4]

Marx himself engaged in a protracted struggle with both Proudhon and the Russian Bakunin; both were fierce anti-Semites who used anti-Semitism also against Marx personally, though the latter could well compete with either adversary in anti-Jewish outbursts. Mikhail Aleksandrovich Bakunin considered the whole Jewish nation as constituting "one exploitative sect, one race of leeches."[5] There was, he claimed, no difference between a Marx and a Rothschild; both came from the same speculating and parasitic stock.[6] Under these circumstances it was hardly surprising that the *Narodnaia volia*—a Russian terrorist organization which leaned heavily on Bakunin's thought—welcomed the persecution of the Russian Jews in the pogrom of 1881 as the beginning of the social revolution, a judgment which testified both to its shortsightedness and to its Jew-hating or, the least, to its nonchalant indifference in the face of undisguised evil.

Friedrich Engels

Friedrich Engels, close collaborator of Karl Marx and with him founder and exponent of Marxist socialism, went to Manchester in 1842 to work in the business firm Ermen and Engels, owned partly by his father. It was Moses Hess, one of the early proponents of socialism and later also known as one of the early theoreticians of Zionism (*Rom und Jerusalem*), who won him over to communism. Soon thereafter Engels met Marx, with whom he was linked from 1844 in a lifelong friendship. After participating in the communist movement in Germany and neighboring countries on the Continent between 1845 and 1849, he returned to Manchester in 1850. Furnishing Marx with means of support, he enabled him to study and write. Later Engels turned his entire attention to political and literary activities; in 1870 he moved to London, where he died in 1895.

Engels had a brilliant mind and knew many languages, including Hebrew. In 1891 he assured Abraham Cahan, a leader of the Jewish labor movement in America, that he could read *laschon hakodesch* (the "holy language")—Hebrew.[7] In many works and articles Engels touched on the question of Jews and Judaism. In a good number of them his own contributions are indistinguishable from those of Marx. Some of them, like his notes relating to the "Jews in Germany," to which Gustav Meyer refers in his biography of Engels, have not been found.[8]

Engels' first remarks about Jews show his objectivity. He was impressed by the poet Karl Isidor Beck, whose Jewish background he underlined, as a "vast talent," even "a genius," though Beck later disappointed him. Yet from the mid-fifties on, Engels apparently coordinated his thought with that of Marx and adopted increasingly Marx's anti-Jewish tone and language, his anti-Semitic witticisms and hostility. In 1844 Marx published the anti-Jewish pamphlet *Zur Judenfrage*, which made a deep impression upon Engels. Marx's tract was largely ignored by contemporary Jews and the Jewish press, though the latter paid considerable attention to the numerous contemporary anti-Jewish pamphlets which flooded the book market, including that by Bruno Bauer, which triggered Marx's brochure. Marx's and Engels' joint work *Die heilige Familie* [The Holy Family] (1845) contained contributions from Marx which constituted a recapitulation of what he had earlier written in *Zur Judenfrage*. In his translation of Charles Fourier, who was well known for his anti-Semitic idiosyncrasies, Engels referred to his anti-Jewish remarks, especially his reference to Jews as "fraudulent bankrupts," without any critical comment whatsoever. In 1846 Engels lauded a notorious anti-Jewish tract.

Writing in a journal of the Chartists, *The Northern Star,* he referred to a worker who had written a brochure against the "head of the system," not King Louis Philippe of Orleans but Rothschild I, "the king of the Jews."[9] According to Engels, he had thus "hit the nail on the head." Actually the anonymous pamphlet was not at all socialist-oriented but rather a petit bourgeois piece of writing.

The Jew appeared in Engels' early writings as trader and usurer, his mother tongue a "terribly distorted German." Such an attack was bound to arouse hostility not only against selected groups among the Jews but against all Jews. In several articles from the year 1848 Engels derided the speaking manner of the Jews from Posen to prove that they were not Germans, though a few years later he considered the Jews to be Germans rather than Slavs. Paraphrasing Ernst Moritz Arndt's "Was ist des Deutschen Vaterland?" (What Is the Fatherland of the German?) he declared that the fatherland of Prince Lichnowski, with whom he had quarreled, reached

> So far as a Polish Jew talks gibberish,
> Lends for usury, falsifies mint and weight.[10]

Engels' exchange of letters with Marx shows that he competed with the latter in his dislike and even contempt for Jews. The question must of course be raised whether his anti-Jewish stance was genuine, rooted in his belief that the Jews were a hopelessly backward and "reactionary" people, or whether it was designed merely to please Marx and his Jewish self-hatred. In any case, Engels, referring to Jewish writers, introduced them as "Jude" (Jew) or in typical anti-Semitic fashion as "Jud" or "Jid." He alluded thus to the known revolutionary Leo Fränkel, "Das Fränkelche ist das richtige Jidche." Jewish names were regularly ridiculed; Moses Hess was once called "Mauses." While Ferdinand Lassalle is dubbed "Ephraim Gescheit" (smart) he was also referred to as "der läppische [foolish] Jud," "Jüdel Braun," "Excellenz Ephraim Gescheit," "Itzig," and numerous other similarly telling epithets.

Engels thus joined Marx in his hostility to Lassalle, pointing to his East European background which he especially disliked. Lassalle, it is conceded, had great talent, "but as a genuine Jew from the Slavic border" he always had pursued his private interests. His "Jewish impudence" was castigated, as was his "Jewish respect for the success of the moment." Though he was politically "one of the most important fellows in Germany," he still was the "Polish Schmuhl." Even Lassalle's premature and tragic death in a duel was commented upon by Engels with coldly hostile words: this could happen only to

Lassalle with his "peculiar mixture of frivolity and sentimentality, Judaism and playing the chivalrous knight." Engels seemed little concerned with the persecution of the Jews in Russia and rather minimized it. However, in speaking of a memoir of Gneisenau of August 21, 1811,[11] which he translated into English, Engels referred to Gneisenau's suggestion that the clergy of all denominations raise before the German people the example of the Jews in the era of the Maccabees and call upon them to follow their example.

FRIEDRICH ENGELS AGAINST ANTI-SEMITISM

As Edmund Silberner showed in his thorough study *Sozialisten zur Judenfrage*, the year 1878 represented a turning point in Engels' attitude toward the Jews. The waves of anti-Semitism which then began to sweep over Germany apparently compelled him to rethink especially the problem of anti-Semitism, of Judaism and the Jews. It was in that year that Engels published his *Anti-Dühring*, referring there to the "ridiculously exaggerated Jew-hating which Herr Dühring exhibits on every occasion"—as if a less exaggerated, a kind of "reasonable" amount of Jew-hating would have been acceptable. Engels declared Jew-hating "if not a specifically Prussian, certainly a specifically East-Elbian quality." While Dühring claimed freedom from all prejudices and superstitions, Engels accused him of being "himself deeply rooted in personal bias," since he called the popular prejudice against the Jews which reached back to medieval bigotry a "judgment of nature" (*Natururteil*), itself based on "natural grounds" (*Naturgründe*).[12]

Yet it was not a newly awakened friendship for the Jews which led Engels to take up the cudgel against Eugen Dühring. He did it, as will be seen, for the sake of Karl Marx, against whom Dühring had directed a frontal attack as a Jew, and for the sake of the cause of socialism itself, which was irretrievably tied up with Marx's untarnished image.

Attacks against Marx "the Jew" were by no means uncommon in the nineteenth-century world of socialism. The Russian revolutionary anarchist Bakunin, Marx's rival in the First International, had repeatedly given expression to his raging anti-Semitism. In view of Bakunin's popularity among German and Russian socialists, his anti-Semitic inroads could not be taken lightly by either Marx or Engels. To the gloating onlooker Eugen Dühring, the dispute between Marx and Bakunin was the indisputable expression of "a racial conflict in the International." Bakunin's revulsion against the "Jewish blood and the German scholarly ballast" of Marx was "understandable." Marx was told by the racial anti-Semite Dühring that the "consistent Judaism" within him was the source of his shortcomings. Engels, while attempting to avoid giving publicity to such "low-type [*hundskommunen*] attacks" against Marx, was, in view of their widespread character, compelled to acknowledge that they had been made and accused Dühring of "megalomania and irresponsibility."[13] Dühring, separated from the University of Berlin in 1877, was obsessed with the triad of enemies—professors, Jews, and particularly Jewish socialists (*Sozialjudodemokraten*)—and therefore became increasingly vituperative against Judaism. He accused Marx and Lassale of having debased socialism and Marx of having taken all parts of his theoretical system from the "Mosaic theory." Marx had "the known impertinence of his people, although himself of the Judaic tribe, to ridicule Jewish opponents in purely doctrinal polemics on account of their Jewish descent. . . . Thus he apparently disavowed his own blood." Yet this did not prevent him from forming his "international clan essentially with descendants of Judaism" and from creating "a kind of *Alliance Israélite.*" The German Social Democrats aimed at the enslavement and exploitation of the people in the interest of "leading Jews and Jewish fellow travelers." Dühring called for struggle against the Jewish race, which was exploitive, criminal, and incorrigible. For the moment he merely recommended strict separation, not annihilation of the Jews; later, however, he asserted that the Jewish question could only be solved through "killing and extermination."

Following these and other "theoretical" outbursts, anti-Semitic disturbances took place during the summer of 1881 throughout Germany, especially in Pomerania. When Eduard Bernstein, later the father of socialist revisionism, sent Engels contemporary anti-Semitic pamphlets, Engels judged them extremely foolish and childish.[14] He seemed to believe that the government had initiated the anti-Semitic movement to help conservatives in the impending election. He was pleased that the *Sozialdemokrat* treated the movement with contempt and did not judge it to constitute an imminent threat. He quoted the report of a Social Democratic writer, Carl Hirsch, according to whom the Germans had "a natural dislike for the Jews" but in whose view the hatred of the government by the workers and other segments of the population was "by far more lively."[15] From the thought of unambiguously denouncing anti-Semitism, Engels was still far away. Engels and German socialists generally were reluctant to come to grips with anti-Semitism, with the "natural dislike" of many Germans for the Jews, fearful of having socialism identified with philo-Semitism and suffering a debacle at the polls.

Yet soon Engels began to mount heavier guns. On May 9, 1890, the Vienna *Arbeiter-Zeitung* published, with the writer's consent, portions of a letter from Engels, addressed to an unknown recipient in Vienna, dated April 19, 1890.[16] The recipient, a noted Austrian Social Democrat, perhaps Engelbert Pernerstorfer, must have entertained anti-Semitic inclinations—for which Pernerstorfer was known. Thus he was warned: "Whether you would not accomplish more misfortune than good with anti-Semitism, I must leave to your consideration." And Engels continued: "Anti-Semitism is the sign of a backward culture and therefore is to be found only in Prussia, Austria, and Russia. If one would wish to promote anti-Semitism here in England or in America one would be simply laughed at, and Mr. Drumont in Paris causes with his writings—which intellectually are far superior to those of the German anti-Semites—only a somewhat ineffective momentary sensation." Who were the anti-Semites in Prussia? Junkers, who with an income of 10,000 marks spend 20,000 and thus fall victims to usurers, and the petite bourgeoisie, small merchants and artisans, who are doomed through competition with big capital; they too raised their voices in the anti-Semitic chorus. Yet if capital annihilated these reactionary classes, "it was merely fulfilling its historic function and doing salutary work, whether it was Semitic or Aryan, circumcised or baptized; it was merely helping the backward Prussians and Austrians to move forward." Only there, Engels asserted, where no strong class of capitalists and no strong proletariat existed, only where production was still in the hands of peasants, landlords, artisans, and similar classes originating in the Middle Ages, only there was capital preeminently Jewish and only there existed anti-Semitism. In North America, he pointed out, there was not a single Jew among the millionaires, and in the British Isles the English Rothschild was a man of modest means. Anti-Semitism, Engels continued, was nothing but "the reaction of medieval, sinking social strata against modern society" and served "only reactionary purposes under seemingly socialist cover." It was "a deviation of feudal socialism and we cannot have anything to do with it." Anti-Semitism was both a symptom of backwardness and its cause. Engels wished "us Germans, among whom I include the Viennese, a rather lively development of the capitalist economy, by no means getting stuck in the mire and remaining stationary."

The letter was clearly designed to dissuade Austrian socialists from entertaining the apparently widespread belief that anti-Semitism was a stepping stone toward socialism, tactically useful and likely to speed the coming of the ideal socialist society. Hardboiled socialist tacticians, however, pushing morality aside and adopting a policy of Machiavellianism, looked upon anti-Semitism as an allegedly anticapitalist phenomenon, wilfully ignoring or nonchalantly overlooking its openly proclaimed and undisguised character as an anti-Jewish movement; they claimed to understand anti-Semitism better than the anti-Semites themselves. Over-sophisticated tacticians of the class struggle and sometimes more or less open anti-Semites, they persuaded themselves that anti-Semitism could be harnessed to the socialist chariot. In the event they should prove to be mistaken, it would be only a tactical error.

Engels, in 1890 at least, held "that anti-Semitism falsifies the entire situation. It does not even know the Jews whom it shouts down. Otherwise it would know that here in England and in America, thanks to Eastern European anti-Semites, and in Turkey, thanks to the Spanish Inquisition, there are thousands and thousands of Jewish proletarians; and it is these Jewish workers who are the worst exploited and most miserable. We here in England have had during the last twelve months three strikes of Jewish workers, and now we are to promote anti-Semitism to battle capitalism?"

It is not quite clear why Engels omitted to mention in this context the large Jewish working class in Eastern Europe. Still, he stressed now the existence of a Jewish proletariat and pointed to the obligation of socialists to acknowledge it as well as the leading role of Jewish intellectuals in the world of socialism. While he had previously drawn attention to tactical and scientific considerations against the use of anti-Semitism as a weapon in the struggle for socialism, Engels now added a new consideration, the existence of a Jewish proletariat. Besides, no doubt in view of the proliferation of anti-Semitism and its increasingly anti-socialist propaganda, tactical considerations forced socialism to enter the arena against anti-Semitism. Not for the sake of the Jews, but for the sake of its own survival, socialism had to strike back at anti-Semitism, which denounced socialism itself as "Jewish," pointed an accusing finger at its Jewish leaders, and tried to lure the workers away from the socialist camp.

After 1890 Engels no longer conspicuously attacked the Rothschilds alone but also criticized non-Jewish capitalists. He praised the leaders of the Jewish workers of America such as Abraham Cahan and promised to write the preface to a Yiddish edition of the Communist Manifesto. Now Engels criticized English dock workers for their protest against the immigrant Russian Jews, voicing his own sympathy for them as mere "foreign paupers." Toward the end of 1894 he warned French socialists not to make pie-in-the-sky promises to peasants and artisans and thus bring the party down "to the level of the noisiest [*Radau*] anti-Semitism." Such peasants and artisans belonged to the anti-Semites; they would learn there "what the truth of their shining phrases was and which melodies the violins play which hang in the anti-Semitic heaven."[17]

Everything Engels said or wrote about the Jews after 1890 had a different ring. Some have surmised that it was Engels' discovery of a Jewish proletariat that made him change his opinion. Perhaps the death of Marx and the removal of the influence of his Jewish self-hatred made Engels return to his earlier objective or at least to a neutral attitude toward the Jews. Against this view, however, is the fact that the turning point in Engels' judgment about Jews and anti-Semitism appears to have been the year 1878, when Marx was still living.

Most likely, the unusual strong waves of anti-Semitism which then swept across all of Europe and affected even the more advanced Western European countries, such as France, brought Friedrich Engels and modern socialism in its entirety face to face not only with questions of abstract justice but also with the actual depth of anti-Semitism among the plain people and the workers that socialist propaganda sought to reach. Anti-Semitism squarely posed for some socialists the question of whether it was not perhaps advisable to sacrifice the Jews—including Jewish socialist intellectuals—to the greater cause of advancing socialism; Engels and other socialist leaders were compelled to take a position.

In his letter to the Vienna *Arbeiter-Zeitung* quoted above, Engels had also remarked that, other considerations aside, "we owe the Jews too much. Aside from Börne and Heine, Marx was of pure Jewish descent [*stockjüdischem Blut*]; Lassalle was a Jew. Many of our best people are Jews. My friend Victor Adler, who now pays for his dedication to the cause of the proletariat in prison in Vienna, Eduard Bernstein, the editor of the London *Sozialdemokrat,* Paul Singer, one of our best deputies in the *Reichstag*—people of whose friendship I am proud, and all Jews! I myself have been made a Jew by the *Gartenlaube,* and in any case, if I had to choose, I would rather be a Jew than 'Herr von . . . '!"[18]

German Socialism: Ambivalence and Inconsistency

The eighties were years of rising anti-Semitism in Germany and Austria and also in Russia, following the assassination of Tsar Alexander II in 1881. The movement in Germany was led by Adolf Stöcker; in Austria, Pan-Germans, led by Georg von Schönerer, and Christian Socials, headed by Karl Lueger, later the mayor of Vienna, competed with each other in virulent anti-Semitism. On both sides of the Inn River, Jews in general and Jewish socialist leaders in particular were attacked and vilified in order to detach the working masses from the socialist parties. Under these circumstances a counterattack against the anti-Semites was a means of self-defense for socialists rather than a purely humanitarian and politically selfless move. The Social Democratic Party took great pains not to appear philo-Semitic; it never was and never became so. German and Austrian Jews who joined the Social Democratic Party found no pro-Jewish haven but a port in which their talents, dedication, and individual contributions to the party and the cause of socialism were given recognition. They in turn tended to ignore the clearly audible anti-Semitic rumblings among the rank and file and even some of the leadership.

Whatever may have prompted Engels to abandon the anti-Jewish views so long jointly expressed with Marx, after 1878 he turned to fighting anti-Semitism and battled it more courageously and consistently than many other socialists, Jewish and non-Jewish. In 1890 he rejected Jew-hating in an unambiguous manner. Yet the international Socialist Congress in Brussels in 1891, fearful of being labeled philo-Semitic, passed a rather lukewarm resolution in regard to anti-Semitism. At their party congress in Cologne in 1893 the German Social Democrats, even more inconsistent, went so far às to ascribe to anti-Semitism, in spite of its reactionary character, a revolutionary function.[19] They found a healthy revolutionary core in the rotten, reactionary anti-Semitic apple! The danger of applying Marxist dialectics in a reckless, if not thoughtless, manner should have been apparent to even less sophisticated men.

Among the German socialists after Lassalle there continued a strong current of anti-Jewish sentiment, which had of course been encouraged by Marx, Engels, and Ferdinand Lassalle. Thus the traditional anti-Jewish feelings of the Germans were not permitted to die away but received fresh nourishment. Other Germans, opposed to socialism, strengthened anti-Semitism by blaming Jewish leadership for the socialist movement.

As early as 1862 Moses Hess had lamented the anti-Jewish mood among German socialists. Indeed, a number of prominent German socialists, including Johann Baptist von Schweitzer, presiding officer of the *Allgemeiner Deutscher Arbeiterverein,* his disciple Wilhelm Hasselmann, editor of the Lassallean *Social-Demokrat* and *Neuer Social-Demokrat,* Richard Calwer, economist and editor of the party paper *Braunschweiger Volksfreund,* and the noted socialist historian Franz Mehring, treated the topic of Jews and Judaism with distinct bias. August Bebel and Wilhelm Liebknecht on the other hand led the party's struggle against political anti-Semitism, which appeared as a mounting threat to socialism itself. Others, such as Eduard Bernstein, the leader of revisionism and himself a Jew, and Karl Kautsky expressed sharp opposition to all Jewish national endeavors, not only to Zionism but to any program holding out the promise of preservation of a separate Jewish national culture.

The prominent leaders of German socialism, with the exception of Moses Hess, propagated prompt and complete assimilation of the German Jews. They therefore opposed separate organizations of Jewish workers, since in their view assimilation would thus merely be delayed. In regard to early and ultimate assimilation of the Jews and their submergence among the German people, virtually all Germans, except a handful of racists who toyed with murderous thoughts, were agreed: the Jews were ultimately to disappear among the Germans. Germans who shared this view ranged from the extreme Right to moderate conservatives, liberals, radical democrats, and socialists at the extreme Left.

For a long time many Social Democrats clung to the notion that anti-Semitism, in the end, might serve the cause of socialism. On January 9, 1881, the *Sozialdemokrat,* confronting the anti-Semitic agitation, voiced its relative "equanimity" in regard to it. Anti-Semitism, after all, revealed a high degree of social dissatisfaction; though it was currently channeled into the wrong outlets, it might survive the "anti-Semitic deception and ultimately do us good." And after the anti-Semitic outbursts in Pomerania, the paper wrote (August 18, 1881) that "today" Jews were killed, "to-morrow," however, logically, it will be the turn of the court preacher, the Chancellor, the kings, the Kaiser. Glancing also into the Russian future and applying the same "dialectical" thought process, the paper gave similar assurances in connection with the Russian pogroms, though these disturbed many. Today the Jews, to-morrow the Tsar! Here, moral insensitivity and political myopia were surpassing each other!

At the party congress in Berlin in 1892 the planned report by August Bebel, *Sozialdemokratie und Antisemitismus* [Social Democracy and Anti-Semitism], was postponed for lack of time, but the Party adopted by a great majority a resolution against anti-Semitism which he had prepared. It was at the next party congress in Köln in 1893 that Bebel finally delivered his talk. The Jews, he explained, were on the average no better and no worse than the "so-called Christians."[20] Some of their characteristics had less to do with race than with the merchant trade to which one had forced them. Other less desirable qualities were partly qualities of race, partly the product of historical discrimination, and would only disappear after a long period of equality and mixing of the Jews with the rest of the population. It was significant that many Jews stood in the forefront of all progressive movements, were humanitarian-minded and willing to sacrifice, and could thus serve as models to their Christian persecutors. Anti-Semitism was no solution to the social question but was used by the bourgeoisie as a means of deflecting popular dissatisfaction. Nevertheless, in the end, "with all its dirty and base motives," anti-Semitism would serve only the Social Democrats. The erroneous concept of the historic "usefulness" of anti-Semitism cropped up here again.

The same view was voiced by Franz Mehring, who paraded this thesis as the "ABC of our social historic development," and by Wilhelm Liebknecht, who expressed it thus: "Yes, the anti-Semites plow and sow, and we Social Democrats shall harvest."[21] An editorial of the *Vorwärts* a few days after startling electoral successes by the anti-Semites called anti-Semitism "the last phase of a dying capitalist society" and considered it, in spite of its admitted hostility to culture, "a bearer of culture against its will." This view was reinforced by a widely known saying, erroneously ascribed to Bebel, "anti-Semitism is the socialism of the fools." Still, the concept embedded in it corresponded to views of Bebel and other socialists and seemed to suggest that one should pity the "fools" and educate them, if possible, to make them recognize that not just Jewish capitalists but capitalists *per se* were their real enemy; if the Jews got hurt in the meantime, this was regrettable but historically unavoidable, and, in any case, they would thus render a service to progress and a sacrifice for humanity!

The views on anti-Semitism of Bebel and the German socialists found final expression in the resolution already submitted to the Congress the year before and now unanimously adopted in Cologne. Anti-Semitism, the resolution stated, originated in the dissatisfaction of certain bourgeois groups and was directed merely against "the Jewish exploiters." (Since it was aimed against all Jews, this view was patently false.) It was hostile to progress. But in spite of its reactionary character and against its will, it would—Bebel's earlier idea emerged here again—have ultimately revolutionary consequences, since the aroused petit bourgeois and small peasant elements "must" come to the recognition that the entire class of capitalists, not merely its Jewish segment, was their enemy. The key question why the ultimate conclusion must by necessity lead to the realization that capitalism *per se* was the foe was never satisfactorily answered. Wishful thinking replaced cold analysis.

Bebel himself later had serious doubts in regard to anti-Semitism being a mere stepping-stone toward socialism, when Russian pogroms erupted in 1904–1905. For the first time he saw anti-Semitism "in its ugliest and most repulsive form, . . . resting, in accordance with its character, upon the lowest drives and instincts" of backward social elements whose "moral depredation"[22] terrified him.

Austrian Socialism and Anti-Semitic Inroads

Anti-Semitism had even deeper roots in the Austrian Empire than in the German *Reich*. More Jews lived in the Habsburg Empire than in Germany; they also were less Germanized, and religious and even ethnic consciousness was more pronounced among them. In the middle 1880s Karl Kautsky, later leading theoretician of German democratic socialism but then still in Austria, wrote in a letter to Friedrich Engels dated June 23, 1884, that "we [Austrian Socialists] have trouble in keeping our own people from fraternizing with the anti-Semites. The latter are now our most dangerous foes, more dangerous than in Germany, because they present themselves as oppositional and democratic, and thus meet the instincts of the workers halfway."[23] And a few months later, in another letter to Engels, Kautsky freely admitted that "a new enemy has sprung up in anti-Semitism, which is assuming colossal dimensions and has won over a large part of the petit bourgeois elements—including some very 'radical' ones—that up to now have been on our side." Such petit bourgeois instincts were very strong even among the workers, and therefore "our leaders have encountered every conceivable difficulty in keeping the masses from deserting to the anti-Semites."[24]

Kautsky's letters clearly illuminated the situation and explained also the ambiguous attitude of Austrian socialism to the Jews and the anti-Semitic movement. Fighting against the anti-Semitic "enemy," Austrian socialism took opportunistic account of the widespread anti-Jewish feelings among the Austrian population, including the Austrian workers, and for apparent propagandistic reasons tried to avoid the philo-Semitic label which anti-Semites were only too willing to attach to it. Many Jewish leaders of the party, including Victor Adler and other baptized and unbaptized Jews, followed in Karl Marx's path of Jewish self-hatred; this seemed to them the means to establish their own credibility on the Jewish question and also seemed to serve the party's interests. Though the Austrian Social Democratic Party was divided into six autonomous national groups, German, Czech, Polish, Ruthenian, Slovenian, and Italian, the Jewish group, in spite of the socialist nationalities program adopted at the party congress at Brünn (1899), was not recognized on the ground that the Jews were not a nation.

Victor Adler himself, as his socialist biographer concedes, was not free from anti-Jewish prejudice,[25] in which his friend Engelbert Pernerstorfer may have confirmed him. Both men were active early in the *Deutschnationaler Verein* (German national club). In 1883 Pernerstorfer left the Austro-German national movement when its anti-Semitism became more pronounced. Nevertheless, his contemporaries, friend and foe, seem agreed as to his anti-Semitism. And later on Nazi, socialist, and communist publicists all shared the view that he had a pronounced personal dislike for the Jews. At the party congress in 1898 he pontificated that Schönerer's preachings about anti-Semitism were "something almost beyond discussion, because it is simply true, namely that the Jews are Jews [laughter]."[26] And in further justification of Schönerer he referred to Karl Marx, who in the pamphlet *Zur Judenfrage* had said everything many decades earlier "in a much wittier and better way." Altogether, Pernerstorfer displayed an ambiguous attitude toward the Jews, a "half-anti-Semitism," as a contemporary called it.

The ambiguous attitude of Pernerstorfer and of many German Social Democratic leaders underlines the precarious position of the Jews in Central Europe toward the end of the nineteenth century. They had few steady and trustworthy friends even at the Left, which ideologically might have been expected to extend the hand of friendship to all joining its ranks and working toward the creation of a new, just social order, irrespective of national, cultural, and religious origins and continuing ties.

An Overview

The century and a half of German and German-Jewish history assessed here from the particular angle of the German judgment on Jews and Judaism covers an era of the most radical change in the life and thought of Germans and Jews. It was an era marked by substantive improvements for both but also one which created new tensions between them, a period which shattered some prejudices but also one which generated new differences and disputes and deepened old biases. With the remnants of religious anti-Semitism, which the Enlightenment had never completely conquered, a new social, economic, national hatred of Jews and, ultimately, a racially tainted anti-Semitism joined forces.

While religious dissension and hate receded somewhat in German public life in this period, it was increasingly replaced by ethnic consciousness and affinity and dislike for alien national groups—an unfortunate by-product of the growth of German national feelings. Nineteenth-century German nationalism on the whole was long a progressive force, but it already contained infectious and dangerously divisive concepts. Religious prejudice and hatred were occasionally shown the front door, but national and racial hatred and social envy and bitterness aiming especially at the Jews reentered Germany's national life by storming through the back door. The Jew continued to serve his historic role of scapegoat. Anti-Semitism did not retreat from the German scene, neither in the era of the Enlightenment nor in the War of Liberation, the era of Romanticism, the *Vormärz,* or subsequent periods. But in an increasingly liberal age most Germans and Jews, partly relying on the concept of the irrepressible march of social and cultural progress and partly prompted by wishful thinking, tended to minimize the undercurrent of anti-Semitism, in spite of warning signals. It must be acknowledged that the most dire prophecies in regard to the future of the German Jews seemed, given all the circumstances, utterly unbelievable; yet they actually fell short of the unspeakable barbarity of mass annihilation that darkened the twentieth century. Abolition of emancipation or expulsion could not be rationally expected, not even at the very height of the anti-Semitic frenzy during the late nineteenth century.

While that century saw the falling of one legal barrier after the other, resistance to the Jews, though pushed back in some sectors of the extended German-Jewish front, remained strong in others. The unceasing debate and political struggle for and against emancipation was accompanied by the continuous publication of anti-Jewish tracts, pamphlets, and treatises of a theological, legal, social, and political nature throughout the eighteenth and nineteenth centuries— a genuine flood which had no counterpart in any other European country. Anti-Semitism may not have been a phenomenon peculiar to Germany and Central Europe, but German *Gründlichkeit* and passion gave it a unique character. German professors and theologians, who to an unusual extent were its disseminators, furnished it with academic and civic respectability. Thus not only the mob and some of the privileged social classes, traditionally conservative and cool if not hostile to the Jews, but also the influential rising middle layer of German society and sectors of the German intelligentsia were susceptible to, if not originators of, anti-Jewish propaganda. The numerous anti-Semitic attacks by the forces of ultraconservatism and reaction, generously supported by a fair representation of liberal, democratic, and even radical Germans, cast an ominous shadow upon the Jews and raised questions as to their future in Germany.

Every progress of German Jewry was quickly followed by the massing of new threatening clouds. Even the Jews' indisputable advance along cultural, economic, and social lines of development, their increasing participation in the literary, political, and social life of the German nation, and their growing assimilation to German *Kultur* did not diminish but paradoxically increased German hostility toward them. Most striking, of course, was the rise of political anti-Semitism after the unification of the *Reich,* after the fulfillment of the age-old desires for national and political unity. Strangely enough, after having reached the long desired plateau of the national state, Germany hurried to ascend the higher peaks of extreme nationalism and domination over non-German peoples beyond the borders of the *Reich*; and simultaneously voices demanding the return of the Jews to the ghetto became shriller.

From the days when Germany had struggled for its liberation from the Napoleonic yoke to the day of the Franco-Prussian War, the ideology of nationalism had been closely intertwined with liberalism and democracy and had also decisively influenced the nascent socialist movement. Bismarck himself and conservative forces in general had swung around to giving nationalism support in order thus to obtain a broader popular base. The most diverse, if not contrary, political ideologies in the German linguistic and cultural realm were all closely wedded to nationalism and the nation-state.

The nineteenth-century nation-state granted minorities toleration but not necessarily permanent toleration; it rather expected subordination, acquiescence to a less than equal civic status, speedy assimilation and ultimate merger. The nation-state, though most vigorously propagated and promoted by liberal and democratic circles and aiming at the creation of a progressive society, was by its very nature the antithesis of a multinational structure, of a genuinely liberal state, or of a pluralistic society. It insisted on the final conformity and submergence of ethnically and culturally different groups. In spite of bitterly opposing each other in policies on the Jews, the noted historians Treitschke and Mommsen supported the same fundamental theoretical concept, the nation-state. What separated them and made them engage in ideological combat with each other was not the ultimate goal, complete assimilation of the Jews and their disappearance as a distinct group, but merely ends and means, tact and tactics; Treitschke criticized and attacked them, while Mommsen defended the equality they had attained.

The nation-state was plainly intolerant of national minorities and fearful of perennial religious and national pluralism. Religious and territorial pluralism was the historical calamity of the German people. The eighteenth-century German demand for the disappearance of the obstinate Jew was partly the result of continuing religious bias; in a later stage it was the result of the new prejudices and the tactical imperatives of the Enlightenment, which, in its fight against Christianity and the Holy Scriptures, carried on a diversionary struggle against a target proven useful for centuries—Judaism. The nineteenth-century German demand finally for the assimilation and ultimate merger of the Jews with the Germans sprang also from the seemingly progressive, liberal, and national program for a strong, unitary, homogenous nation. It aimed at the demise of all territorial, cultural, national, and religious peculiarities and differences. Victory did not make the Germans satisfied but rather led them to raise their sights; it made them more demanding and many of them more intolerant. The German Jews' position in the seventies was endangered to an alarming extent. Immediately after their full legal emancipation, attained in 1869, and the establishment of full equality in Austria in 1867, Jewish emancipation surprisingly was put back on the agenda, and the dispute reached a startling crescendo.

That the German Jews of the period constituted, in spite of growing and deepening assimilation, a nationality, in addition to being held together by religious bonds, is beyond doubt. Yet many Germans, usually the more liberal ones, and most Jews did not and could not accept this view. Most Germans found the permanent coexistence of two nationalities, Germans and Jews, not to mention that of other minorities within their political confines, intolerable and considered assimilation, the ultimate demise of Judaism in all its national aspects, imperative and inevitable. The concept of a pluralistic society was anathema to nineteenth-century German political thought.

Public opinion held that any alien nationality on German soil had the duty to work toward its own cultural and national extinction; it considered belonging to an "alien nationality" a flaw. Those Germans who declared Jews outsiders, a foreign "nationality," happened to be usually those who looked upon them with hostile eyes, were opposed to their equality, and wished to burden them with new discriminatory regulations. On the other hand, those Germans who considered them merely a religious association wished thus to give expression to their thought that the Jews were nationally Germans, just as Protestants or Catholics were.

Jews themselves shared these views, probably because they were also convinced that any acknowledgment of the Jewish people as a nationality would place obstacles on their road to complete assimilation, Germanization, equality, and a happy life in Germany. But by the end of the nineteenth century, with the growth of anti-Semitism in Germany, Austria, and much of the rest of Europe, as well as the emergence of Zionism and the rise of a national movement among Europe's Jews, the outlook of both Jews and Gentiles had undergone radical changes. While continuing along the road to cultural assimilation, the Jews insisted on remaining Jews, nurturing their own national and religious culture and identity. Having become more self-confident and assertive, Jews began to demand national-cultural rights, while at the same time continuing to battle for the implementation of political equality.

Much has been written about the inconsistencies and weaknesses of German liberalism, democracy, and socialism—all of which became apparent in the nineteenth century and again, after 1918, in the Weimar Republic—to explain the relative ease with which National Socialism conquered Germany. The inconsistencies and weaknesses of all these political movements revealed themselves also in their policies on the Jews. The reluctance in regard to Jewish emancipation, if not outright opposition to it, on the part of liberal historians and politicians such as K. Rotteck, C. Welcker, and F. Dahlmann in the 1830s, of numerous liberal and radical theologians, such as Paulus, Bruno Bauer, and others, and of liberal playwrights and poets in the *Vormärz,* is a striking phenomenon. The waves of the revolution of 1848–1849 drowned out the voices of reaction as well as those of "liberal" and radical democratic anti-Semitism, but after their retreat it became apparent that anti-Semitic prejudice had survived. And though the next two decades brought about the complete legal emancipation of the Jews in Central Europe, the marked rise of anti-Semitism after the unification of Germany deeply disturbed the Jews and their German friends and those who had nourished the notion that the status of equality, once attained by the Jews, was inviolable and irreversible.

After the "mad year" of 1848–1849, conservatism revived the concept of the German-Christian state of Frederick William IV, refurbished by a Jewish convert, Friedrich Julius Stahl, and thus held the Jews at bay. But in the camp of those parties which did not share the conservative creed, German Jews could count on few steadfast friends. Liberal, democratic, and even socialist movements looked askance at German Jewry in its entirety. Increasingly, political parties and religious groups opened their door to individual Jews, but the price tag attached to their acceptance was excessively high: either outright baptism or, at the least, willingness to completely relinquish Jewish identity, irrespective of whether it was primarily religious, cultural, or national in character. The German Jew was to shed his Judaic heritage, cease to be a Jew, and eagerly embrace Germandom, for the sake of his individual salvation, the simultaneous "solution" of the Jewish question, and German *Kultur,* which could not and should not become intermixed with alien accretions.

While German political liberalism toward the end of the nineteenth century became a somewhat more consistent champion of Jewish equality than it had been in earlier days, German Catholicism showed that anti-Semitism had made deep inroads in its ranks. German socialism, treading the path of the anti-Judaism of Marx himself, was long anxious to pursue a "neutral" course between anti-Semitism and philo-Semitism, being susceptible to tactical rather than to ideological and ethical imperatives.

It is probably impossible to escape the conclusion that anti-Semitism, as treated in this study, had sunk deep roots in Germany. There were few Germans who in the course of their lives did not pass through some extended anti-Semitic phase and many who never escaped its grip. The prejudices of the past still lay heavily on the eighteenth- and nineteenth-century German mind, and it required great force of intellect and character to overcome them. Numerous Germans remained for life prisoners of their prejudicial notions; others overcame them to some extent; few liberated themselves completely.

It must of course be conceded that Jews were not free from prejudices either. But since they were a small oppressed minority, the target of criticism and discrimination rather than the source, they became the victims rather than the perpetrators of injury. It must also be admitted that German prejudices, whether national, religious, social, racial, or any other kind, were not confined only to Jews but affected German thought in regard to Poles, Czechs, Frenchmen, Englishmen, and members of numerous other nationalities. But the Jews were the favored, proximate, and most vulnerable target, a convenient scapegoat for the Germans, plagued and frustrated as they were by the mounting economic, social, and political problems of a rapidly changing domestic order. Under these circumstances, the portrait of the German Jew frequently mirrored the distorted vision of the German artist.

The depth of anti-Semitic sentiments in this era did not necessarily make the anti-Semitic paranoia of the Third *Reich* and the annihilation of German and much of European Jewry a foregone conclusion. Historically, the catastrophe which befell German Jewry was probably not unavoidable. Hitler's seizure of power, though substantially helped by vicious anti-Semitic propaganda, exploiting the anti-Jewish thought and feelings of broad masses of the German people, was not brought about by anti-Semitism alone. But racial anti-Semitism coupled with Hitler's megalomania and demonic character, the fanaticism of his following, and totalitarian control over a largely submissive, authoritarian-minded people steeped in anti-Semitic tradition, produced the Holocaust.

Is it justified to point the finger of accusation at all those who in times past have expressed anti-Semitic feelings and thoughts? No doubt many of the German Jew-haters of earlier times might have recoiled from the mass murder of the Jews that the Nazis later committed. Few of them could have anticipated the "final solution," unprecedented in history and unsurpassed in its barbarism and inhumanity. On the other hand, it seems only fair to hold each man responsible for what he said, wrote, and recommended. The historian must present and analyze as objectively as possible the persistent as well as the changing thoughts and moods of the Germans on Jews and Judaism, trying to avoid either inflating or belittling their significance.

Notes

Foreword

1. *Jean Pauls Briefwechsel mit seinem Freunde Osmund,* April 15 and April 23, 1795, ed. Fleischmann (Munich, 1863).
2. H. Treitschke, "Ein Wort über unser Judentum" and "Noch einige Bemerkungen zur Judenfrage," in *Preussische Jahrbücher* (December 1879 and January 1880), *Der Berliner Antisemitismusstreit,* ed. Boehlich (1965).
3. H.S. Chamberlain, *Foundations of the Nineteenth Century* (New York, 1912), vol. 1, p. 353.
4. A. Hitler, *Mein Kampf* (New York, 1939), pp. 253 and 335; and *Adolf Hitler spricht* . . . (Leipzig, 1934), p. 18.

Chapter One

1. J.G. Zimmermann, *Von dem Nationalstolze* (Frankfurt, 1781), pp. 88–89.
2. A. Arneth, *Maria Theresia und Joseph II: Ihre Correspondenz,* vol. 2, pp. 157–165; also vol. 3, pp. 351–352, Denkschrift des Kaisers Joseph über den Zustand der österreichischen Monarchie (1765).
3. A. Přibram, *Urkunden und Akten zur Geschichte der Juden in Wien* (Vienna, 1918), vol. 1, pp. 494–500.
4. Ibid.
5. Ibid., p. 592, decree of August 15, 1788.
6. G. Wolf, *Geschichte der Juden in Wien* (Vienna, 1876), p. 56.
7. Ibid., p. 86; see also J.M. Jost, *Geschichte der Israeliten.* . . . (Berlin, 1828), vol. 9, pp. 27–28.
8. A. Fournier, "Joseph II," *Allgemeine Deutsche Biographie,* vol. 14, p. 553.
9. Přibram, *Urkunden,* December 21, 1781.
10. Ibid., vol. 1, p. 516, rescript of March 31, 1782.

11. Ibid., rescript of June 18, 1784.

12. Ibid., vol. 1, p. 498.

13. Ibid., decree of March 3, 1782.

14. Quoted by V. Bibl, *Kaiser Joseph II* (Vienna, 1943), p. 221.

15. Wolf, *Geschichte der Juden,* p. 79.

16. Přibram, *Urkunden,* December 19, 1781.

17. Quoted by Wolf, *Geschichte der Juden,* p. 82.

18. Ibid., pp. 270–271.

19. L. Geiger, *Geschichte der Juden in Berlin* (Berlin, 1871), p. 52.

20. Ibid., p. 55.

21. G.H.T. Liebe, *Das Judentum in der deutschen Vergangenheit* (Leipzig, 1903), p. 95.

22. R. Koser, *Friedrich der Grosse* (Stuttgart, 1901), vol. 2, p. 190.

23. Quoted by H. Jungfer, *Die Juden unter Friedrich dem Grossen* (Leipzig, 1880), p. 21.

24. Koser, *Friedrich der Grosse,* vol. 2, p. 191.

25. V. Valentin, *Friedrich der Grosse* (Berlin, 1927), p. 118.

26. *Jewish Encyclopedia* (New York, 1901), vol. 2, p. 330.

27. J.D.E. Preuss, *Friedrich der Grosse* (Berlin, 1832), vol. 1, p. 289.

28. S.M. Dubnow, *Weltgeschichte des jüdischen Volkes* (Berlin, 1929), vol. 8, p. 21; see also R. Mahler, *A History of Modern Jewry, 1780–1815* (London, 1971), pp. 229f.

29. Koser, *Friedrich der Grosse,* vol. 2, October 29, 1757.

30. Preuss, *Friedrich der Grosse,* vol. 1, p. 289.

31. O. Hintze, *Die Hohenzollern und ihr Werk* (Berlin, 1917), p. 356.

32. O. Hintze, *Die preussische Seidenindustrie im achtzehnten Jahrhundert . . .* (Berlin, 1892), vol. 3, p. 296.

33. Quoted by Jungfer, *Die Juden,* p. 27.

34. M. Bär, *Westpreussen unter Friedrich dem Grossen* (Leipzig, 1909), p. 422.

35. Valentin, *Friedrich der Grosse,* p. 53.

36. Bär, *Westpreussen,* pp. 439f.

37. C. Frantz, *Der Nationalliberalismus und die Judenherrschaft* (Munich, 1844), p. 4.

38. S. Stern-Täubler, *Der preussische Staat und die Juden* (Berlin, 1925), part 3, p. 2.

39. C. Barthélmess, *Histoire philosophique de l'Académie de Prusse . . .* (Paris, 1850), p. 227.

40. Quoted by S. Stern, *Geschichte des Judentums von Mendelssohn . . .* (Breslau, 1870), p. 312.

41. Barthélmess, *Histoire philosophique,* p. 227; for a different evaluation, see A. Altmann's monumental biography *Moses Mendelssohn,* pp. 265, 276.

42. Quoted in *Antisemitenspiegel* (2d edition), p. 311.

43. F.V. Oppeln-Bronikowsky, ed., *Gespräche Friedrichs des Grossen* (1919), pp. 306 f.

44. C.W. Dohm, *Über die bürgerliche Verbesserung der Juden* (Berlin, 1783), pp. 38–39.

45. Dohm's work prompted Moses Mendelssohn to publish two books of his own. Mendelssohn's German translation of the work *Rescue of the Jews* by Manasseh Israel appeared in 1782. Mendelssohn's other work was entitled *Jerusalem, or Religious Power and Judaism*.

46. Dohm, *Über die bürgerliche Verbesserung*, vol. 2, pp. 15–16; for the following, see ibid., pp. 34, 21, 38–39, 114, 112, 116–117, 199–200 and vol. 2, 15–16, 295, Preface and Appendix.

47. H.F. Diez, *Über die Juden* (Leipzig, 1783), p. 8.

48. *Allgemeine Deutsche Bibliothek*, vol. 50, pp. 301–311.

49. Quoted by Dohm, *Über die bürgerliche Verbesserung*, vol. 2, p. 89 and pp. 108–109.

50. *Ephemeriden der Menschheit*, vol. 1, pp. 404–425.

51. Quoted by Dohm, *Über die bürgerliche Verbesserung*, vol. 2, pp. 21–71, especially p. 36.

52. K. Rotteck and C. Welcker, eds., *Encyclopädie der Staatswissenschaften* (Altona, 1837), vol. 4, p. 448.

53. Diez, *Über die Juden*, pp. 13–14.

54. Michaelis, quoted by Dohm, *Über die bürgerliche Verbesserung*, vol. 2, see p. 68.

55. See Note 48.

56. See Note 52.

57. See Note 53.

Chapter Two

1. J.G. Zimmermann, *Von dem Nationalstolze* (Frankfurt, 1781), p. 77.

2. J.C. Gottsched, *Gesammelte Reden* (Leipzig, 1749).

3. J.G. Herder, *Briefe, das Studium der Theologie betreffend*, part 1, letter 12.

4. D. Diderot, *Encyclopédie* (Lausanne, 1781), vol. 14, p. 245.

5. A. Hertzberg, *The French Enlightenment and the Jews* (1968), p. 299.

6. Ibid., p. 286.

7. Preface to Voltaire's *Dictionnaire Philosophique, Oeuvres complètes*, ed. Moland (Paris, 1877), vol. 1, p. xii.

8. Diderot, *Oeuvres complètes* (Paris, 1875), vol. 15, p. 378.

9. Herder, see Note 9.

10. H. Heine, *Confessio Judaica*, ed. Bieber (Berlin, 1925), p. 27; also p. 92.

11. G.W.F. Hegel, *Fragmente theologischer Studien*, pp. 490–492.

12. C.F. Gellert, *Leben der schwed. Gräfin von G., Sämtliche Schriften* (Hildesheim, 1968), vol. 4, pp. 348f., 381f., 394–396.

13. J.T. Hermes, *Sophiens Reise von Memel nach Sachsen.* Deutsche Literatur der Aufklärung, ed. Brüggemann (Leipzig, 1941), vol. 13.

14. G.W. Rabener, *Satiren* (1773), part 4, pp. 398–422.

15. F.G. Klopstock, "An den Kaiser," *Sämtliche Werke* (Leipzig, 1855), vol. 4, pp. 262–263.

16. Klopstock, *Der Tod Adams,* ibid., vol. 6, pp. v–vi.

17. S. Gessner, *Der Tod Abels* (Zürich, 1758), Preface.

18. Klopstock, *Salomo, Sämtliche Werke,* vol. 7, p. 10.

19. Ibid., *Die deutsche Gelehrtenrepublik,* vol. 8, p. 278.

20. Ibid., *Der Messias,* vol. 1, p. 122.

21. Ibid., vol. 1, p. 123.

22. Herder, *Sämtliche Werke* (1803), part 2, pp. 45f.

23. Klopstock, *Sämtliche Werke,* vol. 1, p. 216.

24. C.F.D. Schubart, "Der ewige Jude," *Gesammelte Schriften und Schicksale* (Stuttgart, 1839), vol. 4, pp. 65–69; see also pp. 333–335.

25. "Das Leben Fausts," *Maler Müllers Werke* (Heidelberg, 1825), vol. 2, pp. 47–48; pp. 69–70.

26. C.M. Wieland, *Der Teutsche Merkur* (1775), 3d Quarter, pp. 213–220.

27. Kobler, *Juden und Judentum in deutschen Briefen,* January 28, 1773.

28. *Der goldene Spiegel . . . , Wielands Werke* (Leipzig, 1824), part 2, vol. 17, pp. 240–241.

29. Ibid., pp. 242–243.

30. Ibid., vol. 16, p. 44.

31. Ibid., p. 296.

32. "Aufsätze, welche sich auf die französische Revolution von 1789 beziehen . . . , " ibid., vol. 41, p. 217; also Biach, *Biblische Sprache und biblische Motive in Wielands Oberon* (Brüx, 1897), pp. 5–8.

33. J.H. Voss, *Erinnerungen aus meinem Jugendleben,* pp. 18–21.

34. J.H. Voss, *Luise, Deutsche Nationalliteratur,* vol. 49, p. 15, verse 335; see also *Briefe* (Hildesheim, 1971), vol. 1, pp. 18–20.

35. G.C. Lichtenberg, "Timorus . . . , " *Vermischte Schriften,* Meisterwerke deutscher Dichter (Vienna, 1817), vol. 23–27, III, 49–114.

36. To Ramberg, May 18, 1795.

37. M. Claudius, "Moses Mendelssohn an die Freunde Lessings," *Sämtliche Werke* (Hamburg, 1789), vol. 5, p. 203.

38. C.F. Nicolai, *Leben und Meinungen . . . ,* Deutsche Literatur der Aufklärung, ed. Brüggemann (Leipzig, 1938), vol. 15, p. 15.

39. Ibid., pp. 209–216. For favorable remarks about the Jews, see Nicolai's *Beschreibung der königlichen Residenzstädte . . . ,* (Berlin, 1769), vol. 1, pp. 206–208, 248; vol. 2, pp. 500f.

40. Quoted by A. Kohut, *Geschichte der deutschen Juden* (Berlin, 1898), p. 763.

41. W. Ramler, Prologue to Shakespeare's *Merchant of Venice, Kürschners Deutsche Nationalliteratur,* vol. 45, pp. 262–267.

42. It was the pastor Goeze who had accused Lessing of having accepted a thousand talers from the Jews. *Lessings Werke,* eds. Lachmann and Muncker, vol. 13, pp. 389–411.

43. F. Mehring, *Die Lessinglegende* (Stuttgart, 1922), p. 217.

44. A. Stöcker, *Dreizehn Jahre Hofprediger und Politiker* (Berlin, 1895), pp. 41f.

45. E.K. Dühring, *Die Judenfrage als . . . Kulturfrage* (Karlsruhe, 1881), p. 11; see also the reference on p. 67 to Lessing's "admixture of Jewish blood."

46. G. Feder, *Die Juden* (Munich, 1933), p. 47.

47. J. Nadler, *Literaturgeschichte der deutschen Stämme . . .* (Regensburg, 1932), vol. 3, pp. 175–177.

48. G.E. Lessing, *Die Juden, Sämtliche Schriften,* eds. Lachmann and Munckner (Stuttgart, 1927), vol. 1, part 3.

49. G.E. Lessing, *Rettung des Cardanus.* Ibid., vol. 5, pp. 310–333.

50. G.E. Lessing, *Nathan der Weise, Sämtliche Schriften,* vol. 3. About Lessing's relationship with Mendelssohn, see A. Altmann, *Moses Mendelssohn* (University of Alabama: 1973).

51. G.E. Lessing, "Erziehung des Menschengeschlechtes," *Sämtliche Schriften,* vol. 13, pp. 415–436, paragraphs 8, 15–16, 18, 23, 32, 85–86.

52. F. Schnabel in *Deutsche Geschichte im neunzehnten Jahrhundert,* vol. 4, p. 504, asserted that Hamann was anti-Semitic, "for Mendelssohn had taught that Judaism and Enlightenment belonged together." See Altmann, *Moses Mendelssohn,* pp. 197–199, 638–642.

53. J.G. Hamann, *Schriften und Briefe,* ed. Petri (Hanover, 1878), vol. 2, p. 3.

54. Ibid., vol. 1, p. 111.

55. Ibid., vol. 3, p. 128.

56. Ibid., pp. 128–129.

57. Ibid., vol. 2, p. 108.

58. Ibid., vol. 1, p. 347; vol. 2, p. 117.

59. Hamann, *Schriften und Briefe,* May 29, 1759; vol. 1, p. 193; vol. 2, p. 373; for other remarks on Jews, see vol. 1, pp. 47–48, 52, 100.

60. H.S. Chamberlain, *Grundlagen des 19. Jahrhunderts,* chapter 5. The anti-Semitic writer O. Kernholt, in *Vom Ghetto zur Macht* (Leipzig, 1921), p. 266, also counted Herder among the opponents of the Jews, but felt compelled to make the strongly qualifying observation that his hostility against the Jews was somewhat "peculiar," since he showed them a "certain benevolence."

61. J.G. Herder, "Die Bekehrung der Juden . . . , " in *Adrastea,* a magazine almost entirely written by Herder. See *Herders Werke,* ed. Kurz, vol. 24, pp. 61f.

62. *Vom Geist der hebräischen Poesie, Herders Sämtliche Werke,* ed. Suphan, vol. 11, pp. 213–468.

63. Herder, *Vom Geist des Christentums, Christliche Schriften,* ed. Müller, part 12, p. 117; likewise *Briefe, das Studium der Theologie betreffend, Sämtliche Werke,* ed. Suphan, vol. 10, letter 12.

64. Ibid., letter 4.

65. Herder, *Blätter der Vorzeit, Sämtliche Werke*, ed. Suphan, Preface, pp. iii–iv.

66. *Älteste Urkunde des Menschengeschlechtes, Herders Werke*, ed. Suphan, vols. 6–7.

67. Herder, *Vom Geist der hebräischen Poesie, Sämtliche Werke*, ed. Suphan, vol. 11, p. 222.

68. *Stimmen der Völker in Liedern, Herders Werke*, ed. Kurz, vol. 8, Introduction.

69. Herder, *Ideen zur Philosophie der Geschichte der Menschheit* (Leipzig, 1821), vol. 2, pp. 59–68; also chapters 12, book 3; 16, book 5; 17, book 3.

70. Herder, *Briefe das Studium der Theologie betreffend, Sämtliche Werke*, ed. Suphan, part 1, letter 12.

71. Herder, *Briefe zur Beförderung der Humanität*, Kürschners Deutsche Nationalliteratur (Greifen, 1947), letter 115.

72. Ibid., letter 116.

73. Ibid., 7th compilation.

74. Herder, "Bekehrung der Juden," *Adrastea*.

75. Herder, *Ideen zur Philosophie*, pp. 294–295.

76. See Note 74.

77. Herder, *Vom Geist des Christentums*, pp. 75–77.

78. See Note 74.

79. Herder, *Ideen zur Philosophie*, p. 294.

80. Herder, *Briefe zur Beförderung der Humanität*, Deutsche Nationalliteratur, 10th compilation, pp. 565–566.

81. See Note 74.

82. Herder, "Ëbraer," *Ideen zur Philosophie*.

83. Herder, *Briefe zur Beförderung der Humanität*, 10th compilation, no. 119.

84. Ibid., 5th compilation.

85. Herder, *Ideen zur Philosophie*, pp. 59, 66–68.

86. Nadler, *Literaturgeschichte*, vol. 4, p. 7.

87. See Note 74.

88. See Note 86.

89. Herder, *Vom Geist des Christentums*, pp. 75–78.

90. Ibid., pp. 99–100, 117.

91. Ibid., pp. 163, 109, 156–157.

92. Herder, *Früchte aus den sogenannten goldenen Zeitaltern des achtzehnten Jahrhunderts*, ed. Müller, pp. 263–264.

Chapter Three

1. H. Holtzhauer, ed., *Dichtung und Wahrheit, Goethes Werke* (Berlin and Weimar, 1966), vol. 8, p. 293.

2. *Briefwechsel zwischen Goethe und Zelter* (Berlin, 1834), vol. 5, p. 3, January 24, 1828.

3. H. Houben, ed., *Gespräche mit Eckermann,* March 14, 1830.

4. Holtzhauer, ed., *Dichtung und Wahrheit,* vol. 8, p. 26.

5. "Weltliteratur" in "Epigrammatisch," *Gedichte.*

6. "Zum Divan," ibid.

7. Goethe, *Faust,* part 1, *Werke,* V, verses 2478f.

8. Goethe, *Faust,* part 2, ibid., verses 258f.

9. Goethe, *Balladen, Werke,* I, 130.

10. Goethe, *Clavigo,* Buencos, 3d act, Guilbert's dwelling.

11. *Eckermann,* October 7, 1828; also October 20.

12. L. Geiger, *Die Juden und die deutsche Literatur* (1910), pp. 81–102.

13. Goethe, *Sprüche in Prosa, Werke* (Weimarisches Hoftheater), vol. 13.

14. Goethe, Rezensionen in *Die Frankfurter Gelehrten-Anzeiger,* ibid., vol. 28, p. 25.

15. Eckermann; a similar thought is also expressed by Goethe in the following: "The Germans are pretty good people; if they act as individuals they go far." (*Gespräche mit Eckermann,* vol. 1, p. 241.)

16. A. Sydow, ed., *Wilhelm und Caroline von Humboldt in ihren Briefen* (Berlin, 1906), November 19, 1808.

17. According to Eckermann, on May 3, 1827, Goethe said it would still be several centuries before people could say about the Germans: "It has been a long time since they were barbarians." Another time Goethe asserted that the Germans lacked good taste and intellectual freedom (*Goethes Werke, Weimarisches Hoftheater*), vol. 13, p. 150. The Germans could not rid themselves of philistinism. (*Eckermann,* December 16, 1828.)

18. L. Geiger, *Die Juden,* op. cit., pp. 81–102.

19. W.F. Biedermann, ed., *Goethes Gespräche* (Leipzig, 1925), vol. 3, p. 282.

20. *Eckermann,* June 6, 1831.

21. Biedermann, *Gespräche,* vol. 1, p. 494 (May 30, 1807).

22. W. Bode, ed., *Goethe: Meine Religion, mein politischer Glaube* (Berlin, 1899), p. 69.

23. Holtzhauer, ed., *Dichtung und Wahrheit,* vol. 8, pp. 159–160.

24. *Briefwechsel zwischen Goethe und Zelter,* vol. 2, p. 22 (May 30, 1812); see also Goethe's previous letter of May 19, 1812, p. 21.

25. B. Brentano, *Goethes Briefwechsel mit einem Kinde,* ed. Grimm, p. 111, Jan. 2, 1808.

26. Ibid., pp. 123–124, April 3, 1808.

27. Ibid., p. 128, April 20, 1808.

28. *Goethe-Jahrbuch,* vol. 16, pp. 4, 7.

29. Quoted by N. Waldmann, *Goethe and the Jews* (New York, 1934), p. 79.

30. *Werke* (Weimar), vol. 31, p. 276, February 25, 1802.

31. *Goethes Sämtliche Werke* (Insel-Verlag), vol. 12, pp. 475f.

32. Holtzhauer, ed., *Dichtung und Wahrheit*, vol. 9, pp. 130–131.
33. Ibid., vol. 8, p. 200.
34. J.W. v. Goethe, *Wilhelm Meisters Wanderjahre*, Cotta, vol. 9, book 3, chapter 11.
35. R. Eberhard, *Goethe und das alte Testament*, pp. 161–170.
36. See Note 34, vol. 9, book 2, chapter 2.
37. Holtzhauer, ed., *Dichtung und Wahrheit*, vol. 8, pp. 159–160.
38. See Note 22.
39. See Note 37.
40. J.W. v. Goethe, *West-östlicher Divan* (Die Hebräer), *Werke* (Weimar), vol. 14, pp. 130–131.
41. Holtzhauer, ed., *Dichtung und Wahrheit*, vol. 8, p. 293.
42. Ibid.
43. Quoted by Eberhard, *Goethe*, p. 171.
44. Ibid., p. 174.
45. J.W. v. Goethe, "Israel in der Wüste," *Werke* (Weimar), vol. 14, p. 230.
46. *Eckermann*, February 1, 1827.
47. H. Hirzel, ed., *Briefe von Goethe an Lavater* (Leipzig, 1833), p. 144, July 29, 1782.
48. Holtzhauer, ed., *Dichtung und Wahrheit*, vol. 8, p. 150.
49. Ibid., pp. 149–150.
50. J.W. v. Goethe, *Italienische Reise*, March 1, 1788.
51. J.W. v. Goethe, *Hermann und Dorothea*, *Werke* (Weimar), vol. 3, (Polyhymnia, der Weltbürger).
52. *Eckermann*, October 7, 1828.
53. Holtzhauer, ed., *Dichtung und Wahrheit*, vol. 8, p. 152.
54. Among many treatments, see V. Hehn, "Goethe und die Sprache der Bibel," *Gedanken über Goethe* (Berlin, 1900), pp. 390–405.
55. Goethe, *West-östlicher Divan* (Die Hebräer), *Werke* (Weimar), vol. 14, pp. 130–131.
56. Ibid., Mahmud von Gasna, p. 152.
57. F.W. Riemer, "Über die Juden," *Mitteilungen über Goethe*, part 1, pp. 427–434.; Riemer himself was by no means a friend of the Jews. On one occasion he called them "parasite-like."
58. Bode, ed., *Goethe: Meine Religion* . . . , p. 69.
59. G.L. Kriegk, *Deutsche Kulturbilder aus dem achtzehnten Jahrhundert* (Leipzig, 1874), pp. 263–517; see also N. Waldmann, *Goethe and the Jews* (New York, 1934), pp. 201, 288 and chapter "Goethe, Attorney of Jews."
60. Riemer, *Mitteilungen über Goethe*.
61. Ibid.
62. *Eckermann*, January 29, 1827; February 12, 1829.
63. Ibid., March 14, 1830.
64. J. Bab, *Goethe und die Juden* (Berlin, 1926), p. 17.
65. Holtzhauer, ed., *Dichtung und Wahrheit*, vol. 8, p. 209.

66. Ibid., p. 296.
67. J.W. v. Goethe, *Briefe* (Weimar, 1891), vol. 7, p. 183, February 21, 1786.
68. Holtzhauer, ed., *Dichtung und Wahrheit,* vol. 9, p. 242.
69. Ibid., pp. 241–243. According to Sulpiz Boisserée in 1815, Goethe always carried Spinoza's *Ethics* with him. Goethe joyfully acknowledged, Eckermann related (February 28, 1831), how much the views of that "great thinker" had satisfied the needs of his youth. He had found himself in Spinoza and through him was able to gain strength.
70. Riemer, *Mitteilungen über Goethe.*
71. *Goethes Unterhaltung mit dem Kanzler Fr. v. Müller* (1898), p. 100, September 23, 1823.
72. Koch, *Goethe und die Juden,* p. 31.
73. Bode, ed., *Goethe: Meine Religion . . . ,* p. 69.
74. A. Hitler, *Mein Kampf,* pp. 211, 341.
75. E.K. Dühring, *Die Judenfrage als . . . Kulturfrage* (Karlsruhe, 1881). The "view" that held Goethe to be a Jew was most elaborately expressed in the work of Hans Hermann, *Das Sanatorium der freien Liebe* (1903).
76. H.S. Chamberlain, *Die Grundlagen . . . ,* p. 342. Chamberlain's reproach was primarily directed against T. Fritsch, editor of numerous editions of the *Antisemitenkatechismus.* Nevertheless, both men were one in asserting Goethe's hostility against the Jews. Adolf Hitler, in *Mein Kampf* (Munich, 1939), p. 341, quoted Goethe approvingly in connection with his opposition to mixed marriages.
77. *Das Jahrmarktsfest zu Plundersweilen, Werke* (Weimar), vol. 16.
78. *Zwei ältere Szenen aus dem Jahrmarktsfest . . . ,* ibid., vol. 30, pp. 247–249.
79. Holtzhauer, ed., *Dichtung und Wahrheit,* vol. 9, pp. 249–250.
80. Quoted by L. Geiger, *Die Juden und die deutsche Literatur,* pp. 125–160.
81. F. Jonas, ed., *Schillers Briefe* (Stuttgart, 1896), vol. 4, p. 67.
82. E. Kühnemann, *Schiller* (Munich, 1908), p. 75.
83. K. Goedeke, ed., *Die Räuber, Schillers Sämtliche Schriften* (Stuttgart, 1867), vol. 2, act 1, scene 2. Spiegelberg's proposition that the robbers become Jews, that the "establishment of a Jewish kingdom" be considered, and that all Jews be "called" to Palestine, is mockingly discarded by Karl Moor. The scoundrel Spiegelberg is thus pictured by Schiller as a braggard and an aimless dreamer in whose head arise the most curious plans. Since the grandiose schemer was a typical figure in contemporary comedies, Spiegelberg's foregoing references to Palestine and conversion do not necessarily support the thesis of his supposed Jewish origin. At times Spiegelberg inverts the German word order in a way peculiar to the Jewish jargon; yet it seems natural that he who desires to settle in Palestine as a pretended descendant of Herod, a king of the returning Jews, should wish to prove a knowledge of Yiddish.

84. I. Minor, *Schiller: Sein Leben und seine Werke* (Berlin, 1890), p. 320.

85. K. Berger, *Schiller: Sein Leben und seine Werke* (Munich, 1909), vol. 2, p. 47.

86. F. Schiller, *Die Räuber,* Preface.

87. G. Mann, ed., "Was heisst und zu welchem Ende studiert man Universalgeschichte?" *Schillers Werke* (1966), vol. 4.

88. Goedeke, ed., "Die Sendung Mosis," *Schillers Sämtliche Schriften,* vol. 9, pp. 100–124, esp. p. 102.

89. Geiger, *Die deutsche Literatur,* and O. Frankl, *Schiller in seinen Beziehungen zu den Juden,* failed to see the full significance of this important passage, while Jew-haters for apparent reasons were hardly interested in elaborating upon it.

90. B. Decius (Reinhold), *Die hebräischen Mysterien oder die älteste religiöse Freimaurerei* (Leipzig, 1789). Reinhold's early theological training in Austria may have laid the foundation for his hostility against the Jews, but these views were apparently strengthened from an unexpected source, from reading Voltaire whom he quoted in the foregoing brochure (p. 51). Reinhold considered the Israelites "savages roaming around in deepest ignorance" (56). He pilloried the "inhumanity of the [Jewish] character devoid of intellect and heart" which, "for the honor of mankind, cannot be found in any other people" (28).

91. See Note 88.

92. Anti-Semitic writers have claimed Schiller as one of their illustrious forerunners without furnishing more than the most spurious evidence. Julius Langbehn, *Rembrandt als Erzieher* (Leipzig, 1896), pp. 347–352, and other Jew-haters such as G. Feder, *Die Juden* (Munich, 1933), pp. 46; Count Reventlov, *Judas Kampf* . . . (Berlin, 1937), p. 218; and H. Naudh (Nordmann), *Die Juden und der Deutsche Staat* (1861) all asserted Schiller's enmity against the Jews. However in 1933, the anti-Jewish literary historian A. Bartels, who disliked Schiller, discovered in his work something "un-German, even un-Germanic" and promptly attributed it to his "Celtic blood admixture" (*Einführung in das deutsche Schrifttum für deutsche Menschen,* p. 146).

93. *Jean Pauls Briefwechsel mit seinem Freunde Osmund,* Fleischmann, ed., Oct. 30, 1794; see especially the following pages: 1, 3, 14, 17, 19, 23, 35, 59, 82, 318–319.

94. *Jean Pauls Briefwechsel mit seiner Frau und Christian Otto,* p. 294. See also *Jean Paul: Ein Lebensroman in Briefen,* ed. Hartung, p. 298. For Jean Paul's relations with individual Jews, see C. v. Varnhagen, *Rahel: Ein Buch des Andenkens* . . .

95. "Über die Religionen in der Welt," *Jean Pauls Werke, Kürschners Nationalliteratur,* vol. 130, pp. 12–16.

96. Numerous anti-Semitic writers have asserted that Kant was an enemy of the Jews: T. Fritsch, *Antisemitenkatechismus* (1893), p. 45; A. Rosenberg, *Der Mythus des zwanzigsten Jahrhunderts* (1939), p. 697; and A. Stöcker, *Das moderne Judentum in Deutschland* . . . (1880), p. 17.

97. Kant, *Die Religion innerhalb der Grenzen* . . . , *Gesamtausgabe,* vol. 6, pp. 300–304.

98. H. Cohen, *Die inneren Beziehungen der Kant'schen Lehre zum Judentum,* p. 41, in *28. Bericht der Lehranstalt für die Wissenschaft des Judentums,* Berlin, 1910.

99. I. Kant, *Anthropologie in pragmatischer Hinsicht abgefasst, Gesamtausgabe,* ed. Rosenkranz (Leipzig, 1842), vol. 10, pp. 218–219.

100. I. Kant, *Der Streit der Fakultäten,* ibid., vol. 1, pp. 252–253.

101. L. Bendavid, *Etwas zur Charakteristik der Juden* (Leipzig, 1793), pp. 55, 64–66.

102. I. Kant, *Pädagogik, Gesamtausgabe,* vol. 10, pp. 386–387: "Man . . . is nothing but what education makes of him."

103. Quoted by H. Elsenhaus, *Kants Rassentheorie* (Leipzig, 1904); see also Kant's "Rassen der Menschen," *Gesamtausgabe,* vol. 10, p. 41: "All deviations . . . still presuppose one *original kind*" [italics by Kant].

104. A. Kohut, *Gekrönte und ungekrönte Judenfreunde* (Berlin, 1913), in discussing Kant confines himself to his personal relations with individual Jews.

105. Letter of May 26, 1789, *Kants Gesammelte Schriften* (Berlin, 1922), vol. 2, pp. 48–54.

106. I. Kant, *Gesamtausgabe,* vol. 10, pp. 530–531, March 28, 1794.

107. See Note 105.

108. See Note 106, letter of August 7, 1797.

109. F.W. Schubert, ed., *I. Kant: Briefe, Erklärungen, Fragmente und sein Nachlass* (Leipzig, 1842), p. 5, February 7, 1766.

110. Letter of August 20, 1777, vol. 1, p. 211.

111. Quoted by S.M. Dubnow, *Weltgeschichte des jüdischen Volkes* (Berlin, 1929).

112. F.H.J. Jacobi, *Werke* (Leipzig, 1825), vol. 6, pp. 3 and 142.

113. For Kant's relationship with Mendelssohn, see A. Altmann, *Moses Mendelssohn* (Univ. of Alabama: 1973), pp. 73, 118f., 125f.

114. D. Friedländer, *Beitrag zur Geschichte der Verfolgung der Juden* (Berlin, 1820), p. 20.

115. I. Kant, "Rezension von Schulz' Anleitung zur Sittenlehre," *Gesamtausgabe,* vol. 5, p. 339.

116. I. Kant, "Zum ewigen Frieden," ibid., vol. 5, p. 443.

117. Ibid., vol. 5, pp. 442–443.

118. I. Kant, "Was ist Aufklärung?" ibid., vol. 1, p. 417.

Chapter Four

1. W.F. Grattenauer, *Wider die Juden;* also *Erklärung an das Publikum über meine Schrift* . . . (Berlin, 1803). For Jewish replies, see Graetz, *Volkstümliche Geschichte der Juden* (Vienna, 1923), vol. 3, pp. 539–541.

2. H. v. Boyen, *Denkwürdigkeiten und Erinnerungen, 1771–1813* (Stuttgart, 1899), pp. 47–48.

3. Ibid., pp. 46–47.

4. Quoted by G. Freund, *Die Emanzipation der Juden in Preussen . . .* (Berlin, 1912), vol. 1, p. 122.

5. H. v. Treitschke, *Geschichte des deutschen Volkes im neunzehnten Jahrhundert* (Leipzig, 1890), vol. 2, p. 417; he then wrote, still in an objective manner, about the role of the Jews in the War of Liberation.

6. January 4, 1815, quoted by J.M. Jost, *Geschichte der Israeliten seit der Zeit der Maccabäer bis auf unsere Tage* (Berlin, 1828), vol. 10, pp. 178–181.

7. See the testimony of the Minister of War, Lieutenant General von Cosel, in the *Herrenkurie* of the Prussian United Diet on June 15, 1847.

8. Quoted by L. Geiger, *Die deutschen Juden und der deutsche Krieg* (Berlin, 1915), p. 8.

9. Cited in the magazine *Sulamith,* vol. 4, pp. 367f.

10. *Goethe-Jahrbuch* (1895), vol. 16, pp. 4, 7.

11. A. Sydow, ed., *Wilhelm und Caroline von Humboldt in ihren Briefen* (Berlin, 1906), vol. 4, March 29, 1816.

12. Meisner and Geerg, eds., *E.M. Arndt: Ein Lebensbild in Briefen,* p. 124, July 8, 1815.

13. F. Schnabel, *Deutsche Geschichte im neunzehnten Jahrhundert* (Freiburg, 1929), vol. 3, p. 412.

14. E.C. Corti, *Der Aufstieg des Hauses Rothschild* (New York, 1928), vol. 1, pp. 160–161, also 167.

15. Treitschke, *Geschichte,* vol. 2, p. 389.

16. Ibid.

17. K.B.A. Sessa, *Unser Verkehr* (the original title of the farce was *Die Judenschule*).

18. F. Rühs, *Über die Ansprüche der Juden an das deutsche Bürgerrecht* (Berlin, 1816), pp. v, 33–39.

19. F. Fries, "Über die Gefährdung des Wohlstandes und des Charakters der Deutschen durch die Juden," *Heidelberger Jahrbücher der Literatur,* (1816), pp. 10, 12, 18, 21–33.

20. Quoted by Graetz, *Volkstümliche Geschichte,* vol. 3, p. 573.

21. Hundt von Radowsky, *Die Judenschule* (London, 1822), vol. 1, pp. 19, 25, 29.

22. H.E.G. Paulus, *Die jüdische Nationalabsonderung nach Ursprung, Folgen und Besserungsmitteln* (Heidelberg, 1831), p. 3. The Jews, the author asserted, were not entitled to citizenship, merely to "protection as subjects." They formed not only a religious association, but also a distinct ethnic group. Paulus tried to defend himself against the accusation of religious intolerance; however, he was apparently less sensitive to the possible reproach of national intolerance. While he dismissed the Jews' demand for equality, he wanted the government to act "in a more Christian way" (p. 148). He advised the Jews to embrace Christianity.

23. J.L.K. Klüber, *Übersicht der diplomatischen Verhandlungen des Wiener Kongresses* (Frankfurt a.M., 1816), part 3, p. 390.

24. Treitschke, *Geschichte,* vol. 2, p. 421.

25. Sterling, "The Hep-Hep Riots in Germany, 1819," *Historia Judaica* (1950), no. 2, p. 150.

26. See Note 24.

27. A. v. Feuerbach, October 31, 1813, cited in *Deutsche Romanzeitung,* 1881, pp. 701f.

28. H. v. Treitschke, "Ein Wort über unser Judentum," *Preussische Jahrbücher,* November 1879–January 1880.

29. H. v. Treitschke, *Geschichte des deutschen Volkes im neunzehnten Jahrhundert* (Leipzig, 1890), vol. 2, p. 528.

30. K. Varnhagen v. Ense, *Denkwürdigkeiten des eigenen Lebens* (Leipzig, 1871), vol. 6, pp. 153–154.

Chapter Five

1. F. Meinecke, *Von Stein zu Bismarck* (Berlin, 1911), p. 35.

2. A. Stern, *Geschichte der preussischen Reformzeit 1807–1815* (Leipzig, 1885), p. 228.

3. M. Lehmann, *Freiherr vom Stein* (Leipzig, 1905), vol. 1, p. 301.

4. Ibid. The German socialist August Bebel, in his book *Sozialdemokratie und Antisemitismus* (Berlin, 1894), expressed the opinion that the part played by the Jews in the destruction of peasant property was infinitely small compared to that of the German Junkers, that the former "operated like moles where the others were lions."

5. G.H. Pertz, *Das Leben des Ministers Freiherrn vom Stein* (Berlin, 1855), vol. 1, p. 152. Pertz, the earliest biographer of Stein, appears to have swallowed the latter's anti-Semitism; see pp. 325–326.

6. J.R. Seeley, *Life and Times of Stein* (Boston, 1879), vol. 1, p. 493; see also G. Ritter, *Stein: Eine politische Biographie* (Stuttgart, 1931).

7. Stein, *Lebensbeschreibungen* . . . in Pertz, *Vom Steins Leben,* vol. 7, pp. 2 and 170.

8. C.T. Perthes, *Friedrich Perthes Leben* (Gotha, 1861), vol. 1, pp. 257–258.

9. I. Freund, *Die Emanzipation der Juden in Preussen* . . . (Berlin, 1912), vol. 1, pp. 109f.; also vol. 2, chapter 6.

10. Pertz, *Vom Steins Leben,* vol. 1, pp. 325–327.

11. Lehmann, *Freiherr vom Stein,* vol. 1, pp. 524–525.

12. Ibid.

13. Stern, *Geschichte der preussischen Reformzeit,* p. 234.

14. Freund, *Emanzipation,* vol. 1, p. 118.

15. Stern, *Geschichte,* p. 228. The Jewish historian S.M. Dubnow— *Weltgeschichte des jüdischen Volkes* (Berlin, 1929), vol. 9, p. 208—saw in

Stein an opponent of the Jews, since he, like Schrötter, wished to annihilate the Jewish nationality. While there can be little doubt about Stein's anti-Semitism, many German Christians who had the same objective in mind— destruction and disappearance of the Jewish people—could well qualify as friends of the Jews, though not of Judaism, either as a religion or as a nationality. In fairness, Stein should not be judged on the basis of the concept of a culturally and ethnically pluralistic society which seemed then irreconcilable with the contemporary thought about the national movement for freedom and independence and the creation of a national state. Granting, or withholding and opposing, civil and political equality is in general a better yardstick for measuring the extent of friendship, hostility, or indifference of individual Germans toward the Jews.

How did German historians of the early twentieth century judge vom Stein's attitude toward the Jews? The anti-Semitic historian W. Grau—*Die Judenfrage in der deutschen Geschichte* (Leipzig, 1937), p. 25—speaks of Stein's "implacable enmity" against the Jews, yet regrets that Stein "did not put it into action." In the anti-Semitic pamphlet by E. Herdieckerhoff— *Freiherr vom und zum Stein und die Juden* (Munich, 1931)—Stein is pictured as an irreconcilable opponent of the Jews. When Erich Botzenhart wrote his work *Die Staats-und Reformideen des Freiherrn vom Stein* (1927) and his biography *Freiherr vom Stein* (1931), he did not consider Stein's attitude toward the Jews significant enough to merit special attention. However, when he later edited Stein's works under the auspices of the Nazi government, Stein appeared properly as an incontestable foe of the Jews. See *Freiherr vom Stein: Briefwechsel, Denkschriften und Aufzeichnungen,* vol. 5, p. xi.

16. R. Schwemer, *Geschichte der freien Stadt Frankfurt a.M.* (Frankfurt, 1910), vol. 1, p. 262.

17. Lehmann, *Freiherr vom Stein,* vol. 3, p. 332.

18. Schwemer, *Geschichte,* vol. 1, p. 107.

19. Ibid., vol. 1, p. 264, May 28, 1814.

20. Ibid., vol. 1, p. 108; also vol. 1, p. 264; see further the letter of September 7, 1814, as cited by C.A. Buchholz, *Aktenstücke,* p. 42, and *Freiherr vom Stein: Briefwechsel . . .* (Berlin, 1931), vol. 4, p. 482.

21. Ibid., vol. 6, p. 410.

22. Cited by M.J. Kohler, *Jewish Rights at the Congress of Vienna (1814–1815) and Aix-la-Chapelle,* pp. 33–34, November 4, 1814.

23. Ibid. Smidt, the anti-Semitic representative of the city of Bremen at the Congress of Vienna and also frequent spokesman for all Hanseatic cities in Jewish affairs, suggested to the municipal authorities of Bremen in a report of January 3, 1816 the bestowal of honorary citizenship upon Stein (Schwemer, *Geschichte,* vol. 1, p. 383). Yet it is uncertain whether the suggestion resulted from Stein's generally friendly attitude to the Hanseatic cities or only from his support in Jewish affairs.

24. *Wilhelm und Caroline Humboldt in ihren Briefen,* vol. 4, April 9, 1816.

25. J. Körner, ed., *Briefe von und an Friedrich und Dorothea Schlegel* (Berlin, 1926), p. 48.

26. F. Meinecke, *Vom Stein zu Bismarck* (Berlin, 1911), p. 35.

27. Quoted by Pertz, *Vom Steins Leben,* vol. 4, letter of March 28, 1820 to the later Archbishop of Cologne, Count Spiegel.

28. Quoted by Seeley, *Life and Times,* vol. 2, pp. 470–471, letter of August 21, 1821 to Gagern.

29. Quoted by Pertz, *Vom Steins Leben,* vol. 5, p. 603; see also letter of October 1821 to Minister Schuckmann.

30. Ibid., vol. 5, p. 670; see also the remarks of November 5, 1822, quoted by Herdieckerhoff, *Freiherr vom Stein,* p. 27.

31. *Achendorffsche Schriften. Der erste westfälische Landtag,* p. 65.

32. L. v. Ranke, *Denkwürdigkeiten des Staatskanzlers Fürsten von Hardenberg . . .* (Leipzig, 1877), vol. 4, p. 248.

33. Schwemer, *Geschichte,* vol. 1, pp. 399–410, October 22, 1817.

34. *Wilhelm und Caroline von Humboldt . . . ,* February 4, 1815.

35. Quoted in its entirety by Freund, *Die Emanzipation,* vol. 2.

36. Ibid., vol. 1, p. 165.

37. A. Ernst, ed., *Denkwürdigkeiten von Heinrich und Amalie von Beguélin . . .* (Berlin, 1892), p. 250. See also "Von den Ursachen des Verfalls des preussischen Staates," in *F.A.L. von der Marwitz: Ein märkischer Edelmann im Zeitalter der Befreiungskriege* (Berlin, 1913), vol. 2, pp. 1 and 98. The anti-Semitic writer O. Kernholt, however, refused to consider Hardenberg a "venal instrument" (*Vom Ghetto zur Macht,* p. 80).

38. Ranke, *Denkwürdigkeiten,* Memoir of September 12, 1807, "Über die Reorganisation des preussischen Staates," vol. 4, pp. 82f., 85; also vol. 4, p. 114; see also Stern, *Abhandlungen,* pp. 228–262.

39. Ibid., pp. 240–241, also Ranke, *Denkwürdigkeiten,* vol. 4, Appendix, p. 57.

40. C. Meyer, *Preussens innere Politik in Ansbach und Bayreuth . . . ,* containing the memoir of Hardenberg, p. 59.

41. Ibid., p. 149, no. 182.

42. Ibid., p. 189, no. 220.

43. Quoted by Freund, *Die Emanzipation,* November 26, 1810, vol. 2, pp. 319–320.

44. Ibid., vol. 1, p. 181, and Urkunden, vol. 2, pp. 332f. and 368f.; see also Stern, *Abhandlungen,* p. 251.

45. Freund, *Die Emanzipation,* Urkunden, vol. 2, p. 451.

46. R. Mahler, *Jewish Emancipation: A Selection of Documents* (New York, 1941); see also *Gesetzsammlung für die königlichen Preussischen Staaten* (Berlin, 1812), no. 5, pp. 17–22.

47. *F.A.L. von der Marwitz . . . ,* vol. 2, part 2, pp. 3f., 20–21.

48. Ibid., vol. 2, part 1, pp. 333–334; in some of his other writings Marwitz raged against the government, the "usurers" (vol. 2, p. 337), the "money-oligarchs" (319), the "government of the homeless" (327), without,

however, always including the Jews; yet references to Jews, to Koreff, especially to Jewish army contractors (591) appear frequently. Hardenberg was
accused of "selling the domains to Jews for a very low price" (535) and his
government was repeatedly criticized for being "favorably inclined to usurers" (594). In another connection, however, it emerges clearly that bankers
and usurers were to Marwitz synonymous words (vol. 2, p. 337). Marwitz
often placed the interests of his class ahead of those of his people. Hardenberg once told the king that Marwitz and his Junker friends fought for their
own "privileges," yet gave themselves an air of "speaking as representatives
for the people" (vol. 2, p. 24).

49. W. v. Humboldt's memoir on the emancipation of the Jews is reprinted in full in Freund, *Die Emanzipation,* vol. 2, pp. 269–291.

50. *Wilhelm and Caroline von Humboldt in ihren Briefen,* vol. 4, pp.
454–455, January 13, 1815.

51. *Sulamith,* vol. 4, pp. 367–368.

52. Schwemer, *Geschichte,* vol. 1, pp. 399–401, October 22, 1817.

53. J.K.L. Klüber, *Übersicht der diplomatischen Verhandlungen des
Wiener Kongresses* (Frankfurt a.M., 1816), vol. 1, part 4, pp. 77–80; likewise
vol. 6, pp. 415–418.

54. Schwemer, *Geschichte,* vol. 1, p. 268.

55. Ibid., vol. 1, p. 280.

56. Quoted in *Antisemitenhammer,* pp. 578–579.

57. Varnhagen v. Ense, *Denkwürdigkeiten* . . . (1871), vol. 7, pp. 151–
153.

58. Schwemer, *Geschichte,* vol. 1, pp. 401–402.

59. A. Kohut, *Alexander von Humboldt und das Judentum,* p. 95, January 2, 1835.

60. Ibid., p. 65. Alexander v. Humboldt's testimony contradicts the
supposition of B. Gebhardt, editor of the writings of Wilhelm v. Humboldt,
that Moses Mendelssohn had taken no influence upon the education of the
Humboldt brothers. The testimony is supported by A. Dove (*Allgemeine
Deutsche Biographie,* vol. 13, p. 339), the literary historian R. Haym (*Wilhelm von Humboldt: Ein Lebensbild und Charakter,* p. 10), and M. Kayserling (*Moses Mendelssohn,* pp. 422, 426).

61. Freund, *Die Emanzipation,* vol. 2, pp. 269–291; also W. v. Humboldt, *Politische Denkschriften,* in *Gesammelte Werke,* ed. Gebhardt (Berlin,
1903), vol. 10, part 1, pp. 97–115.

62. Like Humboldt, Hardenberg pointed repeatedly to the necessity
for a solution to the Jewish question in terms of equality in all German
states, not merely in Prussia, and recommended it especially to the Hanseatic cities in 1815, extolling the Prussian example. To a considerable extent
Hardenberg and Wilhelm von Humboldt agreed that equality of the Jews
should not be brought about in a piecemeal fashion, but immediately and
completely.

63. *Wilhelm und Caroline von Humboldt in ihren Briefen,* June 4, 1815.

64. Ibid., March 29, 1816.

65. Quoted by L. Geiger, *Die deutschen Juden und der deutsche Krieg, Die Kriegspolitischen Einzelschriften,* vol. 3 (Berlin, 1915), p. 22.

66. *Wilhelm und Caroline v. Humboldt in ihren Briefen,* March 29, 1816.

67. Ibid., April 9, 1816.

68. Ibid., April 19, 1816.

69. Ibid., April 30, 1816.

70. Ibid., June 3, 1815.

71. Ibid., February 4, 1815.

72. *Briefwechsel zwischen Caroline Humboldt, Rahel und Varnhagen* (Weimar, 1896), June 26, 1815.

73. Ibid.

74. *Ausgewählte Briefe des Feldmarschalls Lebrecht von Blücher* (Leipzig, n.d.), July 10, 1818.

75. H. Delbrück, *Das Leben des Feldmarschalls Grafen Neidhardt von Gneisenau* (Berlin, 1894), vol. 2, p. 354.

76. Quoted in F. Kobler, *Juden und Judentum in deutschen Briefen* (Vienna, 1935), pp. 209–210.

77. G.H. Pertz, *Das Leben des Feldmarschalls Grafen von Gneisenau* (Berlin, 1864), vol. 1, p. 637.

78. Memoir of the *Allgemeines Kriegsdepartment* of November 27, 1808 in Freund, *Die Emanzipation.*

79. Meinecke, *Von Stein zu Bismarck,* p. 24.

80. H. v. Boyen, *Denkwürdigkeiten und Erinnerungen, 1771–1813* (Stuttgart, 1899), pp. 46–47.

Chapter Six

1. H. Graetz in *Geschichte der Juden,* vol. 9, or *History of the Jews* (Philadelphia, 1956), vol. 5, pp. 461–468, speaks of Fichte's "Jew-baiting" (*Judenfressen*); similarly S.M. Dubnow, *Neueste Geschichte des jüdischen Volkes, 1789–Gegenwart* (Berlin, 1920), vol. 1. p. 203. See also F. Rühs and W.F. Grattenauer, *Erklärung an das Publikum . . .* (Berlin, 1803), pp. 34–35.

2. *Adolf Hitler spricht . . .* (Leipzig, 1934), p. 18, July 28, 1922: "Our German Fichte," Hitler said, had shared the knowledge "that the Jew is an alien particle, different in his nature, which is entirely harmful to the Aryan," and "that Judaism as nationality opposes us as a deadly enemy, always and unceasingly." W. Maser in *Hitlers Mein Kampf* (Munich, 1966), p. 82 holds that it could not be proven in a clearcut fashion to what extent Hitler was indebted to Fichte and Treitschke. Fichte appears also as a mortal foe of Judaism to A. Rosenberg, *Die Spur des Juden . . .* (Munich, 1939), p. 79; to T. Fritsch, *Antisemitenkatechismus* (1893), pp. 43–44; A. Stöcker, *Das moderne Judentum in Deutschland . . .* (Berlin, 1880), p. 17; and other anti-Semites. However, an opponent of the Jews, who judged Fichte's utterances

about the Jews "cruel," was the German nationalist historian and later anti-Semite Heinrich von Treitschke, *Geschichte des deutschen Volkes im 19. Jahrhundert* (Leipzig, 1890), vol. 2, p. 419.

3. J.G. Fichte, *Beiträge zur Berichtigung des Urteils des Publikums über die Französische Revolution* . . . , *Fichtes Sämtliche Werke* (Berlin, 1845–1846), vol. 6, pp. 149–153, also 147–148.

4. H. Houben, "Fichte," *Verbotene Literatur* (Berlin, 1924), vol. 2, pp. 92–100.

5. E.L. Schaub on Fichte's relations to Jews, *The Philos. Review,* vol. 49 (New York, 1940) concluded that anti-Semitism claimed Fichte unjustifiably; see also J. Levy, *Fichte und die Juden* (12 pages).

6. W.M. McGovern, *From Luther to Hitler* (Boston, 1941), p. 231, also 239.

7. Fichte, *Beiträge,* vol. 6, p. 177.

8. *J.G. Fichtes Leben und literarischer Briefwechsel,* letter to Reinhold, p. 223. Fichte pleaded therein with Reinhold for "patience" for the work of the previous summer. He had "written it down just to satisfy the publisher. Judge it from this viewpoint."

9. *Gerichtliche Verantwortungsschrift* . . . , p. 93; see also *J.G. Fichtes Leben,* pp. 223–224.

10. H. Schulz, ed., *Aus Fichtes Leben: Briefe und Mitteilungen* . . . (Berlin, 1918); see also O. Rothermel, *Fichte und Schlegel* (Giessen, 1934), on Fichte's relations with the Schlegels. That F. Schlegel dedicated to Fichte in 1804 his edition in three volumes of *Fragmente aus Lessings Briefen und Werken* shows not only the intimacy of their relationship but also that Fichte, whatever his views on the Jews in 1793, had later come closer to the views of Lessing. According to R. Haym, *Die Romantische Schule,* p. 241, Friedrich Schlegel's understanding of Lessing had been awakened by Fichte.

11. *J.G. Fichte: Briefwechsel,* September 1799.

12. Ibid., September 13, 1800.

13. Ibid., September 30, 1794.

14. Ibid., October 16, 1794. "Your letter of September 30," Maimon replied to Fichte, "was very agreeable to me. The assurance of friendship by a man of such acumen and systematic intellect is very precious to me. . . . " In another letter Maimon thanked Fichte for sending him his *Wissenschaftslehre.*

15. Ibid., letter to Reinhold; see also the letter dated March 1795.

16. Ibid., p. 48.

17. Ibid., October 30, 1816, vol. 2, p. 246.

18. Ibid., July 10, 1807.

19. J.G. Fichte, *Aphorismen über Religion und Deismus, Sämtliche Werke,* vol. 5, p. 3.

20. J.G. Fichte, *Kritik aller Offenbarung,* ibid., vol. 5, p. 134.

21. Fichte's sermon of March 25, 1786, in Runze, *Neue Fichte-Funde.* . . . (Gotha, 1919), p. 82.

22. Von Reitzenstein, *Maurerische Klassiker,* vol. 1, p. 95.

23. Quoted in *Clemens Brentanos Werke*, ed. Preitz, vol. 3; see the editor's introduction to Brentano's *Der Philister*. . . .

24. J.G. Fichte, *Die Grundzüge des gegenwärtigen Zeitalters*, in *Sämtliche Werke*, vol. 7, p. 99.

25. Ibid., pp. 174–175.

26. Ibid.

27. Ibid., p. 137.

28. J.G. Fichte, *Politische Fragmente, 1807–1813, Sämtliche Werke*, vol. 7, pp. 600–601.

29. J.G. Fichte, *Die Staatslehre* . . . , ibid., vol. 4, p. 501.

30. Ibid., vol. 4, p. 578.

31. Quoted in *Clemens Brentanos Werke*, ed. Preitz, vol. 3; see the editor's introduction.

32. *Briefe an Fr. Baron de la Motte-Fouqué* (Berlin, 1848); Hitzig's letters of April 15 and 20, 1811, and Fouqué's, April. Also Fichte's *Sämtliche Werke*, vol. 8, pp. 468–471, January 18, 1812.

33. M. Lenz, *Geschichte der kgl. Friedrich Wilhelm Universität zu Berlin* (Halle a.d. Saale, 1910), vol. 1, pp. 402–403.

34. J.G. Fichte, *Politische Fragmente*, vol. 7, p. 573.

35. It is not impossible that vom Stein influenced Arndt in his attitude toward the Jews. Arndt collaborated with Stein not only in St. Petersburg. During the War of Liberation he came to Frankfurt a.M., where he met Stein again. In the old Imperial city the Jewish question was in the foreground of political discussion.

36. E.M. Arndt, "Über den deutschen Studentenstaat," *Schriften für und an seine lieben Deutschen* (Leipzig, 1855), vol. 2, pp. 235–293.

37. O.F. Scheuer, *Burschenschaft und Judenfrage* (Berlin, 1927), p. 9.

38. Ibid., p. 6. The students at Jena demanded the exclusion of Jews probably after the Wartburg festival, under the influence of the "black ones" from Giessen (H. Haupt, *Die Jenaische Burschenschaft*, p. 42).

39. Scheuer, *Burschenschaft*, p. 14.

40. E. Müsebeck, *Arndts Stellung zu den Reformen des studentischen Lebens* (Munich, 1919), p. 17.

41. H. Leo, *Meine Jugendzeit* (Gotha, 1880), pp. 145–146, 166–167.

42. C. Brentano, *Der Philister* . . . , *Clemens Brentanos Werke* (ed., Preitz), vol. 3.

43. E.M. Arndt, "Noch etwas über die Juden," *Ein Blick aus der Zeit auf die Zeit* (1814), pp. 180–201.

44. A writer of National Socialist persuasion, K. Hildebrandt, regretted that Arndt did not display "unlimited hate against the Jew" ("E.M. Arndts Rassebegriff," in *Rasse*, 1938, p. 338); in 1815 Arndt believed that the German people could "absorb the relatively small number of Jews. But he definitely rejected any further admixture of Jewish blood." See also F. Hertz, "Das Problem des Nationalcharakters bei E.M. Arndt," in *Forschungen zur Völkerpsychologie und Soziologie* (Leipzig, 1927), vol. 3.

45. Arndt, *Ein Blick aus der Zeit,* pp. 180–201.

46. Ibid.

47. E.M. Arndt, *Erinnerungen aus meinem äusseren Leben* (Leipzig, 1840), pp. 129–130.

48. E.M. Arndt, *Ein Lebensbild in Briefen,* p. 124, July 8, 1815.

49. Ibid., p. 209, June 3, 1819.

50. Ibid., p. 449. See also Arndt's mention of the Professor of History Georg Benjamin Mendelssohn of the University of Bonn, a grandson of Moses Mendelssohn. Arndt's private letters of the year 1818 also record long, difficult negotiations for the purpose of purchasing a "Jewish house" (pp. 172–174). In spite of many an aggravating moment Arndt did not make any anti-Semitic remarks.

51. E.M. Arndt, *Schriften für seine lieben Deutschen,* vol. 4, pp. 55f.

52. R. Huch, *Stein* (Vienna, 1925), pp. 130–131.

53. Arndt, *Erinnerungen* . . . , p. 11; also p. 39.

54. F. Meinecke, *Von Stein zu Bismarck,* pp. 5f.

55. F. Hertz, "Das Problem des Nationalcharakters . . ."; see No. 44.

56. Laag, *Die religiöse Entwicklung E.M. Arndts* (1926), pp. 44–63; see also W. Bülck, *Christentum und Deutschtum bei Arndt* . . . (Gütersloh, 1937).

57. E.M. Arndt, *Versuche in vergleichender Völkergeschichte* (Leipzig, 1844), p. 19.

58. E.M. Arndt, *Ein Lebensbild* . . . , p. 97.

59. K. Hildebrand, *Junges Deutschland* (1841), p. 338.

60. See Note 58.

61. Ibid.

62. P.R.E. Viereck, *Metapolitics: From the Romantics to Hitler* (New York, 1941), p. 87: "The nationalism of Jahn's movement was partly—and only partly—linked with anti-Semitism. Occasionally tolerant, Jahn vented at other times the coarsest sort of fury upon all Jewry." E. Neuendorff, *Turnvater Jahn* (Jena, 1928), pp. 25, 86, and K. Bungardt, *Jahn als Begründer einer völkisch-politischen Erziehung* (Würzburg, 1938), on the other hand, show by implication that the Jewish question played a very minor role in the totality of his political thinking.

63. Scheuer, *Burschenschaft und Judenfrage,* p. 9.

64. F.L. Jahn, *Kleine Schriften* (Leipzig, 1906), p. 26.

Chapter Seven

1. H. Heine, "Gedanken und Einfälle," *Heines Sämtliche Werke,* ed. Ortmann, vol. 12, p. 8.

2. J. and W. Grimm, "Der Jude im Dorn," *Kinder- und Hausmärchen* (Stuttgart, 1912), no. 110; see also J. Bolte and G. Policka, *Anmerkungen zu den Kinder- und Hausmärchen der Brüder Grimm* (Leipzig, 1915), vol. 2, p. 490.

3. A. Arnim and C. Brentano, *Des Knaben Wunderhorn* (Berlin, 1909); see also "Das neue Jerusalem," "David," and "Die Judentochter."

4. *W. und C. v. Humboldt in ihren Briefen*, vol. 4, April 30, 1816.

5. *Die Mutter der Makkabäer* (last scene), *Dramen von Z. Werner* (Leipzig, 1936).

6. H. Zschokke, *Selbstschau* (Aarau, 1842), p. 135.

7. A. Müller, *Die Elemente der Staatskunst*, ed. Baxa (Berlin, 1809), Lecture 11.

8. L. Tieck, *Erinnerungen aus dem Leben des Dichters*, ed. Koepke, (Leipzig, 1855), vol. 2, p. 245.

9. F. Schleiermacher, *Über die Religion, Gesammelte Werke* (1843), vol. 1, pp. 421–424.

10. F. Schleiermacher, *Aphorismen zur Kirchengeschichte, Gesammelte Werke*, vol. 11, p. 48, also p. 633.

11. W. v. Humboldt, *Politische Denkschriften, Gesammelte Werke*, ed. Gebhardt (Berlin, 1903), vol. 10; also Freund, *Die Emanzipation*, vol. 2, pp. 269–291.

12. The Nazi historian W. Grau was not quite satisfied with the type of opposition to the Jews which German Romanticism exhibited (*Die Judenfrage in der deutschen Geschichte*, Leipzig, 1937, p. 24): "The Romantic thinking on the Jews was as such deeper than that of the enlightened Dohm and of the liberal Humboldt, yet still more unfortunate. . . . Through the conception of the Christian state one thought to keep away the Jew as Jew from the German people, only to win him as a Christian for the German folkdom."

13. A. Arnim, *Halle und Jerusalem, Sämtliche Werke*, ed. Grimm (Berlin, 1857), vol. 16.

14. F. Rühs, *Über die Ansprüche der Juden* . . . (Berlin, 1815), pp. 35–36.

15. Cited by W. Roscher, *Geschichte der Nationalökonomie in Deutschland* (Munich, 1874), p. 770; see also F. Schnabel, *Deutsche Geschichte im 19. Jahrhundert* (Freiburg, 1929), vol. 1, p. 471.

16. Quoted by H. Grätz, *Volkstümliche Geschichte der Juden* (Leipzig, 1923), vol. 3, pp. 568–569.

17. Quoted by Roscher, *Geschichte*, pp. 923–924.

18. *Tagebücher, Aus dem Nachlasse Varnhagens von Ense*, vol. 3, p. 92; and vol. 1, pp. 44–45.

19. *Aus dem Nachlasse Varnhagens . . . Briefwechsel zwischen Varnhagen und Rahel* (Leipzig, 1875), vol. 2, p. 38 (January 18, 1810); vol. 2, p. 97 (November 1, 1810); vol. 3, p. 5 (March 13, 1813).

20. Fontane, *Aus dem Nachlass*, "Die Märker und das Berlinertum," vol. 3, pp. 295–313, especially pp. 306–307.

21. B. Brentano, *Die Günderode* (Grünberg, 1840), vol. 2, pp. 207–213.

22. Quoted by J. Fürst, *Henriette Herz: Ihr Leben und ihre Erinnerungen* (Berlin, 1858), pp. 167–169.

23. *Aus Schleiermachers Leben in Briefen*, vol. 1, p. 194.

24. Ibid., vol. 1, p. 194, October 15, 1798.

25. Ibid., vol. 1, pp. 207–208, March 23, 1799.

26. Ibid.

27. F. Schleiermacher, *Briefe bei Gelegenheit der politisch-theologischen Aufgabe und des Sendschreiben jüdischer Hausväter. Von einem Prediger ausserhalb Berlins, Gesammelte Werke* (Berlin, 1846), vol. 5, pp. 1–39.

28. W. v. Humboldt, *Politische Denkschriften, Gesammelte Werke,* vol. 10, pp. 97–115.

29. Schleiermacher, *Über Religion, Gesammelte Werke,* vol. 1, pp. 421–424.

30. Friedländer, *Sendschreiben* . . . (Berlin, 1799).

31. *Beantwortung des Sendschreibens* . . . *an mich, den Probst Teller* (Berlin, 1799). Teller expressed the "heartfelt wish" that "through our printed correspondence there may blossom forth the recognition of the equal and basic human dignity of your brethren."

32. F. Schleiermacher, *Briefe bei Gelegenheit.* . . .

33. Jewish historians have offered a varied assessment of Schleiermacher's attitude to Jews and Judaism. L. Geiger in *Geschichte der Juden in Berlin,* p. 121, held Schleiermacher's attitude to the Jews not an unfriendly one, but remarked about his *Briefe bei Gelegenheit* . . . : "The tone is not that of a reply to men of equal standing." H. Grätz in *Volkstümliche Geschichte der Juden* (1923), vol. 3, p. 518, called Schleiermacher a "deeper character," but one who "overestimated" Christianity as compared with Judaism. Grätz definitely erred when he placed him into the same category with Fichte in 1793, during the latter's anti-Semitic outbursts. S.M. Dubnow in *Neueste Geschichte des jüdischen Volkes* (1920), vol. 1, pp. 203–204, apparently followed Grätz in his comparison of Schleiermacher's "anti-Semitism" with that of Fichte.

34. F. Schlegel, *Lessings Geist aus seinen Schriften* (Leipzig, 1810), vol. 3, pp. 16 and 153.

35. F. Schlegel, *Geschichte der alten und der neuen Literatur, Sämtliche Werke* (Leipzig, 1822), vol. 1, pp. 142–174, especially 145–151.

36. J. Bleyer, "Bemerkungen über die Frankfurter Angelegenheiten," *Friedrich Schlegel am Bundestage in Frankfurt* (Munich, 1913), pp. 139–144.

37. J. Körner, ed., *Briefe von und an Friedrich und Dorothea Schlegel* (Berlin, 1926), pp. 207 and 538. In a letter of April 22, 1816, Schlegel wrote from Frankfurt to Sulpiz Boisserée: "On the 12th Prof. Welcker from Giessen took along with him the copies of the work 'The Civil Rights of the Israelites for Thibaud, etc.' " (p. 207). The editor, Körner, commented that it probably was "a more recent writing whose author or editor may have been F. Schlegel," and stressed in this connection Schlegel's interest in the emancipation endeavors of Frankfurt's Jewry. In a postscript to a letter by Dorothea to Melchior Boisserée of May 1816, Schlegel requested a reply to "my very urgent[!] inquiry whether the package addressed to Sulpiz and taken from here by Prof. Welcker from Giessen on April 12—which contained several copies of the memoir in behalf of the Israelites of Frankfurt for Thibaud etc.—had duly arrived" (p. 538).

38. *Novalis's Werke,* ed. Scholz (Stuttgart, 1924), vol. 1, p. 350.

39. Ibid., vol. 1, p. 76; also pp. 345–346, 393. In his work *Die Christenheit oder Europa,* which contains the political pronunciamento of Romanticism, Novalis did not specifically mention the Jews. Whether, in accordance with the spirit and ideas of his book, the Jews were to become free citizens of this unified Christian Europe is uncertain. See also Novalis, *Gesammelte Werke,* ed. Seelig, vol. 4, p. 224: Judaism, it is said here, "is diametrically opposite to Christianity." Yet it is evident from the context that what Novalis calls "Judaism" is in some measure the basis of all theologies. We were, he continued, "in a way still in the Old Testament. The New Testament is to us still a book with seven seals."

40. A. W. Schlegel, "Die Warnung," *Sämtliche Werke* (Leipzig, 1847), vol. 1, pp. 223–228.

41. W. Zirus, *Ahasverus, der ewige Jude* (Berlin, 1930), remarked that German Romanticism was the first to take "loving care" of Ahasver; see also the favorable presentation of Ahasver by Achim von Arnim in *Halle und Jerusalem,* otherwise a sharp opponent of the Jews.

Chapter Eight

1. E. Plitt, ed., *Schelling: Leben in Briefen* (Leipzig, 1870), vol. 1, p. 22.

2. Ibid., p. 26.

3. Ibid., p. 30.

4. Ibid., p. 202.

5. Ibid., p. 317.

6. E.K. Dühring, *Die Judenfrage,* pp. 52–53.

7. L. Trost and F. Leist, eds., *König Maximilians II von Bayern und Schellings Briefwechsel* (Stuttgart, 1890), p. 160, November 13, 1848.

8. Plitt, ed., *Schellings Leben,* vol. 1, p. 215, February 12, 1849.

9. Ibid., vol. 1, pp. 244–245, March 8, 1853.

10. R. Koepke, ed., *Ludwig Tieck: Erinnerungen aus dem Leben des Dichters nach dessen . . . Mitteilungen* (Leipzig, 1855), vol. 2, p. 245; for Tieck, however, as an admirer of Rahel Levin, see *Aus dem Nachlasse Varnhagens von Ense: Briefe von Chamisso, Gneisenau, . . . L. Tieck* (Leipzig, 1871), vol. 1, pp. 239f.

11. R. Koepke, ed., *Ludwig Tieck: Erinnerungen,* vol. 2, p. 123.

12. B. Brentano, *Goethes Briefwechsel . . . ,* p. 111, January 2, 1808; pp. 123–124, April 3, 1808.

13. B. Brentano, *Goethes Briefwechsel mit einem Kinde* (Berlin, 1881), p. 125. On the whole this work cannot be considered a truly reliable account as far as Goethe's and Bettina's personal relations were concerned (see K.H. Strobl, *Bettina von Arnim,* Leipzig, 1926, pp. 113–116). Yet there is no reason for assuming that Bettina's views on Jews and Judaism are not those

which she presented here. Also, Goethe's views on the Jews, as pictured by Bettina, are virtually identical with his opinions about them in other contexts (see also the noted Goethe expert L. Geiger, *Die Juden und die deutsche Literatur*).

14. Ibid., p. 122, March 30, 1808. Varnhagen v. Ense, *Vermischte Schriften* (Leipzig, 1875), vol. 2, p. 112, maintained that Bettina, a daughter of Frankfurt a.M., had grown up there hating the Jews. Whatever her earliest sentiments in regard to them may have been, Bettina was considered by all to be an ardent advocate for and friend of the Jews. She appears as such also in her relationship with Goethe. Even the anti-Semitic writer K. Krüger, *Berliner Romantik und Berliner Judentum* (Bonn, 1939), in the end admitted that no trace of anti-Semitism could be found in her works.

15. Brentano, *Goethes Briefwechsel*, pp. 129–130.

16. B. Brentano, *Die Günderode* (Grünberg, 1840), vol. 2, pp. 207–213.

17. Ibid., vol. 2, p. 236.

18. Ibid., vol. 2, p. 87; see also *Goethes Briefwechsel*, p. 110, November 17, 1807: "The new schools don't interest me as much as the Jewish Institute which I often visit." Her interest in Jewish children appears also in *Gespräche mit Dämonen, Sämtliche Schriften* (Berlin, 1853). She commiserated with the poor Jewish children who, in the narrow Jewish quarters, had hardly enough air to breathe.

19. *Aus dem Nachlasse Varnhagens von Ense. Briefe an Stägemann*, pp. 345–346, September 10, 1840.

20. A. Bartels, *Kritiker und Kritikaster* (Leipzig, 1903), p. 113. Before Bartels, H.S. Chamberlain in *Goethe* (1912) had already vilified the Brentanos, "the forerunners of Jewish decadence" (p. 20, also p. 691).

21. *Der Philister . . . , Clemens Brentanos Werke*, ed. Preitz, vol. 3, pp. 271–318.

22. Ibid. Still, ancient Judaism was already ossified.

23. Ibid.

24. Brentano fell short of being a man of heroic proportions. In the fall of 1811 Varnhagen wrote to Dorothea Schlegel about Clemens (*Briefe von und an Friedrich und Dorothea Schlegel*, pp. 138–139): "How many, many blows he would already have received, if his complete cowardice had not disarmed every anger."

25. R. Huch, *Die Romantik: Ausbreitung, Blütezeit und Verfall*, 1951, p. 620.

26. K. Krüger, *Berliner Romantik und Berliner Judentum*, p. 94.

27. R. Steig, *Arnim* (Leipzig, 1911), vol. 1, p. 18.

28. According to Krüger, anti-Semitism was the cause of Clemens Brentano's withdrawal from Dorothea Schlegel and Rahel Levin. One could with equal justification take his numerous attempts to establish or resume relations with them, and the subsequent periods of closeness, as proof of his irrepressible urge for companionship and friendship with Jews.

29. *Aus dem Nachlasse Varnhagens von Ense: Biographische Portraits* (Leipzig, 1871), p. 63; see "Clemens Brentano," pp. 59–117.

30. Krüger, *Berliner Romantik*, p. 101.

31. *Aus dem Nachlasse. Biographische Portraits*, p. 110, August 14, 1813.

32. *Aus dem Nachlasse Varnhagens: Briefwechsel zwischen Varnhagen und Rahel*, vol. 2, p. 236, February 1, 1812.

33. Krüger, *Romantik*, pp. 81f., June 1813; pp. 95, 98, August 9, 1813.

34. *Brentanos Gesammelte Werke*, ed. Schüddekopf, vol. 9, pp. 416–417.

35. Krüger, *Romantik*, p. 116.

36. R. Steig, *Kleists Berliner Kämpfe* (1901), p. 630.

37. Krüger, *Romantik*, p. 116. See also Diehl and W.S.J. Kreiten, *Clemens Brentano* (Freiburg i.B., 1878, laudatory). Brentano himself spoke of his "very intimate relationship" with Philipp Veit (vol. 2, p. 421). According to the authors, Brentano's earlier differences with Dorothea in Frankfurt were long forgotten. "God had shown both mercy and had led them to the same altar and cross" (vol. 2, p. 436).

38. *Blätter aus dem Tagebuch einer Ahnfrau, Gesammelte Schriften*, ed. Brentano (Frankfurt, 1852), vol. 4, pp. 99 and 121–123.

39. K. Varnhagen von Ense, "Achim von Arnim und Moritz Itzig," *Vermischte Schriften* (Leipzig, 1875), part 3, pp. 112–117. Regarding Arnim's hostility to the Jews he wrote: "Arnim had adopted anti-Semitism and expressed it in his way in odd jokes and often in crude mischief" (p. 112); see also R. Steig, *Arnim*, vol. 1, p. 53. K. Krüger, *Romantik*, asserted that Arnim, compared with his Romantic and anti-Semitic friends, had "been the most severe in his rejection of Judaism." Yet even Arnim occasionally visited Jewish houses. In the social gatherings at Rahel's he met numerous Jews and also entertained relations with several Jewish publishers (p. 122).

40. Steig, *Arnim*, vol. 3, p. 611.

41. Ibid., vol. 3, p. 69.

42. Quoted by H. Uffo-Lenz, *Das Volkserlebnis bei . . . Arnim* (Berlin, 1938). Though the author acknowledged Arnim's "deep-seated anti-Semitism" (p. 94), which had emerged "more aggressively" during the War of Liberation, he, writing in 1938, did not approve of the limited anti-Semitism of the Romantic era: "The racial consciousness of the German people was at the time of Arnim hardly awakened" (p. 93). Arnim did "not really come to grips with the Jewish menace," Uffo-Lenz remarked in deep disappointment, adding: "Arnim was not a fighting character." This also became clear from his refusal to engage in a duel with the Jew Moritz Itzig, who challenged him, as recounted in the following (no. 43).

43. Varnhagen related the story of this quarrel in *Vermischte Schriften*, pp. 112–117, in a manner hardly flattering to Arnim. The anti-Semitic literary historian R. Steig rejected Varnhagen's account because of his friendship for the Jews (*Kleists Berliner Kämpfe*, pp. 632f., 635–636) and referred to another document, *Carl von Röder: Erinnerungen aus seinem Leben;* the latter, however, is hardly more favorable to Arnim. See also L. Geiger, *Frankfurter Zeitung*, February 8, 1893.

44. R. Huch, *Die Romantik: Ausbreitung, Blütezeit und Verfall* (Tübingen, 1951), p. 308.

45. Varnhagen made Arnim the same reproach (*Vermischte Schriften,* vol. 18, p. 116). This painful experience, Varnhagen remarked, had merely confirmed Arnim in the "bitterness of his anti-Semitism." According to Rahel, Alexander von der Marwitz, during the struggle between Arnim und Itzig, had expressed himself in favor of the latter. The incident had given Ludwig Robert, Rahel Levin's brother, the idea for a tragedy, *Die Macht der Verhältnisse,* wherein, however, the problem was dealt with in general terms. Arnim, Varnhagen conceded, did not have an ignoble nature. He blamed him, however, for his "lazy acceptance of traditional prejudices" (p. 117).

46. H. v. Kleist, *Gesammelte Werke,* eds. Minde-Pouet, Steig, and Schmidt (Leipzig), vol. 5, p. 196.

47. Ibid., vol. 5, pp. 399 and 432. For Madame Cohen's salons, see Varnhagen, *Denkwürdigkeiten,* vol. 2, pp. 73–79.

48. Kleist, *Gesammelte Werke,* vol. 5, p. 432, October 24, 1811.

49. H. Sembdner, *Die Berliner Abendblätter H. v. Kleists* (Berlin), p. 7.

50. Ibid.

51. *Kleists Werke,* ed. Siegen (Leipzig, 1914), vol. 1, p. 118. "The thoroughly honest Kleist," Siegen remarked, "had probably no idea how his patriotism was continually abused for the benefit of this predominantly noble Fronde"; see also H. Meyer-Benfey, *Kleists Leben und Werke* (Göttingen, 1911), p. 377: "At Rahel's he went in and out to the end—he apparently was not affected by the anti-Semitic tendency of the Table Company."

52. R. Steig (*Kleists Berliner Kämpfe,* p. 505) claimed to know that Kleist's poem "Der Weltlauf" "was aimed at Jewish usurers"! Just as baseless is Steig's assumption that the "Zuschrift eines Predigers an den Herausgeber der *Berliner Abendblätter*"—in which an innocent reference is made to a Jewish "collector" of the name of David—proved Kleist's anti-Semitism, (p. 517).

Actually, the *Berliner Abendblätter* appeared in the press of Hitzig, a converted Jew, who had guaranteed Kleist an annual salary of five hundred talers. Krüger (*Romantik*) was unable to reconcile Kleist's special friendship with Rahel and Hitzig with his simultaneous membership in the Table Company, and remained puzzled about his "strangely ambiguous attitude." Actually, membership in the Christian-German Table Company was hardly convincing evidence of unqualified anti-Semitism. Among other members of the fraternity were for instance the martial poet Stägemann, who was very friendly toward Jews, and the once bitterly anti-Semitic philosopher Fichte, who had radically changed his views on the Jews. A study by P. Eberhard, *Die politischen Anschauungen der christlich-deutschen Tischgesellschaft* (Erlangen, 1937), shows that anti-Semitism, while unquestionably alive among many members of the Table Company and in some cases taking on even virulent forms, was not generally shared.

53. H. v. Kleist, "Katechismus der Deutschen, "*Sämtliche Werke und Briefe,* ed. Sembdner, vol. 2, pp. 350–360.

54. Ibid.

55. H. Houben, "Bericht," Berliner Gesellschaft für deutsche Literatur, 1904.

56. Plan for "Zerstörung von Jerusalem," W. Herzog, *H. v. Kleist* (Munich, 1914), p. 616.

57. H. v. Kleist, "Appell an die Deutschen," in *Politische Schriften des Jahres 1809, Sämtliche Werke,* ed. Sembdner, vol. 2.

58. J. Baxa, *Adam Müller: Ein Lebensbild* . . . (Jena, 1930), p. 77.

59. Ibid., p. 78.

60. C. Schmitt, *Politische Romantik* (Munich, 1925), p. 66.

61. Krüger, *Romantik,* p. 88.

62. See Note 60.

63. R. Kohler, ed., *Adam Müller. Nachschriften zur Staatsphilosophie* (Munich, 1923), p. 63.

64. Ibid., p. 68.

65. A. Müller, *Die Elemente der Staatskunst* (Berlin, 1809), part 3, lecture 11; see also the edition by Baxa (1922), vol. 1, pp. 215f., vol. 2, pp. 353f.

66. Müller, *Elemente,* vol. 2, p. 112; see also for the following.

67. Varnhagen had hinted at Müller's supposed neglect of duty while consul in Leipzig (*Galerie von Bildnissen aus Rahels Umgebung* . . . , vol. 2, p. 147; see also "Adam Müller," *Vermischte Schriften,* vol. 2, pp. 68–75).

68. Krüger found in the Varnhagen collection an essay by A. Müller with an unquestionably anti-Jewish tendency. It had been published in the *Allgemeine Zeitung* (no. 69, June 11, 1816).

69. *Deutsche Staatsanzeigen,* Leipzig, 1816, vol. 1, p. 297.

70. Letter to Metternich, dated December 12, 1815, in Stern, *Abhandlungen,* p. 21.

71. Müller, *Elemente,* pp. 21f. L. Sauzin (*Adam Heinrich Müller: Sa vie et son oeuvre,* p. 554) referred to the inconsistencies in Adam Müller's attitude to the Jews: "Anti-Semitism is somewhat surprising if one considers that the *Abendblätter* came from Hitzig's press and that Müller in *Pallas* and in the *Elements* had praised the Jewish people as a model of an organic nation."

72. Ibid.

73. Savigny's review of D.B.W. Pfeiffer's *Ideas about a New Civil Legislation for German States* (Göttingen, 1815) in F.C. von Savigny, *Vom Beruf unserer Zeit für Gesetzgebung und Rechtswissenschaft* (Heidelberg, 1843), pp. 172–178.

74. A. Dove, "L. v. Ranke," *Allgemeine Deutsche Biographie,* vol. 27.

75. E. Fueter, *Geschichte der neueren Historiographie* (Munich, 1911), p. 292.

76. E. Schulin, *Die weltgeschichtliche Erfassung des Orients bei Hegel und Ranke* (Göttingen, 1858), p. 174.

77. Ibid.

78. L. v. Ranke, *Neue Briefe* (1838), p. 255.

79. L. v. Ranke, *Päpste,* pp. 373f., quoted by Schulin, *Erfassung,* p. 177.

80. L. v. Ranke, *Weltgeschichte*, vol. 1, pp. 42–43.

81. Ibid., p. 76.

82. Ranke, *Weltgeschichte, Biographie*, p. 419, April 30, 1828.

Chapter Nine

1. C. Brentano, *Victoria und ihre Geschwister, Gesammelte Schriften* (Frankfurt, 1852), vol. 7, p. 279.

2. R. Arnold, *Das deutsche Drama* (Munich, 1925), pp. 518f.

3. "Gockel und Hinkel," *Brentanos Gesammelte Werke*, ed. Schüddekopf, vol. 12; "Das Märchen vom Schneider Siebentot auf einen Schlag," *Gesammelte Werke*, vol. 11. See also Glockner, *Brentano als Märchenerzähler*.

4. "Gockel und Hinkel" in *Deutsche Literatur*, ed. Kluckhohn, pp. 88, 131.

5. *Romanzen vom Rosenkranz, Gesammelte Werke*, vol. 4, p. 28.

6. A. v. Arnim, *Halle und Jerusalem, Sämtliche Werke*, ed. Grimm, vol. 16.

7. The contemporary critic F. Schlegel read this drama of Arnim with "regret": "One should let such fungi die by themselves" (R. Arnold, *Das deutsche Drama*, p. 518).

8. *Armut, Reichtum und Busse der Gräfin Dolores, Arnims Werke*, ed. Grimm (Berlin, 1840), vol. 7, pp. 326, 337.

9. *Isabella von Ägypten, Werke* (Berlin, 1839), vol. 1, pp. 101, 105, 125, 129, 150.

10. A.F. v. Droste-Hülschoff, *Die Judenbuche, Deutscher Novellenschatz* (Munich, 1871), vol. 24, pp. 51–128.

11. J.P. Hebel, "Die Juden," in *Vermischte Aufsätze, Sämtliche Werke* (Karlsruhe, 1834), vol. 8.

12. A human trait also characterizes stories of the *Schatzkästlein* (see the edition by H. Trog, *Schelmen-, Scherz- und Judengeschichten*, Zürich, 1925). In the Epilogue the editor asserts that Hebel did not feel "any prejudice or enmity" against the Jews and portrayed "their good sides and other ones" (p. 62). In some of the stories the Jew appears greedy and at times a cheater. But other people are hardly more favorably painted. Again in other stories, the Jew seems especially smart and pleasant, as in "Einträglicher Rätselhandel."

13. "Der grosse Sanhedrin zu Paris," *Schatzkästlein* . . . , ed. Behagel, *Kürschners Deutsche Nationalliteratur*, vol. 142, pp. 93–94, No. 50.

14. D. Grabbe, *Napoleon oder die hundert Tage* (Frankfurt a.M., 1831). In the comedy *Scherz, Satire, Ironie* . . . , Grabbe spoke deprecatingly of "Jewish youths" whose "education consists of eating pork." They "pose as critical judges and not only raise peddlers of cheap things to the stars, but even injure honest men with their praises." Grabbe, admittedly, ridiculed not

only the Jewish critic. The literary historian Biese remarked, "In order to mock everything, the author introduces into this piece the devil, his grandmother, even himself, nothing . . . remains unharmed," *Deutsche Literaturgeschichte* (Munich, 1930), vol. 3, p. 22.

15. W. Hauff, *Mitteilungen des Satan* (see "Mein Besuch in Frankfurt"), *Kürschners Deutsche Nationalliteratur*, vol. 157, pp. 146f., 160.

16. W. Hauff, "Jud Süss," *Sämtliche Werke* (Stuttgart, n.d.), vol. 1, pp. 167–224, esp. p. 224.

17. A. Chamisso, *Peter Schlemihls wundersame Geschichte, Sämtliche Werke*, ed. Gottschall (Berlin, n.d.), vol. 1, pp. 413–465.

18. In the poem "Die Sonne bringt es an den Tag" a murder committed against an old Jew is unearthed twenty years later and the murderer suffers punishment. The poem "Baal Teschuba" focuses on the story of a sinner, ibid., vol. 1, pp. 162, 310; see also vol. 1, p. 60.

19. A. Chamisso, "Der neue Ahasverus," *Sämtliche Werke*, vol. 1, p. 150.

20. A. Chamisso, "Abba Glosk Leczeka," *Werke*, vol. 1, p. 202.

21. A. Platen-Hallermünde, *Der romantische Ödipus, Gesammelte Werke* (Stuttgart, 1848), vol. 4, pp. 91–191.

22. Ibid., "Nathan," *Epigramme*, vol. 2, p. 198.

23. Ibid., "Auf Golgatha," vol. 1, pp. 211–215.

24. F. Rückert, "Der nächtliche Gang."

25. "Vom Bäumlein, das andere Blätter hat gewollt," *Rückerts Werke*, ed. Laistner, vol. 2, p. 165; the anti-Semitic claim concerning this poem is asserted by W. Stapel, *Literatenwäsche* (Berlin, 1930).

26. F. Rückert, "Lessing," *Werke*, vol. 1, p. 177.

27. F. Rückert, "Bekehrungseifer," ibid., vol. 1, pp. 138–139.

28. *Die Epigonen*, in *K. Immermanns Gesammelte Werke*, ed. Maync (Leipzig, 1936), vol. 3, pp. 384–392; see also 422, vol. 4, pp. 60–62.

29. Ibid., vol. 2, pp. 349–356.

30. Ibid., vol. 3, p. 369.

31. See several references to Jews and Judaism in Immermann's *Münchhausen, Gesammelte Werke*, vol. 1, pp. 31–32.

Chapter Ten

1. A. Příbram, *Urkunden und Akten zur Geschichte der Juden in Wien* (Vienna, 1918), vol. 1, pp. cxxix–cxxxi.

2. Ibid., Resolution, January 22, 1820.

3. F. Hebbel, "Der Jude an den Christen," *Sämtliche Werke*, ed. Stern (Leipzig, 1898), vol. 7, p. 45.

4. E.C. Corti, *Der Aufstieg des Hauses Rothschild*, vol. 1, p. 421.

5. C.L.W. Metternich, "Über die Judenfrage in Österreich," *Nachgelassene Schriften* (1880–1884), vol. 3, pp. 181–182.

6. E.C. Corti, *The Reign of the House of Rothschild* (New York, 1928), vol. 1, p. 20.

7. Metternich, *Nachgelassene Schriften,* vol. 6, pp. 92, 491.

8. Ibid., vol. 6, Melanie Metternich, Diary, July 10, 1843.

9. Corti, *Rothschild,* pp. 243–247.

10. Ibid., pp. 46–49.

11. G. Brandes, "Börne," *Hauptströmungen der Literatur des neunzehnten Jahrhunderts* (Leipzig, 1898), vol. 6, p. 65.

12. Metternich, *Nachgelassene Schriften,* vol. 6, Melanie Metternich, Diary, January 26, 1838.

13. Ibid., Metternich to Apponyi, vol. 5, February 13, 1834.

14. Ibid.

15. *Briefe von und an Brinkmann,* p. 218, also pp. 97–99.

16. Ibid., September 19, 1804.

17. Corti, *Rothschild,* vol. 1, p. 218; on Gentz's relations with the Rothschilds, see also Varnhagen, *Denkwürdigkeiten,* vol. 5, p. 350.

18. Corti, *Rothschild,* vol. 1, pp. 222–223.

19. Ibid., pp. 223f.

20. Ibid., pp. 362–366.

21. Quoted by L. Geiger, *Das junge Deutschland* (Berlin, 1907), p. 195; also E. Guglia, *Friedrich von Gentz* (Vienna, 1901), p. 35.

22. *Lenaus Werke* (Berlin), eds. Blödau and Hempel, vol. 1, pp. 63, 159.

23. N. Lenau, "Der arme Jude," *Werke,* vol. 1, p. 257.

24. "Der Rothschildsbronnen," *Lyrische Nachlese,* vol. 2, p. 393.

25. "Der arme Jude"; the poor Jew emphatically rejects baptism. Lying near a cross, he freezes to death in the bitter winter cold.

26. N. Lenau, *Werke, Faust (Waldgespräch),* vol. 2, pp. 76–79.

27. Ibid., *Savonarola (Tubal),* vol. 2, pp. 151–157.

28. A. Grün, *Schutt (Fünf Ostern), Gesammelte Werke* (Berlin, 1902), ed. Frankl, vol. 3, pp. 125f.

29. See Grün, ibid., "Sein Bild" (Joseph II), vol. 2, pp. 369–370.

30. *Grillparzers Sämtliche Werke* (Leipzig, 1903), ed. Necker, vol. 12, p. 104, also vol. 14, p. 33.

31. About Grillparzer and the Jews see Frankl, *Zur Biographie Franz Grillparzers;* according to the Jewish author, who was a friend of Grillparzer, the latter knew both the vices and virtues of the Jews (p. 10). S. Lublinsky (*Jüdische Charaktere bei Grillparzer, Hebbel und Ludwig*) actually did not come to grips with the question of the attitude to the Jews of either Grillparzer or the other playwrights.

32. *Grillparzers Werke,* ed. Necker, vol. 2, p. 236.

33. Ibid., vol. 2, p. 237.

34. Ibid., vol. 2, p. 226.

35. Ibid., "Xenien," vol. 2, p. 127.

36. "Des Kaisers Bildsäule," *Gedichte,* vol. 1, pp. 152–153.

37. Ibid., "Sprüche," vol. 2, p. 228.

38. "Die Jahrhunderte der Kreuzzüge," *Historische und politische Studien,* ibid., vol. 14, pp. 40–42.

39. *Comedias de Lope de Vega, Studien zum spanischen Theater,* ibid., vol. 13, p. 105.

40. Ibid., *Tagebuch auf der Reise nach Deutschland,* vol. 16, p. 175.

41. Ibid., vol. 16, p. 180.

42. Ibid., p. 178.

43. Ibid., *Tagebuch auf der Reise nach Frankreich und England,* vol. 16, p. 214.

44. Ibid., *Selbstbiographie,* vol. 12, p. 130; see also *Tagebuch . . . Frankreich,* vol. 16, p. 242.

45. Ibid., *Studien zur deutschen Literatur,* vol. 14, pp. 94f.

46. Ibid., *Selbstbiographie,* vol. 12, p. 140; see also *Tagebuch . . . Frankreich,* vol. 16, pp. 219, 237.

47. Ibid., *Die Jüdin von Toledo* (Act 1), vol. 7, p. 116.

48. Ibid. (Act 2), vol. 7, pp. 122–123.

49. Ibid. (Act 5), vol. 7, p. 165.

50. "La hermosa Ester," in *Dramaturgische Dichtungen, Studien zum spanischen Theater,* vol. 13, p. 33.

51. Ibid., *Comedias de Lope de Vega, Studien zum spanischen Theater,* vol. 13, p. 105.

52. Ibid., *Aus einem unvollendeten Drama Esther,* vol. 8, pp. 10–42. Grillparzer appears to have begun working on Esther in 1829.

53. Letter to Frau Auguste v. Littrow-Bischoff of May 1868, quoted in ibid., vol. 8, pp. 6–7.

54. Letter to Kuh, December 18, 1856, *Hebbels Sämtliche Briefe* (Berlin, 1919), ed. Werner, vol. 5, p. 353. For Hebbel's relations with Börne, see E. Kuh, *Biographie Hebbels* (Vienna, 1877), vol. 1, pp. 422–472 and vol. 2, p. 432; for his correspondence with S. Engländer, J. Glaser, and E. Kulka, see *Hebbels Briefwechsel mit Freunden,* ed. Bamberg. For Hebbel's attitude toward the Jews, see A. Biach, *Hebbel und die Juden* (Brüx, 1897), and E. Kulka, *Erinnerungen an Friedrich Hebbel* (1878), especially p. 16 and pp. 60–69.

55. Hebbel, *Briefe,* vol. 4, pp. 52–53, September 1, 1847.

56. "Der Jude an den Christen," *Hebbels Sämtliche Werke,* ed. Stern (Leipzig, 1898), vol. 7, p. 45.

57. Hebbel, *Werke,* ed. Werner, vol. 14, p. 334 (December 13, 1843), *Tagebücher,* ed. Bamberg.

58. Ibid., vol. 14, p. 250 (May 20, 1843).

59. *Augsburger Allgemeine Zeitung,* August 7, 1848. The anti-Semitic literary historian Bartels (*Einführung in das deutsche Schrifttum,* 1933) praised Hebbel for his political reports to the *Augsburger Allgemeine Zeitung.* They were of "historic significance" and showed allegedly his "very sound German nationalist views." Bartels was obviously unaware of Hebbel's foregoing pro-Jewish article for that paper. See also Bartels, *Hebbel und die Juden. Das literarische Judentum seiner Zeit* (1922).

60. Hebbel, *Werke,* ed. Werner, vol. 12.

61. Hebbel, *Sämtliche Werke,* ed. Stern, *Tagebücher,* vol. 11, p. 127, January 10, 1852.

62. *Hebbels Briefwechsel mit Freunden* (Berlin, 1892), vol. 2, pp. 116–117, December 18, 1856.

63. Hebbel, *Werke,* ed. Stern, *Tagebücher,* vol. 11, p. 127, January 10, 1852.

64. A. Bartels, *Hebbel und die Juden* (Munich, 1922), p. 32. In spite of Hebbel's close relations with Jews, Bartels claimed the playwright "deep in his heart remained alien" to the Jews, even hostile. The few critical utterances by Hebbel must of course be juxtaposed with as many, if not even more, critical remarks by Hebbel on other peoples, including the Germans.

65. *Hebbels Briefwechsel* . . . , vol. 2, pp. 116–117.

66. Hebbel, *Briefe,* ed. Werner, vol. 1, p. 137, December 19, 1836.

67. See Note 65, vol. 1, pp. 168–169; see also the letters to E. Lensing, October 3 and 22, 1843.

68. Ibid., *Buch der Lieder von Heine, Kritische Schriften,* vol. 10, pp. 43–45; also vol. 11, p. 55.

69. Hebbel, *Werke,* ed. Stern, *Genoveva* (2nd act, 5th scene), vol. 1, p. 95.

70. Ibid., vol. 1, p. 94.

71. *Hebbels Briefwechsel mit Freunden* . . . , letter to Dingelstedt, September 2, 1851, vol. 2, p. 15.

72. Hebbel, *Werke,* ed. Werner, *Ein Steinwurf* . . . , vol. 3, pp. 345f., also pp. 376–377.

73. See Note 72.

Chapter Eleven

1. "Börnes Leben," *Gutzkows Werke* (1872), vol. 12, p. 236.

2. C. Schlosser, *Weltgeschichte für das deutsche Volk,* vol. 16, p. 20; in vol. 1, however, he held that the Jews were the most important people of the Orient.

3. A. Grün, *Schutt, Gesammelte Werke* (Berlin), vol. 3, pp. 125f.

4. "Der Rothschildsbronnen," *Lenaus Werke,* eds. Hempel and Bloedau (Berlin), vol. 2, p. 393.

5. *Münchhausen, Immermanns Gesammelte Werke* (Leipzig, 1936), vol. 1. pp. 31–32; also Gutzkow, "Rothschild," *Gesammelte Werke,* vol. 2, pp. 170–191.

6. F. Dingelstedt, *Lieder eines kosmopolitischen Nachtwächters. Sämtliche Werke,* vol. 8, pp. 49–57.

7. H. v. Fallersleben, "An Israel," *Unpolitische Lieder, Gesammelte Werke* (Berlin, 1893), vol. 4, pp. 207–208.

8. G. Büchner, "Wozzeck," *Gesammelte Werke* (Zürich, 1944).

9. W. Hauff, *Mitteilungen aus den Memoiren des Satan, Kürschners Deutsche Nationalliteratur,* vol. 15, pp. 146, 160.

10. Grün, *Schutt.*

11. K. Beck, "Der Trödeljude," *Lieder vom armen Mann* (Prague, 1846), pp. 51–61.

12. E. Beurmann, *Frankfurter Bilder* (Mainz, 1835).

13. The letter is cited by L. Geiger, *Das junge Deutschland* (Berlin, 1907), p. 187.

14. Quoted by H. Houben, *Gutzkowfunde* (Berlin, 1901), p. 195.

15. *Jeune Allemagne,* p. 12.

16. Quoted by Houben, *Gutzkowfunde,* p. 199.

17. T. Mundt, *Madonna, Unterhaltungen mit einer Heiligen* (Leipzig, 1835), pp. 152–153; see also "Rahel und ihre Zeit," *Charaktere und Situationen* (Weimar, 1837), part 1, pp. 213–272.

18. A. v. Württemberg, "Ahasver und Bonaparte," *Sämtliche Gedichte* (Stuttgart), pp. 216–260, also p. 7.

19. *Jeune Allemagne,* p. 27.

20. Cited by Houben, *Gutzkowfunde,* p. 266.

21. Mundt, *Madonna,* pp. 152–153.

22. K. Gutzkow, *Börne, Gesammelte Werke* (1845), vol. 6, pp. 36–37.

23. Hauff, *Mitteilungen,* p. 146.

24. See Note 21.

25. W. Müller, "Der ewige Jude," *Gedichte* (Halle an der Saale, n.d.), pp. 51–52.

26. *Rückblicke auf mein Leben, Gutzkows Werke,* ed. Müller, vol. 4, pp. 89–90.

27. Mundt, *Madonna,* p. 158.

28. E. Sterling, *Der Judenhass* (Frankfurt, 1969), pp. 152–153.

Chapter Twelve

1. *G. Riessers Gesammelte Schriften* (Frankfurt a.M.), vol. 4, p. 114.

2. Quoted by Houben, "Karl Gutzkow und das Judentum," *Gutzkowfunde,* p. 195.

3. *Literaturblatt,* 1833, no. 4, p. 102, nos. 120 and 121.

4. Ibid.

5. Ibid., 1837, no. 112.

6. Quoted by Houben, *Gutzkowfunde,* p. 119, April 30, 1837; see also *G. Riessers Gesammelte Werke,* vol. 1, pp. 237 and 129.

7. G. Riesser, *Jüdische Briefe zur Abwehr und zur Verständigung, Gesammelte Schriften,* vol. 4, p. 58.

8. *Literaturblatt,* October 26, 1835, no. 110, "Unmoralische Literatur."

9. Houben, *Gutzkowfunde*, p. 172.

10. *Literaturblatt*, October 26, 1835.

11. The noted Jewish author Berthold Auerbach remarked in a letter to Riesser that Menzel "always fought valiantly for the cause of the Jews, though many almost incomprehensible . . . inconsequences occurred thereby" (Houben, *Gutzkowfunde*, pp. 165f.). Similarly J. Weil in his pamphlet *Das junge Deutschland und die Juden* (Frankfurt a.M., 1836), p. 5, while blaming Menzel for his anti-Semitic attacks, contrasted them with his earlier, friendlier remarks about the Jews.

12. *Literaturblatt*, 1837, p. 93, "Schriften über Juden." Menzel also appears as a foe of the Jews in his *Geschichte der deutschen Literatur* (1836 edition, even more so in the edition of 1858–1859, vol. 3, p. 467). His point of view in the *Geschichte der letzten vierzig Jahre* (Stuttgart, 1859) is also anti-Semitic.

13. E. Schuppe, *Der Burschenschafter Wolfgang Menzel* (Frankfurt a.M., 1952), especially pp. 102–111.

14. Quoted by Houben, *Gutzkowfunde*, p. 161. This is an excellent monograph on Gutzkow's relation to Judaism by a noted German literary historian. Most of the articles in which Gutzkow discussed the Jewish question appeared during the years 1837–1843 in the *Telegraph für Deutschland*, which he edited first in Frankfurt and after 1838 in Hamburg. Almost none of these articles has been included in his *Gesammelte Werke*.

15. K. Immermann, *Münchhausen, Kürschners Deutsche Nationalliteratur*, vols. 159 and 160.

16. *Telegraph*, August 1838, nos. 124 and 128.

17. *Uriel Acosta, Gutzkows Werke* (Berlin, 1872), *Dramatische Werke*, vol. 2.

18. K. Gutzkow, *Rückblicke auf mein Leben* (Berlin, 1875), pp. 48–49.

19. K. Gutzkow, *Götter, Helden, Don Quixote* (Hamburg, 1838), pp. 19f.

20. *Börnes Leben, Gutzkows Werke*, vol. 12, pp. 205–431, especially pp. 232–236.

21. Ibid., p. 38.

22. K. Gutzkow, *Aus der Knabenzeit, Gesammelte Werke* (Frankfurt, 1845), vol. 1, p. 38.

23. Quoted by Houben, *Gutzkowfunde*, p. 236.

24. K. Gutzkow, "Religion und Christianity . . ." *Gesamtbild unseres Jahrhunderts, Säkularbilder, Gesammelte Werke*, p. 444.

25. *Telegraph*, March 8, 1841, no. 47.

26. Ibid., 134/8.

27. G. Riesser, *Jüdische Briefe* (1842), vol. 2, p. 108.

28. *Telegraph*, 1842, no. 4.

29. Ibid.

30. See Note 25.

31. However, in another passage quoted before, Gutzkow said, "Let them [the Jews] also become police officers, judges, ministers."

32. Houben noted in conclusion "that, in his later age, Gutzkow believed himself to be slighted, even persecuted by the Jews," yet Houben attributed this "merely to his mental condition which after 1865 produced numerous similar phenomena" (p. 280).

33. "Juden und Emanzipation," *Säkularbilder, Gesammelte Werke,* vol. 8, pp. 404–412.

34. H. Marggraf, *Deutschlands jüngste Literaturepoche* (Leipzig, 1839), pp. 215–264.

35. H. Laube, *Die Krieger, Das junge Europa* (Mannheim, 1837).

36. G. Kühne, "Moses Mendelssohn," *Gesammelte Schriften,* vol. 4.

37. Pückler-Muskau, *Tutti Frutti: Aus den Papieren eines Verstorbenen* (Stuttgart, 1834), vol. 1, pp. 221f.

38. F.C. Dahlmann, *Die Politik* (Leipzig, 1847), 1968 edition, pp. 302–303.

39. F.C. Dahlmann, *Kleine Schriften und Reden,* pp. 373–74. The latter statement is much more positive than preceding ones.

40. K. Rotteck, *Gesammelte und nachgelassene Schriften nebst Biographie und Briefwechsel* (Pforzheim, 1843), vol. 4, p. 350.

41. Ibid., vol. 4, p. 352; J. Weil, *Das junge Deutschland* . . . (Frankfurt a.M., 1836), p. 4, refers to Rotteck's unfavorable opinions about the Jews.

42. K.T. Welcker, *Die vollkommene und ganze Pressfreiheit* (Freiburg, 1830), p. 72. Bopp in the seventh volume of the *Staatslexikon,* edited by Rotteck and Welcker, concluded his article on "Judenschutz und Judenabgabe": "The history of the remaining European states is likewise a monument to the suppression of a homeless people, which was forced to submit to the often deceiving protection of alien peoples, counted among the most civilized ones. What morale of the great teacher History! One may also say of a people: Woe him who needs alien protection" (pp. 671–672).

Chapter Thirteen

1. E. Simon, *Jüdische Rundschau,* "Hegel und die Juden," November 13, 1931.

2. *Hegels theologische Jugendschriften,* ed. Nohl, pp. 153, 214–218, 258–260. See also Hegel, *Early Theological Writings,* trans. Knox, pp. 145–150, 177–179, 182–205. The young Hegel's views about Jews and Judaism apparently were especially influenced by Kant, whose opinions about Jewish religion were unfavorable. The Jews, Hegel wrote, were "overwhelmed by a burden of statutory commands" and showed "slavish obedience to laws" (Nohl, p. 153); see also Knox, p. vi.

3. Ibid.

4. *Hegels Werke, Vorlesungen über die Philosophie der Geschichte,* ed. Gans, vol. 9, pp. 201–204.

5. *Philosophie der Religion,* ibid., vol. 12a, pp. 69–72.

6. *Philosophie der Geschichte,* ibid., vol. 15.

7. *Vorlesungen über die Ästhetik,* ibid., vol. 10, pp. 368–411, especially pp. 369–371.

8. *Geschichte der Philosophie,* ibid., vol. 15, pp. 368–411.

9. Grillparzer, *Selbstbiographie, Sämtliche Werke,* ed. Necker, vol. 12, p. 112.

10. *Hegels Werke,* vol. 17, p. 535.

11. K. Rosenkranz, *Das Leben Hegels* (Berlin, 1844), p. 362.

12. *Grundlinien der Philosophie des Rechts, Hegels Werke,* ed. Gans, vol. 8, pp. 270, 338–339.

13. *Philosophie der Geschichte, Hegels Werke,* vol. 9, p. 397.

14. *Philosophie des Rechtes,* part 3, subsection 3, "Der Staat" (English version, transl. Knox, Oxford, 1942) p. 169.

15. L. Feuerbach, *Das Wesen des Christentums, Sämtliche Werke* (Leipzig, 1851), vol. 7, pp. 161–173, chaps. 12–13.

16. L. Feuerbach, *Vorlesungen über das Wesen der Religion, Sämtliche Werke,* vol. 8, pp. 9–10; see also on Spinoza, *Geschichte der neueren Philosophie, Sämtliche Werke,* vol. 4, pp. 298–392.

17. Ibid., vol. 8, p. 64.

18. Ibid., p. 171.

19. Ibid.

20. B. Bauer, *Die Judenfrage* (Braunschweig, 1843); N. Rotenstreich ("For and against Emancipation: The Bruno Bauer Controversy," *Leo Baeck Yearbook,* 1959, vol. 4) leans over backward in favor of Bauer.

21. F.W. Ghillany, *Das Judentum und die Kritik* (Nuremberg, 1844).

22. K. Grün, *Die Judenfrage: Gegen Bruno Bauer* (Darmstadt, 1844), pp. 61–66, 77–81, 96 and 121.

23. K. Marx, *Zur Judenfrage;* English version in *Karl Marx: Early Texts,* ed. McLellan (New York, 1971), especially pp. 110–114.

24. Ibid.

Chapter Fourteen

1. A. Kohut, *Alexander von Humboldt und das Judentum* (Leipzig, 1871), p. 65.

2. W. Freund, *Zur Judenfrage in Deutschland* (Breslau, 1844), p. 25, February 7, 1843.

3. Kohut, *Humboldt,* pp. 125–126.

4. Ibid., pp. 176–177, 99f.

5. A. Humboldt, *Kosmos* (Stuttgart, 1870), vol. 2, pp. 28–30.

6. Kohut, *Humboldt,* pp. 58–59.

7. Ibid., p. 60; in a letter to Varnhagen Humboldt spoke of the "shocking Jew-law" (*A. v. Humboldt in seinem Briefwechsel mit Varnhagen,* Leipzig, 1860, pp. 109f.).

8. Kohut, *Humboldt,* p. 125.

9. Ibid., p. 157.

10. F. Dingelstedt, *Lieder eines kosmopolitischen Nachtwächters, Sämtliche Werke* (Berlin, 1871), vol. 8, pp. 49–51.

11. "Nachtwächters Weltgang," "Zwei Gassen in Frankfurt," "Die Judengasse," "Goethe und Börne." T. Fritsch in his *Antisemitenkatechismus* suppressed the philo-Semitic lines in Dingelstedt's foregoing *Lieder*.

12. H. v. Fallersleben, "An Israel," *Unpolitische Lieder, Gesammelte Werke* (Berlin, 1893), vol. 4, pp. 207–208.

13. Fallersleben, "Israel," ibid., vol. 4, p. 47.

14. "Kreuzigung," *Freiligraths Werke* (Berlin, 1856), ed. Zaunert, vol. 1, pp. 194–196.

15. List, *Schriften, Reden, Briefe,* eds. Goeser and Sonntag (Berlin, 1932), 9 vols., vol. 8, pp. 451–453.

16. Ibid., p. 456.

17. Ibid., p. 448.

18. F. Schnabel, *Deutsche Geschichte im 19. Jahrhundert* (Freiburg, 1929), vol. 3, p. 351; List, Schnabel remarked, was "inclined to acknowledge to the producers a higher rank than to traders among whom he often observed the strong participation of Jewry with disgust." Schnabel adduced no source for his assertion and his observation must be qualified. As List wrote: "The national wealth is acquired mainly through manufacture and trade" (*Werke,* vol. 7, p. 379). The young List, though, was anti-Semitically inclined, as his diary of the year 1825 shows (*Werke,* vol. 8, pp. 32–33).

19. Ibid.

20. List, *Werke,* vol. 8, p. 598, November 7, 1841.

21. Ibid., vol. 8, p. 604, March 24, 1842.

22. F. List, *Das nationale System der politischen Ökonomie* (English version, Jena, 1904), p. 140, also p. 430.

23. O. Jöhlinger, *Bismarck und die Juden* (1921), p. 5.

24. *Preussische Versammlung,* 32d sitting, June 14 and 15, 1847.

25. Ibid., June 25, 1847.

26. E. Cohen, *Erinnerungen an Bismarck,* p. 326.

Chapter Fifteen

1. *Der Jude* (Altona), vol. 1, p. 100.

2. E.C. Corti, *Der Aufstieg des Hauses Rothschild,* vol. 1, p. 255.

3. F. Grillparzer, *Erinnerungen aus dem Jahre 1848, Werke,* ed. Necker, vol. 16, p. 328.

4. E.M. Arndt, *Ein Lebensbild in Briefen,* p. 450.

5. Treitschke, *Deutsche Geschichte,* vol. 5, p. 212.

6. Quoted by J. Janssen, *Zeit- und Lebensbilder* (Freiburg i B., 1876), vol. 2, pp. 192f.

7. R. Wagner, *Das Judentum in der Musik,* R. Wagner's *Prose Works,* transl. Ellis, vol. 3, pp. 81f.

8. C. Frantz, *Der Nationalliberalismus* (Munich, 1844), p. 56.

9. Cited in *Mitteilungen des Vereins zur Abwehr des Antisemitismus,* 1896, pp. 282–283.

10. *Preussisches Abgeordnetenhaus,* March 4, 1862.

11. C.J. v. Bunsen, *Zeichen der Zeit* (Leipzig, 1885), vol. 1, p. 42.

12. See Note 10.

13. Fontane, *Der deutsche Krieg in 1866* (Berlin, 1871), vol. 1, p. 143.

14. O. Jöhlinger, *Bismarck und die Juden* (1921), pp. 91–110.

15. T. Billroth, *Über das Lehren . . . der medizinischen Wissenschaften* (Vienna, 1876), pp. 148–154.

16. L. Gerlach to Niebuhr, June 3, 1857, cited in *Deutsche Revue,* November 1888.

17. Quoted by A. Kohut on Schopenhauer, *Gekrönte und ungekrönte Judenfreunde,* pp. 119–125.

18. K. Gutzkow, *Rückblicke auf mein Leben,* pp. 69–70.

19. Nietzsche, *Complete Works,* ed. Levy, vol. 8, p. 87.

20. Freytag, "Der Streit über das Judentum in der Musik," *Grenzboten,* 1969, no. 22.

21. Cited by C. Houben, *Gutzkowfunde,* pp. 228–229.

22. H. Helfert, *Die Wiener Journale von 1848* (Vienna, 1887), p. 111.

23. Uhland, cited by A. Kohut, *Judenfreunde,* pp. 181–82.

24. H. v. Treitschke, "Ein Wort über unser Judentum," *Preussische Jahrbücher,* November 1879.

25. W. Raabe, *Die Kinder von Finkenrode, Sämtliche Werke,* ed. Klennen.

26. G. Freytag, *Die Journalisten, Gesammelte Werke* (Leipzig, 1898), vol. 3; see F. Kluge, *Etymologisches Wörterbuch,* 1957, on "Schmock."

27. G. Freytag, *Aufsätze zur Geschichte der Literatur und Kunst, Gesammelte Werke,* vol. 16, pp. 9–20.

28. *Neue Freie Presse,* Vienna, May 21, 1893.

29. Dahn, cited by H. Bahr, *Der Antisemitismus. . . .* (Berlin, 1894), p. 71.

30. G. Keller, "Die missbrauchten Liebesbriefe," *Die Leute von Seldwyla, Gesammelte Werke* (Zürich, 1947), vol. 5, p. 123.

31. D.F. Strauss, *Lessings Nathan der Weise* (Berlin, 1864), p. 12.

Chapter Sixteen

1. M. Harden, *Die Zukunft,* no. 31, 1893.

2. Bismarck, June 15, 1847.

3. Bismarck, to Ann Puttkamer, June 18, 1847.

4. *Preussen im Bundestag,* report no. 218, December 5, 1853.

5. Quoted by Jöhlinger, *Bismarck,* p. 22.

6. W.H. Riehl, *Die bürgerliche Gesellschaft* (Stuttgart, 1856), pp. 336–338.

7. L.A. v. Rochau, *Grundsätze der Realpolitik,* pp. 115, 336–339.

8. *Neues Conversations-, Staats-, und Gesellschafts-Lexikon,* ed. Wagener (1859), vol. 1, p. 18.

9. I.H. Ritter, *Beleuchtung der Wagener'schen Schrift* (Berlin, 1857), pp. 10–11, 16.

10. B. Bauer, "Die Juden als Fremde," *Neues Conversations-Lexikon,* vol. 1, pp. 1–7; see also Rotenstreich, *Leo Baeck Yearbook,* vol. 4, p. 28, on B. Bauer.

11. Treitschke, *Deutsche Geschichte,* vol. 5, pp. 55, 414–416.

12. F.J. Stahl, *Der christliche Staat und sein Verhältnis zu Deismus und Judentum* (1847), pp. 6, 31, 42, 44; see also Kann, "Friedrich Julius Stahl . . . " *Leo Baeck Yearbook,* vol. 7, 1967, pp. 55f.

13. Rochau, *Realpolitik,* p. 336.

Chapter Seventeen

1. *Parerga und Paralipomena, Schopenhauers Sämtliche Werke* (Wiesbaden, 1950), vol. 7, p. 239.

2. Ibid., vol. 6, p. 40.

3. Ibid., p. 241.

4. Ibid., p. 357.

5. "Über das Fundament der Moral" (ibid.), vol. 5, p. 382.

6. Ibid., "Über Religion," *Parerga,* vol. 8, p. 340.

7. Ibid., *Die Welt als Wille . . . ,* vol. 4, p. 667.

8. Ibid., *Parerga,* "Über den Selbstmord," vol. 7, p. 284.

9. Ibid., *Fragmente zur Geschichte der Philosophie,* vol. 6, pp. 128–129; also *Parerga,* vol. 7, p. 276.

10. Ibid., *Die Welt,* vol. 4, p. 276.

11. Ibid., *Fragmente,* vol. 6, pp. 128–129.

12. Ibid., *Parerga,* vol. 7, p. 280.

13. Hegel, *Vorlesungen über die Philosophie der Geschichte,* vol. 9, pp. 201–204.

14. A. Schopenhauer, *Parerga* (Über Religion), vol. 7, pp. 327–328, also p. 240. Hitler quoted Schopenhauer twice in *Mein Kampf* (1939, pp. 253 and 335), both times as witness that the great Germans had been enemies of the Jews. He ignored the fact that Schopenhauer favored mixed marriages rather than considering them a "racial disgrace" and that he approved of conversion and assimilation and, with some qualifications, looked upon "equal rights" for the Jews as a demand for elementary justice. A remark of Schopenhauer about the Jews as "great masters in lying" (*Werke,* vol. 7, p. 328) was twice referred to by Hitler. But this remark of Schopenhauer was followed by praise of the Old Testament. It is true that this praise in turn followed Schopenhauer's criticism that Nebuchadnezzar treated the Jewish people "too leniently," since it "revered a God who donated or promised it the countries of its neighbors." Apparently, Schopenhauer was here concerned with a general criticism

454 *Notes for Chapter Seventeen*

of an immoderate, inflated nationalism, avid for the lands of other peoples, a nationalism for which the ancient Jews, in his opinion, offered an illustration. He concluded: "May every people which reveres a God who makes the neighbors' lands 'countries of promise' find in due time its Nebuchadnezzar and its Antiochus Epiphanes in addition, and may no further mercy be shown to it!" Hitler, understandably enough, did not quote this passage. In any case, Schopenhauer's concern was a universal one; he was not obsessed with the racist notion of the "evil" of one people, the Jews, but feared the evil potentiality of all. Therefore I do not share Werner Maser's view (*Hitlers Mein Kampf*, 1966) that Hitler "was partly influenced" by Schopenhauer (p. 248, also 81); Maser, incidentally, did not find sufficient evidence to make similar claims in regard to Fichte's and Treitschke's (p. 82) possible influence on Hitler.

15. Schopenhauer, *Werke, Parerga*, vol. 7, pp. 327–328.
16. Ibid., pp. 240, 328.
17. Ibid., p. 328.
18. Ibid., *Welt als Wille*, vol. 2, p. 269; *Parerga*, vol. 7, p. 357.
19. Ibid., *Fragmente*, vol. 6, p. 129.
20. Ibid., *Parerga*, vol. 7, p. 240.
21. Ibid., vol. 7, p. 326.
22. Ibid., letter to Lindner, November 3, 1858.
23. Kohut (*Gekrönte und ungekrönte Judenfreunde*) discussed Schopenhauer's personal relations with Jews rather than offering an analysis of his views about Jews and Judaism. For a more detailed anti-Semitic analysis of Schopenhauer's opinions than the two cursory references by Hitler, see M. Gröner, *Schopenhauer und die Juden*, vol. 1 of *Deutschlands führende Männer und das Judentum*. The author of this pamphlet, which appeared after World War I, was anxious to picture Schopenhauer, who actually despised all nationalism, as a representative of the "Aryan Weltanschauung" (p. 38). His "frivolity," however, and his "smiling about the Jewish question" (p. 18) disturbed her. She had to admit that Schopenhauer thought little of Protestantism and the Reformation and saw in both merely a relapse into "Jewish" tendencies.
24. F. Nietzsche, *Gesammelte Werke*, ed. Musarion, vol. 11, p. 108.
25. E. Newman, *The Life of Richard Wagner* (New York, 1949), vol. 2, p. 218.
26. Ibid., pp. 230–231.
27. Ibid., pp. 179–180.
28. G. Freytag, "Der Streit über das Judentum in der Musik," *Die Grenzboten*, 1869, no. 22.
29. Nietzsche, *Der Fall Wagner, Werke*, vol. 8, pp. 1–51.
30. Newman, *Wagner*, Wagner's origins, Appendix 2, vol. 2, pp. 608–619.
31. Ibid., vol. 1, p. 5.
32. Wagner, *Das Judentum in der Musik (Judaism in Music*, R. *Wagner's Prose Works*, transl. Ellis, vol. 3, pp. 77–132, especially pp. 80f.).
33. Letter to Marie Muchanoff, January 1869, *Prose Works*, p. 120.

34. See Note 32. Pp. 84f.

35. Ibid., pp. 85f.

36. K. Grunsky, *R. Wagner und die Juden* (Munich, 1922).

37. See Note 32. P. 7; also Newman, *Wagner,* vol. 1, pp. 275–276.

38. See Note 33.

39. Letter to Tausig, April 1869, *Richard Wagners Briefe* . . . (Leipzig, 1905), p. 405.

40. Letter to Meyerbeer, 1837, cited by Newman, *Wagner,* vol. 1, pp. 603–607.

41. To Meyerbeer, December 19, 1841, *Richard Wagners Briefe,* p. 16.

42. *Judaism in Music,* p. 96.

43. Grunsky, *Wagner,* p. 69. The anti-Semitic author H.S. Chamberlain (*Wagner,* 1901, pp. 224–229) wrote thus: "The Jews themselves with their keen talents belonged almost everywhere to the first who guessed Wagner's artistic genius, and among the critics who gained their reputation by their silly vilifications of the great master were also many gentiles."

44. Grunsky, *Wagner,* p. 18.

45. Newman, *Wagner,* vol. 4, pp. 636–637.

46. Ibid., p. 638.

47. Wagner, *Prose,* vol. 4, p. 166; P.R.E. Viereck, *Metapolitics* (New York, 1941), p. 104.

48. Wagner, *Prose,* vol. 4, p. 166.

49. Wagner, "Modern," *Bayreuther Blätter,* no. 3, March 1879, pp. 59–63; *Prose,* vol. 4, pp. 54, 60; vol. 6, p. 43; Wagner, *Mein Leben* (Munich, 1911), vol. 1, p. 282.

50. See Adolf Fröbel, quoted by Newman, *Wagner,* vol. 4, p. 104.

51. Wagner, *Prose,* vol. 6, pp. 266–269, 276–279.

52. To Angelo Neumann, February 23, 1881; on his relations with Wagner, see Newman, *Wagner,* vol. 4, p. 650.

53. Ibid., vol. 4, p. 626.

54. It is indeed ironic that R. Wagner and H.S. Chamberlain, both foes of the Jews, were introduced to each other by Jews.

55. Newman, *Wagner,* vol. 2, pp. 612–613; reference is made here to Kreowski and Fuchs, *Richard Wagner in der Karikatur,* p. 138.

56. E.K. Dühring, *Die Judenfrage als . . . Kulturfrage* (Karlsruhe, 1881), p. 75.

57. Monod, quoted by Newman, *Wagner,* vol. 4, p. 700.

58. Freytag, "Der Streit über das Judentum in der Musik," *Die Grenzboten,* 1869, no. 22, *Gesammelte Werke,* vol. 16, pp. 321–326.

Chapter Eighteen

1. G. Freytag, *Soll und Haben, Gesammelte Werke* (Leipzig, 1898), vol. 5.

2. Freytag, *Erinnerungen*, ibid., vol. 1, pp. 602–603; see also B. Auerbach, *Das Judentum und die . . . Literatur*, pp. 551–553.

3. Ibid., pp. 573–574; about *Die Journalisten*, p. 593.

4. *Mitteilungen des Vereins zur Abwehr des Antisemitismus*, 1895.

5. G. Freytag, *Bilder aus der deutschen Vergangenheit*, "Jesuiten und Juden," *Werke*, vol. 20, pp. 348–386, also 389.

6. Freytag, *Bilder*, "Aus den Kreuzzügen," vol. 17, pp. 431f., especially pp. 475–476. According to Philippsohn (*Neueste Geschichte des jüdischen Volkes*, 1910), Freytag "freely recanted the accusations" that he made against the Jews in *Soll und Haben*. Also in later years he married Frau Strakosch, a Jew. He rejected the idea of her conversion to Christianity, just because of the contemporary anti-Semitic agitation. When his stepson began to attend school, Freytag wrote a letter to the teacher requesting permission for his son to receive religious instruction in Hebrew at home. The letter to the teacher, May 6, 1892, is quoted in *Mitteilungen des Vereines zur Abwehr des Antisemitismus*, 1895.

7. F. Dahn, *Der Kampf um Rom* (Leipzig, 1901), vol. 1, pp. 373–374.

8. Ibid., vol. 2, p. 230.

9. Ibid., vol. 2, p. 245.

10. "Die Jüdin."

11. Letter to Karpeles, see Index, *Antisemitenhammer*.

12. F. Reuter, *Aus meiner Stromzeit* (Ut mine Stromtid), *Werke*, ed. Seelman, vols. 2 and 3.

13. F. Reuter, *Werke*, *Schurr-Murr* (Meine Vaterstadt Stavenhagen), vol. 6, pp. 139–144. However, because of a passage in his novel *Franzosentid* (*Werke*, vol. 3) Reuter was proclaimed by the *Antisemitische Korrespondenz* (January 27, 1899) as an enemy of the Jews. It is a perjuring Jew in this novel who is supposed to prove the novelist's hostility against the Jews. Yet this Jew appears in close companionship with the shady Gentile businessman Müller Voss (*Franzosentid, Werke*, vol. 3, p. 455).

14. K.T. Goedertz, ed., *Ungedruckte Briefe Reuters*, March 24, 1867.

15. L. Schücking, *Die drei Freier*, ed. Heller (Boston, 1904).

16. Köster, ed., *Briefwechsel zwischen T. Storm und G. Keller*, p. 115, August 14, 1881, and Keller's reply, pp. 119–120, August 16, 1881; see also Keller, *Briefe und Tagebücher*, ed. Ermatinger, vol. 3, pp. 361–362.

17. Storm's close friend in early years was L. Loewe, later machine manufacturer and representative in the *Reichstag*. Storm was also an intimate friend of the novelist poet Paul Heyse, who was of partly Jewish ancestry, and with Emil Kuh, biographer and friend of Hebbel.

18. *T. Storm: Ein Bild seines Lebens* (Berlin, 1912), vol. 1, pp. 96–98.

19. "Crucifixus," *Storms Werke* (Meyers Klassiker-Ausgaben), vol. 1, p. 106.

20. *Der Hungerpastor. Raabe Sämtliche Werke*, ed. Klemm, vol. 1, pp. 216–218.

21. *Die Chronik der Sperlingsgasse*, ibid., vol. 1, p. 170.

22. *Die Leute aus dem Walde*, ibid., vol. 5, pp. 241–255.

23. *Der heilige Born*, ibid., vol. 3, pp. 336–337.

24. *Die Hollunderblüte*, ibid., vol. 5, pp. 594–627.

25. *Frau Salome, in Krähenfelder Geschichten*, ibid., vol. 4, pp. 314–421.

26. "Höxter und Corvey," *Krähenfelder Gesch.*, ibid., vol. 4, pp. 107–212. For a thorough treatment of the image of Jews and Judaism in Raabe's creative work, see J. Bass, "Die Juden bei Wilhelm Raabe," *Monatsschrift für Geschichte und Wissenschaft des Judentums*, 1910, p. 641. See also *Raabe, Nachlese*, vol. 6, p. 519, "Berthold Auerbachs Deutsche Volkslieder für das Jahr 1859." In this review Raabe called Auerbach "a brave German master." On p. 572 he contrasted the "narrow Christian-German accumulation of money" with the "great Jewish financial world view."

27. *Kellers Gesammelte Werke*, "Nationalität" (Zürich, 1947), vol. 9, p. 123.

28. *Der grüne Heinrich, Werke*, vol. 2, pp. 70–73 (chs. 6 and 7).

29. Quoted by H.M. Kriesi, *G. Keller als Politiker* (Leipzig, 1918), p. 305; also in Keller, *Nachgelassene Schriften* (Ungedruckter Entwurf des Mandates . . .).

30. D.F. Strauss, *Lessings Nathan der Weise, Gesammelte Schriften* (Bonn, 1876), vol. 2, p. 82.

31. A. Diesterweg, *Preussisches Abgeordnetenhaus*, March 4, 1862.

32. *Die Makkabäer, Ludwigs Werke*, ed. Schweizer, vol. 5. The anti-Semitic literary historian Adolf Bartels deplored the fact that Otto Ludwig "had not completed another drama of an appealing subject" (*Einführung in das deutsche Schrifttum*, 1933, p. 364). Actually, Ludwig began working on still another drama, likewise touching Jewish history, *Jud Süss*, which, unfortunately, has remained a mere fragment.

33. *Jud Süss* or *Der Jakobsstab, Ludwigs Werke*, vol. 4.

34. "Menetekel," *E. Geibels Werke*, vol. 2, p. 234.

35. *Heroldsrufe*, "Ein Psalm wider Babel," ibid., vol. 2, pp. 391f.; also "Zwei Psalmen," ibid., vol. 2, pp. 284f.

36. "Auf Felix Mendelssohn-Bartholdys Tod," ibid., vol. 2, pp. 326f.

37. "Judas Ischariot," ibid., vol. 2, pp. 409–415.

38. A. Schack, "Nächte des Orients," *Werke* (Stuttgart, 1874).

39. Singer, *Briefe berühmter christlicher Zeitgenossen* . . . , p. 93.

40. "Deutschland," *Gesammelte Gedichte, J.v. Scheffels Sämtliche Werke* (Leipzig).

Chapter Nineteen

1. M. Busch, *Unser Reichskanzler* (1881), vol. 1, p. 33.

2. Ibid., vol. 1, p. 153.

3. M. Harden, "Prinz Bismarck und der Antisemitismus," *Die Zukunft*, no. 31, 1893.

4. Quoted by O. Jöhlinger, *Bismarck und die Juden* (1921), pp. 31–32.

5. O. v. Mohl, *Fünfzig Jahre Reichsdienst* (1920).

6. Quoted by H. Poschinger, *Bismarck-Portefeuille* (Stuttgart, 1900), vol. 2, p. 21.

7. Berliner Kongress, 8. Protokoll, June 28, 1878.

8. E. Cohen, *Erinnerungen an Bismarck*, p. 304.

9. H. Oncken, *Lassalle* (Stuttgart, 1904), p. 53.

10. Reichstag, September 17, 1879.

11. Jöhlinger, *Bismarck*, p. 63.

12. "Hermann Schulze-Delitzsch und Eduard Lasker," *Jahrbuch für Gesetzgebung*, 1882, vol. 2.

13. *Deutsche Tageszeitung*, January 19, 1898, quoted by Jöhlinger, *Bismarck*, pp. 187–188.

14. Ibid., pp. 91f., 126.

15. L. v. Ballhausen, *Bismarck-Erinnerungen* (Stuttgart, 1920), p. 217.

16. A. Stöcker, *Dreizehn Jahre Hofprediger* . . . , pp. 17–18; also Jöhlinger, *Bismarck*, pp. 28–29.

17. M. Busch, *Tagebücher* (1898), vol. 3, p. 155.

18. Jöhlinger, *Bismarck*, pp. 135–136.

19. Ibid., p. 168.

20. Letter to Prince Wilhelm, January 6, 1888, ibid., p. 170.

21. *Norddeutsche Allgemeine Zeitung*, September 25, 1885.

22. Jöhlinger, *Bismarck*, p. 140.

23. *Die Hamburger Nachrichten*, September 28, 1895, also October 15, 1896.

24. Jöhlinger, *Bismarck*, pp. 183–184; see also the interview of Bismarck with a South German politician in Kissingen, which was published in the Vienna *Neue Freie Presse*, Jöhlinger, *Bismarck*, pp. 185–186.

25. H. v. Treitschke, *Deutsche Geschichte* . . . (Leipzig, 1890), vol. 3, p. 46; vol. 4, pp. 159 and 511, 553–558.

26. H. Liebeschütz, "Treitschke und Mommsen . . ." *Leo Baeck Yearbook* (1962), vol. 7, p. 173.

27. H. v. Petersdorff, *Die Vereine deutscher Studenten* (Leipzig, 1895), pp. 10–26, 58, 128, 140.

28. H. v. Treitschke, "Ein Wort über unser Judentum," *Preussische Jahrbücher*, November, 1879.

29. Bresslau and Grätz, see W. Boehlich, ed. *Der Antisemitismusstreit* (Frankfurt a.M., 1965).

30. Ibid.

31. T. Mommsen, "Auch ein Wort über unser Judentum" (Berlin, 1880).

32. Some of the most important writings, in addition to the foregoing, were Treitschke's *Deutsche Geschichte des neunzehnten Jahrhunderts*, "Noch einige Bemerkungen zur Judenfrage," *Preussische Jahrbücher*, January 10, 1880; Frantz's *Der Nationalliberalismus und die Judenherrschaft;* Dühring's, *Die Judenfrage als Rassen-, Sitten- und Kulturfrage;* E. v. Hart-

mann's *Das Judentum in Gegenwart und Zukunft;* P. de Lagarde, *Deutsche Schriften* and *Ausgewählte Schriften;* and J. Langbehn, *Rembrandt als Erzieher.*

33. J. Burckhardt, *Briefe,* pp. 455–456, to Preen, December 23, 1882, and pp. 428–429, January 2, 1880.

34. *Nietzsches Werke* (Leipzig, 1899), vol. 2, pp. 353f. (If not otherwise listed in the following notes, this edition was used.)

35. F. Nietzsche (Musarion), quoted by W.A. Kaufmann, *Nietzsche* . . . . (1950), p. 261; the author is indebted to Kaufmann's penetrating study of Nietzsche's philosophy.

36. Nietzsche, *Werke,* vol. 8, pp. 108–109.

37. Ibid., vol. 7, p. 77.

38. Nietzsche (Musarion), vol. 16, p. 371.

39. Nietzsche (Musarion), vol. 16, p. 373.

40. Nietzsche, *Werke,* vol. 7, p. 217.

41. Nietzsche (Musarion), vol. 16, pp. 373f.

42. Nietzsche (Musarion), *Wille zur Macht,* p. 960.

43. Ibid., vol. 16, pp. 373f.

44. Ibid.

45. Ibid., vol. 16, p. 391.

46. A. Bäumler, *Nietzsche der Philosoph und Politiker* (Leipzig, 1931), pp. 8, 63.

47. Kaufmann, *Nietzsche,* pp. 4, 48–49.

48. Nietzsche (Musarion), vol. 11, p. 300.

49. Nietzsche, vol. 7, pp. 313, 317.

50. Nietzsche (Kröner's edition), vol. 78, p. 126.

51. Nietzsche, vol. 8, p. 250.

52. Ibid., vol. 7, pp. 335–336.

53. Ibid., vol. 7, pp. 313, 315; and vol. 8, p. 310.

54. R.N. Lonsbach, *Friedrich Nietzsche und die Juden* (Stockholm, 1939), p. 35.

55. Nietzsche (Kröner's edition), vol. 78, p. 127.

56. Nietzsche (Musarion), vol. 10, p. 67.

57. Ibid., vol. 19, p. 261.

58. Ibid.

59. Nietzsche, *Werke und Briefe* (1933), vol. 2, nos. 377, 430, 443.

60. Ibid., no. 460; cf. no. 271 to Overbeck.

61. Kaufmann, *Nietzsche,* p. 33.

62. Nietzsche, vol. 8, p. 39.

63. Kaufmann, *Nietzsche,* pp. 39–40.

64. Nietzsche, *Ecce Homo* (1908), vol. 1, p. 4.

65. Nietzsche (Kröner's), vol. 78, p. 584.

66. Ibid., vol. 77, p. 266; vol. 78, p. 239; and vol. 73, p. 405.

67. G. Brandes, *An Essay on Aristocratic Radicalism* (1914).

68. Nietzsche, vol. 7, p. 220.

69. Nietzsche, vol. 7, p. 217.

70. Nietzsche, vol. 5, p. 284.

71. Nietzsche, vol. 2, p. 354.

72. Nietzsche (Kröner's), vol. 78, p. 559, and vol. 83, p. 406.

73. See the Paneth letter to his bride in the Nietzsche biography by Elizabeth Förster-Nietzsche; for Paneth see also C.A. Bernouilli, *Franz Overbeck und Friedrich Nietzsche* (Jena, 1908), pp. 359–362.

74. F. Mess, *Nietzsche als Gesetzgeber* (Leipzig, 1930), p. 112.

Chapter Twenty

1. *Allgemeine Zeitung des Judentums,* 1879, p. 229; and 1884, p. 382, quoted by J. Toury, *Die politischen Orientierungen der Juden in Deutschland* . . . (Tübingen, 1966), p. 252.

2. *Allgemeine Zeitung des Judentums,* 1884, p. 326, and *Israelitisches Familienblatt,* 1898, no. 2, pp. 2f., quoted by Toury, *Orientierungen,* pp. 253–254.

3. *Die Judenfrage im preussischen Abgeordnetenhause,* Hänel, p. 25; for the other speeches see the entire proceedings.

4. P.J. Proudhon, *Césarisme et Christianisme* (Paris, 1883), vol. 1, p. 139.

5. M.A. Bakunin, *Gesammelte Werke* (1924), vol. 3, p. 208.

6. Ibid., vol. 3, pp. 208–209; see also Silberner, *Sozialisten zur Judenfrage,* 1962, to whose pioneering study the author is indebted, pp. 390–391.

7. For the following, see Silberner, *Sozialisten,* on Engels, pp. 143–159.

8. G. Mayer, *Friedrich Engels* (1934), vol. 2, p. 455.

9. *Marx-Engels Werke* (Berlin, 1959), vol. 4, p. 29.

10. Silberner, *Sozialisten,* pp. 147–150f.; also for the following.

11. Engels, *Notes on War,* p. 107.

12. Silberner, *Sozialisten,* p. 151 and *Anti-Dühring* (1971), p. 123; see also Mayer, *Engels,* pp. 262–292.

13. *Marx-Engels Gesamtausgabe,* part 3, Briefwechsel zwischen Marx und Engels (Berlin, 1931), vol. 4, p. 433.

14. *Eduard Bernsteins Briefwechsel mit Fr. Engels* (1970), pp. 28–29, August 17, 1881.

15. Ibid., Bernstein to Engels, pp. 27–28, July 23, 1881.

16. *Arbeiter-Zeitung,* Vienna, May 9, 1890.

17. V. Adler, *Aufsätze, Reden und Briefe* (1922), vol. 1, pp. 6–8.

18. See Note 16.

19. *Sozialdemokratischer Parteitag* (Cologne, 1893), p. 224; for the following see Silberner, *Sozialisten,* pp. 181–230.

20. A. Bebel, *Sozialdemokratie und Antisemitismus* (Berlin, 1906), pp. 31f.

21. Quoted by Silberner, *Sozialisten,* p. 205.

22. Bebel, *Sozialdemokratie,* pp. 36–38.

23. K. Kautsky, *Aus der Frühzeit des Marxismus* (Prague, 1935), p. 122.

24. Letter of December 22, 1884, ibid., p. 160.

25. M. Ermers, *Victor Adler* (Vienna, 1932), pp. vi and 126.

26. *Sozialdemokratischer Parteitag, 1898, Verhandlungen,* p. 80; see also Silberner, "Austrian Social Democracy and the Jewish Problem," *Historia Judaica* (New York, 1951), pp. 131–133.

Bibliography

Reference Works

Baron, S.W. *Bibliography of Jewish Social Studies 1938–1939*. New York, 1941.

Burckhart, A.A.H., and Stern, M. *Aus der Zeitschriftenliteratur zur Geschichte der Juden in Deutschland.*

Duker, A.G. "Selected Bibliography on Jewish Emancipation and Counter-Emancipation," in *Emancipation and Counter-Emancipation*. New York, 1974.

Eichstädt, V. *Bibliographie zur Geschichte der Judenfrage*, Vol. 1: 1750–1848.

Encyclopedia Judaica (in English). 16 vols. Jerusalem, 1972.

Encyclopedia Judaica (in German). 10 vols., A–L. Berlin, 1928–1934.

Encyclopedia of Zionism and Israel. 2 vols. New York, 1971.

German Jewry: Its History, Life and Culture. The Wiener Library Catalogue Series No. 3. London, 1958.

Haenzyklopedia Haivrit. Jerusalem.

The Jewish Encyclopedia. 12 vols. New York, 1901–1906.

The New Standard Jewish Encyclopedia. 1 vol. New York, 1970.

The Universal Jewish Encyclopedia. 10 vols. New York, 1939–1943.

Jüdisches Lexikon: Ein enzyklopädisches Handbuch des jüdischen Wissens. 5 vols. Berlin, 1927–1930.

Kirsch, G. *Schriften zur Geschichte der Juden: Eine Bibliographie der in Deutschland und der Schweiz 1922–1955 erschienenen Dissertationen.* 1959.

Melzer, J. *Deutsch-jüdisches Schicksal: Wegweiser durch das Schrifttum der letzten 15 Jahre, 1945–1960*. Cologne, 1960.

Rothschild, M. *Jewish Social Studies Cumulative Index 1939–1964*. New York, 1967.

Rotteck, K., and Welcker, C., eds. *Encyclopädie der Staatswissenschaften*. Altona, 1837.

Shunami, S. *Maftesh Hamaftehot* (Bibliography of Jewish Bibliographies). Revised and enlarged edition. Jerusalem, 1965.

Sigilla Veri (Semi-Kürschner, anti-Semitic dictionary). Erfurt, 1929.

462

Periodicals and Newspapers

Allgemeine Zeitung des Judentums.
American Jewish Historical Quarterly.
American Political Science Review.
Antisemitische Korrespondenz.
Antisemitisches Jahrbuch.
Antisemitismus.
Arbeiter-Zeitung. Vienna.
Augsburger Allgemeine Zeitung.
Austrian History Yearbook.
Bulletin des Leo Baeck Instituts.
Deutsch-Französische Jahrbücher.
Deutsch-Soziale Blätter.
Deutsche Literatur.
Deutsche Revue.
Deutsche Romanzeitung.
Deutsche Staatsanzeigen.
Deutsches Recht.
Ephemeriden der Menschheit.
Frankfurter Zeitung.
Germania Judaica.
Germanisch-Romanische Monatshefte.
Germanisch-Romanische Monatsschriften.
Grenzboten.
Hamburger Nachrichten.
Heidelberger Jahrbücher der Literatur.
Historia Judaica.
Historische Zeitschrift.
Israelitisches Familienblatt.
Jahrbuch für Gesetzgebung.
The Jewish Quarterly.
The Jewish Quarterly Review.
Jewish Social Studies.
Journal of the History of Ideas.
Der Jude. Altona.
Jüdische Rundschau.
Mitteilungen des Vereins zur Abwehr des Antisemitismus.
Monatsschrift für Geschichte und Wissenschaft des Judentums.
Mindensches Intelligenzblatt.
Neue Freie Presse.
Norddeutsche Allgemeine Zeitung.
The Philosophical Review.
Preussische Jahrbücher.
Révue hébdomadaire.
Schmollers Jahrbücher für Gesetzgebung.
Sprache und Kultur der Germanischen und Romanischen Völker.

Sulamith.
Der Teutsche Merkur.
Vierteljahrshefte für Zeitgeschichte.
Vossische Zeitung.
Der Weltkampf.
Zeitschrift für Deutsche Bildung.
Zeitschrift für die Gesamten Staatswissenschaften.
Zeitschrift für die Geschichte der Juden in Deutschland.
Die Zukunft.

General Works, Comprehensive Histories, and Surveys

(A few books listed under "Secondary Sources" belong also in this category).

Baron, S.W. "The Jewish Question in the Nineteenth Century." In *Journal of Modern History*. March 1938.
———. *Modern Nationalism and Religion*. New York, 1947.
———. *A Social and Religious History of the Jews*. 3 vols. New York, 1937.
Biese, A. *Deutsche Literaturgeschichte*. 3 vols. Munich, 1930.
Brandes, G. *Hauptströmungen der Literatur des neunzehnten Jahrhunderts*. Vol. 6: *Das junge Deutschland*. Leipzig, 1898.
Castle, E. *Deutsch-österreichische Literaturgeschichte*. 3 vols. Vienna, 1930.
Droz, J. *Le Romanticisme Allemand et l'Etat*. Paris, 1966.
Dubnow, S.M. *Neueste Geschichte des jüdischen Volkes*. 10 vols. Berlin, 1920.
———. *Weltgeschichte des jüdischen Volkes*. 10 vols. Berlin, 1925–1929.
Elbogen, I. *Geschichte der Juden in Deutschland*. Berlin, 1935.
Finkelstein, L., ed. *The Jews: Their History, Culture and Religion*. 2 vols. Philadelphia, 1960.
Graetz, H. *Geschichte der Juden*. 11 vols. in 13 parts. 4th ed., n.d.
———. *History of the Jews*. 6 vols. Philadelphia, 1956.
———. *Volkstümliche Geschichte der Juden*. 3 vols. Vienna and Leipzig, 1923.
Grunwald, M. *Vienna*. Philadelphia, 1934.
Hamerow, T. *The Social Foundations of German Unification 1858–1871*. Princeton, 1969.
Hettner, H. *Geschichte der deutschen Literatur im achtzehnten Jahrhundert*. Leipzig, 1928.
Holborn, H. *History of Modern Germany*. 3 vols. New York, 1964–1969.
Jost, J.M. *Geschichte der Israeliten seit der Zeit der Maccabäer bis auf unsere Tage*. 9 vols. Berlin, 1828.
Kastein, J. (Katzenstein). *Eine Geschichte der Juden*. Berlin, 1931.
Kaznelson, S. *Juden im deutschen Kulturbereich: Ein Sammelwerk*. Berlin, 1962.

Kober, A. "Die Geschichte der deutschen Juden in der historischen Forschung der letzten 35 Jahre." In *Zeitschrift für die Geschichte der
Juden in Deutschland.* Vol. 1. 1929.

The Leo Baeck Institute Yearbook. London, 1956. (Continuing series).

Margolis, M., and Marx, A. *A History of the Jewish People.* Philadelphia,
1927.

Mikoletzky, H.L. *Österreich: Das grosse achtzehnte Jahrhundert.* Vienna
and Munich, 1967.

Pessès, A. *L'Image des juifs dans la littérature romantique française.* Paris,
1964–1965.

Philipp, A. *Die Juden und das Wirtschaftsleben: Eine antikritische bibliogra-
phische Studie zu Werner Sombart.* Strasbourg, 1929.

Philippsohn, M. *Neueste Geschichte des jüdischen Volkes.* 3 vols. Frankfurt
and Leipzig, 1910.

Roth, C. *A Bird's-Eye View of Jewish History.* Cincinnati, 1935.

Sachar, H.M. *The Course of Modern Jewish History.* Cleveland, 1958.

Scherr, J. *Deutsche Kultur- und Sittengeschichte.* Leipzig, 1858.

Schnabel, F. *Deutsche Geschichte im neunzehten Jahrhundert.* 4 vols. Freiburg, 1929.

Sombart, W. *The Jews and Modern Capitalism.* Glencoe, 1951.

Stern, S. *Geschichte des Judentums von Mendelssohn bis auf die neuere Zeit.*
Breslau, 1870.

Troeltsch, E. *Deismus: Schriften.* Vol. 4. Aachen, 1965.

Primary Sources

Achendorffsche Schriften. Der erste westfälische Landtag. N.d.

Aktenmässige Darstellung des Bürgerrechts der Israeliten zu Frankfurt a.M.
Rödelheim, 1816.

Antisemitenhammer. Anthologie aus der Weltliteratur. J. Schrattenholz (ed.).
Düsseldorf, 1894.

*Antisemitenspiegel. Die Antisemiten im Lichte des Christentums, des Rechts
und der Wissenschaft.* Danzig, 1900.

Anzengruber, L. *Briefe von L. Anzengruber.* A. Bettelheim (ed.). Stuttgart
and Berlin, 1902.

D'Argens, J.E. *Lettres juives.* La Haye, 1736–1737.

Arndt, E.M. *Ansichten und Aussichten der deutschen Geschichte.* Leipzig,
1814.

————. *Ein Blick aus der Zeit auf die Zeit.* Germanien, 1814.

————. *Einleitung zur historischen Charakterbildung.* Berlin, 1810.

————. *E.M. Arndt: Ein Lebensbild in Briefen.* Meisner and Geerg (eds.).
1848.

————. *Erinnerungen aus meinem äusseren Leben.* Leipzig, 1840.

————. "Über den deutschen Studentenstaat." In *Schriften an und für seine
lieben Deutschen.* 4 vols. Leipzig, 1845–1855.

———. *Das verjüngte oder vielmehr das verjüngende Deutschland.* Bonn, 1848.

———. *Versuch in vergleichender Völkergeschichte.* Leipzig, 1844.

Arnim, A. von. *Armut, Reichtum und Busse der Gräfin Dolores. Werke.* 21 vols. Grimm (ed.). Berlin, 1840.

———. *Halle und Jerusalem. Sämtliche Werke.* Vol. 16. Berlin, 1857.

———. *Isabella von Ägypten. Werke.* Berlin, 1839.

Arnim, A. and Brentano, C. *Des Knaben Wunderhorn.* Berlin, 1909.

Ascher, S. *Eisenmenger der Zweite: Nebst einem vorangesetzten Sendschreiben an Herrn Professor Fichte in Jena.* Berlin, 1794.

———. *Die Wartburgfeier.* Leipzig, 1818.

Auerbach, B. *Das Judentum und die neueste deutsche Literatur.* Stuttgart, 1836.

Auerbach, L. *Das Judentum und seine Bekenner in Preussen.* Berlin, 1890.

Bahr, H. *Der Antisemitismus: Ein internationales Interview.* Berlin, 1894.

Bamberg, F., ed. *Hebbels Briefwechsel mit Freunden und berühmten Zeitgenossen.* Berlin, 1892.

———. *Hebbels Tagebücher mit Vorwort.* 2 vols. Berlin, 1885–1887.

Baron, S.W. *Unveröffentlichte Aktenstücke zur Judenfrage auf dem Wiener Kongress (1814–1815).* Vienna and Berlin, 1920.

Bauer, B. *Die Judenfrage.* Braunschweig, 1843.

———. *Vollständige Geschichte der Parteikämpfe in Deutschland, 1842–46.* Charlottenburg, 1847.

Bebel, A. *Sein Leben in Dokumenten.* Hirsch (ed.). 1968.

———. *Sozialdemokratie und Antisemitismus.* Berlin, 1894.

Beck, K. *Lieder vom armen Mann.* Prague, 1846.

Beguélin, H. *Denkwürdigkeiten von Heinrich und Amalie von Beguélin aus den Jahren 1807–1813.* Ernst (ed.). Berlin, 1892.

Bein, A. "Der moderne Antisemitismus und seine Bedeutung für die Judenfrage," in *Vierteljahrshefte für Zeitgeschichte.* 1958.

Bendavid, L. *Etwas zur Charakteristik der Juden.* Leipzig, 1793.

———. *Selbstbiographie.* Berlin, 1806.

Bernouilli, J. *De la réforme politique des juifs.* Berlin, 1782.

Bernstein, E. *Briefwechsel mit Friedrich Engels.* Hirsch (ed.). Assen, 1870.

Beurmann, E. *Frankfurter Bilder.* Mainz, 1835.

Billroth, T. *Über das Lehren und Lernen der medizinischen Wissenschaften.* Vienna, 1876.

Bismarck, O. v. *Die politischen Reden des Fürsten Bismarck.* Kohl (ed.). 14 vols. 1847–1852.

Blücher, L. von. *Ausgewählte Briefe des Feldmarschalls Lebrecht von Blücher.* Schulze (ed.). Leipzig, n.d.

Bodenstedt, F. *Erinnerungen aus meinem Leben.* Berlin, 1888–1890.

Boehlich, W., ed. *Der Berliner Antisemitismusstreit 1879–1880.* Frankfurt a.M., 1965.

Bolte, J., and Policka, G. *Anmerkungen zu den Kinder- und Hausmärchen der Brüder Grimm.* 2 vols. Leipzig, 1915.

Bopp, A. "Judenschutz und Judenabgabe," in *Staatslexikon*. Vol. 7. Rotteck und Welcker (eds.).

Boyen, H. von. *Denkwürdigkeiten und Erinnerungen, 1771–1813*. Stuttgart, 1899.

Brand, T. *Die Judenfrage in Preussen*. Breslau, 1842.

Braun, J.W. *Lessing im Urteile seiner Zeitgenossen aus den Jahren 1747–1781*. 2 vols. Berlin, 1884–1893.

Brentano, B. *Gespräche mit Dämonen. Sämtliche Schriften*. Berlin, 1853.

―――. *Goethes Briefwechsel mit einem Kinde*. Grimm (ed.). Berlin, 1881.

―――. *Die Günderode*. Grünberg and Leipzig, 1840.

Brentano, C. *Blätter aus dem Tagebuch einer Ahnfrau. Gesammelte Schriften*. Frankfurt, 1852.

―――. "Gockel und Hinkel," in *Gesammelte Werke*. Vol. 12. Schüddekopf (ed.). Munich and Leipzig, 1914.

―――. "Das Märchen vom Schneider Siebentot auf einen Schlag," in *Gesammelte Werke*. Vol. 11, Schüddekopf (ed.).

―――. *Der Philister in und nach der Geschichte*, in *Clemens Brentanos Werke*. Vol. 3. Preitz (ed.).

―――. *Romanzen vom Rosenkranz. Gesammelte Werke*. Vol. 4. Schüddekopf (ed.).

―――. *Victoria und ihre Geschwister. Gesammelte Schriften*. Vol. 7. Frankfurt.

Buchholz, C.A. *Aktenstücke die Verbesserung des bürgerlichen Zustandes der Israeliten betreffend*. Tübingen, 1815.

Büchner, G. *Wozzeck. Gesammelte Werke*. Seelig (ed.). Zürich, 1944.

Buesching, A.F. *Geschichte der jüdischen Religion*. Berlin, 1779.

Bunsen, C.J. von. *Zeichen der Zeit*. 2 vols. Leipzig, 1885.

Burckhardt, J. *Kultur der Renaissance*. 3d edition. Geiger (ed.). Leipzig, 1877–1878.

―――. "Der schwarze Tod," in *Wanderer in der Schweiz*. 1838.

Busch, M. *Bismarck: Some Secret Pages of His History. (Tagebücher)*. New York, 1970.

―――. *Unser Reichskanzler*, 2 vols. Leipzig, 1884.

Chamisso, A. *Peter Schlemihls wundersame Geschichte. Sämtliche Werke*. Gottschall (ed.). Berlin and Leipzig, n.d.

Claudius, M. "Moses Mendelssohn und die Freunde Lessings," *Sämtliche Werke*. Hamburg, 1789.

Cohen, E. *Erinnerungen an Bismarck*.

Cohen, H. *Jüdische Schriften*. 2 vols. Berlin, 1924.

Dahlmann, F.C. *Die Politik*. Leipzig, 1847.

―――. *Kleine Schriften und Reden*. Stuttgart, 1886.

Dahn, F. *Der Kampf um Rom*. 4 vols. Leipzig, 1901.

―――. *Die Könige der Germanen*. Munich and Würzburg, 1862–1866.

Decius, B. (Reinhold) *Die hebräischen Mysterien oder die älteste religiöse Freimaurerei*. Leipzig, 1789.

Diderot, D. *Encyclopédie*. 2d ed. Lausanne and Berne, 1781.

————. *Oeuvres complètes.* Paris, 1875.

Diest-Daber, O. von. *Bismarck und Bleichröder: Deutsches Rechtsbewusstsein und die Gleichheit vor dem Gesetze.* N.d.

Diez, H.F. *Über die Juden.* Leipzig, 1783.

Dingelstedt, F. *Lieder eines kosmopolitischen Nachtwächters. Sämtliche Werke.* Vol. 8. Berlin, 1871.

————. *Literarisches Bilderbuch.* Berlin, 1878.

Dohm, C.W. *Denkwürdigkeiten meiner Zeit.* 5 vols. Hannover, 1814–1819.

————. *Über die bürgerliche Verbesserung der Juden.* Berlin-Stettin, 1781–1783.

Döllinger, I. von. *Die Juden in Europa.* Berlin, 1924.

Droste-Hülshoff, A.F. v. *Die Judenbuche. Deutscher Novellenschatz.* Vol. 24. Heyse (ed.). Munich, 1871.

Droysen, J.G. *Johann Gustav Droysen: Briefwechsel.* Hübner (ed.). Berlin, 1929.

Dühring, E.K. *Die Judenfrage als Rassen-, Sitten- und Kulturfrage.* Karlsruhe, 1881.

————. *Die Überschätzung Lessings und dessen Anwaltschaft für die Juden.* Leipzig, 1906.

Ebner-Eschenbach, M. v. *Der Kreiphysikus. Gesammelte Schriften.* "Dorf- und Schlossgeschichten." Berlin, 1905.

Eckardt, J.D. von. *Lebenserinnerungen.* Leipzig, 1910.

Edler, C.F. *Stimmen der preussischen Provinzialstände des Jahres 1845 über die Emanzipation der Juden.* Berlin, 1845.

Engels, F. *Anti-Dühring (Herr Eugen Dührings Umwälzung der Wissenschaft).* Frankfurt a.M., 1971.

————. *Notes on War.* Vienna, 1923.

Engels, F., and Marx, K. *Die heilige Familie.* Frankfurt a.M., 1845.

Ernst, L. *Die Juden, die verjudeten Christlich-Sozialen und die Deutschnationalen.* Leipzig, 1896.

Fallersleben, H. v. *Unpolitische Lieder. Gesammelte Werke.* Vol. 7. Gerstenberg (ed.). Berlin, 1890–1893.

Feuerbach, A. Oct. 31, 1813, quoted in *Deutsche Romanzeitung.* Nov. 1881.

Fichte, J.G.

————. *Aus Fichtes Leben: Briefe und Mitteilungen zu einer künftigen Sammlung von Fichtes Briefwechsel.* Schulz (ed.). Berlin, 1918.

————. *Fichtes sämtliche Werke.* Fichte (ed.). 8 vols. Berlin, 1845–1846.

————. *J.G. Fichte: Briefwechsel.* Leipzig, 1925.

————. *Leben und literarischer Briefwechsel.* Fichte (ed.). Sulzbach, 1830.

Fontane, T. *Der deutsche Krieg in 1866.* 2 vols. in 1. Berlin, 1871.

————. "Die Märker und das Berlinertum," *Aus dem Nachlass.* Ettlinger (ed.). 3 vols. Berlin, 1908.

Förster-Nietzsche, E. *Das Leben Friedrich Nietzsches.* 3 vols. Leipzig, 1895–1904.

Frantz, C. *Ahasverus oder die Judenfrage.* Berlin, 1844.

————. *Der Nationalliberalismus und die Judenherrschaft.* Munich, 1844.

Freiligrath, F. *Ein Dichterleben in Briefen.* 2 vols. Buechner (ed.). Schauen-burg, Lahr, 1881.

——. *Werke.* Zaunert (ed.). Berlin, 1856.

Freund, W. *Zur Judenfrage in Deutschland: Vom Standpunkt des Rechts und der Gewissensfreiheit.* Breslau, 1844.

Freytag, G. "Eine Pfingstbetrachtung," in *Neue Freie Presse.* Vienna, May 21, 1893.

——. *Gesammelte Werke.* 22 vols. Leipzig, 1896–1898.

——. "Der Streit über das Judentum in der Musik," *Aufsätze zur Ge-schichte, Literatur und Kunst. Gesammelte Werke.* Vol. 16. Leipzig, 1896–1898.

Friedländer, D. *Beitrag zur Geschichte der Verfolgung der Juden.* Berlin, 1820.

——. *Sendschreiben an Seine Hochwürden, Herrn Oberkonsistorialrat und Probst Teller zu Berlin, von einigen Hausvätern jüdischer Religion.* Berlin, 1799.

Fries, F. *Bekehret euch!* Heidelberg, 1814.

——. *Politik oder philosophische Staatslehre.* Jena, 1848.

——. "Über die Gefährdung des Wohlstandes und des Charakters der Deutschen durch die Juden," in *Heidelberger Jahrbücher der Literatur.* 1815.

——. *Vom deutschen Bund und deutscher Staatsverfassung.* Heidelberg, 1816.

Fritsch, T., ed. *Antisemitenkatechismus.* Leipzig, 1892.

——. *Handbuch der Judenfrage.* Updated. Leipzig, 1938.

Geibel, E. *Emanuel Geibels Werke.* Schacht (ed.). Leipzig, 1915.

——. *Heroldsrufe.* Stuttgart, 1871.

Geiger, A. "Bruno Bauer und die Juden," in *Wissenschaftliche Zeitschrift für jüdische Theologie.* 1844.

——. "Der Kampf christlicher Theologen gegen die bürgerliche Gleichstel-lung der Juden," in *Nachgelassene Schriften.*

Gellert, C.F. *Leben der schwedischen Gräfin von G. Sämtliche Schriften.* 10 parts in 5 vols. Hildesheim, 1968.

Gerlach, L. v. Letter to von Niebuhr, in *Deutsche Revue.* November 1888.

Gesetzsammlung für die königlichen Preussischen Staaten. No. 5. Berlin, 1812.

Gessner, S. *Der Tod Abels.* Zürich, 1758.

Ghillany, F.W. *Die Judenfrage. Eine Beigabe zu Bruno Bauers Abhandlung über diesen Gegenstand.* Nuremberg, 1843.

——. *Das Judentum und die Kritik, oder es bleibt bei den Menschenopfern der Hebräer und bei der Notwendigkeit einer zeitgemässen Reform des Judentums.* Nuremberg, 1844.

Goerres, J.V. *Politische Schriften.* Goerres (ed.). Munich, 1854.

——. *Die Teutschen Volksbücher.* Heidelberg, 1803.

Goethe, J.W. v. *Briefe von Goethe an Lavater.* Hirzel (ed.). Leipzig, 1833.

——. *Briefwechsel zwischen Goethe und Zelter.* Berlin, 1834.

————. *Dichtung und Wahrheit, Werke.* 11 vols. Hellen (ed.).

————. *Gespräche mit Eckermann.* Houben (ed.). Leipzig, 1925.

————. *Goethes Gespräche.* Biedermann (ed.). Leipzig, 1889–1891.

————. *Goethe-Handbuch.* Zeitler (ed.). Stuttgart, 1916.

————. *Goethe-Jahrbuch.* Vol. 16.

————. *Goethe: Meine Religion, mein politischer Glaube.* Bode (ed.). Berlin, 1899.

————. *Goethes Unterhaltung mit dem Kanzler Fr. v. Müller.* Burckhardt (ed.). 1898.

————. *Sämtliche Werke.* Ernst (ed.).

————. *Werke.* Holtzhauer (ed.). Berlin-Weimar, 1966.

————. *Werke.* Weimar. Hoftheater.

Gotthelf, J. *Uli der Knecht.* Berlin, 1891.

Gottsched, J.C. *Gesammelte Reden.* Leipzig, 1749.

Grabbe, D. *Napoleon oder die hundert Tage.* Frankfurt a.M., 1831.

————. *Scherz, Satire, Ironie und tiefere Bedeutung.* Leipzig, n.d.

Grattenauer, W.F. *Erklärung an das Publikum über meine Schrift: "Wider die Juden."* Berlin, 1803.

Grillparzer, F. *Sämtliche Werke.* Sauer (ed.). 20 vols. in 10 vols. Cotta, 1883.

————. *Sämtliche Werke.* Necker (ed.). 16 vols. Leipzig, 1903.

Grimm, J., and Grimm, W. *Briefwechsel zwischen Jakob und Wilhelm Grimm.* 1881.

————. *Briefwechsel zwischen Jakob und Wilhelm Grimm, Dahlmann und Gervinus.* 2 vols. Berlin, 1885.

————. *Kinder- und Hausmärchen.* Stuttgart and Berlin, 1912.

Grün, A. (von Auersperg). *Schutt. Gesammelte Werke.* Vol. 3. Frankl (ed.). Berlin, 1902.

Grün, K. *Die Judenfrage: Gegen Bruno Bauer.* Darmstadt, 1844.

Gutzkow, K. *Aus der Knabenzeit.* Frankfurt a.M., 1852.

————. *Börnes Leben.* Jena, 1872.

————. *Fritz Ellrodt.* 1870.

————. *Götter, Helden, Don Quixote.* Hamburg, 1838.

————. "Juden und Emanzipation," in *Säkularbilder. Gesammelte Werke.* Vol. 8. Frankfurt.

————. *König Saul.* 1839.

————. "Rothschild," in *Öffentliche Charaktere.* Hamburg, 1835.

————. *Rückblicke auf mein Leben.* Berlin, 1875.

————. *Der Sadduzäer von Amsterdam. Gesammelte Werke.* Vol. 1. Leipzig, 1911.

————. *Uriel Acosta. Werke.* Berlin, 1872.

————. *Zur Geschichte unserer Zeit. Werke.* Vol. 20. 1845.

Gutzkow, K., ed. *Telegraph für Deutschland.* 1837–1843.

Haller, K.L. von. *Restauration der Staatswissenschaften.* 6 vols. Winterthur, 1816–1825.

Hamann, J.G. *Hamann, Schriften und Briefe.* Petri (ed.). 2 vols. Hanover, 1878.

————. *Sämtliche Werke*. Nadler (ed.). 5 vols. Vienna, 1952.

Hamerling, R. *Ahasverus in Rom*. Hamburg, 1885.

————. *Blätter im Winde*. Hamburg and Leipzig, 1888.

————. *Homunculus*. Hamburg and Leipzig, 1888.

————. *Stationen meiner Lebenspilgerschaft*. Hamburg, 1889.

Hartmann, E. von. *Das Judentum in Gegenwart und Zukunft*. Leipzig, 1885.

Hartung, E. *Jean Paul: Ein Lebensroman in Briefen*. Munich, 1925.

Hauff, W. *Jud Süss. Sämtliche Werke*. 6 vols. Stuttgart, n.d.

————. *Mitteilungen aus den Memoiren des Satan. Kürschners Deutsche Nationalliteratur*. Vol. 157.

Haym, R., ed. *Briefe von Wilhelm von Humboldt and Georg H.L. Nicolovius*. Berlin, 1894.

Hebbel, F. *Agnes Bernauer. Sämtliche Werke*. Stern (ed.). 12 vols. Leipzig, 1898.

————. *Augsburger Allgemeine Zeitung*. August 7, 1848.

————. *Hebbels Briefwechsel mit Freunden und berühmten Zeitgenossen*. Bamberg (ed.). 2 vols. Berlin, 1892.

————. *Sämtliche Briefe*. Werner (ed.). Berlin, 1919.

————. *Sämtliche Werke*. Werner (ed.). 25 vols. Bern, 1970.

————. *Tagebücher*. Bamberg (ed.). In *Sämtliche Werke,* Werner (ed.). 4 vols. 1887.

Hebel, J.P. *Hebels Werke: Schatzkästlein des rheinischen Hausfreundes*. Behagel (ed.). *Kürschners Deutsche Nationalliteratur*. Vol. 142.

Hegel, G.W.F. *Gesammelte Werke*. Gans (ed.). 18 vols. Berlin, 1837.

————. *Hegel: Early Theological Writings*. Knox (trans.). Chicago, 1948.

————. *Hegels theologische Jugendschriften*. Nohl (ed.). Tübingen, 1907.

————. *Sämtliche Werke*. Bousman and Glockner (eds.). 20 vols. Stuttgart, 1940.

————. *Vorlesungen über die Philosophie der Geschichte*. Michelet (ed.). Berlin, 1844.

Heine, H. *Heine, Heinrich. Confessio Judaica*. Bieber (ed.). Berlin, 1925.

Herder, J.G. *Adrastea. Werke*. Vol. 24. Kurz (ed.).

————. *Älteste Urkunde des Menschengeschlechtes. Werke*. Suphan (ed.). Vols. 6 and 8.

————. *Blätter der Vorzeit. Sämtliche Werke*. Tübingen, 1807.

————. *Briefe, das Studium der Theologie betreffend. Sämtliche Werke*. Vol. 10. Suphan (ed.).

————. *Briefe zur Beförderung der Humanität. Kürschners Deutsche Nationalliteratur*. Greifen, 1947.

————. *Früchte aus den sogenannten goldenen Zeitaltern des achtzehnten Jahrhunderts*. Müller (ed.). Tübingen, 1809.

————. *Ideen zur Philosophie der Geschichte der Menschheit*. Leipzig, 1821.

————. *Stimmen der Völker in Liedern. Werke*. Vol. 8. Kurz (ed.).

————. *Vom Geist des Christentums. Christliche Schriften*. Müller (ed.).

————. *Vom Geist der ebräischen Poesie. Sämtliche Werke*. Vol. 11. Suphan (ed.).

Hermes, T.T. *Sophiens Reise von Memel nach Sachsen*. Deutsche Literatur der Aufklärung. Vol. 13. Brüggemann (ed.). Leipzig, 1941.

Hildebrand, K. *Junges Deutschland*. 1841.

Hippel, T.G. von. *Vorwärts oder rückwarts in der Judenfrage*. 1842.

Hirsch, S. *Das Judentum, der christliche Staat und die moderne wissenschaftliche Kritik*. 1843.

Hitler, A. *Adolf Hitler spricht: Ein Lexikon des Nationalsozialismus*. Leipzig, 1934.

————. *Mein Kampf*. Fay (ed.). New York and Munich, 1939.

Hitzig, J.E. *Aus Hoffmanns Leben und Nachlass*. Berlin, 1823.

Hoffmann, E.T.A. *Werke*. Ellinger (ed.). Berlin, 1912.

d'Holbach, P.T. *L'Esprit du Judaisme*. London, 1770.

Holst, J. *Judentum*. Mainz, 1821.

Holtze, F., ed. *Brautwahl*. Schriften des Vereins für die Geschichte Berlins. Vol. 43. Berlin, 1910.

Humboldt, A. von. *Alexander von Humboldts Briefe an Christian Karl Josias von Bunsen*. Leipzig, 1869.

————. *Alexander von Humboldt in seinem Briefwechsel mit Varnhagen*. Leipzig, 1860.

————. *Kosmos*. 4 vols. Stuttgart, 1870.

Humboldt, Caroline von. *Briefwechsel zwischen Karoline Humboldt, Rahel und Varnhagen*. Leitzmann (ed.). Weimar, 1896.

Humboldt, W. von. *Briefe von W. v. Humboldt an G.H.L. Nicolovius*. Haym (ed.). Berlin, 1894.

————. *Politische Denkschriften. Gesammelte Werke*. Gebhardt (ed.). Berlin, 1903.

————. *Wilhelm und Caroline von Humboldt in ihren Briefen*. Sydow (ed.). 7 vols. Berlin, 1906.

————. *Wilhelm von Humboldts Briefe an K.G. v. Brinkmann*. Leitzmann (ed.). Leipzig, 1939.

Immermann, K. *Die Epigonen. Gesammelte Werke*. Vol. 3. Maync (ed.). Leipzig, 1936.

————. *Münchhausen. Gesammelte Werke*. Vol. 1. Maync (ed.). Leipzig and Vienna, 1936.

Israel, M. *Rescue of the Jews*. Mendelssohn (trans.). 1782.

Jacobi, F.H.J. *Werke*. 6 vols. Leipzig, 1825.

Jacoby, J. *Über das Verhältnis des königlichen preussischen Oberregierungsrates Herrn Streckfuss zur Emanzipation der Juden*. Hamburg, 1833.

Jahn, F.L. *Deutsches Volkstum*. Frankfurt, 1810.

————. *Kleine Schriften*. Leipzig, 1906.

Jensen, W. *Die Juden von Köln.* Berlin, 1897.

Jeune Allemagne. *Die Jeune Allemagne in Deutschland*. Stuttgart bei Lieschning, 1836.

Die Juden. *Die Juden in Deutschland.* Vol. 2: Die Juden als Soldaten. Vom Kommittee zur Abwehr antisemitischer Angriffe. 1896.

Die Judenfrage. *Die Judenfrage im preussischen Abgeordnetenhause.* Abdruck stenographischer Berichte vom 20 und 22. Nov. 1880. Bresslau, 1880.

Judenverfolgungen. *Judenverfolgungen und Emanzipation.* Berlin, 1848.

Kant, I. *Gesamtausgabe.* Rosenkranz (ed.). 14 vols. Leipzig, 1842.

———. *I. Kant: Briefe, Erklärungen, Fragmente und sein Nachlass.* Schubert (ed.). Leipzig, 1842.

———. *Werke.* Cohen and Cassirer (eds.). Berlin, 1923.

Kautsky, K. *Aus der Frühzeit des Marxismus.* Prague, 1935.

Kayser, J.F. *Über die Autonomie der Juden.* Giessen, 1739.

Keller, G. *Gesammelte Werke.* 10 vols. Zürich, 1947.

———. *Gottfried Keller. Briefe und Tagebücher.* Vol. 3. Ermatinger (ed.).

———. *Nachgelassene Schriften.* 1862.

Keudell, F.M.L.R. *Fürst und Fürstin Bismarck: Erinnerungen aus den Jahren 1846–1872.* Berlin, 1872.

Kleist, H. von. *Gesammelte Werke.* Minde-Pouet, Steig, and Schmidt (eds.). 5 vols. Leipzig.

Klopstock, F.G. *Sämtliche Werke.* 10 vols. Leipzig, 1855.

Klüber, J.L.K. *Übersicht der diplomatischen Verhandlungen des Wiener Kongresses.* Frankfurt a.M., 1816.

Kobler, F. *Juden und Judentum in deutschen Briefen seit drei Jahrhunderten.* Vienna, 1935.

———. *Jüdische Geschichte in Briefen aus Ost und West.* Vienna, 1938.

Kohler, R. *Adam Müller: Schriften zur Staatsphilosophie.* Munich, 1923.

Kölbele, J.B. *Begebenheiten der Jungfer Meyern, eines jüdischen Frauenzimmers von ihr selbst beschrieben.* 2 pts. Frankfurt a.M., 1766.

Kommittee. *Kommittee zur Abwehr antisemitischer Angriffe. Die Juden in Deutschland.* 1896.

Körner, T. *Briefe und Lieder aus dem Feld.* Munich, n.d.

———. *Sämtliche Werke.* Macke (ed.). Berlin, 1908.

Kosegarten, C. *Ansichten für den deutschen Staatenbund.* 1816.

Krug, W.T. *Die Politik der Christen und die Politik der Juden.* Leipzig, 1832.

———. *Über das Verhältnis verschiedener Religionsparteien zum Staat und über die Emanzipation der Juden.* Jena, 1828.

Kühne, G. "Moses Mendelssohn," in *Gesammelte Schriften.* Vol. 4.

———. *Karnival in Berlin.* Braunschweig, 1843.

Kulke, E. *Erinnerungen an Friedrich Hebbel.* Vienna, 1878.

Lagarde, P. de (Bötticher). *Ausgewählte Schriften.*

———. *Deutsche Schriften.* 1878.

Langbehn, J. *Rembrandt als Erzieher.* 44th edition. Leipzig, 1896.

Laube, H. *Erinnerungen 1841–1881.* Vienna, 1882.

———. *Die Krieger. Das junge Europa.* 4 vols. Mannheim, 1833–1837.

Lenau, N. *Lenaus Werke.* Blödau and Hempel (eds.). Berlin.

Leo, H. *Meine Jugendzeit.* Gotha, 1880.

Lessing, G.E. *Ernst und Falk: Gespräche für Freimaurer. Sämtliche Schriften.* Muncker (ed.). Vol. 13.

——. *Die Juden. Sämtliche Schriften.* Vol. 1. Lachmann (ed.). Stuttgart, 1886–1924.

——. *Nathan der Weise. Sämtliche Schriften.* Lachmann and Muncker (eds.). Vol. 13.

Lichtenberg, G.C. *Aphorismen.* Berlin, 1902.

——. "Timorus," in *Vermischte Schriften.* Lichtenberg and Kries (eds.). Vienna, 1817.

Lips, M.A. *Über die künftige Stellung der Juden in den deutschen Bundesstaaten.* Erlangen, 1819.

List, F. *Schriften, Reden, Briefe.* Goeser and Sonntag (eds.). 9 vols. Berlin, 1932.

Löwenstein, L.H. *Stimmen berühmter Christen über den damaszener Blutprozess.* Frankfurt, 1843.

Ludwig, O. *Werke.* Schweizer (ed.). Leipzig, 1891.

Mahler, R. *Jewish Emancipation: A Selection of Documents.* New York, 1941.

Maier, J.C. *Stark, de Judaeorum tolerantia legum series temporum ordine digesta.* 1782.

Maimon, S. *Lebensgeschichte.* Berlin, 1792–1793.

Marggraf, H. *Deutschlands jüngste Literatur- und Culturepoche.* Leipzig, 1839.

Marr, W. *Der Judenspiegel.* Hamburg, 1863.

——. *Der Sieg des Judentums über das Germanentum.* 1879.

Marwitz, F.A.L. v. d. *F.A.L. von der Marwitz: Ein märkischer Edelmann im Zeitalter der Befreiungskriege.* Meusel (ed.). Berlin, 1913.

Marx, K. *Zur Judenfrage* (first appeared in *Deutsch-Französische Jahrbücher,* 1843).

Maximilian II. *König Maximilians II von Bayern und Schellings Briefwechsel.* Trost and Leist (eds.). Stuttgart, 1890.

Mémoires. *Mémoires sur l'état des Israélites, dédiés et réprésentés à leur majestés imperiales et royales, réunies au Congrès d'Aix-la-Chapelle.* Paris, 1819.

Mendelssohn, M. *Jerusalem, or Religious Power and Judaism.* 1782.

Mendelssohn-Bartholdy, F. *Briefe von Gentz an Pilat.* Leipzig, 1868.

Menzel, W. *Geschichte der deutschen Literatur.* 1836 (also 1858–1859).

——. *Geschichte der letzten vierzig Jahre.* Stuttgart, 1859.

Menzel, W., ed. *Literaturblatt* (especially 1833–1837).

Metternich-Winneburg, C.L.W. (Freiherr von). *Aus Metternichs nachgelassenen Papieren.* 8 vols. 1884.

Meyer, E. *Gegen Ludwig Börne.* Altona, 1831.

Mirabeau, H.G.V.R. (Le Comte de). *De la monarchie prussienne sous Frédéric le Grand.* 8 vols. London, 1788.

——. "Memorial to Frederick William II," *Secret Memoirs of the Court of Berlin.* 1901.

————. *Sur Moses Mendelssohn, sur la réforme politique des Juifs et en particulier sur la révolution tentée, en leur faveur en 1753, dans la Grande Bretagne.* 1787.

Mitteilungen. *Mitteilungen des Vereins zur Abwehr des Antisemitismus*, especially 1891, 1895, 1896.

Mohl, O. v. *Fünfzig Jahre Reichsdienst.* 1920.

Mohl, R. *Das Staatsrecht des Königreiches Württemberg.* Tübingen, 1829–1831.

Möser, J. *Briefe aus Virginien über die allgemeine Toleranz. Sämtliche Werke.* Abeken (ed.).

————. *Patriotische Phantasien. Sämtliche Werke.* Abeken (ed.)

Mommsen, T. *Auch ein Wort über unser Judentum.* Berlin, 1880.

————. *Römische Geschichte.* 5 vols. in 4. Berlin, 1903–1904.

Montesquieu, C.L. de. *Oeuvres complètes.* Caillot (ed.). Paris, 1949.

Mosen, J. *Ahasver. Werke.* Leipzig, 1880.

Motte-Fouqué, A. de la. *Briefe an Fr. Baron de la Motte-Fouqué.* Berlin, 1848.

Müller, A. *Die Elemente der Staatskunst.* Berlin, 1809.

————. *Nachschriften zur Staatsphilosophie.* Kohler (ed.). Munich, 1923.

Müller, F. Mahler. *Mahler Müllers Werke.* 3 vols. Heidelberg, 1825.

Müller, W. "Der ewige Jude," *Gedichte.* Halle an der Saale, n.d.

Mundt, T. *Charaktere und Situationen.* Wismar, 1837.

————. *Madonna. Unterhaltungen mit einer Heiligen.* Leipzig, 1835.

Nationalversammlung. *Stenographischer Bericht über die Verhandlungen der deutschen konstituierenden Nationalversammlung zu Frankfurt a.M.* 9 vols. Wigard (ed.).

Nestroy, J.N. *Judith und Holofernes. Sämtliche Werke.* 12 vols. Brukner and Rommel (eds.). Vienna, 1924–1930.

Nicolai, C.F. *Beschreibung der königlichen Residenzstädte.* 2 vols. Berlin, 1769.

————. *Leben und Meinungen des Magisters Sebaldus Nothanker.* Brüggemann (ed.). Leipzig, 1938.

Nietzsche, F. *F. Nietzsche, Paul Rée, Lou von Salomé.* Frankfurt a.M., 1970.

————. *Gesammelte Werke.* 23 vols. Musarion (ed.). 1920–1929.

Nordmann, H. (Naudh). *Die Juden und der deutsche Staat.* 1861.

Novalis, F. (von Hardenberg). *Die Christenheit oder Europa. Novalis Werke.* Vol. 1. Scholz (ed.). Stuttgart, 1924.

Oppeln-Bronikowski, F.V., ed. *Gespräche Friedrichs des Grossen.* 1919.

Paulus, H.E.G. *Die jüdische Nationalabsonderung nach Ursprung, Folgen und Besserungsmitteln.* Heidelberg, 1831.

Perthes, C.T. *Friedrich Perthes Leben nach dessen schriftlichen und mündlichen Mitteilungen aufgezeichnet.* Gotha, 1861.

————. *Memoirs of F. Perthes.* Edinburgh, 1857.

Pertz, G.H. *Das Leben des Ministers Freiherrn vom Stein.* 6 vols. in 7. Berlin, 1849–1855.

Pestalozzi, H. *Figuren zu meinem ABC-Buch. Sämtliche Werke.* Vol. 9. Buchenau (ed.). Berlin, 1881.

——. *Meine Nachforschungen. Sämtliche Werke.* Vol. 12. Spranger and Stettbacher (eds.). Buchenau, 1881.

Petersdorff, H. v. *Die Vereine deutscher Studenten. Zwölf Jahre akademische Kämpfe.* Leipzig, 1895.

Platen-Hallermünde, Graf, A. *Epigramme. Gesammelte Werke.* Stuttgart and Tübingen, 1848.

——. *Der romantische Ödipus. Gesammelte Werke.* 5 vols. Stuttgart and Tübingen, 1848.

Poschinger, H.V. *Bismarck-Portefeuille.* 5 vols. Stuttgart, 1898–1900.

Preuss, J.D.E. *Friedrich der Grosse.* 4 vols. Berlin, 1832.

Preussen. *Der erste Vereinigte Landtag in Berlin 1847.* Berlin, 1847.

Přibram, A. *Urkunden und Akten zur Geschichte der Juden in Wien.* 2 vols. Vienna and Leipzig, 1918.

Proudhon, P.J. *Césarisme et Christianisme.* Paris, 1883.

Pückler-Muskau, Prince. *Tutti-Frutti: Aus den Papieren eines Verstorbenen.* 5 vols. Stuttgart, 1834.

Raabe, W. *Raabe-Lexikon.* Spiero (ed.).

——. *Sämtliche Werke.* Hoppe and Carstenn (eds.). 20 vols. Göttingen, 1970.

Rabener, G.W. *Satiren.* 1773.

Radowsky, Hundt von. *Die Judenschule.* London, 1822.

Ramler, K.W. Prologue to Shakespeare's *Merchant of Venice. Kürschners Deutsche Nationalliteratur.* Vol. 45.

Ranke, L. v. *Biographie* in *Sämtliche Werke.* Vols. 53 and 54. Leipzig, 1867–1870.

——. *Weltgeschichte.* 9 vols. in 4. Leipzig, 1896.

——. *Denkwürdigkeiten des Staatskanzlers Fürsten von Hardenberg vom Jahre 1806 bis zum Jahre 1813.* 5 vols. Leipzig, 1877.

Reinach, T. *Textes d'auteurs grecs et romains relatifs au judaisme.* Paris, 1895.

Reuter, F. *Aus meiner Stromzeit. Werke.* Seelman (ed.). 7 vols. Leipzig-Vienna, n.d.

——. *Franzosentid, Werke.* Vol. 3.

——. *Ungedruckte Briefe.* Goedertz (ed.).

Richter, J.P.F. (Jean Paul). *Jean Pauls Briefwechsel mit seinem Freunde Osmund.* Munich, 1863.

——. *Jean Pauls Briefwechsel mit seiner Frau und Christian Otto.* 1902.

——. *Jean Paul: Ein Lebensroman in Briefen.* Hartung (ed.). N.d.

——. "Über die Religionen in der Welt," in *Jean Pauls Werke.* Nerrlich (ed.). *Kürschners Deutsche Nationalliteratur.*

Riehl, W.H. *Die bürgerliche Gesellschaft.* Stuttgart and Augsburg, 1856.

——. *Die Naturgeschichte des deutschen Volkes.* Ipsen (ed.). Leipzig, 1935.

Riemer, F.W. *Mitteilungen über Goethe.* Berlin, 1913.

Ritter, I.H. *Beleuchtung der Wagener'schen Schrift: Das Judentum und der Staat.* Berlin, 1857.

Rochau, L.A. von. *Grundsätze der Realpolitik.* 1853.

Röder, C. von. *Erinnerungen aus seinem Leben: Carl von Röder.*

Roscher, W. *Geschichte der Nationalökonomie in Deutschland.* Munich, 1874.

————. "Die Lage der Juden im Mittelalter vom Gesichtspunkt der ökonomischen Politik gesehen," in *Zeitschrift für die gesamten Staatswissenschaften,* 1875; abridged in English, *Historia Judaica.* Vol. 6. 1944.

Rosegger, P.K. *Mein Weltleben oder wie es dem Waldbauernbuben bei den Stadtleuten erging.* Leipzig, 1898.

————. *Persönliche Erinnerungen an Robert Hamerling.* Vienna, 1893.

Roselius, L., ed. *Fichte für heute.* Bremen and Berlin, 1938.

Rotteck, K. *Gesammelte und nachgelassene Schriften nebst Biographie und Briefwechsel.* 5 vols. Pforzheim, 1843.

Rückert, F. *Nachgelassene Gedichte Friedrich Rückerts.* Rückert and Spiegel (eds.). Vienna, 1877.

————. *Werke.* Laistner (ed.). 6 vols. N.d.

Ruge, A. *Briefwechsel und Tagebuchblätter.* Nerrlich (ed.). Berlin, 1886.

Rühs, F. *Über die Ansprüche der Juden an das deutsche Bürgerrecht.* 2d printing. Berlin, 1815.

Savigny, F.C. v. *Vom Beruf unserer Zeit für Gesetzgebung und Rechtswissenschaft.* Heidelberg, 1843.

Schack, A. Freiherr v. *Nächte des Orients. Werke.* Vol. 9. Stuttgart, 1874.

Scheffel, J.V. von. *Gesammelte Gedichte. Sämtliche Werke.* 10 vols. Francke (ed.). Leipzig, n.d.

Schelling, F.W. *Schelling: Leben in Briefen.* 3 vols. Plitt (ed.). Leipzig, 1869–1870.

Schiller, F. *Sämtliche Schriften,* Goedeke (ed.). Stuttgart, 1867. 17 vols.

————. *Schillers Briefe.* Jonas (ed.). Stuttgart, 1892–1896.

Schlegel, A.W. *Sämtliche Werke.* Boecking (ed.). Leipzig, 1847.

Schlegel, F. *Briefe von und an Friedrich und Dorothea Schlegel.* Körner (ed.). Berlin, 1926.

————. *Fragmente aus Lessings Briefen und Werken.* 3 vols. Leipzig, 1804.

————. *Geschichte der alten und neuen Literatur. Sämtliche Werke.* Vienna, 1822.

————. *Lessings Geist aus seinen Schriften.* 3 vols. Leipzig, 1810.

Schleiermacher, F. *Aphorismen zur Kirchengeschichte. Gesammelte Werke.* 31 vols. Reimer (ed.). Berlin, 1843.

————. *Aus Schleiermachers Leben in Briefen.* 4 vols. Berlin, n.d.

————. *Briefe bei Gelegenheit der politisch-theologischen Aufgabe und des Sendschreibens jüdischer Hausväter. Von einem Prediger ausserhalb Berlins. Gesammelte Werke.* 1846.

————. *Über die Religion. Gesammelte Werke.* Vol. 1, part 1.

Schlosser, F.C. *Weltgeschichte in zusammenhängender Erzählung.* Frankfurt, 1821.

Schmid, X. v. *Die patriotischen Wünsche und Vorschläge zur bürgerlichen Verbesserung der Israeliten.* 1819.

Schönerer, G. v. *Gesammelte Werke.* Pichl (ed.). Berlin, 1938.

Schopenhauer, A. *Gesammelte Werke.* Frischeisen-Köhler (eds.). N.d.

———. *Sämtliche Werke.* Frauenstädt and Hübscher (eds.), Wiesbaden.

Schrattenholz, J., ed. *Antisemitenhammer.* Düsseldorf, 1894.

Schubart, C.F.D. "Der ewige Jude," in *Gesammelte Schriften und Schicksale.* Vol. 4. Stuttgart, 1839.

Schücking, L. *Abkehr von der Emanzipation.* N.d.

———. *Die drei Freier.* Heller (ed.). Boston, 1904.

Sessa, K.B.A. *Unser Verkehr* (original title, *Die Judenschule*). Leipzig, Reclam Nr. 129.

Springer, A., ed. *Protokolle des Verfassungsausschusses im österreichischen Reichstag 1848–49.* 1849.

Stahl, F.J. *Der christliche Staat und sein Verhältnis zu Deismus und Judentum.* 1847.

Steig, R. *Arnim.*

Stein, K.F., Baron vom. *Freiherr vom Stein: Briefwechsel, Denkschriften und Aufzeichnungen.* Botzenhart (ed.). Berlin, 1931.

Stenographische Berichte über die Verhandlungen der deutschen konstitutionellen Nationalversammlung zu Frankfurt am Main. Wigard (ed.). 9 vols. 1848–1850.

Stern, A. *Abhandlungen und Aktenstücke zur Geschichte der preussischen Reformzeit 1807–1815.* Leipzig, 1885.

Steub, L. *Altbayrische Culturbilder.* 1869.

Stieglitz, H. *Selbstbiographie.* Gotha, 1865.

Stöcker, A. *Dreizehn Jahre Hofprediger und Politiker.* 1890.

———. *Das moderne Judentum in Deutschland, besonders in Berlin.* Berlin, 1880.

Storm, T. *Auf der Universität.* Vol. 2. New York, 1886.

———. *Briefwechsel zwischen T. Storm und G. Keller.* Köster (ed.). Berlin, 1904.

———. "Kruzifixus," Meyers Klassiker-Ausgaben. Vol. 1. Leipzig and Vienna.

———. *Theodor Storm: Ein Bild seines Lebens.* Storm (ed.). Berlin, 1912.

Strauss, D.F. *Lessings Nathan der Weise.* Berlin, 1864.

Teller, P. *Beantwortung des Sendschreibens einiger jüdischer Hausväter an mich.* Berlin, 1799.

Tieck, L. *Erinnerungen aus dem Leben des Dichters.* Koepke (ed.). Leipzig, 1855.

———. *Nachgelassene Schriften.* Leipzig, 1855.

Toussenel, A. *Les juifs, rois de l'époque.* Paris, 1845–1846.

Treitschke, H. v. *Deutsche Kämpfe.* 1896.

———. "Ein Wort über unser Judentum," in *Preussische Jahrbücher,* Nov. 1879; a second article appeared in the January issue of 1880.

————. *Geschichte des deutschen Volkes im neunzehnten Jahrhundert.* 5 vols. Leipzig, 1879–1890. (There is an English version of four volumes.)

————. *Politik. Vorlesungen.* 1899.

Varnhagen v. Ense, K. *Aus dem Nachlasse Varnhagen: Briefwechsel zwischen Varnhagen und Rahel.* 6 vols. Leipzig, 1874–1875.

————. *Aus dem Nachlasse Varnhagens von Ense. Briefe an Stägemann, Metternich und Bettina von Arnim.* Leipzig, 1865.

————. *Aus dem Nachlasse Varnhagens von Ense: Briefe von Chamisso, Gneisenau, Haugwitz, W. v. Humboldt, Prinz Louis Ferdinand, Rückert, Tieck.* 2 vols. Leipzig, 1867.

————. *Aus dem Nachlasse von Varnhagens von Ense. Biographische Portraits. Nebst Briefen von Koreff, Clemens Brentano.* Leipzig, 1871.

————. *Denkwürdigkeiten des eigenen Lebens.* 6 vols. Leipzig, 1871.

————. *Denkwürdigkeiten und vermischte Schriften.* Leipzig, 1843–1859.

————. *Galerie von Bildnissen aus Rahels Umgebung und Briefwechsel.* 2 vols. Berlin, 1836.

———— *Précis historique sur l'état des Israélites du royaume des pays bas.*

————. *Tagebücher. Aus dem Nachlasse.* Leipzig, 1861.

Varnhagen v. Ense, K., ed. "Achim v. Arnim und Moritz Itzig," in *Vermischte Schriften.* Leipzig, 1875.

————. *Rahel: Ein Buch des Andenkens an ihre Freunde.* Berlin, 1834.

Voss, J. v. *Die Hep Heps in Franken und anderen Orten.* Berlin, 1819.

————. *Das Judenkonzert in Krakau.* Neue Possen und Marionettenspiele. Berlin, 1816.

————. *Der travestierte Nathan,* in *Die Fortsetzungen und Travestien von Lessings Nathan der Weise.* Stümke (ed.). Berlin, 1904.

Voss, J.H. v. *Briefe,* Ed. Voss, Hildesheim, New York, 1971.

Wackenroder, W.H. *Herzensergiessungen eines Klosterbruders.* Berlin, 1797.

Wagener, H. *Das Judentum und der Staat: Eine historisch-politische Skizze zur Orientierung über die Judenfrage.* 1857.

————. *Staats- und Gesellschaftslexikon.* Vol. 1. Berlin, 1859.

Wagner, R. *Bayreuther Blätter,* especially 1878–1881.

————. *Judaism in Music, R. Wagner's Prose Works.* Ellis (trans.).

————. *Das Judentum in der Musik.* Leipzig, 1869.

————. *Mein Leben.* 2 vols. Munich, 1911.

————. "Modern," in *Bayreuther Blätter.* Vol. 1, no. 3. March 1879.

————. *Richard Wagners Briefe.* Altmann (ed.). Leipzig, 1915.

————. *Wagner-Lexikon.* Glasenapp and Stein (eds.). Stuttgart, 1883.

Wahrmund, A. *Das Gesetz des Nomadentums und die heutige Judenherrschaft.* Munich, 1919.

Weil, J. *Das junge Deutschland und die Juden.* Frankfurt a.M., 1836.

Weininger, O. *Geschlecht und Charakter.* Vienna and Leipzig, 1905.

Welcker, K.T. *Die vollkommene und ganze Pressfreiheit.* Freiburg, 1830.

Werner, Z. *Die Mutter der Makkabäer. Dramen.* Kluckhohn (ed.). Leipzig, 1936.

Wertheimer, J. v. *Die Juden von Österreich vom Standpunkt des Rechts und des Staatsvorteiles*. 2 vols. 1842.
Wieland, C.M. *Aufsätze, welche sich auf die französische Revolution von 1789 beziehen* in *Wielands Werke*. Gruber (ed.). Leipzig, 1824.
———. "Gedanken über das Schicksal der Juden," in *Der Teutsche Merkur*. 1775, 3d Quarter.
———. *Der goldene Spiegel oder die Könige von Scheschian*. *Wielands Werke*. Vols. 16–17.
Württemberg, A. Graf von. *Sämtliche Gedichte*. Stuttgart.
Zedlitz, J.C. Freiherr. "Die Wanderungen des Ahasverus," in *Gedichte*. Stuttgart, 1859.
Zimmermann, J.G. *Vom Nationalstolze*. Frankfurt and Leipzig, 1781.
Zschokke, H. "Erinnerungen an Heinrich Pestalozzi," in *Prometheus für Licht und Recht*. Aarau, 1832; also Zschokke, *Sämtliche Schriften*. Vol. 42.
———. *Selbstschau*. Aarau, 1842.

Secondary Sources

Adler H. *Die Juden in Deutschland von der Aufklärung bis zum Nationalsozialismus*. Munich, 1960.
Altmann, A. *Moses Mendelssohn*. University of Alabama, 1973.
Anstett, J.J. "Paul de Lagarde," in *The Third Reich*. Unesco, London, 1955.
Antonowytsch, N. *F.L. Jahn: Ein Beitrag zur Geschichte der Anfänge des deutschen Nationalismus*. Berlin, 1933.
Arendt, H. *The Origins of Totalitarianism*. New York, 1951.
———. *Privileged Jews*. New York, 1946.
———. *Rahel Varnhagen*. Munich, 1959 (English edition, London, 1957).
Arneth, A.R. v. *Geschichte Maria Theresias*. 10 vols. Vienna, 1881.
———. *Maria Theresia und Joseph II: Ihre Correspondenz*. 3 vols. Vienna, 1867.
Arnold, R. *Das deutsche Drama*. Munich, 1925.
Avineri, S. "Marx and Jewish Emancipation," in *Journal of the History of Ideas*. 1964.
Bab, J. *Goethe und die Juden*. Berlin, 1926.
Ballhausen, L. v. *Bismarck Erinnerungen*. Stuttgart, 1920.
Bär, M. *Westpreussen unter Friedrich dem Grossen*. Publikat. Kgl. Preuss. Staatsarchive. Vols. 83 and 84. Leipzig, 1909.
Bartels, A. *Einführung in das deutsche Schrifttum für deutsche Menschen*. Leipzig, 1933.
———. *Goethe*. Munich, 1912.
———. *Hebbel*. Leipzig, Reclam, n.d.
———. *Hebbel und die Juden. Das literarische Judentum seiner Zeit*. Munich, 1922.

———. *Kritiker und Kritikaster*. Leipzig, 1903.

———. *Lessing und die Juden*. Leipzig, 1934.

Barnikol, E. "Bruno Bauers Kampf gegen Religion und Christentum und die Spaltung der vormärzlichen preussischen Opposition," in *Zeitschrift für Kirchengeschichte*. Vol. 46. 1928.

Baron, S.W. "The Impact of the Revolution of 1848 on Jewish Emancipation," in *Emancipation and Counter-Emancipation*. Duker and Ben-Horin (eds.). New York, 1974.

———. "The Jewish Question in the Nineteenth Century," in *Journal of Modern History*. Vol. 10. 1938.

———. *Die Judenfrage auf dem Wiener Kongress*. Vienna and Berlin, 1920.

Barthélmess, C. *Histoire philosophique de l'Académie de Prusse depuis Leibniz jusqu'à Schelling, particulièrement sous Frédéric le Grand*. Paris, 1850.

Barzilay, I. "The Jew in the Literature of the Enlightenment," in *Jewish Social Studies*. Vol. 18. October 1950.

Bass, J. "Die Juden bei Wilhelm Raabe," in *Monatsschrift für Geschichte und Wissenschaft des Judentums*. 1910.

Bauer, W. "Treitschke und die Juden," in *Der Weltkampf*. May–August, 1944.

———. "Zur Judenfrage als gesamtdeutscher Angelegenheit zu Beginn des neunzehnten Jahrhunderts," in *Gesamtdeutsche Vergangenheit*. Munich, 1938.

Bäumler, A. *Nietzsche der Philosoph und Politiker*. Leipzig, 1931.

Baxa, J. *Adam Müller: Ein Lebensbild aus den Befreiungskriegen und aus der deutschen Restauration*. Jena, 1930.

Bein, A. "Der moderne Antisemitismus und seine Bedeutung für die Judenfrage," in *Vierteljahrshefte für Zeitgeschichte*. 1958.

Bender, C. *From Luther to Hitler: Why Anti-Semitism Is Indigenous to the German People*. Montreal, 1938.

Bender, H. *Aufklärung und Judenemanzipation im Werden*. Hamburg. Jan. 1, 1938.

———. *Der Kampf um die Judenemanzipation in Deutschland im Spiegel der Flugschriften 1815–1820*. Jena, 1939.

Benedikt, E. *Kaiser Joseph II., 1741–1790*. Vienna, 1947.

Berger, K. *Schiller: sein Leben und seine Werke*. 2 vols. Munich, 1909.

Bergmann, E. *Fichte und der Nationalsozialismus*. Breslau, 1933.

Bergmann, H. "Eduard von Hartmann und die Judenfrage in Deutschland," in *Leo Baeck Yearbook*. Vol. 5. 1960.

Bernard, P.P. *Jesuits and Jacobins: Enlightenment and Enlightened Despotism in Austria*. Urbana, Chicago, 1971.

———. "Joseph II and the Jews: The Origins of the Toleration Patent of 1782," in *Austrian History Yearbook, 1968–1969*, vols. 4–5, 1970.

Bernouilli, C.A., ed. *Christentum und Kultur*. 1919.

———. *Franz Overbeck und Friedrich Nietzsche*. 2 vols. Jena, 1908.

Bestermann, T. *Voltaire*. New York, 1969.

Biach, A. *Biblische Sprache und biblische Motive in Wielands Oberon.* Brüx, 1897.

———. *Friedrich Hebbel und die Juden.* Brüx, 1897.

Bibl, V. *Kaiser Josef II.* Vienna and Leipzig, 1943.

Bleyer, J. *Friedrich Schlegel am Bundestage in Frankfurt.* Munich and Leipzig, 1913.

Blome, H. *Der Rassengedanke in der deutschen Romantik und seine Grundlagen im achtzehnten Jahrhundert.* Berlin, 1943.

Bloom, S. "Karl Marx and the Jews," in *Jewish Social Studies.* Vol. 4. 1942.

Blüher, H. *Secessio Judaica.* Berlin, 1922.

Botzenhart, E. *Freiherr vom Stein.* Münster in Westfalen, 1931.

———. *Der politische Aufstieg des Judentums von der Emancipation bis zur Revolution, 1848.*

———. *Die Staats- und Reformideen des Freiherrn vom Stein.* Tübingen, 1927.

Bouchet, M. *Le sentiment national en Allemagne.* Paris, 1947.

Brandes, G. *An Essay on Aristocratic Radicalism.* 1914.

Brentano, L. *Der Judenhass.* Berlin, 1924.

Brod, M. *Heinrich Heine.* Amsterdam, 1934.

Brunschwig, H. *Enlightenment and Romanticism in Eighteenth Century Prussia.* Chicago, 1974.

Bülck, W. *Christentum und Deutschtum bei Arndt, Bismarck und H. St. Chamberlain und heutigen Dichtern.* Gütersloh, 1937.

Bürger-Prinz, H., and Segel, A. *Julius Langbehn, der Rembrandtdeutsche: Eine psychopathologische Studie.* Leipzig, 1940.

Bungardt, K. *F.L. Jahn als Begründer einer völkisch-politischen Erziehung.* Würzburg, 1938.

Burdach, K. "Faust und Moses," in *Sitzungsberichte der königlich-preussischen Akademie der Wissenschaften.* Berlin, 1912.

Busch, M. *Unser Reichskanzler.* 1881.

Bussmann, W. *Treitschke, sein Welt- und Geschichtsbild.* Göttingen, 1952.

Byrnes, J. *Anti-Semitism in Modern France.* New Jersey, 1950.

Cahnmann, W. "Adolf Fischhof and His Jewish Followers," in *Leo Baeck Yearbook.* Vol. 4. 1959.

Carlebach, S. *Geschichte der Juden in Lübeck und Moisling.* Lübeck, 1898.

Carrington, H. *Die Figur des Juden in der dramatischen Literatur des achtzehnten Jahrhunderts.* Heidelberg, 1897.

Chamberlain, H.S. *Foundations of the Nineteenth Century.* 2 vols. New York, 1912.

———. *Die Grundlagen des neunzehnten Jahrhundert.* 2 vols. Munich, 1909.

Charmatz, R. *Adolf Fischhof.* Stuttgart, 1910.

Claassen, J.J.G. *Hamanns Leben und Werk.* Gütersloh, 1878.

Cohen, H. *Die inneren Beziehungen der Kant'schen Lehre zum Judentum.* Berlin, 1910.

———. "Ein Bekenntnis in der Judenfrage," in *Jüdische Schriften.* 2 vols. Berlin, 1924.

————. "Betrachtungen über Schmollers Angriff," in *Jüdische Schriften.*

————. "Heinrich Heine und das Judentum," in *Jüdische Schriften.*

————. "Virchow und die Juden," in *Jüdische Schriften.*

Corti, E.C. Conte. *Der Aufstieg des Hauses Rothschild.* Leipzig, 1927. See also English version. New York, 1928.

Coudenhove-Kalergi, R.N. v. *Anti-Semitism Throughout the Ages.* Westport, Conn., 1972.

Deeg, H.P. *Hofjuden,* 1939.

Delbrück, H. *Das Leben des Feldmarschalls Grafen Neidhardt von Gneisenau.* 2 vols. in 1. Berlin, 1894.

Dietz, E. *Die deutsche Burschenschaft in Heidelberg.* Heidelberg, 1894.

Dilthey, W. *Das achtzehnte Jahrhundert und die geschichtliche Welt. Schriften.* Vol. 3. Leipzig and Berlin, 1927.

————. *Das Leben Schleiermachers.* Berlin, 1870.

————. "Schleiermacher," in *Allgemeine Deutsche Biographie.* Vol. 31.

————. *Studien zur Geschichte des deutschen Geistes. Gesammelte Schriften.* Vol. 3.

Dorpalen, A. *Heinrich von Treitschke.* New Haven, 1957.

Dove, A. "Wilhelm von Humboldt," in *Allgemeine Deutsche Biographie.* Vol. 13.

Droz, J. *Le romanticisme allemand et l'état.* Paris, 1966.

Eberhard, P. *Die politischen Anschauungen der christlich-deutschen Tischgesellschaft.* Erlangen, 1937.

Eberhard, R. *Goethe und das alte Testament.* Vienna, 1932.

Eckert, F. *Der Bolschewismus von seinen Anfängen bis Lenin.* Munich, 1924.

Eckstein, A. *Der Kampf der Juden um ihre Emanzipation in Bayern.* Fürth, 1905.

Elbogen, J., and Sterling, E. *Die Geschichte der Juden in Deutschland.* Hamburg, 1959.

Eloesser, A. *Vom Ghetto nach Europa: Das Judentum im geistigen Leben des neunzehnten Jahrhunderts.* Berlin, 1936.

Elsenhaus, H. *Kants Rassentheorie.* Leipzig, 1904.

Emmerlich, H. *Das Judentum bei Voltaire.* Breslau, 1930.

Ermers, M. *Victor Adler.* Vienna, 1932.

Esser, H. *Die jüdische Weltpest.* Munich, 1939.

Falb, A. *Luther und die Juden.* Munich, 1921.

Feder, G. *Die Juden.* Munich, 1933.

Fournier, A. "Joseph II." *Allgemeine Deutsche Biographie.* Vol. 14.

Frank, W. *Hofprediger Stöcker und die christlich-soziale Arbeiterbewegung.* Berlin, 1928.

Frankl, O. *Schiller in seinen Beziehungen zu den Juden.* Leipzig, 1905.

Franz, G. *Liberalismus: Die deutschliberale Bewegung in der Habsburger Monarchie.* Munich, 1955.

Freund, I. *Die Emanzipation der Juden in Preussen unter besonderer Berücksichtigung des Gesetzes vom 11. März, 1812.* 2 vols. Berlin, 1912.

Friedländer, D.M.H. *Das Leben und Wirken der Juden in Österreich in vormärzlichen Zeiten.* Vienna, 1911.

Friedländer, F. *Das Leben Gabriel Riessers.* Berlin, 1926.

Fueter, E. *Geschichte der neueren Historiographie.* Munich, 1911.

Fürst, J. *Henriette Herz: Ihr Leben und ihre Erinnerungen.* Berlin, 1858.

Ganzer, K.R. *Richard Wagner.* Munich, 1934.

———. "Richard Wagner und das Judentum," in *Forschungen zur Judenfrage.* Vol. 3.

Gebhardt, J. "Karl Marx and Bruno Bauer," in *Politische Ordnung und menschliche Existenz.* Munich, 1962.

———. *Politik und Eschatologie: Studien zur Geschichte der Hegel'schen Schule in den Jahren 1830–1840.* Munich, 1963.

Geiger, A. "Der Kampf der christlichen Theologen gegen die bürgeriche Gleichstellung der Juden," in *Wissenschaftliche Zeitschrift für jüdische Theologie.* Vol. 1. 1835.

Geiger, L. *Aus Chamissos Frühzeit.* Berlin, 1905.

———. *Berlin 1688–1840: Geschichte des geistigen Lebens der preussischen Hauptstadt.* Berlin, 1893–1895.

———. *Die deutschen Juden und der deutsche Krieg.* Die Kriegspolitischen Einzelschriften, vol. 3. Berlin, 1915.

———. *Dichter und Frauen.* Berlin, 1896.

———. *Die Juden und die deutsche Literatur.* 1910.

———. "Die Juden und die deutsche Literatur des 16. Jahrhunderts," in *Zeitschrift für die Geschichte der Juden in Deutschland.* 3 vols. Braunschweig, 1883.

———. *Geschichte der Juden in Berlin.* Berlin, 1871.

———. *Das junge Deutschland.* Berlin, 1907.

———. *Das junge Deutschland und die preussische Zensur.* Berlin, 1900.

Glöckner, K. *Brentano als Märchenerzähler.* Jena, 1937.

Goldstein, J. *Rasse und Politik.* Schlüchtern, 1921.

Graetz, H. "Voltaire und die Juden," in *Monatsschrift für die Geschichte und Wissenschaft des Judentums.* 1868.

Grau, W. *Die Judenfrage in der deutschen Geschichte.* Leipzig and Berlin, 1937.

Graupe, H.M. *Die Entstehung des modernen Judentums: Geistesgeschichte der deutschen Juden, 1650–1942.* Hamburg, 1969.

Grenzmann, W. "Nietzsche and National-Socialism," in *The Third Reich.* London, 1955.

Gronau, W. *Chr. W. Dohm nach seinem Wollen und Handeln.* Lemgo, 1824.

Gröner, M. *Schopenhauer und die Juden.* Deutschland's führende Männer und das Judentum. Vol. 1. Munich, 1920.

Grosser, D. *Grundlagen und Struktur der Staatslehre Friedrich Julius Stahls.* Cologne, 1963.

Grünhagen, C. *Schlesien unter Friedrich dem Grossen.* Breslau, 1890.

Grunsky, K. *R. Wagner und die Juden.* Munich, 1922.

Grunwald, M. *Österreichische Juden in den Befreiungskriegen*. Leipzig, 1908.

———. *History of the Jews in Vienna*. Philadelphia, 1936.

Guglia, E. *Friedrich von Gentz*. Vienna, 1901.

Gurian, W. "Antisemitismus in Modern Germany," in *Essays on Antisemitism*. Pinson (ed.). New York, 1946.

———. "Das Judentum und die Aufklärung des 19. Jahrhunderts," in M. Österreicher, *Die Erfüllung*. Vienna, 1936.

Hahn, J. *Julius von Voss*. Berlin, 1910.

Hartenstein, J.G. *Juden in der Geschichte Leipzigs*. Berlin, 1938.

Härtle, H. *Nietzsche und der Nationalsozialismus*. Munich, 1937.

Haupt, H. *Die Jenaische Burschenschaft*. 1904.

Häusser, L. *Deutsche Geschichte vom Tode Friedrichs des Grossen bis zum deutschen Bund*. 4 vols. Berlin, 1861–1863.

Haussherr, H. *Hardenberg: Eine politische Biographie*. 3 vols. Cologne, 1935.

Haym, R., ed. *Die Romantische Schule*. Berlin, 1870.

———. *Wilhelm von Humboldt: Ein Lebensbild und Charakter*. Berlin, 1856.

Heckel, J. "Der Einbruch des jüdischen Geistes in das deutsche Staats- und Kirchenrecht durch Friedrich Julius Stahl," in *Historische Zeitschrift*. Vol. 155. February and March 1937.

Hehn, V. *Gedanken über Goethe*. Berlin, 1900.

Heiden, K. *Der Führer: Hitler's Rise to Power*. Boston, 1944.

Helfert, H. *Geschichte der österreichischen Revolution*. Freiburg, 1907.

———. *Die Wiener Journale von 1848*. Vienna, 1887.

Herdieckerhoff, E. *Freiherr vom und zum Stein und die Juden*. Deutschlands führende Männer und das Judentum. Vol. 6. Munich, 1931.

Hermann, H. *Das Sanatorium der freien Liebe*. 1903.

Hertz, F. *Nationalgeist und Politik*. Zürich, 1937.

———. "Das Problem des Nationalcharakters bei E.M. Arndt," in *Forschungen zur Völkerpsychologie und Soziologie*. Vol. 3. Leipzig, 1927.

Herzog, W. *Heinrich von Kleist*. Munich, 1914.

Heuss, A. *Theodor Mommsen und das neunzehnte Jahrhundert*. Kiel, 1956.

Hildebrandt, K. "E.M. Arndts Rassebegriff," in *Rasse*. 1938.

Hintze, O. *Die Hohenzollern und ihr Werk*. 7th edition. Berlin, 1917.

———. *Die preussische Seidenindustrie im achtzehnten Jahrhundert und ihre Begründung durch Friedrich den Grossen*. 3 vols. *Acta Borussica*. Berlin, 1892.

Hoffmann, H. *Die Religion im Leben und Denken Pestalozzis*. Bern, 1944.

Holzknecht, G. *Ursprung und Herkunft der Reformideen des Kaisers Josef II auf kirchlichem Gebiete*. Innsbruck, 1914.

Holzmann, M. *Ludwig Börne: Sein Leben und sein Wirken, nach den Quellen dargestellt*. Berlin, 1888.

Houben, H. "Fichte," in *Verbotene Literatur von der klassischen Zeit bis zur Gegenwart*. Berlin, 1924.

———. *Gutzkowfunde*. Berlin, 1901.

———. *Jungdeutscher Sturm und Drang*. Leipzig, 1911.

Huch, R. *Die Romantik: Blütezeit, Ausbreitung und Verfall.* Leipzig, 1951.
———. *Stein.* Vienna and Leipzig, 1924–1925.
Isaac, J. *The Teaching of Contempt: Christian Roots of Anti-Semitism.* Weaver (transl.). New York, 1964.
Jahrbuch "H. Schulze-Delitzsch und Eduard Lasker," in *Jahrbuch für Gesetzgebung.* Vol. 2. 1882.
Janssen, J. *Zeit- und Lebensbilder.* 4th edition. Freiburg i.B., 1876.
Jászi, O. *The Dissolution of the Habsburg Monarchy.* 1929.
Jöhlinger, O. *Bismarck und die Juden.* 1921.
Judenfrage. *Die Judenfrage im preussischen Abgeordnetenhause.* Abdruck stenograph. Berichte vom 20. und 22. November 1880. Breslau, 1880.
Judengesetzgebung. "Die Judengesetzgebung Friedrichs des Grossen," in *Deutsches Recht.* Vol. 8, no. 1–2. Jan. 15, 1938.
Jungfer, H. *Die Juden unter Friedrich dem Grossen.* Leipzig, 1880.
Kahn, L.W. "Fortschrittsglaube und Kulturkritik im bürgerlichen Roman: Gustav Freytag und Wilhelm Raabe," in *Corona.* Durham, 1941.
Kaim, I. *Ein Jahrhundert der Judenemanzipation und deren christliche Verteidiger.* Überblick über die Literatur und Geschichte. Leipzig, 1869.
Kampmann, W. *Deutsche und Juden.* 1963.
Kann, R.A. "Friedrich Julius Stahl," in *Leo Baeck Institute Yearbook.* Vol. 7. 1967.
———. *A Study in Austrian Intellectual History.* London, 1960.
Kant, I. "Kant und das Judentum," in *Zeitschrift für Religion und Geschichte.* Vol. 12. 1961.
Katz, J. *Emancipation and Assimilation: Studies in Modern Jewish History.* Westmead, Farnborough, 1972.
———. *Out of the Ghetto: The Social Background of Jewish Emancipation 1770–1870.* Cambridge, 1973.
———. *The Role of Religion in Modern Jewish History.* Cambridge, 1975.
Kaufmann, D., and Freudenthal, M. *Die Familie Gomperz.* Frankfurt a.M., 1902.
Kaufmann, F.W. "Fichte and National Socialism," in *American Political Science Review.* June, 1942.
Kaufmann, W.A. *Nietzsche: Philosopher, Psychologist, Anti-Christ.* Princeton, 1968.
Kaulla, R. *Der Liberalismus und die deutschen Juden.* 1928.
Kayserling, M. *Die jüdischen Frauen in der Geschichte, Literatur und Kunst.* Leipzig, 1879.
———. *Moses Mendelssohn: Sein Leben und seine Werke.* Leipzig, 1888.
Keil, R. *Wiener Freunde 1784–1808.* Vienna, 1883.
Keipert, H. *Behandlung der Judenfrage im Unterricht.* 1937.
Kernholt, O. *Vom Ghetto zur Macht: Die Geschichte des Aufstieges der Juden auf dem deutschen Boden.* Leipzig and Berlin, 1921.
Kober, A. "The French Revolution and the Jews in Germany," in *Jewish Social Studies.* Vol. 7. 1945.
———. "Die Geschichte der Juden in der historischen Forschung der letzten

35 Jahre," in *Zeitschrift für die Geschichte der Juden in Deutschland.* Vols. 1–4.

Koch, F. "Goethe und die Juden," paper read at Forschungsabteilung Judenfrage des Reichsinstituts für Geschichte des neuen Deutschlands. May 13, 1937.

Koch, T., ed. *Porträts deutsch-jüdischer Geistesgeschichte.* Cologne, 1961.

Kogan, N. *Pestalozzis religiöse Haltung und die Rolle der Religion in seiner Pädagogik.* Danzig, 1936.

Kohler, M.J. *Jewish Rights at the Congress of Vienna (1814–1815) and Aix-la-Chapelle.* 1918.

Kohn, H. *The Idea of Nationalism: A Study in Its Origins and Background.* New York, 1944.

Kohut, A. *Alexander von Humboldt und das Judentum.* Leipzig, 1871.

———. *Berühmte israelitische Männer und Frauen in der Kulturgeschichte der Menschheit.* 2 vols. Leipzig, 1900–1901.

———. *Gekrönte und ungekrönte Judenfreunde.* Berlin, 1913.

———. *Geschichte der deutschen Juden.* Berlin, 1898.

———. *Herder und die Humanitätsbestrebungen der Neuzeit.* Berlin, 1870.

Korff, H.A. *Voltaire im literarischen Deutschland des achtzehnten Jahrhunderts.* 2 vols. Heidelberg, 1917.

Koser, R. *Friedrich der Grosse.* 4 vols. Stuttgart and Berlin, 1901.

Kramer, A. *Die Juden und ihre gesellschaftlichen Ansprüche an die Staaten.* Regensburg, 1816.

Kreowski, E., and Fuchs, E. *Richard Wagner in der Karikatur.* Berlin, 1907.

Kreysig, F. *Vorlesungen über den deutschen Roman der Gegenwart.* Berlin, 1871.

Kriegk, G.L. *Deutsche Kulturbilder aux dem achtzehnten Jahrhundert.* 2 vols. Leipzig, 1874.

Kreiten, W.S.J. and Diehl, B. *Clemens Brentano.* Freiburg i.B., 1878.

Kriesi, H.M. *Gottfried Keller als Politiker.* Leipzig, 1918.

Krüger, J. *Friedrich Schlegels Bekehrung zu Lessing.* Weimar, 1913.

Krüger, K. *Berliner Romantik und Berliner Judentum.* Bonn, 1939.

———. "Adam Müller," in *Zeitschrift für deutsche Bildung.* March, 1939.

Kuh, E. *Biographie Hebbels.* 2 vols. Vienna, 1877.

Kühnemann, E. *Schiller.* Munich, 1908.

Laag, H. *Die religiöse Entwicklung E.M. Arndts.* 1926.

Lasher-Schlitt, D. *Grillparzer's Attitude to the Jews.* New York, 1936.

Laube, H. *Erinnerungen 1841–1881.* Vienna, 1882.

———. *Die Krieger: Das junge Europa.* 4 vols. Mannheim, 1833–1837.

Lees, A. *Revolution and Reflection: Intellectual Change in Germany during the 1850's.* The Hague, 1974.

Lehmann, M. *Freiherr vom Stein.* 3 vols. Leipzig, 1905.

Lehrmann, C. *L'élement juif dans la littérature française.* Paris, 1960.

Lenz, M. *Geschichte der kgl. Friedrich Wilhelm Universität zu Berlin.* 5 vols. Halle a.d. Saale, 1910.

Lessing, T. *Deutschland und seine Juden.* Prag and Karlin, 1933.

Levy, A. *Geschichte der Juden in Sachsen.* Berlin, 1901.

Levy, J. *Fichte und die Juden.* Berlin, 1924.

Lewin, A. *Geschichte der badischen Juden, 1783–1909.* Karlsruhe, 1909.

Lewkowitz, A. *Das Judentum und die geistigen Strömungen des neunzehnten Jahrhunderts.* Breslau, 1935.

Liebe, G.H.T. *Das Judentum in der deutschen Vergangenheit.* Leipzig, 1903.

Liebeschütz, H. "Das Judentum im Geschichtsbild Jacob Burckhardts," in *Leo Baeck Yearbook.* Vol. 4. 1959.

————. *Das Judentum im deutschen Geschichtsbild von Hegel bis Max Weber.* Tübingen, 1967.

————. "Treitschke und Mommsen on Jewry and Judaism," in *Leo Baeck Yearbook.* Vol. 7, 1962.

Liptzin, S. *Germany's Stepchildren.* Philadelphia, 1944.

Littman, E. "Saul Ascher," in *Leo Baeck Yearbook.* Vol. 5. 1960.

Lonsbach, R.N. *Friedrich Nietzsche und die Juden.* Stockholm, 1939.

Lowenthal, M. *The Jews of Germany.* Philadelphia, 1936.

Lublinsky, S. *Jüdische Charaktere bei Grillparzer, Hebbel und Ludwig.* Berlin, 1899.

Mahler, R. *A History of Modern Jewry: 1780–1815.* London, 1971.

Mann, G. *Secretary of Europe: The Life of Friedrich Gentz, Enemy of Napoleon.* New Haven, 1946.

Mann, T. *Leiden und Grösse der Meister.* Berlin, 1935.

Marcus, R. *The Rise and Destiny of the German Jew.* Cincinnati, 1934.

Maser, W. *Hitlers Mein Kampf.* Munich, 1966.

Massing, P.W. *Rehearsal for Destruction: A Study of Political Anti-Semitism in Imperial Germany.* New York, 1949.

————. *Vorgeschichte des politischen Antisemitismus.* Frankfurt, 1959.

Mayer, G. *Friedrich Engels.* 1934.

Mayer, S. *Die Wiener Juden.* Vienna, 1918.

McGovern, W.M. *From Luther to Hitler.* Boston, 1941.

Mehring, F. *Karl Marx: Geschichte seines Lebens.* Leipzig, 1918.

————. *Die Lessinglegende.* Stuttgart, 1922.

Meinecke, F. *Vom Stein zu Bismarck.* Berlin, 1911.

————. *Weltbürgertum und Nationalstaat.* Munich, 1911.

Mess, F. *Nietzsche als Gesetgeber.* Leipzig, 1930.

Meyer, C. *Preussens innere Politik in Ansbach und Bayreuth in den Jahren 1792–1797.* Historische Studien. Vol. 49. Eberling (ed.).

Meyer, H.O. *Felix Dahn.* Leipzig, 1913.

Meyer, M. *The Origins of the Modern Jew.* Wayne State, 1967.

Meyer-Benfey, H. *Kleists Leben und Werke.* Göttingen, 1911.

Mickniewicz, B. *Stahl und Bismarck.* Berlin, 1913.

Minor, I. *Schiller: Sein Leben und seine Werke.* 2 vols. Berlin, 1890.

Modder, E. *The Jew in the Literature of England to the End of the Nineteenth Century.* Philadelphia, 1939.

Morris, M. *Der junge Goethe.* Leipzig, 1909.

Mosse, G.L. *The Crisis of German Ideology*. New York, 1964.
———. "The Image of the Modern Jew in German Popular Culture: Felix Dahn and Gustav Freytag," in *Leo Baeck Yearbook*. Vol. 2. 1957.
Much, Willi (Buchnow). *Fünfzig Jahre antisemitische Bewegung*. Munich, 1937.
Mugsch, W. *Josef Nadlers Literaturgeschichte*. Bern, 1956.
Müller, F. *Zweitausend Jahre Judentum in Deutschland*. Special edition of *Die Praxis der Landesschule*. Berlin, n.d.
Müsebeck, E. *Arndts Stellung zu den Reformen des studentischen Lebens*. Munich, 1919.
Na'aman, S. *Lassalle*. Hanover, 1970.
Nadler, J. *Literaturgeschichte der deutschen Stämme und Landschaften*. 4 vols. Regensburg, 1929–1932.
Neher, W. *Arnold Ruge als Politiker und politischer Schriftsteller*. Heidelberg, 1933.
Neubaur, L. *Die Sage vom ewigen Juden*. Leipzig, 1893.
Neuendorff, E. *Turnvater Jahn: Sein Leben und sein Werk*. Jena, 1928.
Neumann, F.L. *Behemoth: The Structure and Practice of National Socialism*. New York, 1944.
Newman, E. *The Life of Richard Wagner*. 4 vols. New York, 1944–1949.
Oehler, R. *Friedrich Nietzsche und die deutsche Zukunft*. Leipzig, 1935.
Oncken, H. *Historisch-politische Aufsatze*. 2 vols. Munich, 1914.
———. *Lassalle*. Stuttgart, 1904.
———. "Ludwig Bamberger," in *Preussische Jahrbücher*. 1900.
Oppeln-Bronikowski, F. v. *Antisemitismus?* Charlottenburg, 1920.
———. *David Ferdinand Koreff: Serapionsbruder, Magnetiseur, Geheimrat und Dichter*. Berlin and Leipzig, 1928.
Osborne, S. *Germany and Her Jews*. London, 1939.
Padover, S. *The Revolutionary Emperor*. London, 1934.
Parkes, J. *Antisemitism*. Chicago, 1963.
———. *Lewis Way and His Time: The Transactions of the Jewish Society of England*. Vol. 20. 1964.
Pertz, G.H. *Das Leben des Feldmarschalls Grafen von Neithardt von Gneisenau*. 5 vols. Berlin, 1864.
Pessès, A. *L'Image du juif dans la littérature romantique française*. Paris, 1964–1965.
Pfeil, Graf von. *Welt als Geschichte*. Vol. 21. 1961.
Philippsohn, G. *Die Judenfrage von Bruno Bauer*. 1843.
Philippsohn, J. "Constantin Frantz," in *Leo Baeck Yearbook*. Vol. 13. 1968.
Philippsohn, M. "Der Anteil der Juden an den Befreiungskriegen," in *Wissenschaft des Judentums*. Vols. 1 and 2. 1906.
Poliakov, L. *Du Christ au Juifs de Cour*. Paris, 1955.
———. *Histoire de l'antisémitisme de Voltaire à Wagner*. Paris, 1968.
Popper-Lynkeus, J. *Fürst Bismarck und der Antisemitismus*. Vienna and Leipzig, 1925.

Prinz, A. "New Perspectives on Marx as a Jew," in *Leo Baeck Yearbook*. Vol. 15. 1970.

Proelss, J. *Das Junge Deutschland*. Stuttgart, 1892.

Pulzer, G.J. *The Rise of Political Antisemitism in Germany and Austria*. London and New York, 1964.

Pundt, A. G. *Arndt and the Nationalist Awakening in Germany*. New York, 1935.

Rahmer, R. *Heinrich von Kleist als Mensch und Dichter*. 1908.

Reinharz, J. *Fatherland or Promised Land: The Dilemma of the German Jew, 1893–1914*. Ann Arbor, 1975.

Reininger, R. *Kant: Seine Anhänger und seine Gegner*. Munich, 1923.

Reissner, H.G. *Eduard Gans: Ein Leben im Vormärz*. 1965.

Reuss, F. *Christian Wilhelm Dohms "Über die bürgerliche Verbesserung der Juden" und deren Einwirkung auf die gebildeten Stände Deutschlands*. Kaiserslautern, 1891.

Reventlov, Count. *Judas Kampf und Niederlage in Deutschland*. Berlin, 1937.

Rhyn, H. am, O. *Die Kulturgeschichte des Judentums*. Jena, 1892.

Richter, K.A. "Wegbereiter der Judenemanzipation," in *Der Weltkampf*. Vol. 15. 1938.

Riehl-Reinöhl, O. *Joseph II als Reformator auf kirchlichen Gebiete*. 1881.

Rinott, M. "Gabriel Riesser: Fighter for Jewish Emancipation," in *Leo Baeck Yearbook*. Vol. 12. 1968.

Ritter, G. *Stein: Eine politische Biographie*. Stuttgart-Berlin, 1931.

Ritter, I.H. *Beleuchtung der Wagener'schen Schrift: Das Judentum und der Staat*. Berlin, 1857.

Rosenberg, A. *Die Spur des Juden im Wandel der Zeiten*. Munich, 1939.

Rosenberg, H. *Grosse Depression und Bismarckzeit*. Berlin, 1967.

Rosenkranz, K. *Das Leben Hegels*. Berlin, 1844.

Rozenzweig, F. *Hegel und der Staat*. 1920.

Rotenstreich, N. "For and against Emancipation: The Bruno Bauer Controversy," in *Leo Baeck Yearbook*. Vol. 4. 1959.

———. "Hegel's Image of Judaism," in *Jewish Social Studies*. New York, 1953.

———. *The Recurring Pattern: Studies in Anti-Judaism in Modern Thought*. London, 1963.

Rothermel, O. *Fichte und Schlegel*. Giessen, 1934.

Rürup, R. *Emanzipation und Antisemitismus*. Göttingen, 1975.

———. "Jewish Emancipation and Bourgeois Society," in *Leo Baeck Yearbook*. Vol. 14. 1969.

———. "Die Judenemanzipation in Baden," in *Zeitschrift für die Geschichte des Oberrheins*. Vol. 114. 1969.

Rüthnik, R. *Bürgermeister Smidt und die Juden*. Bremen, 1934.

Sandvoss, E. *Hitler und Nietzsche*. Göttingen, 1969.

Sauzin, L. *Adam Heinrich Müller: Sa vie et son oeuvre*. Paris, 1937.

————. "The Political Thoughts of Constantin Frantz," in *The Third Reich*. Unesco, London, 1955.

Schaub, E.L. "Fichte and the Jews," in *The Philos. Review*. Vol. 49. New York, 1940.

Schay, R. *Juden in der deutschen Politik*. Berlin, 1929.

Scherer, J.E. *Die Rechtsverhältnisse der Juden in den deutsch-österreichischen Ländern*. Leipzig, 1901.

Scheuer, O.F. *Burschenschaft und Judenfrage*. Berlin, 1927.

Scheuermann, S. *Der Kampf der Frankfurter Juden um ihre Gleichberechtigung (1815–1824)*. Kollmünz, 1933.

Schlegel-Veit, Dorothea. "Dorothea Schlegel-Veit," in *Allgemeine Deutsche Biographie*. Vol. 31.

Schmidt, E. *Lessing: Geschichte seines Lebens und seiner Schriften*. 2 vols. Berlin, 1899.

Schmidt, H.D. "The Terms of Emancipation, 1781–1812," in *Leo Baeck Yearbook*. 1956.

Schmidt, W.A. *Geschichte der deutschen Verfassungsfrage während der Deutschen Befreiungskriege und des Wiener Kongresses*. Stern (ed.). Stuttgart, 1890.

Schmitt, C. *Politische Romantik*. Munich and Leipzig, 1925.

Schmoller, G. *Grundriss der allgemeinen Volkswirtschaftslehre*. Leipzig, 1900–1904.

Schochow, W. *Deutsch-jüdische Geschichtswissenschaft*. Berlin, 1969.

Schoeps, H.J. *Das andere Preussen*. Stuttgart, 1952.

————. "Die ausserchristliche Religion bei Hegel," in *Zeitschrift für Religion und Geschichte*. Vol. 7. 1955.

Schorsch, I. "German Anti-Semitism in the Light of the Postwar Historiography," in *Leo Baeck Yearbook*. Vol. 19. 1974.

————. *Jewish Reactions to German Anti-Semitism, 1870–1914*. New York, 1972.

Schulin, E. *Die weltgeschichtliche Erfassung des Orients bei Hegel und Ranke*. Göttingen, 1958.

Schuppe, E. *Der Burschenschafter Wolfgang Menzel*. Frankfurt a.M., 1952.

Schwemer, R. *Geschichte der freien Stadt Frankfurt a.M.* Frankfurt, 1910.

Seebass, F. "Clemens Brentano in der neuren Forschung," in *Germanisch-Romanische Monatsschriften*. Heidelberg, September 1931.

Seeley, J.R. *Life and Times of Stein*. 2 vols. Boston, 1879.

Sembdner, H. *Die Berliner Abendblätter Heinrich von Kleists: Ihre Quellen und ihre Redaktion*. Schriften der Kleistgesellschaft. Vol. 19. Berlin.

Silberner, E. "The Anti-Semitic Tradition in Modern Socialism," in *Scripta Hierosolymitana*. Bachi (ed.). Jerusalem, 1956.

————. "Anti-Semitism and Philosemitism in the Socialist International," in *Judaism*. Vol. 2. 1953.

————. "Austrian Social Democracy and the Jewish Problem," in *Historia Judaica*. New York, 1951.

————. "British Socialism and the Jews," in *Historia Judaica*. Vol. 14. 1952.

————. "French Socialism and the Jewish Question, 1865–1914" in *Historia Judaica*. Vol. 16. 1954.

————. "Friedrich Engels and the Jews," in *Jewish Social Studies*. Vol. 9. 1949.

————. "German Social Democracy and the Jewish Problem prior to World War I," in *Historia Judaica*. Vol. 15. 1953.

————. "The Jew-Hatred of Mikhail Aleksandrovich Bakunin," in *Historia Judaica*. Vol. 14. 1952.

————. *Johann Jacoby: Politiker und Mensch*. Bonn, 1976.

————. *Moses Hess: Geschichte seines Lebens*. Leiden, 1966.

————. *Sozialisten zur Judenfrage: Ein Beitrag zur Geschichte des Sozialismus vom Anfang des neunzehnten Jahrhunderts bis 1914*. Berlin, 1962.

————. "Was Marx an Anti-Semite?" in *Historia Judaica*. April 1949.

Simon, E. "Hegel und die Juden," in *Jüdische Rundschau*. Berlin, Nov. 3, 1931.

Singer, I. *Berlin, Wien und der Antisemitismus*. Vienna, 1882.

Snyder, L.L. *German Nationalism: The Tragedy of a People*. Harrisburg, 1952.

Sombart, W. *Die Zukunft der Juden*. 1912.

Sorgel, A. *Ahasverdichtungen seit Goethe*.

————. *The Jews and Modern Capitalism*. 1951.

Spiel, H. *Fanny von Arnstein oder die Emanzipation*. 1962.

Springer, R. *Dahlmann*. 2 vols. Leipzig, 1870–1872.

Srbik, H. Ritter von. *Metternich: Der Staatsmann und der Mensch*. 2 vols. Munich, 1925.

————. "Die Wiener Revolution in sozialgeschichtlicher Bedeutung," in *Schmollers Jahrbücher für Gesetzgebung*. Vol. 43.

Stamm, E. *Constantin Frantz: Schriften und Leben*. 1907.

————. *Constantin Frantz, 1857–1866*. 1930.

Stapel, W. *Literatenwäsche*. Berlin, 1930.

Steig, R. *Achim von Arnim und die Gebrüder Grimm*. Berlin, 1904.

————. *Arnim*. Leipzig, 1911.

————. *Kleists Berliner Kämpfe*. 1901.

————. *Neue Kunde zu Heinrich von Kleist*. Berlin, 1909.

Stein, L. *The Racial Thinking of Richard Wagner*. New York, 1950.

Sterling, E. *Er ist wie Du: Aus der Frühgeschichte des Antisemitismus in Deutschland, 1815–1850*. Munich, 1956.

————. "The Hep Hep Riots in Germany 1819," in *Historia Judaica*. No. 2. 1950.

————. *Der Judenhass: Die Anfänge des politischen Antisemitismus in Deutschland*. Frankfurt, 1969.

————. *Kulturelle Entwicklung im Judentum von der Aufklärung bis zur Gegenwart*. Berlin, 1969.

Stern, A. *Der Einfluss der französischen Revolution auf das deutsche Geistesleben*. Stuttgart und Berlin, 1928.

——. *Geschichte Europas seit den Verträgen von 1815.* Vol. 1. Berlin, 1894–1924.

——. *Geschichte der preussischen Reformzeit 1807–1815.* Leipzig, 1885.

Stern, F. *The Politics of Cultural Despair.* Berkeley, 1961.

Stern, S. *The Court Jew.* Philadelphia, 1950.

Stern-Täubler, S. "Early German Socialism and Jewish Emancipation," in *Historia Judaica.*

——. "The Jew in Transition from Ghetto to Emancipation," in *Historia Judaica.* Vol. 2. 1940.

——. *Der preussische Staat und die Juden.* Berlin, 1925 (1938).

——. "Principles of German Policy towards the Jews at the Beginning of the Modern Era," in *Leo Baeck Yearbook.* Vol. 1. 1956.

Stohl, A. *Freiherr Carl von Savigny.* 2 vols. Berlin, 1927–1929.

Stuemke, H., ed. *Die Fortsetzungen und Nachahmungen und Travestien von Lessings "Nathan der Weise."* Berlin, 1904.

Sybel, H. v. *Kleine Schriften.* Vol. 1. 1852.

Tal, U. *Christians and Jews in the "Second Reich."* Ithaca, 1975.

Teweles, H. *Goethe und die Juden.* Hamburg, 1925.

Tharaud, J. and Tharaud, J. "Juifs allemands du 18e siècle," in *Revue hébdomadaire.* Paris, 1929.

Theune, B. *Volk und Nation bei Jahn, Rotteck, Welcker und Dahlmann.* Berlin, 1937.

Thieme, K., ed. *Judenfeindschaft: Darstellung und Analysen.* Frankfurt a.M. and Hamburg, 1963.

Tietze, H. *Die Juden Wiens.* Vienna, 1933.

Toury, J. *Die politischen Orientierungen der Juden in Deutschland.* Tübingen, 1966.

Trog, H., ed. *Schelmen-, Scherz- und Judengeschichten.* Zürich, 1925.

Tröltsch, E. *Deismus. Schriften.* Vol. 4.

Uffo-Lenz, H. *Das Volkserlebnis bei Ludwig Achim von Arnim.* Berlin, 1938.

Unger, R. *Hamann und die Aufklärung.* 2 vols. Jena, 1931.

Unna, I. *Die Stellung Schopenhauers zum Judentum.* Frankfurt a.M., 1928.

Valentin, V. *Friedrich der Grosse.* Berlin, 1927.

——. *Geschichte der deutschen Revolution.* Berlin, 1931.

Valvajec, F. *Die Entstehung der politischen Strömungen in Deutschland, 1770–1815.* Munich, 1951.

——. *Der Josephinismus zur geistigen Entwicklung Österreichs im 18. und 19. Jahrhundert.* Munich-Brünn-Vienna, 1944.

Viereck, P.R.E. *Metapolitics: From the Romantics to Hitler.* New York, 1941.

Waldman, N. *Goethe and the Jews.* New York and London, 1934.

Waldkraut, E. "Germanentum und Judentum im Lebenswerke Bruno Bauers," in *Weltkampf.* Sept.-Dec. 1944.

Wawrzinek, K. *Antisemitenparteien (1873–1890).* Historische Studien. Vol. 168. 1927.

——. *Entstehung der deutschen Antisemitenparteien.* Berlin, 1926.

Westernhagen, C. v. *Nietzsche, Juden, Antijuden.* Weimar, 1936.

Westphal, O. *Feinde Bismarcks.* 1930.

Wickert, L. *Theodor Mommsen: Eine Biographie.* 1919.

Winkler, W. "W. Menzels Bedeutung in den geistigen Auseinandersetzungen des 19. Jahrhunderts," in *Sprache und Kultur der germanischen und romanischen Völker.* Vol. 25. German. Reihe, Breslau, 1938.

Winter, E. *Frühliberalismus in der Donaumonarchie.* Berlin, 1938.

Witte, J.H. *Salomon Maimon.* Berlin, 1876.

Wolf, G. *Geschichte der Juden in Wien.* Vienna, 1876.

———. *Judentaufen in Österreich.* Vienna, 1863.

Wöninger, A.T. *Preussens erster Reichstag.* N.d.

Wurzer, W.S. *Nietzsche und Spinoza.* Freiburg i.B., 1974.

Ziegler, T. *Die geistigen und sozialen Strömungen des neunzehnten Jahrhunderts.* Berlin, 1911.

Ziekursch, J. *Politische Geschichte des neuen Deutschen Kaiserreiches.* 3 vols. Frankfurt a.M., 1925–1930.

Zimmermann, W. "Die Gestalt des Juden in der deutschen Dichtung der Aufklärung," in *Zeitschrift für Deutschkunde.* 1940.

Zimmern, R. "Der Jude Kants," in *Deutsche Revue.* March 1878.

Zirus, W. *Ahasverus: Der ewige Jude.* Berlin and Leipzig, 1930.

Zweig, A. *Insulted and Exiled.* London, 1937.

Index

502   *Index*